Consolidated Ontario Business Corporations Act, Related Statutes and Regulations 2015

38th Edition

Contributing Editor:
Angelin Soosaipillai, B.A., LL.B.

Current to Ontario Gazette Vol. 148:5 (January 31, 2015)
E-laws current to O. Reg. 27/15

CARSWELL®

∞ The paper used in this publication meets the minimum requirements of American National Standard for Information Sciences — Permanence of Paper for Printed Library Materials, ANSI Z39.48-1984.

A cataloguing record for this publication is available from Library and Archives Canada.

ISSN 1202-029X

ISBN 978-0-7798-6520-8

Printed in the United States by Thomson Reuters.

TELL US HOW WE'RE DOING
Scan the QR code to the right with your smartphone to send your comments regarding our products and services. Free QR Code Readers are available from your mobile device app store. You can also email us at carswell.feedback@thomsonreuters.com

CARSWELL, A DIVISION OF THOMSON REUTERS CANADA LIMITED

One Corporate Plaza
2075 Kennedy Road
Toronto, Ontario
M1T 3V4

Customer Relations
Toronto 1-416-609-3800
Elsewhere in Canada/U.S. 1-800-387-5164
Fax 1-416-298-5082
www.carswell.com
Contact www.carswell.com/contact

INTRODUCTION

The statutes and regulations in this 38th edition of the *Consolidated Ontario Business Corporations Act, Related Statutes and Regulations* have been updated to the Ontario Gazette Vol. 148:5 (January 31, 2015). E-laws current to O. Reg. 27/15.

The following amendments and revisions are included in this edition:

- Ontario Regulation 665/05 — Health Profession Corporations (under the *Business Corporations Act*, R.S.O. 1990, c. B.16), as amended by O. Reg. 263/14;
- The addition of Forms under the *Limited Partnerships Act*, R.S.O. 1990, Chapter L.16, including Form 3 — Declaration and Form 4 — Power of Attorney;
- Updated version of Registration Form 1 — Sole Proprietorship/Partnership under the *Business Names Act*, R.S.O. 1990, c. B.17; and
- An updated Table of Concordance.

Proposed amendments to legislation which have not been proclaimed in force as of the publication date of this edition are in gray-shaded text.

This consolidation reproduces only the official English language version of the legislation.

It is hoped that this consolidation will provide to be a useful desktop reference for all who study or have a special interest in this area of law.

Summary Table of Contents

TABLE OF CONTENTS

BUSINESS CORPORATIONS ACT

PART I — DEFINITIONS AND APPLICATION

PART II — INCORPORATION

PART III — CORPORATE FINANCE

PART XII — AUDITORS AND FINANCIAL STATEMENTS

PART XIII — INVESTIGATION

PART XIV — FUNDAMENTAL CHANGES

PART XV — COMPULSORY ACQUISITIONS

PART XVI — LIQUIDATION AND DISSOLUTION

62 — General

Names

Subsidiary Body Corporate Holding Shares of Holding Corporation

Shareholder Proposals

Form of Documents

Designating Officers

"Resident Canadian" Class of Persons Prescribed

Proxies and Proxy Solicitation Form of Proxy

Management Information Circular

Dissident's Information Circular

Contents Of Dissident's Information Circular

Information Circulars — General

Financial Statements In Information Circular

Audit Exemption

Auditors and Financial Statements

General

INFORMATION SHEETS — MINISTRY OF GOVERNMENT SERVICES, COMPANIES AND PERSONAL PROPERTY SECURITY BRANCH

BUSINESS NAMES ACT

121/91 — GENERAL

122/91 — Restrictions Respecting Names

General

Prohibited Usage

Restrictions

Exceptions

Commencement

18/07 — Refund of Fee for Electronic Application for New Registration

BNA Forms

Business Records Protection Act

Business Regulation Reform Act, 1994

442/95 — General

Designation of Acts

Unified Form

Filing under the Private Career Colleges Act, 2005

Filing Format

Business Identifier

Disclosure of Tax Information

Compensation

Business Information

Corporations Act

Part I — Corporations, Incorporation and Name

PART II — COMPANIES

PART VI — WINDING UP

SCHEDULE — CONVERSION OF JOINT STOCK LIFE COMPANIES INTO MUTUAL COMPANIES

181 — GENERAL

NAMES

CAPITAL

OBJECTS

MISCELLANEOUS

Corporations Information Act

182 — General

Schedule — Fees

CIA Forms

Extra-Provincial Corporations Act

365 — General

Names

Licences

Delegation of Duties

Fees

Refunds

Exemptions

Schedule — Fees

245/05 — FORMS

EPCA FORMS

LIMITED PARTNERSHIPS ACT

TABLE OF CONCORDANCE OF BUSINESS CORPORATIONS ACTS

Editor: Annamarie M. Bergen,
Legal Information Specialist, Osler, Hoskin & Harcourt LLP

This table concords the *Canada Business Corporations Act* (CBCA) with the corporations Acts of the provinces as well as those of Northwest Territories, Nunavut and Yukon. The Table of Concordance follows the numerical order of the sections/subsections of the CBCA, and for the most part the marginal notes used in the CBCA. Where provincial sections/subsections do not read the same or similar to a CBCA provision, but have a similar *concept/subject* to the CBCA section/subsection, those provincial sections/subsections will be provided in *italics*.

Every effort is being made for accuracy, however this is a *work in progress*; its accuracy will improve with each update. This iteration (Revision 1A) is current to March 2015.

Should you find any anomalies or wish to provide feedback on enhancements to the Concordance, please e-mail the Editor at abeditor@shaw.ca or abergen@osler.com

Annamarie Bergen
March 2015

[*Please see the next page for the list of legislation concorded to, as well as the currency for each jurisdiction*].

Legislation:

Canada (CA): *Canada Business Corporations Act*, R.S.C. 1985, c. C-44[1]

Ontario (ON): *Business Corporations Act*, R.S.O. 1990, c. B.16[2]

Alberta (AB): *Business Corporations Act*, R.S.A. 2000, c. B-9[3]

British Columbia (BC): *Business Corporations Act*, S.B.C. 2002, c. 57[4]

Manitoba (MB): *Corporations Act*, C.C.S.M. c. C225[5]

New Brunswick (NB): *Business Corporations Act*, S.N.B. 1981, c. B-9.1[6]

Newfoundland and Labrador (NL): *Corporations Act*, R.S.N.L. 1990, c. C-36[7]

Northwest Territories (NWT): *Business Corporations Act*, S.N.W.T. 1996, c. 19[8]

Nova Scotia (NS): *Companies Act*, R.S.N.S. 1989, c. 81[9]

Nunavut (NU): *Business Corporations Act*, S.N.W.T. (Nu.) 1996, c. 19[10]

Prince Edward Island (PEI): *Companies Act*, R.S.P.E.I. 1988, c. C-14[11]

Quebec (QC): *Business Corporations Act*, R.S.Q., c. S-31.1[12]

Saskatchewan (SK): *Business Corporations Act*, R.S.S. 1978 c. B-10[13]

Yukon (YK): *Business Corporations Act*, R.S.Y. 2002, c. 20[14]

---

[1]Canada — Current to 2015, c. 3, s. 12.

[2]Ontario — Current to 2011, c. 1, Sched. 5, s. 1 [NOTE: Sched. 2, s. 1 not in force at date of publication].

[3]Alberta — Current to 2014, c. 13, s. 49; 2014, c. 17, s. 57.

[4]British Columbia — Current to 2012, c. 12, ss. 1–38.

[5]Manitoba — Current to 2014, c. 32, s. 4.

[6]New Brunswick — Current to 2014, c. 50. [NOTE: S.N.B. 2013, c. 32, s. 5 not in force at date of publication].

[7]Newfoundland and Labrador — Current to 2010, c. 31, s. 6.

[8]Northwest Territories — Current to 2014, c. 31, s. 2.

[9]Nova Scotia — Current to 2013, c. 3, s. 2.

[10]Nunavut — Current to 2013, c. 20, s. 4.

[11]Prince Edward Island — Current to 2012, c. 8, s. 1; 2012, c. 17, s. 2.

[12]Quebec — Current to 2013, c. 18, ss. 100, 101.

[13]Saskatchewan — Current to 2014, c. 19, s. 33.

[14]Yukon — No amendments. [NOTE: S.Y. 2010, c. 8 and S.Y. 2012, c. 8, s. 2 to come into force on May 1, 2015. These changes are NOT reflected in Rev. 1A (March 2015). They will be reflected in the next revision].

	CAN	ON	AB	BC	MB	NB	NL	NS	NU	NWT	PE	QC	SK	YK
INTERPRETATION AND APPLICATION														
Definitions														
"affairs"	2(1)	1(1)	1(a)		1(1)	1(1)	2(a)		1	1		2	2(1)(a)	1
"affiliate"	2(1)	1(1)	1(b)	1(1)	1(1)	1(1)	2(b)		1	1		2	2(1)(b)	1
"articles"	2(1)	1(1)	1(d)	1(1)	1(1)	1(1)	2(c)	2(1)(a)	1	1			2(1)(c)	1
"associate"	2(1)	1(1)	1(e)	192(1)	1(1)	1(1)	2(d)		1	1			2(1)(d)	1
"auditor"	2(1)	1(1)	1(f)	1(1)	1(1)	1(1)	2(e)	2(1)(aa)	1	1			2(1)(e)	1
"beneficial interest"	2(1)	1(1)	1(g)		1(1)	1(1)	2(f)		1	1			2(1)(f)	1
"beneficial ownership" "beneficially own" (BC)	2(1)	1(1)	1(h)	1(1)	1(1)				1	1			2(1)(f.1)	1
"body corporate"	2(1)	1(1)	1(i)		1(1)	1(1)	2(g)	2(1)(ab)	1	1			2(1)(g)	1
"call"	2(1)													
"corporation"	2(1)	1(1)	1(l)	1(1)	1(1)	1(1)	2(i)		1	1			2(1)(j)	1
"court"	2(1)	1(1)	1(m)	1(1)	1(1)	1(1)	2(j)	2(1)(d)	1	1		2	2(1)(k)	
"court of appeal"	2(1)								1	1				
"debt obligation"	2(1)	1(1)	1(n)		1(1)	1(1)	2(k)		1	1			2(1)(l)	1
"Director"	2(1)	1(1)			1(1)	1(1)					1(b)		2(1)(m)	
"director" "directors" and "board of directors"	2(1)	1(1)	1(o)	1(1)	1(1)	1(1)	2(l)	2(1)(f)	1	1			2(1)(n)	1

	CAN	ON	AB	BC	MB	NB	NL	NS	NU	NWT	PE	QC	SK	YK
"distributing corporation"	2(1)		1(p)				2(m)		1	1			2(1)(o)	1
"entity"	2(1)													
"going-private transaction"	2(1)	*190(1)*												
"incorporator"	2(1)	1(1)	1(s)	1(1)	1(1)		2(p)		1	1			2(1)(q)	1
"individual"	2(1)	1(1)	1(t)		1(1)	1(1)	2(q)		1	1			2(1)(r)	1
"liability"	2(1)	1(1)	1(u)		1(1)	1(1)	2(r)		1	1			2(1)(s)	1
"mandatary"	2(1)													
"Minister"	2(1)	1(1)	1(v)		1(1)		2(s)		1	1	1(d)		2(1)(t)	
"officer"	2(1)	1(1)										2		
"ordinary resolution" "resolution" (QC)	2(1)	1(1)	1(w)	1(1)	1(1)	1(1)	2(t)		1	1		2	2(1)(v)	1
"person"	2(1)	1(1)	1(x)		1(1)	1(1)	2(u)		1	1			2(1)(w)	1
"personal representative"	2(1)	1(1)												
"prescribed"	2(1)	1(1)	1(y)		1(1)	1(1)	2(v)						2(1)(x)	1
"put"	2(1)													
"redeemable share"	2(1)	1(1)	1(aa)		1(1)	1(1)	2(w)		1	1		2	2(1)(y)	1
"resident Canadian" "resident of Canada" (MB)	2(1)	1(1)	1(dd)		1(1)		2(y)		1	1			2(1)(aa)	
"security"	2(1)	1(1)	1(ee)		1(1)	1(1)	2(z)	2(1)(nba)	1	1		2	2(1)(bb)	1
"security interest"	2(1)	1(1)	1(ff)	1(1)	1(1)	1(1)	2(aa)		1	1			2(1)(cc)	1
"send"	2(1)	1(1)	1(gg)	1(1)	1(1)	1(1)	2(bb)		1	1			2(1)(dd)	1
"series"	2(1)	1(1)	1(hh)		1(1)	1(1)	2(cc)	2(1)(nc)	1	1			2(1)(ee)	1
"special resolution"	2(1)	1(1)	1(ii)	1(1)	1(1)	1(1)	2(ee)		1	1		2	2(1)(ff)	1
"squeeze-out transaction"	2(1)													

Table of Concordance of Business Corporations Acts

	CAN	ON	AB	BC	MB	NB	NL	NS	NU	NWT	PE	QC	SK	YK
"unanimous shareholder agreement"	2(1)	1(1)	1(jj)		1(1)	1(1)	2(ff)		1	1			2(1)(gg)	1
Interpretation														
Affiliated bodies corporate	2(2)	1(4)	2(1)	2(1)	1(2)	1(2)	7(1), 7(2)	2(2)	2(1)	2(1)	1.1(a) 1.1(b)		2(2)	2(1)
Control	2(3)	1(5)	2(2)	2(3)	1(3)	1(3)	8	2(3)	2(2)	2(2)	1.1(c)		2(3)	2(2)
Holding body corporate	2(4)	1(3)	2(3)	2(4)	1(4)	1(4)	9(1)	2(5)	2(3)	2(3)	1.1(d)		2(4)	2(3)
Subsidiary body corporate	2(5)	1(2)	2(4)	2(2)	1(5)	1(5)	9(2)	2(4)	2(4)	2(4)	1.1(e)		2(5)	2(4)
Exemptions — on application by corporation	2(6)		*3(3)*						*3(3)*	*3(3)*				
Exemptions — classes of corporations	2(7)		*3(3)*						*3(3)*	*3(3)*				
Infants	2(8)													
Application														
Application of Act	3(1)	2(1), 2(2)	1.[illegible]	3	2(1)	2(1)	4(1)	138(1)				1	3(1)	5(1), 5(2), 5(3), 5(4), 5(5)
Certain Acts do not apply	3(3)	2(3)			*3(1), 3(2)*	2(2), 2(7), 2(8)	5						4	
Limitations on business that may be carried on	3(4), 3(5)								16(3)	16(3)				
Purposes of Act														

	CAN	ON	AB	BC	MB	NB	NL	NS	NU	NWT	PE	QC	SK	YK
Purposes	4						*3*							
INCORPORATION														
Incorporators	5(1)	4(1), 4(2)	5	*10(1)*	5(1), 5(2)	3(1)	11(1), 11(2)	9	5	5		3, 4	5(1)	7
Bodies corporate	5(2)	4(1)		*10(1)*		3(2)	11(1)		5	5		4	5(2)	7
Articles of incorporation	6(1)	5(1)	6(1)	*10(2), 10(3), 11, 12*	6(1)	4(1)	12(1)	*10, 11*	6(1)	6(1)	6	5	6(1)	8(1)
Additional provisions in articles	6(2)	5(3)	6(2)		6(2)	4(2)	12(2)	*20*	6(2)	6(2)	7	6	6(2)	8(2)
Special majorities	6(3)	5(4)	6(3)		6(3)	4(3)	13(1)		6(3)	6(3)		7	6(3)	8(3)
Idem (Votes to remove director)	6(4)	5(5)	6(4)		6(4)	4(4)	13(2)		6(4)	6(4)		7	6(4)	8(4)
Delivery of articles of incorporation	7	6	7(1)	*13(1)*	7	5	14	25	7	7	*8*	8, 9	7	9(1), 9(2)
Certificate of incorporation	8(1)	6	8	13(2), *13(3)*	8	6	15	26(1)	8	8	*10*	10	8	10
Exemption — failure to comply with Act	8(2)											474		
Effect of certificate	9	7	9(1)	*17, 18*	9	7(1), 7(2)	16		9(1), 9(2)	9(1), 9(2)		10	9	11(1), 11(2)

	CAN	ON	AB	BC	MB	NB	NL	NS	NU	NWT	PE	QC	SK	YK
Name of corporation	10(1)	10(1)	10(1)	23	10(1)	8(1)	17(1)	*10, 11, 12, 80*	10(1), 10(2)	10(1), 10(2)	84	*16, 18*	10(1)	12(1), 12(2), 12(3)
Saving for "S.C.C."	10(1.1)	—	—	—	—	—	—	—	—	—	—	—	—	—
Exemption	10(2)					8(2)	17(2)						10(2)	
Alternate name Alternative name outside Canada	10(3), 10(4)	10(2), 10(2.1), *10(3)*, 10(4)	10(5), 10(5), 10(7)	25	10(2). 10(3)	8(3), 8(4)	18, 19	15, 80(3)	10(4), 10(5), 10(6)	10(4), 10(5), 10(6)		20, 22	10(4), 10(5)	12(5), 12(6)
Publication of name	10(5)	10(5)	10(8)	27(1)	10(4)	8(5)	35(1), 35(2)	80(1)	10(7)	10(7)		19	267(1)	12(7)
Other name	10(6)	11(2)	10(3), 10(9), 10(10)		10(5)	8(6)		80(7)	10(8)	10(8)		21	267(2)	12(8), 12(9)
Reserving name	11(1)			22	11(1)	9(1)	403		11(2)	11(2)	12(1)	17	292	13(1)
Designating number	11(2)	8(1), *8(2) to 8(5)*	11		11(2)	9(2)	20		11(1)	11(1)	10(2.1)	23	11	13(2)
Prohibited names	12(1)	9(1)	12(1)	*24*	*12(2), 12(3), 12(4), 12(5)*	10(1)	21, *404*	16(1)	12(1)	12(1)	9(1)	16	12(1)	14(1)
Directing change of name / Idem	12(2), 12(4)	12(1)	13(1)	28(1), 28(2)	12(7), 12(8)	10(2)	22, 23(2)	16(2)	13(1)	13(1)		24, 25	12(2), 12(4)	15(1)
Undertaking to dissolve or change name	12(4.1)	*12(2), 12(3)*	12(2)		12(6)	10(4), 10(5)			12(3)	12(3)		25		14(2)
Revoking name	12(5)		13(3)		12(6), 12(9)	10(3)	24		13(3)	13(3)		24, 27	12(5)	15(3)

	CAN	ON	AB	BC	MB	NB	NL	NS	NU	NWT	PE	QC	SK	YK
Certificate of amendment	13(1)		14(1)		13(1)	11(1)	25(1)		13(4)(a)	13(4)(a)		28	13(1)	16(1)
Effect of certificate	13(2)		14(2)		13(2)	11(2)	25(2)		13(4)(b)	13(4)(b)		28	13(2)	16(2)
Personal liability	14(1)	21(1)	15(2)	20(2)	14(1)	12(1)	26(1)		14(1)	14(1)			14(1)	17(2)
Pre-incorporation and pre-amalgamation contracts	14(2)	21(2)	15(3)	20(3), 20(4)	14(2)	12(2)	26(2)		14(2)	14(2)			14(2)	17(3)
Application to court	14(3)	21(3)	15(5)	20(5), 20(6), 20(7)	14(3)	12(3)	26(3), 26(4)		14(3)	14(3)			14(3)	17(5)
Exemption from personal liability	14(4)	21(4)	15(6)	20(8)	14(4)	12(4)	26(5)		14(4)	14(4)			14(4)	17(6)
CAPACITY AND POWERS														
Capacity of a corporation	15(1)	15	16(1)	30	15(1)	13(1)	27(1)	26(8)	15(1)	15(1)			15(1)	18(1)
Idem (Activities throughout Canada)	15(2)													
Extra-territorial capacity	15(3)	16	16(2)	32	15(2)	13(2)	27(2)	26(13), 26(14), 26(15)	15(2)	15(2)			15(2)	18(2)
Powers of a corporation	16(1)	17(1)	17(1)		16(1)	14(1)	27(3)		16(1)	16(1)	*14, 15, 20*		16(1)	19(1)
Restricted business or powers	16(2)	17(2)	17(2)	33(1)	16(2)	14(2)	28	26(12)	16(2)	16(2)			16(2)	19(2)
Rights preserved	16(3)	17(3)	17(3)	33(2)	16(3)	14(3)	29		16(4)	16(4)			16(3)	19(3)

	CAN	ON	AB	BC	MB	NB	NL	NS	NU	NWT	PE	QC	SK	YK
No constructive notice	17	18	13	421	17	15	30	31	17	17		12	17	20
Authority of directors, officers and agents	18	19	19	146	18	16	31	30	18	18		13, 14	18	21
REGISTERED OFFICE AND RECORDS														
Registered office	19(1)	14(1)	20(1)	34(1)	19(1)	17(1)	33(1)	79(1)	19(1)	19(1)	67(1)	29	19(1)	22(1)
Notice of registered office	19(2)		20(2)			17(2)	34(1)	79(2)	19(2)	19(2)	67(1)		19(2)	22(2)
Change of address	19(3)	14(3)	20(3)	35(1), 35(2)	19(3)	17(3)	33(2)	79(2)	19(3)	19(3)	67(2)	30	19(3.2)	22(3)
Notice of change of address	19(4)		20(5)		19(4)	17(4)	34(2)	79(2)	19(5)	19(5)		30	19(4)	22(5)
Corporate records	20(1)	140(1)	21(1)	*42*	20(1)	18(1)	36	*42(1), 88, 89, 120*	21(1)	21(1)	50	31	20(1)	23(1)
Directors records	20(2)	140(2)	21(5)	*42*, 196(1)	20(2)	18(2)	37(1)		21(2)	21(2)		34	20(2)	23(5)
Retention of accounting records	20(2.1)	140(2)							21(9)	21(9)		34	20(2)	
Records of continued corporations	20(3)	140(3)	21(5)			18(3)	39		21(6)	21(6)			20(3)	23(6)
Place of records	20(4), 20(5), 20(5.1)	144(1), 144(2), 144(3), *144(4)*	21(7), 21(8), 21(8.1)	196(2), 196(3)	20(3), 20(4), 20(5)	18(4)	37(2), 38		21(7), 21(8)	21(7), 21(8)		35, 36	20(4), 20(5)	23(7), 23(8)

	CAN	ON	AB	BC	MB	NB	NL	NS	NU	NWT	PE	QC	SK	YK
Offence	20(6)		21(9)	426(1) 428(1)	20(9)			42(2)	21(10)	21(10)			20(6)	23(9)
Access to corporate records	21(1)	145(1)	23(1), 23(3)	*46*	21(1)	19(1), 19(3)	42(1)	29(1), 43, 90	22(1), 22(3), 22(4)	22(1), 22(3), 22(4)	52	32	21(1), 21(1.1)	24(1), 24(3), 24(4)
Requirement for affidavit — securities register	21(1.1)													
Copies of corporate records	21(2)	145(2)	23(2)	48(2)	21(2)	19(2)	42(2)		22(1), 22(2)	22(1), 22(2)		32	21(2)	24(2)
Shareholder lists	21(3)	146(1), 146(2)	23(5)	49(1), 49(2), 49(4)	21(3)		43(1)		22(5)	22(5)		41	21(3)	24(5)
Supplemental lists / When supplemental lists to be provided	21(4), 21(5)	146(3), 146(4)	23(6), 23(7)	49(5), 49(6), 49(7)	21(4), 21(5)		43(2), 43(3)		22(8), 22(9)	22(8), 22(9)		42	21(4), 21(5)	24(6), 24(7)
Holders of options	21(6)	146(5)	23(8)		21(6)		44		22(10)	22(10)		42	21(6)	24(8)
Contents of affidavit / statutory declaration	21(7), 21(8)	146(6), 146(7)	23(9), 23(10)	49(2)	21(7), 21(8)		43(4), 43(5)		22(6), 22(7)	22(6), 22(7)		40	21(7), 21(8)	24(9), 24(10)
Use of information or list	21(9)	146(8)	23(11)	49(3)	21(9)		45		22(11)	22(11)		40	21(9)	24(11)
Offence	21(10)	258(1)(b)	23(12)	426(1), 428(1)	21(10)		503		22(12)	22(12)		491	21(10)	24(12)
Form of records	22(1)	*139(1)*, 276(1)	24(1)	44(2)	22(1)	20(1)	40	89(4)	23(1)	23(1)		37	22(1)	25(1)
Precautions	22(2)	*139(2)*	24(3)	44(4)	22(2)	20(2)	41	89(5)	23(3)	23(3)		37	22(2)	25(3)
Offence	22(3)		24(4)		22(3)		502		23(4)	23(4)			22(3)	25(4)
Corporate seal	23(1)	13	25(1)						24(1)	24(1)	14			26(1)

	CAN	ON	AB	BC	MB	NB	NL	NS	NU	NWT	PE	QC	SK	YK
Validity of unsealed document	23(2)		25(2)	*194(1)*	23	21	32	155	24(4)	24(4)	60		23	26(2)
CORPORATE FINANCE														
Shares	24(1)	22(1)	26(1)	*52(1)(a)*	24(1)	22(1)	46(1)		25(1)	25(1)	13(1)	43, 46	24(1)	27(1)
Transitional	24(2)	22(2)	26(2)				46(2)		25(2)	25(2)			24(2)	27(2)
Rights attached to shares	24(3)	22(3)	26(3)	*58*	24(4)	22(2)	47		25(3)	25(3)		47	24(3)	27(3)
Rights to classes of shares	24(4)	22(4)	26(4)	*59*	24(3)	22(3)	48		25(4)	25(4)		44, 45	24(4)	27(4)
Issue of shares	25(1)	23(1)	27(1)	62	25(1)	23(1)	49		27(2)	27(2)	*32, 33, 34, 35*	52	25(1)	28(1)
Shares non-assessable	25(2)	23(2)	27(2)		25(2)	23(4)	51		27(3)	27(3)			25(2)	28(2)
Consideration	25(3)	23(3)	27(3)	64(2), 64(3)	25(3)	23(5)	50(1)		27(4)	27(4)		54	25(3)	28(3)
Consideration other than money	25(4)	*23(4),* 23(5)	27(4)	64(5)	25(4)	23(6)	50(2)		27(5)	27(5)			25(4)	28(4)
Definition of "property"	25(5)	23(6)	27(5)	64(1)	25(5)	24	50(3)		27(1)	27(1)		54	25(5)	28(5)
Stated capital account	26(1)	24(1)	28(1)	*72*	26(1)	25(1)	52(1)		28(1)	28(1)	*13(2)*	68	26(1)	29(1)
Entries in stated capital account	26(2)	24(2)	28(2)		26(2)	25(2)	52(2)		28(2)	28(2)		69	26(1.1)	29(2)
Exception for non-arm's length transactions	26(3)	24(3)	28(3)		26(3)	25(4)	52(3)		28(3)	28(3)		70	26(1.2)	29(3)

	CAN	ON	AB	BC	MB	NB	NL	NS	NU	NWT	PE	QC	SK	YK
Limit on addition to a stated capital account	26(4)	24(4)	28(4)		26(4)	25(5)	52(4)						26(1.3)	29(4)
Constraint on addition to a stated capital account	26(5)	24(6)	28(5)		26(5)	25(6)	52(5)		28(6)	28(6)		100	26(1.4)	29(5)
Other additions to stated capital	26(6)	24(5)	28(6), 28(7)		26(6), 26(7)	25(7)	52(6)		28(4), 28(5)	28(4), 28(5)			26(1.5)	29(6), 29(7)
Transitional	26(7), 26(8), 26(9)		28(8), 28(9)		26(9), 26(10), 26(11)	25(8), 25(9), 25(10)	52(7), 52(8), 52(9)		28(7), 28(8)	28(7), 28(8)			26(2), 26(3), 26(4)	29(8), 29(9)
Restriction	26(10)	24(9)	28(11)		26(12)	25(11)	52(10)		28(10)	28(10)			26(5)	29(11)
Exception for an open-end mutual fund	26(11)	24(10)	28(12)		26(13)	25(12)	53(1)		28(11)	28(11)			26(6)	29(12)
Definition of "open-end mutual fund"	26(12)	24(11)	28(13)		26(14)	25(13)	53(2)		28(12)	28(12)			26(7)	29(13)
Shares in series	27(1)	25(1)	29(1)	60(1), 60(2)	27(1)	26(1)	54(1)		29(1)	29(1)		45	27(1)	30(1)
Series participation	27(2)	25(2)	29(2)	60(7)	27(2)	26(2)	54(2)		29(2)	29(2)		50	27(2)	30(2)
Restrictions on series	27(3)	25(3)	29(3)	60(6)	27(3)	26(3)	54(3)		29(3)	29(3)			27(3)	30(3)
Amendment of articles	27(4)	25(4)	29(5)		27(4)	26(4)	54(4)		29(5)	29(5)		45	27(4)	30(5)
Certificate of amendment	27(5)	25(5)	29(6)		27(5)	26(5)	54(5)		29(6)	29(6)			27(5)	30(6)
Effect of certificate	27(6)		29(7)		27(6)		54(6)		29(7)	29(7)			27(6)	30(7)
Pre-emptive right	28(1)	26	30(1)		28(1)	27(2)	55(1)	19A(1)	30(1)	30(1)		55	28(1)	31(1)
Exception	28(2)		30(2)		28(2)	27(7)	55(2)	19A(2)	30(2)	30(2)		55	28(2)	31(2)
Options and rights	29(1)	27(1)	31(1)		29(1)	28(1)	56(1)		31(1)	31(1)		56	29(1)	32(1)
Transferable rights	29(2)	27(2)	31(2)		29(2)	28(2)	56(2)		31(2)	31(2)			29(2)	32(2)

	CAN	ON	AB	BC	MB	NB	NL	NS	NU	NWT	PE	QC	SK	YK
Reserved shares	29(3)	27(3)	31(3)		29(4)	28(3)	57		31(3)	31(3)		57	29(3)	32(3)
Corporation holding its own shares	30(1)	28(1)	32(1)		30(1)	29(1)	58(1)		32(1)	32(1)	88.1(1)	86	30(1)	33(1)
Subsidiary holding shares of its parent	30(2)	28(2)	32(3)		30(2)	29(2)	58(2)		32(2)	32(2)	88.1(2)	88	30(2)	33(3)
Exception	31(1), 31(2)	29(1), 29(3)	33(1), 33(2)		31(1), 31(2)	30(1), 30(2)	59(1), 59(2)		33(1), 33(2)	33(1), 33(2)	88.2(1) 88(2)		31(1), 31(2)	34(1), 34(2)
Exception — subsidiary acquiring shares	31(3)	29(2)												
Exception — conditions precedent	31(4)	29(9)												
Conditions subsequent	31(5)	29(10)												
Non-compliance with conditions	31(6)	29(11)												
Exception relating to Canadian ownership	32(1)	29(4)					60(1)						31.1(1)	
Prohibited transfers	32(2)	29(5)					60(2)						31.1(2)	
Offence	32(3)	258(1)(a)					60(3)						31.1(3)	
Directors of corporation	32(4)						60(4)						31.1(4)	
Where shares are transferred	32(5)	29(6)					60(5)						31.1(5)	
Transfer not void, voidable or null	32(6)	29(7)					60(6)						31.1(6)	
Voting shares	33(1)	29(8)	33(3)		31(4)	30(3)	61, 66		34	34	88.3		31.2	34(3)

	CAN	ON	AB	BC	MB	NB	NL	NS	NU	NWT	PE	QC	SK	YK
Subsidiary body corporate	33(2)	29(8)	33(4)	*177*	31(4)									
Acquisition of corporation's own shares	34(1)	30(1)	34(1)	*77*	32(1)	31(1)	62(1)	51(5)	35(1)	35(1)	88.4(1)	93	32(1)	35(1)
Limitation	34(2)	30(2)	34(2)	78(1)	32(2)	31(2)	62(2)	51(6)	35(2)	35(2)	88.4(2)	95, 96	32(2)	35(2)
Alternative acquisition of corporation's own shares	35(1), 35(2)	31(1), 31(2)	35(1), 35(2)		33(1), 33(2)	32(1), 32(2)	63(1), 63(2)	51(7)	37(1), 37(3)	37(1), 37(3)	88.5(1) 88.5(2)		33(1), 33(2)	36(1), 36(2)
Limitation	35(3)	31(3)	35(3)		33(3)	32(3)	63(3)	51(8)	37(2)	37(2)	88.5(3)		33(3)	36(3)
Redemption of shares	36(1)	32(1)	36(1)	*77*	34(1)	33(1)	64(1)	51(9)	38(1)	38(1)	88.6(1)	94	34(1)	37(1)
Limitation	36(2)	32(2)	36(2)	*79*	34(2)	33(2)	64(2)	51(10)	38(2)	38(2)	88.6(2)		34(2)	37(2)
Gift or legacy of shares	37	33	37(1)(a), 37(2)	75(b)	35	34	65		39(1), 39(2)	39(1), 39(2)		99	35	38(1), 38(2)
Other reduction of stated capital	38(1)	34(1)	38(1)	*74*	36(1)	35(1)	67(1)	57	40(1)	40(1)		101	36(1)	39(1)
Contents of special resolution	38(2)	34(3)	38(2)		36(2)	35(2)	67(2)		40(2)	40(2)			36(2)	39(2)
Limitation	38(3), 38(5)	34(4)	38(3), 38(5)	74(1.1)	36(3), 36(5)	35(3), 35(5)	67(3), 67(5)		40(3), 40(5)	40(3), 40(5)		101	36(3)	39(3), 39(5)
Recovery	38(4)	34(5)	38(4)		36(4)	35(4)	67(4)		40(4)	40(4)		102	36(4)	39(4)

	CAN	ON	AB	BC	MB	NB	NL	NS	NU	NWT	PE	QC	SK	YK
Adjustment of stated capital account	39(1), 39(2), 39(3), 39(4)	35(1), 35(2), 35(3), 35(4)	39(1), 39(2), 39(3), 39(4)		37(1), 37(2), 37(3), 37(4)	36(1), 36(2), 36(3), 37(2)	68(1), 68(2), 68(3), 68(4)	51(13)	41(1), 41(2), 41(3), 41(4)	41(1), 41(2), 41(3), 41(4)		*71, 72,* 73	37(1), 37(2), 37(3), 37(4)	40(1), 40(2), 40(3), 40(4)
Stated capital of inter-convertible shares	39(5)	35(5)	39(5)		37(5)	37(3)	68(5)		41(5)	41(5)		74	37(4.1)	40(5)
Cancellation or restoration of shares	39(6)	35(6)	39(6)	82(1)	37(6)	36(4)	69	51(12)	41(6)	41(6)		85	37(5), 37(5.1)	40(6)
Exception	39(7)	35(7)(a)	39(7)		37(7), 37(9)	36(5)	70		41(7)	41(7)			37(6)	40(7)
Idem (Deemed not to have purchased)	39(8)	35(7)(b)					71						37(7), 37(7.1)	
Conversion or change of shares	39(9)	*35(8)*	39(8)	*76*	37(8)	37(4)	72(1)		41(8)	41(8)			37(7.2)	40(8)
Effect of change of shares on number of unissued shares	39(10)	*35(8)*	39(9)		37(9)	37(5)	72(2)		41(9)	41(9)			37(8)	40(9)
Repayment	39(11)	44(2)	40(1)		37(10)	38(3)	73(1)		42(1)	42(1)			37(9)	41(1)
Acquisition and reissue of debt obligations	39(12)	44(3)	40(2)		37(11)	38(4)	73(2)		42(2)	42(2)			37(10)	41(2)
Enforcement of contract to buy shares	40(1)	36(1), *36(2)*	41(1), 41(2)		38(1), 38(2)	39(1), 39(2)	74(1), 74(2)	*114*	43(1), 43(2)	43(1), 43(2)		*97*	38(1), 38(2)	42(1), 42(2)
Status of contracting party	40(2)	36(3)	41(3)		38(3)	39(3)	74(3)		43(3)	43(3)		97	38(3)	42(3)
Commission for sale of shares	41	37	42	67(1)	39	40	75	110(1)	44	44		58	39	43
Dividends	42	38(3)	43	*70(2)*	40	41	76		45(1)	45(1)	62	104	40	44

	CAN	ON	AB	BC	MB	NB	NL	NS	NU	NWT	PE	QC	SK	YK
Form of dividend	43(1)	38(1)	44(1)	70(1)	41(1)	42(1)	77(1)		45(2)	45(2)		103	41(1)	45(1)
Adjustment of stated capital account	43(2)	38(2)	44(2)		41(2)	42(2)	77(2)		45(3)	45(3)			41(2)	45(2)
Shareholder immunity	45(1)	92(1)	46(1)	87(1)	43(1)	44(1)	81		47(1)	47(1)	57	224	43(1)	47(1)
Lien or hypothec on shares	45(2)	40(1)	46(2)		43(2)	44(2)	82(1)		47(2)	47(2)			43(2)	47(2)
Enforcement of lien or hypothec	45(3)	40(3)	46(3)		43(3)	44(3)	82(2)		47(3)	47(3)			43(3)	47(3)
SALE OF CON-STRAINED SHARES														
Sale of constrained shares by corporation	46(1)	45(1)					83(1)						43.1(1)	
Obligations of directors in sale	46(2)	45(2)					83(2)						43.1(2)	
Effect of sale	46(3)	45(3)					83(3)						43.1(3)	
Application	46(4)	45(4)					83(4)						43.1(4)	
Proceeds of sale to be trust fund	47(1)	45(5)					84(1)						43.2(1), 43.2(2)	
Costs of administration	47(2)	45(6)					84(2)						43.2(3)	
Appointment of trust company	47(3)	45(7)					84(3)						43.2(4)	
Discharge of corporation and trust company	47(4)	45(8)					84(4)						43.2(5)	
Vesting in Crown	47(5)	45(9)					84(5)						43.2(6)	

	CAN	ON	AB	BC	MB	NB	NL	NS	NU	NWT	PE	QC	SK	YK
Escheats Act applies	47(6)												43.2(7)	
SECURITY CERTIFI-CATES, REGISTERS AND TRANSFERS														
Interpretation and General														
Application of Part	48(1)	53	47	106.1	44	45.1	85	33	48	48			44	48(1)
"adverse claim"	48(2)													48(2)
"bearer"	48(2)													48(2)
"bona fide purchaser"	48(2)													48(2)
"broker"	48(2)													48(2)
"delivery"	48(2)													48(2)
"fiduciary"	48(2)													48(2)
"fungible"	48(2)													48(2)
"genuine"	48(2)													48(2)
"good faith"	48(2)													48(2)
"holder"	48(2)													48(2)
"issuer"	48(2)													48(2)
"overissue"	48(2)													48(2)
"purchaser"	48(2)													48(2)
"security" or "security certificate"	48(2)													48(2)
"transfer"	48(2)													48(2)
"trust indenture"	48(2)	46(1)												48(2)
"unauthorized"	48(2)													48(2)
"valid"	48(2)													48(2)

	CAN	ON	AB	BC	MB	NB	NL	NS	NU	NWT	PE	QC	SK	YK
Negotiable instruments	48(3)													48(3)
Registered form	48(4)													48(4)
Order form	48(5)													48(5)
Bearer form	48(6)													48(6)
Guarantor for issuer	48(7)													48(7)
Rights of holder	49(1)		48(1)	107(3)	45(1)	47(1)	87(1)		49(1)	49(1)			45(1)	49(1)
Maximum fee for certificate by regulation	49(2)	54(5)	48(2)	107(3)	45(2)	47(2)	87(2)		49(2)	49(2)			45(2)	49(2)
Joint holders	49(3)	54(6)	48(3)	108	45(3)	47(3)	87(3)		49(3)	49(3)		63	45(3)	49(3)
Signatures	49(4)	55(1), 55(2)	48(4), 48(5)	110(1), 110(2)	45(4)	47(4)	87(4)		49(4), 49(5)	49(4), 49(5)		62	45(4)	49(4)
Continuation of signature	49(6)	55(3)	48(6)	110(3)	45(6)	47(6)	87(6)		49(6)	49(6)			45(6)	49(6)
Contents of share certificate	49(7)	56(1)	48(7)	57(1)	45(7)	47(7)	88		49(7)	49(7)		63, 65	45(7)	49(7)
Restrictions	49(8)				45(9)									49(8)
Limit on restriction	49(9)	*42(1)*	48(9)				91		49(9)	49(9)			45(8.1)	49(9)
Notation of constraint	49(10)	56(8)					90(1)		49(11)	49(11)			45(8.2)	
Failure to note	49(11)						90(2)		49(12)	49(12)			45(8.3)	
Transitional	49(12)				45(10)	47(9)			49(10)	49(10)				49(10)
Particulars of class	49(13)	56(2)	48(10)		45(11)	47(10)	92(1)		49(13)	49(13)		*65*	45(10)	49(11)
Duty	49(14)	56(7)	48(11)	*57(4)*	45(12)	47(11)	92(2)		49(14)	49(14)			45(11)	49(12)
Fractional share	49(15)	57(1)	48(12)	*69(1)*	45(13)	47(12)	93(1)		49(15)	49(15)		51	45(12)	49(13)
Scrip certificates	49(16)	57(2)	48(13)		45(14)	47(13)	93(2)		49(16)	49(16)			45(13)	49(14)
Holder of fractional share	49(17)	57(3)	48(14)	*69(2)*	45(15)	47(14)	94		49(17)	49(17)		51	45(14)	49(15)

	CAN	ON	AB	BC	MB	NB	NL	NS	NU	NWT	PE	QC	SK	YK
Holder of scrip certificate	49(18)	57(4)	48(15)		45(16)	47(15)	95		49(18)	49(18)			45(15)	49(16)
Securities records	50(1)	*141(1)*	49(1)	111(1)	46(1)	48(1)	96	Third Sched., s. 11(1)	50(1)	50(1)	50	33	46(1)	50(1)
Central and branch registers	50(2)	142(a)	49(3)	111(3)	46(2)	48(2)	97	Third Sched., s. 11(2)	50(2)	50(2)			46(2)	50(2)
Place of register	50(3)	143(1)	21(2)	111(4)	46(3)	48(3)	98	Third Sched., s. 11(3)	21(3)	21(3)			46(3)	23(2)
Effect of registration	50(4)	143(2)	49(4)	111(5)	46(4)		99		50(3)	50(3)			46(4)	50(3)
Branch register	50(5)	143(3)	49(5)	111(6)	46(5)	48(4)	100(1)	Third Sched., s. 11(4)	50(4)	50(4)			46(5)	50(4)
Central register	50(6)	143(4)	49(6)	111(7)	46(6)	48(5)	100(2)	Third Sched., s. 11(5)	50(5)	50(5)			46(6)	50(5)
Destruction of certificates	50(7)	143(5)	49(7)		46(7)	48(6)	101		50(6)	50(6)			46(7)	50(6)
Dealings with registered holder	51(1)	67(1)	50(1)		47(1)	49(1)	102(1)		51(1)	51(1)			47(1)	51(1)
Constructive registered holder	51(2)	67(2)	50(2)	*115, 118*	47(2)	49(2)	102(2)		51(2)	51(2)	49		47(2)	51(2)
Permissible registered holder	51(3)	67(3)	50(3)	*115*	47(3)		102(3)		51(3)	51(3)			47(3)	51(3)
Immunity of corporation	51(4)	67(4)	50(4)		47(4)	49(5)	103		51(4)	51(4)			47(4)	51(4)
Persons less than 18 years of age	51(5)	67(5)	50(5)		47(5)		104		51(5)	51(5)			47(5)	51(5)

	CAN	ON	AB	BC	MB	NB	NL	NS	NU	NWT	PE	QC	SK	YK
Joint holders	51(6)	67(6)	50(6)		47(6)	49(6)	105		51(6)	51(6)			47(6)	51(6)
Transmission of securities	51(7)	67(7)	50(7)	*118*	47(7)	49(7)	106(1)		51(7)	51(7)			47(7)	51(7)
Excepted transmissions	51(8)	67(8)	50(8)		47(8)	49(8)	106(2)	41(3)	51(8)	51(8)			47(8)	51(8)
Right of corporation	51(9)	67(9)	50(9)	*119*	47(9)	49(9)	106(3)	41(4)	51(9)	51(9)			47(9)	51(9)
Overissue	52(1)													52(1)
Retroactive validation	52(2)	58(1)	51(1)		48(1)		107(1)		52(1)	52(1)			48(1)	52(2)
Payment not a purchase or redemption	52(3)	58(2)	51(3)		48(3)		107(3)		52(3)	52(3)			48(3)	52(4)
Burden of proof	53													53
Securities fungible	54													54
Issue — Issuer														
Notice of defect	55(1)													55(1)
Purchaser for value	55(2)													55(2)
Lack of genuineness	55(3)													55(3)
Ineffective defences	55(4)													55(4)
Staleness as notice of defect	56													56
Unauthorized signature	57													57
Completion or alteration	58(1)													58(1)

	CAN	ON	AB	BC	MB	NB	NL	NS	NU	NWT	PE	QC	SK	YK
Enforceability	58(2)													58(2)
Warranties of agents	59(1)													59(1)
Limitation of liability	59(2)													59(2)
Purchase														
Title of purchaser	60(1)													60(1)
Title of *bona fide* purchaser	60(2)													60(2)
Limitation of the purchase	60(3)													60(3)
Deemed notice of adverse claim	61(1)													61(1)
Notice of fiduciary duty	61(2)													61(2)
Staleness as notice of adverse claim	62													62
Warranties to issuer	63(1)													63(1)
Warranties to purchaser	63(2)													63(2)
Warranties of intermediary	63(3)													63(3)
Warranties of pledgee	63(4)													63(4)
Warranties of broker	63(5)													63(5), 63(6), 63(7)

	CAN	ON	AB	BC	MB	NB	NL	NS	NU	NWT	PE	QC	SK	YK
Right to compel endorsement	64													64
Definition of "appropriate person"	65(1)													65(1)
Determining "appropriate person"	65(2)													65(2)
Endorsement	65(3)													65(3)
Special or blank	65(4)													65(4)
Blank endorsement	65(5)													65(5)
Special endorsement	65(6)													65(6)
Right of holder	65(7)													65(7)
Immunity of endorser	65(8)													65(8)
Partial endorsement	65(9)													65(9)
Failure of fiduciary to comply	65(10)													65(10)
Effect of endorsement without delivery	66													66
Endorsement in bearer form	67													67
Effect of unauthorized endorsement	68(1)													68
Liability of issuer	68(2)													

	CAN	ON	AB	BC	MB	NB	NL	NS	NU	NWT	PE	QC	SK	YK
Warranties of guarantor of signature	69(1)													69(1)
Limitation of liability	69(2)													69(2)
Warranties of guarantor of endorsement	69(3)													69(3)
Extent of liability	69(4)													69(4)
Constructive delivery of a security	70(1)													70(1)
Constructive ownership	70(2)													70(2)
Ownership of part of fungible bulk	70(3)													70(3)
Notice to broker	70(4)													70(4)
Delivery of security	71(1)													71(1)
Duty to deliver	71(2)													71(2)
Delivery to broker	71(3)													71(3)
Right to reclaim possession	72(1)													72(1)
Recovery if unauthorized endorsement	72(2)													72(2)
Remedies	72(3)													72(3)
Right to requisites for registration	73(1)													73(1)
Rescission of transfer	73(2)													73(2)

	CAN	ON	AB	BC	MB	NB	NL	NS	NU	NWT	PE	QC	SK	YK
Seizure of security	74													74
No liability for acts in good faith	75													75
Registration														
Duty to register transfer	76(1)													76(1)
Liability for delay	76(2)													76(2)
Assurance that endorsement effective	77(1)													77(1)
Definition of "guarantee of the signature"	77(2)													77(2)
Standards	77(3)													77(3)
Definition of "evidence of appointment or incumbency"	77(4)					*49(3)*								77(4)
Standards	77(5)													77(5)
No notice to issuer	77(6)													77(6)
Notice from excess documentation	77(7)													77(7)
Limited duty of inquiry	78(1)													78(1)
Discharge of duty	78(2)													78(2)
Inquiry into adverse claims	78(3)													78(3)
Duration of notice	78(4)													78(4)

	CAN	ON	AB	BC	MB	NB	NL	NS	NU	NWT	PE	QC	SK	YK
Limitation of issuer's liability	79(1)													79(1)
Duty of issuer in default	79(2)													79(2)
Notice of lost or stolen security	80(1)			*109*										80(1)
Duty of issuer to issue a new security	80(2)													80(2)
Duty to register transfer	80(3)													80(3)
Right of issuer to recover	80(4)													80(4)
Rights and obligations	81(1)													81(1)
Notice to agent or mandatary	81(2)													81(2)
TRUST INDENTURES														
"event of default"	82(1)	46(1)	81(1)	90	77(1)		145		82(1)	82(1)			77(1)	82(1)
"trustee"	82(1)	46(1)	81(1)	90	77(1)		145		82(1)	82(1)			77(1)	82(1)
"trust indenture"	82(1)	46(1)	81(1)	90	77(1)		145		82(1)	82(1)			77(1)	82(1)
Application	82(2)	*46(2)*	81(2)	*91(1), 91(2)*	77(2)		146(1)		82(2)	82(2)			77(2)	82(2)
Exemption	82(3)	46(4)		*91(3)*			146(2)							
Conflict of interest	83(1)	48(1)	82(1)	92(2)	78(1)		147(1)		83(1)	83(1)			78(1)	83(1)
Eliminating conflict of interest	83(2)	48(2)	82(2)	92(3)	78(2)		147(2)		83(2)	83(2)			78(2)	83(2)
Validity	83(3)	48(3)	82(3)	92(4)	78(3)		147(3)		83(3)	83(3)			78(3)	83(3)
Removal of trustee	83(4)	48(4)	82(4)	92(5)	78(4)		147(4)		83(4)	83(4)			78(4)	83(4)

	CAN	ON	AB	BC	MB	NB	NL	NS	NU	NWT	PE	QC	SK	YK
Qualification of trustee	84	46(3)	83	92(1)	79		148		84	84			79	84
List of security holders	85(1)	52(1)	84(1)	93(1)	80(1)		149(1)		85(1)	85(1)			80(1)	85(1)
Duty of issuer	85(2)	52(2)	84(2)	94	80(2)		149(2)		85(2)	85(2)			80(2)	85(2)
Corporate applicant	85(3)	52(4)	84(3)		80(3)		149(3)		85(4)	85(4)			80(3)	85(3)
Contents of statutory declaration	85(4)	52(3)	84(4)	93(2)	80(4)		149(4)		85(3)	85(3)			80(4)	85(4)
Use of list	85(5)	52(5)	84(5)	93(4)	80(5)		149(5)		85(5)	85(5)			80(5)	85(5)
Offence	85(6)	258(1)(b)	84(6)		80(6)				85(6)	85(6)			80(6)	85(6)
Evidence of compliance	86(1)	49(1)	85(1)	95	81(1)		150(1)		86(1)	86(1)			81(1)	86(1)
Duty of issuer or guarantor	86(2)		85(2)	95	81(2)		150(2)		86(2)	86(2)			81(2)	86(2)
Contents of declaration, etc.	87	49(2)	86	96	82		151		87	87			82	87
Further evidence of compliance	88	49(3)	87	96(d)	83		152		88	88			83	88
Trustee may require evidence of compliance	89(1)	49(5)	88(1)	97(1)	84(1)		153		89(1)	89(1)			84(1)	89(1)
Certificate of compliance	89(2)	49(4)	88(2)	97(2)	84(2)		154		89(2)	89(2)			84(2)	89(2)
Notice of default	90	51(1), *51(2)*	89	98	85		155		90	90			85	90

	CAN	ON	AB	BC	MB	NB	NL	NS	NU	NWT	PE	QC	SK	YK
Duty of care	91	47(1)	90	99	86		156		91	91			86	91
Reliance on statements	92	49(6)	91	100	87		157		92	92			87	92
No exculpation	93	47(2)	92	101	88		158		93	93			88	93
RECEIVERS, RECEIVER-MANAGERS AND SEQUESTRATORS														
Functions of receiver or sequestrator	94		93		89	52	159	71	94	94				94
Functions of receiver-manager	95		94		90	53	160	72	95	95				95
Directors' powers cease	96		95	105	91	54	161	73	96	96			91	96
Duty to act	97		95		92	55	162	74	97	97				97
Duty under instrument or act	98		97		93	56	163	75	98	98				98
Duty of care	99		98		94	57	164	76	99	99				99
Directions given by court	100		99		95	58	165	77	100	100				100

	CAN	ON	AB	BC	MB	NB	NL	NS	NU	NWT	PE	QC	SK	YK
Duties of receiver, receiver-manager or sequestrator	101		100	106	96(1)	59	166	78	101(1)	101(1)				101
DIRECTORS AND OFFICERS														
Duty to manage or supervise management	102(1)	115(1)	101(1)	136(1)	97(1)	60(1)	167		102(1)	102(1)	21(1), 28	112	97(1)	102(1)
Number of directors	102(2)	115(2), 115(3)	101(2)	120	97(2)	60(2), 60(3)	168	93	102(2), 102(3)	102(2), 102(3)	21(2)	106	97(2)	102(2)
By-laws	103(1)	116(1)	102(1)		98(1)	61(1)	170(1)		103(1)	103(1)		113	98(1)	103(1)
Shareholder approval	103(2)	116(2)	102(2)		98(2)	61(2)	170(2)		103(2)	103(2)		113	98(2)	103(2)
Effective date	103(3)	116(3)	102(3)		98(3)	61(3)	170(3)		103(3)	103(3)		113	98(3)	103(3)
Idem (rejection)	103(4)	116(4)	102(4)		98(4)	61(4)	170(4)		103(4)	103(4)		114	98(4)	103(4)
Shareholder proposal	103(5)	*116(5)*	102(5)		98(5)	61(5)	170(5)		103(5)	103(5)			98(5)	103(5)
Organization meeting	104(1)	117(1)	104(1)		99(1)	62(1)	171(1)		105(1)	105(1)		11	99(1)	105(1)
Exception	104(2)	117(3)	104(2)		99(2)	62(2)	171(3)		105(2)	105(2)			99(1.1)	105(2)
Calling meeting	104(3)	117(4)	104(3)		99(3)	62(3)	171(2)		105(3)	105(3)		11	99(2)	105(3)
Qualifications of directors	105(1)	118(1)	105(1)	124(1), 124(2)	100(1)	63(1)	172		106(1)	106(1)		108	100(1)	106(1)
Further qualifications	105(2)	118(2)	105(2)	125	100(2)	63(2)	173		106(2)	106(2)	23	109	100(2)	106(2)
Residency etc.	105(3) 105(3.1) 105(3.2) 105(3.3) 105(4)	118(3)	105(3)		100(3) 100(3.1)		174(1), 174(3), 174(4)						100(3), 100(3.1)	

	CAN	ON	AB	BC	MB	NB	NL	NS	NU	NWT	PE	QC	SK	YK
Notice of directors	106(1)		106(1)			64(1)	175(1)	*94*	107(1)	107(1)			101(1)	107(1)
Term of office	106(2)	119(1)	106(2)	*121(1)*	101(1)	64(2)	175(2)		107(2)	107(2)	*22*	107	101(2)	107(2)
Election of directors	106(3)	119(4)	106(3)		101(2)		175(3)	*First Sched., Table A, ss. 116–120*	107(3)	107(3)	*24*	110	101(3)	107(3)
Staggered terms	106(4)	119(5)	106(5)		101(3)		175(4)		107(4)	107(4)		110	101(4)	107(5)
No stated terms	106(5)	119(6)	106(6)		101(4)		175(5)		107(5)	107(5)		110	101(5)	107(6)
Incumbent directors	106(6)	119(7)	106(7)		101(5)	64(3)	175(6)		107(6)	107(6)	*26*		101(6)	107(7)
Vacancy among candidates	106(7)	119(8)	106(8)		101(6)	64(4)	175(7)		107(7)	107(7)		110	101(7)	107(8)
Appointment of directors	106(8)	*124(2)*	106(4)	122(2), 122(3)					112(6)	112(6)		153	101(9)	107(4)
Election or appointment as director	106(9)	119(9), 119(10), 119(11)	105(5)	122(4), *123*		63(3)			106(3)	106(3)			101(10)	106(3)
Cumulative voting	107	120	107		102	65, 70(2)	176		108	108		111	102	108
Ceasing to hold office	108(1)	121(1)	108(1)	128(1)	103(1)	66(1)	177		109(1)	109(1)		142	103(1)	109(1)
Effective date of resignation	108(2)	121(2)	108(2)	128(2)	103(2)	66(2)	178		109(2)	109(2)		142	103(2)	109(2)
Removal of directors	109(1)	122(1)	109(1)	128(3)	104(1)	67(1)	179(1)	*First Sched., Table A, s. 114(d)*	110(1)	110(1)		144	104(1)	110(1)

	CAN	ON	AB	BC	MB	NB	NL	NS	NU	NWT	PE	QC	SK	YK
Exception	109(2)	122(2)	109(2)	128(4)	104(2)	67(2)	179(2)		110(2)	110(2)		144	104(2)	110(2)
Vacancy	109(3)	122(3)	109(3)	130	104(3)	67(3)	179(3)		110(3)	110(3)		144	104(3)	110(3)
Resignation (or removal)	109(4)	115(4)			114.1(1)									
Exception	109(5)	115(5)			114.1(2)									
Attendance at meeting	110(1)	123(1)	110(1)		105(1)	68	180(1)		111(1)	111(1)		*150*	105(1)	111(1)
Statement of director	110(2)	123(2)	110(2)		105(2)		180(2)		111(2)	111(2)		*150*	105(2)	111(2)
Circulating statement	110(3)	123(3)	110(3)		105(3)		180(3)		111(3)	111(3)			105(3)	111(3)
Immunity	110(4)	123(4)	110(4)		105(4)		180(4)		111(4)	111(4)			105(4)	111(4)
Filling vacancy	111(1)	124(1)	111(1)	*130, 131*	106(1)	69(1)	181(1)		112(1)	112(1)	*25(e)*	145	106(1)	112(1)
Calling meeting	111(2)	124(3)	111(2)	134(1)	106(2)	69(2)	181(2)		112(2)	112(2)		146	106(2)	112(2)
Class director	111(3)	124(4)	111(3)	132	106(3)	69(3)	181(3)		112(3)	112(3)		147	106(3)	112(3)
Shareholders filling vacancy	111(4)	124(5)	111(4)	*131(a)(ii), 132*	106(4)	69(4)	181(4)		112(4)	112(4)		148	106(4)	112(4)
Unexpired term	111(5)	124(6)	111(5)	133	106(5)	69(5)	181(5)		112(5)	112(5)		149	106(5)	112(5)
Number of directors	112(1)	125(1)	112(1)		107	70(1)	182(1)		113(1)	113(1)	*27*	151, 152	107(1)	113(1)
Election of directors where articles amended	112(2)		112(2)				182(2)		113(2)	113(2)			107(2)	113(2)
Notice of change of director or director's address	113(1)		113(1)	127	108(1)	71(1)	183(1)	*98(1), 98(2)*	114(1)	114(1)			108(1)	114(1)
Director's change of address	113(1.1)		113(1.1)											

	CAN	ON	AB	BC	MB	NB	NL	NS	NU	NWT	PE	QC	SK	YK
Application to court	113(2)		113(2)		108(2)	71(2)	183(2)		114(2)	114(2)			108(2)	114(2)
Meeting of directors	114(1)	*126(1), 126(2)*	114(1)		109(1)	72(1), 72(2)	184(1)	*First Sched., Table A, ss. 129–134*	115(1)	115(1)		134	109(1)	115(1)
Quorum	114(2)	*126(3), 126(4), 126(5)*	114(2)		109(2)	72(3)	184(2)	*First Sched., Table A, s. 129*	115(2)	115(2)		138	109(2)	115(2)
Canadian directors present at meetings	114(3)		114(3)		109(3)		184(3)						109(3)	
Exception	114(4)		114(4)		109(4)		184(4)						109(4)	
Notice of meeting	114(5)	*126(8), 126(9)*	114(5)		109(5)		185(1)		115(3)	115(3)		135	109(5)	115(3)
Waiver of notice	114(6)	126(10)	114(6)		109(6)	72(5)	185(2)		115(4)	115(4)		136	109(6)	115(4)
Adjournment	114(7)	126(11)	114(7)		109(7)	72(6)	186		115(5)	115(5)		141	109(7)	115(5)
One director meeting	114(8)	126(12)	114(8)	140(4)	109(8)	72(7)	187		115(6)	115(6)		140	109(8)	115(6)
Participation	114(9)	126(13)	114(9)	140(1), 140(2)	109(9), 109(10)	72(8)	188(1), 188(2)		115(7)	115(7)		137	109(9)	115(7)
Delegation	115(1)	127(1)	115(1)		110(1)	73(1)	189(1)		116(1)	116(1)			110(1)	116(1)
Limits on authority	115(3)	127(3)	115(3)		110(3)	73(2)	189(3)		116(2)	116(2)		118	110(3)	116(2)
Validity of acts of directors and officers	116	128	116(1)	143	111	74	190	97	117	117			111	117

	CAN	ON	AB	BC	MB	NB	NL	NS	NU	NWT	PE	QC	SK	YK
Resolution in lieu of meeting	117(1)	129(1)	117(1)	140(3)	112(1)	75(1)	191(1)	91(1)	118(1)	118(1)		140	112(1)	118(1)
Filing resolution	117(2)	129(2)	117(3)	140(6)	112(2)	75(2)	191(2)	91(2)	118(2)	118(2)		140	112(2)	118(2)
Evidence	117(3)													
Directors' liability	118(1)	130(1)	118(1)	*154(2)*	113(1)	76(1)	192		119(1)	119(1)	*83, 88.7*	155	113(1)	119(1)
Further directors' liabilities	118(2)	130(2)	118(3)	154(1)	113(2)	76(2)	193		119(3)	119(3)		156	113(2)	119(3)
Contribution	118(3)	130(3)	118(4)	156(1)	113(3)	76(3)	194		119(4)	119(4)			113(3)	119(4)
Recovery	118(4)	130(4)	118(5)		113(4)	76(4)	195(1)		119(5)	119(5)		157	113(4)	119(5)
Order of court	118(5)	130(5)	118(6)	156(2)	113(5)	76(5)	195(2)		119(6)	119(6)		157	113(5)	119(6)
No liability	118(6)	130(6)	118(7)	154(4)	113(6)	76(6)	196	*153*	119(7)	119(7)		155	113(6)	120(1)
Limitation	118(7)		118(9)	154(9)	113(7)	76(7)	197		119(8)	119(8)			113(7)	120(3)
Liability of directors for wages	119(1)	131(1)	119(1)		114(1)				120(1)	120(1)		154	114	121(1)
Conditions precedent to liability	119(2)	131(2)	119(3)		114(2)				120(3)	120(3)		154		
Limitation	119(3)		119(4)		114(3)				120(4)	120(4)				
Amount due after execution	119(4)	131(3)	119(5)		114(4)				120(5)	120(5)				
Subrogation of director	119(5)	131(4)	119(6)		114(5)				120(6)	120(6)				121(2)
Contribution	119(6)	131(5)	119(7)		114(6)				120(7)	120(7)				121(3)
Disclosure of interest	120(1)	132(1)	120(1)	*147 to 153*	115(1)	77(1)	198(1)	*99*	121(1)	121(1)		122	115(1)	122(1)

	CAN	ON	AB	BC	MB	NB	NL	NS	NU	NWT	PE	QC	SK	YK
Time of disclosure for director	120(2)	132(2)	120(2)	*147 to 153*	115(2)	77(2)	198(2)		121(2)	121(2)		124	115(2)	122(2)
Time of disclosure for officer	120(3)	132(3)	120(4)	*147 to 153*	115(3)	77(3)	198(3)		121(4)	121(4)		125	115(3)	122(3)
Time of disclosure for director or officer	120(4)	132(4)	120(5)	*147 to 153*	115(4)	77(4)	198(4)		121(5)	121(5)		126	115(4)	122(4)
Voting	120(5)	132(5)	120(6)	*149(2)*	115(5)	77(5)	198(5)		121(6)	121(6)		127	115(5)	122(5)
Continuing disclosure	120(6)	132(6)	*120(7)*	*147 to 153*	115(6)	77(6)	199		121(7)	121(7)		*123*	115(6)	122(6)
Access to disclosures	120(6.1)													
Avoidance standards	120(7)	132(7)	120(8)	*148(1), 148(2)*	115(7)	77(7)	200		121(8)	121(8)			115(7)	122(7)
Confirmation by shareholders	120(7.1)	132(8)	120(8.1)	*148(1), 148(2)*									*115(8.1)*	
Application to court	120(8)	132(9)	120(9)	*150*	115(8)	77(8)	201		121(9)	121(9)		131	115(8)	122(8)
Officers	121	133	121	141(1), 141(2)	116	78	202		122	122		116	116	123
Duty of care of directors and officers	122(1)	134(1)	122(1)	142(1)(a), 142(1)(b)	117(1)	79(1)	203(1)		123(1)	123(1)		119	117(1)	124(1)
Duty to comply	122(2)	134(2)	122(2)	142(1)(c), 142(1)(d)	117(2)	79(2)	203(2)		123(2)	123(2)			117(2)	124(2)
No exculpation	122(3)	134(3)	122(3)	142(3)	117(3)	79(3)	203(3)		123(3)	123(3)		120	117(3)	124(3)
Dissent	123(1)	135(1)	123(1)	154(5)	118(1)	80(1)	204(1)		124(1)	124(1)		139	118(1)	125(1)
Loss of right to dissent	123(2)	135(2)	123(2)	154(6)	118(2)	80(2)	204(2)		124(2)	124(2)		139	118(2)	125(2)
Dissent of absent director	123(3)	135(3)		154(7), 154(8)	118(3)		204(3)					139	118(3)	

	CAN	ON	AB	BC	MB	NB	NL	NS	NU	NWT	PE	QC	SK	YK
Defence — reasonable diligence	123(4)	135(4)	123(3)	157(1)	118(4)								*117(4)*	
Defence — good faith	123(5)			157(1)	118(5)	80(3)			124(3)	124(3)		121	118(4)	125(3)
Indemnification	124(1)	136(1)	124(1)	*160, 163*	119(1)	81(1)	205(1)	*First Sched., Table A, s. 204*	125(1)	125(1)	64	159	119(1)	126(1)
Advance of costs	124(2)	136(2)	124(3.1)	*162*								159	119(2)	
Limitation	124(3)	136(3), 136(4)	124(1)	*163*	119(1)	81(1)	205(2)		125(1)	125(1)		159	119(1)	126(1)
Indemnification in derivative actions	124(4)	136(4.1)	124(2)		119(2)	81(2)	206		125(2)	125(2)		161	119(3)	126(2)
Right to indemnity	124(5)	136(4.2)	124(3)		119(3)	81(3)	207		125(3)	125(3)			119(4)	126(3)
Insurance	124(6)	136(4.3)	124(4)	165	119(4)	81(4)	208		125(4)	125(4)		162	119(5)	126(4)
Application to court	124(7)	136(5)	124(5)	*164*	119(5)	81(5)	209(1)		125(5)	125(5)			119(6)	126(5)
Notice to Director	124(8)				119(6)	81(6)	209(2)		125(6)	125(6)			119(7)	
Other notice	124(9)	136(6)	124(6)		119(7)	81(7)	209(3)		125(6)	125(6)			119(8)	126(6)
Remuneration	125	137	125(1)		120	82	210	*First Sched., Table A, s. 111*	126(1)	126(1)		117	120	127(1)
INSIDER TRADING														
"business combination"	126(1)	138(4)	129		125(4)	83(4)	212(3)		127(1)	127(1)			123	131
"insider"	126(1)	138(1)	126(b)	192(1)	125(1)	83(1)	211(1)		127(1)	127(1)			121	128
"officer"	126(1)								127(1)	127(1)				

Table of Concordance of Business Corporations Acts

	CAN	ON	AB	BC	MB	NB	NL	NS	NU	NWT	PE	QC	SK	YK
"share" "voting share" (AB, YK)	126(1)		126(c)				211(2)		127(1)	127(1)				128
Further interpretation	126(2)	138(2)	127		125(2)	83(2)	212(1)		127(2)	127(2)			122(1)	129
Prohibition of short sale	130(1)													
Calls and puts	130(2)													
Exception	130(3)													
Offence	130(4)													
Definitions — "insider"	131(1)	138(1)	126(b)	192(1)	125(1)	83(1)	211(1)		127(1)	127(1)			121	128
Expanded definition of "security"	131(2)													
Deemed insiders	131(3), 131(3.1)				*125(3)*									
Insider trading — compensation to persons	131(4)	*138(5)(a)*	130(1)(a)	192(2), 192(3)(a)	125(5)(a)	83(5)	213(a)		128(1)(a)	128(1)(a)			124	132(1)
Insider trading — compensation to corporation	131(5)	138(5)(b)	130(1)(b)	192(3)(b)	125(5)(b)		213(b)		128(1)(b)	128(1)(b)			124	132(1)
Tipping — compensation to persons	131(6)													
Tipping — compensation to corporation	131(7)													
Measure of damages	131(8)													
Liability	131(9)													
Limitation	131(10)		130(2)	192(4)	125(6)	83(6)	214		128(2)	128(2)			125	132(2)
SHAREHOLDERS														
Place of meetings	132(1)	93(1)	131(1)	166	126(1)	84(1)	215(1)		133(1)	133(1)		164	126(1)	133(1)

	CAN	ON	AB	BC	MB	NB	NL	NS	NU	NWT	PE	QC	SK	YK
Meeting outside Canada / province	132(2)	93(1)	131(2), *131(4)*	166	126(2), *126(3)*	84(2), *84(3)*	215(2), 216		133(2)	133(2)		164	126(2), 126(3)	133(2)
Exception	132(3)		131(2)		126(2)	84(2)	215(3)		133(2)	133(2)			126(2)	133(2)
Participation in meeting by electronic means	132(4)	*93(2)*, 94(2)	131(3)		126(4), 126(5)	85(3)			133(3)	133(3)			126(2.1)	133(3)
Meeting held by electronic means	132(5)		131(3.1)		126.1									
Calling annual meetings	133(1)	94(1)(a)	132(1)(a)	182(1)	127(a)	85(1)(a)	217(a)	83(1)	134(1)(a)	134(1)(a)		163	127	134(1)
Calling special meetings	133(2)	94(1)(b)	132(1)(b)		127(b)	85(1)(b)	217(b)	*84*	134(1)(b)	134(1)(b)		207	127	134(1)
Order to delay calling of annual meeting	133(3)		132(2)	*182(2)*		85(2)			134(2)	134(2)				134(2)
Fixing record date	134(1)	95(1)	133(1)	171(1), *171(2)*	128(1)	86(1)	218(1)		135(1)	135(1)		169	128(1)	135(1)
No record date fixed	134(2)	95(3)	133(3)	171(3)	128(3)	86(3)	219		135(3)	135(3)			128(3)	135(3)
When record date fixed	134(3)	95(4)	133(4)		128(4)		220		135(4)	135(4)			128(4)	135(4)
Notice of meeting	135(1)	96(1)	134(1)	169(1)	129(1)	87(1)	221(1)		136(1)	136(1)	*25*	165	129(1)	136(1)
Exception — not a distributing corporation / shareholders not registered	135(1.1), 135(2)	96(2)	134(3)		129(2)	87(2)	221(2)		136(2)	136(2)			129(2)	136(3)
Adjournment	135(3)	96(3)	134(4)		129(3)		221(3)		136(3)	136(3)		190	129(3)	136(4)
Notice of adjourned meeting	135(4)	96(4)	134(5)		129(4)	87(3)	221(4)		136(4)	136(4)		190	129(4)	136(5)
Business	135(5)	96(5)	134(6)		129(5)	87(4)	222(1)		136(5)	136(5)			129(5)	136(6)
Notice of business	135(6)	96(6)	134(7)		129(6)	87(5)	222(2)		136(6)	136(6)		167	129(6)	136(7)

	CAN	ON	AB	BC	MB	NB	NL	NS	NU	NWT	PE	QC	SK	YK
Waiver of notice	136	98	135	170(1), 170(3)	130	88	223(1), 223(2)		137	137		168	130	137
Proposals	137(1)	99(1)	136(1)	*187*	131(1)	89(1)	224	Third Sched., s. 9(1)	138(2)	138(2)		194	131(1)	138(1)
Persons eligible to make proposals	137(1.1)		136(1.1)(a), 136(1.1)(b)	188(1)								195		
Information to be provided	137(1.2)		136(1.1)(c)	188(1)(d)								196		
Information not part of proposal	137(1.3)		136(1.2)	188(3)										
Proof may be required	137(1.4)													
Information circular	137(2)	99(2)	136(2)		131(2)	89(2)	225(1)	Third Sched., s. 9(2)	138(3)	138(3)			131(2)	138(2)
Supporting statement	137(3)	99(3), 99(3.1)	136(3)	*189(1), 189(2)*	131(3)	89(3)	225(2)	Third Sched., s. 9(3)	138(4)	138(4)		197	131(3)	138(3)
Nomination for director	137(4)	99(4)	136(4)		131(4)	89(4)	226(1), 226(2)	Third Sched., s. 9(4)	138(5)	138(5)		198	131(4)	138(4)
Exemptions	137(5)	99(5)	136(5)	189(5)	131(5)	89(5)	227	Third Sched., s. 9(5)	138(6)	138(6)		200	131(5)	138(5)
Refusal to include proposal / Notice of refusal	137(5.1), 137(7)	99(7)	136(7)	191(1)	131(7)	89(7)	229	Third Sched., s. 9(7)	138(8)	138(8)		201, 203	131(7)	138(7)

	CAN	ON	AB	BC	MB	NB	NL	NS	NU	NWT	PE	QC	SK	YK
Immunity	137(6)	99(6)	136(6)	190	131(6)	89(6)	228	Third Sched., s. 9(6)	138(7)	138(7)		202	131(6)	138(6)
Person may apply to court	137(8)	99(8)	136(8)	191(2), 191(3)	131(8)	89(8)	230	Third Sched., s. 9(8)	138(9)	138(9)		204	131(8)	138(8)
Corporation's application to court	137(9)	99(9)	136(9)	191(4)	131(9)	89(9)	231	Third Sched., s. 9(9)	138(10)	138(10)		205	131(9)	138(9)
Director entitled to notice	137(10)	99(10)			131(10)	89(10)	232	Third Sched., s. 9(10)					131(10)	
List of shareholders entitled to receive notice	138(1)	100(1)	137(1)	*112*	132(1)	90(1)	233(1)		139(1)	139(1)			132(1)	139(1)
Voting list	138(2), 138(3)		137(2), 137(3)		132(2), 132(3)	90(2), 90(3)	233(2), 233(3)						132(2), 132(3)	*139(2), 139(3)*
Entitlement to vote	138(3.1)	100(2)	137(2), 137(3)		132(2), 132(3)	90(2), 90(3)	233(2), 233(3)		139(2)	139(2)			132(2), 132(3)	*139(2), 139(3)*
Examination of list	138(4)	100(4)	137(4)		132(4)	90(4)	234		139(4)	139(4)			132(4)	139(4)
Quorum	139(1)	101(1)	138(1)	172(1)	133(1)	92(1)	235(1)		140(1)	140(1)		176	133(1)	140(1)
Opening quorum sufficient	139(2)	101(2)	138(2)		133(2)	92(2)	235(2)		140(2)	140(2)			133(2)	140(2)
Adjournment	139(3)	101(3)	138(3)	172(2)	133(3)	92(3)	235(3)		140(3)	140(3)		176	133(3)	140(3)
One shareholder meeting	139(4)	101(4)	138(4)	172(3)	133(4)	92(4)	235(4)		140(4)	140(4)		177	133(4)	140(4)
Right to vote	140(1)	102(1)	139(1)	173(1)		93(1)	236		141(1)	141(1)		179	134(1)	141(1)
Representative	140(2)	102(2)	139(2)		134(1)	93(2)	237(1)	86(1)	141(2)	141(2)			134(2)	141(2)

	CAN	ON	AB	BC	MB	NB	NL	NS	NU	NWT	PE	QC	SK	YK
Powers of representative	140(3)	102(3)	139(3)		134(2)	93(3)	237(2)	86(2)	141(3)	141(3)	59		134(3)	141(3)
Joint shareholders	140(4)	102(4)	139(4)		134(3)	93(4)	238(1), 238(2)		141(4)	141(4)		182	134(4)	141(4)
Voting	141(1)	103(1)	140(1)	173(2)	135(1)	94(1)	239(1)		142(1)	142(1)	25	183	135(1)	142(1)
Ballot	141(2)	103(2)	140(2)	173(4)	135(2)	94(2)	239(2)		142(2)	142(2)		183	135(2)	142(2)
Electronic voting	141(3)		140(4)	*174(1), 174(2)*	135(3)							183		
Voting while participat-ing electronically	141(4)		140(5)	*174(1), 174(2)*	135(4)							184		
Resolution in lieu of meeting	142(1)	104(1)	141(1), 141(2)	*180*	136(1)	95(1), 95(2)	240(1)	92(1)	143(1)	143(1)		178	136(1)	143(1), 143(2)
Filing resolution	142(2)	104(2)	141(3)		136(2)	95(3)	240(2)	92(2)	143(2)	143(2)		178	136(2)	143(3)
Evidence	142(3)	103(3)	140(3)	173(3)								185	135(2)	
Requisition of meeting	143(1)	105(1)	142(1)	167(1), 167(2)	137(1)	96(1)	241(1)	84(1)	144(1)	144(1)		208	137(1)	144(1)
Form	143(2)	105(2)	142(2)	*167(3), 167(4)*	137(2)	96(2)	241(2)	84(2)	144(2)	144(2)		208	137(2)	144(2)
Directors calling meeting	143(3)	105(3)	142(3)	*167(5)*	137(3)	96(3)	241(3)	84(4)	144(3)	144(3)		209	137(3)	144(3)
Shareholder calling meeting	143(4)	105(4)	142(4)	167(8)	137(4)	96(4)	241(4)	84(3)	144(4)	144(4)		209	137(4)	144(4)
Procedure	143(5)	105(5)	142(5)	*167(9)*	137(5)	96(5)	241(5)	84(5)	144(5)	144(5)			137(5)	144(5)
Reimbursement	143(6)	105(6)	142(6)	167(10)	137(6)	96(6)	241(6)		144(6)	144(6)		210	137(6)	144(6)
Meeting called by court	144(1)	106(1)	143(1)	186(1), 186(2)	138(1)	97(1)	242(1)		145(1)	145(1)		193	138(1)	145(1)

	CAN	ON	AB	BC	MB	NB	NL	NS	NU	NWT	PE	QC	SK	YK
Varying quorum	144(2)	106(2)	143(2)	186(3)	138(2)	97(2)	242(2)		145(2)	145(2)		193	138(2)	145(2)
Valid meeting	144(3)	106(3)	143(3)		138(3)	97(3)	242(3)		145(3)	145(3)			138(3)	145(3)
Court review of election	145(1)	107(1)	144(1)		139(1)	98(1)	243(1)		146(1)	146(1)		454	139(1)	146(1)
Powers of court	145(2)	107(2)	144(2)		139(2)	98(2)	243(2)		146(2)	146(2)		455	139(2)	146(2)
Pooling agreement	145.1	108(1)	145	175	140(1)	99(1)	244		147	147			140(1)	147
Unanimous shareholder agreement	146(1)	108(2)	*146(1)*		140(2)	99(2)	245(1)		*148(1)*	*148(1)*		213	140(2)	148(1)
Declaration by single shareholder	146(2)	108(3)			140(3)	99(3)	245(2)					213	140(2.1)	
Constructive party	146(3)	108(4)			140(4)	99(4)	245(3)(a)					218	140(3)	
When no notice given	146(4)	*108(7)(c)*	*146(4)*				245(5)					218		*148(4)*
Rights of shareholder	146(5)	108(5)	146(7)		140(5)	99(5)	245(8)		148(7)	148(7)		214	140(4)	148(7)
Discretion of shareholders	146(6)	108(5.1)										220		
PROXIES														
"form of proxy"	147	109	147(a)		141		246(1)(a)	85A(b)	149	149			141(a)	149
"intermediary"	147													
"proxy"	147	109	147(b)	1	141		246(1)(b)	85A(d)	149	149			141(b)	149
"solicit" or "solicitation"	147	109	147(d)		141		246(1)(d) 246(2)	85A(e)	149	149			141(d)	149
"solicitation by or on behalf of the management of a corporation"	147	109	147(e)		141		246(1)(e)	85A(f)	149	149			141(e)	149

	CAN	ON	AB	BC	MB	NB	NL	NS	NU	NWT	PE	QC	SK	YK
Appointing proxyholder	148(1)	110(1)	148(1)		142(1)	91(1)	247(1)	85B(1)	150(1)	150(1)		170, 171	142(1)	150(1)
Execution or signing of proxy	148(2)	*110(2)*	148(2)		142(2)	91(2)	247(2)	85B(2)	150(2)	150(2)		172	142(2)	150(2)
Validity of proxy	148(3)	*110(2.1)*	148(3)		142(3)	91(3)	247(3)		150(3)	150(3)			142(3)	150(3)
Revocation of proxy	148(4)	110(4), 110(4.1)	148(4)		142(4)	91(4)	248	85B(4)	150(4)	150(4)			142(4)	150(4)
Deposit of proxies	148(5)	110(5)	148(5)		142(5)	91(5)	249	85B(5)	150(5)	150(5)		167	142(5)	150(5)
Mandatory solicitation	149(1)	111	149(1)		143(1)		250	85C	151(1)	151(1)			143(1)	151(1)
Exception	149(2)		*149(2)*		143(2)				151(2)	151(2)			143(2)	151(2)(a)
Offence	149(3)	258(1)(c)	149(4)		143(3)				151(4)	151(4)			143(3)	151(4)
Officers, etc. of corporations	149(4)	258(2)	149(5)		143(4)				151(5)	151(5)			143(4)	151(5)
Soliciting proxies	150(1)	112(1)	150(1)		144(1)		251	85D(1)	152(1)	152(1)			144(1)	152(1)
Exception	150(1.1), 150(1.2)	112(1.1), 112(1.2)	150(2)						152(2)	152(2)				*152(2)*
Copy to Director	150(2)	112(2)	150(3)		144(2)		252	85D(2)	152(3)	152(3)			144(2)	152(3)
Offence	150(3)	258(1)(d)	150(4)		144(3)				152(4)	152(4)			144(3)	152(4)
Officers, etc. of bodies corporate	150(4)	258(2)	150(5)		144(4)				152(5)	152(5)			144(4)	152(5)
Exemption	151(1)	113	151		145		253	85E	153	153			145	153
Publication	151(2)													
Attendance at meeting	152(1)	114(1)	152(1)		146(1)		254(1)	85F(1)	154(1)	154(1)			146(1)	154(1)
Right of a proxyholder	152(2)	114(2)	152(2)		146(2)		254(2)	85F(2)	154(2)	154(2)			146(1.1)	154(2)

	CAN	ON	AB	BC	MB	NB	NL	NS	NU	NWT	PE	QC	SK	YK
Show of hands	152(3)	114(3)	152(3)		146(3)			85F(3)	154(3)	154(3)			146(1.2)	154(3)
Offence	152(4)	258(1)(e)	152(4)		146(4)		508		154(4)	154(4)			146(2)	154(4)
Duty of intermediary	153(1)		153(1)		147(1)		255(1)		155(1)	155(1)			147(1)	155(1)
Restriction on voting	153(2)		153(2)		147(2)		255(2)		155(2)	155(2)			147(2)	155(2)
Copies	153(3)		153(3)		147(3)		255(3)		155(3)	155(3)			147(3)	155(3)
Instructions to intermediary	153(4)		153(4)		147(4)		255(4)		155(4)	155(4)			147(4)	155(4)
Beneficial owner as proxyholder	153(5)		153(5)		147(5)		255(5)		155(5)	155(5)			147(5)	155(5)
Validity	153(6)		153(6)		147(6)		255(6)		155(6)	155(6)			147(6)	155(6)
Limitation	153(7)		153(7)		147(7)		256		155(7)	155(7)			147(7)	155(7)
Offence	153(8)		153(8)		147(8)		509(1)		155(8)	155(8)			147(8)	155(8)
Officers, etc. of bodies corporate	153(9)		153(9)		147(9)		509(2)		155(9)	155(9)			147(9)	155(9)
Restraining order	154(1)	253(2)	154		148(1)		257(1), 257(2)		156	156			148(1)	156
Notice to Director	154(2)				148(2)		257(3)						148(2)	
FINANCIAL DISCLOSURE														
Annual financial statements	155(1)	154(1)	155(1)	*185, 198(2), 198(3), 198(4)*	149(1)	100(1)	258(1)	121(1)	157(1)	157(1)	*79*	225	149(1)	157
Exception	155(2)		155(2)		149(2)	100(2)	258(2)		157(2)	157(2)			149(2)	

	CAN	ON	AB	BC	MB	NB	NL	NS	NU	NWT	PE	QC	SK	YK
Exemption	156		156(2)		*150(1), 150(2)*		259	*123, 124*	158	158			*150(1), 150(2)*	158
Consolidated statements	157(1)	*157(1)*	157(1)		151(1)	101(1)	260(1)	Third Sched., s. 10(1)	159(1)	159(1)		228	151(1)	159(1)
Examination	157(2)	*157(1)*	157(2)		151(2)	101(2)	260(2)	Third Sched., s. 10(2)	159(2)	159(2)		228	151(2)	159(2)
Barring examination	157(3)	157(2)	157(3)		151(3)	101(3)	260(3)	Third Sched., s. 10(3)	159(3)	159(3)		229	151(3)	159(3)
Notice to Director	157(4)		157(4)		151(4)		260(4)	Third Sched., s. 10(4)	159(4)	159(4)			151(4)	159(4)
Approval of financial statements	158(1)	*159(1)*	158(1)	199(1)	152(1)	102(1)	261(1)	122(2)	160(1)	160(1)		227	152(1)	160(1)
Condition precedent	158(2)	159(2)	158(2)	199(2)	152(2)	102(2)	261(2)	122(3)	160(2)	160(2)		227	152(2)	160(2)
Copies to shareholders	159(1)	154(3)	159(1)	*185(2), 185(3)*	153(1)	103(1)	262	121(3)	161(1)	161(1)			153(1)	161(1)
Offence	159(2)		159(2)		153(3)		510		161(2)	161(2)			153(2)	161(2)
Copies to Director	160(1)		160(1)		154(1)		263(1)		162(1)	162(1)			154(1)	162(1)
Subsidiary corporation exemption	160(2)		160(3)				263(3)		162(3)	162(3)				162(3)
Offence	160(3)		160(4)		154(7)		511		162(4)	162(4)			154(3)	162(4)

	CAN	ON	AB	BC	MB	NB	NL	NS	NU	NWT	PE	QC	SK	YK
Qualification of auditor	161(1)	152(1)	161(1)	206(2)	155(1)	104(1)	264(1)	119A(1)	163(1)	163(1)			155(1)	163(1)
Independence	161(2)	152(2)	161(2)	206(3)	155(2)	104(2)	264(2)	119A(2)	163(2)	163(2)			155(2)	163(2)
Business partners	161(2.1)		161(2.1)											
Duty to resign	161(3)	152(3)	161(3)	208(1), 208(2)	155(3)	104(3)	264(3)	119A(3)	163(3)	163(3)			155(3)	163(3)
Disqualification order	161(4)	152(4)	161(4)	208(3)	155(4)	104(4)	264(4)	119A(4)	163(4)	163(4)			155(4)	163(4)
Exemption order	161(5)		161(5)	208(4)	155(5)	104(5)	264(5)	119A(5)	163(5)	163(5)			155(5)	163(5)
Appointment of auditor	162(1)	149(1)	162(1)	204(2)	156(1)	105(1)	265(1)	117(1)	164(1)	164(1)		231	156(1)	164(1)
Eligibility	162(2)		162(2)		156(2)	105(2)	265(2)		164(2)	164(2)			156(2)	164(2)
Incumbent auditor	162(3)	149(2)	162(3)	204(3)	156(3)	105(5)	265(3)	117(4)	164(3)	164(3)			156(3)	164(3)
Remuneration	162(4)	149(7)	162(4)	207	156(4)	105(4)	265(4)	117(5)	164(4)	164(4)		232	156(4)	164(4)
Dispensing with auditor	163(1)	148(a)	163(1)	203(2)	157(1)		266(1)	118	165(1)	165(1)		239	157(1)	165(1)
Limitation	163(2)	148(b)	163(2)	203(3)	157(2)		266(2)		165(2)	165(2)		239	157(2)	165(2)
Unanimous consent	163(3)		163(3)	203(2)	157(3)		266(3)	118	165(3)	165(3)		239	157(3)	165(3)
Ceasing to hold office	164(1)		164(1)		158(1)	106(1)	257(1)		166(1)	166(1)		234	158(1)	166(1)
Effective date of resignation	164(2)	150	164(2)		158(2)	106(2)	257(2)	117(11)	166(2)	166(2)		235	158(2)	166(2)
Removal of auditor	165(1)	149(4)	165(1)	209(1)(a)	159(1)	107(1)	258(1)	117(6)	167(1)	167(1)		236	159(1)	167(1)
Vacancy	165(2)	149(4)	165(2)	209(1)(b)	159(2)	107(2)	258(2)	117(6)	167(2)	167(2)		236	159(2)	167(2)
Filling vacancy	166(1)		166(1)	204(4)	160(1)	108(1)	259(1)	117(2)	168(1)	168(1)		237	160(1)	168(1)
Calling meeting	166(2)		166(2)		160(2)	108(2)	259(2)		168(2)	168(2)		237	160(2)	168(2)

	CAN	ON	AB	BC	MB	NB	NL	NS	NU	NWT	PE	QC	SK	YK
Shareholders filling vacancy	166(3)		166(3)		160(3)	108(3)	269(3)		168(3)	168(3)		238	160(3)	168(3)
Unexpired term	166(4)		166(4)		160(4)	108(4)	269(4)		168(4)	168(4)			160(4)	168(4)
Court appointed auditor	167(1)	149(8)	167(1)	204(5)	161(1)		270(1)	117(9)	169(1)	169(1)			161(1)	169(1)
Exception	167(2)		167(2)		161(2)		270(2)		169(2)	169(2)			161(2)	169(2)
Right to attend meeting	168(1)	151(1)	168(1)	219(1)	162(1)	109(1)	271	119(1)	170(1)	170(1)			162(1)	170(1)
Duty to attend	168(2)	151(2)	168(2)	214(1), 214(3)	162(2)	109(2)	272(1)	119(2)	170(2)	170(2)		166	162(2)	170(2)
Notice to corporation	168(3)	151(3)	168(3)		162(3)	109(3)	272(2)	119(3)	170(3)	170(3)			162(3)	170(3)
Offence	168(4)	258(1)(h)	168(4)		162(4)		512		170(4)	170(4)			162(4)	170(4)
Statement of auditor	168(5)		168(5)	*209(4), 209(5)*	162(5)	109(5)	273(1)		170(5)	170(5)			162(5)	170(5)
Other statements	168(5.1)		168(5.1)	*209(6)*										
Circulating statement	168(6)		168(6)		162(6)	109(6)	273(2)		170(6)	170(6)			162(6)	170(6)
Replacing auditor	168(7)	151(4)	168(7)	211(1)	162(7)	109(7)	273(3)	119(4)	170(7)	170(7)			162(7)	170(7)
Exception	168(8)	151(5)	168(8)	211(2)	162(8)	109(8)	273(4)	119(5)	170(8)	170(8)			162(8)	170(8)
Effect of non-compliance	168(9)				162(9)	109(9)	273(5)		170(9)	170(9)			162(9)	
Examination	169(1)	153(1)	169(1)	212(1)	163(1)	110(1)	274(1)	119B(1)	171(1)	171(1)			163(1)	171(1)
Reliance on other auditor	169(2)		169(2)	212(2)(a)	163(2)	110(2)	274(2)		171(2)	171(2)			163(2)	171(2)
Reasonableness	169(3)		169(3)		163(3)	110(3)	274(3)		171(3)	171(3)			163(3)	171(3)
Application	169(4)		169(4)	212(2)(b)	163(4)	110(4)	274(4)		171(4)	171(4)			163(4)	171(4)
Right to information	170(1)	153(5)	170(1)	217(1)	164(1)	111(1)	275(1)	119B(6)	172(1)	172(1)		233	164(1)	172(1)

	CAN	ON	AB	BC	MB	NB	NL	NS	NU	NWT	PE	QC	SK	YK
Idem (Information from subsidiaries)	170(2)	153(6)	170(2)	218	164(2)	111(2)	275(2)	119B(7)	172(2)	172(2)		233	164(2)	172(2)
No civil liability	170(3)		170(3)						172(3)	172(3)				
Audit committee	171(1)	158(1)	171(1), 171(2)	224(1), 224(2)	165(1)		276(1)		173(1), 173(2)	173(1), 173(2)			165(1)	173(1), 173(2)
Exemption	171(2)	158(1.1)	171(3)		165(2)		276(2)						165(2)	173(3)
Duty of committee	171(3)	158(2)	171(4)	*225, 226*	165(3)		276(3)		173(3)	173(3)			165(3)	173(4)
Auditor's attendance	171(4)	158(3)	171(5)	224(5)	165(4)		276(4)	*119B(9)*	173(4)	173(4)			165(4)	173(5)
Calling meeting	171(5)	158(4)	171(6)		165(5)		276(5)		173(5)	173(5)			165(5)	173(6)
Notice of errors	171(6)	153(2)	171(7)	216(1)	165(6)		277(1)	119B(3)	173(6)	173(6)			165(6)	173(7)
Error in financial statements	171(7)	153(3)	171(8)	216(3)	165(7)		277(2)	119B(4)	173(7)	173(7)			165(7)	173(8)
Duty of directors	171(8)	153(4)	171(9)	216(4), *216(5)(b)*	165(8)		277(3)	119B(5)	173(8)	173(8)			165(8)	173(9)
Offence	171(9)	*258(1)(j)*	171(10)		165(9)		513		173(9)	173(9)			165(9)	173(10)
Qualified privilege (defamation)	172	151(7)	172	220	166	112	278	119B(7), 119B(8)	174	174			166	174
FUNDAMENTAL CHANGES														
Amendment of articles	173(1)	168(1)	173(1)	*54, 58, 60*	167(1)	113(1)	279(1)	*19, 23*	176(1)	176(1)	*17*	240, 241	167(1)	177(1)
Termination	173(2)	168(3)	173(2)		167(8)	113(2)	279(2)		176(2)	176(2)		241	167(2)	177(2)
Amendment of number name	173(3)	168(4)	173(3)		167(5)(b)	113(3)	279(4)		176(3)	176(3)			167(3)	177(3)

	CAN	ON	AB	BC	MB	NB	NL	NS	NU	NWT	PE	QC	SK	YK
Constraints on shares	174(1)	42(2)	174(1)		168(1)		280(1)		26(1)	26(1)			168(1)	176(2)
Exception	174(2)	42(3)					280(2)		26(2)	26(2)			168(2)	
Limitation on ownership of shares	174(3)	42(4)					280(3)						168(3)	
Change or removal of constraint	174(4)		174(2)		168(2)		280(4)						168(4)	176(3)
Termination	174(5)		174(3)		168(3)		280(5)						168(5)	176(4)
Regulations	174(6)		174(4)		168(4)		281		26(3)	26(3)			168(6)	176(5)
Validity of acts	174(7)		174(5)		168(5)		282		26(4)	26(4)			168(7)	176(6)
Proposal to amend	175(1)	169(1)	175(1)		169(1)	114(1)	283(1)		177(1)	177(1)			169(1)	177(1)
Notice of amendment	175(2)	169(2)	175(2)		169(2)	114(2)	283(2)		177(2)	177(2)			169(2)	177(2)
Class vote	176(1)	170(1)	176(1)		170(1)	115(1)	284(1)		178(1)	178(1)			170(1)	178(1)
Exception	176(2)	170(5)							178(2)	178(2)			170(1.1)	
Deeming provision	176(3)	170(6)							178(3)	178(3)			170(1.2)	
Limitation	176(4)	170(2)	176(2)		170(2)	115(2)	284(2)		178(4)	178(4)			170(2)	178(2)
Right to vote	176(5)	170(3)	176(3)		170(3)	115(3)			178(5)	178(5)			170(3)	178(3)
Separate resolutions	176(6)	170(4)	176(4)		170(4)	115(4)	284(3)		178(6)	178(6)			170(4)	178(4)
Delivery of articles	177(1)	171(1)	177(1)		171(1)	116(1)	285(1)		179(1)	179(1)			171(1)	179(1)
Reduction of stated capital	177(2)	171(2)	177(3)		171(2)	116(2)	285(2)		179(3)	179(3)			171(2)	179(3)
Certificate of amendment	178	172	178		172	117	286(1)		180	180			172	180

	CAN	ON	AB	BC	MB	NB	NL	NS	NU	NWT	PE	QC	SK	YK
Effect of certificate	179(1)		179(1)		173(1)	118(1)	286(2)		181(1)	181(1)		245	173(1)	181(1)
Rights preserved	179(2)		179(2)		173(2)	118(2)	286(3)		181(2)	181(2)			173(2)	181(2)
Restated articles	180(1)	173(1)	180(1)		174(1)	119(1)	287(1)		182(1)	182(1)			174(1)	182(1)
Delivery of articles	180(2)	173(2)	180(3)		174(2)	119(2)	287(2)		182(2)	182(2)			174(2)	182(2)
Restated certificate	180(3)	173(3)	180(4)		174(3)	119(3)	287(3)		182(3)	182(3)			174(3)	182(3)
Effect of certificate	180(4)	173(4)	180(5)		174(4)	119(4)	287(4)		182(4)	182(4)			174(4)	182(4)
Amalgamation	181	174	181	269	175(1)	120	288	134(1)	183	183	77(1)	276	175	183(1)
Amalgamation agreement	182(1)	175(1)	182(1)	270(1), 270(2)	176(1)	121(1)	289(1)	134(2), 134(3)	184(1)	184(1)	77(2)	277	176(1)	184(1)
Cancellation	182(2)	175(2)	182(2)	270(3)	176(2)	121(2)	289(2)		184(2)	184(2)			176(2)	184(2)
Shareholder approval	183(1)	176(1)	183(1)	*271*	177(1)	122(1)	290(1)	134(4)	185(1)	185(1)	77(3)	278	177(1)	185(1)
Notice of meeting	183(2)	176(2)	183(2)		177(2)	122(2)	290(2)		185(2)	185(2)		278	177(2)	185(2)
Right to vote	183(3)	*176(3)*	183(3)		177(3)	122(3)			185(3)	185(3)			177(3)	185(3)
Class vote	183(4)	176(3)	183(4)		177(4)	122(4)	290(3)		185(4)	185(4)			177(4)	185(4)
Shareholder approval	183(5)	176(4)	183(5)		177(5)	122(5)	290(4)	134(4)	185(5)	185(5)		279	177(5)	185(5)
Termination	183(6)	176(5)	183(6)		177(6)	122(6)	290(5)		185(6)	185(6)		280	177(6)	185(6)
Vertical short-form amalgamation	184(1)	177(1)	184(1)	273	178(1)	123(1)	291	134(23)	186(1)	186(1)		282	178(1)	186(1)
Horizontal short-form amalgamation	184(2)	177(2)	184(2)	274	178(2)	123(2)	292	134(24)	186(2)	186(2)		281	178(2)	186(2)
Sending of articles	185(1)	178(1)	185(1)	*275*	179(1)	124(1)	293(1)	134(9)	187(1)	187(1)	*77(4)*	*283*	179(1)	187(1)

	CAN	ON	AB	BC	MB	NB	NL	NS	NU	NWT	PE	QC	SK	YK
Attached declarations	185(2)	178(2)	185(2)		179(2)	124(2)	293(2)	134(10B)	187(2)	187(2)		*284*	179(2)	187(2)
Adequate notice	185(3)	178(3)	185(3)		179(3)	124(3)	293(3)		187(3)	187(3)			179(3)	187(3)
Certificate of amalgamation	185(4)	178(4)	185(4)	*281*	179(4)	124(4)	294(1)	134(10)	187(4)	187(4)		*286*	179(4)	187(4)
Effect of certificate	186	179	186	*282*	180	125	294(2)	*134(11), 134(12)*	188	188	*77(4)*	*286*	180	188
Amalgamation under other federal Acts	186.1													
Continuance (import)	187(1)	180(1)	188(1)	*302, 303*	181(1)	126(1)	295(1)	*133(1)*	190(1)	190(1)	85(1)	288	181(1)	190(1)
Amendments in articles of continuance	187(2)	*180(3)*	188(2)		181(3)	*126(3)*	295(2)		190(2)	190(2)		*289*	181(2)	190(2)
Articles of continuance	187(3)	180(2)	188(3)	*307*	181(4)	126(2)	295(3)					*289*	181(3)	190(3)
Certificate of continuance	187(4)	180(4)	188(4)		181(5)	126(4)	296(1)		190(3)	190(3)	85(3)		181(4)	190(4)
Effect of certificate	187(5)	180(5)	188(5)	*305*	181(7)	126(5)	296(2)	*133(3)*	190(4)	190(4)	85(4)	293	181(5)	190(5)
Copy of certificate	187(6)	180(6)	188(6)		181(8)	126(6)	296(3)		190(6)	190(6)		295	181(6)	190(6)
Rights preserved	187(7)	180(7)	188(7)	*305, 306*	181(9)	126(7)	297(1)	*133(4)*	190(7)	190(7)	85(5)	*294*	181(7)	190(7)
Issued shares	187(8)	180(8)	188(8)		181(10)	126(8)	298(1)		190(8)	190(8)		*296*	181(8)	190(8)
Exception in case of convertible shares	187(9)		188(9)		181(11)		298(2)		190(9)	190(9)			181(9)	190(9)
Definition of "share"	187(10)		188(10)		181(12)	126(9)	298(3)		190(10)	190(10)			181(10)	190(10)
Where continued reference to par value shares permissible	187(11)		188(11)				297(2)		190(11)	190(11)			181(11)	190(11)

	CAN	ON	AB	BC	MB	NB	NL	NS	NU	NWT	PE	QC	SK	YK
Limitation	187(12)		188(12)				297(3)		190(12)	190(12)			181(12) 181(13)	190(12)
Continuance — other jurisdictions	188(1)	181(1)	189(1)	308	182(1)	127(1)	299(1)	133(5)	191(1)	191(1)	86(1)	297	182(1)	191(1)
Continuance — other federal Acts	188(2)													
Notice of meeting	188(3)	181(2)	189(2)		182(4)	127(2)	299(2)		191(2)	191(2)			182(3)	191(2)
Right to vote	188(4)		189(3)		182(5)	127(3)			191(3)	191(3)			182(4)	191(3)
Shareholder approval	188(5)	181(3)(a)	189(4)		182(6)	127(4)	299(3)		191(4)	191(4)	86(2)	298	182(5)	191(4)
Termination	188(6)	181(5)	189(5)		182(7)	127(5)	299(4)		191(5)	191(5)		298	182(6)	191(5)
Discontinuance	188(7)		189(6)		182(8)	127(6)	301(1)	133(7)	191(6)	191(6)	86(4)	*300*	182(7)	191(6)
Notice deemed to be articles	188(8)		189(7)		182(9)		301(3)		191(7)	191(7)			182(7.1)	191(7)
Rights preserved	188(9)	*181(8)*	189(8)	311(3)	182(10)	127(7)	301(2)	133(8)	191(8)	191(8)	86(5)	*300*	182(8)	191(8)
Prohibition	188(10)	181(9)	189(9)	310	182(11)	127(8)	300(2)	133(6)	191(9)	191(9)	86(6)		182(9)	191(9)
Borrowing powers	189(1)	184(1)	103(1)		183(1)		302(1)	Third Sched., s. 13	104(1)	104(1)	78(i)	115	183(1)	
Delegation of borrowing powers	189(2)	184(2)	103(2)		183(2)		302(2)		104(2)	104(2)			183(1.1)	
Extraordinary sale, lease or exchange	189(3)	184(3)	190(1)		183(3)	130(1)	303(1)		192(1)	192(1)			183(2)	192(1)
Notice of meeting	189(4)	184(4)	190(2)		183(4)	130(2)	303(2)		192(2)	192(2)			183(3)	192(2)
Shareholder approval	189(5), 189(8)	184(5), 184(7)	190(3), 190(6)		183(5), 183(7)	130(3), 130(6)	303(3), 303(5)		192(3), 192(6)	192(3), 192(6)			183(4), 183(7)	192(3), 192(6)
Right to vote	189(6)	*184(6)*	190(4)		183(6)	130(4)			192(4)	192(4)			183(5)	192(4)

	CAN	ON	AB	BC	MB	NB	NL	NS	NU	NWT	PE	QC	SK	YK
Class vote	189(7)	*184(6)*	190(5)			130(5)	303(4)		192(5)	192(5)			183(6)	192(5)
Termination	189(9)	184(8)	190(7)		183(8)	130(7)	303(6)		192(7)	192(7)			183(8)	192(7)
Rights to dissent	190(1)	185(1)	191(1)	*238*	184(1)	131(1)	304(1)	Third Sched., s. 2(1)	193(1)	193(1)			184(1)	193(1)
Further right	190(2)	*185(2)*	191(2)		184(2)	131(2)	304(2), 304(3)	Third Sched., s. 2(2)	193(2)	193(2)			184(2)	193(2)
If one class of shares	190(2.1)	185(2.1)												
Payment for shares	190(3)	185(4)	191(3)		184(3)	131(3)	304(4)	Third Sched., s. 2(4)	193(3)	193(3)			184(3)	193(3)
No partial dissent	190(4)	185(5)	191(4)		184(4)	131(4)	304(5)	Third Sched., s. 2(5)	193(4)	193(4)			184(4)	193(4)
Objection	190(5)	185(6)	191(5)		184(5)	131(5)	304(6)	Third Sched., s. 2(6)	193(5)	193(5)			184(5)	193(5)
Notice of resolution	190(6)	185(8)			184(6)	131(6)	304(7)	Third Sched., s. 2(7)					184(6)	
Demand for payment	190(7)	185(10)			184(7)	131(7)	305(1)	Third Sched., s. 2(8)					184(7)	
Share certificate	190(8)	185(11)			184(8)	131(8)	305(2)	Third Sched., s. 2(9)					184(8)	
Forfeiture	190(9)	185(12)			184(9)	131(9)	305(3)	Third Sched., s. 2(10)					184(9)	

	CAN	ON	AB	BC	MB	NB	NL	NS	NU	NWT	PE	QC	SK	YK
Endorsing certificate	190(10)	185(13)			184(10)	131(10)	305(4)	Third Sched., s. 2(11)					184(10)	
Suspension of rights	190(11)	185(14)			184(11)	131(11)	306	Third Sched., s. 2(12)					184(11)	
Offer to pay	190(12)	185(15)	191(7), 191(9)(b)		184(12)	131(12)	307(1)	Third Sched., s. 2(13)	*193(7)*	*193(7)*			184(12)	*193(7)*
Same terms	190(13)	185(16)	191(9)(a)		184(13)	131(13)	307(2)	Third Sched., s. 2(14)	*193(9)*	*193(9)*			184(13)	193(9)(a)
Payment	190(14)	185(17)			184(14)	131(14)	307(3)	Third Sched., s. 2(15)					184(14)	
Corporation may apply to court	190(15)	185(18)	*191(6)*		184(15)	131(15)	308(1)	Third Sched., s. 2(16)	*193(6)*	*193(6)*			184(15)	*193(6)*
Shareholder application to court	190(16)	185(19)	*191(6)*		184(16)	131(16)	308(2)	Third Sched., s. 2(17)	*193(6)*	*193(6)*			184(16)	*193(6)*
Venue	190(17)				184(17)								184(17)	
No security for costs	190(18)	185(20)	191(11)		184(18)		309(1)	Third Sched., s. 2(18)	193(11)(a)	193(11)(a)			184(18)	193(11)(a)
Parties	190(19)	*185(22), 185(23)*	*191(12)*		184(19)	131(18), 131(19)	309(2)	Third Sched., s. 2(19)	*193(12)*	*193(12)*			184(19)	*193(12)*
Powers of court	190(20)	185(24)	*191(13)*		184(20)	131(20)	310(1)	Third Sched., s. 2(20)	*193(13)*	*193(13)*			184(20)	*193(13)*

	CAN	ON	AB	BC	MB	NB	NL	NS	NU	NWT	PE	QC	SK	YK
Appraisers	190(21)	185(25)			184(21)	131(21)	310(2)	Third Sched., s. 2(21)					184(21)	
Final order	190(22)	185(26)			184(22)	131(22)	310(3)	Third Sched., s. 2(22)					184(22)	
Interest	190(23)	185(27)	191(17)		184(23)	131(23)	311	Third Sched., s. 2(23)	193(17)	193(17)			184(23)	193(17)
Where corporation unable to pay	190(24), 190(25)	185(28), 185(29)	191(18), 191(19)		184(24), 184(25)	131(24), 131(25)	312(1), 312(2)	Third Sched., s. 2(24), 2(25)	193(18), 193(19)	193(18), 193(19)			184(24), 184(25)	193(18), 193(19)
Limitation	190(26)	185(30)	191(20)		184(26)	131(26)	313	Third Sched., s. 2(26)	193(20)	193(20)			184(26)	193(20)
Definition of "reorganization" "order for reorganization" (AB, NU, NWT, YK)	191(1)	186(1)	192(1)		185(1)	132(1)	314(1)		194(1)	194(1)			185(1)	194(1)
Powers of court	191(2)	186(2)	192(2)		185(2)	132(2)	314(2)		194(2)	194(2)		411	185(2)	194(2)
Further powers	191(3)	186(3)	192(3)		185(3)	132(3)	314(3)		194(3)	194(3)		411	185(3)	194(3)
Articles of reorganization	191(4)	186(4)	192(4)		185(4)	132(4)	314(4)		194(4)	194(4)		412	185(4)	194(4)
Certificate of reorganization	191(5)	186(5)	192(5)		185(5)	132(5)	314(5)		194(5)	194(5)			186(1)	194(5)
Effect of certificate	191(6)		192(6)		185(6)	132(6)	314(6)		194(6)	194(6)			186(2)	194(6)
No dissent	191(7)	186(6)	192(7)		185(7)	132(7)	314(7)		194(7)	194(7)			186(3)	194(7)

	CAN	ON	AB	BC	MB	NB	NL	NS	NU	NWT	PE	QC	SK	YK
Definition of "arrangement"	192(1)	182(1)	193(1)		185(1)	128(1)	315(1)		195(1)	195(1)		415	186.1(1)	195(1)
Where corporation insolvent	192(2)				185(8)		315(2)						186.1(2)	
Application to court for approval of arrangement	192(3)		193(2), 193(3)		185(9)	128(2), 128(3)	315(3)		195(2), 195(3)	195(2), 195(3)		414	186.1(3)	*195(2), 195(3)*
Powers of court	192(4)	182(5)	193(4)		185(10)	128(4)	315(4)	Third Sched., s. 3	195(4)	195(4)		416	186.1(4)	195(4)
Notice to Director	192(5)		193(8)		185(11)	128(5)	315(5)		195(8)	195(8)			186.1(5)	195(8)
Articles of arrangement	192(6)	183(1)	193(10)		185(12)	129(1)	315(6)		195(10)	195(10)		*418, 419*	186.1(6)	*195(10)*
Certificate of arrangement	192(7)	183(2)	193(11)		185(13)	129(2)	315(7)		195(11)	195(11)			186.1(7)	195(11)
Effect of certificate	192(8)		193(12)		185(14)		315(8)		195(12)	195(12)		420	186.1(8)	195(12)
GOING-PRIVATE TRANSACTIONS AND SQUEEZE-OUT TRANSACTIONS														
Going-private transactions	193	*190*												
Squeeze-out transactions	194											223		
COMPULSORY AND COMPELLED ACQUISITIONS														
"dissenting offeree"	206(1)	187(2)	194(a)			133(1)	316(a)		196	196			187(a)	196
"offer"	206(1)		194(b)				316(b)		196	196			187(b)	196
"offeree"	206(1)	187(2)	194(c)				316(c)		196	196			187(c)	196

	CAN	ON	AB	BC	MB	NB	NL	NS	NU	NWT	PE	QC	SK	YK
"offeree corporation"	206(1)	187(2)	194(d)				316(d)		196	196			187(d)	196
"offeror"	206(1)	187(2)	194(e)				316(e)		196	196			187(e)	196
"share"	206(1)		194(f)				316(f)		196	196		399	187(f)	196
"take-over bid"	206(1)	187(2)	194(g)				316(g)		196	196			187(g)	196
Right to acquire	206(2)	188(1)	195(2)			133(2)	317		197(2)	197(2)		398	188	197(2)
Notice	206(3)	188(2)	196(1)			133(3)	318		198(1)	198(1)		*401*	189	198(1)
Notice of adverse claim	206(4)	188(3)	196(2)			133(4)	319		198(2)	198(2)			190	198(2)
Share certificate	206(5)	188(4)	197(1)			133(5)	320		199(1)	199(1)			191	199(1)
Deemed election	206(5.1)	188(2)(d)	196(1)(d)			133(3)(d)	318(d)		198(1)(d)	198(1)(d)			189(d)	198(1)(d)
Payment	206(6)	188(5)	197(2)			133(6)	321		199(2)	199(2)		403	192	199(2)
Consideration	206(7)	188(6)	198(1)			133(7)	322		200(1)	200(1)		404	193	200(1)
When corporation is offeror	206(7.1)	*188(7)*												
Duty of offeree corporation	206(8)	188(11)	198(2)			133(8)	323		200(2)	200(2)			194	200(2)
Application to court	206(9)	188(13)	199(1)			133(9)	324(1)		201(1)	201(1)		407	195(1)	201
Idem	206(10)	188(14)	199(2)			133(10)	324(2)		201(2)	201(2)			195(2)	
Status of dissenter if no court application	206(11)	188(15)	199(3)				324(3)		201(3)	201(3)		407	195(3)	
Venue	206(12)						325						196	
No security for costs	206(13)	188(16)	200			133(11)	326		202	202			197	202
Parties	206(14)	188(17)	201			133(12)	327		203	203			198	203
Powers of court	206(15)	188(18)	202			133(13)	328(1)		204	204			199(1)	204
Appraisers	206(16)	188(19)	203			133(14)	328(2)		205	205			199(2)	205
Final order	206(17)	188(20)	204			133(15)	328(3)		206	206			199(3)	206
Additional powers	206(18)	188(21)	205			133(16)	329		207(1)	207(1)		409	200	207

	CAN	ON	AB	BC	MB	NB	NL	NS	NU	NWT	PE	QC	SK	YK
Obligation to acquire shares	206.1(1)					133(17)								
Conditions	206.1(2)													
LIQUIDATION AND DISSOLUTION														
Definition of "court"	207													
Application	208(1)	*192*				*135(1)*	*330(1)*		*209(2)*	*209(2)*			*201(1)*	
Staying proceeding	208(2)		207	313		135(2)	330(2)		209(1)	209(1)			201(2)	209
Revival	209(1)	*241(5)*	208(1)	*355–368*	200	136(1)	331(1)		210(1)	210(1)	73(1)	365	202(1)	210(1)
Articles of revival	209(2)	241(6)	208(2)			136(3)	331(2)		210(2)	210(2)			202(2)	210(2)
Certificate of revival	209(3)	*241(7)*	208(3)		202(1)	136(4)	331(3)		210(3)	210(3)	73(2)		202(3)	210(3)
Date of revival	209(3.1)		208(4)			136(5)	331(4)		210(4)	210(4)	73(3)	370	202(4)	210(4)
Rights preserved	209(4)				202(2)		331(4)		210(4)	210(4)	73(3)		202(4)	210(4)
Legal actions	209(5)													
Defintion of "interested person"	209(6)		206.1											
Dissolution before commencing business	210(1)		211(1)		203(1)	137(1)	332		212(1)	212(1)	*74*	316	203(1)	212(1)
Dissolution if no property	210(2)		211(2)		203(2)	137(2)	333		212(2)	212(2)			203(2)	212(2)
Dissolution where property disposed of	210(3)		211(3)		203(3)	137(3)	334		212(3)	212(3)			203(2.1)	212(3)
Articles of dissolution	210(4)		211(4)		203(4)	137(4)	335(1)		212(4)	212(4)			203(3)	212(4)
Certificate of dissolution	210(5)	239	211(5)		203(5)	137(5)	335(2)		212(5)	212(5)			203(4)	212(5)

	CAN	ON	AB	BC	MB	NB	NL	NS	NU	NWT	PE	QC	SK	YK
Effect of certificate	210(6)		211(6)		203(6)	137(6)	335(3)		212(6)	212(6)			203(5)	212(6)
Proposing liquidation and dissolution	211(1)	*193(1)*	212(1)	*313–318, 319–323*	204(1)	138(1)	336(1)		213(1)	213(1)		*304–307, 308–311*	204(1)	213(1)
Notice of meeting	211(2)		212(2)		204(2)	138(2)	336(2)		213(2)	213(2)			204(2)	213(2)
Shareholders resolution	211(3)		212(3)		204(3)	138(3)	336(3)		213(3)	213(3)			204(3)	213(3)
Statement of intent to dissolve	211(4)		212(4)		204(4)	138(4)	337(1)		213(4)	213(4)			204(4)	213(4)
Certificate of intent to dissolve	211(5)		212(5)		204(5)	138(5)	337(2)		213(5)	213(5)			204(5)	213(5)
Effect of certificate	211(6)		212(6)		204(6)	138(6)	337(3)		213(6)	213(6)			204(6)	213(6)
Liquidation	211(7)		212(7)		204(7)	138(7)	337(4)		213(7)	213(7)			204(7)	213(7)
Supervision by court	211(8)		212(8)		204(8)	138(8)	338(1)		213(8)	213(8)		351	204(8)	213(8)
Notice to Director	211(9)		212(9)		204(9)	138(9)	338(2)		213(9)	213(9)			204(9)	213(9)
Revocation	211(10)		212(10)		204(10)	138(10)	339(1)		213(10)	213(10)			204(10)	213(10)
Certificate of revocation of intent to dissolve	211(11)		212(11)		204(11)	138(11)	339(2)		213(11)	213(11)			204(11)	213(11)
Effect of certificate	211(12)		212(12)		204(12)	138(12)	339(3)		213(12)	213(12)			204(12)	213(12)
Right to dissolve	211(13)		212(13)		204(13)	138(13)	340(1)		213(13)	213(13)			204(13)	213(13)
Articles of dissolution	211(14)		212(14)		204(14)	138(14)	340(2)		213(13)	213(13)			204(14)	213(14)
Certificate of dissolution	211(15)		212(15)		204(15)	138(15)	340(3)		213(14)	213(14)			204(15)	213(15)
Effect of certificate	211(16)		212(16)		204(16)	138(16)	340(4)		213(15)	213(15)			204(16)	213(16)
Dissolution by Director	212(1)	*240(1)*	213(1)	*422*	205(1)	139(1)	341(1)	*136, 137*	214(1)	214(1)	72(1)		205(1)	214(1)
Publication	212(2)		213(2)		205(2), 205(3)	139(2), 139(2.1) 139(2.2)	341(2)		214(2), 214(3), 214(4)	214(2), 214(3), 214(4)	72(2)		205(2)	214(2)

	CAN	ON	AB	BC	MB	NB	NL	NS	NU	NWT	PE	QC	SK	YK
Certificate of dissolution	212(3)		213(3)		205(5)	139(3)	341(3)		214(6)	214(6)	72(3)		205(3)	214(3)
Exception — non-payment of incorporation fee	212(3.1)													
Effect of certificate	212(4)		213(4)		205(6)	139(4)	341(4)		214(7)	214(7)	72(4)		205(4)	214(4)
Grounds for dissolution	213(1)		214(1)	*324–326*	206(1)	140(1)	342(1)		215(1)	215(1)		462	206(1)	215(1)
Notice to Director	213(2)		214(2)		206(2)	140(2)	342(2)		215(2)	215(2)			206(2)	215(2)
Dissolution order	213(3)		214(3)		206(3)	140(3)	342(3)		215(3)	215(3)		464	206(3)	215(3)
Certificate	213(4)		214(4)		206(4)	140(4)	342(4)		215(4)	215(4)			206(4)	215(4)
Effect of certificate	213(5)		214(5)		206(5)	140(5)	342(5)		215(5)	215(5)		467	206(5)	215(5)
Further grounds	214(1), 214(3)	207(1)	215(1), 215(3)		207(1), 207(3)	141(1), 141(3)	343(1), 343(3)		216(1), 216(3)	216(1), 216(3)		463	207(1), 207(3)	216(1), 216(3)
Alternative order	214(2)	207(2)	215(2)		207(2)	141(2)	343(2)		216(2)	216(2)			207(2)	216(2)
Application for supervision	215(1)		216(1)		208(1)	142(1)	344(1)		217(1)	217(1)			208(1)	217(1)
Court supervision	215(2)		216(2)		208(2)	142(2)	344(2)		217(2)	217(2)			208(2)	217(2)
Application to court	216(1)		217(1)		209(1)	143(1)	345(1)		218(1)	218(1)			209(1)	218(1)
Show cause order	216(2)		217(2)		209(2)	143(2)	345(2)		218(2)	218(2)			209(2)	218(2)
Powers of court	216(3)		217(3)		209(3)	143(3)	345(3)		218(3)	218(3)			209(3)	218(3)
Publication	216(4)		217(4)		209(4)	143(4)	345(4)		218(4)	218(4)			209(4)	218(4)
Person responsible	216(5)		217(5)		209(5)	143(5)	345(5)		218(5)	218(5)			209(5)	218(5)
Powers of court	217	*209*	218	*324–326, 342*	210	144(1)	346		219	219		*363*	210	219

	CAN	ON	AB	BC	MB	NB	NL	NS	NU	NWT	PE	QC	SK	YK
Effect of order	218	*213*	219		211	144(2)	347		220	220			211	220
Cessation of business and powers	219(1)		220(1)	*344–349*	212(1)	145(1)	348(1)		221(1)	221(1)			212(1)	221(1)
Delegation by liquidator	219(2)		220(2)		212(2)	145(2)	348(2)		221(2)	221(2)			212(2)	221(2)
Appointment of liquidator	220(1)	*210(1)*	221(1)	*324(4)*	213(1)	146(1)	349(1)		222(1)	222(1)		*325–333*	213(1)	222(1)
Vacancy	220(2)	*210(3)*	221(2)		213(2)	146(2)	349(2)		222(2)	222(2)			213(2)	222(2)
Duties of liquidator	221		222(1)	*330*	214	147	350		223	223		*334–339*	214	223
Powers of liquidator	222(1)	223(1)	223(1)	*334*	215(1)	148(1)	351(1)		224(1)	224(1)			215(1)	224(1)
Due diligence	222(2)	*223(4)*	222(2), 223(2)		215(2)	148(2)	351(2)		224(2)	224(2)			215(2)	224(2)
Application for examination	222(3)		223(3)		215(3)	148(3)	351(3)		224(3)	224(3)			215(3)	224(3)
Power of court	222(4)		223(4)		215(4)	148(4)	351(4)		224(4)	224(4)			215(4)	224(4)
Costs of liquidation	223(1)	222	224(1)	*341*	216(1)	149(1)			225(1)	225(1)			216(1)	225(1)
Final accounts	223(2)		224(2)	*342*	216(2)	149(2)	352(1)		225(2)	225(2)		*339–340*	216(2)	225(2)
Shareholder application	223(3)		224(3)		216(3)	149(3)	352(2)		225(3)	225(3)			216(3)	225(3)
Publication	223(4)		224(4)		216(4)	149(4)	352(3)		225(4)	225(4)			216(4)	225(4)
Final order	223(5)		224(5)		216(5)	149(5)	352(4)		225(5)	225(5)			216(5)	225(5)
Delivery of order	223(6)		224(6)		216(6)	149(6)	352(5)		225(6)	225(6)			216(6)	225(6)
Certificate of dissolution	223(7)		224(7)	345	216(7)	149(7)	352(6)		225(7)	225(7)			216(7)	225(7)

	CAN	ON	AB	BC	MB	NB	NL	NS	NU	NWT	PE	QC	SK	YK
Effect of certificate	223(8)	*241(4)*	224(8)	344(1)	216(8)	149(8)	352(7)		225(8)	225(8)			216(8)	225(8)
Right to distribution in money	224(1)		225(1)	336(1), 336(2)	217(1)	150(1)	353(1)		226(1)	226(1)			217(1)	226(1)
Powers of court	224(2)		225(2)		217(2)	150(2)	353(2)		226(2)	226(2)			217(2)	226(2)
Custody of records	225(1)	*236(1), 236(2)*	225(1)	*351*	218(1)	151(1)	354		227(1)	227(1)			218(1)	227(1)
Offence	225(2)	*258(1)(j)*	225(2)		218(2)		514		227(2)	227(2)			218(2)	227(2)
Definition of "shareholder"	226(1)	243(3)	226(1)		219(1)	152(1)	355(1)		228(1)	228(1)			219(1)	228(1)
Continuation of actions	226(2)	242(1)	226(2)	346(1)	219(2)	152(2)	355(2)		228(2)	228(2)			219(2)	228(2)
Service	226(3), 226(3.1)	242(2)	226(3)		219(3)	152(3)	355(3)		228(3)	228(3)			219(3)	228(3)
Reimbursement	226(4)	243(1)	226(4)		219(4)	152(4)	355(4)		228(4)	228(4)			219(4)	228(4)
Representative action	226(5)	243(2)	226(5)		219(5)	152(5)	355(5)		228(5), 228(6)	228(5), 228(6)			219(5)	228(5)
Unknown claimants	227(1)	*238(3), 238(4)*	228(1)	337	220(1)	153(1)	356(1)		229(1)	229(1)			220(1)	229(1)
Constructive satisfaction	227(2)		228(2)		220(2)	153(2)	356(2)		229(2)	229(2)			220(2)	229(2)
Recovery	227(3)	*238(6)*	228(3)		220(3)	153(3)	356(3)		229(3)	229(3)			220(3)	229(3)
Vesting in Crown	228(1)	244(1)	229(1)	344(2)	221(1)	154(1)	357(1)		230(1)	230(1)	75		221(1)	230(1)
Return of property on revival	228(2)		229(2)	*368*	221(2)	154(2)	357(3)		230(2)	230(2)			221(2)	230(2)

	CAN	ON	AB	BC	MB	NB	NL	NS	NU	NWT	PE	QC	SK	YK
INVESTIGATION														
Investigation	229(1)	161(1)	231(1)	*248(1)*	222(1)	155(1)	359(1)	*115, 116*	232(1)	232(1)		421	222(1)	232(1)
Grounds	229(2)	161(2)	231(2)	*248(3)*	222(2)	155(2)	359(2)		232(2)	232(2)		422	222(2)	232(2)
Notice to Director	229(3)	161(3)			222(3)	155(3)	359(3)						222(3)	
No security for costs	229(4)	161(4)	231(3)		222(4)	155(4)	359(4)		232(3)	232(3)			222(4)	232(3)
Hearings *in camera*	229(5)	*161(5)*	231(4)		222(5)	155(5)	359(5)		232(4)	232(4)		421	222(5)	232(4)
Consent to publish proceedings required	229(6)	161(6)	231(5)		222(6)	155(6)	359(6)		232(5)	232(5)		424	222(6)	232(5)
Powers of court	230(1)	162(1)	232(1)		223(1)	156(1)	360(1)		233(1)	233(1)		425	223(1)	233(1)
Copy of report	230(2)	162(2)	232(2)	253(1)	223(2)	156(2)	360(2)		233(2)	233(2)			223(2)	233(2)
Power of inspector	231(1)	163(1)	233(1)	*251*	224(1)	157(1)	361(1)		234(1)	234(1)		426	224(1)	234(1)
Exchange of information	231(2)	163(2)	233(2)		224(2)	157(2)	361(2)		234(2)	234(2)		432	224(1.1)	234(2)
Court order	231(3)	163(3)	233(3)		224(3)	157(3)	361(3)		234(3)	234(3)		429	224(2)	234(3)
Hearing *in camera*	232(1)	164(1)	234(1)		225(1)	158(1)	362(1)		235(1)	235(1)		430	225(1)	235(1)
Right to counsel	232(2)	164(2)	234(2)	251(3)	225(2)	158(2)	362(2)		235(2)	235(2)		431	225(2)	235(2)
Criminating statements	233		235		226	159	363		236	236		427	226	236
Absolute privilege (defamation)	234	165	236	255	227	160	364		237	237			227	237
Information respecting ownership and control	235(1)				228(1)		365(1)						228(1)	

	CAN	ON	AB	BC	MB	NB	NL	NS	NU	NWT	PE	QC	SK	YK
Presumption	235(2)				228(2)		365(2)						228(2)	
Publication	235(3)													
Offence	235(4)				228(3)								228(3)	
Officers, etc., of bodies corporate	235(5)				228(4)								228(4)	
Solicitor-client privilege or professional secrecy	236	166	237	252	229	161	366		238	238			229	238
Inquiries	237	167			230	162	367						230	
APPORTIONING AWARD OF DAMAGES	237.1 to 237.9													
REMEDIES, OFFENCES AND PUNISHMENT														
“action”	238	245	239(a)		231	163	368(a)	Third Sched., s. 7(5)	240	240			231	240
“complainant”	238	245	239(b)	232(1)	231	163	368(b)	Third Sched., s. 7(5)	240	240			231	240
Commencing derivative action	239(1)	246(1)	240(1)	232(2)	232(1)	164(1)	369(1)	Third Sched., s. 4(1)	241(1)	241(1)	*70, 71*	445	232(1)	241(1)
Conditions precedent	239(2)	246(2)	240(2)	233(1)	232(2)	164(2)	369(2)	Third Sched., s. 4(2)	241(2)	241(2)		446	232(2)	241(2)

	CAN	ON	AB	BC	MB	NB	NL	NS	NU	NWT	PE	QC	SK	YK
Powers of court	240	247	241	233(3), 233(4)	233	165	370	Third Sched., s. 4(3)	242	242		447	233	242
Application to court re oppression	241(1)	248(1)	242(1)		234(1)	166(1)	371(1)	Third Sched., s. 5(1)	243(1)	243(1)		450	234(1)	243(1)
Grounds	241(2)	248(2)	242(2)	227(2)	234(2)	166(2)	371(2)	Third Sched., s. 5(2)	243(2)	243(2)		450	234(2)	243(2)
Powers of court	241(3)	248(3)	242(3)	227(3)	234(3)	166(3)	371(3)	Third Sched., s. 5(3)	243(3)	243(3)		451	234(3)	243(3)
Duty of directors	241(4)	248(4)	242(5), 242(6)		234(4)	166(4)	371(4)	Third Sched., s. 5(4)	243(5), 243(6)	243(5), 243(6)			234(4)	243(5)
Exclusion	241(5)	248(5)	242(7)		234(5)	166(5)	371(5)						234(5)	243(7)
Limitation	241(6)	248(6)			234(6)	166(6)	371(6)	Third Sched., s. 5(5)	243(7)	243(7)			234(6)	
Alternative order	241(7)		242(8)		234(7)	166(7)	371(7)		243(9)	243(9)			234(7)	243(8)
Evidence of shareholder approval not decisive	242(1)	249(1)	243(1)		235(1)	167(1)	372(1)	Third Sched., s. 7(1)	244(1)	244(1)			235(1)	244(1)
Court approval to discontinue	242(2)	249(2)	243(2)	*233(5), 233(6)*	235(2)	167(2)	372(2)	Third Sched., s. 7(2)	244(2)	244(2)			235(2)	244(2)

	CAN	ON	AB	BC	MB	NB	NL	NS	NU	NWT	PE	QC	SK	YK
No security for costs	242(3)	249(3)	243(3)		235(3)	167(3)	373(1)	Third Sched., s. 7(3)	244(3)	244(3)			235(3)	244(3)
Interim costs	242(4)	249(4)	243(4)		235(4)	167(4)	373(2)	Third Sched., s. 7(4)	244(4), 244(5)	244(4), 244(5)			235(4)	244(4)
Application to court to rectify records	243(1)	250(1)	244(1)	230(2)	236(1)	168(1)	374(1)		245(1)	245(1)		456	236(1)	245(1)
Notice to Director	243(2)		244(2)		236(2)	168(2)	374(2)		245(2)	245(2)			236(2)	245(2)
Powers of court	243(3)	250(2)	244(3)	230(3)	236(3)	168(3)	374(3)		245(3)	245(3)		457	236(3)	245(3)
Application for directions	244		245		237	169	375		246	246			237	246
Notice of refusal by Director	245(1)	251(1)	246(1)		238(1)	170(1)	376(1)		247(1)	247(1)			238(1)	247(1)
Deemed refusal	245(2)	251(2)	246(2)		238(2)	170(2)	376(2)		247(2)	247(2)			238(2)	247(2)
Appeal from Director's decision	246	252(1)	247(1)		239	171	377		248	248			239(1)	248(1)
Restraining or compliance order	247	253(1)	248	228(2), 228(3)	240	172	378	Third Sched., s. 6	249	249			240	249
Summary application to court	248	*254*	249	*235*	241	173	379		250	250			241	250

	CAN	ON	AB	BC	MB	NB	NL	NS	NU	NWT	PE	QC	SK	YK
Appeal of final order Appeal with leave	249(1), 249(2)	255	250			174	380			251			242	
Offences with respect to reports	250(1)	256(2)	251(1)	427(1)	242(1)	175(1)			252(1)	252(1)		*493*	300(1)	251(1)
Officers, etc., of bodies corporate	250(2)	256(3)	251(2)	427(2)	242(2)	175(2)			252(2)	252(2)			301	251(2)
Immunity	250(3)	256(4)	251(3)	427(3)	242(3)	175(3)			252(3)	252(3)			300(2)	251(3)
Offence	251	*258(1)(j)*	252	*426*	243			*150*	253	253			302	252
Order to comply	252(1)		253(1)		244	176(1)			254(1)	254(1)			303(1)	253(1)
Limitation period	252(2)	259(1), 259(2)	253(2)		245(1)	176(4)			254(2)	254(2)			303(2)	253(2)
Civil remedy not affected	252(3)	261	253(3)		245(2)	176(5)			254(3)	254(3)			303(3)	253(3)
DOCUMENTS IN ELECTRONIC OR OTHER FORM	252.1 to 252.7													
GENERAL														
Notice to directors and shareholders	253(1)	262(1)	255(1)	*6–9*	246(1)	177(1)	385(1)		256(1)	256(1)			247(1)	255(1)
Effect of notice	253(2)	262(3)	255(2)		246(2)	177(2)	385(2)		256(2)	256(2)			247(2)	255(3)
Deemed receipt	253(3)	262(2)	255(3)		246(3)	177(3)	386		256(3)	256(3)			248	255(4)
Undelivered notices	253(4)	262(4)	255(4)		246(4)	177(4)	387		256(4)	256(4)			249	255(6)

Table of Concordance of Business Corporations Acts

	CAN	ON	AB	BC	MB	NB	NL	NS	NU	NWT	PE	QC	SK	YK
Notice to and service on a corporation	254	*263(1)*	256(1), 256(3)	*6–9*	247	178(1)	402(1)	*154*	257(1), 257(2)	257(1), 257(2)	*68*		*269*	*256(1), 256(2)*
Waiver of notice	255	264(1)	258(1)	*7(4)*	248	179	388		259	259			250	258
Certificate of Director	256(1)	265(2)	259(1)		249(1)	180(1)	399(2)	*28*	260(1)	260(1)			*286(1)*	259(1)
Evidence	256(2)	265(3)	259(2)		249(2)	180(2)	399(3)		260(3)	260(3)			286(3)	259(2)
Certificate of corporation	257(1)	266(1)	260(1)		250(1)	181(1)	389		261(1)	261(1)			251(1)	260(1)
Proof	257(2)	266(2)	260(2)		250(2)	181(2)	390		261(2)	261(2)			251(2)	260(2)
Security certificate	257(3)	266(3)	260(3)		250(3)	181(3)	391		261(3)	261(3)			253	260(3)
Copies	258	267(1)	261		251	182	392		262(1)	262(1)			254	261
Content and form of notices and documents	258.1													
Exemption	258.2								264	264				
Proof required by Director	259(1)	*268(1)*	262		252(1)	183(1)	396(1)		265	265			289	262
Form of proof	259(2)	*268(1)*	262		252(2)	183(2)	396(2)		265	265			289	262
Appointment of Director	260	278	263(1)	*400*	253	184(1), 184(1.1)	381(1)	*3*	266(1)	266(1)	2		279(1), 279(2)	*263(1)*

	CAN	ON	AB	BC	MB	NB	NL	NS	NU	NWT	PE	QC	SK	YK
Regulations	261(1)	272	266	432	254(1)	185(1)	409	*7*	267	267	81, 82	489	304	265
Incorporation by reference	261(2)													
Incorporated material is not a regulation	261(3)													
Fee to be paid before service performed	261.1	*271.1(2)*		431				*5(1), 6*						
Definition of "statement"	262(1)		267(1)		255(1)	186(1)	393(1)		268(1)	268(1)			255(1)	266(1)
Filing of articles and statements	262(2)	273(1)	267(2)		255(2)	186(2)	393(2)		268(2)	268(2)			255(2)	266(2)
Date of certificate	262(3), 262(5)	273(2), *273(5)*	267(3), 267(5)		255(3), 255(4)	186(3)	393(3), 393(5)		268(3), 268(4)	268(3), 268(4)			255(3), 255(5)	266(3), 266(5)
Signature	262.1(1)	265(4)	267(4)		255(6)		393(4)		260(2)	260(2)			255(4)	266(4)
Authority to sign notices	262.1(2)													
Execution of documents	262.1(3)													
Annual return	263		268(1)			187(1)	408(1)		270(2)	270(2)	*80(1)*		273	267(1)
Certificate	263.1(1)		268(2)		*256*	*187(2)*			271(1)	271(1)				
Director may refuse to issue certificate of existence	263.1(2)													
Alteration	264		269		257	188	394						256	268

	CAN	ON	AB	BC	MB	NB	NL	NS	NU	NWT	PE	QC	SK	YK
Corrections at request of Director	265(1)	*275(1)*	270(1)	*414, 420*	258(3)	189(1)	395(1)		272(1)	272(1)	*10(3)*	*246–256*	257(1)	269(1)
No prejudice	265(2)													
Corrections at the request of the corporation	265(3)											*257–260*		
Application to court	265(4)		270(4)		258(4)									
Notice to Director	265(5)				258(6)									
Director may require surrender of document	265(6)				258(7), 258(8)									
Date of corrected document	265(7)	275(2)	270(2)		258(9)	189(2)	395(2)		272(2)	272(2)			257(2)	269(2)
Notice	265(8)				258(10)	189(3)	395(3)						257(3)	
Cancellation of articles by Director	265.1(1)											*265–270*		
No prejudice	265.1(2)													
Request to Director to cancel articles	265.1(3)													
Application to court	265.1(4)													
Notice to Director	265.1(5)													
Return of certificate	265.1(6)													
Inspection	266(1)	270(1)	271(1)	*416*	259(1)	190(1)	384(1)	*4*	273(1)	273(1)			*284*	270
Copies	266(2)	270(2)	271(2)		259(2)	190(2)	384(2)	*4*	273(2)	273(2)				271
Records of Director	267(1)	276(1)	272(1)	*412*	260(1)	191(1)	383(1)		274(1)	274(1)				272
Obligation to furnish	267(2)	276(2)	272(3)		260(2)	191(3)	397		274(2)	274(2)			285(1)	273

	CAN	ON	AB	BC	MB	NB	NL	NS	NU	NWT	PE	QC	SK	YK
Retention of records	267(3)	276(3)			260(3)	191(5)	398						285(2)	
Form of publication	267.1								275	275				
Definition of "charter"	268(1)		276(c)			192(1)								
Amendment of charter	268(2), 268(2.1)					192(2)							258(1)	
Change of class rights	268(3)					192(3)								
Authorizing continuance	268(4), 268(4.1)					192(4)							258(1.1)	
Financial institutions	268(4.2)													
No dissent	268(5)					192(5)								
Discretionary continuance	268(6)													
Fees	268(8)													
Special Act no longer applicable	268(8.1)													
Idem	268(9)													
Continuance prohibited	268(10)													
Exception for railway companies	268(11)													

BUSINESS CORPORATIONS ACT

R.S.O. 1990, c. B.16 [s. 152(5) not in force at date of publication. Repealed 2004, c. 19, s. 3(4); s. 274 not in force at date of publication. Repealed 2006, c. 21, Sched. F, s. 10.1(1).], as am. S.O. 1993, c. 16, s. 2; 1994, c. 17, s. 30; 1994, c. 27, s. 71; 1998, c. 18, Sched. E, ss. 20–32; 1999, c. 6, s. 3; 1999, c. 12, Sched. F, ss. 1–9; 2000, c. 26, Sched. B, s. 3; 2000, c. 42, Sched., ss. 1, 2; 2001, c. 8, ss. 1, 2; 2001, c. 9, Sched. D, s. 2; 2001, c. 23, s. 6; 2002, c. 8, Sched. I, s. 2; 2002, c. 22, s. 8; 2002, c. 24, Sched. B, ss. 25, item 2, 27; 2004, c. 8, s. 46; 2004, c. 16, Sched. D, s. 1, Table (Fr.); 2004, c. 19, s. 3; 2004, c. 31, Sched. 4; 2005, c. 5, s. 4; 2005, c. 28, Sched. B, s. 1; 2006, c. 8, ss. 106–122; 2006, c. 9, Sched. A; 2006, c. 19, Sched. G, s. 2; 2006, c. 21, Sched. F, s. 10.1(1); 2006, c. 34, Sched. B; 2007, c. 7, Sched. 7, s. 181; 2008, c. 19, Sched. V, s. 1; 2009, c. 33, Sched. 17, s. 1; 2010, c. 1, Sched. 1, s. 12; 2010, c. 6, Sched. A, s. 69, Sched. C, s. 67; CTS 30 AU 10 – 1; 2010, c. 16, Sched. 5, s. 1, Sched. 8, s. 1 [Sched. 5, s. 1 not in force at date of publication.]; 2011, c. 1, Sched. 2, s. 1(1)–(11), (12) (Fr.), (13) (Fr.), (14)–(19), Sched. 5, s. 1 [Sched. 2, s. 1 not in force at date of publication.].

PART I — DEFINITIONS AND APPLICATION

1. (1) Definitions — In this Act,

"affairs" means the relationships among a corporation, its affiliates and the shareholders, directors and officers of such bodies corporate but does not include the business carried on by such bodies corporate;

"affiliate" means an affiliated body corporate within the meaning of subsection (4);

"articles" means the original or restated articles of incorporation, articles of amendment, articles of amalgamation, articles of arrangement, articles of continuance, articles of dissolution, articles of reorganization, articles of revival, letters patent, supplementary letters patent, a special Act and any other instrument by which a corporation is incorporated;

"associate", where used to indicate a relationship with any person, means,

(a) any body corporate of which the person beneficially owns, directly or indirectly, voting securities carrying more than 10 per cent of the voting rights attached to all voting securities of the body corporate for the time being outstanding,

(b) any partner of that person,

(c) any trust or estate in which the person has a substantial beneficial interest or as to which the person serves as trustee or in a similar capacity,

(d) any relative of the person, including the person's spouse, where the relative has the same home as the person, or

(e) any relative of the spouse of the person where the relative has the same home as the person;

"auditor" includes a partnership of auditors;

Proposed Amendment — 1(1) "auditor"

"auditor" includes a partnership of auditors and an auditor that is incorporated;
2011, c. 1, Sched. 2, s. 1(1) [Not in force at date of publication.]

"beneficial interest" or **"beneficial ownership"** includes ownership through a trustee, legal representative, agent or other intermediary and, in the case of a security, includes the interest of an entitlement holder, as defined in the *Securities Transfer Act, 2006*, with respect to that security, but does not include the interest of an entitlement holder that is a securities intermediary, as defined in the *Securities Transfer Act, 2006*, that has established a security entitlement, as defined in the *Securities Transfer Act, 2006*, in favour of its entitlement holder with respect to that security;

"body corporate" means any body corporate with or without share capital and whether or not it is a corporation to which this Act applies;

"certified copy" means,

(a) in relation to a document of a corporation, a copy of the document certified to be a true copy by an officer thereof,

(b) in relation to a document issued by a court, a copy of the document certified to be a true copy under the seal of the court and signed by the registrar thereof,

(c) in relation to a document in the custody of the Director, a copy of the document certified to be a true copy by the Director and signed by the Director or by such officer of the Ministry as is designated by the regulations;

"Commission" means the Ontario Securities Commission;

"corporation" means a body corporate with share capital to which this Act applies;

"corporation number" means the number assigned by the Director to a corporation in accordance with subsection 8(1) and "number" in relation to a corporation means the corporation number of that corporation;

"court" means the Superior Court of Justice;

"day" means a clear day and a period of days shall be deemed to commence the day following the event that began the period and shall be deemed to terminate at midnight of the last day of the period except that if the last day of the period falls on a Sunday or holiday the period shall terminate at midnight of the day next following that is not a Sunday or holiday;

"debt obligation" means a bond, debenture, note or other similar obligation or guarantee of such an obligation of a body corporate, whether secured or unsecured;

"Director" means the Director appointed under section 278;

"director" means a person occupying the position of director of a corporation by whatever name called, and "directors" and "board of directors" include a single director;

"electronic signature" means an identifying mark or process that is,

(a) created or communicated using telephonic or electronic means,

(b) attached to or associated with a document or other information, and

(c) made or adopted by a person to associate the person with the document or other information, as the case may be.

"endorse" includes imprinting a stamp on the face of articles or other document sent to the Director;

"financial statement" means a financial statement referred to in section 154;

"incorporator" means a person who signs articles of incorporation;

"individual" means a natural person, but does not include a partnership, unincorporated association, unincorporated syndicate, unincorporated organization, trust, or a natural person in his or her capacity as trustee, executor, administrator or other legal representative;

"interim financial statement" means a financial statement referred to in section 160;

"liability" includes a debt of a corporation arising under section 36, subsection 185(29) or clause 248(3)(f) or (g);

"Minister" means the Minister of Consumer and Business Services or such other member of the Executive Council to whom the administration of this Act may be assigned;

"Ministry" means the Ministry of the Minister;

"non-resident corporation" means a corporation incorporated in Canada before the 27th day of April, 1965, and that is not deemed to be resident in Canada for the purposes of the *Income Tax Act* (Canada) by subsection 250(4) of that Act;

"number name" means the name of a corporation that consists only of its corporation number followed by the word "Ontario" and one of the words or abbreviations provided for in subsection 10(1);

"offering corporation" means a corporation that is offering its securities to the public within the meaning of subsection (6) and that is not the subject of an order of the Commission deeming it to have ceased to be offering its securities to the public;

"officer" means an officer designated under section 133 and includes the chair of the board of directors, a vice-chair of the board of directors, the president, a vice-president, the secretary, an assistant secretary, the treasurer, an assistant treasurer and the general manager of a corporation, and any other individual designated an officer of a corporation by by-law or by resolution of the directors or any other individual who performs functions for a corporation similar to those normally performed by an individual occupying any such office;

"ordinary resolution" means a resolution that is submitted to a meeting of the shareholders of a corporation and passed, with or without amendment, at the meeting by at least a majority of the votes cast;

"person" includes an individual, sole proprietorship, partnership, unincorporated association, unincorporated syndicate, unincorporated organization, trust, body corporate, and a natural person in his or her capacity as trustee, executor, administrator, or other legal representative;

"personal representative", where used with reference to holding shares in that capacity, means an executor, administrator, estate trustee, guardian, tutor, trustee, receiver or liquidator or the curator, guardian for property or attorney under a continuing power of attorney with authority for a person who is mentally incapable of managing his or her property;

"prescribed" means prescribed by the regulations;

"redeemable share" means a share issued by a corporation,

(a) that the corporation may purchase or redeem upon the demand of the corporation, or

(b) that the corporation is required by its articles to purchase or redeem at a specified time or otherwise upon the demand of a shareholder;

"registered form" means registered form as defined in the *Securities Transfer Act, 2006*;

"registered office" means the office of a corporation located at the address specified in its articles or in the notice most recently filed by the corporation under subsection 14(3);

Proposed Amendment — 1(1) "registered office"

"registered office" means the office of a corporation located at the address specified in its articles or in the notice most recently filed by the corporation under the *Corporations Information Act*;

2011, c. 1, Sched. 2, s. 1(2) [Not in force at date of publication.]

"regulations" means the regulations made under this Act;

"related person", where used to indicate a relationship with any person, means,

(a) any spouse, son or daughter of that person,

(b) any relative of the person or of the person's spouse, other than an individual referred to in clause (a), who has the same home as the person, or

(c) any body corporate of which the person and any of the persons referred to in clause (a) or (b) or the partner or employer of the person, or any combination, beneficially own, directly or indirectly, voting securities carrying more than 50 per cent of the voting rights attached to all voting securities of the body corporate for the time being outstanding;

"resident Canadian" means an individual who is,

(a) a Canadian citizen ordinarily resident in Canada,

(b) a Canadian citizen not ordinarily resident in Canada who is a member of a prescribed class of persons, or

(c) a permanent resident within the meaning of the *Immigration Act* (Canada) and ordinarily resident in Canada;

"same-sex partner" [Repealed 2005, c. 5, s. 4(4).]

"security" means a share of any class or series of shares or a debt obligation of a body corporate;

"security certificate" means a certificate evidencing a security;

"security interest" means an interest in or charge upon the property of a body corporate by way of mortgage, hypothec, pledge or otherwise, to secure payment of a debt or performance of any other obligation of the body corporate;

"send" includes deliver or mail;

"senior officer" means,

(a) the chair of the board of directors, a vice-chair of the board of directors, the president, a vice-president, the secretary, the treasurer or the general manager of a corporation or any other individual who performs functions for a corporation similar to those normally performed by an individual occupying any such office, and

(b) each of the five highest paid employees of a corporation, including any individual referred to in clause (a);

"series", in relation to shares, means a division of a class of shares;

"special resolution" means a resolution that is,

(a) submitted to a special meeting of the shareholders of a corporation duly called for the purpose of considering the resolution and passed, with or without amendment, at the meeting by at least two-thirds of the votes cast, or

(b) consented to in writing by each shareholder of the corporation entitled to vote at such a meeting or the shareholder's attorney authorized in writing;

"spouse" means a person to whom the person is married or with whom the person is living in a conjugal relationship outside marriage;

"telephonic or electronic means" means telephone calls or messages, facsimile messages, electronic mail, transmission of data or information through automated touch-tone telephone systems, transmission of data or information through computer networks, any other similar means or any other prescribed means.

"unanimous shareholder agreement" means an agreement described in subsection 108(2) or a declaration of a shareholder described in subsection 108(3);

"uncertificated security" means an uncertificated security as defined in the *Securities Transfer Act, 2006*;

"voting security" means any security other than a debt obligation of a body corporate carrying a voting right either under all circumstances or under some circumstances that have occurred and are continuing;

"warrant" means any certificate or other document issued by a corporation as evidence of conversion privileges or options or rights to acquire securities of the corporation.

(2) Interpretation: subsidiary body corporate — For the purposes of this Act, a body corporate shall be deemed to be a subsidiary of another body corporate if, but only if,

(a) it is controlled by,

(i) that other, or

(ii) that other and one or more bodies corporate each of which is controlled by that other, or

(iii) two or more bodies corporate each of which is controlled by that other; or

(b) it is a subsidiary of a body corporate that is that other's subsidiary.

(3) Holding body corporate — For the purposes of this Act, a body corporate shall be deemed to be another's holding body corporate if, but only if, that other is its subsidiary.

(4) Affiliated body corporate — For the purposes of this Act, one body corporate shall be deemed to be affiliated with another body corporate if, but only if, one of them is the subsidiary of the other or both are subsidiaries of the same body corporate or each of them is controlled by the same person.

(5) Control — For the purposes of this Act, a body corporate shall be deemed to be controlled by another person or by two or more bodies corporate if, but only if,

(a) voting securities of the first-mentioned body corporate carrying more than 50 per cent of the votes for the election of directors are held, other than by way of security only, by or for the benefit of such other person or by or for the benefit of such other bodies corporate; and

(b) the votes carried by such securities are sufficient, if exercised, to elect a majority of the board of directors of the first-mentioned body corporate.

(6) Offering securities to public — For the purposes of this Act, a corporation is offering its securities to the public only where,

(a) in respect of any of its securities a prospectus or statement of material facts has been filed under the *Securities Act* or any predecessor thereof, or in respect of which a prospectus has been filed under *The Corporations Information Act*, being chapter 72 of the Revised Statutes of Ontario, 1960, or any predecessor thereof, so long as any of such securities are outstanding or any securities into which such securities are converted are outstanding; or

(b) any of its securities have been at any time since the 1st day of May, 1967, listed and posted for trading on any stock exchange in Ontario recognized by the Commission regardless of when such listing and posting for trading commenced,

except that where, upon the application of a corporation, the Commission is satisfied, in its discretion, that to do so would not be prejudicial to the public interest, the Commission may order, subject to such terms and conditions as the Commission may impose, that the corporation shall be deemed to have ceased to be offering its securities to the public.

(7) Execution of documents — Any articles, notice, resolution, requisition, statement or other document required or permitted to be executed by more than one person for the purposes of this Act may be executed in several documents of like form each of which is executed by one or more of such persons, and such documents, when duly executed by all persons required or permitted, as the case may be, to do so, shall be deemed to constitute one document for the purposes of this Act.

1994, c. 27, s. 71(1); 1999, c. 6, s. 3; 1999, c. 12, Sched. F, s. 1; 2000, c. 26, Sched. B, s. 3(1), (2); 2001, c. 9, Sched. D, s. 2(1), (2); 2005, c. 5, s. 4; 2006, c. 8, s. 106; 2006, c. 34, Sched. B, s. 1

2. (1) Application — This Act, except where it is otherwise expressly provided, applies to every body corporate with share capital,

(a) incorporated by or under a general or special Act of the Parliament of the former Province of Upper Canada;

(b) incorporated by or under a general or special Act of the Parliament of the former Province of Canada that has its registered office and carries on business in Ontario; or

(c) incorporated by or under a general or special Act of the Legislature,

but this Act does not apply to a corporation within the meaning of the *Loan and Trust Corporations Act* except as provided by that Act.

(2) Idem — Despite *The Railways Act*, being chapter 331 of the Revised Statutes of Ontario, 1950, and subject to subsection 168(6), this Act applies to a body corporate with share capital that is a company as defined in that Act but that is not engaged in constructing or operating a railway, street railway or incline railway.

(3) Idem — This Act does not apply to a body corporate with share capital that,

(a) is a company within the meaning of the *Corporations Act* and has objects in whole or in part of a social nature;

(b) is a corporation to which the *Co-operative Corporations Act* applies;

(c) is a corporation that is an insurer within the meaning of subsection 141(1) of the *Corporations Act*; or

(d) is a corporation to which the *Credit Unions and Caisses Populaires Act* applies.

PART II — INCORPORATION

3. (1) [Repealed 2000, c. 42, Sched., s. 1.]

(2) Incorporation — A corporation may be incorporated under this Act with its powers restricted by its articles to lending and investing money on mortgage of real estate or otherwise, or with its powers restricted by its articles to accepting and executing the office of liquidator, receiver, assignee, trustee in bankruptcy or trustee for the benefit of creditors and to accepting the duty of and acting generally in the winding up of corporations, partnerships and estates, other than estates of deceased persons, and shall not by reason thereof be deemed to be a corporation within the meaning of the *Loan and Trust Corporations Act,* but the number of its shareholders, exclusive of persons who are in the employment of the corporation, shall be limited by its articles to five, and no such corporation shall issue debt obligations except to its shareholders, or borrow money on the security of its property except from its shareholders, or receive money on deposit or offer its securities to the public.

2000, c. 42, Sched., s. 1

3.1 (1) Definitions — In this section and in sections 3.2, 3.3 and 3.4,

"member" means a member of a profession governed by an Act that permits the profession to be practised through a professional corporation;

"professional corporation" means a corporation incorporated or continued under this Act that holds a valid certificate of authorization or other authorizing document issued under an Act governing a profession.

(2) Professions — Where the practice of a profession is governed by an Act, a professional corporation may practise the profession if,

(a) that Act expressly permits the practice of the profession by a corporation and subject to the provisions of that Act; or

(b) the profession is governed by an Act named in Schedule 1 of the *Regulated Health Professions Act, 1991*, one of the following Acts or a prescribed Act:

1. *Certified General Accountants Act, 2010.*
2. *Chartered Accountants Act, 2010.*
3. *Law Society Act.*
4. *Social Work and Social Service Work Act, 1998.*
5. *Veterinarians Act.*

(3) Regulations — The Lieutenant Governor in Council may make regulations prescribing Acts for the purposes of clause (2)(b).

2000, c. 42, Sched., s. 2; 2010, c. 6, Sched. A, s. 69, Sched. C, s. 67

3.2 (1) Application of Act — This Act and the regulations apply with respect to a professional corporation except as otherwise set out in this section and sections 3.1, 3.3 and 3.4 and the regulations.

(2) Conditions for professional corporations — Despite any other provision of this Act but subject to subsection (6), a professional corporation shall satisfy all of the following conditions:

1. All of the issued and outstanding shares of the corporation shall be legally and beneficially owned, directly or indirectly, by one or more members of the same profession.
2. All officers and directors of the corporation shall be shareholders of the corporation.
3. The name of the corporation shall include the words "Professional Corporation" or "Société professionnelle" and shall comply with the rules respecting the names of professional corporations set out in the regulations and with the rules respecting names set out in the regulations or bylaws made under the Act governing the profession.
4. The corporation shall not have a number name.
5. The articles of incorporation of a professional corporation shall provide that the corporation may not carry on a business other than the practice of the profession but this paragraph shall not be construed to prevent the corporation from carrying on activities related to or ancillary to the practice of the profession, including the investment of surplus funds earned by the corporation.

(2.1) Deemed compliance — A professional corporation that has a name that includes the words "société professionnelle" shall be deemed to have complied with the requirements of subsection 10(1).

(3) Corporate acts not invalid — No act done by or on behalf of a professional corporation is invalid merely because it contravenes this Act.

(4) Voting agreements void — An agreement or proxy that vests in a person other than a shareholder of a professional corporation the right to vote the rights attached to a share of the corporation is void.

(5) Unanimous shareholder agreements void — Subject to subsection (6) a unanimous shareholder agreement in respect of a professional corporation is void unless each shareholder of the corporation is a member of the professional corporation.

(6) Special rules, health profession corporations — The Lieutenant Governor in Council may make regulations,

(a) exempting classes of health profession corporations, as defined in section 1(1) of the *Regulated Health Professions Act, 1991*, from the application of subsections (1) and (5) and such other provisions of this Act and the regulations as may be specified and prescribing terms and conditions that apply with respect to the health profession corporations in lieu of the provisions from which they are exempted;

(b) exempting classes of the shareholders of those health profession corporations from the application of subsections 3.4(2), (4) and (6) and such other provisions of this Act and the regulations as may be specified and prescribing rules that apply with respect to the shareholders in lieu of the provisions from which they are exempted;

(c) exempting directors and officers of those health profession corporations from the application of such provisions of this Act and the regulations as may be specified and prescribing rules that apply with respect to the directors and officers in lieu of the provisions from which they are exempted.

2000, c. 42, Sched., s. 2; 2002, c. 22, s. 8; 2004, c. 19, s. 3(1); 2005, c. 28, Sched. B, s. 1

3.3 (1) **Consequences of occurrence of certain events** — Despite any other Act, a professional corporation's certificate of authorization or other authorizing document remains valid and the corporation does not cease to be a professional corporation despite,

(a) the death of a shareholder;

(b) the divorce of a shareholder;

(c) the bankruptcy or insolvency of the corporation;

(d) the suspension of the corporation's certificate of authorization or other authorizing document; or

(e) the occurrence of such other event or the existence of such other circumstance as may be prescribed.

(2) **Invalidity of certificate** — Subject to the regulations, a certificate of authorization or other authorizing document becomes invalid and the corporation ceases to be a professional corporation on the revocation of the certificate.

(3) **Regulations** — For the purposes of subsection (1), the Lieutenant Governor in Council may make regulations,

(a) prescribing events and circumstances for the purposes of clause (1)(e);

(a.1) providing that, despite clause (1)(a), (b), (c), (d) or (e), whichever applies, a professional corporation's certificate of authorization or other authorizing document ceases to be valid and the corporation ceases to be a professional corporation because of a failure to meet the terms and conditions described in the regulation;

(a.2) prescribing terms and conditions that apply with respect to the events and circumstances referred to in clauses (1)(a), (b), (c), (d) and (e);

(a.3) prescribing exceptions to the events and circumstances referred to in clauses (1)(a), (b), (c), (d) and (e);

(b) prescribing the manner in which shares of a shareholder are to be dealt with on the occurrence of any event mentioned in clauses (1)(a) to (e), the time within which they are to be dealt with and any other matter related to dealing with the shares.

(4) **Name change** — A corporation that ceases to be a professional corporation shall change its name to remove from it the word "professional" or "professionnelle".

2000, c. 42, Sched., s. 2; 2001, c. 8, s. 1; 2001, c. 23, s. 6

3.4 (1) **No limit on professional liability** — Subsection 92(1) shall not be construed as limiting the professional liability of a shareholder of a professional corporation under an Act governing the profession for acts of the shareholder or acts of employees or agents of the corporation.

(2) **Deemed acts** — For the purposes of professional liability, the acts of a professional corporation shall be deemed to be the acts of the shareholders, employees or agents of the corporation, as the case may be.

(3) **Professional liability** — The liability of a member for a professional liability claim is not affected by the fact that the member is practising the profession through a professional corporation.

(4) **Joint and several liability** — A person is jointly and severally liable with a professional corporation for all professional liability claims made against the corporation in respect of errors and omissions that were made or occurred while the person was a shareholder of the corporation.

(5) **Same** — The liability of a member under subsection (4) cannot be greater than his or her liability would be in the circumstances if he or she were not practising through the professional corporation.

(6) **Same, partnerships and limited liability partnerships** — If a professional corporation is a partner in a partnership or limited liability partnership, the shareholders of the corporation have the same liability in respect of the partnership or limited liability partnership as they would have if the shareholders themselves were the partners.

2000, c. 42, Sched., s. 2; 2001, c. 8, s. 2

4. (1) **Articles of incorporation** — One or more individuals or bodies corporate or any combination thereof may incorporate a corporation by signing articles of incorporation and complying with section 6.

(2) **Idem** — Subsection (1) does not apply to an individual who,

(a) is less than eighteen years of age;

(b) has been found under the *Substitute Decisions Act, 1992* or under the *Mental Health Act* to be incapable of managing property or who has been found to be incapable by a court in Canada or elsewhere; or

(c) has the status of bankrupt.

2006, c. 34, Sched. B, s. 2

5. (1) **Contents of articles** — Articles of incorporation shall follow the prescribed form and shall set out the prescribed information.

(2) **Director's consent** — The corporation shall keep at its registered office address the consent, in the prescribed form, to act as a first director,

(a) of each individual who is named in the articles as a first director and who is not an incorporator; and

(b) of each individual who is named in the articles as a first director and who is an incorporator, if the articles are sent to the Director in a prescribed electronic format and the electronic signature of the individual is not set out on the articles under clause 273(4)(a) because the regulations provide that the signature is not required.

(2.1) **Inspection of consent** — Upon request and without charge, the corporation shall permit a director, shareholder or creditor to inspect a consent mentioned in subsection (2) during the normal business hours of the corporation and to make a copy.

(3) **Provisions in articles** — The articles may set out any provisions permitted by this Act or permitted by law to be set out in the by-laws of the corporation.

(4) **Where articles, etc., prevail** — Subject to subsection (5), if a greater number of votes of directors or shareholders are required by the articles or a unanimous shareholder agree-

ment than are required by this Act to effect any action, the provisions of the articles or of the unanimous shareholder agreement prevail.

(5) **Votes to remove director** — The articles shall not require a greater number of votes of shareholders to remove a director than the number specified in section 122.

1994, c. 27, s. 71(2); 1999, c. 12, Sched. F, s. 2; 2006, c. 19, Sched. G, s. 2; 2006, c. 34, Sched. B, s. 2

6. Certificate of incorporation — An incorporator shall send to the Director articles of incorporation and, upon receipt of the articles, the Director shall endorse thereon, in accordance with section 273, a certificate which shall constitute the certificate of incorporation.

7. Certificate of incorporation — A certificate of incorporation is conclusive proof that the corporation has been incorporated under this Act on the date set out in the certificate, except in a proceeding under section 240 to cancel the certificate for cause.

8. (1) Assignment of number — Every corporation shall be assigned a number by the Director and such number shall be specified as the corporation number in the certificate of incorporation and in any other certificate relating to the corporation endorsed or issued by the Director.

(2) **Idem** — Where no name is specified in the articles that are delivered to the Director, the corporation shall be assigned a number name.

(3) **Idem** — Where, through inadvertence or otherwise, the Director has assigned to a corporation a corporation number or number name that is the same as the number or name of any other corporation previously assigned, the Director may, without holding a hearing, issue a certificate of amendment to the articles of the corporation changing the number or name assigned to the corporation and, upon the issuance of certificate of amendment, the articles are amended accordingly.

(4) **Idem** — Where for any reason the Director has endorsed a certificate on articles that sets out the corporation number incorrectly, the Director may substitute a corrected certificate that bears the date of the certificate it replaces.

(5) **Idem** — The file number that was assigned to each corporation by the Minister prior to the 29th day of July, 1983 shall be deemed to be that corporation's number.

9. (1) Name prohibition — Subject to subsection (2), a corporation shall not have a name,

(a) that contains a word or expression prohibited by the regulations;

(b) that is the same as or, except where a number name is proposed, similar to,

(i) the name of a known,

(A) body corporate,

(B) trust,

(C) association,

(D) partnership,

(E) sole proprietorship, or

(F) individual,

whether in existence or not, or

(ii) the known name under which any body corporate, trust, association, partnership, sole proprietorship, or individual, carries on business or identifies himself, herself or itself,

if the use of that name would be likely to deceive; or

(c) that does not meet the requirements prescribed by the regulations.

(2) **Exception to subs. (1)** — A corporation may have a name described in clause (1)(b) upon complying with conditions prescribed by the regulations.

(3) **Documents filed** — There shall be filed with the Director such documents relating to the name of the corporation as may be prescribed by the regulations.

10. (1) **Use of "Limited", "Limitée", etc.** — The word "Limited", "Limitée", "Incorporated", "Incorporée" or "Corporation" or the corresponding abbreviations "Ltd.", "Ltée", "Inc." or "Corp." shall be part, in addition to any use in a figurative or descriptive sense, of the name of every corporation, but a corporation may be legally designated by either the full or the abbreviated form.

(2) **Languages** — Subject to this Act and the regulations, a corporation may have a name that is,

(a) English only;

(b) French only;

(c) one name that is a combination of English and French; or

(d) one name in English and one name in French that are equivalent but are used separately.

(2.1) **Same** — A corporation that has a name described in clause (2)(d) may be legally designated by its English name or its French name.

(3) **Idem** — For the purposes of subsections (1) and (2), only letters from the Roman alphabet or Arabic numerals or a combination thereof, together with such punctuation marks and other marks as are permitted by regulation, may form part of the name of a corporation.

(4) **Idem** — Subject to the provisions of this Act and the regulations, a corporation may have in its articles a special provision permitting it to set out its name in any language and the corporation may be legally designated by that name.

(5) **Idem** — Despite subsection (4), a corporation shall set out its name in legible characters in all contracts, invoices, negotiable instruments and orders for goods or services issued or made by or on behalf of the corporation and in all documents sent to the Director under this Act.

1994, c. 27, s. 71(3); 2010, c. 16, Sched. 8, s. 1

11. (1) **Unauthorized use of "Limited", etc.** — No person, while not incorporated, shall trade or carry on a business or undertaking under a name in which "Limited", "Incorporated" or "Corporation" or any abbreviation thereof, or any version thereof in another language, is used.

(2) **Idem** — Where a corporation carries on business or identifies itself to the public by a name or style other than as provided in the articles, that name or style shall not include the word "Limited", "Incorporated", or "Corporation" or any abbreviation thereof or any version thereof in another language.

12. (1) Change of name if objectionable — If a corporation, through inadvertence or otherwise, has acquired a name contrary to section 9 or 10, the Director may, after giving the corporation an opportunity to be heard, issue a certificate of amendment to the articles changing the name of the corporation to a name specified in the certificate and, upon the issuance of the certificate of amendment, the articles are amended accordingly.

(1.1) Written hearing — A hearing referred to in subsection (1) shall be in writing in accordance with the rules made by the Director under the *Statutory Powers Procedure Act*.

(2) Failure to perform undertaking — Where an undertaking to dissolve or change its name is given by a corporation and the undertaking is not carried out within the time specified, the Director may, after giving the corporation an opportunity to be heard, issue a certificate of amendment to the articles changing the name of the corporation to a name specified in the certificate and, upon the issuance of a certificate of amendment, the articles are amended accordingly.

(3) Idem — Where an undertaking to dissolve or change its name is given by a person who is not a corporation and the undertaking is not carried out within the time specified, the Director may, after giving the corporation that acquired the name by virtue of such undertaking an opportunity to be heard, issue a certificate of amendment to the articles changing the name of the corporation to a name specified in the certificate and, upon the issuance of the certificate, the articles are amended accordingly.

1998, c. 18, Sched. E, s. 20; 2004, c. 19, s. 3(2)

13. Corporate seal — A corporation may, but need not, have a corporate seal.

14. (1) Registered office — A corporation shall at all times have a registered office in Ontario at the location specified in its articles, in a resolution made under subsection (3) or in a special resolution made under subsection (4).

(2) Idem — The head office of every corporation incorporated prior to the 29th day of July, 1983 shall be deemed to be the registered office of the corporation.

(3) Change of location — A corporation may by resolution of its directors change the location of its registered office within a municipality or geographic township.

(4) Change of municipality, etc. — A corporation may by special resolution change the municipality or geographic township in which its registered office is located to another place in Ontario.

(5) Validity — Failure to file as set out in subsection (3) or (4) does not affect the validity of the resolution.

Proposed Repeal — 14(5)

(5) [Repealed 2011, c. 1, Sched. 2, s. 1(3). Not in force at date of publication.]

1994, c. 27, s. 71(4), (5); 2000, c. 26, Sched. B, s. 3(3)

15. Corporate powers — A corporation has the capacity and the rights, powers and privileges of a natural person.

16. Capacity to act outside Ontario — A corporation has the capacity to carry on its business, conduct its affairs and exercise its powers in any jurisdiction outside Ontario to the extent that the laws of such jurisdiction permit.

17. (1) Corporate power not dependent on by-law — It is not necessary for a by-law to be passed in order to confer any particular power on the corporation or its directors.

(2) Power limited by articles, etc. — A corporation shall not carry on any business or exercise any power that it is restricted by its articles from carrying on or exercising, nor shall the corporation exercise any of its powers in a manner contrary to its articles.

(3) Acting outside powers — Despite subsection (2) and subsection 3(2), no act of a corporation including a transfer of property to or by the corporation is invalid by reason only that the act is contrary to its articles, by-laws, a unanimous shareholder agreement or this Act.

18. Where notice is not deemed — No person is affected by or is deemed to have notice or knowledge of the contents of a document concerning a corporation by reason only that the document has been filed with the Director or is available for inspection at an office of the corporation.

19. Indoor management rule — A corporation or a guarantor of an obligation of a corporation may not assert against a person dealing with the corporation or with any person who has acquired rights from the corporation that,

(a) the articles, by-laws or any uninamous shareholder agreement have not been complied with;

(b) the persons named in the most recent notice filed under the *Corporations Information Act*, or named in the articles, whichever is more current, are not the directors of the corporation;

(c) the location named in the most recent notice filed under subsection 14(3) or named in the articles, whichever is more current, is not the registered office of the corporation;

Proposed Amendment — 19(c)

(c) the location named in the most recent notice filed under the *Corporations Information Act* or named in the articles, whichever is more current, is not the registered office of the corporation;

2011, c. 1, Sched. 2, s. 1(4) [Not in force at date of publication.]

(d) a person held out by a corporation as a director, an officer or an agent of the corporation has not been duly appointed or does not have authority to exercise the powers and perform the duties that are customary in the business of the corporation or usual for such director, officer or agent;

(e) a document issued by any director, officer or agent of a corporation with actual or usual authority to issue the document is not valid or not genuine; or

(f) a sale, lease or exchange of property referred to in subsection 184(3) was not authorized,

except where the person has or ought to have, by virtue of the person's position with or relationship to the corporation, knowledge to that effect.

2006, c. 34, Sched. B, s. 3

20. [Repealed 2006, c. 34, Sched. B, s. 4.]

21. (1) Contract prior to corporate existence — Except as provided in this section, a person who enters into an oral or written contract in the name of or on behalf of a corporation before it comes into existence is personally bound by the contract and is entitled to the benefits thereof.

(2) Adoption of contract by corporation — A corporation may, within a reasonable time after it comes into existence, by any action or conduct signifying its intention to be bound thereby, adopt an oral or written contract made before it came into existence in its name or on its behalf, and upon such adoption,

(a) the corporation is bound by the contract and is entitled to the benefits thereof as if the corporation had been in existence at the date of the contract and had been a party thereto; and

(b) a person who purported to act in the name of or on behalf of the corporation ceases, except as provided in subsection (3), to be bound by or entitled to the benefits of the contract.

Proposed Addition — 21(2.1)

(2.1) Assignment, etc., of contract before adoption — Until a corporation adopts an oral or written contract made before it came into existence, the person who entered into the contract in the name of or on behalf of the corporation may assign, amend or terminate the contract subject to the terms of the contract.

2011, c. 1, Sched. 2, s. 1(5) [Not in force at date of publication.]

(3) Non-adoption of contract — Except as provided in subsection (4), whether or not an oral or written contract made before the coming into existence of a corporation is adopted by the corporation, a party to the contract may apply to a court for an order fixing obligations under the contract as joint or joint and several or apportioning liability between the corporation and the person who purported to act in the name of or on behalf of the corporation, and, upon such application, the court may make any order it thinks fit.

(4) Exception to subs. (1) — If expressly so provided in the oral or written contract referred to in subsection (1), a person who purported to act in the name of or on behalf of the corporation before it came into existence is not in any event bound by the contract or entitled to the benefits thereof.

PART III — CORPORATE FINANCE

22. (1) Shares — Shares of a corporation shall be in registered form and shall be without nominal or par value.

(2) Idem — Shares with nominal or par value of a corporation incorporated before the 29th day of July, 1983 shall be deemed to be shares without nominal or par value.

(3) Rights of shareholders — Where a corporation has only one class of shares, the rights of the holders thereof are equal in all respects and include the rights,

(a) to vote at all meetings of shareholders; and

(b) to receive the remaining property of the corporation upon dissolution.

(4) Idem — The articles may provide for more than one class of shares and where they so provide,

(a) the rights, privileges, restrictions and conditions attaching to the shares of each class shall be set out therein; and

(b) each of the rights set out in subsection (3) shall be attached to at least one class of shares, but both such rights are not required to be attached to any one class.

(5) Saving provision — Despite subsection (4), the right of the holders of a class of shares to one vote for each share at all meetings of shareholders other than meetings of the holders of another class of shares, or to receive the remaining property of the corporation upon dissolution, need not be set out in the articles.

(6) Shares within a class equal — Except as provided in section 25, each share of a class shall be the same in all respects as every other share of that class.

(7) Same rights, etc. — The articles may provide that two or more classes of shares or two or more series within a class of shares may have the same rights, privileges, restrictions and conditions.

2006, c. 34, Sched. B, s. 5

23. (1) Issuance of shares — Subject to the articles, the by-laws, any unanimous shareholder agreement and section 26, shares may be issued at such time and to such persons and for such consideration as the directors may determine.

(2) Shares non-assessable — Shares issued by a corporation are non-assessable and the holders are not liable to the corporation or to its creditors in respect thereof.

(3) Fully-paid shares — A share shall not be issued until the consideration for the share is fully paid in money or in property or past service that is not less in value than the fair equivalent of the money that the corporation would have received if the share had been issued for money.

(4) Value determined by directors — The directors shall, in connection with the issue of any share not issued for money, determine,

(a) the amount of money the corporation would have received if the share had been issued for money; and

(b) either,

(i) the fair value of the property or past service in consideration of which the share is issued, or

(ii) that such property or past service has a fair value that is not less than the amount of money referred to in clause (a).

(5) Idem — In determining the value of property or past service, the directors may take into account reasonable charges and expenses of organization and reorganization and payments for property and past service reasonably expected to benefit the corporation.

(6) Interpretation of property — For the purposes of subsection (3) and of subsection 24(3), a document evidencing indebtedness of a person to whom shares are to be issued, or of any other person not dealing at arm's length with such person within the meaning of that term in the *Income Tax Act* (Canada), does not constitute property.

24. (1) Separate capital account — A corporation shall maintain a separate stated capital account for each class and series of shares it issues.

(2) Idem — A corporation shall add to the appropriate stated capital account in respect of any shares it issues the full amount of the consideration it receives as determined by the directors which, in the case of shares not issued for money, shall be the amount determined by the directors in accordance with clause 23(4)(a) or, if a determination is made by the directors in accordance with subclause 23(4)(b)(i), the amount so determined.

(3) Exceptions — Despite subsection (2) and subsection 23(3), a corporation may, subject to subsection (4), add to the stated capital accounts maintained for the shares of classes or series the whole or any part of the consideration that it receives in exchange if the corporation issues shares,

(a) in exchange for,

(i) property of a person who immediately before the exchange did not deal with the corporation at arm's length within the meaning of that term in the *Income Tax Act* (Canada),

(ii) shares of, or another interest in, a body corporate that immediately before the exchange, or that because of the exchange, did not deal with the corporation at arm's length within the meaning of that term in the *Income Tax Act* (Canada), or

(iii) property of a person who, immediately before the exchange, dealt with the corporation at arm's length within the meaning of that term in the *Income Tax Act* (Canada), if the person, the corporation and all holders of shares in the class or series of shares so issued consent to the exchange; or

(b) under an agreement referred to in subsection 175(1) or an arrangement referred to in clause (c) or (d) of the definition of "arrangement" in subsection 182(1) or to shareholders of an amalgamating corporation who receive the shares in addition to or instead of securities of the amalgamated corporation.

(3.1) Consent not required — The consent referred to in subclause (3)(a)(iii) is not required if the issuance of the shares does not result in a decrease in the value of the stated capital account maintained for the class or series divided by the number of shares in the class or series.

(4) Addition to stated capital account — On the issue of a share, a corporation shall not add to a stated capital account in respect of the share an amount greater than the amount referred to in subsection (2).

(5) Stated capital at time of coming into force or continuance — Despite subsection (2), on the 29th day of July, 1983 or at such time thereafter as a corporation has been continued under this Act, as the case may be, the amount in the stated capital account maintained by a corporation in respect of each class or series of shares then issued shall be equal to the aggregate amount paid up on the shares of each such class or series of shares immediately prior thereto, and, after such time, a corporation may, upon complying with subsection (6), add to the stated capital account maintained by it in respect of any class or series of shares any amount it has credited to a retained earnings or other surplus account.

(6) Additions to stated capital account — Where a corporation proposes to add any amount to a stated capital account that it maintains in respect of a class or series of shares otherwise than under subsection 38(2), the addition to the stated capital account must be approved by special resolution if,

(a) the amount to be added,

(i) was not received by the corporation as consideration for the issue of shares, or

(ii) was received by the corporation as consideration for the issue of shares but does not form part of the stated capital attributable to such shares; and

(b) the corporation has outstanding shares of more than one class or series.

(7) **Idem** — Where a class or series of shares of a corporation would be affected by the addition of an amount to any stated capital account under subsection (6) in a manner different from the manner in which any other class or series of shares of the corporation would be affected by such action, the holders of the differently affected class or series of shares are entitled to vote separately as a class or series, as the case may be, on the proposal to take the action, whether or not such shares otherwise carry the right to vote.

(8) **Expressed in one or more currencies** — Stated capital accounts of a corporation may be expressed in one or more currencies.

(9) **Reduction in stated capital** — A corporation shall not reduce its stated capital or any stated capital account except in the manner provided in this Act.

(10) **Non-application of Act** — The provisions of this Act relating to stated capital do not apply to an open-end mutual fund.

(11) **Definition** — For the purposes of this section,

"open-end mutual fund" means an offering corporation that carries on only the business of investing the consideration it receives for the shares it issues, and all or substantially all the shares of which are redeemable upon the demand of the holders of such shares.

2006, c. 34, Sched. B, s. 6

25. (1) **Special shares in series** — The articles, subject to the limitations set out in them,

(a) may authorize the issue of any class of shares in one or more series and may fix the number of shares in, and determine the designation, rights, privileges, restrictions and conditions attaching to the shares of, each series; and

(b) may, where the articles authorize the issue of any class of shares in one or more series, authorize the directors to fix the number of shares in, and to determine the designation, rights, privileges, restrictions and conditions attaching to the shares of each series.

(2) **Proportionate abatement** — If any amount,

(a) of cumulative dividends, whether or not declared, or declared non-cumulative dividends; or

(b) payable on return of capital in the event of the liquidation, dissolution or winding up of a corporation,

in respect of shares of a series is not paid in full, the shares of the series shall participate rateably with the shares of all other series of the same class in respect of,

(c) all accumulated cumulative dividends, whether or not declared, and all declared non-cumulative dividends; or

(d) all amounts payable on return of capital in the event of the liquidation, dissolution or winding up of the corporation,

as the case may be.

(3) **No priority of shares of same class** — No rights, privileges, restrictions or conditions attached to a series of shares authorized under this section shall confer upon the shares of a series a priority in respect of,

(a) dividends; or

(b) return of capital in the event of the liquidation, dissolution or winding up of the corporation,

over the shares of any other series of the same class.

(4) **Articles designating special shares** — Where, in respect of a series of shares, the directors exercise the authority conferred on them, before the issue of shares of such series, the directors shall send to the Director articles of amendment in the prescribed form designating such series.

(5) **Certificate re special shares** — On receipt of articles of amendment designating a series of shares under subsection (4), the Director shall endorse thereon, in accordance with section 273, a certificate which shall constitute the certificate of amendment.

26. **Pre-emptive rights** — If it is so provided in the articles or a unanimous shareholder agreement, no shares of a class or series shall be issued unless the shares have first been offered to the shareholders of the corporation holding shares of that class or series or of another class or series on such terms as are provided in the articles or unanimous shareholder agreement.

27. (1) **Conversion privileges, etc.** — A corporation may issue warrants as evidence of conversion privileges or options or rights to acquire securities of the corporation, and shall set out the conditions thereof,

(a) in certificates evidencing the securities to which the conversion privileges, options or rights are attached; or

(b) in separate certificates or other documents.

(2) **Idem** — Conversion privileges and options or rights to purchase securities of a corporation may be made transferable or non-transferable, and options or rights to purchase may be made separable or inseparable from any securities to which they are attached.

(3) **Corporation to maintain sufficient reserve** — Where a corporation has granted privileges to convert any securities, other than shares issued by the corporation, into shares of the corporation or has issued or granted options or rights to acquire shares of the corporation and where the articles limit the number of authorized shares, the corporation shall reserve and continue to reserve sufficient authorized shares to meet the exercise of such conversion privileges, options and rights.

28. (1) **Subsidiaries not to hold shares of holding bodies corporate** — Except as provided in subsection (2) and sections 29 to 32, a corporation,

(a) shall not hold shares in itself or in its holding body corporate; and

(b) shall not permit any of its subsidiary bodies corporate to hold shares of the corporation.

(2) **Disposal of shares** — A corporation shall cause a subsidiary body corporate of the corporation that holds shares of the corporation to sell or otherwise dispose of those shares within five years from the date the body corporate became a subsidiary of the corporation.

29. (1) **Exception to s. 28** — A corporation may in the capacity of a legal representative hold shares in itself or in its holding body corporate unless it or the holding body corporate or a subsidiary of either of them has a beneficial interest in the shares.

(2) **Idem** — A corporation may permit a subsidiary body corporate to hold shares of the corporation in the capacity of a legal representative unless the corporation or the subsidiary body corporate or a subsidiary of either of them has a beneficial interest in the shares.

(3) **Idem** — A corporation may hold shares in itself or in its holding body corporate by way of security for the purposes of a transaction entered into by it in the ordinary course of a business that includes the lending of money.

(4) **Exception relating to Canadian ownership** — A corporation may, for the purpose of assisting the corporation or any of its affiliates or associates to qualify under any prescribed Act of Canada or a province or ordinance of a territory to receive licences, permits, grants, payments or other benefits by reason of attaining or maintaining a specified level of Canadian ownership or control, hold shares in itself that,

(a) are not restricted for the purpose of assisting the corporation or any of its affiliates or associates to so qualify; or

(b) are shares into which shares held under clause (a) were converted by the corporation that are restricted for the purpose of assisting the corporation to so qualify and that were not previously held by the corporation.

(5) **Prohibited transfers** — A corporation shall not transfer shares held under subsection (4) to any person unless the corporation is satisfied, on reasonable grounds, that the ownership of the shares as a result of the transfer would assist the corporation or any of its affiliates or associates to achieve the purpose set out in subsection (4).

(6) **Where shares are transferred** — Where shares held under subsection (4) are transferred by a corporation, subsections 23(1), (3), (4), (5) and (6), clause 127(3)(c) and subsection 130(1) apply, with such modifications as the circumstances require, in respect of the transfer as if the transfer were an issue.

(7) **Transfer not void** — No transfer of shares by a corporation shall be void or voidable solely because the transfer is in contravention of subsection (5).

(8) **Corporation holding shares in itself** — A corporation holding shares in itself or in its holding body corporate or a subsidiary body corporate of a corporation holding shares of the corporation shall not vote or permit those shares to be voted unless the corporation or subsidiary body corporate, as the case may be,

(a) holds the shares in the capacity of a legal representative; and

(b) has complied with section 49 of the *Securities Act* where that section is applicable.

(9) **Exception, conditions precedent** — A corporation may permit any of its subsidiary bodies corporate to acquire shares of the corporation through the issuance of those shares by the corporation to the subsidiary body corporate if, before the acquisition takes place, the conditions prescribed for the purposes of this subsection are met.

(10) Conditions subsequent — After the acquisition has taken place under the purported authority of subsection (9), the conditions prescribed for the purposes of this subsection shall be met.

(11) Non-compliance with conditions — If a corporation permits a subsidiary body corporate to acquire shares of the corporation under the purported authority of subsection (9) and either,

(a) one or more of the conditions prescribed for the purposes of subsection (9) were not met; or

(b) one or more of the conditions prescribed for the purposes of subsection (10) were not met or have ceased to be met,

then, despite subsections 17(3) and 24(2), the prescribed consequences apply in respect of the acquisition of the shares and their issuance.

2006, c. 34, Sched. B, s. 7

30. (1) Purchase of issued shares permitted — Subject to subsection (2) and to its articles, a corporation may purchase or otherwise acquire any of its issued shares or warrants.

(2) Where prohibited — A corporation shall not make any payment to purchase or otherwise acquire shares issued by it if there are reasonable grounds for believing that,

(a) the corporation is or, after the payment, would be unable to pay its liabilities as they become due; or

(b) after the payment, the realizable value of the corporation's assets would be less than the aggregate of,

(i) its liabilities, and

(ii) its stated capital of all classes.

31. (1) Where s. 30(2) does not apply — Despite subsection 30(2) but subject to subsection (3) of this section and to its articles, a corporation may purchase or otherwise acquire shares issued by it to,

(a) settle or compromise a debt or claim asserted by or against the corporation;

(b) eliminate fractional shares; or

(c) fulfil the terms of a non-assignable agreement under which the corporation has an option or is obliged to purchase shares owned by a current or former director, officer or employee of the corporation.

(2) Idem — Despite subsection 30(2), a corporation may purchase or otherwise acquire shares issued by it to,

(a) satisfy the claim of a shareholder who dissents under section 185; or

(b) comply with an order under section 248.

(3) Restriction on payment — A corporation shall not make any payment to purchase or acquire under subsection (1) shares issued by it if there are reasonable grounds for believing that,

(a) the corporation is or, after the payment, would be unable to pay its liabilities as they become due; or

(b) after the payment, the realizable value of the corporation's assets would be less than the aggregate of,

(i) its liabilities, and

(ii) the amount required for the payment on a redemption or in a liquidation of all shares where the holders have the right to be paid before the holders of the shares to be purchased or acquired, to the extent that the amount has not been included in its liabilities.

2006, c. 34, Sched. B, s. 8

32. (1) **Redemption of shares** — Despite subsection 30(2) and subsection 31(3), but subject to subsection (2) and to its articles, a corporation may purchase or redeem any redeemable shares issued by it at prices not exceeding the redemption price thereof stated in the articles or calculated according to a formula stated in the articles.

(2) **Restriction on redemption** — A corporation shall not make any payment to purchase or redeem any redeemable shares issued by it if there are reasonable grounds for believing that,

(a) the corporation is or, after the payment, would be unable to pay its liabilities as they become due; or

(b) after the payment, the realizable value of the corporation's assets would be less than the aggregate of,

(i) its liabilities, and

(ii) the amount that would be required to pay the holders of shares that have a right to be paid, on a redemption or in a liquidation, rateably with or before the holders of the shares to be purchased or redeemed, to the extent that the amount has not been included in its liabilities.

2006, c. 34, Sched. B, s. 9

33. **Donation of share** — A corporation may accept from any shareholder a share of the corporation surrendered to it as a gift, but may not extinguish or reduce a liability in respect of an amount unpaid on any such share except in accordance with section 34.

34. (1) **Reduction of liability re unpaid share: stated capital** — Subject to subsection (4), a corporation may by special resolution,

(a) extinguish or reduce a liability in respect of an amount unpaid on any share; or

(b) reduce its stated capital for any purpose including, without limiting the generality of the foregoing, for the purpose of,

(i) distributing to the holders of issued shares of any class or series of shares an amount not exceeding the stated capital of the class or series, or

(ii) declaring its stated capital to be reduced by,

(A) an amount that is not represented by realizable assets, or

(B) an amount otherwise determined in respect of which no amount is to be distributed to holders of issued shares of the corporation.

(2) **Right to vote where reduction under subs. (1)** — Where a class or series of shares of a corporation would be affected by a reduction of stated capital under clause (1)(b) in a manner different from the manner in which any other class or series of shares of the corpora-

tion would be affected by such action, the holders of the differently affected class or series of shares are entitled to vote separately as a class or series, as the case may be, on the proposal to take the action, whether or not the shares otherwise carry the right to vote.

(3) **Account to be reduced specified** — A special resolution under this section shall specify the stated capital account or accounts from which the reduction of stated capital effected by the special resolution will be made.

(4) **Restriction on reduction** — A corporation shall not take any action to extinguish or reduce a liability in respect of an amount unpaid on a share or to reduce its stated capital for any purpose other than the purpose mentioned in sub-subclause (1)(b)(ii)(A) if there are reasonable grounds for believing that,

(a) the corporation is or, after the taking of such action, would be unable to pay its liabilities as they become due; or

(b) after the taking of such action, the realizable value of the corporation's assets would be less than the aggregate of its liabilities.

(5) **Application for order where improper reduction** — A creditor of a corporation is entitled to apply to the court for an order compelling a shareholder or other recipient,

(a) to pay to the corporation an amount equal to any liability of the shareholder that was extinguished or reduced contrary to this section; or

(b) to pay or deliver to the corporation any money or property that was paid or distributed to the shareholder or other recipient as a consequence of a reduction of capital made contrary to this section.

(6) [Repealed 2002, c. 24, Sched. B, s. 25, item 2.]

(7) **Class action** — Where it appears that there are numerous shareholders who may be liable under this section, the court may permit an action to be brought against one or more of them as representatives of the class and, if the plaintiff establishes a claim as creditor, may make an order of reference and add as parties in the referee's office all such shareholders as may be found, and the referee shall determine the amount that each should contribute towards the plaintiff's claim, which amount may not, in the case of any particular shareholder, exceed the amount referred to in subsection (5), and the referee may direct payment of the sums so determined.

(8) **Shareholder holding shares in fiduciary capacity** — No person holding shares in the capacity of a personal representative and registered on the records of the corporation as a shareholder and therein described as the personal representative of a named person is personally liable under this section, but the person named is subject to all liabilities imposed by this section.

(9) **S. 130, does not apply** — This section does not affect any liability that arises under section 130.

2002, c. 24, Sched. B, s. 25, item 2

35. (1) **Amount deducted from account upon purchase, etc., of shares** — Upon a purchase, redemption or other acquisition by a corporation under section 30, 31, 32, 40 or 185 or clause 248(3)(f) of shares or fractions thereof issued by it, the corporation shall deduct from the stated capital account maintained for the class or series of shares of which the shares purchased, redeemed or otherwise acquired form a part, an amount equal to the result obtained by multiplying the stated capital of the shares of that class or series by the number of shares of that class or series or fractions thereof purchased, redeemed or otherwise acquired, divided by the number of issued shares of that class or series immediately before the purchase, redemption or other acquisition.

(2) **Idem** — A corporation shall deduct the amount of a payment made by the corporation to a shareholder under clause 248(3)(g) from the stated capital account maintained for the class or series of shares in respect of which the payment was made.

(3) **Adjustment in stated capital account** — A corporation shall adjust its stated capital account or accounts in accordance with any special resolution referred to in subsection 34(3).

(4) **Idem** — Upon a change under section 168, 186 or 248 of issued shares of a corporation, or upon a conversion of such shares pursuant to their terms, into shares of another class or series, the corporation shall,

(a) deduct from the stated capital account maintained for the class or series of shares changed or converted an amount equal to the result obtained by multiplying the stated capital of the shares of that class or series by the number of shares of that class or series changed or converted, and dividing by the number of issued shares of that class or series immediately before the change or conversion; and

(b) add the result obtained under clause (a) and any additional consideration received pursuant to the change or conversion to the stated capital account maintained or to be maintained for the class or series of shares into which the shares have been changed or converted.

(5) **Idem** — For the purpose of subsection (4) and subject to its articles, where a corporation issues two classes or series of shares and there is attached to each class or series a right to convert a share of the one class or series into a share of the other class or series, the amount of stated capital attributable to a share in either class or series is the amount obtained when the sum of the stated capital of both classes or series of shares is divided by the number of issued shares of both classes or series of shares immediately before the conversion.

(6) **Status of shares purchased, etc.** — Shares of any class or series or fractional shares issued by a corporation and purchased, redeemed or otherwise acquired by it shall be cancelled or, if the articles limit the number of authorized shares of the class or series, may be restored to the status of authorized but unissued shares of the class.

(7) **Interpretation** — For the purposes of this section,

(a) a corporation holding shares in itself as permitted by subsections 29(1) and (2) shall be deemed not to have purchased, redeemed or otherwise acquired the shares; and

(b) a corporation holding shares in itself under clause 29(4)(a) shall be deemed not to have purchased, redeemed or otherwise acquired the shares at the time they were acquired, but,

(i) any of those shares that are held by the corporation at the expiration of two years, and

(ii) any shares into which any of those shares were converted by the corporation and held under clause 29(4)(b) that are held by the corporation at the expiration of two years after the shares from which they were converted were acquired,

shall be deemed to have been acquired at the expiration of the two years.

(8) **Conversion of shares** — Where shares of a class or series are changed under section 168, 186 or 248, or converted pursuant to their terms, into the same or another number of

shares of another class or series, such shares become the same in all respects as the shares of the class or series respectively into which they are changed or converted and, if the articles limit the number of shares of either of such classes or series, the number of authorized shares of such class or series is changed and the articles are amended accordingly.

36. (1) Contract with corporation re purchase of its shares — A contract with a corporation providing for the purchase of shares of the corporation by the corporation is specifically enforceable against the corporation except to the extent that the corporation cannot perform the contract without thereby being in breach of section 30, 31 or 32.

(2) Idem — In any action brought on a contract referred to in subsection (1), the corporation has the burden of proving that performance thereof is prevented by section 30, 31 or 32.

(3) Enforcement of contract — Until the corporation has fulfilled all of its obligations under a contract referred to in subsection (1), the other party to the contract retains the status of a claimant entitled to be paid as soon as the corporation is lawfully able to do so or, in a liquidation, to be ranked subordinate to the rights of creditors and to the rights of holders of any class of shares whose rights were in priority to the rights given to the holders of the class of shares being purchased, but in priority to the rights of other shareholders.

2006, c. 34, Sched. B, s. 10

37. Commission on sale of shares — The directors may authorize the corporation to pay a reasonable commission to any person in consideration of the person's purchasing or agreeing to purchase shares of the corporation from the corporation or from any other person, or procuring or agreeing to procure purchasers for any such shares.

38. (1) Declaration of dividends — Subject to its articles and any unanimous shareholder agreement, the directors may declare and a corporation may pay a dividend by issuing fully paid shares of the corporation or options or rights to acquire fully paid shares of the corporation and, subject to subsection (3), a corporation may pay a dividend in money or property.

(2) Stock dividend — If shares of a corporation are issued in payment of a dividend, the corporation may add all or part of the value of those shares to the stated capital account of the corporation maintained or to be maintained for the shares of the class or series issued in payment of the dividend.

(3) When dividend not to be declared — The directors shall not declare and the corporation shall not pay a dividend if there are reasonable grounds for believing that,

(a) the corporation is or, after the payment, would be unable to pay its liabilities as they become due; or

(b) the realizable value of the corporation's assets would thereby be less than the aggregate of,

(i) its liabilities, and

(ii) its stated capital of all classes.

2006, c. 34, Sched. B, s. 11

39. (1) Corporations with wasting assets — Despite anything in this Act, a corporation,

(a) that for the time being carries on as its principal business the business of operating a producing mining, gas or oil property owned and controlled by it;

(b) that has at least 75 per cent of its assets being of a wasting character; or

(c) that is incorporated for the purpose of acquiring the assets or a substantial part of the assets of a body corporate and administering such assets for the purpose of converting them into cash and distributing the cash among the shareholders of the corporation,

may declare and pay dividends out of the funds derived from the operations of the corporation.

(2) Extent of impairment of capital — The powers conferred by subsection (1) may be exercised even though the value of the net assets of the corporation may be thereby reduced to less then its stated capital of all classes if the payment of the dividends does not reduce the value of its remaining assets to an amount insufficient to meet all the liabilities of the corporation, exclusive of its stated capital of all classes.

(3) Special resolution — The powers conferred by subsection (1) may be exercised only under the authority of a special resolution.

40. (1) Lien on share — The articles or by-laws of a corporation or, in the case of a corporation other than an offering corporation, a unanimous shareholder agreement, may provide that the corporation has a lien on a share registered in the name of a shareholder or the shareholder's legal representative for a debt of that shareholder to the corporation, including an amount unpaid in respect of a share issued by a body corporate on the date it was continued under this Act.

(2) Exception — Subsection (1) does not apply to any class or series of shares listed and posted for trading on a stock exchange in or outside Canada.

(3) Enforcement of lien — A corporation may enforce a lien referred to in subsection (1) in accordance with its articles, by-laws or unanimous shareholder agreement.

2006, c. 8, s. 107

41. Shares personal property — The shares of a corporation are personal property.

42. (1) Restrictions on transfer, etc. — An offering corporation shall not impose restrictions on the transfer or ownership of shares of any class or series except such restrictions as are authorized by its articles.

(2) No public offer if transfer, etc., restricted — exceptions — A corporation that has imposed restrictions on the transfer or ownership of a class or series of its shares shall not offer any of its shares of that class or series, or any shares convertible into shares of that class or series, to the public unless the restrictions are necessary,

(a) by or under any Act of Canada or Ontario as a condition to the obtaining, holding or renewal of authority to engage in any activity necessary to its undertaking;

(b) for the purpose of achieving or preserving its status as a Canadian body corporate for the purpose of any Act of Canada or Ontario;

(c) to limit to a specified level the ownership of its shares by any prescribed class of person for the purpose of assisting the corporation or any of its affiliates or associates to qualify under the *Securities Act* or similar legislation of a province or territory to obtain, hold or renew registration, or to qualify for membership in a stock exchange in Ontario recognized as such by the Commission; or

(d) to attain or to maintain a specified level of Canadian ownership or control for the purpose of assisting the corporation or any of its affiliates or associates to qualify to receive licences, permits, grants, payments or other benefits under any prescribed Act of Canada or a province or ordinance of a territory.

(3) **Application of subs. (2)(c), (d)** — Nothing in clauses (2)(c) or (d) authorizes a corporation to impose restrictions on the transfer or ownership of shares of any class or series of which any shares are outstanding unless,

(a) in the case of restrictions in respect of a class, the shares of the class; or

(b) in the case of restrictions in respect of a series, the shares of the series,

are already subject to restrictions for the purpose described in clause (2)(c) or (d).

(4) **Idem** — A corporation may,

(a) limit the number of its shares that may be owned; or

(b) prohibit the ownership of its shares,

by any person whose ownership would adversely affect the ability of the corporation or any of its affiliates or associates to attain or maintain a level of Canadian ownership or control specified in its articles that equals or exceeds a specified level referred to in clause (2)(d).

1994, c. 27, s. 71(6); 2006, c. 8, s. 108

43. Bearer debt obligations — Nothing in this Act prohibits the issue of debt obligations in bearer form.

44. (1) **Irredeemable debt obligation** — A condition contained in a debt obligation or in an instrument for securing a debt obligation is not invalid by reason only that the debt obligation is thereby made irredeemable or redeemable only on the happening of a contingency, however remote, or on the expiration of a period, however long.

(2) **Debt obligations** — Debt obligations issued, pledged, hypothecated or deposited by a corporation are not redeemed by reason only that the indebtedness evidenced by the debt obligations or in respect of which the debt obligations are issued, pledged, hypothecated or deposited is repaid.

(3) **Idem** — Debt obligations issued by a corporation and purchased, redeemed or otherwise acquired by it may be cancelled or, subject to any applicable trust indenture or other agreement, may be reissued, pledged or hypothecated to secure any obligation of the corporation then existing or thereafter incurred, and any such acquisition and reissue, pledge or hypothecation is not a cancellation of the debt obligations.

Part IV — Sale of Restricted Shares

45. (1) **Sale of restricted shares by corporation** — A corporation that has restrictions on the issue, transfer or ownership of its shares of any class or series may, for any of the purposes set out in clauses (a) to (c), sell, under the conditions and after giving the notice that may be prescribed, as if it were the owner of the shares, any of those restricted shares that are owned, or that the directors determine in the manner that may be prescribed may be owned, contrary to the restrictions in order to,

(a) assist the corporation or any of its affiliates or associates to qualify under the *Securities Act* or similar legislation of a province or territory to obtain, hold or renew a registration, or to qualify for membership in a stock exchange in Ontario recognized as such by the Commission, by reason of limiting to a specified level the ownership of its shares by any prescribed class of persons;

(b) assist the corporation or any of its affiliates or associates to qualify under any prescribed law of Canada or of a province or territory to receive licences, permits, grants, payments or other benefits by reason of attaining or maintaining a specified level of Canadian ownership or control; or

(c) assist the corporation to comply with a prescribed law.

(2) **Obligations of directors in sale** — Where shares are to be sold by a corporation under subsection (1), the directors of the corporation shall select the shares for sale in good faith and in a manner that is not unfairly prejudicial to, and does not unfairly disregard the interests of, the holders of the shares in the restricted class or series taken as a whole.

(3) **Effect of sale** — Where shares are sold by a corporation under subsection (1), the owner of the shares immediately prior to the sale shall, by that sale, be divested of the owner's interest in the shares, and the person who, but for the sale, would be the registered holder of the shares or a person who satisfies the corporation that, but for the sale, such person could properly be treated as the registered holder of the shares under section 67 shall, from the time of the sale, be entitled to receive only the net proceeds of the sale, together with any income earned thereon from the beginning of the month next following the date of the receipt by the corporation of the proceeds of the sale, less any taxes thereon and any costs of administration of a trust fund constituted under subsection (5) in relation thereto.

(4) **S. 67(4–6) apply** — Subsections 67(4), (5) and (6) apply in respect of the person who is entitled under subsection (3) to receive the proceeds of a sale of shares under subsection (1) as if the proceeds were a security and the person were a registered holder of the security.

(5) **Proceeds of sale to be trust fund** — The proceeds of a sale by a corporation under subsection (1) constitute a trust fund in the hands of the corporation for the benefit of the person entitled under subsection (3) to receive the proceeds of the sale, and any such trust fund may be commingled by the corporation with other such trust funds and shall be invested in such manner as may be prescribed.

(6) **Cost of administration** — Reasonable costs of administration of a trust fund referred to in subsection (5) may be deducted from the trust fund and any income earned thereon.

(7) **Appointment of trust corporation** — Subject to this section, a corporation may transfer any trust fund referred to in subsection (5) and the administration thereof, to a trust company in Canada registered as such under the laws of Canada, a province or a territory, and the corporation is thereupon discharged of all further liability in respect of the trust fund.

(8) **Discharge of corporation and trust corporation** — A receipt signed by a person entitled under subsection (3) to receive the proceeds of a sale that constitute a trust fund under subsection (5) shall be a complete discharge of the corporation and of any trust corporation to which a trust fund is transferred under subsection (7), in respect of the trust fund and income earned thereon paid to the person.

(9) **Forfeit to Crown** — A trust fund described in subsection (5) together with any income earned thereon, less any taxes thereon and costs of administration, that has not been claimed, by a person entitled under subsection (3) to receive the proceeds of a sale that constitute the trust fund for a period of ten years after the date of the sale is forfeited to the Crown.

2006, c. 34, Sched. B, s. 12

PART V — INDENTURE TRUSTEES

46. (1) Definitions — In this Part,

"event of default" means an event specified in a trust indenture on the occurrence of which,

(a) a security interest constituted by the trust indenture becomes enforceable, or

(b) the principal, interest and other money payable thereunder become or may be declared to be payable before the date of maturity,

but the event is not an event of default until all conditions prescribed by the trust indenture in connection with such event for the giving of notice or the lapse of time or otherwise have been satisfied;

"trust indenture" means any deed, indenture or other instrument, including any supplement or amendment thereto, made by a body corporate under which the body corporate issues or guarantees debt obligations and in which a person is appointed as trustee for the holders of the debt obligations issued or guaranteed thereunder;

"trustee" means any person appointed as trustee under the terms of a trust indenture to which a body corporate is a party and includes any successor trustee, whether or not the person is a trust corporation authorized to carry on business in Ontario.

(2) Application of this Part — This Part applies to a trust indenture, whether entered into before or after the 29th day of July, 1983, if, in respect of any debt obligations outstanding or guaranteed thereunder or to be issued or guaranteed thereunder, a prospectus or securities exchange issuer or take-over bid circular has been filed under the *Securities Act* or any predecessor thereof or in respect of which a prospectus has been filed under *The Corporations Information Act*, being chapter 72 of the Revised Statutes of Ontario, 1960, or any predecessor thereof.

(3) Resident trustee — The person appointed as trustee under a trust indenture, or at least one of such persons if more than one is so appointed, shall be resident or authorized to do business in Ontario.

(4) Exemption by Commission — Where, upon the application of a body corporate incorporated otherwise than under the laws of Canada, a province or a territory, the Commission is satisfied that to do so would not be prejudicial to the public interest, the Commission may exempt, subject to such terms and conditions as the Commission may impose, a trust indenture from this Part.

47. (1) Duty of trustee — A trustee in exercising the trustee's powers and discharging the trustee's duties shall,

(a) act honestly and in good faith with a view to the best interests of the holders of the debt obligations issued under the trust indenture; and

(b) exercise the care, diligence and skill of a reasonably prudent trustee.

(2) Exculpatory clauses — No term of a trust indenture or of any agreement between a trustee and the holders of debt obligations issued thereunder or between the trustee and the issuer or guarantor shall operate so as to relieve a trustee from the duties imposed upon the trustee in subsection (1).

48. (1) Conflict of interest — No person shall be appointed as trustee if there is a material conflict of interest between the person's role as trustee and the person's role in any other capacity.

(2) Idem — A trustee shall, within ninety days after becoming aware that a material conflict of interest exists,

(a) eliminate such conflict of interest; or

(b) resign from office.

(3) Validity not affected — If, despite this section, a trustee has a material conflict of interest, the validity and enforceability of the trust indenture under which the trustee has been appointed, of the security interest constituted by or under such trust indenture and of the securities issued under such trust indenture are not affected in any manner whatsoever by reason only of the existence of such material conflict of interest.

(4) Replacing trustee — If a trustee contravenes subsection (1) or (2), any interested person may apply to the court for an order that the trustee be replaced, and the court may make an order on such terms as it thinks fit.

49. (1) Evidence of compliance — An issuer or a guarantor of debt obligations issued or to be issued under a trust indenture, before doing any act referred to in clause (a), (b), (c) or (d), shall furnish the trustee with evidence of compliance with the conditions in the trust indenture relating to,

(a) the issue, certification and delivery of debt obligations under the trust indenture;

(b) the release or release and substitution of property subject to a security interest constituted by the trust indenture;

(c) the satisfaction and discharge of the trust indenture; or

(d) the taking of any other action to be taken by the trustee at the request of or on the application of the issuer or guarantor.

(2) Idem — Evidence of compliance as required by subsection (1) shall consist in each case of,

(a) a statutory declaration or certificate made by a director or an officer of the issuer or guarantor stating that the conditions referred to in that section have been complied with in accordance with the terms of the trust indenture; and

(b) where the trust indenture requires compliance with conditions that are subject to review,

(i) by legal counsel, an opinion, and

(ii) by an auditor or accountant, an opinion or report of the auditor of the issuer or guarantor, or any accountant licensed under the *Public Accounting Act, 2004* or comparable legislation of the jurisdiction in which the accountant practises, based on the examinations or enquiries required to be made under the trust indenture,

in each case approved by the trustee, that the conditions have been complied with in accordance with the terms of the trust indenture.

(3) Idem — The evidence of compliance referred to in subsection (2) shall include a statement by the person giving the evidence,

(a) declaring that the person has read and understands the conditions of the trust indenture described in subsection (1);

(b) describing the nature and scope of the examination or investigation upon which the person based the statutory declaration, certificate, opinion or report; and

(c) declaring that the person has made such examination or investigation as the person believes necessary to enable the person to make the statements or give the opinions contained or expressed therein.

(4) **Certificate of issuer or guarantor** — At least once in each twelve-month period beginning on the date debt obligations are first issued under the trust indenture and at any other reasonable time upon the demand of a trustee, the issuer or guarantor of debt obligations issued under a trust indenture shall furnish the trustee with a certificate that the issuer or guarantor has complied with all requirements contained in the trust indenture that, if not complied with, would, with the giving of notice, lapse of time or otherwise, constitute an event of default, or, if there has been failure to so comply, giving particulars thereof.

(5) **Evidence of compliance** — Upon the demand of a trustee, the issuer or guarantor of debt obligations issued under a trust indenture shall furnish the trustee with evidence in such form as the trustee may require as to compliance with any condition therein relating to any action required or permitted to be taken by the issuer or guarantor under the trust indenture or as a result of any obligation imposed by the trust indenture.

(6) **Reliance on opinions** — A trustee is not in contravention of subsection 47(1) if he relies in good faith upon statements contained in a statutory declaration, certificate, opinion or report that complies with this Act or the trust indenture.

2004, c. 8, s. 46

50. **Trustee not to be receiver** — A trustee under a trust indenture and any related person to the trustee shall not be appointed a receiver or receiver and manager or liquidator of the assets or undertaking of the issuer or guarantor of the debt obligations under the trust indenture.

51. (1) **Notice of events of default** — The trustee shall be required to give to the holders of debt obligations issued under the trust indenture, within a reasonable time but not exceeding thirty days after the trustee becomes aware of the occurrence thereof, notice of every event of default arising under the trust indenture unless the trustee in good faith determines that the withholding of the notice is in the best interests of the holders of the debt obligations and so advises the issuer or guarantor in writing.

(2) **Idem** — Where notice of the occurrence of an event of default under a trust indenture is given under subsection (1) and the default is thereafter cured, notice that the default is no longer continuing shall be given by the trustee to the holders of the debt obligations within a reasonable time, but not exceeding thirty days, after the trustee becomes aware that the default has been cured.

52. (1) **Where list of debt obligation holders to be furnished** — Any person, upon payment to a trustee of a reasonable fee therefor, may require the trustee to furnish, within ten days after delivering to the trustee the statutory declaration referred to in subsection (3), a list setting out,

(a) the names and addresses of the registered holders of the outstanding debt obligations;

(b) the principal amount of outstanding debt obligations owned by each such holder; and

(c) the aggregate principal amount of debt obligations outstanding,

as shown on the records maintained by the trustee on the day that the statutory declaration is delivered to the trustee.

(2) Information to be furnished to trustee — Upon the demand of a trustee, the issuer of debt obligations shall furnish the trustee with the information required to enable the trustee to comply with subsection (1).

(3) Statutory declaration — The statutory declaration required under subsection (1) shall state,

(a) the name and address of the person requiring the trustee to furnish the list and, if the person is a body corporate, the address for service thereof; and

(b) that the list will not be used except as permitted under subsection (5).

(4) Idem — If the person requiring the trustee to furnish a list under subsection (1) is a body corporate, the statutory declaration required under that subsection shall be made by a director or officer of the body corporate.

(5) Use of list — No person shall use a list obtained under this section except in connection with,

(a) an effort to influence the voting of the holders of debt obligations;

(b) an offer to acquire debt obligations; or

(c) any other matter relating to the debt obligations or the affairs of the issuer or guarantor thereof.

PART VI — CORPORATE SECURITIES

[Heading amended 2006, c. 8, s. 109.]

53. Application of *Securities Transfer Act, 2006* — Except as otherwise provided in this Act, the transfer or transmission of a security is governed by the *Securities Transfer Act, 2006*.

2006, c. 8, s. 110

54. (1) Certificated or uncertificated securities — A security issued by a corporation may be represented by a security certificate or may be an uncertificated security.

(2) Uncertificated securities — Unless otherwise provided by the corporation's articles, the directors of a corporation may provide by resolution that any or all classes and series of its shares or other securities shall be uncertificated securities, provided that such resolution shall not apply to securities represented by a certificate until such certificate is surrendered to the corporation.

(3) Notice to holder of uncertificated security — Within a reasonable time after the issuance or transfer of an uncertificated security, the corporation shall send to the registered owner of the uncertificated security a written notice containing the information required to be stated on a share certificate pursuant to subsections 56(1) and (2).

(4) Parity of rights — Except as otherwise expressly provided or authorized by law, the rights and obligations of the registered owners of uncertificated securities and the rights and obligations of the holders of certificated securities of the same class and series shall be identical.

(5) **Fee** — A corporation may charge a fee, not exceeding the prescribed amount, for a security certificate issued in respect of a transfer.

(6) **Joint holders** — A corporation required to issue a security certificate is not required to issue more than one security certificate in respect of securities held jointly by several persons, and delivery to one of several joint holders is sufficient delivery to all.

(7) **Definition** — In this section,

"certificated security" means a certificated security as defined in the *Securities Transfer Act, 2006.*

2006, c. 8, s. 111

55. (1) **Signing of security certificates** — A security certificate shall be signed by at least one of the following persons:

1. A director or officer of the corporation.
2. A registrar, transfer agent or branch transfer agent of the corporation, or an individual on their behalf.
3. A trustee who certifies it in accordance with a trust indenture.

(2) **Same** — A signature required by subsection (1) may be printed or otherwise mechanically reproduced on the security certificate.

(3) **Same** — If a security certificate contains a printed or mechanically reproduced signature of a person, the corporation may issue the security certificate even if the person has ceased to be a director or an officer of the corporation, and the security certificate is as valid as if the person were a director or an officer at the date of its issue.

2006, c. 8, s. 112

56. (1) **Contents of share certificate** — There shall be stated on the face of each share certificate issued by a corporation,

(a) the name of the corporation;

(b) the words "Incorporated under the law of the Province of Ontario", "Subject to the *Ontario Business Corporations Act*" or words of like effect;

(c) the name of the person to whom it was issued; and

(d) the number and class of shares and the designation of any class or series that the certificate represents.

(2) **Idem** — Where a corporation is authorized to issue shares of more than one class or series, the corporation shall legibly state on each share certificate issued by it,

(a) the rights, privileges, restrictions and conditions attached to the shares of each class and series that exists when the share certificate is issued; or

(b) that the class or series of shares that it represents has rights, privileges, restrictions or conditions attached thereto and that the corporation will furnish to a shareholder, on demand and without charge, a full copy of the text of,

(i) the rights, privileges, restrictions and conditions attached to that share and to each class authorized to be issued and to each series in so far as the same have been fixed by the directors, and

(ii) the authority of the directors to fix the rights, privileges, restrictions and conditions of subsequent series, if applicable.

(3)-(5) [Repealed 2006, c. 8, s. 113(2).]

(6) Par value share certificate — A share certificate issued,

(a) prior to the 29th day of July, 1983 by a corporation; or

(b) prior to the date of the certificate of continuance by a body corporate continued under section 180,

does not contravene this Act merely because the certificate refers to the share or shares represented thereby as having a nominal or par value.

(7) Information to be furnished by corporation — Where a share certificate issued by a corporation contains the statement mentioned in clause (2)(b), the corporation shall furnish to a shareholder on demand and without charge a full copy of the text of,

(a) the rights, privileges, restrictions and conditions attached to that class authorized to be issued and to that series in so far as the same have been fixed by the directors; and

(b) the authority of the directors to fix the rights, privileges, restrictions and conditions of subsequent series, if applicable.

(8) Notice of restrictions — Where the articles of a corporation restrict the issue, transfer or ownership of shares of any class or series for a purpose set out in clause 42(2)(c) or (d), the restriction or a reference to it shall be noted conspicuously on every share certificate of the corporation evidencing a share that is subject to the restriction if the certificate is issued after the day on which the share becomes subject to the restriction under this Act and any reference to the restriction shall include a statement that the corporation will furnish to a shareholder, on demand and without charge, a full copy of the text of the restriction.

(9) Furnishing text of restrictions — Where a share certificate of a corporation contains a reference to a restriction under subsection (8), the corporation shall furnish to a shareholder, on demand and without charge, a full copy of the text of the restriction.

(10) [Repealed 2006, c. 8, s. 113(2).]

2006, c. 8, s. 113

57. (1) Certificate for fractional share or scrip certificates — A corporation may issue a certificate for a fractional share or may issue in place thereof scrip certificates in bearer form that entitle the holder to receive a certificate for a full share by exchanging scrip certificates aggregating a full share.

(1.1) Same — A corporation may issue the fractional share described in subsection (1) as an uncertificated security registered or recorded in records maintained by or on behalf of the corporation or by or on behalf of a registrar, transfer agent, branch transfer agent or issuing or other authenticating agent of the corporation by the making of an appropriate entry in the records of the corporation or its registrar, transfer agent, branch transfer agent or other issuing or authenticating agent.

(2) Scrip certificates — The directors may attach conditions to any scrip certificates issued by a corporation or its registrar, transfer agent, branch transfer agent or other issuing or authenticating agent, including conditions that,

(a) the scrip certificates become void if not exchanged for a certificate, or an uncertificated security, representing a full share before a specified date; and

(b) any shares for which such scrip certificates are exchangeable may, despite any pre-emptive right, be issued by the corporation to any person and the proceeds thereof distributed rateably to the holders of the scrip certificates.

(3) **Rights of holder of fractional share** — A holder of a fractional share issued by a corporation is not entitled to exercise voting rights or to receive a dividend in respect of the fractional share unless,

(a) the fractional share results from a consolidation of shares; or

(b) the articles of the corporation otherwise provide.

(4) **Rights of holder of scrip certificate** — A holder of a scrip certificate is not entitled to exercise voting rights or to receive a dividend in respect of the scrip certificate.

2006, c. 8, s. 114

58. (1) **Overissue** — When there has been an overissue within the meaning of the *Securities Transfer Act, 2006* and the corporation subsequently amends its articles or trust indenture to increase any maximum number of securities to a number equal to or in excess of the maximum number of securities previously authorized plus the amount of the securities over-issued, the securities so overissued, and any act taken by any person in reliance upon the validity of such overissued securities, are valid from the date of their issue.

(2) **Non-application of ss. 30, 31, 32, 35** — A purchase or payment in accordance with subsection 67(2) or (3) of the *Securities Transfer Act, 2006* is not a purchase or payment to which section 30, 31, 32 or 35 of this Act applies.

(3) [Repealed 2006, c. 8, s. 115.]

2006, c. 8, s. 115

59-66 [Repealed 2006, c. 8, s. 116]

67. (1) **Effect of registration** — An issuer or a trustee defined in subsection 46(1) may, subject to sections 95, 96 and 100, treat the registered holder of a security as the person exclusively entitled to vote, to receive notices, to receive any interest, dividend or other payments in respect of the security, and otherwise to exercise all the rights and powers of a holder of the security.

(2) **Representatives, etc., may exercise rights of security holder** — A corporation whose articles or unanimous shareholder agreement restrict the right to transfer its securities shall, and any other corporation may, treat a person referred to in clause (a), (b) or (c) as a registered security holder entitled to exercise all the rights of the security holder that the person represents, if that person furnishes evidence as described in section 87 of the *Securities Transfer Act, 2006* to the corporation that the person is,

(a) the executor, administrator, estate trustee, heir or legal representative of the heirs, of the estate of a deceased security holder;

(b) a guardian, attorney under a continuing power of attorney with authority, guardian of property, committee, trustee, curator or tutor representing a registered security holder who is a minor, a person who is incapable of managing his or her property or a missing person; or

(c) a liquidator of, or a trustee in bankruptcy for, a registered security holder.

(3) Rights where ownership devolves by operation of law — If a person upon whom the ownership of a security devolves by operation of law, other than a person referred to in subsection (2), furnishes proof of the person's authority to exercise rights or privileges in respect of a security of the corporation that is not registered in the person's name, the corporation shall treat the persons as entitled to exercise those rights or privileges.

(4) Corporation has no duty to enforce performance — A corporation is not required to inquire into the existence of, or see to the performance or observance of, any duty owed to a third person by a registered holder of any of its securities or by anyone whom it treats, as permitted or required by this section, as the owner or registered holder thereof.

(5) Repudiation by minor — If a minor exercises any rights of ownership in the securities of a corporation, no subsequent repudiation or avoidance is effective against the corporation.

(6) Joint holders — Where a security is issued to several persons as joint holders, upon satisfactory proof of the death of one joint holder, the corporation may treat the surviving joint holders as owner of the security.

(7) Registration of executor, etc. — Subject to any applicable law of Canada or a province of Canada relating to the collection of taxes, a person referred to in clause (2)(a) is entitled to become a registered holder or to designate a registered holder, if the person deposits with the corporation or its transfer agent,

(a) the original grant of probate or of letters of administration, or a copy thereof certified to be a true copy by,

(i) the court that granted the probate or letters of administration,

(ii) a trust corporation incorporated under the laws of Canada or a province, or

(iii) a lawyer or notary acting on behalf of the person; or

(b) in the case of transmission by notarial will in the Province of Quebec, a copy thereof authenticated under the laws of that Province,

together with,

(c) an affidavit or declaration of transmission made by the person stating the particulars of the transmission;

(d) the security certificate that was owned by the deceased holder,

(i) in case of a transfer to the person, with or without the endorsement of that person, and

(ii) in case of a transfer to any other person, endorsed in accordance with section 29 of the *Securities Transfer Act, 2006*; and

(e) any assurance the issuer may require under section 87 of the *Securities Transfer Act, 2006*.

(8) Idem — Despite subsection (7), if the laws of the jurisdiction governing the transmission of a security of a deceased holder do not require a grant of probate or of letters of administration in respect of the transmission, a legal representative of the deceased holder is entitled, subject to any applicable law of Canada or a province of Canada relating to the collection of taxes, to become a registered holder or to designate a registered holder, if the legal representative deposits with the corporation or its transfer agent,

(a) any security certificate that was owned by the deceased holder; and

(b) reasonable proof of the governing laws, the deceased holder's interest in the security and the right of the legal representative or the person the legal representative designates to become the registered holder.

(9) Recording in security register — Deposit of the documents required by subsection (7) or (8) empowers a corporation or its transfer agent to record in a securities register the transmission of a security from the deceased holder to a person referred to in clause (2)(a) or to such person as that person may designate and, thereafter, to treat the person who thus becomes a registered holder as the owner of those securities.

2006, c. 8, s. 117; 2006, c. 34, Sched. B, s. 13

68–91 [Repealed 2006, c. 8, s. 118.]

PART VII — SHAREHOLDERS

92. (1) Shareholders' liability limited — The shareholders of a corporation are not, as shareholders, liable for any act, default, obligation or liability of the corporation except under subsection 34(5), subsection 108(5) and section 243.

Proposed Amendment — 92(1)

(1) Shareholders' liability limited — The shareholders of a corporation are not, as shareholders, liable for any act, default, obligation or liability of the corporation except under subsections 34(5), 108(5) and 130(5) and section 243.

2011, c. 1, Sched. 2, s. 1(6) [Not in force at date of publication.]

(2) Shares subject to call — The provisions of the *Corporations Act* relating to the liability of a holder of shares that are not fully paid and to the enforcement of such liability apply in respect of shares that were not fully paid,

(a) on the 1st day of January, 1971, in the case of shares of a corporation that then became subject to *The Business Corporations Act* being chapter 53 of the Revised Statutes of Ontario, 1970; or

(b) on the day upon which any other body corporate was continued under *The Business Corporations Act* being chapter 53 of the Revised Statutes of Ontario, 1970, or under this Act, in the case of shares of such other body corporate.

93. (1) Place of meetings — Subject to the articles and any unanimous shareholder agreement, a meeting of shareholders of a corporation shall be held at such place in or outside Ontario as the directors determine or, in the absence of such a determination, at the place where the registered office of the corporation is located.

(2) Meeting by electronic means — A meeting held under subsection 94(2) shall be deemed to be held at the place where the registered office of the corporation is located.

1999, c. 12, Sched. F, s. 4

94. (1) Shareholders' meetings — Subject to subsection 104(1), the directors of a corporation,

(a) shall call an annual meeting of shareholders not later than eighteen months after the corporation comes into existence and subsequently not later than fifteen months after holding the last preceding annual meeting; and

(b) may at any time call a special meeting of shareholders.

(2) Meeting by electronic means — Unless the articles or the by-laws provide otherwise, a meeting of the shareholders may be held by telephonic or electronic means and a shareholder who, through those means, votes at the meeting or establishes a communications link to the meeting shall be deemed for the purposes of this Act to be present at the meeting.

1999, c. 12, Sched. F, s. 5; 2001, c. 9, Sched. D, s. 2(3)

95. (1) Date for determining shareholders — For the purpose of determining shareholders,

(a) entitled to receive payment of a dividend;

(b) entitled to participate in a liquidation or distribution; or

(c) for any other purpose except the right to receive notice of or to vote at a meeting,

the directors may fix in advance a date as the record date for such determination of shareholders, but the record date shall not precede by more than fifty days the particular action to be taken.

(2) Same — For the purpose of determining shareholders entitled to receive notice of a meeting of shareholders, the directors may fix in advance a date as the record date for such determination of shareholders, but the record date shall not precede by more than 60 days or by less than 30 days the date on which the meeting is to be held.

(3) Idem — Where no record date is fixed,

(a) the record date for the determination of shareholders entitled to receive notice of a meeting of shareholders shall be,

(i) at the close of business on the day immediately preceding the day on which the notice is given, or

(ii) if no notice is given, the day on which the meeting is held; and

(b) the record date for the determination of shareholders for any purpose other than to establish a shareholders right to receive notice of a meeting or to vote shall be at the close of business on the day on which the directors pass the resolution relating thereto.

(4) Notice of date — If a record date is fixed, unless notice of the record date is waived in writing by every holder of a share of the class or series affected whose name is set out in the securities register at the close of business on the day the directors fix the record date, notice thereof shall be given, not less than seven days before the date so fixed,

(a) by advertisement in a newspaper published or distributed in the place where the corporation has its registered office and in each place in Canada where it has a transfer agent or where a transfer of its shares may be recorded; and

(b) by written notice to each stock exchange in Canada on which the shares of the corporation are listed for trading.

2006, c. 9, Sched. A, s. 1

96. (1) Notice of shareholders' meetings — Notice of the time and place of a meeting of shareholders shall be sent, in the case of an offering corporation, not less than twenty-one days and, in the case of any other corporation, not less than ten days, but, in either case, not more than fifty days, before the meeting,

(a) to each shareholder entitled to vote at the meeting;

(b) to each director; and

(c) to the auditor of the corporation.

(2) Idem — A notice of a meeting is not required to be sent to shareholders who were not registered on the records of the corporation or its transfer agent on the record date determined under subsection 95(2) or (3), but failure to receive a notice does not deprive a shareholder of the right to vote at the meeting.

(3) Idem — If a meeting of shareholders is adjourned for less than thirty days, it is not necessary, unless the by-laws otherwise provide, to give notice of the adjourned meeting other than by announcement at the earliest meeting that is adjourned.

(4) Idem — If a meeting of shareholders is adjourned by one or more adjournments for an aggregate of thirty days or more, notice of the adjourned meeting shall be given as for an original meeting but, unless the meeting is adjourned by one or more adjournments for an aggregate of more than ninety days, section 111 does not apply.

(5) Special business — All business transacted at a special meeting of shareholders and all business transacted at an annual meeting of shareholders, except consideration of the minutes of an earlier meeting, the financial statements and auditor's report, election of directors and reappointment of the incumbent auditor, shall be deemed to be special business.

(6) Idem — Notice of a meeting of shareholders at which special business is to be transacted shall state or be accompanied by a statement of,

(a) the nature of that business in sufficient detail to permit the shareholder to form a reasoned judgment thereon; and

(b) the text of any special resolution or by-law to be submitted to the meeting.

97. Shareholders' meeting — Subject to this Act or the articles or by-laws of a corporation or a unanimous shareholder agreement,

(a) all questions proposed for the consideration of the shareholders shall be determined by the majority of the votes cast and the chair presiding at the meeting shall not have a second or casting vote in case of an equality of votes;

(b) the chair presiding at a meeting of shareholders may, with the consent of the meeting and subject to such conditions as the meeting decides, adjourn the meeting from time to time and from place to place subject to subsections 96(3) and (4); and

(c) the president or, in his or her absence, a vice-president who is a director shall preside as chair at a meeting of shareholders, but, if there is no president or such a vice-president or if at a meeting none of them is present within fifteen minutes after the time appointed for the holding of the meeting, the shareholders present shall choose a person from their number to be the chair.

98. Waiving notice — A shareholder and any other person entitled to attend a meeting of shareholders may in any manner and at any time waive notice of a meeting of shareholders, and attendance of any such person at a meeting of shareholders is a waiver of notice of the meeting, except where such person attends a meeting for the express purpose of objecting to the transaction of any business on the grounds that the meeting is not lawfully called.

99. (1) Proposal — A registered holder of shares entitled to vote or a beneficial owner of shares that are entitled to be voted at a meeting of shareholders may,

(a) submit to the corporation notice of a proposal; and

(b) discuss at the meeting any matter in respect of which the registered holder or beneficial owner would have been entitled to submit a proposal.

Proposed Addition — 99(1.1), (1.2)

(1.1) Proof of status — If a person claims to be a beneficial owner of shares of a corporation for the purposes of subsection (1), the corporation may require the person to provide proof that the person is a beneficial owner of shares of the corporation.

(1.2) Same — A written statement by a securities intermediary, as defined in the *Securities Transfer Act, 2006*, that a person is a beneficial owner of shares of the corporation is sufficient proof for the purposes of subsection (1.1).

2010, c. 16, Sched. 5, s. 1(1) [Not in force at date of publication.]

(2) Circulating proposal — Where a corporation receives notice of a proposal and the corporation solicits proxies, it shall set out the proposal in the management information circular required by section 112 or attach the proposal thereto.

(3) Statement in support of proposal — If so requested by the person who submits notice of a proposal, the corporation shall include in the management information circular or attach to it a statement in support of the proposal by the person and the name and address of the person.

(3.1) Same — The proposal referred to in subsection (2) and the statement referred to in subsection (3) shall together not exceed the prescribed maximum number of words.

(4) Proposal may include nominations — A proposal may include nominations for the election of directors if the proposal is signed by one or more holders of shares representing in the aggregate not less than 5 per cent of the shares or 5 per cent of the shares of a class or series of shares of the corporation entitled to vote at the meeting to which the proposal is to be presented, but this subsection does not preclude nominations being made at a meeting of shareholders.

(5) Where subss. (2), (3) do not apply — A corporation is not required to comply with subsections (2) and (3) where,

(a) the proposal is not submitted to the corporation at least sixty days before the anniversary date of the last annual meeting, if the matter is proposed to be raised at an annual meeting, or at least sixty days before a meeting other than the annual meeting, if the matter is proposed to be raised at a meeting other than the annual meeting;

(b) it clearly appears that the primary purpose of the proposal is to enforce a personal claim or redress a personal grievance against the corporation or its directors, officers or security holders;

(b.1) it clearly appears that the proposal does not relate in a significant way to the business or affairs of the corporation;

(c) not more than two years before the receipt of the proposal, a person failed to present, in person or by proxy, at a meeting of shareholders, a proposal that, at the person's request, had been included in a management information circular relating to the meeting; or

(d) substantially the same proposal was submitted to shareholders in a management information circular or a dissident's information circular relating to a meeting of shareholders held within two years preceding the receipt of the shareholder's request and the proposal was defeated.

(6) Where no liability — No corporation or person acting on its behalf incurs any liability by reason only of circulating a proposal or statement in compliance with this section.

(7) Notice of refusal — If a corporation refuses to include a proposal in a management information circular, the corporation shall, within 10 days after receiving the proposal, send notice to the person submitting the proposal of its intention to omit the proposal from the management information circular and send to the person a statement of the reasons for the refusal.

(8) Application to court — On the application of a person submitting a proposal who claims to be aggrieved by a corporation's refusal under subsection (7), a court may restrain the holding of the meeting to which the proposal is sought to be presented and make any further order it thinks fit.

(9) Idem — The corporation or any person aggrieved by a proposal may apply to the court for an order permitting the corporation to omit the proposal from the management information circular, and the court, if it is satisfied that subsection (5) applies, may make such order as it thinks fit.

(10) Idem — An applicant under subsection (8) or (9) shall give the Director notice of the application and the Director is entitled to appear and be heard in person or by counsel.

(11) Definition — In this section,

"proposal" means a matter that a registered holder or beneficial owner of shares entitled to be voted proposes to raise at a meeting of shareholders.

2006, c. 34, Sched. B, s. 14

100. (1) List of shareholders — A corporation shall prepare a list of shareholders entitled to receive notice of a meeting, arranged in alphabetical order and showing the number of shares held by each shareholder, which list shall be prepared,

(a) if a record date is fixed under subsection 95(2), not later than ten days after such record date; or

(b) if no record date is fixed,

(i) at the close of business on the day immediately preceding the day on which notice is given, or

(ii) where no notice is given, on the day on which the meeting is held.

(2) Entitlement to vote — A shareholder whose name appears on a list prepared under subsection (1) is entitled to vote the shares shown opposite the shareholder's name at the meeting to which the list relates.

(3) [Repealed 2006, c. 34, Sched. B, s. 15.]

(4) Examination of list — A shareholder may examine the list of shareholders,

(a) during usual business hours at the registered office of the corporation or at the place where its central securities register is maintained; and

(b) at the meeting of shareholders for which the list was prepared.

2006, c. 34, Sched. B, s. 15

101. (1) Quorum — Unless the by-laws otherwise provide, the holders of a majority of the shares entitled to vote at a meeting of shareholders, whether present in person or represented by proxy, constitute a quorum.

(2) Idem — If a quorum is present at the opening of a meeting of shareholders, the shareholders present may, unless the by-laws otherwise provide, proceed with the business of the meeting even if a quorum is not present throughout the meeting.

(3) Idem — If a quorum is not present at the time appointed for a meeting of shareholders, or within such reasonable time thereafter as the shareholders present may determine, the shareholders present may adjourn the meeting to a fixed time and place but may not transact any other business.

(4) Where only one shareholder — If a corporation has only one shareholder, or only one holder of any class or series of shares, the shareholder present in person or by proxy constitutes a meeting.

102. (1) Voting rights — Unless the articles otherwise provide, each share of a corporation entitles the holder thereof to one vote at a meeting of shareholders.

(2) Representative — Where a body corporate or association is a shareholder of a corporation, the corporation shall recognize any individual authorized by a resolution of the directors or governing body of the body corporate or association to represent it at meetings of shareholders of the corporation.

(3) Idem — An individual authorized as set out in subsection (2) may exercise on behalf of the body corporate or association he or she represents all the powers it could exercise if it were an individual shareholder.

(4) Joint shareholders — Unless the by-laws otherwise provide, where two or more persons hold shares jointly, one of those holders present at a meeting of shareholders may in the absence of the others vote the shares, but if two or more of those persons are present, in person or by proxy, they shall vote as one on the shares jointly held by them.

103. (1) Manner of voting — Unless the by-laws otherwise provide, voting at a meeting of shareholders shall be by show of hands, except where a ballot is demanded by a shareholder or proxyholder entitled to vote at the meeting.

(2) Idem — A shareholder or proxyholder may demand a ballot either before or after any vote by show of hands.

(3) Entry in minutes — Unless a ballot is demanded, an entry in the minutes of a meeting of shareholders to the effect that the chair declared a motion to be carried is admissible in evidence as proof of the fact, in the absence of evidence to the contrary, without proof of the number or proportion of the votes recorded in favour of or against the motion.

104. (1) Resolution in lieu of meeting — Except where a written statement is submitted by a director under subsection 123(2) or where representations in writing are submitted by an auditor under subsection 149(6),

(a) a resolution in writing signed by all the shareholders or their attorney authorized in writing entitled to vote on that resolution at a meeting of shareholders is as valid as if it had been passed at a meeting of the shareholders; and

(b) a resolution in writing dealing with all matters required by this Act to be dealt with at a meeting of shareholders, and signed by all the shareholders or their attorney authorized in writing entitled to vote at that meeting, satisfies all the requirements of this Act relating to that meeting of shareholders.

(2) Copy of resolution kept with minutes — A copy of every resolution referred to in subsection (1) shall be kept with the minutes of the meetings of shareholders.

2000, c. 26, Sched. B, s. 3(5), (6)

105. (1) Requisition for shareholders meeting — The holders of not less than 5 per cent of the issued shares of a corporation that carry the right to vote at a meeting sought to be held may requisition the directors to call a meeting of shareholders for the purposes stated in the requisition.

(2) Idem — The requisition referred to in subsection (1) shall state the business to be transacted at the meeting and shall be sent to the registered office of the corporation.

(3) Duty of directors to call meeting — Upon receiving the requisition referred to in subsection (1), the directors shall call a meeting of shareholders to transact the business stated in the requisition unless,

(a) a record date has been fixed under subsection 95(2) and notice thereof has been given under subsection 95(4);

(b) the directors have called a meeting of shareholders and have given notice thereof under section 96; or

(c) the business of the meeting as stated in the requisition includes matters described in clauses 99(5)(b) to (d).

(4) Where requisitionist may call meeting — Subject to subsection (3), if the directors do not within twenty-one days after receiving the requisition referred to in subsection (1) call a meeting, any shareholder who signed the requisition may call the meeting.

(5) Calling of meeting — A meeting called under this section shall be called as nearly as possible in the manner in which meetings are to be called under the by-laws, this Part and Part VIII.

(6) Repayment of expenses — The corporation shall reimburse the shareholders for the expenses reasonably incurred by them in requisitioning, calling and holding the meeting unless the shareholders have not acted in good faith and in the interest of the shareholders of the corporation generally.

106. (1) Requisition by court — If for any reason it is impracticable to call a meeting of shareholders of a corporation in the manner in which meetings of those shareholders may be called or to conduct the meeting in the manner prescribed by the by-laws, the articles and this Act, or if for any other reason the court thinks fit, the court, upon the application of a director or a shareholder entitled to vote at the meeting, may order a meeting to be called, held and conducted in such manner as the court directs and upon such terms as to security for the costs of holding the meeting or otherwise as the court deems fit.

(2) Power of court — Without restricting the generality of subsection (1), the court may order that the quorum required by the by-laws, the articles or this Act be varied or dispensed with at a meeting called, held and conducted under this section.

(3) Effect of meeting — A meeting called, held and conducted under this section is for all purposes a meeting of shareholders of the corporation duly called, held and conducted.

107. (1) Application to court — A corporation, shareholder or director may apply to the court to determine any controversy with respect to an election or appointment of a director or auditor of the corporation.

(2) Idem — Upon an application under this section, the court may make any order it thinks fit including, without limiting the generality of the foregoing,

(a) an order restraining a director or auditor whose election or appointment is challenged from acting pending determination of the dispute;

(b) an order declaring the result of the disputed election or appointment;

(c) an order requiring a new election or appointment and including in the order directions for the management of the business and affairs of the corporation until a new election is held or appointment made; and

(d) an order determining the voting rights of shareholders and of persons claiming to own shares.

108. (1) Agreement between shareholders — A written agreement between two or more shareholders may provide that in exercising voting rights the shares held by them shall be voted as therein provided.

(2) Idem — A written agreement among all the shareholders of a corporation or among all the shareholders and one or more persons who are not shareholders may restrict in whole or in part the powers of the directors to manage or supervise the management of the business and affairs of the corporation.

(3) Unanimous shareholder agreement — Where a person who is the registered holder of all the issued shares of a corporation makes a written declaration that restricts in whole or in part the powers of the directors to manage or supervise the management of the business and affairs of a corporation, the declaration shall be deemed to be a unanimous shareholder agreement.

(4) Party to unanimous shareholder agreement — A transferee of shares subject to a unanimous shareholder agreement shall be deemed to be a party to the agreement.

(5) Where shareholder has power, etc., of director — A shareholder who is a party to a unanimous shareholder agreement has all the rights, powers, duties and liabilities of a director of a corporation, whether arising under this Act or otherwise, including any defences available to the directors, to which the agreement relates to the extent that the agreement restricts the discretion or powers of the directors to manage or supervise the management of the business and affairs of the corporation and the directors are relieved of their duties and liabilities, including any liabilities under section 131, to the same extent.

(5.1) Unanimous shareholder agreement — Nothing in this section prevents shareholders from fettering their discretion when exercising the powers of directors under a unanimous shareholder agreement.

(6) Matter that a unanimous shareholder agreement may provide — A unanimous shareholder agreement may, without restricting the generality of subsection (2), provide that,

(a) any amendment of the unanimous shareholder agreement may be effected in the manner specified therein; and

(b) in the event that shareholders who are parties to the unanimous shareholder agreement are unable to agree on or resolve any matter pertaining to the agreement, the matter may be referred to arbitration under such procedures and conditions as are specified in the unanimous shareholder agreement.

(7) Issuance or shares subject to unanimous shareholder agreement — If a unanimous shareholder agreement is in effect at the time a share is issued by a corporation to a person other than an existing shareholder,

(a) that person shall be deemed to be a party to the agreement whether or not that person had actual knowledge of it when the share was issued;

(b) the issue of the share does not operate to terminate the agreement; and

(c) if that person is a purchaser for value without notice of the agreement, that person may rescind the contract under which the shares were acquired by giving notice to that effect to the corporation within 60 days after the person actually receives a complete copy of the agreement.

(8) Transfer of shares subject to unanimous shareholder agreement — If a unanimous shareholder agreement is in effect when a person who was not otherwise a party to the agreement acquires a share of the corporation, other than under subsection (1),

(a) the person who acquired the share shall be deemed to be a party to the agreement whether or not that person had actual knowledge of it when he or she acquired the share; and

(b) neither the acquisition of the share nor the registration of that person as a shareholder operates to terminate the agreement.

(9) Notice of objection — If a person referred to in subsection (8) is a purchaser for value without notice of the unanimous shareholder agreement and the transferor's share certificate, if any, did not contain a reference to the unanimous shareholder agreement, the transferee may, within 60 days after he or she actually receives a complete copy of the agreement, send to the corporation and the transferor a notice of objection.

(10) Rights of transferee — If a person sends a notice of objection under subsection (9), that person is entitled to,

(a) rescind the contract under which the shares were acquired by giving notice to that effect to the corporation and the transferor within 60 days after the transferee actually receives a complete copy of the unanimous shareholder agreement; or

(b) demand that the transferor pay the transferee the fair value of the shares held by the transferee, determined as of the close of business on the day on which the transferor delivers the notice of objection to the corporation, in which case subsections 185(4), (18) and (19) apply, with the necessary modifications, as if the transferor were the corporation.

Proposed Amendment — 108(10)(b)

(b) demand that the transferor pay the transferee the fair value of the shares held by the transferee, determined as of the close of business on the day on which the transferee delivers the notice of objection to the corporation, in which case subsections 185(4), (18) and (19) apply, with the necessary modifications, as if the transferor were the corporation.

2011, c. 1, Sched. 2, s. 1(7) [Not in force at date of publication.]

(11) Deficiency — A transferee who is entitled to be paid the fair value of the transferee's shares under clause (10)(b) also has the right to recover from the transferor the amount by which the value of the consideration paid for those shares exceeds their fair value.

2006, c. 8, s. 119; 2006, c. 34, Sched. B, s. 16

PART VIII — PROXIES

109. Definitions — In this Part,

"dissident's information circular" means the circular referred to in clause 112(1)(b);

"form of proxy" means a form that is in written or printed format or a format generated by telephonic or electronic means and that becomes a proxy when completed and signed in writing or electronic signature by or on behalf of a shareholder;

"management information circular" means the circular referred to in clause 112(1)(a);

"proxy" means a completed and signed form of proxy by means of which a shareholder has appointed a proxyholder to attend and act on a shareholder's behalf at a meeting of shareholders;

"solicit" and **"solicitation"** include,

(a) a request for a proxy whether or not accompanied by or included in a form of proxy,

(b) a request to execute or not to execute a form of proxy or to revoke a proxy,

(c) the sending of a form of proxy or other communication to a shareholder under circumstances reasonably calculated to result in the procurement, withholding or revocation of a proxy, and

(d) the sending of a form of proxy to a shareholder under section 111, but do not include,

(e) the sending of a form of proxy in response to an unsolicited request made by or on behalf of a shareholder,

(f) the performance of administrative acts or professional services on behalf of a person soliciting a proxy,

(g) the sending of material under section 49 of the *Securities Act*,

(h) a solicitation by a person in respect of shares of which the person is the beneficial owner,

(i) a public announcement, as prescribed, by a shareholder of how the shareholder intends to vote and the reasons for that decision,

(j) a communication, other than a solicitation by or on behalf of the management of the corporation, that is made to shareholders in any circumstances that may be prescribed.

"solicitation by or on behalf of the management of a corporation" means a solicitation by any person under a resolution or the instructions of the directors of that corporation or a committee of such directors.

1999, c. 12, Sched. F, s. 6; 2006, c. 34, Sched. B, s. 17

110. (1) Proxies — Every shareholder entitled to vote at a meeting of shareholders may by means of a proxy appoint a proxyholder or one or more alternate proxyholders, who need not be shareholders, as the shareholders nominee to attend and act at the meeting in the manner, to the extent and with the authority conferred by the proxy.

(2) Signature — Subject to subsection (4.2), a proxy must be signed,

(a) in writing or by electronic signature by the shareholder or an attorney who is authorized by a document that is signed in writing or by electronic signature; or

(b) if the shareholder is a body corporate, by an officer or attorney of the body corporate duly authorized.

(2.1) Expiry — A proxy appointing a proxyholder to attend and act at a meeting or meetings of shareholders of an offering corporation ceases to be valid one year from its date.

(3) Form of proxy — Every form of proxy shall comply with the regulations.

(4) Revocation — A shareholder may revoke a proxy,

(a) by depositing an instrument in writing that complies with subsection (4.1) and that is signed by the shareholder or by an attorney who is authorized by a document that is signed in writing or by electronic signature;

(b) by transmitting, by telephonic or electronic means, a revocation that complies with subsection (4.1) and that, subject to subsection (4.2), is signed by electronic signature; or

(c) in any other manner permitted by law.

(4.1) Time of revocation — The instrument or the revocation must be received,

(a) at the registered office of the corporation at any time up to and including the last business day preceding the day of the meeting, or any adjournment of it, at which the proxy is to be used; or

(b) by the chair of the meeting on the day of the meeting or an adjournment of it.

(4.2) Electronic signature — A shareholder or an attorney may sign, by electronic signature, a proxy, a revocation of proxy or a power of attorney authorizing the creation of either of them if the means of electronic signature permits a reliable determination that the document was created or communicated by or on behalf of the shareholder or the attorney, as the case may be.

(5) Time limit for deposit — The directors may by resolution fix a time not exceeding forty-eight hours, excluding Saturdays and holidays, preceding any meeting or adjourned meeting of shareholders before which time proxies to be used at that meeting must be deposited with the corporation or an agent thereof, and any period of time so fixed shall be specified in the notice calling the meeting.

1999, c. 12, Sched. F, s. 7

111. Mandatory solicitation of proxy — The management of an offering corporation shall, concurrently with or prior to sending notice of a meeting of shareholders, send a form of proxy to each shareholder who is entitled to receive notice of the meeting.

112. (1) Information circular — No person shall solicit proxies in respect of an offering corporation unless,

(a) in the case of solicitation by or on behalf of the management of the corporation, a management information circular in prescribed form, either as an appendix to or as a separate document accompanying the notice of the meeting; or

(b) in the case of any other solicitation, a dissident's information circular in prescribed form,

is sent to the auditor of the corporation, to each shareholder whose proxy is solicited and, if clause (b) applies, to the corporation.

(1.1) Exception — Despite subsection (1), a person may solicit proxies, other than by or on behalf of the management of the corporation, without sending a dissident's information circular, if the total number of shareholders whose proxies are solicited is 15 or fewer, two or more joint holders being counted as one shareholder.

(1.2) Same — Despite subsection (1), a person may solicit proxies, other than by or on behalf of the management of the corporation, without sending a dissident's information circular, if the solicitation is, in the prescribed circumstances, conveyed by public broadcast, speech or publication.

(2) Filing copy — A person, upon sending a management or dissident's information circular, shall concurrently file with the Commission,

(a) in the case of a management information circular, a copy thereof together with a copy of the notice of meeting, form of proxy and of any other documents for use in connection with the meeting; and

(b) in the case of a dissident's information circular, a copy thereof together with a copy of the form of proxy and of any other documents for use in connection with the meeting.

2006, c. 34, Sched. B, s. 18

113. Exemption order re ss. 111, 112 — Upon the application of any interested person, the Commission may, if satisfied in the circumstances of the particular case that there is adequate justification for so doing, make an order, on such terms and conditions as the Commission may impose, exempting, in whole or in part, any person from the requirements of section 111 or from the requirements of section 112.

114. (1) Proxyholder — A person who solicits a proxy and is appointed proxyholder shall attend in person or cause an alternate proxyholder to attend the meeting in respect of which the proxy is given and comply with the directions of the shareholder who appointed the person.

(2) Rights of proxyholder — A proxyholder or an alternate proxyholder has the same rights as the shareholder who appointed him or her to speak at a meeting of shareholders in respect of any matter, to vote by way of ballot at the meeting and, except where a proxyholder or an alternate proxyholder has conflicting instructions from more than one shareholder, to vote at such a meeting in respect of any matter by way of a show of hands.

(3) Vote — Despite subsections (1) and (2), where the chair of a meeting of shareholders declares to the meeting that, to the best of his or her belief, if a ballot is conducted, the total number of votes attached to the shares represented at the meeting by proxy required to be voted against what will be the decision of the meeting in relation to any matter or group of matters is less than 5 per cent of all the votes that might be cast at the meeting on such ballot, and where a shareholder, proxyholder or alternate proxyholder does not demand a ballot,

(a) the chair may conduct the vote in respect of that matter or group of matters by a show of hands; and

(b) a proxyholder or alternate proxyholder may vote in respect of that matter or group of matters by a show of hands.

PART IX — DIRECTORS AND OFFICERS

115. (1) Duties — Subject to any unanimous shareholder agreement, the directors shall manage or supervise the management of the business and affairs of a corporation.

(2) Board of directors — A corporation shall have a board of directors which shall consist of,

(a) in the case of a corporation that is not an offering corporation, at least one individual; and

(b) in the case of a corporation that is an offering corporation, not fewer than three individuals.

(3) Idem — At least one-third of the directors of an offering corporation shall not be officers or employees of the corporation or any of its affiliates.

(4) Deemed directors — Where all of the directors have resigned or have been removed by the shareholders without replacement, any person who manages or supervises the management of the business and affairs of the corporation shall be deemed to be a director for the purposes of this Act.

(5) Exceptions — Subsection (4) does not apply to,

(a) an officer who manages the business of the corporation under the direction or control of a shareholder or other person;

(b) a lawyer, accountant or other professional who participates in the management of the corporation solely for the purposes of providing professional services; or

(c) a trustee in bankruptcy, receiver, receiver-manager or secured creditor who participates in the management of the corporation or exercises control over its property solely for the purposes of enforcement of a security agreement or administration of a bankrupt's estate, in the case of a trustee in bankruptcy.

1994, c. 27, s. 71(11), (12)

116. (1) By-laws by resolution — Unless the articles, the by-laws or a unanimous shareholder agreement otherwise provide, the directors may, by resolution, make, amend or repeal any by-laws that regulate the business or affairs of a corporation.

(2) Confirmation by shareholders — Where the directors make, amend or repeal a by-law under subsection (1), they shall submit the by-law, amendment or repeal to the shareholders at the next meeting of shareholders, and the shareholders may confirm, reject or amend the by-law, amendment or repeal.

(3) Effective date — Where a by-law is made, amended or repealed under subsection (1), the by-law, amendment or repeal is effective from the date of the resolution of the directors until it is confirmed, confirmed as amended or rejected by the shareholders under subsection (2) or until it ceases to be effective under subsection (4) and, where the by-law is confirmed or confirmed as amended, it continues in effect in the form in which it was so confirmed.

(4) Rejection, etc. — If a by-law or an amendment or repeal of a by-law is rejected by the shareholders, or if the directors do not submit the by-law, amendment or repeal to the shareholders as required under subsection (2), the by-law, amendment or repeal ceases to be effective on the date of such rejection or on the date of the meeting of shareholders at which it should have been submitted, as the case may be, and no subsequent resolution of the directors to make, amend or repeal a by-law having substantially the same purpose or effect is effective until it is confirmed or confirmed as amended by the shareholders.

(5) By-law re shareholder proposal — If a shareholder proposal to make, amend or repeal a by-law is made in accordance with section 99 and is adopted by shareholders at a meeting, the by-law, amendment or repeal is effective from the date of its adoption and requires no further confirmation.

(6) By-law need not be so described — A by-law need not be described as a by-law in a resolution referred to in this section.

117. (1) First directors meeting — After incorporation, a meeting of the directors of a corporation shall be held at which the directors may,

(a) make by-laws;

(b) adopt forms of security certificates and corporate records;

(c) authorize the issue of securities;

(d) appoint officers;

(e) appoint one or more auditors to hold office until the first annual or special meeting of shareholders;

(f) make banking arrangements; and

(g) transact any other business.

(2) Resolution in writing — Any matter referred to in subsection (1) may be dealt with by the directors by a resolution in writing in accordance with subsection 129(1).

(3) Where subs. (1) does not apply — Subsection (1) does not apply to a body corporate that is an amalgamated corporation under section 178 or that is continued under section 180.

(4) Calling meeting — An incorporator or a director may call the meeting of directors referred to in subsection (1) by giving not less than five days notice thereof to each director stating the time and place of the meeting.

118. (1) Director disqualification — The following persons are disqualified from being a director of a corporation:

1. A person who is less than eighteen years of age.

2. A person who has been found under the *Substitute Decisions Act, 1992* or under the *Mental Health Act* to be incapable of managing property or who has been found to be incapable by a court in Canada or elsewhere.

3. A person who is not an individual.
4. A person who has the status of bankrupt.

(2) **Holding shares** — Unless the articles otherwise provide, a director of a corporation is not required to hold shares issued by the corporation.

(3) **Residency** — At least 25 per cent of the directors of a corporation other than a non-resident corporation shall be resident Canadians, but where a corporation has less than four directors, at least one director shall be a resident Canadian.

2006, c. 34, Sched. B, s. 19

119. (1) **First directors** — Each director named in the articles shall hold office from the date of endorsement of the certificate of incorporation until the first meeting of shareholders.

(2) **Resignation** — Until the first meeting of shareholders, the resignation of a director named in the articles shall not be effective unless at the time the resignation is to become effective a successor has been elected or appointed.

(3) **Idem** — The first directors of a corporation named in the articles have all the powers and duties and are subject to all the liabilities of directors.

(4) **Election of directors** — Subject to clause 120(a), shareholders of a corporation shall elect, at the first meeting of shareholders and at each succeeding annual meeting at which an election of directors is required, directors to hold office for a term expiring not later than the close of the third annual meeting of shareholders following the election.

(5) **Term for directors** — It is not necessary that all directors elected at a meeting of shareholders hold office for the same term.

(6) **Idem** — A director not elected for an expressly stated term ceases to hold office at the close of the first annual meeting of shareholders following his or her election.

(7) **Idem** — Despite this section, if directors are not elected at a meeting of shareholders the incumbent directors continue in office until their successors are elected.

(8) **Failure to elect required number of directors** — If a meeting of shareholders fails to elect the number of directors required by the articles or by section 125 by reason of the disqualification, incapacity or death of one or more candidates, the directors elected at that meeting, if they constitute a quorum, may exercise all the powers of the directors of the corporation pending the holding of a meeting of shareholders in accordance with subsection 124(3).

(9) **Consent required** — Subject to subsection (10), the election or appointment of a director under this Act is not effective unless the person elected or appointed consents in writing before or within 10 days after the date of the election or appointment.

(10) **Later consent** — If the person elected or appointed consents in writing after the time period mentioned in subsection (9), the election or appointment is valid.

(11) **Exception** — Subsection (9) does not apply to a director who is re-elected or re-appointed where there is no break in the director's term of office.

1994, c. 27, s. 71(13), (14); 1999, c. 12, Sched. F, s. 8

120. Cumulative voting for directors — Where the articles provide for cumulative voting,

(a) each shareholder entitled to vote at an election of directors has the right to cast a number of votes equal to the number of votes attached to the shares held by the shareholder multiplied by the number of directors to be elected, and the shareholder may cast all such votes in favour of one candidate or distribute them among the candidates in any manner;

(b) a separate vote of shareholders shall be taken with respect to each candidate nominated for director unless a resolution is passed unanimously permitting two or more persons to be elected by a single resolution;

(c) if a shareholder has voted for more than one candidate without specifying the distribution of the shareholder's votes among the candidates, the shareholder is deemed to have distributed the shareholder's votes equally among the candidates for whom the shareholder voted;

(d) if the number of candidates nominated for director exceeds the number of positions to be filled, the candidates who receive the least number of votes shall be eliminated until the number of candidates remaining equals the number of positions to be filled;

(e) each director ceases to hold office at the close of the first annual meeting of shareholders following his or her election;

(f) a director may not be removed from office if the votes cast against the director's removal would be sufficient to elect him or her and such votes could be voted cumulatively at an election at which the same total number of votes were cast and the number of directors required by the articles were then being elected;

(g) the number of directors required by the articles may not be decreased if the votes cast against the motion to decrease would be sufficient to elect a director and such votes could be voted cumulatively at an election at which the same total number of votes were cast and the number of directors required by the articles were then being elected; and

(h) the articles shall require a fixed number and not a minimum and maximum number of directors.

121. (1) When director ceases to hold office — A director of a corporation ceases to hold office when he or she,

(a) dies or, subject to subsection 119(2), resigns;

(b) is removed in accordance with section 122; or

(c) becomes disqualified under subsection 118(1).

(2) Idem — A resignation of a director becomes effective at the time a written resignation is received by the corporation or at the time specified in the resignation, whichever is later.

122. (1) Removal of directors — Subject to clause 120(f), the shareholders of a corporation may by ordinary resolution at an annual or special meeting remove any director or directors from office.

(2) Idem — Where the holders of any class or series of shares of a corporation have an exclusive right to elect one or more directors, a director so elected may only be removed by an ordinary resolution at a meeting of the shareholders of that class or series.

(3) Idem — Subject to clauses 120(a) to (d), a vacancy created by the removal of a director may be filled at the meeting of the shareholders at which the director is removed or, if not so filled, may be filled under section 124.

123. (1) Entitlement of director — A director of a corporation is entitled to receive notice of and to attend and be heard at every meeting of shareholders.

(2) Idem — A director who,

(a) resigns;

(b) receives a notice or otherwise learns of a meeting of shareholders called for the purpose of removing him or her from office; or

(c) receives a notice or otherwise learns of a meeting of directors or shareholders at which another person is to be appointed or elected to fill the office of director, whether because of the resignation or removal of the director or because his or her term of office has expired or is about to expire,

is entitled to submit to the corporation a written statement giving the reasons for the director's resignation or the reasons why he or she opposes any proposed action or resolution, as the case may be.

(3) Distribution of statement — Upon receiving a statement under subsection (2), a corporation shall forthwith send a copy of the statement to every shareholder entitled to receive notice of meetings of shareholders unless the statement is included in or attached to a management information circular required by section 112.

(4) No liability — No corporation or person acting on its behalf incurs any liability by reason only of circulating a director's statement in compliance with subsection (3).

2004, c. 19, s. 3(3)

124. (1) Vacancies — Despite subsection 126(6), but subject to subsections (2), (4) and (5) of this section, a quorum of directors may fill a vacancy among the directors, except a vacancy resulting from,

(a) an increase in the number of directors otherwise than in accordance with subsection (2), or in the maximum number of directors, as the case may be; or

(b) a failure to elect the number of directors required to be elected at any meeting of shareholders.

(2) Appointment of directors subsequent to annual meeting — Where a special resolution passed under subsection 125(3) empowers the directors of a corporation the articles of which provide for a minimum and maximum number of directors to determine the number of directors, the directors may not, between meetings of shareholders, appoint an additional director if, after such appointment, the total number of directors would be greater than one and one-third times the number of directors required to have been elected at the last annual meeting of shareholders.

(3) Election of directors to make quorum — If there is not a quorum of directors, or if there has been a failure to elect the number of directors required by the articles or by section 125, the directors then in office shall forthwith call a special meeting of shareholders to fill the vacancy and, if they fail to call a meeting or if there are no directors then in office, the meeting may be called by any shareholder.

(4) **Where elected by class of shareholders** — Where the holders of any class or series of shares of a corporation have an exclusive right to elect one or more directors and a vacancy occurs among those directors,

(a) subject to subsection (5), the remaining directors elected by that class or series may fill the vacancy except a vacancy resulting from an increase in the number of directors for that class or series or from a failure to elect the number of directors for that class or series; or

(b) if there are no such remaining directors, any holder of shares of that class or series may call a meeting of the holders thereof for the purpose of filling the vacancy.

(5) **Idem, where no quorum** — The articles may provide that a vacancy among the directors shall only be filled by a vote of the shareholders, or by a vote of the holders of any class or series of shares having an exclusive right to elect one or more directors if the vacancy occurs among the directors elected by that class or series.

(6) **Term** — A director appointed or elected to fill a vacancy holds office for the unexpired term of the director's predecessor.

125. (1) **Change in number of directors** — A corporation may increase or decrease the number, or the minimum or maximum number, of its directors in accordance with clause 168(1)(m), but no decrease in the number of directors shall shorten the term of an incumbent director.

(2) **Articles amendment** — Where a corporation has increased or decreased the number of directors by special by-law under a predecessor of this Act, the special by-law shall be deemed to constitute an amendment to its articles.

(3) **Number of directors** — Where a minimum and maximum number of directors of a corporation is provided for in its articles, the number of directors of the corporation and the number of directors to be elected at the annual meeting of the shareholders shall be such number as shall be determined from time to time by special resolution or, if the special resolution empowers the directors to determine the number, by resolution of the directors.

(4) **Idem** — Where no resolution has been passed under subsection (3), the number of directors of the corporation shall be the number of directors named in its articles.

(5), (6) [Repealed 1998, c. 18, Sched. E, s. 22.]

1994, c. 27, s. 71(15); 1998, c. 18, Sched. E, s. 22

126. (1) **Place of meetings** — Subject to subsection (2), a meeting of the board of directors shall be held at the place where the registered office of the corporation is located.

(2) **Exceptions** — Where the by-laws of the corporation so provide, a meeting of the board of directors may be held at any place within or outside Ontario, but, except where the corporation is a non-resident corporation or the articles or the by-laws otherwise provide, in any financial year of the corporation a majority of the meetings of the board of directors shall be held at a place within Canada.

(3) **Quorum** — Subject to the articles or by-laws and subsection (4), a majority of the number of directors or minimum number of directors required by the articles constitutes a quorum at any meeting of directors, but in no case shall a quorum be less than two-fifths of the number of directors or minimum number of directors, as the case may be.

(4) Idem — Where a corporation has fewer than three directors, all directors must be present at any meeting of directors to constitute a quorum.

(5) Idem — Subject to the articles or by-laws, where there is a vacancy or vacancies in the board of directors, the remaining directors may exercise all the powers of the board so long as a quorum of the board remains in office.

(6), (7) [Repealed 2006, c. 34, Sched. B, s. 20.]

(8) Calling meeting of directors — In addition to any other provision in the articles or by-laws of a corporation for calling meetings of directors, a quorum of the directors may, at any time, call a meeting of the directors for the transaction of any business the general nature of which is specified in the notice calling the meeting.

(9) Notice — In the absence of any other provision in that behalf in the by-laws of the corporation, notice of the time and place for the holding of the meeting called under subsection (8) shall be given to every director of the corporation by sending the notice ten days or more before the date of the meeting to each director's latest address as shown on the records of the corporation.

(10) Waiver of notice — A director may in any manner and at any time waive a notice of a meeting of directors and attendance of a director at a meeting of directors is a waiver of notice of the meeting, except where a director attends a meeting for the express purpose of objecting to the transaction of any business on the grounds that the meeting is not lawfully called.

(11) Adjourned meeting — Notice of an adjourned meeting of directors is not required to be given if the time and place of the adjourned meeting is announced at the original meeting.

(12) Where one director — Where a corporation has only one director, that director may constitute a meeting.

(13) Meeting by telephone, etc. — Unless the by-laws otherwise provide, if all the directors of a corporation present at or participating in the meeting consent, a meeting of directors or of a committee of directors may be held by means of such telephone, electronic or other communication facilities as permit all persons participating in the meeting to communicate with each other simultaneously and instantaneously, and a director participating in such a meeting by such means is deemed for the purposes of this Act to be present at that meeting.

(14) Place of meeting by telephone — If a majority of the directors participating in a meeting held under subsection (13) are then in Canada, the meeting shall be deemed to have been held in Canada.

2006, c. 34, Sched. B, s. 20

127. (1) Delegation by directors — Subject to the articles or by-laws, directors of a corporation may appoint from their number a managing director or a committee of directors and delegate to such managing director or committee any of the powers of the directors.

(2) [Repealed 2006, c. 34, Sched. B, s. 21(2).]

(3) Limitations on authority — Despite subsection (1), no managing director and no committee of directors has authority to,

(a) submit to the shareholders any question or matter requiring the approval of the shareholders;

(b) fill a vacancy among the directors or in the office of auditor or appoint or remove any of the chief executive officers, however designated, the chief financial officer, however designated, the chair or the president of the corporation;

(c) subject to section 184, issue securities except in the manner and on the terms authorized by the directors;

(d) declare dividends;

(e) purchase, redeem or otherwise acquire shares issued by the corporation;

(f) pay a commission referred to in section 37;

(g) approve a management information circular referred to in Part VIII;

(h) approve a take-over bid circular, directors' circular or issuer bid circular referred to in Part XX of the *Securities Act*;

(i) approve any financial statements referred to in clause 154(1)(b) of the Act and Part XVIII of the *Securities Act*;

(i.1) approve an amalgamation under section 177 or an amendment to the articles under subsection 168(2) or (4); or

(j) adopt, amend or repeal by-laws.

1994, c. 27, s. 71(16); 2006, c. 34, Sched. B, s. 21

128. Validity of acts of directors and officers — An act done by a director or by an officer is not invalid by reason only of any defect that is thereafter discovered in his or her appointment, election or qualification.

129. (1) Resolutions in writing — A resolution in writing, signed by all the directors entitled to vote on that resolution at a meeting of directors or a committee of directors, is as valid as if it had been passed at a meeting of directors or a committee of directors.

(2) Copy to be kept — A copy of every resolution passed under subsection (1) shall be kept with the minutes of the proceedings of the directors or committee of directors.

130. (1) Liability of directors — Directors of a corporation who vote for or consent to a resolution authorizing the issue of a share for a consideration other than money contrary to section 23 are jointly and severally liable to the corporation to make good any amount by which the consideration received is less than the fair equivalent of the money that the corporation would have received if the share had been issued for money on the date of the resolution.

(2) Idem — Directors of a corporation who vote for or consent to a resolution authorizing,

(a) [Repealed 2006, c. 34, Sched. B, s. 22(1).]

(b) a purchase, redemption or other acquisition of shares contrary to section 30, 31 or 32;

(c) a commission contrary to section 37;

(d) a payment of a dividend contrary to section 38;

(e) a payment of an indemnity contrary to section 136; or

(f) a payment to a shareholder contrary to section 185 or 248,

are jointly and severally liable to restore to the corporation any amounts so distributed or paid and not otherwise recovered by the corporation.

(3) **Joint liability** — A director who has satisfied a judgment rendered under this section is entitled to contribution from the other directors who voted for or consented to the unlawful act upon which the judgment was founded.

(4) **Application to court** — A director liable under subsection (2) is entitled to apply to the court for an order compelling a shareholder or other recipient to pay or deliver to the director any money or property that was paid or distributed to the shareholder or other recipient contrary to section 30, 31, 32, 37, 38, 136, 185 or 248.

(5) **What court may order** — In connection with an application under subsection (4), the court may, if it is satisfied that it is equitable to do so,

(a) order a shareholder or other recipient to pay or deliver to a director any money or property that was paid or distributed to the shareholder or other recipient contrary to section 30, 31, 32, 37, 38, 136, 185 or 248;

(b) order a corporation to return or issue shares to a person from whom the corporation has purchased, redeemed or otherwise acquired shares; or

(c) make any further order it thinks fit.

(6) **Exception to subs. (1)** — A director is not liable under subsection (1) if the director proves that he or she did not know and could not reasonably have known that the share was issued for a consideration less than the fair equivalent of the money that the corporation would have received if the share bad been issued for money.

(7) [Repealed 2002, c. 24, Sched. B, s. 25, item 2.]

2002, c. 24, Sched. B, s. 25, item 2; 2006, c. 34, Sched. B, s. 22

131. (1) **Directors' liability to employees for wages** — The directors of a corporation are jointly and severally liable to the employees of the corporation for all debts not exceeding six months' wages that become payable while they are directors for services performed for the corporation and for the vacation pay accrued while they are directors for not more than twelve months under the *Employment Standards Act*, and the regulations thereunder, or under any collective agreement made by the corporation.

(2) **Limitation of liability** — A director is liable under subsection (1) only if,

(a) the corporation is sued in the action against the director and execution against the corporation is returned unsatisfied in whole or in part; or

(b) before or after the action is commenced, the corporation goes into liquidation, is ordered to be wound up or makes an authorized assignment under the *Bankruptcy and Insolvency Act* (Canada), or a receiving order under that Act is made against it, and, in any such case, the claim for the debt has been proved.

(3) **Idem** — Where execution referred to in clause (2)(b) has issued, the amount recoverable from a director is the amount remaining unsatisfied after execution.

(4) **Rights of director who pays debt** — Where a director pays a debt under subsection (1) that is proved in liquidation and dissolution or bankruptcy proceedings, the director is entitled to any preference that the employee would have been entitled to, and where a judgment has been obtained the director is entitled to an assignment of the judgment.

(5) **Idem** — A director who has satisfied a claim under this section is entitled to contribution from the other directors who were liable for the claim.

2002, c. 24, Sched. B, s. 27(1)

132. (1) Disclosure: conflict of interest — A director or officer of a corporation who,

(a) is a party to a material contract or transaction or proposed material contract or transaction with the corporation; or

(b) is a director or an officer of, or has a material interest in, any person who is a party to a material contract or transaction or proposed material contract or transaction with the corporation,

shall disclose in writing to the corporation or request to have entered in the minutes of meetings of directors the nature and extent of his or her interest.

(2) By director — The disclosure required by subsection (1) shall be made, in the case of a director,

(a) at the meeting at which a proposed contract or transaction is first considered;

(b) if the director was not then interested in a proposed contract or transaction, at the first meeting after he or she becomes so interested;

(c) if the director becomes interested after a contract is made or a transaction is entered into, at the first meeting after he or she becomes so interested; or

(d) if a person who is interested in a contract or transaction later becomes a director, at the first meeting after he or she becomes a director.

(3) By officer — The disclosure required by subsection (1) shall be made, in the case of an officer who is not a director,

(a) forthwith after the officer becomes aware that the contract or transaction or proposed contract or transaction is to be considered or has been considered at a meeting of directors;

(b) if the officer becomes interested after a contract is made or a transaction is entered into, forthwith after he or she becomes so interested; or

(c) if a person who is interested in a contract or transaction later becomes an officer, forthwith after he or she becomes an officer.

(4) Where contract or transaction does not require approval — Despite subsections (2) and (3), where subsection (1) applies to a director or officer in respect of a material contract or transaction or proposed material contract or transaction that, in the ordinary course of the corporation's business, would not require approval by the directors or shareholders, the director or officer shall disclose in writing to the corporation or request to have entered in the minutes of meetings of directors the nature and extent of his or her interest forthwith after the director or officer becomes aware of the contract or transaction or proposed contract or transaction.

(5) Director not to vote — A director referred to in subsection (1) shall not attend any part of a meeting of directors during which the contract or transaction is discussed and shall not vote on any resolution to approve the contract or transaction unless the contract or transaction is,

(a) one relating primarily to his or her remuneration as a director of the corporation or an affiliate;

(b) one for indemnity or insurance under section 136; or

(c) one with an affiliate.

(d) [Repealed 2006, c. 34, Sched. B, s. 23(1).]

(5.1) Remaining directors deemed quorum — If no quorum exists for the purpose of voting on a resolution to approve a contract or transaction only because a director is not permitted to be present at the meeting by reason of subsection (5), the remaining directors shall be deemed to constitute a quorum for the purposes of voting on the resolution.

(5.2) Shareholder approval — Where all of the directors are required to make disclosure under subsection (1), the contract or transaction may be approved only by the shareholders.

(6) Continuing disclosure — For the purposes of this section, a general notice to the directors by a director or officer disclosing that he or she is a director or officer of or has a material interest in a person, or that there has been a material change in the director's or officer's interest in the person, and is to be regarded as interested in any contract made or any transaction entered into with that person, is sufficient disclosure of interest in relation to any such contract or transaction.

(7) Effect of disclosure — Where a material contract is made or a material transaction is entered into between a corporation and a director or officer of the corporation, or between a corporation and another person of which a director or officer of the corporation is a director or officer or in which he or she has a material interest,

(a) the director or officer is not accountable to the corporation or its shareholders for any profit or gain realized from the contract or transaction; and

(b) the contract or transaction is neither void nor voidable,

by reason only of that relationship or by reason only that the director is present at or is counted to determine the presence of a quorum at the meeting of directors that authorized the contract or transaction, if the director or officer disclosed his or her interest in accordance with subsection (2), (3), (4) or (6), as the case may be, and the contract or transaction was reasonable and fair to the corporation at the time it was so approved.

(8) Confirmation by shareholders — Despite anything in this section, a director or officer, acting honestly and in good faith, is not accountable to the corporation or to its shareholders for any profit or gain realized from any such contract or transaction by reason only of his or her holding the office of director or officer, and the contract or transaction, if it was reasonable and fair to the corporation at the time it was approved, is not by reason only of the director's or officer's interest therein void or voidable, where,

(a) the contract or transaction is confirmed or approved by special resolution at a meeting of the shareholders duly called for that purpose; and

(b) the nature and extent of the director's or officer's interest in the contract or transaction are disclosed in reasonable detail in the notice calling the meeting or in the information circular required by section 112.

(9) Court setting aside contract — Subject to subsections (7) and (8), where a director or officer of a corporation fails to disclose his or her interest in a material contract or transaction in accordance with this section or otherwise fails to comply with this section, the corporation or a shareholder of the corporation, or, in the case of an offering corporation, the Commission may apply to the court for an order setting aside the contract or transaction and directing that the director or officer account to the corporation for any profit or gain realized and upon such application the court may so order or make such other order as it thinks fit.

2006, c. 34, Sched. B, s. 23

133. Officers — Subject to the articles, the by-laws or any unanimous shareholder agreement,

(a) the directors may designate the offices of the corporation, appoint officers, specify their duties and delegate to them powers to manage the business and affairs of the corporation, except, subject to section 184, powers to do anything referred to in subsection 127(3);

(b) a director may be appointed to any office of the corporation; and

(c) two or more offices of the corporation may be held by the same person.

134. (1) Standards of care, etc., of directors, etc. — Every director and officer of a corporation in exercising his or her powers and discharging his or her duties to the corporation shall,

(a) act honestly and in good faith with a view to the best interests of the corporation; and

(b) exercise the care, diligence and skill that a reasonably prudent person would exercise in comparable circumstances.

(2) Duty to comply with Act, etc. — Every director and officer of a corporation shall comply with this Act, the regulations, articles, by-laws and any unanimous shareholder agreement.

(3) Cannot contract out of liability — Subject to subsection 108(5), no provision in a contract, the articles, the by-laws or a resolution relieves a director or officer from the duty to act in accordance with this Act and the regulations or relieves him or her from liability for a breach thereof.

2006, c. 34, Sched. B, s. 24

135. (1) Consent of director at meeting — A director who is present at a meeting of directors or committee of directors is deemed to have consented to any resolution passed or action taken thereat unless the director,

(a) requests that his or her dissent be or his or her dissent is entered in the minutes of the meeting;

(b) sends a written dissent to the secretary of the meeting before the meeting is terminated; or

(c) sends a dissent by registered mail or delivers it to the registered office of the corporation immediately after the meeting is terminated.

(2) Idem — A director who votes for or consents to a resolution is not entitled to dissent under subsection (1).

(3) Idem — A director who was not present at a meeting at which a resolution was passed or action taken is deemed to have consented thereto unless within seven days after becoming aware of the resolution the director,

(a) causes his or her dissent to be placed with the minutes of the meeting; or

(b) sends his or her dissent by registered mail or delivers it to the registered office of the corporation.

(4) Reasonable diligence defence — A director is not liable under section 130 and has complied with his or her duties under subsection 134(2) if the director exercised the care, diligence and skill that a reasonably prudent person would have exercised in comparable circumstances, including reliance in good faith on,

(a) financial statements of the corporation represented to him or her by an officer of the corporation or in a written report of the auditor of the corporation to present fairly the financial position of the corporation in accordance with generally accepted accounting principles;

(b) an interim or other financial report of the corporation represented to him or her by an officer of the corporation to present fairly the financial position of the corporation in accordance with generally accepted accounting principles;

(c) a report or advice of an officer or employee of the corporation, where it is reasonable in the circumstances to rely on the report or advice; or

(d) a report of a lawyer, accountant, engineer, appraiser or other person whose profession lends credibility to a statement made by any such person.

2006, c. 34, Sched. B, s. 25

136. (1) Indemnification — A corporation may indemnify a director or officer of the corporation, a former director or officer of the corporation or another individual who acts or acted at the corporation's request as a director or officer, or an individual acting in a similar capacity, of another entity, against all costs, charges and expenses, including an amount paid to settle an action or satisfy a judgment, reasonably incurred by the individual in respect of any civil, criminal, administrative, investigative or other proceeding in which the individual is involved because of that association with the corporation or other entity.

(2) Advance of costs — A corporation may advance money to a director, officer or other individual for the costs, charges and expenses of a proceeding referred to in subsection (1), but the individual shall repay the money if the individual does not fulfil the conditions set out in subsection (3).

(3) Limitation — A corporation shall not indemnify an individual under subsection (1) unless the individual acted honestly and in good faith with a view to the best interests of the corporation or, as the case may be, to the best interests of the other entity for which the individual acted as a director or officer or in a similar capacity at the corporation's request.

(4) Same — In addition to the conditions set out in subsection (3), if the matter is a criminal or administrative action or proceeding that is enforced by a monetary penalty, the corporation shall not indemnify an individual under subsection (1) unless the individual had reasonable grounds for believing that the individual's conduct was lawful.

(4.1) Derivative actions — A corporation may, with the approval of a court, indemnify an individual referred to in subsection (1), or advance moneys under subsection (2), in respect of an action by or on behalf of the corporation or other entity to obtain a judgment in its favour, to which the individual is made a party because of the individual's association with the corporation or other entity as described in subsection (1), against all costs, charges and expenses reasonably incurred by the individual in connection with such action, if the individual fulfils the conditions set out in subsection (3).

(4.2) Right to indemnity — Despite subsection (1), an individual referred to in that subsection is entitled to indemnity from the corporation in respect of all costs, charges and expenses reasonably incurred by the individual in connection with the defence of any civil, criminal, administrative, investigative or other proceeding to which the individual is subject because of the individual's association with the corporation or other entity as described in subsection (1), if the individual seeking an indemnity,

(a) was not judged by a court or other competent authority to have committed any fault or omitted to do anything that the individual ought to have done; and

(b) fulfils the conditions set out in subsections (3) and (4).

(4.3) **Insurance** — A corporation may purchase and maintain insurance for the benefit of an individual referred to in subsection (1) against any liability incurred by the individual,

(a) in the individual's capacity as a director or officer of the corporation; or

(b) in the individual's capacity as a director or officer, or a similar capacity, of another entity, if the individual acts or acted in that capacity at the corporation's request.

(5) **Application to court** — A corporation or a person referred to in subsection (1) may apply to the court for an order approving an indemnity under this section and the court may so order and make any further order it thinks fit.

(6) **Idem** — Upon an application under subsection (5), the court may order notice to be given to any interested person and such person is entitled to appear and be heard in person or by counsel.

2006, c. 34, Sched. B, s. 26

137. **Remuneration of directors** — Subject to the articles, the by-laws or any unanimous shareholder agreement, the directors of a corporation may fix the remuneration of the directors, officers and employees of the corporation.

PART X — INSIDER LIABILITY

138. (1) **Definitions** — In this Part,

"corporation" means a corporation that is not an offering corporation;

"insider" means, with respect to a corporation,

(a) the corporation,

(b) an affiliate of the corporation,

(c) a director or officer of the corporation,

(d) a person who beneficially owns, directly or indirectly, more than 10 per cent of the voting securities of the corporation or who exercises control or direction over more than 10 per cent of the votes attached to the voting securities of the corporation,

(e) a person employed or retained by the corporation, or

(f) a person who receives specific confidential information from a person described in this definition or in subsection (3), including a person described in this clause, and who has knowledge that the person giving the information is a person described in this definition or in subsection (3), including a person described in this clause;

"security" includes a warrant.

(2) **Insider** — For the purposes of this Part,

(a) a director or officer of a body corporate that is an insider of a corporation is deemed to be an insider of the corporation;

(b) a director or officer of a body corporate that is a subsidiary is deemed to be an insider of its holding corporation;

(c) a person is deemed to own beneficially, voting securities beneficially owned by a body corporate controlled by the person directly or indirectly; and

(d) a body corporate is deemed to own beneficially, voting securities beneficially owned by its affiliates.

(3) **Idem** — For the purposes of this Part,

(a) where a body corporate becomes an insider of a corporation, or enters into a business combination with a corporation, a director or an officer of the body corporate or a shareholder of the body corporate who is a person referred to in clause (d) of the definition of "insider" in subsection (1) is deemed to have been an insider of the corporation for the previous six months or for such shorter period as he or she was a director, an officer or such a shareholder of the body corporate; and

(b) where a corporation becomes an insider of a body corporate or enters into a business combination with a body corporate, a director or an officer of the body corporate or a shareholder of the body corporate who is a person referred to in clause (d) of the definition of "insider" in subsection (1) is deemed to have been an insider of the corporation for the previous six months or for such shorter period as he or she was a director, an officer or such a shareholder of the body corporate.

(4) **Business combination** — In subsection (3), **"business combination"** means an acquisition of all or substantially all the property of one body corporate by another or an amalgamation of two or more bodies corporate.

(5) **Liability of insider** — An insider who, in connection with a transaction in a security of the corporation or any of it affiliates, makes use of any specific confidential information for the insider's own benefit or advantage that, if generally known, might reasonably be expected to affect materially the value of the security,

(a) is liable to compensate any person for direct loss suffered by that person as a result of the transaction, unless the information was known or in the exercise of reasonable diligence should have been known to that person; and

(b) is accountable to the corporation for any direct benefit or advantage received or receivable by the insider as a result of the transaction.

(6) [Repealed 2002, c. 24, Sched. B, s. 25, item 2.]

2002, c. 24, Sched. B, s. 25, item 2

PART XI — BOOKS AND RECORDS

139. (1) Records — Where this Act requires a record to be kept by a corporation, it may be kept in a bound or looseleaf book or may be entered or recorded by any system of mechanical or electronic data processing or any other information storage device.

(2) **Guard against falsification of records** — The corporation shall,

(a) take adequate precautions, appropriate to the means used, for guarding against the risk of falsifying the information recorded; and

(b) provide means for making the information available in an accurate and intelligible form within a reasonable time to any person lawfully entitled to examine the records.

(3) Admissibility of records in evidence — The bound or looseleaf book or, where the record is not kept in a bound or looseleaf book, the information in the form in which it is made available under clause (2)(b) is admissible in evidence as proof, in the absence of evidence to the contrary, of all facts stated therein, before and after dissolution of the corporation.

(4) False information — No person shall remove, withhold or destroy information required by this Act or the regulations to be recorded, or,

(a) record or assist in recording any information in a record; or

(b) make information purporting to be accurate available in a form referred to in clause (2)(b),

knowing it to be untrue.

140. (1) Records — A corporation shall prepare and maintain, at its registered office or at such other place in Ontario designated by the directors,

(a) the articles and the by-laws and all amendments thereto, and a copy of any unanimous shareholder agreement known to the directors;

(b) minutes of meetings and resolutions of shareholders;

(c) a register of directors in which are set out the names and residence addresses, while directors, including the street and number, if any, of all persons who are or have been directors of the corporation with the several dates on which each became or ceased to be a director; and

(d) a securities register complying with section 141.

(2) Idem — In addition to the records described in subsection (1), a corporation shall prepare and maintain,

(a) adequate accounting records; and

(b) records containing minutes of meetings and resolutions of the directors and any committee thereof,

but, provided the retention requirements of any taxing authority of Ontario, the government of Canada or any other jurisdiction to which the corporation is subject have been satisfied, the accounting records mentioned in clause (a) need only be retained by the corporation for six years from the end of the last fiscal period to which they relate.

(3) Idem — For the purposes of clause (1)(b) and subsection (2), where a body corporate is continued under this Act, "records" includes similar records required by law to be maintained by the body corporate before it was so continued.

141. (1) Securities register — A corporation shall prepare and maintain at its registered office, or at any other place in Ontario designated by the directors, a securities register in which it records the securities issued by it in registered form, showing with respect to each class or series of securities,

(a) the names, alphabetically arranged of persons who,

(i) are or have been within six years registered as shareholders of the corporation, the address including the street and number, if any, of every such person while a holder, and the number and class of shares registered in the name of such holder,

(ii) are or have been within six years registered as holders of debt obligations of the corporation, the address including the street and number, if any, of every such person while a holder, and the class or series and principal amount of the debt obligations registered in the name of such holder, or

(iii) are or have been within six years registered as holders of warrants of the corporation, other than warrants exercisable within one year from the date of issue, the address including the street and number, if any, of every such person while a registered holder, and the class or series and number of warrants registered in the name of such holder; and

(b) the date and particulars of the issue of each security and warrant.

(2) **Register of transfers** — A corporation shall cause to be kept a register of transfers in which all transfers of securities issued by the corporation in registered form and the date and other particulars of each transfer shall be set out.

(3) [Repealed 2006, c. 8, s. 120.]

2006, c. 8, s. 120

142. Transfer agents — For each class of securities and warrants issued by it, a corporation may appoint,

(a) a trustee, transfer agent or other agent to keep the securities register and the register of transfers and one or more persons or agents to keep branch registers; and

(b) a registrar, trustee or agent to maintain a record of issued security certificates and warrants,

and, subject to section 48, one person may be appointed for the purposes of both clauses (a) and (b) in respect of all securities and warrants of the corporation or any class or classes thereof.

143. (1) Where registers to be kept — The securities register and the register of transfers shall be kept at the registered office of a corporation or at such other places in Ontario designated by the directors, and the branch register or registers of transfers may be kept at such offices of the corporation or other places, either within or outside Ontario, designated by the directors.

(2) **Valid registration** — Registration of the transfer of a security or warrant of a corporation in the register of transfers or a branch register of transfers is a complete and valid registration for all purposes.

(3) **Entry in branch transfer register** — In each branch register of transfers there shall be recorded only the particulars of the transfers of securities or warrants registered in that branch register of transfers.

(4) **Entry in register of transfers** — Particulars of every transfer of securities and warrants registered in every branch register of transfers shall be recorded in the register of transfers.

(5) **Documents not required to be produced** — A corporation or a person appointed under section 142 is not required to produce,

(a) any security certificate or warrant that is not in registered form; or

(b) any security certificate or warrant that is in registered form after six years,

(i) in the case of a share certificate, from the date of its cancellation,

(ii) in the case of a warrant, from the date of its transfer or exercise, whichever occurs first, or

(iii) in the case of a certificate representing a debt obligation, from the date of cancellation of such certificate.

144. (1) Records open to examination by directors — The records mentioned in sections 140 and 141 shall, during normal business hours of a corporation, be open to examination by any director and shall, except as provided in sections 140 and 143 and in subsections (2) and (3) of this section, be kept at the registered office of the corporation.

(2) Records of account at branch — A corporation may keep at any place where it carries on business such parts of the accounting records as relate to the operations, business and assets and liabilities of the corporation carried on, supervised or accounted for at such place, but there shall be kept at the registered office of the corporation or such other place as is authorized under this section such records as will enable the directors to ascertain quarterly with reasonable accuracy the financial position of the corporation.

(3) Off-site records — A corporation may keep all or any of the records mentioned in subsection (1) at a place other than the registered office of the corporation if the records are available for inspection during regular office hours at the registered office by means of a computer terminal or other electronic technology.

(4) Rescission of orders made under subs. (3) — The Director may by order upon such terms as the Director thinks fit rescind any order made under subsection (3) or any order made by the Lieutenant Governor in Council or the Minister under a predecessor of that subsection.

1994, c. 27, s. 71(17)

145. (1) Examination of records by shareholders and creditors — Registered holders of shares, beneficial owners of shares and creditors of a corporation, their agents and legal representatives may examine the records referred to in subsection 140(1) during the usual business hours of the corporation, and may take extracts from those records, free of charge, and, if the corporation is an offering corporation, any other person may do so upon payment of a reasonable fee.

(2) Copy — A registered holder or beneficial owner of shares of a corporation is entitled upon request and without charge to one copy of the articles and by-laws and of any unanimous shareholder agreement.

2006, c. 34, Sched. B, s. 27

146. (1) List of shareholders — Registered holders, beneficial owners of shares and creditors of a corporation, their agents and legal representatives and, if the corporation is an offering corporation, any other person, upon payment of a reasonable fee and upon sending to the corporation or its transfer agent the statutory declaration referred to in subsection (6), may require the corporation or its transfer agent to furnish a basic list setting out the names of the registered holders of shares of the corporation, the number of shares of each class and series owned by each registered holder and the address of each of them, all as shown on the records of the corporation.

(2) Idem — The basic list referred to in subsection (1) shall be furnished to the applicant as soon as is practicable and, when furnished, shall be as current as is practicable having regard to the form in which the securities register of the corporation is maintained, but, in any case, shall be furnished not more than ten days following the receipt by the corporation or its transfer agent of the statutory declaration referred to in subsection (1) and shall be made up to a date not more than ten days before the date on which it is actually furnished.

(3) **Supplemental lists** — A person requiring a corporation to supply a basic list may, if the person states in the statutory declaration referred to in subsection (1) that the person requires supplemental lists, require the corporation or its agent upon payment of a reasonable fee to furnish supplemental lists setting out any changes from the basic list in the names or addresses of the registered holders of the corporation's shares and the number of shares owned by each registered holder for each business day following the date to which the basic list is made up.

(4) **Idem** — The corporation or its agent shall furnish a supplemental list required under subsection (3),

(a) on the date the basic list is furnished, where the information relates to changes that took place prior to that date; and

(b) on the business day following the day to which the supplemental list relates, where the information relates to changes that take place on or after the date the basic list is furnished.

(5) **List of option holders** — A person requiring a corporation to supply a basic or supplemental list may also require the corporation to include in that list the name and address of any known holder of an option or right to acquire shares of the corporation.

(6) **Statutory declaration** — The statutory declaration required under subsection (1) shall state,

(a) the name and address including the street and number, if any, of the applicant and whether the applicant is a registered holder, beneficial owner, creditor or any other person referred to in the subsection;

(b) the name and address including street and number, if any, for service of the body corporate if the applicant is a body corporate; and

(c) that the basic list and any supplemental lists shall be used only as permitted under subsection (8).

(7) **Idem** — If the applicant is a body corporate, the statutory declaration shall be made by a director or officer of the body corporate.

(8) **Use of list** — A list of registered holders obtained under this section shall not be used by any person except in connection with,

(a) an effort to influence the voting by registered holders of the corporation;

(b) an offer to acquire shares of the corporation; or

(c) any other matter relating to the affairs of the corporation.

2006, c. 34, Sched. B, s. 28

146.1 (1) **Proof of status** — Before providing a document referred to in sections 145 or 146 to a person who claims to be a beneficial owner of shares of the corporation, a corporation may require the person to provide proof that the person is a beneficial owner.

(2) Same — A written statement by a securities intermediary, as defined in the *Securities Transfer Act, 2006*, that a person is a beneficial owner is sufficient proof for the purposes of subsection (1).

2006, c. 34, Sched. B, s. 29

147. Trafficking in lists — No person shall offer for sale or sell or purchase or otherwise traffic in a list or a copy of a list of all or any of the holders of securities or warrants of a corporation.

PART XII — AUDITORS AND FINANCIAL STATEMENTS

148. Exemption from audit requirements — In respect of a financial year of a corporation, the corporation is exempt from the requirements of this Part regarding the appointment and duties of an auditor if,

(a) the corporation is not an offering corporation; and

(b) all of the shareholders consent in writing to the exemption in respect of that year.

1994, c. 27, s. 71(18); 1998, c. 18, Sched. E, s. 23

149. (1) Auditors — The shareholders of a corporation at their first annual or special meeting shall appoint one or more auditors to hold office until the close of the first or next annual meeting, as the case may be, and, if the shareholders fail to do so, the directors shall forthwith make such appointment or appointments.

(2) Idem — The shareholders shall at each annual meeting appoint one or more auditors to hold office until the close of the next annual meeting and, if an appointment is not so made, the auditor in office continues in office until a successor is appointed.

(3) Casual vacancy — The directors may fill any casual vacancy in the office of auditor, but, while such vacancy continues, the surviving or continuing auditor, if any, may act.

(4) Removal of auditor — The shareholders may, except where the auditor has been appointed by order of the court under subsection (8), by resolution passed by a majority of the votes cast at a special meeting duly called for the purpose, remove an auditor before the expiration of the auditor's term of office, and shall by a majority of the votes cast at that meeting appoint a replacement for the remainder of the auditor's term.

(5) Notice to auditor — Before calling a special meeting for the purpose specified in subsection (4) or an annual or special meeting where the board is not recommending the reappointment of the incumbent auditor, the corporation shall, fifteen days or more before the mailing of the notice of the meeting, give to the auditor,

(a) written notice of the intention to call the meeting, specifying therein the date on which the notice of the meeting is proposed to be mailed; and

(b) a copy of all material proposed to be sent to shareholders in connection with the meeting.

(6) Right of auditor to make representations — An auditor has the right to make to the corporation, three days or more before the mailing of the notice of the meeting, representations in writing, concerning,

(a) the auditor's proposed removal as auditor;

(b) the appointment or election of another person to fill the office of auditor; or

(c) the auditor's resignation as auditor,

and the corporation, at its expense, shall forward with the notice of the meeting a copy of such representations to each shareholder entitled to receive notice of the meeting.

(7) **Remuneration** — The remuneration of an auditor appointed by the shareholders shall be fixed by the shareholders, or by the directors if they are authorized so to do by the shareholders, and the remuneration of an auditor appointed by the directors shall be fixed by the directors.

(8) **Appointment by court** — If a corporation does not have an auditor, the court may, upon the application of a shareholder or the Director, appoint and fix the remuneration of an auditor to hold office until an auditor is appointed by the shareholders.

(9) **Notice of appointment** — The corporation shall give notice in writing to an auditor of the auditor's appointment forthwith after the appointment is made.

150. **Resignation of auditor** — A resignation of an auditor becomes effective at the time a written resignation is sent to the corporation or at the time specified in the resignation, whichever is later.

151. (1) **Auditor may attend shareholders' meetings** — The auditor of a corporation is entitled to receive notice of every meeting of shareholders and, at the expense of the corporation, to attend and be heard thereat on matters relating to auditor's duties.

(2) **Auditor's attendance may be required** — If any director or shareholder of a corporation, whether or not the shareholder is entitled to vote at the meeting, gives written notice, not less than five days or more before a meeting of shareholders, to the auditor or a former auditor of the corporation, the auditor or former auditor shall attend the meeting at the expense of the corporation and answer questions relating to the auditor's duties.

(3) **Notice to corporation** — A director or shareholder who sends a notice referred to in subsection (2) shall send concurrently a copy of the notice to the corporation.

(4) **Replacing auditor** — No person shall accept appointment or consent to be appointed as auditor of a corporation if the person is replacing an auditor who has resigned, been removed or whose term of office has expired or is about to expire until the person has requested and received from that auditor a written statement of the circumstances and the reasons why, in that auditor's opinion, that auditor is to be replaced.

(5) **Idem** — Despite subsection (4), a person otherwise qualified may accept appointment or consent to be appointed as auditor of a corporation if, within fifteen days after making the request referred to in that subsection, the person does not receive a reply.

(6) **Idem** — Any interested person may apply to the court for an order declaring an auditor to be disqualified and the office of auditor to be vacant if the auditor has not complied with subsection (4), unless subsection (5) applies with respect to the appointment of the auditor.

(7) **Statement by auditor privileged** — Any oral or written statement or report made under this Act by the auditor or former auditor of the corporation has qualified privilege.

152. (1) **Disqualification as auditor** — Subject to subsection (5), a person is disqualified from being an auditor of a corporation if the person is not independent of the corporation, all of its affiliates, or of the directors or officers of the corporation and its affiliates.

(2) Independence — For the purposes of this section,

(a) independence is a question of fact; and

(b) a person is deemed not to be independent if the person or the person's business partner,

(i) is a business partner, director, officer or employee of the corporation or any of its affiliates, or a business partner of any director, officer or employee of the corporation or any of its affiliates,

(ii) beneficially owns directly or indirectly or exercises control or direction over a material interest in the securities of the corporation or any of its affiliates, or

(iii) has been a receiver, receiver and manager, liquidator or trustee in bankruptcy of the corporation or any of its affiliates within two years of the person's proposed appointment as auditor of the corporation.

Proposed Addition — 152(2.1)

(2.1) Business partners — For the purposes of subsection (2), a person's business partner includes a shareholder of the person.

2011, c. 1, Sched. 2, s. 1(8) [Not in force at date of publication.]

(3) Resignation by auditor — An auditor who becomes disqualifed under this section shall, subject to subsection (5), resign forthwith upon becoming aware of such disqualification.

(4) Application to court — An interested person may apply to the court for an order declaring an auditor to be disqualified under this section and the office of auditor to be vacant.

(5) [Repealed without coming into force 2004, c. 19, s. 3(4).]

(6) [Repealed 2004, c. 19, s. 3(4).]

2004, c. 19, s. 3(4)

153. (1) Examination by auditor — An auditor of a corporation shall make such examination of the financial statements required by this Act to be placed before shareholders as is necessary to enable the auditor to report thereon and the auditor shall report as prescribed and in accordance with generally accepted auditing standards.

(2) Reporting error — A director or an officer of a corporation shall forthwith notify the audit committee and the auditor or the former auditor of any error or misstatement of which he or she becomes aware in a financial statement that the auditor or the former auditor has reported upon if the error or misstatement in all the circumstances appears to be significant.

(3) Idem — If the auditor or former auditor of a corporation is notified or becomes aware of an error or misstatement in a financial statement upon which he or she has reported, and if in his or her opinion the error or misstatement is material, the auditor or former auditor shall inform each director accordingly.

(4) Amendment of auditor's report — When under subsection (3) the auditor or former auditor informs the directors of an error or misstatement in a financial statement, the directors shall within a reasonable time,

(a) prepare and issue revised financial statements; or

(b) otherwise inform the shareholders.

(5) Right of access — Upon the demand of an auditor of a corporation, the present or former directors, officers, employees or agents of the corporation shall furnish such,

(a) information and explanations; and

(b) access to records, documents, books, accounts and vouchers of the corporation or any of its subsidiaries,

as are, in the opinion of the auditor, necessary to enable the auditor to make the examination and report required under this section and that the directors, officers, employees or agents are reasonably able to furnish.

(6) Furnishing information — Upon the demand of the auditor of a corporation, the directors of the corporation shall,

(a) obtain from the present or former directors, officers, employees and agents of any subsidiary of the corporation the information and explanations that the present or former directors, officers, employees and agents are reasonably able to furnish and that are, in the opinion of the auditor, necessary to enable the auditor to make the examination and report required under this section; and

(b) furnish the information and explanations so obtained to the auditor.

(7) Idem — Any oral or written communication under this section between the auditor or former auditor of a corporation and its present or former directors, officers, employees or agents or those of any subsidiary of the corporation, has qualified privilege.

154. (1) Information to be laid before annual meeting — The directors shall place before each annual meeting of shareholders,

(a) in the case of a corporation that is not an offering corporation, financial statements for the period that began on the date the corporation came into existence and ended not more than six months before the annual meeting or, if the corporation has completed a financial year, the period that began immediately after the end of the last completed financial year and ended not more than six months before the annual meeting;

(b) in the case of a corporation that is an offering corporation, the financial statements required to be filed under the *Securities Act* and the regulations thereunder relating separately to,

(i) the period that began on the date the corporation came into existence and ended not more than six months before the annual meeting or, if the corporation has completed a financial year, the period that began immediately after the end of the last completed financial year and ended not more than six months before the annual meeting, and

(ii) the immediately preceding financial year, if any;

(c) the report of the auditor, if any, to the shareholders; and

(d) any further information respecting the financial position of the corporation and the results of its operations required by the articles, the by-laws or any unanimous shareholder agreement.

(2) Auditor's report — Except as provided in subsection 104(1), the report of the auditor to the shareholders shall be open to inspection at the annual meeting by any shareholder.

(3) Copy of documents to shareholders, offering corporations — Not less than 21 days before each annual meeting of shareholders or before the signing of a resolution under clause 104(1)(b) in lieu of the annual meeting, an offering corporation shall send a copy of the documents referred to in this section to all shareholders who have informed the corporation that they wish to receive a copy of those documents.

(4) Non-offering corporations — Not less than 10 days before each annual meeting of shareholders or before the signing of a resolution under clause 104(1)(b) in lieu of the annual meeting, a corporation that is not an offering corporation shall send a copy of the documents referred to in this section to all shareholders other than those who have informed the corporation in writing that they do not wish to receive a copy of those documents.

2006, c. 34, Sched. B, s. 30

155. Preparation of financial statements — The financial statements required under this Act shall be prepared as prescribed by regulation and in accordance with generally accepted accounting principles.

156. Filing by offering corporation — An offering corporation shall prepare and file with the Commission the financial statements required under Part XVIII of the *Securities Act*.

157. (1) Financial statements of subsidiaries — True copies of the latest financial statements of each subsidiary of a holding corporation shall be kept on hand by the holding corporation at its registered office and shall be open to examination by the shareholders of the holding corporation and their agents and legal representatives who may make extracts therefrom free of charge on request during the normal business hours of the holding corporation.

(2) Application to court — A corporation may, within fifteen days after a request to examine under subsection (1), apply to the court for an order barring the right of any person to so examine, and the court may, if satisfied that such examination would be detrimental to the corporation or a subsidiary body corporate, bar such right and make any further order it thinks fit.

158. (1) Audit committee — A corporation that is an offering corporation shall, and any other corporation may, have an audit committee composed of not fewer than three directors of the corporation, a majority of whom are not officers or employees of the corporation or any of its affiliates, to hold office until the next annual meeting of the shareholders.

(1.1) Exemption — The Commission may, on the application of a corporation, authorize the corporation to dispense with an audit committee, and the Commission may, if satisfied that the shareholders will not be prejudiced, permit the corporation to dispense with an audit committee on any reasonable conditions that the Commission thinks fit.

(2) Idem — An audit committee shall review the financial statements of the corporation and shall report thereon to the board of directors of the corporation before such financial statements are approved under section 159.

(3) Auditor may attend committee meetings — The auditor of a corporation is entitled to receive notice of every meeting of the audit committee and, at the expense of the corporation, to attend and be heard thereat, and, if so requested by a member of the audit committee, shall attend every meeting of the committee held during the term of office of the auditor.

(4) Calling meetings of committee — The auditor of a corporation or a member of the audit committee may call a meeting of the committee.

(5) Right of auditor to be heard — The auditor of a corporation shall be entitled to attend at the expense of the corporation and be heard at meetings of the board of directors of the corporation on matters relating to the auditor's duties.

2006, c. 34, Sched. B, s. 31

159. (1) Approval by directors — The financial statements shall be approved by the board of directors and the approval shall be evidenced by the signature at the foot of the balance sheet by two of the directors duly authorized to sign or by the director where there is only one, and the auditor's report, unless the corporation is exempt under section 148, shall be attached to or accompany the financial statements.

Proposed Amendment — 159(1)

(1) Approval by directors — The financial statements shall be approved by the board of directors and the approval shall be evidenced by the signature at the foot of the balance sheet of any director authorized to sign, and the auditor's report, unless the corporation is exempt under section 148, shall be attached to or accompany the financial statements.

2010, c. 16, Sched. 5, s. 1(2) [Not in force at date of publication.]

(2) Publishing, etc., copies of financial statements — A corporation shall not issue, publish or circulate copies of the financial statements referred to in section 154 unless the financial statements are,

(a) approved and signed in accordance with subsection (1); and

(b) accompanied by the report of the auditor of the corporation, if any.

160. (1) Interim financial statement — Within 60 days after the date that an interim financial statement required to be filed under the *Securities Act* and the regulations made under that Act is prepared, an offering corporation shall send a copy of the interim financial statement to all shareholders who have informed the corporation that they wish to receive a copy.

(2) Address — The interim financial statement referred to in subsection (1) shall be sent to a shareholder's latest address as shown on the records of the corporation.

2006, c. 34, Sched. B, s. 32

PART XIII — INVESTIGATION

161. (1) Investigation — A registered holder or a beneficial owner of a security or, in the case of an offering corporation, the Commission may apply, without notice or on such notice as the court may require, to the court for an order directing an investigation to be made of the corporation or any of its affiliates.

(2) Idem — Where, upon an application under subsection (1), it appears to the court that,

(a) the business of the corporation or any of its affiliates is or has been carried on with intent to defraud any person;

(b) the business or affairs of the corporation or any of its affiliates are or have been carried on or conducted, or the powers of the directors are or have been exercised, in a manner that is oppressive or unfairly prejudicial to, or that unfairly disregards, the interests of a security holder;

(c) the corporation or any of its affiliates was formed for a fraudulent or unlawful purpose or is to be dissolved for a fraudulent or unlawful purpose; or

(d) persons concerned with the formation, business or affairs of the corporation or any of its affiliates have in connection therewith acted fraudulently or dishonestly,

the court may order an investigation to be made of the corporation and any of its affiliates.

(3) **Notice** — If a registered holder or a beneficial owner of a security makes an application under subsection (1) and the corporation is an offering corporation, the applicant shall give the Commission reasonable notice of the application and the Commission is entitled to appear and be heard in person or by counsel.

(4) **Security for costs not required** — An applicant under this section is not required to give security for costs.

(5) **Closed hearing** — The hearing of an application made without notice under this section shall be closed to the public.

(6) **No publication without consent** — No person may publish anything relating to an application under this section except with the authorization of the court or the written consent of the corporation being investigated.

1994, c. 27, s. 71(19); 2006, c. 34, Sched. B, s. 33

162. (1) **Matters that may be covered by court order** — In connection with an investigation under this Part, the court may make any order it thinks fit including, without limiting the generality of the foregoing,

(a) an order to investigate;

(b) an order appointing and fixing the remuneration of an inspector or replacing an inspector;

(c) an order determining the notice to be given to any interested person, or dispensing with notice to any person;

(d) an order authorizing an inspector to enter any premises in which the court is satisfied there might be relevant information, and to examine anything and make copies of any document or record found on the premises;

(e) an order requiring any person to produce documents or records to the inspector;

(f) an order authorizing an inspector to conduct a hearing, administer oaths and examine any person upon oath, and prescribing rules for the conduct of the hearing;

(g) an order requiring any person to attend a hearing conducted by an inspector and to give evidence upon oath;

(h) an order giving directions to an inspector or any interested person on any matter arising in the investigation;

(i) an order requiring an inspector to make an interim or final report to the court;

(j) an order determining whether a report of an inspector should be made available for public inspection and ordering that copies be sent to any person the court designates;

(k) an order requiring an inspector to discontinue an investigation;

(l) an order requiring the corporation to pay the costs of the investigation.

(2) **Inspector's report** — An inspector shall send to the Director and, where an offering corporation is involved, the Commission, a copy of every report made by the inspector under

this Part which, subject to clause (1)(j), shall be placed on the corporation file for public inspection.

163. (1) Powers of inspector — An inspector under this Part has the powers set out in the order appointing the inspector.

(2) Idem — In addition to the powers set out in the order referred to in subsection (1), an inspector appointed to investigate a corporation may furnish to, or exchange information and otherwise co-operate with, any public official in Canada or elsewhere who is authorized to exercise investigatory powers and who is investigating, in respect of the corporation, any allegation of improper conduct that is the same as, or similar to, the conduct described in subsection 161(2).

(3) Production of order — An inspector shall produce upon request to an interested person a copy of any order made under subsection 162(1).

164. (1) Closed hearing — Any interested person may apply to the court for an order that a hearing conducted under this Part be closed to the public and for directions on any matter arising in the investigation.

(2) Right to counsel — A person whose conduct is being investigated or who is being examined at a hearing conducted by an inspector under this Part has a right to be represented by counsel.

165. Privileged statements — Any oral or written statement or report made by an inspector or any other person in an investigation under this Part has absolute privilege.

166. Solicitor-client privilege — Nothing in this Part shall be construed to affect the privilege that exists in respect of communications between a solicitor and his or her client.

167. Inquiries by Director — The Director may make inquiries of any person relating to compliance with this Act.

PART XIV — FUNDAMENTAL CHANGES

168. (1) Amendments — Subject to sections 170 and 171, a corporation may from time to time amend its articles to add, change or remove any provision that is permitted by this Act to be, or that is, set out in its articles, including without limiting the generality of the foregoing, to,

(a) change its name;

(b) [Repealed 1994, c. 27, s. 71(20).]

(c) add, change or remove any restriction upon the business or businesses that the corporation may carry on or upon the powers that the corporation may exercise;

(d) add, change or remove any maximum number of shares that the corporation is authorized to issue or any maximum consideration for which any shares of the corporation are authorized to be issued;

(e) create new classes of shares;

(f) [Repealed 1994, c. 27, s. 71(20).]

(g) change the designation of all or any of its shares, and add, change or remove any rights, privileges, restrictions and conditions, including rights to accrued dividends, in respect of all or any of its shares, whether issued or unissued;

(h) change the shares of any class or series, whether issued or unissued, into a different number of shares of the same class or series or into the same or a different number of shares of other classes or series;

(i) divide a class of shares, whether issued or unissued, into series and fix the number of shares in each series and the rights, privileges, restrictions and conditions thereof;

(j) authorize the directors to divide any class of unissued shares into series and fix the number of shares in each series and the rights, privileges, restrictions and conditions thereof;

(k) authorize the directors to change the rights, privileges, restrictions and conditions attached to unissued shares of any series;

(l) revoke, diminish or enlarge any authority conferred under clauses (j) and (k);

(m) subject to sections 120 and 125, increase or decrease the number, or minimum or maximum number, of directors; and

(n) add, change or remove restrictions on the issue, transfer or ownership of shares of any class or series.

(2) Idem — Where the directors are authorized by the articles to divide any class of unissued shares into series and determine the designation, rights, privileges, restrictions and conditions thereof, they may authorize the amendment of the articles to so provide.

(3) Revocation of resolution — The directors of a corporation may, if so authorized by a special resolution effecting an amendment under this section, revoke the resolution without further approval of the shareholders at any time prior to the endorsement by the Director of a certificate of amendment of articles in respect of such amendment.

(4) Change of number name — Despite subsection (1), where a corporation has a number name, the directors may amend its articles to change that name to a name that is not a number name.

(5) Authorization — An amendment under subsection (1) shall be authorized by a special resolution and an amendment under subsection (2) or (4) may be authorized by a resolution of the directors.

(6) Special Act corporations excepted — This section does not apply to a corporation incorporated by special Act, except that a corporation incorporated by special Act, including a corporation to which *The Railways Act*, being chapter 331 of the Revised Statutes of Ontario, 1950, applies, may under this section amend its articles to change its name.

1994, c. 27, s. 71(20)

169. (1) Proposal to amend articles — The directors or any shareholder who is entitled to vote at an annual meeting of shareholders may, in accordance with section 99, make a proposal to amend the articles.

Proposed Amendment — 169(1)

(1) **Proposal to amend articles** — A registered holder of shares entitled to vote, or a beneficial owner of shares that are entitled to be voted, at an annual meeting of shareholders may, in accordance with section 99, make a proposal to amend the articles.

2010, c. 16, Sched. 5, s. 1(3) [Not in force at date of publication.]

(2) **Idem** — Notice of a meeting of shareholders at which a proposal to amend the articles is to be considered shall set out the proposed amendment and, where applicable, shall state that a dissenting shareholder is entitled to be paid the fair value of his shares in accordance with section 185, but failure to make that statement does not invalidate an amendment.

170. (1) **Authorization for variation of rights of special shareholders** — The holders of shares of a class or, subject to subsection (2), of a series are, unless the articles otherwise provide in the case of an amendment referred to in clause (a), (b) or (e), entitled to vote separately as a class or series upon a proposal to amend the articles to,

(a) increase or decrease any maximum number of authorized shares of such class or series, or increase any maximum number of authorized shares of a class or series having rights or privileges equal or superior to the shares of such class or series;

(b) effect an exchange, reclassification or cancellation of the shares of such class or series;

(c) add to, remove or change the rights, privileges, restrictions or conditions attached to the shares of such class or series and, without limiting the generality of the foregoing,

(i) remove or change prejudicially rights to accrued dividends or rights to cumulative dividends,

(ii) add, remove or change prejudicially redemption rights or sinking fund provisions,

(iii) reduce or remove a dividend preference or a liquidation preference, or

(iv) add, remove or change prejudicially conversion privileges, options, voting, transfer or pre-emptive rights, or rights to acquire securities of a corporation;

(d) add to the rights or privileges of any class or series of shares having rights or privileges equal or superior to the shares of such class or series;

(e) create a new class or series of shares equal or superior to the shares of such class or series, except in the case of a series under section 25;

(f) make any class or series of shares having rights or privileges inferior to the shares of such class or series equal or superior to the shares of such class or series;

(g) effect an exchange or create a right of exchange of the shares of another class or series into the shares of such class or series; or

(h) add, remove or change restrictions on the issue, transfer or ownership of the shares of such class or series.

(2) **Idem** — The holders of a series of shares of a class are entitled to vote separately as a series under subsection (1) only if such series is affected by an amendment in a manner different from other shares of the same class.

(3) **Idem** — Subsection (1) applies whether or not shares of a class or series otherwise carry the right to vote.

(4) Idem — A proposed amendment to the articles referred to in subsection (1) is adopted when the shareholders have approved the amendment by a special resolution of the holders of the shares of each class or series entitled to vote thereon.

(5) Exception — Subsection (1) does not apply in respect of a proposal to amend the articles to add a right or privilege for a holder to convert shares of a class or series into shares of another class or series that is subject to restrictions described in clause 42(2)(d) but is otherwise equal to the class or series first mentioned.

(6) Deeming provision — For the purpose of clause (1)(e), a new class of shares, the issue, transfer or ownership of which is to be restricted by an amendment to the articles for the purpose of clause 42(2)(d) that is otherwise equal to an existing class of shares shall be deemed not to be equal or superior to the existing class of shares.

171. (1) Articles of amendment sent to Director — Articles of amendment in prescribed form shall be sent to the Director.

(2) Application of s. 34(4), (5) — If an amendment effects or requires a reduction of stated capital, subsections 34(4) and (5) apply.

(3) Change of name — No corporation shall change its name if,

(a) the corporation is unable to pay its liabilities as they become due; or

(b) the realizable value of the corporation's assets is less than the aggregate of its liabilities.

172. Certificate of amendment — Upon receipt of articles of amendment, the Director shall endorse thereon in accordance with section 273 a certificate of amendment.

173. (1) Restated articles of incorporation — The directors may at any time restate the articles of incorporation as amended.

(2) Idem — Restated articles of incorporation in prescribed form shall be sent to the Director.

(3) Restated certificate of incorporation — Upon receipt of restated articles of incorporation, the Director shall endorse thereon in accordance with section 273 a certificate which shall constitute the restated certificate of incorporation.

(4) Idem — Restated articles of incorporation supersede the original articles of incorporation and all amendments thereto.

174. Amalgamation — Two or more corporations, including holding or subsidiary corporations, may amalgamate and continue as one corporation.

175. (1) Amalgamation agreement — Where corporations propose to amalgamate, each such corporation shall enter into an agreement setting out the terms and means of effecting the amalgamation and, in particular, setting out,

(a) the provisions that are required to be included in articles of incorporation under section 5;

(b) subject to subsection (2), the basis upon which and manner in which the holders of the issued shares of each amalgamating corporation are to receive,

(i) securities of the amalgamated corporation,

(ii) money, or

(iii) securities of any body corporate other than the amalgamated corporation,

in the amalgamation;

(c) the manner of payment of money instead of the issue of fractional shares of the amalgamated corporation or of any other body corporate the securities of which are to be received in the amalgamation;

(d) whether the by-laws of the amalgamated corporation are to be those of one of the amalgamating corporations and the address where a copy of the proposed by-laws may be examined; and

(e) such other details as may be necessary to perfect the amalgamation and to provide for the subsequent management and operation of the amalgamated corporation.

(2) **Shares of amalgamating corporation held by another** — Where shares of one of the amalgamating corporations are held by or on behalf of another of the amalgamating corporations, the amalgamation agreement shall provide for the cancellation of such shares upon the amalgamation becoming effective without any repayment of capital in respect thereof, and no provision shall be made in the agreement for the conversion of such shares into shares of the amalgamated corporation.

176. (1) **Submission of amalgamation agreement** — The directors of each amalgamating corporation shall submit the amalgamation agreement for approval at a meeting of the shareholders of the amalgamating corporation of which they are directors and, subject to subsection (3), of the holders of shares of each class or series entitled to vote thereon.

(2) **Notice of meeting** — The notice of the meeting of shareholders of each amalgamating corporation shall include or be accompanied by,

(a) a copy or summary of the amalgamation agreement; and

(b) a statement that a dissenting shareholder is entitled to be paid the fair value of the shares in accordance with section 185, but failure to make that statement does not invalidate an amalgamation.

(3) **Voting by class, etc.** — The holders of a class or series of shares of an amalgamating corporation, whether or not they are otherwise entitled to vote, are entitled to vote separately as a class or series in respect of an amalgamation if the amalgamation agreement contains a provision that, if contained in a proposed amendment to the articles, would entitle such holders to vote separately as a class or series under section 170.

(4) **Adoption of amalgamation agreement** — An amalgamation agreement is adopted when the shareholders of each amalgamating corporation have approved of the amalgamation by a special resolution of the holders of the shares of each class or series entitled to vote thereon.

(5) **Termination of agreement** — An amalgamation agreement may provide that at any time before the endorsement of a certificate of amalgamation the agreement may be terminated by the directors of an amalgamating corporation, despite approval of the agreement by the shareholders of all or any of the amalgamating corporations.

177. (1) Amalgamation of holding corporation and its subsidiary — A holding corporation and one or more of its subsidiary corporations may amalgamate and continue as one corporation without complying with sections 175 and 176, if

(a) the amalgamation is approved by a resolution of the directors of each amalgamating corporation;

(a.1) all of the issued shares of each amalgamating subsidiary corporation are held by one or more of the other amalgamating corporations; and

(b) the resolutions provide that,

(i) the shares of each amalgamating subsidiary corporation shall be cancelled without any repayment of capital in respect thereof,

(i.1) the by-laws of the amalgamated corporation shall be the same as the by-laws of the amalgamating holding corporation,

(ii) except as may be prescribed, the articles of amalgamation shall be the same as the articles of the amalgamating holding corporation, and

(iii) no securities shall be issued and no assets shall be distributed by the amalgamated corporation in connection with the amalgamation.

(2) Amalgamation of subsidiaries — Two or more wholly-owned subsidiary corporations of the same holding body corporate may amalgamate and continue as one corporation without complying with sections 175 and 176 if,

(a) the amalgamation is approved by a resolution of the directors of each amalgamating corporation; and

(b) the resolutions provide that,

(i) the shares of all but one of the amalgamating subsidiary corporations shall be cancelled without any repayment of capital in respect thereof,

(i.1) the by-laws of the amalgamated corporation shall be the same as the by-laws of the amalgamating subsidiary corporation whose shares are not cancelled,

(ii) except as may be prescribed, the articles of amalgamation shall be the same as the articles of the amalgamating subsidiary corporation whose shares are not cancelled; and

(iii) the stated capital of the amalgamating subsidiary corporations whose shares are cancelled shall be added to the stated capital of the amalgamating subsidiary corporation whose shares are not cancelled.

1994, c. 27, s. 71(21), (22); 1998, c. 18, Sched. E, s. 24

178. (1) Articles of amalgamation to be sent to Director — Subject to subsection 176(5), after an amalgamation has been adopted under section 176 or approved under section 177, articles of amalgamation in prescribed form shall be sent to the Director.

(2) Director's statement — The articles of amalgamation shall have attached thereto a statement of a director or an officer of each amalgamating corporation stating that,

(a) there are reasonable grounds for believing that,

(i) each amalgamating corporation is and the amalgamated corporation will be able to pay its liabilities as they become due, and

(ii) the realizable value of the amalgamated corporation's assets will not be less than the aggregate of its liabilities and stated capital of all classes;

(b) there are reasonable grounds for believing that,

(i) no creditor will be prejudiced by the amalgamation, or

(ii) adequate notice has been given to all known creditors of the amalgamating corporations;

(c) the grounds upon which the objections of all creditors who have notified the corporation that they object to the amalgamation, setting forth with reasonable particularity the grounds for such objections, are either frivolous or vexatious; and

(d) the corporation has given notice to each person who has, in the manner referred to in clause (c), notified the corporation of an objection to the amalgamation, that,

(i) the grounds upon which the person's objection is based are considered to be frivolous or vexatious, and

(ii) a creditor of a corporation who objects to an amalgamation has the status of a complainant under section 248.

(3) Notice — For the purposes of subsection (2), adequate notice is given if,

(a) a notice in writing is sent to each known creditor having a claim against the corporation that exceeds $2,500, at the last address of the creditor known to the corporation;

(b) a notice is published once in a newspaper published or distributed in the place where the corporation has its registered office; and

(c) each notice states that the corporation intends to amalgamate with one or more specified corporations in accordance with this Act unless a creditor of the corporation objects to the amalgamation within thirty days from the date of the notice.

(4) Certificate of amalgamation — Upon receipt of articles of amalgamation, the Director shall endorse thereon in accordance with section 273 a certificate which shall constitute the certificate of amalgamation.

179. Effect of certificate — Upon the articles of amalgamation becoming effective,

(a) the amalgamating corporations are amalgamated and continue as one corporation under the terms and conditions prescribed in the amalgamation agreement;

(a.1) the amalgamating corporations cease to exist as entities separate from the amalgamated corporation;

(b) the amalgamated corporation possesses all the property, rights, privileges and franchises and is subject to all liabilities, including civil, criminal and quasi-criminal, and all contracts, disabilities and debts of each of the amalgamating corporations;

(c) a conviction against, or ruling, order or judgment in favour or against an amalgamating corporation may be enforced by or against the amalgamated corporation;

(d) the articles of amalgamation are deemed to be the articles of incorporation of the amalgamated corporation and, except for the purposes of subsection 117(1), the certificate of amalgamation is deemed to be the certificate of incorporation of the amalgamated corporation; and

(e) the amalgamated corporation shall be deemed to be the party plaintiff or the party defendant, as the case may be, in any civil action commenced by or against an amalgamating corporation before the amalgamation has become effective.

2004, c. 19, s. 3(5)

180. (1) Articles of continuance — A body corporate incorporated under the laws of any jurisdiction other than Ontario may, if it appears to the Director to be thereunto authorized by the laws of the jurisdiction in which it was incorporated, apply to the Director for a certificate of continuance.

(2) Idem — Articles of continuance in prescribed form shall be sent to the Director together with any other prescribed documents.

(3) Amendments to original articles — The articles of continuance shall make any amendments to the original or restated articles of incorporation, articles of amalgamation, letters patent, supplementary letters patent, a special Act and any other instrument by which the body corporate was incorporated and any amendments thereto necessary to make the articles of continuance conform to the laws of Ontario, and may make such other amendments as would be permitted under this Act if the body corporate were incorporated under the laws of Ontario, provided that at least the same shareholder approval has been obtained for such other amendments as would have been required under this Part if the body corporate were incorporated under the laws of Ontario.

(4) Endorsement of certificate of continuance — Upon receipt of articles of continuance and any other prescribed documents, the Director may, on such terms and subject to such limitations and conditions as the Director considers proper, endorse thereon in accordance with section 273 a certificate which shall constitute the certificate of continuance.

(5) Effect of certificate — Upon the articles of continuance becoming effective,

(a) the body corporate becomes a corporation to which this Act applies as if it had been incorporated under this Act;

(b) the articles of continuance are deemed to be the articles of incorporation of the continued corporation; and

(c) except for the purposes of subsection 117(1), the certificate of continuance is deemed to be the certificate of incorporation of the continued corporation.

(6) Copy of certificate of continuance — The Director shall send a copy of the certificate of continuance to the appropriate official or public body in the jurisdiction in which continuance under the Act was authorized.

(7) Rights, liabilities, etc., preserved — When a body corporate is continued as a corporation under this Act,

(a) the corporation possesses all the property, rights, privileges and franchises and is subject to all the liabilities, including civil, criminal and quasi-criminal, and all contracts, disabilities and debts of the body corporate;

(b) a conviction against, or ruling, order or judgment in favour of or against, the body corporate may be enforced by or against the corporation; and

(c) the corporation shall be deemed to be the party plaintiff or the party defendant, as the case may be, in any civil action commenced by or against the body corporate.

(8) Shares issued before body corporate continued under this Act — A share of a body corporate issued before the body corporate was continued under this Act shall be deemed to have been issued in compliance with this Act and with the provisions of the articles of continuance, irrespective that the share is not fully paid and of any designation, rights, privileges, restrictions or conditions set out on or referred to in the certificate representing the share, and continuance under this section does not deprive a holder of any right or privilege that the holder claims under, or relieve the holder of any liability in respect of, an issued share.

2006, c. 8, s. 121

181. (1) Transfer of Ontario corporations — Subject to subsection (9), a corporation may, if it is authorized by the shareholders and the Director in accordance with this section, apply to the appropriate official or public body of another jurisdiction requesting that the corporation be continued as if it had been incorporated under the laws of that other jurisdiction.

(2) Notice to shareholders — The notice of the meeting of shareholders shall include or be accompanied by a statement that a dissenting shareholder is entitled to be paid the fair value of the shares in accordance with section 185, but failure to make that statement does not invalidate an authorization under clause (3)(a).

(3) Application for continuance — An application for continuance becomes authorized,

(a) by the shareholders when the shareholders voting thereon have approved of the continuance by a special resolution; and

(b) by the Director when, following receipt from the corporation of an application in prescribed form, the Director endorses an authorization on the application.

(4) Authorization by Director — The Director may endorse the authorization if he or she is satisfied that the application is not prohibited by subsection (9).

(5) Abandoning application — The directors of a corporation may, if authorized by the shareholders, abandon an application without further approval of the shareholders.

(6) Time limit to Director's authorization — The authorization of the Director for an application for continuance expires six months after the date of endorsement of the authorization unless, within the six-month period, the corporation is continued under the laws of the other jurisdiction.

(7) Filing instrument of continuance — The corporation shall file with the Director a copy of the instrument of continuance issued to it by the other jurisdiction within sixty days after the date of issuance.

(8) Effective date — This Act ceases to apply to the corporation on the date upon which the corporation is continued under the laws of the other jurisdiction.

(9) Continuance in outside jurisdiction — A corporation shall not apply under subsection (1) to be continued as a body corporate under the laws of another jurisdiction unless those laws provide in effect that,

(a) the property of the corporation continues to be the property of the body corporate;

(b) the body corporate continues to be liable for the obligations of the corporation;

(c) an existing cause of action, claim or liability to prosecution is unaffected;

(d) a civil, criminal or administrative action or proceeding pending by or against the corporation may be continued to be prosecuted by or against the body corporate; and

(e) a conviction against the corporation may be enforced against the body corporate or a ruling, order or judgment in favour of or against the corporation may be enforced by or against the body corporate.

2000, c. 26, Sched. B, s. 3(7)

181.1 (1) Continuation as co-operative corporation — A corporation may, if it is authorized by the shareholders and the Director in accordance with this section, apply under the *Co-operative Corporations Act* to be continued as a co-operative corporation.

(2) Notice to shareholders — The notice of the meeting of shareholders to authorize an application under subsection (1) must include or be accompanied by a statement that a dissenting shareholder is entitled to be paid the fair value of the shares in accordance with section 185 but failure to make that statement does not invalidate an authorization under clause (3)(a).

(3) Authorization — An application for continuance is authorized,

(a) by the shareholders, when the shareholders voting thereon have approved of the continuance by a special resolution; and

(b) by the Director, when, following receipt from the corporation of an application in the prescribed form, the Director endorses an authorization on the application.

(4) Abandoning application — The directors of a corporation may, if authorized by the shareholders, abandon an application without further approval of the shareholders.

(5) Time limit to Director's authorization — The authorization of the Director for an application for continuance expires six months after the date of endorsement of the authorization unless, within the six-month period, the corporation is continued under the *Co-operative Corporations Act*.

(6) Certificate to be filed — The corporation shall file with the Director a copy of the certificate of continuance issued to it under the *Co-operative Corporations Act* within 60 days after the date of issuance.

(7) Act ceases to apply — This Act ceases to apply to the corporation on the date upon which the corporation is continued under the *Co-operative Corporations Act*.

1994, c. 17, s. 30; 2000, c. 26, Sched. B, s. 3(8)

182. (1) Arrangement — In this section, **"arrangement"**, with respect to a corporation, includes,

(a) a reorganization of the shares of any class or series of the corporation or of the stated capital of any such class or series;

(b) the addition to or removal from the articles of the corporation of any provision that is permitted by this Act to be, or that is, set out in the articles or the change of any such provision;

(c) an amalgamation of the corporation with another corporation;

(d) an amalgamation of a body corporate with a corporation that results in an amalgamated corporation subject to this Act;

(e) a transfer of all or substantially all the property of the corporation to another body corporate in exchange for securities, money or other property of the body corporate;

(f) an exchange of securities of the corporation held by security holders for other securities, money or other property of the corporation or securities, money or other property of another body corporate that is not a takeover bid as defined in Part XX of the *Securities Act*;

(g) a liquidation or dissolution of the corporation;

(h) any other reorganization or scheme involving the business or affairs of the corporation or of any or all of the holders of its securities or of any options or rights to acquire any of its securities that is, at law, an arrangement; and

(i) any combination of the foregoing.

(2) Scheme of arrangement — A corporation proposing an arrangement shall prepare, for the approval of the shareholders, a statement thereof setting out in detail what is proposed to be done and the manner in which it is proposed to be done.

(3) Adoption of arrangement — Subject to any order of the court made under subsection (5), where an arrangement has been approved by shareholders of a corporation and by holders of shares of each class or series entitled to vote separately thereon, in each case by special resolution, the arrangement shall have been adopted by the shareholders of the corporation and the corporation may apply to the court for an order approving the arrangement.

(4) Separate votes — The holders of shares of a class or series of shares of a corporation are not entitled to vote separately as a class or series in respect of an arrangement unless the statement of the arrangement referred to in subsection (2) contains a provision that, if contained in a proposed amendment to the articles, would entitle such holders to vote separately as a class or series under section 170 and, if the statement of the arrangement contains such a provision, such holders are entitled to vote separately on the arrangement whether or not such shares otherwise carry the right to vote.

(5) Application to court — The corporation may, at any time, apply to the court for advice and directions in connection with an arrangement or proposed arrangement and the court may make such order as it considers appropriate, including, without limiting the generality of the foregoing,

(a) an order determining the notice to be given to any interested person or dispensing with notice to any person;

(b) an order requiring a corporation to call, hold and conduct an additional meeting of, or to hold a separate vote of, all or any particular group of holders of any securities or warrants of the corporation in such manner as the court directs;

(c) an order permitting a shareholder to dissent under section 185 if the arrangement is adopted;

(d) an order appointing counsel, at the expense of the corporation, to represent the interests of shareholders;

(e) an order that the arrangement or proposed arrangement shall be deemed not to have been adopted by the shareholders of the corporation unless it has been approved by a specified majority that is greater than two-thirds of the votes cast at a meeting of the holders, or any particular group of holders, of securities or warrants of the corporation; and

(f) an order approving the arrangement as proposed by the corporation or as amended in any manner the court may direct, subject to compliance with such terms and conditions, if any, as the court thinks fit,

and to the extent that any such order is inconsistent with this section such order shall prevail.

(6) Procedure — Where a reorganization or scheme is proposed as an arrangement and involves an amendment of the articles of a corporation or the taking of any other steps that could be made or taken under any other provision of this Act, the procedure provided for in this section, and not the procedure provided for in such other provision, applies to such reorganization or scheme.

(7) [Repealed 1994, c. 27, s. 71(23).]

1994, c. 27, s. 71(23)

183. (1) Articles of arrangement sent to Director — After an order referred to in clause 182(5)(f) has been made, articles of arrangement in prescribed form shall be sent to the Director.

(2) Certificate of arrangement — Upon receipt of articles of arrangement the Director shall endorse thereon in accordance with section 273 a certificate which shall constitute the certificate of arrangement.

184. (1) Borrowing powers — Unless the articles or by-laws of or a unanimous shareholder agreement otherwise provide, the articles of a corporation shall be deemed to state that the directors of a corporation may, without authorization of the shareholders,

(a) borrow money upon the credit of the corporation;

(b) issue, reissue, sell or pledge debt obligations of the corporation;

(c) give a guarantee on behalf of the corporation to secure performance of an obligation of any person; and

(d) mortgage, hypothecate, pledge or otherwise create a security interest in all or any property of the corporation, owned or subsequently acquired, to secure any obligation of the corporation.

(2) Delegation of powers — Unless the articles or by-laws of or a unanimous shareholder agreement relating to a corporation otherwise provide, the directors may by resolution delegate any or all of the powers referred to in subsection (1) to a director, a committee of directors or an officer.

(3) Sale, etc., requires approval of shareholders — A sale, lease or exchange of all or substantially all the property of a corporation other than in the ordinary course of business of the corporation requires the approval of the shareholders in accordance with subsections (4) to (8).

(4) Notice — The notice of a meeting of shareholders to approve a transaction referred to in subsection (3) shall be sent to all shareholders and shall include or be accompanied by,

(a) a copy or summary of the agreement of sale, lease or exchange; and

(b) a statement that a dissenting shareholder is entitled to be paid the fair value of the shares in accordance with section 185, but failure to make that statement does not invalidate a sale, lease or exchange referred to in subsection (3).

(5) Shareholders may authorize sale, etc. — At the meeting referred to in subsection (4), the shareholders may authorize the sale, lease or exchange and may fix or authorize the directors to fix any of the terms and conditions thereof.

(6) Right to vote separately — If a sale, lease or exchange by a corporation referred to in subsection (3) would affect a particular class or series of shares of the corporation in a manner different from the shares of another class or series of the corporation entitled to vote on the sale, lease or exchange at the meeting referred to in subsection (4), the holders of such first mentioned class or series of shares, whether or not they are otherwise entitled to vote, are entitled to vote separately as a class or series in respect to such sale, lease or exchange.

(7) When approval effective — The approval of a sale, lease or exchange referred to in subsection (3) is effective when the shareholders have approved the sale, lease or exchange by a special resolution of the holders of the shares of each class or series entitled to vote thereon.

(8) Approval by directors — The directors of a corporation may, if authorized by the shareholders approving a proposed sale, lease or exchange, and subject to the rights of third parties, abandon the sale, lease or exchange without further approval of the shareholders.

1998, c. 18, Sched. E, s. 25; 2006, c. 34, Sched. B, s. 34

185. (1) Rights of dissenting shareholders — Subject to subsection (3) and to sections 186 and 248, if a corporation resolves to,

(a) amend its articles under section 168 to add, remove or change restrictions on the issue, transfer or ownership of shares of a class or series of the shares of the corporation;

(b) amend its articles under section 168 to add, remove or change any restriction upon the business or businesses that the corporation may carry on or upon the powers that the corporation may exercise;

(c) amalgamate with another corporation under sections 175 and 176;

(d) be continued under the laws of another jurisdiction under section 181; or

(e) sell, lease or exchange all or substantially all its property under subsection 184(3),

a holder of shares of any class or series entitled to vote on the resolution may dissent.

(2) Idem — If a corporation resolves to amend its articles in a manner referred to in subsection 170(1), a holder of shares of any class or series entitled to vote on the amendment under section 168 or 170 may dissent, except in respect of an amendment referred to in,

(a) clause 170(1)(a), (b) or (e) where the articles provide that the holders of shares of such class or series are not entitled to dissent; or

(b) subsection 170(5) or (6).

(2.1) One class of shares — The right to dissent described in subsection (2) applies even if there is only one class of shares.

(3) Exception — A shareholder of a corporation incorporated before the 29th day of July, 1983 is not entitled to dissent under this section in respect of an amendment of the articles of the corporation to the extent that the amendment,

(a) amends the express terms of any provision of the articles of the corporation to conform to the terms of the provision as deemed to be amended by section 277; or

(b) deletes from the articles of the corporation all of the objects of the corporation set out in its articles, provided that the deletion is made by the 29th day of July, 1986.

(4) Shareholder's right to be paid fair value — In addition to any other right the shareholder may have, but subject to subsection (30), a shareholder who complies with this section is entitled, when the action approved by the resolution from which the shareholder dissents becomes effective, to be paid by the corporation the fair value of the shares held by the shareholder in respect of which the shareholder dissents, determined as of the close of business on the day before the resolution was adopted.

(5) No partial dissent — A dissenting shareholder may only claim under this section with respect to all the shares of a class held by the dissenting shareholder on behalf of any one beneficial owner and registered in the name of the dissenting shareholder.

(6) Objection — A dissenting shareholder shall send to the corporation, at or before any meeting of shareholders at which a resolution referred to in subsection (1) or (2) is to be voted on, a written objection to the resolution, unless the corporation did not give notice to the shareholder of the purpose of the meeting or of the shareholder's right to dissent.

(7) Idem — The execution or exercise of a proxy does not constitute a written objection for purposes of subsection (6).

(8) Notice of adoption of resolution — The corporation shall, within ten days after the shareholders adopt the resolution, send to each shareholder who has filed the objection referred to in subsection (6) notice that the resolution has been adopted, but such notice is not required to be sent to any shareholder who voted for the resolution or who has withdrawn the objection.

(9) Idem — A notice sent under subsection (8) shall set out the rights of the dissenting shareholder and the procedures to be followed to exercise those rights.

(10) Demand for payment of fair value — A dissenting shareholder entitled to receive notice under subsection (8) shall, within twenty days after receiving such notice, or, if the shareholder does not receive such notice, within twenty days after learning that the resolution has been adopted, send to the corporation a written notice containing,

(a) the shareholder's name and address;

(b) the number and class of shares in respect of which the shareholder dissents; and

(c) a demand for payment of the fair value of such shares.

(11) Certificates to be sent in — Not later than the thirtieth day after the sending of a notice under subsection (10), a dissenting shareholder shall send the certificates representing the shares in respect of which the shareholder dissents to the corporation or its transfer agent.

Proposed Amendment — 185(11)

(11) Certificates to be sent in — Not later than the thirtieth day after the sending of a notice under subsection (10), a dissenting shareholder shall send the certificates, if any, representing the shares in respect of which the shareholder dissents to the corporation or its transfer agent.

2011, c. 1, Sched. 2, s. 1(9) [Not in force at date of publication.]

(12) Idem — A dissenting shareholder who fails to comply with subsections (6), (10) and (11) has no right to make a claim under this section.

(13) Endorsement on certificate — A corporation or its transfer agent shall endorse on any share certificate received under subsection (11) a notice that the holder is a dissenting shareholder under this section and shall return forthwith the share certificates to the dissenting shareholder.

(14) Rights of dissenting shareholder — On sending a notice under subsection (10), a dissenting shareholder ceases to have any rights as a shareholder other than the right to be paid the fair value of the shares as determined under this section except where,

(a) the dissenting shareholder withdraws notice before the corporation makes an offer under subsection (15);

(b) the corporation fails to make an offer in accordance with subsection (15) and the dissenting shareholder withdraws notice; or

(c) the directors revoke a resolution to amend the articles under subsection 168(3), terminate an amalgamation agreement under subsection 176(5) or an application for continuance under subsection 181(5), or abandon a sale, lease or exchange under subsection 184(8),

in which case the dissenting shareholders rights are reinstated as of the date the dissenting shareholder sent the notice referred to in subsection (10), and the dissenting shareholder is entitled, upon presentation and surrender to the corporation or its transfer agent of any certificate representing the shares that has been endorsed in accordance with subsection (13), to be issued a new certificate representing the same number of shares as the certificate so presented, without payment of any fee.

Proposed Amendment — 185(14) closing words

in which case the dissenting shareholders rights are reinstated as of the date the dissenting shareholder sent the notice referred to in subsection (10).

2011, c. 1, Sched. 2, s. 1(10) [Not in force at date of publication.]

Proposed Addition — 185(14.1), (14.2)

(14.1) Same — A dissenting shareholder whose rights are reinstated under subsection (14) is entitled, upon presentation and surrender to the corporation or its transfer agent of any share certificate that has been endorsed in accordance with subsection (13),

(a) to be issued, without payment of any fee, a new certificate representing the same number, class and series of shares as the certificate so surrendered; or

(b) if a resolution is passed by the directors under subsection 54(2) with respect to that class and series of shares,

(i) to be issued the same number, class and series of uncertificated shares as represented by the certificate so surrendered, and

(ii) to be sent the notice referred to in subsection 54(3).

(14.2) Same — A dissenting shareholder whose rights are reinstated under subsection (14) and who held uncertificated shares at the time of sending a notice to the corporation under subsection (10) is entitled,

(a) to be issued the same number, class and series of uncertificated shares as those held by the dissenting shareholder at the time of sending the notice under subsection (10); and

(b) to be sent the notice referred to in subsection 54(3).

2011, c. 1, Sched. 2, s. 1(11) [Not in force at date of publication.]

(15) Offer to pay — A corporation shall, not later than seven days after the later of the day on which the action approved by the resolution is effective or the day the corporation received the notice referred to in subsection (10), send to each dissenting shareholder who has sent such notice,

(a) a written offer to pay for the dissenting shareholder's shares in an amount considered by the directors of the corporation to be the fair value thereof, accompanied by a statement showing how the fair value was determined; or

(b) if subsection (30) applies, a notification that it is unable lawfully to pay dissenting shareholders for their shares.

(16) Idem — Every offer made under subsection (15) for shares of the same class or series shall be on the same terms.

(17) Idem — Subject to subsection (30), a corporation shall pay for the shares of a dissenting shareholder within ten days after an offer made under subsection (15) has been accepted, but any such offer lapses if the corporation does not receive an acceptance thereof within thirty days after the offer has been made.

(18) Application to court to fix fair value — Where a corporation fails to make an offer under subsection (15) or if a dissenting shareholder fails to accept an offer, the corporation may, within fifty days after the action approved by the resolution is effective or within such further period as the court may allow, apply to the court to fix a fair value for the shares of any dissenting shareholder.

(19) Idem — If a corporation fails to apply to the court under subsection (18), a dissenting shareholder may apply to the court for the same purpose within a further period of twenty days or within such further period as the court may allow.

(20) Idem — A dissenting shareholder is not required to give security for costs in an application made under subsection (18) or (19).

(21) Costs — If a corporation fails to comply with subsection (15), then the costs of a shareholder application under subsection (19) are to be borne by the corporation unless the court otherwise orders.

(22) Notice to shareholders — Before making application to the court under subsection (18) or not later than seven days after receiving notice of an application to the court under subsection (19), as the case may be, a corporation shall give notice to each dissenting shareholder who, at the date upon which the notice is given,

(a) has sent to the corporation the notice referred to in subsection (10); and

(b) has not accepted an offer made by the corporation under subsection (15), if such an offer was made,

of the date, place and consequences of the application and of the dissenting shareholder's right to appear and be heard in person or by counsel, and a similar notice shall be given to each dissenting shareholder who, after the date of such first mentioned notice and before termination of the proceedings commenced by the application, satisfies the conditions set out in clauses (a) and (b) within three days after the dissenting shareholder satisfies such conditions.

(23) Parties joined — All dissenting shareholders who satisfy the conditions set out in clauses (22)(a) and (b) shall be deemed to be joined as parties to an application under subsection (18) or (19) on the later of the date upon which the application is brought and the date upon which they satisfy the conditions, and shall be bound by the decision rendered by the court in the proceedings commenced by the application.

(24) Idem — Upon an application to the court under subsection (18) or (19), the court may determine whether any other person is a dissenting shareholder who should be joined as a party, and the court shall fix a fair value for the shares of all dissenting shareholders.

(25) Appraisers — The court may in its discretion appoint one or more appraisers to assist the court to fix a fair value for the shares of the dissenting shareholders.

(26) Final order — The final order of the court in the proceedings commenced by an application under subsection (18) or (19) shall be rendered against the corporation and in favour of each dissenting shareholder who, whether before or after the date of the order, complies with the conditions set out in clauses (22)(a) and (b).

(27) Interest — The court may in its discretion allow a reasonable rate of interest on the amount payable to each dissenting shareholder from the date the action approved by the resolution is effective until the date of payment.

(28) Where corporation unable to pay — Where subsection (30) applies, the corporation shall, within ten days after the pronouncement of an order under subsection (26), notify each dissenting shareholder that is unable lawfully to pay dissenting shareholders for their shares.

(29) Idem — Where subsection (30) applies, a dissenting shareholder, by written notice sent to the corporation within thirty days after receiving a notice under subsection (28), may,

(a) withdraw a notice of dissent, in which case the corporation is deemed to consent to the withdrawal and the shareholder's full rights are reinstated; or

(b) retain a status as a claimant against the corporation, to be paid as soon as the corporation is lawfully able to do so or, in a liquidation, to be ranked subordinate to the rights of creditors of the corporation but in priority to its shareholders.

(30) Idem — A corporation shall not make a payment to a dissenting shareholder under this section if there are reasonable grounds for believing that,

(a) the corporation is or, after the payment, would be unable to pay its liabilities as they become due; or

(b) the realizable value of the corporation's assets would thereby be less than the aggregate of its liabilities.

(31) Court order — Upon application by a corporation that proposes to take any of the actions referred to in subsection (1) or (2), the court may, if satisfied that the proposed action is not in all the circumstances one that should give rise to rights arising under subsection (4), by order declare that those rights will not arise upon the taking of the proposed action, and the order may be subject to compliance upon such terms and conditions as the court thinks fit and, if the corporation is an offering corporation, notice of any such application and a copy of any order made by the court upon such application shall be served upon the Commission.

(32) Commission may appear — The Commission may appoint counsel to assist the court upon the hearing of an application under subsection (31), if the corporation is an offering corporation.

1994, c. 27, s. 71(24); 2006, c. 34, Sched. B, s. 35

186. (1) Definition, reorganization — In this section,

"reorganization" means a court order made under section 248, an order made under the *Bankruptcy and Insolvency Act* (Canada) or an order made under the *Companies Creditors Arrangement Act* (Canada) approving a proposal.

(2) Articles amended — If a corporation is subject to a reorganization, its articles may be amended by the order to effect any change that might lawfully be made by an amendment under section 168.

(3) Auxiliary powers of court — Where a reorganization is made, the court making the order may also,

(a) authorize the issue of debt obligations of the corporation, whether or not convertible into shares of any class or having attached any rights or options to acquire shares of any class, and fix the terms thereof; and

(b) appoint directors in place of or in addition to all or any of the directors then in office.

(4) Articles of reorganization — After a reorganization has been made, articles of reorganization in prescribed form shall be sent to the Director.

(5) Certificate — Upon receipt of articles of reorganization, the Director shall endorse thereon in accordance with section 273 a certificate which shall constitute the certificate of amendment and the articles are amended accordingly.

(6) No dissent — A shareholder is not entitled to dissent under section 185 if an amendment to the articles is effected under this section.

2000, c. 26, Sched. B, s. 3(9)

PART XV — COMPULSORY ACQUISITIONS

187. (1) Application — This Part applies only to an offering corporation.

(2) Definitions In this Part,

"dissenting offeree" means a person to whom a take-over bid or issuer bid is made who does not accept the take-over bid or issuer bid and includes a person who subsequently acquires a security that is the subject of the bid;

"equity security" means any security other than a debt obligation of a corporation;

"issuer bid" means an offer made by a corporation to security holders to purchase, redeem or otherwise acquire any or all of a class of the securities of the corporation, other than where,

(a) the securities to be purchased, redeemed or otherwise acquired are debt securities that are not convertible into equity securities,

(b) the securities are to be purchased, redeemed or otherwise acquired in accordance with the terms and conditions thereof or otherwise agreed to at the time they were issued or subsequently varied by amendment of the documents setting out those terms and conditions, or are acquired to meet sinking fund requirements or from an employee or a former employee of the issuer or of an affiliate, or

(c) the purchases, redemptions or other acquisitions to be made are required by the instrument creating or governing the class of securities or by this Act;

"offeree" means a person to whom a take-over bid or an issuer bid is made;

"offeree corporation" means a corporation whose securities are the subject of a take-over bid;

"offeror" means a person, other than an agent, who makes a take-over bid or an issuer bid;

"take-over bid" means an offer made to security holders of an offeree corporation to purchase directly or indirectly voting securities of the offeree corporation, where the voting securities that are the subject of the offer to purchase, the acceptance of the offer to sell or the combination thereof, as the case may be, together with the securities currently owned by the offeror, its affiliates and associates will carry, in the aggregate, 10 per cent or more of the voting rights attached to the voting securities of the offeree corporation that would be outstanding on exercise of all currently exercisable rights of purchase, conversion or exchange relating to voting securities of the offeree corporation;

"voting security" includes,

(a) a security currently convertible into a voting security or into another security that is convertible into a voting security,

(b) a currently exercisable option or right to acquire a voting security or another security that is convertible into a voting security, or

(c) a security carrying an option or right referred to in clause (b).

188. (1) Take-over or issuer bid — If within 120 days after the date of a take-over bid or an issuer bid, the bid is accepted by the holders of not less than 90 per cent of the securities of any class of securities to which the bid relates, other than securities held at the date of the bid by or on behalf of the offeror, or an affiliate or associate of the offeror, the offeror is entitled, upon complying with this section, to acquire the securities held by dissenting offerees.

(2) Shares of dissenting offeree — An offeror may acquire the securities of any class to which the bid relates that are held by a dissenting offeree by sending, on or before the earlier of the sixtieth day following the termination of the bid and the one hundred and eightieth day following the date of the bid, an offeror's notice to each dissenting offeree stating in substance that,

(a) offerees holding more than 90 per cent of the securities to which the bid relates other than securities held at the date of the bid by or on behalf of the offeror or an affiliate or associate of the offeror have accepted the bid;

(b) the offeror is bound to take up and pay for or has taken up and paid for the securities of the offerees who accepted the bid;

(c) a dissenting offeree is required to elect,

(i) to transfer his, her or its securities to the offeror on the terms on which the offeror acquired the securities of the offerees who accepted the bid, or

(ii) to demand payment of the fair value of his, her or its securities in accordance with subsections (13) to (21) by notifying the offeror within twenty days after receipt of the offeror's notice;

(d) a dissenting offeree who does not notify the offeror in accordance with subclause (c)(ii) is deemed to have elected to transfer his, her or its securities to the offeror on the same terms that the offeror acquired the securities from the offerees who accepted the bid; and

(e) a dissenting offeree must send the certificates representing his, her or its securities to which the bid relates to the offeree corporation or, in the case of an issuer bid, to the offeror within twenty days after the dissenting offeree receives the offeror's notice.

Proposed Amendment — 188(2)(e)

(e) a dissenting offeree must send the certificates, if any, representing his, her or its securities to which the bid relates to the offeree corporation or, in the case of an issuer bid, to the offeror within twenty days after the dissenting offeree receives the offeror's notice.

2011, c. 1, Sched. 2, s. 1(14) [Not in force at date of publication.]

(3) Notice — In the case of a take-over bid, concurrently with sending the offeror's notice under subsection (2), the offeror shall send or deliver to the offeree corporation a copy of the offeror's notice, which constitutes a demand under subsection 88(1) of the *Securities Transfer Act, 2006*, that the offeree corporation not register a transfer with respect to each share held by a dissenting offeree.

(4) Sending in share certificates — A dissenting offeree to whom an offeror's notice is sent under subsection (2) shall, within twenty days after receiving that notice,

(a) send the certificates representing his, her or its securities to which the take-over bid relates to the offeree corporation; or

Proposed Amendment — 188(4)(a)

(a) send the certificates, if any, representing his, her or its securities to which the take-over bid relates to the offeree corporation; or

2011, c. 1, Sched. 2, s. 1(15) [Not in force at date of publication.]

(b) send the certificates representing his, her or its securities to which the issuer bid relates to the offeror.

Proposed Amendment — 188(4)(b)

(b) send the certificates, if any, representing his, her or its securities to which the issuer bid relates to the offeror.

2011, c. 1, Sched. 2, s. 1(16) [Not in force at date of publication.]

(5) Payment by offeror — Within twenty days after the offeror sends an offeror's notice under subsection (2), the offeror shall pay or transfer to the offeree corporation the amount of money or other consideration that the offeror would have had to pay or transfer to all dissenting offerees if they had elected to accept the take-over bid under subclause (2)(c)(i).

(6) Trust funds — An offeree corporation is deemed to hold in trust for dissenting offerees the money or other consideration it receives under subsection (5), and the offeree corporation shall deposit the money in a separate account in a financial institution described in subsection (7.1) and shall place the other consideration in the custody of such a financial institution.

(7) Same — The offeror making an issuer bid is deemed to hold in trust for dissenting offerees the money or other consideration that the offeror would have had to pay or transfer to all dissenting offerees if they had elected to accept the issuer bid under subclause (2)(c)(i) and, within 20 days after the issuer sends an offeror's notice under subsection (2), the issuer shall deposit any such money in a separate account in a financial institution described in subsection (7.1) and shall place the other consideration in the custody of such a financial institution within 20 days after the offeror sends an offeror's notice under subsection (2).

(7.1) Same — A financial institution referred to in subsection (6) or (7) is,

(a) a bank or authorized foreign bank within the meaning of section 2 of the *Bank Act* (Canada);

(b) a corporation registered under the *Loan and Trust Corporations Act*;

(c) a credit union within the meaning of the *Credit Unions and Caisses Populaires Act, 1994*; or

(d) a retail association as defined under the *Cooperative Credit Associations Act* (Canada).

(8) Notice of compliance — Within ten days after the offeror complies with subsection (5) or subsection (7), as the case may be, the offeror shall give notice of the date of such compliance to all dissenting offerees.

(9) Application to court — At any time prior to the thirtieth day following the day upon which the offeror's notice referred to in subsection (2) is sent to dissenting offerees, a dissenting offeree who has demanded payment of the fair value of his, her or its securities in accordance with subclause (2)(c)(ii) may apply to the court for an order requiring the person who has sent the offeror's notice to provide, in such form as the court considers appropriate, such additional security for payment to dissenting offerees of the fair value of their securities as the court may determine to be necessary, pending the determination of such fair value.

(10) Where shares deemed acquired — The securities of all dissenting offerees shall be deemed to have been acquired by the offeror,

(a) where an application under subsection (9) has not been made within the time set out in subsection (9), upon the expiration of that time; or

(b) where an application has been made under subsection (9), upon compliance with the order made in respect of the application.

(11) Duties of offeree corporation — Within ten days after the acquisition of the securities of dissenting offerees under subsection (10) by an offeror who has made a take-over bid, the offeree corporation shall,

(a) issue to the offeror a security certificate in respect of the securities that were held by dissenting offerees;

(b) send to each dissenting offeree who elects to accept the take-over bid terms under subclause (2)(c)(i) and who sends his, her or its security certificates as required under clause (4)(a), the money or other consideration to which the dissenting offeree is entitled; and

(c) send to each dissenting offeree who has not sent his, her or its security certificates as required under clause (4)(a), notice stating in substance that,

(i) the certificates representing the dissenting offeree's securities have been cancelled,

(ii) the offeree corporation or some designated person holds in trust for the dissenting offeree the money or other consideration to which the dissenting offeree is entitled as payment for or in exchange for his, her or its securities, and

(iii) the offeree corporation will, subject to subsections (13) to (21), send that money or other consideration to the dissenting offeree forthwith after receiving his, her or its securities.

Proposed Amendment — 188(11)

(11) Duties of offeree corporation — Within 10 days after the acquisition of the securities of dissenting offerees under subsection (10) by an offeror who has made a take-over bid, the offeree corporation,

(a) shall,

(i) issue to the offeror one or more security certificates in respect of the securities so acquired, or

(ii) if a resolution is passed by the directors under subsection 54(2) with respect to any class and series of securities so acquired, issue to the offeror uncertificated securities in respect of the securities of such class and series so acquired and send the offeror the notice referred to in subsection 54(3); and

(b) shall send to each dissenting offeree who elects to accept the take-over bid terms under subclause (2)(c)(i),

(i) the money or other consideration to which the dissenting offeree is entitled as payment for or in exchange for his, her or its securities, if,

(A) the dissenting offeree's securities were uncertificated, or

(B) the dissenting offeree's securities were represented by security certificates and the dissenting offeree has sent the certificates to the offeree corporation, or

(ii) if the dissenting offeree's securities were represented by security certificates and the dissenting offeree has not sent the certificates to the offeree corporation, a notice stating in substance that,

(A) the certificates representing the dissenting offeree's securities have been cancelled,

(B) the offeree corporation or a designated person holds in trust for the dissenting offeree the money or other consideration to which the dissenting offeree is entitled as payment for or in exchange for his, her or its securities, and

(C) the offeree corporation will, subject to subsections (13) to (21), send that money or other consideration to the dissenting offeree forthwith after receiving the certificates representing the dissenting offeree's securities.

(c) [Repealed 2011, c. 1, Sched. 2, s. 1(17). Not in force at date of publication.]

2011, c. 1, Sched. 2, s. 1(17) [Not in force at date of publication.]

(12) Payment by offeror — Within ten days after the acquisition of the securities of dissenting offerees under subsection (10) by an offeror who has made an issuer bid, the offeror shall,

(a) send to each dissenting offeree who elects to accept the issuer bid terms under subclause (2)(c)(i) and who sends his, her or its security certificates as required under clause (4)(b), the money or other consideration to which the dissenting offeree is entitled; and

(b) send to each dissenting offeree who has not sent his, her or its security certificates as required under clause (4)(b) a notice stating in substance that,

(i) the certificates representing the dissenting offeree's securities have been cancelled,

(ii) the offeror or some designated person holds in trust for the dissenting offeree the money or other consideration to which the dissenting offeree is entitled as payment for or in exchange for his, her or its securities, and

(iii) the offeror will, subject to subsections (13) to (21), send that money or other consideration to the dissenting offeree forthwith after receiving his, her or its securities.

Proposed Amendment — 188(12)

(12) Payment by offeror — Within 10 days after the acquisition of the securities of dissenting offerees under subsection (10) by an offeror who has made an issuer bid, the offeror shall send to each dissenting offeree who elects to accept the issuer bid terms under subclause (2)(c)(i),

(a) the money or other consideration to which the dissenting offeree is entitled as payment for or in exchange for his, her or its securities, if,

(i) the dissenting offeree's securities were uncertificated, or

(ii) the dissenting offeree's securities were represented by security certificates and the dissenting offeree has sent the certificates to the offeror; or

(b) if the dissenting offeree's securities were represented by security certificates and the dissenting offeree has not sent the certificates to the offeror, a notice stating in substance that,

(i) the certificates representing the dissenting offeree's securities have been cancelled,

(ii) the offeror or a designated person holds in trust for the dissenting offeree the money or other consideration to which the dissenting offeree is entitled as payment for or in exchange for his, her or its securities, and

(iii) the offeror will, subject to subsections (13) to (21), send that money or other consideration to the dissenting offeree forthwith after receiving the certificates representing the dissenting offeree's securities.

2011, c. 1, Sched. 2, s. 1(17) [Not in force at date of publication.]

(13) Application to fix fair value — If a dissenting offeree has elected to demand payment of the fair value of his, her or its securities under subclause (2)(c)(ii), the offeror may, in the case of a take-over bid, within twenty days after it has complied with subsection (5) or, in the case of an issuer bid, within twenty days after it has complied with subsection (7), apply to the court to fix the fair value of the securities of that dissenting offeree.

(14) Idem — If an offeror fails to apply to the court under subsection (13), a dissenting offeree may apply to the court for the same purpose within a further period of twenty days.

(15) Where no application — If no application is made to the court under subsection (13) or (14) within the periods set out in those subsections, a dissenting offeree is deemed to have elected to transfer his, her or its securities to the offeror on the same terms that the offeror acquired the securities from offerees who accepted the take-over or issuer bid and, provided that the dissenting offeree has complied with subsection (4), the issuer or the offeree corporation, as the case may be, shall pay or transfer to the dissenting offeree the money or other consideration to which the dissenting offeree is entitled.

(16) Security for costs not required — A dissenting offeree is not required to give security for costs in an application made under subsection (13) or (14).

(17) Parties — Upon an application under subsection (13) or (14),

(a) all dissenting offerees referred to in subclause (2)(c)(ii) whose securities have not been acquired by the offeror shall be joined as parties and are bound by the decision of the court; and

(b) the offeror shall notify each such dissenting offeree of the date, place and consequences of the application and of the dissenting offeree's right to appear and be heard in person or by counsel.

(18) Idem — Upon an application to the court under subsection (13) or (14), the court may determine whether any other person is a dissenting offeree who should be joined as a party, and the court shall fix a fair value for the securities of all dissenting offerees.

(19) Appointment of appraisers — The court may appoint one or more appraisers to assist the court in fixing a fair value for the securities of each dissenting offeree.

(20) Final order — The final order of the court shall be made against the offeror in favour of each dissenting offeree.

(21) What court may order — In connection with proceedings under this section, the court may make any order it thinks fit and, without limiting the generality of the foregoing, it may,

(a) fix the amount of money or other consideration that is required to be held in trust under subsection (6) or (7);

(b) order that the money or other consideration be held in trust by a person other than,

(i) the offeree corporation, or

(ii) in the case of an issuer bid, the offeror corporation;

(c) allow a reasonable rate of interest on the amount payable to each dissenting offeree from the date the dissenting offeree sends his, her or its security certificates under subsection (4) until the date of payment; or

(d) order that any money payable to a dissenting offeree who cannot be found be paid to the Public Guardian and Trustee.

2000, c. 26, Sched. B, s. 3(10); 2006, c. 8, s. 122; 2007, c. 7, Sched. 7, s. 181(1); CTS 30 AU 10 – 1

189. (1) Where corporation required to acquire securities — Where 90 per cent or more of a class of securities of a corporation, other than debt obligations, are acquired by or on behalf of a person, the person's affiliates and the person's associates, then the holder of any securities of that class not counted for the purposes of calculating such percentage shall be entitled in accordance with this section to require the corporation to acquire the holder's securities of that class.

(2) Notice — Every corporation, within thirty days after it becomes aware that security holders are entitled to require it to acquire their securities under subsection (1), shall send a written notice to each such security holder that the security holder may within sixty days after the date of such notice require the corporation to acquire his, her or its securities.

(3) Idem — The notice sent by the corporation under subsection (2) shall,

(a) set out a price that the corporation is willing to pay for the securities;

(b) give the basis for arriving at the price;

(c) state the location where any supporting material used for arriving at the price may be examined and extracts taken therefrom by the security holder or a duly authorized agent; and

(d) state that if the security holder is not satisfied with the price offered by the corporation in the notice, the security holder is entitled to have the fair value of his, her or its securities fixed by the court.

(4) **Election by security holder** — Where a security holder receives a notice under subsection (2) and wishes the corporation to acquire his, her or its securities, the security holder may, within sixty days after the date of the notice,

(a) elect to accept the price offered by the corporation by giving notice of acceptance to the corporation and by forthwith sending his, her or its security certificates to the corporation; or

(b) notify the corporation that the security holder wishes to have the fair value of his, her or its securities fixed by the court.

(5) **Application to fix fair value** — Where a security holder wishes to have the fair value of his, her or its securities fixed by the court, the corporation shall make an application to the court within ninety days after the date of the notice under subsection (2).

(6) **Idem** — If a corporation fails to send notice under subsection (2), a security holder, after giving the corporation thirty days notice of intention so to do, may apply to the court to have the fair value of his, her or its securities fixed.

(7) **Idem** — If a corporation fails to make an application to the court as required under subsection (5), a security holder may make the application.

(8) **Parties** — Upon an application to the court under subsection (5), (6) or (7),

(a) all security holders who have notified the corporation under clause (4)(b) may be joined as parties as the court thinks fit and, if so joined, are bound by the decision of the court; and

(b) the corporation shall notify each security holder entitled to notice under subsection (2) of the date, place and purpose of the application and of the security holder's right to appear and be heard in person or by counsel.

(9) **Idem** — Upon an application to the court under subsection (5), (6) or (7), the court may determine whether any security holders should properly be sent or have been sent notice and whether such security holders should be joined as parties.

(10) **Appointment of appraiser** — The court may appoint one or more appraisers to assist the court in fixing a fair value for the securities.

(11) **Final order** — The final order of the court shall be made against the corporation in favour of each entitled security holder.

(12) **Security not required** — A security holder requesting the court to fix the fair value of his, her or its securities is not required to give security for costs on the application.

(13) **Costs** — The costs under this section shall be on a solicitor and client basis.

Proposed Amendment — 189(13)

(13) **Costs** — The costs under this section shall be on a substantial indemnity basis.

2011, c. 1, Sched. 2, s. 1(18) [Not in force at date of publication.]

190. (1) Definitions — In this section

"affected security" means a participating security of a corporation in which the interest of the holder would be terminated by reason of a going private transaction;

"going private transaction" means an amalgamation, arrangement, consolidation or other transaction carried out under this Act by a corporation that would cause the interest of a holder of a participating security of the corporation to be terminated without the consent of the holder and without the substitution therefor of an interest of equivalent value in a participating security that,

(a) is issued by the corporation, an affiliate of the corporation or a successor body corporate, and

(b) is not limited in the extent of its participation in earnings to any greater extent than the participating security for which it is substituted,

but does not include,

(c) an acquisition under section 188,

(d) a redemption of, or other compulsory termination of the interest of the holder in, a security if the security is redeemed or otherwise acquired in accordance with the terms and conditions attaching thereto or under a requirement of the articles relating to the class of securities or of this Act, or

(e) a proceeding under Part XVI;

"participating security" means a security issued by a body corporate other than a security that is, in all circumstances, limited in the extent of its participation in earnings and includes,

(a) a security currently convertible into such a security, and

(b) currently exercisable warrants entitling the holder to acquire such a security or such a convertible security.

(2) Going private transaction — A corporation that proposes to carry out a going private transaction shall have prepared by an independent, qualified valuer a written valuation indicating a per security value or range of values for each class of affected securities, and,

(a) the valuation shall be prepared or revised as of a date not more than 120 days before the announcement of the going private transaction, with appropriate adjustments for subsequent events other than the going private transaction;

(b) the valuation shall not contain a downward adjustment to reflect the fact that the affected securities do not form part of a controlling interest; and

(c) if the consideration to be received by the holders of the affected securities is wholly or partly other than cash, or a right to receive cash within ninety days after the approval by security holders of the going private transaction, the valuation shall include the valuer's opinion whether the value of each affected security to be surrendered is equal to or greater than the total value of the consideration to be received therefor.

(3) Information circular — The corporation shall send a management information circular to the holders of the affected securities not less than forty days prior to the date of a meeting which shall be called by it to consider that transaction, and the information circular shall contain, in addition to any other required information and subject to any exemption granted under subsection (6),

(a) a summary of the valuation prepared in compliance with subsection (2) and a statement that a holder of an affected security may inspect a copy of the valuation at the registered office of the corporation or may obtain a copy of the valuation upon request and payment of a specified amount sufficient to cover reasonable costs of reproduction and mailing;

(b) a statement of the approval or approvals of holders of affected securities required to be obtained in accordance with this section;

(c) a certificate signed by a senior officer or a director of the corporation certifying that he or she and, to his or her knowledge, the corporation are unaware of any material fact relevant to the valuation prepared in compliance with subsection (2) that was not disclosed to the valuer; and

(d) a statement of the class or classes of affected securities and of the number of securities of each class and, if any securities of any such class are, under paragraph 3 of subsection (4), not to be taken into account in the vote required by subsection (4), a statement of the number thereof and why they are not to be taken into account,

but if all or any portion of a class of affected securities is represented by certificates that are not in registered form, it shall be sufficient to make the information circular available to the holders of such affected securities in the manner provided for in the terms of the securities for sending notice to such holders or otherwise in such manner as may be prescribed.

(4) **Idem** — A corporation shall not carry out a going private transaction unless, in addition to any other required security holder approval, the transaction is approved by the holders of each class of affected securities by a vote in accordance with the following provisions:

1. If the consideration to be received by a holder of an affected security of the particular class is,

    i. payable wholly or partly other than in cash or a right to receive cash within ninety days after the approval of the going private transaction, or

    ii. payable entirely in cash and is less in amount than the per security value or the mid-point of the range of per security values, arrived at by the valuation prepared in compliance with subsection (2),

    then the approval shall be given by a special resolution.

2. In cases other than those referred to in paragraph 1, the approval shall be given by an ordinary resolution.

3. In determining whether the transaction has been approved by the requisite majority, the votes of,

    i. securities held by affiliates of the corporation,

    ii. securities the beneficial owners of which will, consequent upon the going private transaction, be entitled to a per security consideration greater than that available to other holders of affected securities of the same class,

    iii. securities the beneficial owners of which, alone or in concert with others, effectively control the corporation and who, prior to distribution of the information circular, entered into an understanding that they would support the going private transaction,

    shall be disregarded both in determining the total number of votes cast and in determining the number of votes cast in favour of or against the transaction.

(5) **Effect of section** — The rights provided by this section are in addition to any other rights of a holder of affected securities.

(6) Powers of Commission — Upon an application by an interested person, the Commission may, subject to such terms and conditions as it may impose, exempt any person from any requirement of this section where in its opinion to do so would not be prejudicial to the public interest, and the Commission may publish guidelines as to the manner and circumstances in which it will exercise this discretion.

(7) Rights of security holder — A holder of an affected security that is a share of any class of a corporation may dissent from a going private transaction upon compliance with the procedures set out in section 185, in which case the holder shall be entitled to the rights and remedies provided by that section.

PART XVI — LIQUIDATION AND DISSOLUTION

191. Definition — In sections 193 to 236, **"contributory"** means a person who is liable to contribute to the property of a corporation in the event of the corporation being wound up under this Act.

192. Application of ss. 193–205 — Sections 193 to 205 apply to corporations being wound up voluntarily.

193. (1) Voluntary winding up — The shareholders of a corporation may, by special resolution, require the corporation to be wound up voluntarily.

(2) Appointment of liquidator — At such meeting, the shareholders shall appoint one or more persons, who may be directors, officers or employees of the corporation, as liquidator of the estate and effects of the corporation for the purpose of winding up its business and affairs and distributing its property, and may at that or any subsequent meeting fix the liquidators remuneration and the costs, charges and expenses of the winding up.

(3) Review of remuneration by court — On the application of any shareholder or creditor of the corportion or of the liquidator, the court may review the remuneration of the liquidator and, whether or not the remuneration has been fixed in accordance with subsection (2), the court may fix and determine the remuneration at such amount as it thinks proper.

(4) Publication of notice — A corporation shall file notice, in the prescribed form, of a resolution requiring the voluntary winding up of the corporation with the Director within ten days after the resolution has been passed and shall publish the notice in *The Ontario Gazette* within twenty days after the resolution has been passed.

194. Inspectors — The shareholders of a corporation being wound up voluntarily may delegate to any committee of shareholders, contributories or creditors, hereinafter referred to as inspectors, the power of appointing the liquidator and filling any vacancy in the office of liquidator, or may enter into any arrangement with creditors of the corporation with respect to the powers to be exercised by the liquidator and the manner in which they are to be exercised.

195. Vacancy in office of liquidator — If a vacancy occurs in the office of liquidator by death, resignation or otherwise, the shareholders may, subject to any arrangement the corporation may have entered into with its creditors upon the appointment of inspectors, fill such vacancy, and a meeting for that purpose may be called by the continuing liquidator, if any, or by any shareholder or contributory, and shall be deemed to have been duly held if called in the manner prescribed by the articles or by-laws of the corporation, or, in default thereof, in the manner prescribed by this Act for calling meetings of the shareholders of the corporation.

196. Removal of liquidator — The shareholders of a corporation may by ordinary resolution passed at a meeting called for that purpose remove a liquidator appointed under section 193, 194 or 195, and in such ease shall appoint a replacement.

197. Commencement of winding up — A voluntary winding up commences at the time of the passing of the resolution requiring the winding up or at such later time as may be specified in the resolution.

198. Corporation to cease business — A corporation being wound up voluntarily shall, from the commencement of its winding up, cease to carry on its undertaking, except in so far as may be required as beneficial for the winding up thereof, and all transfers of shares, except transfers made to or with the sanction of the liquidator taking place after the commencement of its winding up, are void, but its corporate existence and all its corporate powers, even if it is otherwise provided by its articles or by-laws, continue until its affairs are wound up.

199. No proceedings against corporation after voluntary winding up except by leave — After the commencement of a voluntary winding up,

(a) no action or other proceeding shall be commenced against the corporation; and

(b) no attachment, sequestration, distress or execution shall be put in force against the estate or effects of the corporation,

except by leave of the court and subject to such terms as the court imposes.

200. (1) List of contributories and calls — Upon a voluntary winding up, the liquidator,

(a) shall settle the list of contributories; and

(b) may, before the liquidator has ascertained the sufficiency of the property of the corporation, call on all or any of the contributories for the time being settled on the list of contributories to the extent of their liability to pay any sum that the liquidator considers necessary for satisfying the liabilities of the corporation and the costs, charges and expenses of winding up and for adjusting the rights of the contributories among themselves.

(2) List is proof — A list settled by the liquidator under clause (1)(a) is, in the absence of evidence to the contrary, proof of the liability of the persons named therein to be contributories.

(3) Default on calls — The liquidator in making a call under clause (1)(b) may take into consideration the probability that some of the contributories upon whom the call is made may partly or wholly fail to pay their respective portions of the call.

201. (1) Meetings of corporation during winding up — The liquidator may, during the continuance of the voluntary winding up, call meetings of the shareholders of the corporation for any purpose the liquidator thinks fit.

(2) Where winding up continues more than one year — Where a voluntary winding up continues for more than one year, the liquidator shall call a meeting of the shareholders of the corporation at the end of the first year and of each succeeding year from the commencement of the winding up, and the liquidator shall lay before the meeting an account showing the liquidator's acts and dealings and the manner in which the winding up has been conducted during the immediately preceding year.

202. Arrangements with creditors — The liquidator, with the approval of the shareholders of the corporation or the inspectors, may make such compromise or other arrangement as the liquidator thinks expedient with any creditor or person claiming to be a creditor or having or alleging that he, she or it has a claim, present or future, certain or contingent, liquidated or unliquidated, against the corporation or whereby the corporation may be rendered liable.

203. Power to compromise with debtors and contributories — The liquidator may, with the approval referred to in section 202, compromise all debts and liabilities capable of resulting in debts, and all claims, whether present or future, certain or contingent, liquidated or unliquidated, subsisting or supposed to subsist between the corporation and any contributory, alleged contributory or other debtor or person who may be liable to the corporation and all questions in any way relating to or affecting the property of the corporation, or the winding up of the corporation, upon the receipt of such sums payable at such times and generally upon such terms as are agreed, and the liquidator may take any security for the discharge of such debts or liabilities and give a complete discharge in respect thereof.

204. (1) Power to accept shares, etc., as consideration for sale of property to another body corporate — Where a corporation is proposed to be or is in the course of being wound up voluntarily and it is proposed to transfer the whole or a portion of its business or property to another body corporate, the liquidator, with the approval of a resolution of the shareholders of the corporation conferring either a general authority on the liquidator or an authority in respect of any particular arrangement, may receive, in compensation or in part-compensation for the transfer, cash or shares or other like interest in the purchasing body corporate or any other body corporate for the purpose of distribution among the creditors or shareholders of the corporation that is being wound up in the manner set forth in the arrangement, or may, in lieu of receiving cash or shares or other like interest, or in addition thereto, participate in the profits of or receive any other benefit from the purchasing body corporate or any other body corporate.

(2) Confirmation of sale or arrangement — A transfer made or arrangement entered into by the liquidator under this section is not binding on the shareholders of the corporation that is being wound up unless the transfer or arrangement is approved in accordance with subsections 184(3), (6) and (7).

(3) Where resolution not invalid — No resolution is invalid for the purposes of this section because it was passed before or concurrently with a resolution for winding up the corporation or for appointing the liquidator.

205. (1) Account of voluntary winding up to be made by liquidator to a meeting — The liquidator shall make up an account showing the manner in which the winding up has been conducted and the property of the corporation disposed of, and thereupon shall call a meeting of the shareholders of the corporation for the purpose of having the account laid before them and hearing any explanation that may be given by the liquidator, and the meeting shall be called in the manner prescribed by the articles or by-laws or, in default thereof, in the manner prescribed by this Act for the calling of meetings of shareholders.

(2) **Notice of holding of meeting** — The liquidator shall within ten days after the meeting is held file a notice in the prescribed form with the Director stating that the meeting was held and the date thereof and shall forthwith publish the notice in *The Ontario Gazette*.

(3) **Dissolution** — Subject to subsection (4), on the expiration of three months after the date of the filing of the notice, the corporation is dissolved.

(4) **Extension** — At any time during the three-month period mentioned in subsection (3), the court may, on the application of the liquidator or any other person interested, make an order deferring the date on which the dissolution of the corporation is to take effect to a date fixed in the order, and in such event the corporation is dissolved on the date so fixed.

(5) **Dissolution by court order** — Despite anything in this Act, the court at any time after the affairs of the corporation have been fully wound up may, upon the application of the liquidator or any other person interested, make an order dissolving it, and it is dissolved on the date fixed in the order.

(6) **Copy of extension order to be filed** — The person on whose application an order was made under subsection (4) or (5) shall within ten days after it was made file with the Director a certified copy of the order and forthwith publish notice of the order in *The Ontario Gazette*.

206. **Application of ss. 207–218** — Sections 207 to 218 apply to corporations being wound up by order of the court.

207. (1) **Winding up by court** — A corporation may be wound up by order of the court,

(a) where the court is satisfied that in respect of the corporation or any of its affiliates,

(i) any act or omission of the corporation or any of its affiliates effects a result,

(ii) the business or affairs of the corporation or any of its affiliates are or have been carried on or conducted in a manner, or

(iii) the powers of the directors of the corporation or any of its affiliates are or have been exercised in a manner,

that is oppressive or unfairly prejudicial to or that unfairly disregards the interests of any security holder, creditor, director or officer; or

(b) where the court is satisfied that,

(i) a unanimous shareholder agreement entitled a complaining shareholder to demand dissolution of the corporation after the occurrence of a specified event and that event has occurred,

(ii) proceedings have been begun to wind up voluntarily and it is in the interest of contributories and creditors that the proceedings should be continued under the supervision of the court,

(iii) the corporation, though it may not be insolvent, cannot by reason of its liabilities continue its business and it is advisable to wind it up, or

(iv) it is just and equitable for some reason, other than the bankruptcy or insolvency of the corporation, that it should be wound up; or

(c) where the shareholders by special resolution authorize an application to be made to the court to wind up the corporation.

(2) Court order — Upon an application under this section, the court may make such order under this section or section 248 as it thinks fit.

208. (1) Who may apply — A winding-up order may be made upon the application of the corporation or of a shareholder or, where the corporation is being wound up voluntarily, of the liquidator or of a contributory or of a creditor having a claim of $2,500 or more.

(2) Notice — Except where the application is made by the corporation, four days' notice of the application shall be given to the corporation before the making of the application.

209. Power of court — The court may make the order applied for, may dismiss the application with or without costs, may adjourn the hearing conditionally or unconditionally or may make any interim or other order as is considered just, and upon the making of the order may, according to its practice and procedure, refer the proceedings for the winding up to an officer of the court for inquiry and report and may authorize the officer to exercise such powers of the court as are necessary for the reference.

210. (1) Appointment of liquidator — The court in making the winding-up order may appoint one or more persons as liquidator of the estate and effects of the corporation for the purpose of winding up its business and affairs and distributing its property.

(2) Remuneration — The court may at any time fix the remuneration of the liquidator.

(3) Vacancy — If a liquidator appointed by the court dies or resigns or the office becomes vacant for any reason, the court may by order fill the vacancy.

(4) Notice of appointment — A liquidator appointed by the court under this section shall forthwith give to the Director notice in the prescribed form of the liquidator's appointment and shall, within twenty days after being appointed, publish the notice in *The Ontario Gazette*.

211. Removal of liquidator — The court may by order remove for cause a liquidator appointed by it, and in such case shall appoint a replacement.

212. Costs and expenses — The costs, charges and expenses of a winding up by order of the court shall be assessed by an assessment officer of the Superior Court of Justice.

2001, c. 9, Sched. D, s. 2(4)

213. Commencement of winding up — Where a winding-up order is made by the court without prior voluntary winding-up proceedings, the winding up shall, unless a court otherwise orders, be deemed to commence at the time of the service of notice of the application, and, where the application is made by the corporation, at the time the application is made.

214. Proceedings in winding up after order — Where a winding-up order has been made by the court, proceedings for the winding up of the corporation shall be taken in the same manner and with the like consequences as provided for a voluntary winding up, except that the list of contributories shall be settled by the court unless it has been settled by the liquidator before the winding-up order, in which case the list is subject to review by the court, and except that all proceedings in the winding up are subject to the order and direction of the court.

215. (1) Meetings of shareholders of corporation may be ordered — Where a winding-up order has been made by the court, the court may direct meetings of the shareholders of the corporation to be called, held and conducted in such manner as the court thinks fit for the purpose of ascertaining their wishes, and may appoint a person to act as chair of any such meeting and to report the result of it to the court.

(2) Order for delivery by contributories and others of property, etc. — Where a winding-up order has been made by the court, the court may require any contributory for the time being settled on the list of contributories, or any director, officer, employee, trustee, banker or agent of the corporation to pay, deliver, convey, surrender or transfer forthwith, or within such time as the court directs, to the liquidator any sum or balance, documents, records, estate or effects that are in his, her or its hands and to which the corporation is apparently entitled.

(3) Inspection of documents and records — Where a winding-up order has been made by the court, the court may make an order for the inspection of the documents and records of the corporation by its creditors and contributories, and any documents and records in the possession of the corporation may be inspected in conformity with the order.

216. Proceedings against corporation after court winding up — After the commencement of a winding up by order of the court,

(a) no action or other proceeding shall be proceeded with or commenced against the corporation; and

(b) no attachment, sequestration, distress or execution shall be put in force against the estate or effects of the corporation,

except by leave of the court and subject to such terms as the court imposes.

217. (1) Provision for discharge and distribution by the court — Where the realization and distribution of the property of a corporation being wound up under an order of the court has proceeded so far that in the opinion of the court it is expedient that the liquidator should be discharged and that the property of the corporation remaining in the liquidator's hands can be better realized and distributed by the court, the court may make an order discharging the liquidator and for payment, delivery and transfer into court, or to such person as the court directs, of such property, and it shall be realized and distributed by or under the. direction of the court among the persons entitled thereto in the same way as nearly as may be as if the distribution were being made by the liquidator.

(2) Disposal of documents and records — In such case, the court may make an order directing how the documents and records of the corporation and of the liquidator are to be disposed of, and may order that they be deposited in court or otherwise dealt with as the court thinks fit.

218. (1) Order for dissolution — The court at any time after the business and affairs of the corporation have been fully wound up may, upon the application of the liquidator or any other person interested, make an order dissolving it, and it is dissolved on the date fixed in the order.

(2) Copy of dissolution order to be filed — The person on whose application the order was made shall within ten days after it was made file with the Director a certified copy of the order and shall forthwith publish notice of the order in *The Ontario Gazette*.

219. Application of ss. 220–236 — Sections 220 to 236 apply to corporations being wound up voluntarily or by order of the court.

220. Where no liquidator — Where there is no liquidator,

(a) the court may by order on the application of a shareholder of the corporation appoint one or more persons as liquidator; and

(b) the estate and effects of the corporation shall be under the control of the court until the appointment of a liquidator.

221. (1) Consequences of winding up — Upon a winding up,

(a) the liquidator shall apply the property of the corporation in satisfaction of all its debts, obligations and liabilities and, subject thereto, shall distribute the property rateably among the shareholders according to their rights and interests in the corporation;

(b) in distributing the property of the corporation, debts to employees of the corporation for services performed for it due at the commencement of the winding up or within one month before, not exceeding three months' wages and vacation pay accrued for not more than twelve months, shall be paid in priority to the claims of the ordinary creditors, and such persons are entitled to rank as ordinary creditors for the residue of their claims;

(c) all the powers of the directors cease upon the appointment of a liquidator, except in so far as the liquidator may sanction the continuance of such powers.

(2) Distribution of property — Section 53 of the *Trustee Act* applies with necessary modifications to liquidators.

222. Payment of costs and expenses — The costs, charges and expenses of a winding up, including the remuneration of the liquidator, are payable out of the property of the corporation in priority to all other claims.

223. (1) Powers of liquidators — A liquidator may,

(a) bring or defend any action, suit or prosecution, or other legal proceedings, civil or criminal, in the name and on behalf of the corporation;

(b) carry on the business of the corporation so far as may be required as beneficial for the winding up of the corporation;

(c) sell the property of the corporation by public auction or private sale and receive payment of the purchase price either in cash or otherwise;

(d) do all acts and execute, in the name and on behalf of the corporation, all documents, and for that purpose use the seal of the corporation, if any;

(e) draw, accept, make and endorse any bill of exchange or promissory note in the name and on behalf of the corporation;

(f) raise upon the security of the property of the corporation any requisite money;

(g) take out in the liquidator's official name letters of administration of the estate of any deceased contributory and do in the liquidator's official name any other act that is necessary for obtaining payment of any money due from a contributory or from the contributory's estate and which act cannot be done conveniently in the name of the corporation; and

(h) do and execute all such other things as are necessary for winding up the business and affairs of the corporation and distributing its property.

(2) **Bills of exchange, etc., to be deemed drawn in the course of business** — The drawing, accepting, making or endorsing of a bill of exchange or promissory note by the liquidator on behalf of a corporation has the same effect with respect to the liability of the corporation as if such bill or note had been drawn, accepted, made or endorsed by or on behalf of the corporation in the course of carrying on its business.

(3) **Where money deemed to be due to liquidator** — Where the liquidator takes out letters of administration or otherwise uses the liquidator's official name for obtaining payment of any money due from a contributory, such money shall be deemed, for the purpose of enabling the liquidator to take out such letters or recover such money, to be due to the liquidator rather than to the corporation.

(4) **What liquidator may rely upon** — A liquidator who acts in good faith is entitled to rely upon,

(a) financial statements of the corporation represented to the liquidator by an officer of the corporation or in a written report of the auditor of the corporation to present fairly the financial position of the corporation in accordance with generally accepted accounting principles; or

(b) an opinion, a report or a statement of a lawyer, an accountant, an engineer, an appraiser or other professional adviser retained by the liquidator.

224. **Acts by more than one liquidator** — Where more than one person is appointed as liquidator, any power conferred by sections 193 to 236 on a liquidator may be exercised by such one or more of such persons as may be determined by the resolution or order appointing them or, in default of such determination, by any number of them not fewer than two.

225. **Nature of liability of contributory** — The liability of a contributory creates a debt accruing due from the contributory at the time the contributory's liability commenced, but payable at the time or respective times when calls are made for enforcing such liability.

226. **Liability in case of contributory's death** — If a contributory dies before or after having been placed on the list of contributories, the contributory's personal representative is liable in due course of administration to contribute to the property of the corporation in discharge of the liability of the deceased contributory and shall be a contributory accordingly.

227. (1) **Deposit of money** — The liquidator shall deposit all money that the liquidator has belonging to the corporation and amounting to $100 or more in a financial institution described in subsection (2).

(2) **Financial institutions** — A financial institution referred to in subsection (1) is,

(a) a bank or authorized foreign bank within the meaning of section 2 of the *Bank Act* (Canada);

(b) a corporation registered under the *Loan and Trust Corporations Act*;

(c) a credit union within the meaning of the *Credit Unions and Caisses Populaires Act, 1994*; or

(d) a retail association as defined under the *Cooperative Credit Associations Act* (Canada).

(3) Separate deposit account to be kept; withdrawal from account — Such deposit shall not be made in the name of the liquidator individually, but a separate deposit account shall be kept of the money belonging to the corporation in the liquidator's name as liquidator of the corporation and in the name of the inspectors, if any, and such money shall be withdrawn only by order for payment signed by the liquidator and one of the inspectors, if any.

(4) Liquidator to produce bank pass-book — At every meeting of the shareholders of the corporation, the liquidator shall produce a pass-book, or statement of account showing the amount of the deposits, the dates at which they were made, the amounts withdrawn and the dates of withdrawal, and mention of such production shall be made in the minutes of the meeting, and the absence of such mention is admissible in evidence as proof, in the absence of evidence to the contrary, that the pass-book or statement of account was not produced at the meeting.

(5) Idem — The liquidator shall also produce the pass-book or statement of account whenever so ordered by the court upon the application of the inspectors, if any, or of a shareholder of the corporation.

2002, c. 8, Sched. I, s. 2; 2007, c. 7, Sched. 7, s. 181(2)

228. Proving claim — For the purpose of proving claims, sections 23, 24 and 25 of the *Assignments and Preferences Act* apply with necessary modifications, except that where the word "judge" is used therein, the word "court" as used in this Act shall be substituted.

229. Application for direction — Upon the application of the liquidator or of the inspectors, if any, or of any creditors, the court, after hearing such parties as it directs to be notified or after such steps as the court prescribes have been taken, may by order give its direction in any matter arising in the winding up.

230. (1) Examination of persons as to estate — The court may at any time after the commencement of the winding up summon to appear before the court or liquidator any director, officer or employee of the corporation or any other person known or suspected of having possession of any of the estate or effects of the corporation, or alleged to be indebted to it, or any person whom the court thinks capable of giving information concerning its trade, dealings, estate or effects.

(2) Damages against delinquent directors, etc. — Where in the course of the winding up it appears that a person who has taken part in the formation or promotion of the corporation or that a past or present director, officer, employee, liquidator or receiver of the corporation has misapplied or retained in that person's own hands, or become liable or accountable for, property of the corporation, or has committed any misfeasance or breach of trust in relation to it, the court may, on the application of the liquidator or of any creditor, shareholder or contributory, examine the conduct of that person and order that person to restore the property so misapplied or retained, or for which that person has become liable or accountable, or to contribute such sum to the property of the corporation by way of compensation in respect of such misapplication, retention, misfeasance or breach of trust, or both, as the court thinks just.

231. (1) Proceedings by shareholders — Where a shareholder of the corporation desires to cause any proceeding to be taken that, in the shareholder's opinion, would be for the benefit of the corporation, and the liquidator, under the authority of the shareholders or of the inspectors, if any, refuses or neglects to take such proceeding after being required so to do, the shareholder may obtain an order of the court authorizing the shareholder to take such proceeding in the name of the liquidator or corporation, but at the shareholder's own expense and risk, upon such terms and conditions as to indemnity to the liquidator or corporation as the court prescribes.

(2) Benefits: when for shareholders — Any benefit derived from a proceeding under subsection (1) belongs exclusively to the shareholder causing the institution of the proceeding for the shareholder's benefit and that of any other shareholder who has joined together in causing the institution of the proceeding.

(3) When for corporation — If, before the order is granted, the liquidator signifies to the court the liquidator's readiness to institute the proceeding for the benefit of the corporation, the court shall make an order prescribing the time within which the liquidator is to do so, and in that case the advantage derived from the proceeding, if instituted within such time, belongs to the corporation.

232. Rights conferred by Act to be in addition to other powers — The rights conferred by this Act are in addition to any other right to institute a proceeding against any contributory, or against any debtor of the corporation, for the recovery of any sum due from such contributory or debtor or an estate thereof.

233. Stay of winding up proceedings — At any time during a winding up, the court, upon the application of a shareholder, creditor or contributory and upon proof to its satisfaction that all proceedings in relation to the winding up ought to be stayed, may make an order staying the proceedings altogether or for a limited time on such terms and subject to such conditions as the court thinks fit.

234. (1) Where creditor unknown — Where the liquidator is unable to pay all the debts of the corporation because a creditor is unknown or a creditor's whereabouts is unknown, the liquidator may, by agreement with the Public Guardian and Trustee, pay to the Public Guardian and Trustee an amount equal to the amount of the debt due to the creditor to be held in trust for the creditor, and thereupon subsections 238(5) and (6) apply thereto.

(2) Idem — A payment under subsection (1) shall be deemed to be in satisfaction of the debt for the purposes of winding up.

CTS 30 AU 10 – 1

235. (1) Where shareholder unknown — Where the liquidator is unable to distribute rateably the property of the corporation among the shareholders because a shareholder is unknown or a shareholder's whereabouts is unknown, the share of the property of the corporation of such shareholder may, by agreement with the Public Guardian and Trustee, be delivered or conveyed by the liquidator to the Public Guardian and Trustee to be held in trust for the shareholder, and thereupon subsections 238(5) and (6) apply thereto.

(2) Idem — A delivery or conveyance under subsection (1) shall be deemed to be a distribution to that shareholder of his, her or its rateable share for the purposes of the winding up.

CTS 30 AU 10 – 1

236. (1) Disposal of records, etc., after winding up — Where a corporation has been wound up under sections 192 to 235 and is about to be dissolved, its documents and records and those of the liquidator may be disposed of as it by resolution directs in case of voluntary winding up, or as the court directs in case of winding up under an order.

(2) When responsibility as to custody of records, etc., to cease — After the expiration of five years after the date of the dissolution of the corporation, no responsibility rests on it or the liquidator, or anyone to whom the custody of the documents and records has been committed, by reason that the same or any of them are not forthcoming to any person claiming to be interested therein.

237. Voluntary dissolution — A corporation may be dissolved upon the authorization of,

(a) a special resolution passed at a meeting of the shareholders of the corporation duly called for the purpose or, in the case of a corporation that is not an offering corporation, by such other proportion of the votes cast as the articles provide, but such other proportion shall not be less than 50 per cent of the votes of all the shareholders entitled to vote at the meeting;

(b) the consent in writing of all the shareholders entitled to vote at such meeting; or

(c) all its incorporators or their personal representatives if the corporation has not commenced business and has not issued any shares.

2006, c. 34, Sched. B, s. 36

238. (1) Articles of dissolution where corporation active — For the purpose of bringing the dissolution authorized under clause 237(a) or (b) into effect, articles of dissolution shall follow the prescribed form and shall set out,

(a) the name of the corporation;

(b) that its dissolution has been duly authorized under clause 237(a) or (b);

(c) that it has no debts, obligations or liabilities or its debts, obligations or liabilities have been duly provided for in accordance with subsection (3) or its creditors or other persons having interests in its debts, obligations or liabilities consent to its dissolution;

(d) that after satisfying the interests of creditors in all its debts, obligations and liabilities, if any, it has no property to distribute among its shareholders or that it has distributed its remaining property rateably among its shareholders according to their rights and interests in the corporation or in accordance with subsection (4) where applicable;

(e) that there are no proceedings pending in any court against it.

(f) [Repealed 1994, c. 27, s. 71(25).]

(2) Articles of dissolution where corporation never active — For the purpose of bringing a dissolution authorized under clause 237(c) into effect, articles of dissolution shall follow the prescribed form and shall set out,

(a) the name of the corporation;

(b) the date set out in its certificate of incorporation;

(c) that the corporation has not commenced business;

(d) that none of its shares has been issued;

(e) that dissolution has been duly authorized under clause 237(c);

(f) that it has no debts, obligations or liabilities;

(g) that after satisfying the interests of creditors in all its debts, obligations and liabilities, if any, it has no property to distribute or that it has distributed its remaining property to the persons entitled thereto; and

(h) that there are no proceedings pending in any court against it.

(i) [Repealed 1994, c. 27, s. 71(26).]

(3) **Where creditor unknown** — Where a corporation authorizes its dissolution and a creditor is unknown or a creditor's whereabouts is unknown, the corporation may, by agreement with the Public Guardian and Trustee, pay to the Public Guardian and Trustee an amount equal to the amount of the debt due to the creditor to be held in trust for the creditor, and such payment shall be deemed to be due provision for the debt for the purposes of clause (1)(c).

(4) **Where shareholder unknown** — Where a corporation authorizes its dissolution and a shareholder is unknown or a shareholder's whereabouts is unknown, it may, by agreement with the Public Guardian and Trustee, deliver or convey the shareholder's share of the property to the Public Guardian and Trustee to be held in trust for the shareholder, and such delivery or conveyance shall be deemed to be a distribution to that shareholder of his, her or its rateable share for the purposes of the dissolution.

(5) **Power to convert** — If the share of the property so delivered or conveyed to the Public Guardian and Trustee under subsection (4) is in a form other than cash, the Public Guardian and Trustee may at any time, and within ten years after such delivery or conveyance shall, convert it into cash.

(6) **Payment to person entitled** — If the amount paid under subsection (3) or the share of the property delivered or conveyed under subsection (4) or its equivalent in cash, as the case may be, is claimed by the person beneficially entitled thereto within ten years after it was so delivered, conveyed or paid, it shall be delivered, conveyed or paid to the person, but, if not so claimed, it vests in the Public Guardian and Trustee for the use of Ontario, and, if the person beneficially entitled thereto at any time thereafter establishes the person's right thereto to the satisfaction of the Lieutenant Governor in Council, an amount equal to the amount so vested in the Public Guardian and Trustee shall be paid to the person.

1994, c. 27, s. 71(25), (26); CTS 30 AU 10 – 1

239. (1) **Certificate of dissolution** — Upon receipt of the articles of dissolution, the Director shall endorse thereon in accordance with section 273 a certificate which shall constitute the certificate of dissolution.

(2) **Incorporators to sign articles of dissolution where corporation did not commence business** — Despite clause 273(1)(a), articles of dissolution for the purposes of subsection 238(2) shall be signed by all its incorporators or their personal representatives.

240. (1) **Cancellation of certificate, etc., by Director** — Where sufficient cause is shown to the Director, despite the imposition of any other penalty in respect thereof and in addition to any rights the Director may have under this or any other Act, the Director may, after having given the corporation an opportunity to be heard, by order, upon such terms and conditions as the Director thinks fit, cancel a certificate of incorporation or any other certificate issued or endorsed under this Act or a predecessor of this Act, and,

(a) in the case of the cancellation of a certificate of incorporation, the corporation is dissolved on the date fixed in the order; and

(b) in the case of the cancellation of any other certificate, the matter that became effective upon the issuance of the certificate ceases to be in effect from the date fixed in the order.

(2) Definition — In this section, **"sufficient cause"** with respect to cancellation of a certificate of incorporation includes,

(a) [Repealed 1994, c. 27, s. 71(27).]

(b) failure to comply with subsection 115(2) or subsection 118(3);

(c) [Repealed 1994, c. 27, s. 71(27).]

(d) a conviction of the corporation for an offence under the *Criminal Code* (Canada) or any other federal statute or an offence as defined in the *Provincial Offences Act*, in circumstances where cancellation of the certificate is in the public interest; or

(e) conduct described in subsection 248(2).

1994, c. 27, s. 71(27), (28)

241. (1) Notice of dissolution — Where the Director is notified by the Minister of Finance that a corporation is in default of complying with any of the following Acts, the Director may give notice by registered mail to the corporation or by publication once in *The Ontario Gazette* that an order dissolving the corporation will be issued unless the corporation remedies its default within 90 days after the notice is given:

0.1 *Alcohol and Gaming Regulation and Public Protection Act, 1996.*

1. *Corporations Tax Act.*

2. *Employer Health Tax Act.*

3. *Fuel Tax Act.*

4. *Gasoline Tax Act.*

5. *Land Transfer Tax Act.*

6. *Retail Sales Tax Act.*

6.1 *Taxation Act, 2007.*

7. *Tobacco Tax Act.*

(2) Idem — Where the Director is notified by the Commission that a corporation has not complied with sections 77 and 78 of the *Securities Act*, the Director may give notice by registered mail to the corporation or by publication once in *The Ontario Gazette* that an order dissolving the corporation will be issued unless the corporation complies with sections 77 and 78 of the *Securities Act* within ninety days after the giving of the notice.

(3) Same, non-filing — Where a corporation fails to comply with a filing requirement under the *Corporations Information Act* or fails to pay a fee required under this Act, the Director may give notice in accordance with section 263 to the corporation or by publication once in *The Ontario Gazette* that an order dissolving the corporation will be issued unless the corporation within 90 days after the notice is given, complies with the requirement or pays the fee.

(4) Order for dissolution — Upon default in compliance with the notice given under subsection (1), (2) or (3), the Director may by order cancel the certificate of incorporation and, subject to subsection (5), the corporation is dissolved on the date fixed in the order.

(5) Revival — Where a corporation is dissolved under subsection (4) or any predecessor of it, the Director on the application of any interested person, may, in his or her discretion, on the terms and conditions that the Director sees fit to impose, revive the corporation; upon revival, the corporation, subject to the terms and conditions imposed by the Director and to the rights, if any, acquired by any person during the period of dissolution, shall be deemed for all purposes to have never been dissolved.

(5.1) Time limit for application — The application referred to in subsection (5) shall not be made more than 20 years after the date of dissolution.

(6) Articles of revival — The application referred to in subsection (5) shall be in the form of articles of revival which shall be in prescribed form.

(7) Certificate of revival — Upon receipt of articles of revival and any other prescribed documents, the Director, subject to subsection (5), shall endorse thereon in accordance with section 273 a certificate which shall constitute the certificate of revival.

1993, c. 16, s. 2; 1994, c. 27, s. 71(29), (30); 1998, c. 18, Sched. E, s. 26; 1999, c. 12, Sched. F, s. 9; 2004, c. 31, Sched. 4, s. 1; 2006, c. 34, Sched. B, s. 37; 2008, c. 19, Sched. V, s. 1; 2010, c. 1, Sched. 1, s. 12

242. (1) Actions after dissolution — Despite the dissolution of a corporation under this Act,

(a) a civil, criminal or administrative action or proceeding commenced by or against the corporation before its dissolution may be continued as if the corporation had not been dissolved;

(b) a civil, criminal or administrative action or proceeding may be brought against the corporation, as if the corporation had not been dissolved;

(c) any property that would have been available to satisfy any judgment or order if the corporation had not been dissolved remains available for such purpose; and

(d) title to land belonging to the corporation immediately before the dissolution remains available to be sold in power of sale proceedings.

(1.1) Interpretation — In this section and section 244,

"proceeding" includes a power of sale proceeding relating to land commenced pursuant to a mortgage.

(2) Service after dissolution — For the purposes of this section, the service of any process on a corporation after its dissolution shall be deemed to be sufficiently made if it is made upon any person last shown on the records of the Ministry as being a director or officer of the corporation before the dissolution.

(3) Notice of action — A person who commences an action, suit or other proceeding against a corporation after its dissolution, shall serve the writ or other document by which the action, suit or other proceeding was commenced, on the Public Guardian and Trustee in accordance with the rules that apply generally to service on a party to an action, suit or other proceeding.

(4) Same, power of sale proceeding — A person who commences a power of sale proceeding related to land against a corporation after its dissolution, shall serve a notice of the proceeding on the Public Guardian and Trustee in accordance with the notice requirements in the *Mortgages Act* that apply with respect to a person with an interest in the land recorded in the records of the appropriate land registry office.

1998, c. 18, Sched. E, s. 27

243. (1) Liability of shareholders to creditors — Despite the dissolution of a corporation, each shareholder to whom any of its property has been distributed is liable to any person claiming under section 242 to the extent of the amount received by that shareholder upon the distribution, and an action to enforce such liability may be brought.

(2) Party action — The court may order an action referred to in subsection (1) to be brought against the persons who were shareholders as a class, subject to such conditions as the court thinks fit and, if the plaintiff establishes his, her or its claim, the court may refer the proceedings to a referee or other officer of the court who may,

(a) add as a party to the proceedings before him or her each person who was a shareholder found by the plaintiff;

(b) determine, subject to subsection (1), the amount that each person who was a shareholder shall contribute towards satisfaction of the plaintiff's claim; and

(c) direct payment of the amounts so determined.

(3) Definition — In this section, **"shareholder"** includes the heirs and legal representatives of a shareholder.

2002, c. 24, Sched. B, s. 27(2)

244. (1) Forfeiture of undisposed property — Any property of a corporation that has not been disposed of at the date of its dissolution is immediately upon such dissolution forfeit to and vests in the Crown.

(2) Exception — Despite subsection (1), if a judgment is given or an order or decision is made or land is sold in an action, suit or proceeding commenced in accordance with section 242 and the judgment, order, decision or sale affects property belonging to the corporation before the dissolution, unless the plaintiff, applicant or mortgagee has not complied with subsection 242(3) or (4),

(a) the property shall be available to satisfy the judgment, order or other decision; and

(b) title to the land shall be transferred to a purchaser free of the Crown's interest, in the case of a power of sale proceeding.

(3) Further exception — A forfeiture of land under subsection (1) or a predecessor of subsection (1) is not effective against a purchaser for value of the land if the forfeiture occurred more than 20 years before the deed or transfer of the purchaser is registered in the proper land registry office.

(4) No notice — Despite subsection (2), if a person commences a power of sale proceeding relating to land before the dissolution of a corporation but the sale of the land is not completed until after the dissolution, the person is not required to serve the notice mentioned in subsection 242(4) and title to the land may be transferred to a purchaser free of the Crown's interest.

1994, c. 27, s. 71(31), (32); 1998, c. 18, Sched. E, s. 28

PART XVII — REMEDIES, OFFENCES AND PENALTIES

245. Definitions — In this Part,

"action" means an action under this Act;

"complainant" means,

(a) a registered holder or beneficial owner, and a former registered holder or beneficial owner, of a security of a corporation or any of its affiliates,

(b) a director or an officer or a former director or officer of a corporation or of any of its affiliates,

(c) any other person who, in the discretion of the court, is a proper person to make an application under this Part.

246. (1) Derivative actions — Subject to subsection (2), a complainant may apply to the court for leave to bring an action in the name and on behalf of a corporation or any of its subsidiaries, or intervene in an action to which any such body corporate is a party, for the purpose of prosecuting, defending or discontinuing the action on behalf of the body corporate.

(2) Idem — No action may be brought and no intervention in an action may be made under subsection (1) unless the complainant has given fourteen days' notice to the directors of the corporation or its subsidiary of the complainant's intention to apply to the court under subsection (1) and the court is satisfied that,

(a) the directors of the corporation or its subsidiary will not bring, diligently prosecute or defend or discontinue the action;

(b) the complainant is acting in good faith; and

(c) it appears to be in the interests of the corporation or its subsidiary that the action be brought, prosecuted, defended or discontinued.

(2.1) Notice not required — A complainant is not required to give the notice referred to in subsection (2) if all of the directors of the corporation or its subsidiary are defendants in the action.

(3) Application — Where a complainant on an application made without notice can establish to the satisfaction of the court that it is not expedient to give notice as required under subsection (2), the court may make such interim order as it thinks fit pending the complainant giving notice as required.

(4) Interim order — Where a complainant on an application can establish to the satisfaction of the court that an interim order for relief should be made, the court may make such order as it thinks fit.

2006, c. 34, Sched. B, s. 38

247. Court order — In connection with an action brought or intervened in under section 246, the court may at any time make any order it thinks fit including, without limiting the generality of the foregoing,

(a) an order authorizing the complainant or any other person to control the conduct of the action;

(b) an order giving directions for the conduct of the action;

(c) an order directing that any amount adjudged payable by a defendant in the action shall be paid, in whole or in part, directly to former and present security holders of the corporation or its subsidiary instead of to the corporation or its subsidiary; and

(d) an order requiring the corporation or its subsidiary to pay reasonable legal fees and any other costs reasonably incurred by the complainant in connection with the action.

248. (1) Oppression remedy — A complainant and, in the case of an offering corporation, the Commission may apply to the court for an order under this section.

(2) Idem — Where, upon an application under subsection (1), the court is satisfied that in respect of a corporation or any of its affiliates,

(a) any act or omission of the corporation or any of its affiliates effects or threatens to effect a result;

(b) the business or affairs of the corporation or any of its affiliates are, have been or are threatened to be carried on or conducted in a manner; or

(c) the powers of the directors of the corporation or any of its affiliates are, have been or are threatened to be exercised in a manner,

that is oppressive or unfairly prejudicial to or that unfairly disregards the interests of any security holder, creditor, director or officer of the corporation, the court may make an order to rectify the matters complained of.

(3) Court order — In connection with an application under this section, the court may make any interim or final order it thinks fit including, without limiting the generality of the foregoing,

(a) an order restraining the conduct complained of;

(b) an order appointing a receiver or receiver-manager;

(c) an order to regulate a corporation's affairs by amending the articles or by-laws or creating or amending a unanimous shareholder agreement;

(d) an order directing an issue or exchange of securities;

(e) an order appointing directors in place of or in addition to all or any of the directors then in office;

(f) an order directing a corporation, subject to subsection (6), or any other person, to purchase securities of a security holder;

(g) an order directing a corporation, subject to subsection (6), or any other person, to pay to a security holder any part of the money paid by the security holder for securities;

(h) an order varying or setting aside a transaction or contract to which a corporation is a party and compensating the corporation or any other party to the transaction or contract;

(i) an order requiring a corporation, within a time specified by the court, to produce to the court or an interested person financial statements in the form required by section 154 or an accounting in such other form as the court may determine;

(j) an order compensating an aggrieved person;

(k) an order directing rectification of the registers or other records of a corporation under section 250;

(l) an order winding up the corporation under section 207;

(m) an order directing an investigation under Part XIII be made; and

(n) an order requiring the trial of any issue.

(4) Idem — Where an order made under this section directs amendment of the articles or by-laws of a corporation,

(a) the directors shall forthwith comply with subsection 186(4); and

(b) no other amendment to the articles or by-laws shall be made without the consent of the court, until the court otherwise orders.

(5) Shareholder may not dissent — A shareholder is not entitled to dissent under section 185 if an amendment to the articles is effected under this section.

(6) Where corporation prohibited from paying shareholder — A corporation shall not make a payment to a shareholder under clause (3)(f) or (g) if there are reasonable grounds for believing that,

(a) the corporation is or, after the payment, would be unable to pay its liabilities as they become due; or

(b) the realizable value of the corporation's assets would thereby be less than the aggregate of its liabilities.

1994, c. 27, s. 71(33)

249. (1) Discontinuance and settlement — An application made or an action brought or intervened in under this Part shall not be stayed or dismissed by reason only that it is shown that an alleged breach of a right or duty owed to the corporation or its affiliate has been or may be approved by the shareholders of such body corporate, but evidence of approval by the shareholders may be taken into account by the court in making an order under section 207, 247 or 248.

(2) Idem — An application made or an action brought or intervened in under this Part shall not be stayed, discontinued, settled or dismissed for want of prosecution without the approval of the court given upon such terms as the court thinks fit and, if the court determines that the interests of any complainant may be substantially affected by such stay, discontinuance, settlement or dismissal, the court may order any party to the application or action to give notice to the complainant.

(3) Costs — A complainant is not required to give security for costs in any application made or action brought or intervened in under this Part.

(4) Idem — In an application made or an action brought or intervened in under this Part, the court may at any time order the corporation or its affiliate to pay to the complainant interim costs, including reasonable legal fees and disbursements, for which interim costs the complainant may be held accountable to the corporation or its affiliate upon final disposition of the application or action.

250. (1) Rectifying error in entering, etc., name — Where the name of a person is alleged to be or have been wrongly entered or retained in, or wrongly deleted or wrongly omitted from, the registers or other records of a corporation, the corporation, a security holder of the corporation or any aggrieved person may apply to the court for an order that the registers or records be rectified.

(2) Idem — In connection with an application under this section, the court may make any order it thinks fit including, without limiting the generality of the foregoing,

(a) an order requiring the registers or other records of the corporation to be rectified;

(b) an order restraining the corporation from calling or holding a meeting of shareholders or paying a dividend or making any other distribution or payment to shareholders before the rectification;

(c) an order determining the right of a party to the proceedings to have the party's name entered or retained in, or deleted or omitted from, the registers or records of the corporation, whether the issue arises between two or more security holders, or between the corporation and any security holders or alleged security holders;

(d) an order compensating a party who has incurred a loss.

251. (1) Notice of refusal to file — Where the Director refuses to endorse a certificate on articles or any other document required by this Act to be endorsed with a certificate by the Director before it becomes effective, the Director shall give written notice to the person who delivered the articles or other document of the Director's refusal, specifying the reasons therefor.

(2) Failure to act deemed refusal — Where, within six months after the delivery to the Director of articles or other documents referred to in subsection (1), the Director has not endorsed a certificate on such articles or other document, the Director shall be deemed for the purposes of section 252 to have refused to endorse it.

252. (1) Appeal from Director — A person aggrieved by a decision of the Director,

(a) to refuse to endorse a certificate on articles or on any other document;

(b) to issue or refuse to issue a certificate of amendment under section 12;

(c) to refuse to grant an order under section 144;

(d) to grant or refuse to grant exemption under section 148;

(e) to refuse to endorse an authorization under section 181; or

(f) to issue an order under section 240,

may appeal to the Divisional Court.

(2) Form of appeal — Every appeal shall be by notice of appeal sent by registered mail to the Director within thirty days after the mailing of the notice of the decision.

(3) Certificate of Director — The Director shall certify to the Divisional Court,

(a) the decision of the Director together with a statement of the reasons therefor;

(b) the record of any hearing; and

(c) all written submissions to the Director or other material that is relevant to the appeal.

(4) Representation — The Director is entitled to be heard, by counsel or otherwise, upon the argument of an appeal under this section.

(5) Court order — Where an appeal is taken under this section, the court may by its order direct the Director to make such decision or to do such other act as the Director is authorized and empowered to do under this Act and as the court thinks proper, having regard to the material and submissions before it and to this Act, and the Director shall make such decision or do such act accordingly.

(6) Director may make further decision — Despite an order of the court under subsection (5), the Director has power to make any further decision upon new material or where there is a material change in the circumstances, and every such decision is subject to this section.

253. (1) Orders for compliance — Where a corporation or any shareholder, director, officer, employee, agent, auditor, trustee, receiver and manager, receiver, or liquidator of a corporation does not comply with this Act, the regulations, articles, by-laws, or a unanimous shareholder agreement, a complainant or a creditor of the corporation may, despite the imposition of any penalty in respect of such non-compliance and in addition to any other right the complainant or creditor has, apply to the court for an order directing the corporation or any person to comply with, or restraining the corporation or any person from acting in breach of, any provisions thereof, and upon such application the court may so order and make any further order it thinks fit.

(2) Idem — Where it appears to the Commission that any person to whom section 111 or subsection 112(1) applies has failed to comply with or is contravening either or both of such provisions, despite the imposition of any penalty in respect of such non-compliance or contravention, the Commission may apply to the court and the court may, upon such application, make any order it thinks fit including, without limiting the generality of the foregoing,

(a) an order restraining a solicitation, the holding of a meeting or any person from implementing or acting upon any resolution passed at a meeting, to which such non-compliance with or contravention of section 111 or subsection 112(1) relates;

(b) an order requiring correction of any form of proxy or information circular and a further solicitation; or

(c) an order adjourning the meeting to which such non-compliance with or contravention of section 111 or subsection 112(1) relates.

254. Application made without notice — Where this Act states that a person may apply to the court, that person may apply for injunctive relief without notice as the rules of the court provide.

255. Appeal — An appeal lies to thc Divisional Court from any order made by the court under this Act.

256. (1) Offences — In this section, **"misrepresentation"** means,

(a) an untrue statement of material fact; or

(b) an omission to state a material fact that is required to be stated or that is necessary to make a statement not misleading in the light of the circumstances in which it was made.

(2) Offence, false statements, etc. — Every person who,

(a) makes or assists in making a statement in any material, evidence or information submitted or given under this Act or the regulations to the Director, the Director's delegate or the Commission or any person appointed to make an investigation or audit under this Act that, at the time and in the light of the circumstances under which it is made, is a misrepresentation;

(b) makes or assists in making a statement in any application, articles, consent, financial statement, information circular, notice, report or other document required to be filed with, furnished or sent to the Director or the Commission under this Act or the regulations that, at the time and in the light of the circumstances under which it is made, is a misrepresentation;

(c) fails to file with the Director or the Commission any document required by this Act to be filed with the Director or the Commission; or

(d) fails to observe or to comply with any direction, decision, ruling, order or other requirement made by the Director or the Commission under this Act or the regulations,

is guilty of an offence and on conviction is liable to a fine of not more than $2,000 or to imprisonment for a term of not more than one year, or to both, or, if such person is a body corporate, to a fine of not more than $25,000.

(3) Idem — Where a body corporate is guilty of an offence under subsection (2), every director or officer of such body corporate who, without reasonable cause, authorized, permitted or acquiesced in the offence is also guilty of an offence and on conviction is liable to a fine of not more than $2,000 or to imprisonment for a term of not more than one year, or to both.

(4) Defence — No person is guilty of an offence under clause (2)(a) or (b) if the person did not know and in the exercise of reasonable diligence could not have known that the statement was a misrepresentation.

257. Consent — No proceeding under section 256 shall be commenced except with the consent or under the direction of the Minister.

258. (1) Offence — Every person who,

(a) fails without reasonable cause to comply with subsection 29(5);

(b) without reasonable cause uses a list of holders of securities in contravention of subsection 52(5) or subsection 146(8);

(c) fails without reasonable cause to send a prescribed form of proxy to each shareholder of an offering corporation with notice of a meeting of shareholders in contravention of section 111;

(d) fails without reasonable cause to send an information circular in connection with a proxy solicitation in contravention of subsection 112(1);

(e) being a proxyholder or alternate proxyholder, fails without reasonable cause, to comply with the directions of the shareholder who appointed him or her in contravention of subsection 114(1);

(f) without reasonable cause contravenes section 145;

(g) being a director of a corporation, fails, without reasonable cause, to appoint an auditor or auditors, as the case may be, under subsection 149(1);

(h) being an auditor or former auditor of a corporation fails without reasonable cause to comply with subsection 151(2);

(i) fails without reasonable cause to comply with subsection 154(1); or

(j) otherwise without reasonable cause commits an act contrary to or fails or neglects to comply with any provision of this Act or the regulations,

is guilty of an offence and on conviction is liable to a fine of not more than $2,000 or to imprisonment for a term of not more than one year, or to both, or if such person is a body corporate, to a fine of not more than $25,000.

(2) Idem — Where a body corporate is guilty of an offence under subsection (1), every director or officer of such body corporate who, without reasonable cause, authorized, permitted or acquiesced in such offence is also guilty of an offence and on conviction is liable to a fine of not more than $2,000 or to imprisonment for a term of not more than one year, or to both.

259. (1) Limitation — No proceeding under section 256 or under clause 258(1)(j) for a contravention of section 144 shall be commenced more than two years after the facts upon which the proceedings are based first came to the knowledge of the Director as certified by him or her.

(2) Idem — Subject to subsection (1), no proceeding for an offence under this Act or the regulations shall be commenced more than two years after the time when the subject-matter of the offence arose.

260. Information containing more than one offence — An information in respect of any contravention of this Act may be for one or more offences and no information, summons, warrant, conviction or other proceeding in any prosecution is objectionable as insufficient by reason of the fact that it relates to two or more offences.

261. Civil remedy not affected — No civil remedy for an act or omission is suspended or affected by reason that the act or omission is an offence under this Act.

PART XVIII — GENERAL

262. (1) Notice to directors or shareholders — A notice or document required by this Act, the regulations, the articles or the by-laws to be sent to a shareholder or director of a corporation may be sent by prepaid mail addressed to, or may be delivered personally to,

(a) a shareholder at the shareholder's latest address as shown in the records of the corporation or its transfer agent; and

(b) a director at his or her latest address as shown in the records of the corporation or in the most recent notice filed under the *Corporations Information Act*, whichever is the more current.

(2) Idem — A notice or document sent in accordance with subsection (1) to a shareholder or director of a corporation is deemed to be received by the addressee on the fifth day after mailing.

(3) Director — A director named in the articles or the most recent return or notice filed under the *Corporations Information Act*, or a predecessor thereof, is presumed for the purposes of this Act to be a director of the corporation referred to in the articles, return or notice.

(4) Where notice returned — Where a corporation sends a notice or document to a shareholder in accordance with subsection (1) and the notice or document is returned on three consecutive occasions because the shareholder cannot be found, the corporation is not required to send any further notices or documents to the shareholder until the shareholder informs the corporation in writing of the shareholder's new address.

(5) Application to court — Where it is impracticable or impossible to comply with subsection (1), a person may apply to the court for such order as the court thinks fit.

(6) Electronic communications — A notice or document required or permitted to be sent under this section or section 263 may be sent by electronic means in accordance with the *Electronic Commerce Act, 2000.*

2006, c. 34, Sched. B, s. 39

263. (1) Notice to corporation — Except where otherwise provided in this Act, a notice or document required to be sent to a corporation may be sent to the corporation by prepaid mail at its registered office as shown on the records of the Director or may be delivered personally to the corporation at such office and shall be deemed to be received by the corporation on the fifth day after mailing.

(2) Exception — A notice or other document that is required or permitted by this Act or the regulations to be sent by the Director may be sent by ordinary mail or by any other method, including registered mail, certified mail or prepaid courier, to an address referred to in section 262 or 263 if there is a record by the person who has delivered it that the notice or document has been sent.

(3) Same — A notice or other document referred to in subsection (2) may be sent by telephone transmission of a facsimile of the notice or other document or by any other form of electronic transmission if there is a record that the notice or other document has been sent.

(4) Deemed delivery — A notice or other document sent by mail by the Director shall be deemed to have been received by the intended recipient on the earlier of,

(a) the day the intended recipient actually receives it; or

(b) the fifth business day after it is mailed.

(5) Same — A notice or other document sent by a method referred to in subsection (3) shall be deemed to have been received by the intended recipient on the earlier of,

(a) the day the intended recipient actually receives it; or

(b) the first business day after the day the transmission is sent by the Director.

1994, c. 27, s. 71(34)

264. (1) Waiver of notice and abridgement of times — Where a notice or document is required by this Act or the regulations to be sent, the notice may be waived or the time for the sending of the notice or document may be waived or abridged at any time with the consent in writing of the person entitled thereto.

(2) Electronic communications — The consent of a person entitled to waive the requirement for the sending of a notice or document or to waive or abridge the time for the sending of the notice or the document under subsection (1) may be sent by electronic means in accordance with the *Electronic Commerce Act, 2000.*

2006, c. 34, Sched. B, s. 40

265. (1) Delegation of powers and duties — The Director may delegate in writing any of the Director's duties or powers under this Act to any public servant employed under Part III of the *Public Service of Ontario Act, 2006.*

(2) Execution of certificate of Director — Where this Act requires or authorizes the Director to endorse or issue a certificate or to certify any fact, the certificate shall be signed by the Director or any other person designated by the regulations.

(3) Certificate as evidence — A certificate referred to in subsection (2) or a certified copy thereof, when introduced as evidence in any civil, criminal, or administrative action or proceeding, is, in the absence of evidence to the contrary, proof of the facts so certified without personal appearance to prove the signature or official position of the person appearing to have signed the certificate.

(4) Mechanical reproduction of signature — For the purposes of subsections (2) and (3), any signature of the Director or any signature of an officer of the Ministry designated by the regulations may be printed or otherwise mechanically reproduced.

(5) Non-application — Subsections (2), (3) and (4) do not apply to certificates which are in electronic form.

1994, c. 27, s. 71(35); 2011, c. 1, Sched. 5, s. 1(1)

266. (1) Certificate that may be signed by directors, etc. — A certificate issued on behalf of a corporation stating any fact that is set out in the articles, the by-laws, a unanimous shareholder agreement, the minutes of the meetings of the directors, a committee of directors or the shareholders, or a trust indenture or other contract to which the corporation is a party, may be signed by a director, an officer or a transfer agent of the corporation.

(2) Evidence being proof — When introduced as evidence in any civil, criminal or administrative action or proceeding,

(a) a fact stated in a certificate referred to in subsection (1);

(b) a certified extract from a register of a corporation required to be maintained by this Act; or

(c) a certified copy of minutes or extract from minutes of a meeting of shareholders, directors or a committee of directors of a corporation,

is, in the absence of evidence to the contrary, proof of the facts so certified without proof of the signature or official character of the person appearing to have signed the certificate.

(3) Idem — An entry in a securities register of, or a security certificate issued by, a corporation is, in the absence of evidence to the contrary, proof that the person in whose name the security is registered or whose name appears on the certificate is the owner of the securities described in the register or in the certificate, as the case may be.

267. (1) Copy of document acceptable — Where a notice or document is required to be sent to the Director under this Act, the Director may accept a photostatic or photographic copy thereof.

(2) Exception to subs. (1) — Subsection (1) does not apply to articles, applications or documents filed under subsection 9(3).

268. (1) Proof of affidavit — The Director may require any fact relevant to the performance of the Director's duties under this Act or the regulations to be verified by affidavit or otherwise.

(2) Oaths and affirmations at hearings — For the purpose of holding a hearing under this Act, the Director may administer oaths and affirmations to witnesses and require them to give evidence under oath or affirmation.

269. [Repealed 1994, c. 27, s. 71(36).]

270. (1) Examination, etc., of documents — A person who has paid the required fee is entitled during usual business hours to examine and to make copies of or extracts from any document required by this Act or the regulations to be sent to the Director or the Commission, except a report sent to the Director under subsection 162(2) that the court has ordered not to be made available to the public.

(2) Copies to be furnished — Subject to clause 162(1)(j), the Director or the Commission shall furnish any person with a copy or a certified copy of a document required by this Act or the regulations to be sent to the Director or the Commission.

(3) Privileged documents — Subsections (1) and (2) do not apply in respect of documents and financial statements required, by this Act or the regulations, to be filed with the Director with an application for exemption from the requirements of Part XII of this Act.

1998, c. 18, Sched. E, s. 29

271. Appeal from Commission — Any person aggrieved by a decision of the Commission under this Act may appeal the decision to the Divisional Court and subsection 9(2) to (6) of the *Securities Act* apply to the appeal.

271.1 Powers of Minister — (1) Minister's regulations — The Minister may make regulations,

(a) designating officers of the Ministry for the purposes of endorsing certificates, issuing certificates as to any fact or certifying true copies of documents required or authorized under this Act;

(b) prescribing the punctuation marks and other marks that may form part of a corporate name under subsection 10(3);

(c) respecting the content of a special language provision under subsection 10(4);

(d) prescribing exceptions under section 177;

(e) providing for and governing the filing of documents sent by electronic format, including the manner of determining the date of receipt and the form of electronic signatures;

(f) providing for the waiver of signature requirements, and for requirements for the execution of articles, applications or statements filed with the Director requiring the signature of one or more persons;

(g) providing for the exclusion of any class or classes of documents from being filed in electronic format or by telephone transmission of a facsimile;

(h) prescribing documents that are required to accompany articles and applications made under this Act;

(i) prescribing the form and content of any notices or documents that this Act requires to be filed.

(2) Fees — The Minister may by order require the payment of fees for search reports, copies of documents or information, filing of documents or other services under this Act and may approve the amount of those fees.

1998, c. 18, Sched. E, s. 30; 2011, c. 1, Sched. 5, s. 1(2)

271.2 Director's regulations — The Director may make regulations prescribing forms and providing for their use.

2011, c. 1, Sched. 5, s. 1(3)

272. Regulations — The Lieutenant Governor in Council may make regulations respecting any matter the Lieutenant Governor in Council considers necessary for the purposes of this Act including, without limiting the generality of the foregoing, regulations,

1. respecting names of corporations or classes thereof, the designation, rights, privileges, restrictions or conditions attaching to shares or classes of shares of corporations, or any other matter pertaining to articles or the filing thereof;

2-4 [Repealed 1998, c. 18, Sched. E, s. 31.]

5. [Repealed 2011, c. 1, Sched. 5, s. 1(4).]

6. prescribing the form and content of information circulars and proxies required by Part VIII and the discretionary authority that may be conferred in proxies;

7. prescribing requirements with respect to applications to the Director or the Commission for exemptions permitted by this Act and the practice and procedure thereon;

8. prohibiting the use of any words or expressions in a corporate name;

9. defining any word or expression used in clause 9(1)(b);

10. prescribing requirements for the purposes of clause 9(1)(c);

11. prescribing conditions for the purposes of subsection 9(2);

12. prescribing the documents relating to names that shall be filed with the Director under subsection 9(3);

13. respecting the name of a corporation under subsection 10(2);

14, 15 [Repealed 2011, c. 1, Sched. 5, s. 1(4).]

15.1 prescribing conditions for the purposes of subsections 29(9) and (10);

15.2 prescribing consequences for the purposes of subsection 29(11);

15.3 prescribing conditions, notices, the manner for making determinations and laws for the purposes of subsection 45(1);

15.4 prescribing the maximum number of words for the purposes of subsection 99(3.1);

15.5 prescribing public announcements and circumstances for the purposes of clauses (i) and (j) of the definition of "“solicit” and “solicitation”" in section 109;

15.6 prescribing circumstances for the purpose of clause 112(1.2);

16. prescribing the form of the statutory declarations under subsection 52(1) and subsection 146(1);

16.1 prescribing an amount for the purposes of subclause 148(1)(a)(iii);

Proposed Repeal — 272, para. 16.1

16.1 [Repealed 2011, c. 1, Sched. 2, s. 1(19). Not in force at date of publication.]

17. prescribing the form and content of financial statements and interim financial statements required under this Act;

18. prescribing that, for the purposes of Part XII of this Act, the standards, as they exist from time to time, of a prescribed accounting body shall be followed;

19. prescribing standards to be used by an auditor in making an examination of financial statements required under this Act and the manner in which the auditor shall report thereon;

20. [Repealed 2011, c. 1, Sched. 5, s. 1(4).]

21. prescribing the manner in which notice may be sent under subsection 190(3);

22. [Repealed 2009, c. 33, Sched. 17, s. 1(1).]

23. prescribing Acts of Canada or a province or ordinances of a territory for purposes of sections 29, 42, 45 and 56 and prescribing the notice required under subsection 45(1);

24. prescribing the manner in which the directors of corporations may determine that restricted shares are owned contrary to restrictions under subsection 45(1);

25. prescribing the manner in which funds may be invested under subsection 45(5);

26. prescribing, with respect to a corporation that has imposed restrictions on the issue, transfer or ownership of its shares for a purpose under subsection 42(2),

(i) the disclosure required of the restrictions in documents issued or published by such corporation,

(ii) the duties and powers of the directors to refuse to issue or register transfers of shares in accordance with the articles of the corporation,

(iii) the limitations on voting rights of any shares held contrary to the articles of the corporation, and

(iv) the powers of the directors to require disclosure of beneficial ownership of shares of the corporation and the rights of the corporation and its directors, employees or agents to rely on the disclosure and the effects of the reliance;

27. prescribing persons or classes of persons for the purpose of clause 42(2)(c) and prescribing the manner of computing the ownership of shares of a corporation by persons for such purpose;

28. [Repealed 2009, c. 33, Sched. 17, s. 1(1).]

29. prescribing classes of persons for the purposes of clause (b) of the definition of "resident Canadian" in subsection 1(1);

29.1-29.3 [Repealed 2011, c. 1, Sched. 5, s. 1(4).]

29.4 authorizing the Director to enter into an agreement with any person respecting the use, disclosure, sale or licensing of records required under this Act and prescribing terms and conditions for any such agreement;

30. prescribing any matter referred to in this Act as prescribed by the regulations for which a specific power is not otherwise provided.

1994, c. 27, s. 71(37); 1998, c. 18, Sched. E, s. 31; 2006, c. 34, Sched. B, s. 41; 2009, c. 33, Sched. 17, s. 1(1); 2011, c. 1, Sched. 5, s. 1(4), (5)

273. (1) Where articles to be sent to Director — Where this Act requires that articles relating to a corporation be sent to the Director, unless otherwise specifically provided,

(a) two duplicate originals of the articles shall be signed by a director or an officer of the corporation or, in the case of articles of incorporation, by all incorporators; and

(b) upon receiving duplicate originals of any articles in the prescribed form that have been executed in accordance with this Act, any other required documents and the prescribed fees, the Director shall, subject to his or her discretion as provided in subsection 180(4) and subsection 241(5), and, subject to subsection (2),

(i) endorse on each duplicate original a certificate, setting out the day, month and year of endorsement and the corporation number,

(ii) file a copy of the articles with the endorsement of the certificate thereon, and

(iii) send to the corporation or its representative one duplicate original of the articles with the endorsement of the certificate thereon.

(iv) [Repealed 1994, c. 27, s. 71(38).]

(2) **Date on certificate** — A certificate referred to in subsection (1) shall be dated as of the day the Director receives the duplicate originals of any articles together with all other required documents executed in accordance with this Act and the required fee, or as of any later date acceptable to the Director and specified by the person who submitted the articles or by the court.

(3) **Effective date of articles** — Articles endorsed with a certificate under subsection (1), are effective on the date shown in the certificate even if any action required to be taken by the Director under this Act with respect to the endorsement of the certificate and filing by the Director is taken at a later date.

(4) **Electronic filing** — Despite subsections (1) and (2), if articles relating to a corporation are sent to the Director in a prescribed electronic format,

(a) the articles shall set out an electronic signature of a director or officer of the corporation or, in the case of articles of incorporation, the electronic signature of all incorporators, unless the regulations otherwise provide; and

(b) upon receipt of the articles in the prescribed electronic format completed in accordance with this Act and the required fee, the Director shall, subject to his or her discretion as provided in subsections 180(4) and 241(5), and subject to subsection (5) of this section,

(i) endorse a certificate by making an appropriate entry in an electronic database maintained under section 276, and

(ii) send to the corporation or its representative a copy of the certificate in a form prescribed by the regulations.

(5) **Date of certificate** — A certificate referred to in subsection (4) shall be dated as of the day the Director received the articles in a prescribed electronic format completed in accordance with this Act and the required fee or as of any later date acceptable to the Director and specified by the person who submitted the articles or by the court.

1994, c. 27, s. 71(38), (39); 1998, c. 18, Sched. E, s. 32; 2009, c. 33, Sched. 17, s. 1(2), (3)

273.1 (1) **Electronic filers** — Information that is filed in an electronic format may be filed by a person who is authorized to do so by the Director or by a person who is a member of a class of persons that is authorized to do so.

(2) **Condition** — The Director may attach terms and conditions to an authorization given under subsection (1) and may require any person who applies for an authorization to enter into an agreement governing the making of filings in an electronic format.

1994, c. 27, s. 71(40)

273.2 (1) **Fax filing** — Despite section 273 and subject to the regulations, articles or other documents may be sent in duplicate to the Director by telephone transmission of a facsimile.

(2) **Same** — Where articles or another document are sent to the Director under subsection (1), a required signature may be a facsimile.

1994, c. 27, s. 71(40)

274. [Repealed without coming into force 2006, c. 21, Sched. F, s. 10.1(1).]

275. (1) Where error in respect of certificate — Where a certificate endorsed or issued under this Act or a predecessor of this Act contains an error or where a certificate has been endorsed or issued on articles or any other documents that contain an error,

(a) the corporation, its directors or shareholders may apply to the Director for a corrected certificate and shall surrender the certificate and related articles or documents; or

(b) the corporation shall upon the request of the Director surrender the certificate and related articles or documents,

and, after giving the corporation an opportunity to be heard, where the Director is of the opinion that it is appropriate to so do and is satisfied that such steps have been taken by the corporation as the Director required, the Director shall endorse a corrected certificate.

(2) Date on certificate — A corrected certificate endorsed under subsection (1) may bear the date of the certificate it replaces.

(3) [Repealed 2004, c. 19, s. 3(6).]

(4) Appeal — A decision of the Director under subsection (1) may be appealed to the Divisional Court which may order the Director to change his or her decision and make such further order as it thinks fit.

2004, c. 19, s. 3(6)

276. (1) Records — Records required by this Act to be prepared and maintained by the Director or Commission may be in bound or loose-leaf or electronic form or in photographic film form, or may be entered or recorded by any system of mechanical or electronic data processing or by any other information storage device that is capable of reproducing any required information in an accurate and intelligible form within a reasonable time.

(2) Admission as evidence — When records maintained by the Director or the Commission are prepared and maintained other than in written form,

(a) the Director or the Commission shall furnish any copy required to be furnished under subsection 270(2) in intelligible written or other form; and

(b) a report reproduced from those records, if it is certified by the Director or the Commission or a member thereof, as the case may be, is, without proof of the office or signature thereof, admissible in evidence.

(3) Copy in lieu of document — The Director or Commission, as the case may be, is not required to produce any document where a copy of the document is furnished in compliance with clause (2)(a).

1994, c. 27, s. 71(41)–(43)

277. (1) Deemed amendment — Any provision in articles, by-laws or any special resolution of a corporation that was valid immediately before the 29th day of July, 1983 and that has not been amended in accordance with this Act is deemed to be amended to the extent necessary to bring the terms of the provision into conformity with this Act.

(2) Amendments — A corporation may, by articles of amendment, change the express terms of any provision in its articles to which subsection (1) applies to conform to the terms of the provision as deemed to be amended by that subsection.

(3) **Idem** — A corporation shall not restate its articles under section 173 unless the articles of the corporation are in conformity with this Act and, where the articles have been deemed to be amended under subsection (1), the corporation has amended the express terms of the provisions in its articles in accordance with subsection (2).

(4) **Where s. 185 does not apply** — A shareholder is not entitled to dissent under section 185 in respect of any amendment made for the purpose only of bringing the provisions of articles into conformity with this Act.

278. Appointment of Director — The Minister may appoint a Director to carry out the duties and exercise the powers of the Director under this Act.

ONT. REG. 62 — GENERAL

made under the *Business Corporations Act*

R.R.O. 1990, Reg. 62, as am. O. Reg. 578/91; 594/92; 627/93; 637/94; 293/95; 400/95; 308/96; 561/98; 190/99; 196/99; 288/00; 246/05; 648/05; 59/07; 13/09.

NAMES

1. In this Regulation **"trade-mark"** means a trade-mark as defined in the *Trade-Marks Act* (Canada).

2. (1) "Name" when used in the expression "if the use of that name would be likely to deceive" used in clause 9(1)(b) of the Act includes,

(a) a name that would lead to the inference that the business or activities carried on or intended to be carried on by the corporation under the proposed name and the business or activities carried on by any other person are one business or one activity, whether or not the nature of the business or activity of each is generally the same;

(b) a name that would lead to the inference that the corporation bearing the name or proposed name is or would be associated or affiliated with a person if the corporation and such person are not or will not be associated or affiliated; or

(c) a name whose similarity to the name of a person would lead someone who has an interest in dealing with that person, to deal with the corporation bearing the name in the mistaken belief that they are dealing with the person.

(2) In this section,

(a) **"person"** means a person, whether in existence or not; and

(b) **"use"** means actual use by a person that carries on business in Canada or elsewhere.

3. For the purpose of section 12 of the Act, the matters the Director may consider when determining whether a name is contrary to section 9 of the Act include,

(a) the distinctiveness of the whole or any element of any name or trademark and the extent to which the name or trade-mark has become known;

(b) the length of time the trade-mark or name has been in use;

(c) the nature of the goods or services associated with the trade-mark or the nature of the business carried on under or associated with a name, including the likelihood of any competition among businesses using such a trade-mark or name;

(d) the nature of the trade with which a trade-mark or name is associated, including the nature of the goods or services and the means by which they are offered or distributed;

(e) the degree of similarity between the corporate name and any trade-mark or name in appearance or sound or in the ideas suggested by them; and

(f) the geographic area in Ontario in which the corporate name is likely to be used.

4. A corporation may have a name similar to that of another body corporate where the corporation is not or will not be affiliated with the body corporate if,

(a) that corporate name relates to a corporation that is the successor to the business of the body corporate and the body corporate has ceased or will cease to carry on business under that name; or

(b) the body corporate undertakes in writing to dissolve forthwith or to change its name before the corporation proposing to use the name commences to use it,

and the corporate name sets out in numerals the year of acquisition of the name in parentheses, words, numerals, or initials are added, deleted or substituted, as the case may be, or the name is varied by substituting one of the legal elements required under subsection 10(1) of the Act or their corresponding abbreviations.

5. A corporation may have a name similar to that of another body corporate where the corporation is affiliated with that body corporate.

6. (1) Except as provided in subsection (2) and section 10, no corporation may acquire a name identical to the name or former name of another body corporate, whether in existence or not, unless,

(a) the body corporate was incorporated under the laws of a jurisdiction outside Ontario and has never carried on any activities or identified itself in Ontario; or

(b) at least ten years have elapsed since the body corporate was dissolved or changed its name.

(2) A corporation may acquire a name identical to that of another corporation if a person who is authorized to practise law in Ontario provides a legal opinion stating that,

(a) neither corporation is an offering corporation;

(b) the corporations are affiliated or associated with one another or are controlled by related persons;

(c) the corporation that acquires the name is a successor to the business of the other corporation; and

(d) the other corporation has been dissolved or has changed its name.

O. Reg. 627/93, s. 1; 59/07, s. 1

7. For the purpose of acquisition of a name, the addition or deletion of punctuation marks or other symbols does not make a name different but a name is not identical for the purpose of section 6 if words, numerals or initials are added, deleted or substituted or the legal element of the name is varied by substituting one of the other legal elements required under subsection 10(1) of the Act or their corresponding abbreviations.

O. Reg. 627/93, s. 2

7.1 (1) Subsequent to incorporation, the current corporate name set out in the articles or other documents sent to the Director under the Act shall be identical to,

(a) the name set out in the certificate of incorporation if the name has not been changed; or

(b) the name set out in the most recent certificate changing the name otherwise.

(2) For the purpose of subsection (1), a name is not identical if there is any variation in spacing or punctuation marks or other marks.

O. Reg. 627/93, s. 2

8. A corporation may have a name similar to that of a known,

(a) trust;

(b) association;

(c) partnership; or

(d) sole proprietorship,

or a known name under which any of them carries on business or identifies itself if,

(e) the corporate name relates to a proposed corporation that is the successor to the business carried on under the name and the user of the name has ceased or will cease to carry on business under the name; or

(f) the known trust, association, partnership or sole proprietor undertakes in writing to dissolve forthwith or to change its name before the corporation proposing to use the name commences to use it.

9. A corporate name containing a word that is the same as or similar to the distinctive element of a trade-mark or name of another body corporate shall not for that reason alone be prohibited if,

(a) the body corporate consents to the use of the name; and

(b) the corporate name contains additional words or expressions to differentiate it from the body corporate and other users of the trade-mark or name.

10. The name of a corporation formed by the amalgamation of two or more corporations may be identical to the name of one of its amalgamating corporations, if the name is not a number name.

O. Reg. 627/93, s. 3

11. (1) A corporate name shall not be,

(a) too general;

(b) only descriptive, in any language, of the quality, function or other characterestics of the goods or services in which the corporation deals or intends to deal;

(c) primarily or only the name or surname of an individual who is living or has died within thirty years preceding the date of filing the articles; or

(d) primarily or only a geographic name used alone,

unless the proposed corporate name has been in continuous use for at least twenty years prior to the date of filing the articles or the proposed corporate name has through use acquired a meaning which renders the name distinctive.

(2) A corporate name shall not be primarily or only a combination of punctuation marks or other marks that are permitted under section 20 and the first character of the name shall be a letter of the Roman alphabet or an Arabic numeral.

O. Reg. 246/05, s. 1

12. (1) A corporate name shall not contain a word or expression, an element of which is the family name of an individual whether or not preceded by his or her given name or initials, unless the individual or his or her heir, executor, administrator, assigns or guardian consents in writing to the use of the name and the individual has, had or will have a material interest in the business.

(2) Subsection (1) does not apply where the corporation that will use the proposed name is the successor or affiliate of a person other than an individual that has as an element of its name, the family name, where,

(a) the person consents in writing to the use of the name;

(b) if the proposed name would contravene clause 9(1)(b) of the Act, the person undertakes in writing to dissolve forthwith or change its name to some other name that complies with clause 9(1)(b) of the Act before the corporation proposing to use the name commences to use it; and

(c) the proposed name does not contravene section 6.

13. No word or expression in any language, that is obscene or connotes a business that is scandalous, obscene or immoral or that is otherwise objectionable on public grounds, shall be used in a corporate name.

14. No word, expression or abbreviation, the use of which is prohibited or restricted under an Act or Regulation of the Parliament of Canada or a province or territory of Canada, unless the restriction is satisfied, shall be used in a corporate name.

15. The following words and expressions shall not be used in a corporate name:

1. "Amalgamated", "fusionné" or any other related word or expression in French, unless the corporation is an amalgamated corporation resulting from the amalgamation of two or more corporations.

2. "Architect", "architecte", "architectural", "d'architecture" or any variation thereof, where such word suggests the practice of the profession, except with the written consent of the Council of the Ontario Association of Architects.

3. "Association".

4. [Revoked O. Reg. 190/99, s. 1.]

5. "College", "collège", "institute", "institut", "university" or "université" if the word would lead to the inference that the corporation is a university, college of applied arts and technology or other post-secondary educational institution.

6. "Condominium", "condominial" or any abbreviation or derivation thereof.

7. "Co-operative", "coopérative" or any abbreviation or derivation thereof.

8. "Council" or "conseil".

9. Digits or words that would lead to the inference that the name is a number name.

10. "Engineer", "ingénieur", "engineering", "génie", "ingénierie" or any variation thereof, where such word suggests the practice of the profession, except with the written consent of the Association of Professional Engineers of Ontario.

11. [Repealed O. Reg. 246/05, s. 2.]

12. "Veteran", "ancien combattant" or any abbreviation or derivation thereof unless there has been continuous use of the name for a period of at least twenty years prior to the acquisition of the name.

13. Numerals indicating the year of incorporation unless section 4 applies or it is a year of amalgamation of the corporation.

14. Any word or expression that would lead to the inference that the corporation is not a business corporation to which the Act applies.

O. Reg. 627/93, s. 4; 190/99, s. 1; 246/05, s. 2

16. (1) No word or expression that suggests that a corporation,

(a) is connected with the Crown or the Government of Canada, a municipality, any province or territory of Canada or any department, Ministry, branch, bureau, service, board, agency, commission or activity of any such government or municipality;

(b) is sponsored or controlled by or is associated or affiliated with a university or an association of accountants, architects, engineers, lawyers, physicians, surgeons or any other professional association recognized by the laws of Canada or a province or territory of Canada; or

(c) carries on the business of a bank, loan company, insurance company, trust company, other financial intermediary or a stock exchange that is regulated by a law of Canada or a province or territory of Canada,

shall be used in a corporate name without the consent in writing of the appropriate authority, university or professional association, as the case may be.

(2) No word or expression that suggests that a corporation is connected with a political party or leader of a political party, where the purpose for which the corporation is incorporated is of a political nature, shall be used in a corporate name.

17. No word or expression that misdescribes, in any language,

(a) the business, goods or services in association with which the corporate name is proposed to be used;

(b) the conditions under which goods or services will be produced or supplied or the persons to be employed in the production or supply of these goods or services; or

(c) the place of origin of the goods or services produced or supplied by the corporation,

shall be used in a corporate name.

18. (1) The following documents shall accompany any articles containing a proposed name for a corporation or a change of corporate name:

1. An Ontario biased or weighted computer printed search report for the proposed name from the NUANS automated name search system maintained by the Department of Consumer and Corporate Affairs, Canada dated not more than ninety days prior to the submission of the articles.

2. Any consent or consent and undertaking required under the Act or this Regulation and, if applicable, in the Form prescribed.

(1.1) Despite paragraph 1 of subsection 18(1), if articles containing a proposed name for a corporation are filed with the Director electronically under section 24.1, they shall be accompanied by the NUANS report reference number, the date of the report and the proposed name searched, and not the report itself.

(2) If a proposed name is in an English form and a French form, separate computer-printed search reports shall be provided for the English form and the French form of the name, unless the English and French forms of the name are identical and the legal element required under subsection 10(1) of the Act that is used in the French form of the name is the French version of the legal element used in the English form of the name.

(3) Subsections (1) and (2) apply to an application for revival under section 241 of the Act if the articles change the name of the corporation or at least 10 years have elapsed since the corporation was dissolved.

(4) No name that is identified in a computer printed search report as proposed or otherwise where a computer printed search report is not submitted shall be used as a corporate name by a person other than the one who proposed the name unless a consent in writing has been obtained from the person who first proposed the name.

O. Reg. 627/93, s. 5; 637/94, s. 1; 400/95, s. 1; 288/00, s. 1; 59/07, s. 2

19. [Revoked O. Reg. 400/95, s. 2.]

20. For the purposes of subsection 10(3) of the Act, the following punctuation marks and other marks are the only ones permitted as part of the name of a corporation:

! “ ” << >> # $ % & ’ ( ) * + , - . / \ : ; < = > ? [ ] , ’ ‘ ^ ’’ @

O. Reg. 627/93, s. 6; 246/05, s. 3

21. (1) The name of a corporation shall not exceed 120 characters in length, including punctuation marks and spaces.

(2) The name of a corporation shall be set out in articles or applications filed with the Director in block capital letters and with only one space between each word.

O. Reg. 246/05, s. 4

22. A name set out in the articles pursuant to subsection 10(4) of the Act shall be a direct translation of the corporate name but changes may be made to ensure that the name is idiomatically correct.

22.1 If articles set out an English form and a French form for a name of a corporation, the “/” mark shall separate the two forms of the name.

O. Reg. 627/93, s. 7

SUBSIDIARY BODY CORPORATE HOLDING SHARES OF HOLDING CORPORATION

[Heading amended O. Reg. 59/07, s. 3.]

23. In sections 23.1, 23.2 and 23.3,

“delivery shares” means shares issued by a corporation to one of its subsidiary bodies corporate for the purposes of an acquisition under subsection 29(9) of the Act.

O. Reg. 190/99, s. 2; 59/07, s. 3

23.1 The following conditions are prescribed for the purposes of subsection 29(9) of the Act:

1. The consideration received by the corporation for the delivery shares must be equal to the fair market value of those shares at the time of their issuance.

2. The class of shares of which the delivery shares are a part must be widely held and shares of that class must be actively traded on any of the following stock exchanges in Canada:

    i. The TSX Venture Exchange.

    ii. The Toronto Stock Exchange.

3. The sole purpose of effecting the acquisition by the subsidiary body corporate of delivery shares is to transfer them to the shareholders of another body corporate.

4. Immediately before the acquisition of the delivery shares by the subsidiary body corporate, the other body corporate and its shareholders must deal at arm's length, as determined under the *Income Tax Act* (Canada), with the corporation and the subsidiary body corporate.

5. Immediately before the acquisition of the delivery shares by the subsidiary body corporate, the subsidiary body corporate and the other body corporate must not be resident in Canada for the purposes of the *Income Tax Act* (Canada).

O. Reg. 59/07, s. 3

23.2 The following conditions are prescribed for the purposes of subsection 29(10) of the Act:

1. The subsidiary body corporate shall acquire the delivery shares in trust for the shareholders of the other body corporate, such that the beneficial interest in the delivery shares is acquired by those shareholders and not by the subsidiary body corporate.

2. Immediately after the acquisition of the delivery shares by the subsidiary body corporate, the subsidiary body corporate shall transfer the delivery shares to the shareholders of the other body corporate.

3. Immediately after the transfer of the delivery shares to the shareholders of the other body corporate, the subsidiary body corporate and the other body corporate must not be resident in Canada for the purposes of the *Income Tax Act* (Canada).

4. Immediately after the transfer of the delivery shares to the shareholders of the other body corporate, the other body corporate must be a subsidiary body corporate of the subsidiary body corporate.

O. Reg. 59/07, s. 3

23.3 (1) If a condition prescribed for the purposes of subsection 29(9) or (10) of the Act was not met, the following consequences apply for the purposes of subsection 29(11) of the Act:

1. The corporation shall,

    i. cancel the delivery shares, or

    ii. if the articles of the corporation limit the number of authorized shares, restore the delivery shares to the status of authorized but unissued shares.

2. The corporation shall return the consideration received by it for the delivery shares to the subsidiary body corporate.

3. The corporation shall cancel the entry for the consideration in the stated capital account for the class of shares of which the delivery shares were a part.

(2) The corporation shall fulfil the requirements set out in paragraphs 1, 2 and 3 of subsection (1) within 30 days after the day the unmet condition was required to have been met.

O. Reg. 59/07, s. 3

SHAREHOLDER PROPOSALS

[Heading added O. Reg. 59/07, s. 3.]

23.4 For the purposes of subsection 99(3.1) of the Act, the proposal referred to in subsection 99(2) of the Act and the statement referred to in subsection 99(3) of the Act shall together not exceed 500 words.

O. Reg. 59/07, s. 3

FORM OF DOCUMENTS

24. (1) All documents sent to the Director or filed in the office of the Director including all affidavits, applications, assurances, balance sheets, by-laws, consents, dissents, forms, notices and statements shall be printed, typewritten or reproduced legibly and, in the opinion of the Director, suitable for photographing on microfilm, upon one side of good quality white paper that is,

(a) 210 millimetres by 297 millimetres with a margin of 30 millimetres on the left-hand side; or

(b) 8½ inches by 11 inches, with a margin of 1¼ inches on the left-hand side.

(2) A document consisting of two or more pages shall have no backing or binding, and be stapled in the upper left-hand corner and each page shall be numbered consecutively.

(3) Any document that is sent to the Director shall be on good quality white paper of the size prescribed in subsection (1) that is capable of being endorsed by the Director without smudging.

(4) Articles, applications or statements filed with the Director requiring the signature of one or more persons shall be signed manually by each such person and not by an attorney.

24.1 (1) Only articles of incorporation and their supporting documents may be submitted in electronic format for filing with the Director.

(2) Articles of incorporation and their supporting documents may be submitted in electronic format for filing with the Director if,

(a) the person submits them in a format compatible with the technical requirements established by the Director;

(b) the corporation agrees to keep a paper or electronic copy of the NUANS report referred to in subsection 18(1) and any consent or consent and undertaking required under the Act or the regulations at the corporation's registered office and to permit any person to inspect and copy the documents during the corporation's normal business hours; and

(c) the corporation agrees that, upon receipt of a written notice from the Director, it shall provide the Director or any other person specified in the notice with a copy of any of the documents referred to in clause (b) within the time period set out in the notice.

(3) Articles submitted in electronic format are not required to be signed.

O. Reg. 288/00, s. 2; 246/05, s. 5

24.2 (1) Only restated articles may be submitted to the Director by fax.

(2) Restated articles shall not be submitted to the Director by fax unless the person submitting them has a deposit account in good standing with the Director.

O. Reg. 288/00, s. 2

Designating Officers

25. A director, deputy director or manager of the Ministry whose duties relate to the administration of the Act may sign any certificate required or authorized by the Act.

O. Reg. 13/09, s. 1

"Resident Canadian" Class of Persons Prescribed

26. For the purposes of clause (b) of the definition of "resident Canadian" in subsection 1(1) of the Act, the following classes of persons are prescribed:

1. Full-time employees of the Government of Canada, a province or a territory of Canada or of an agency of any such government or of a federal or provincial crown corporation.

2. Full-time employees of a body corporate,

   (i) of which more than 50 per cent of the voting securities are beneficially owned or over which control or direction is exercised by resident Canadians, or

   (ii) a majority of directors of which are resident Canadians,

   where the principal reason for the residence outside Canada is to act as such employees.

3. Full-time students at a university outside of Canada or at another educational institution outside of Canada recognized by the province.

4. Full-time employees of an international association or organization of which Canada is a member.

5. Persons who were, at the time of reaching their 60th birthday, ordinarily resident in Canada and have been resident outside of Canada since that time.

O. Reg. 400/95, s. 3

Proxies and Proxy Solicitation Form of Proxy

27. (1) A form of proxy required by section 111 and subsection 112(2) of the Act to be sent to shareholders and to be filed with the Commission shall indicate in bold-face type,

(a) the meeting at which it is to be used; and

(b) whether the proxy is solicited by or on behalf of the management of the offering corporation,

and shall provide a designated blank space for dating the form of proxy and if the date is not inserted in the space the proxy shall be deemed to be dated on the day on which it is mailed.

(2) A form of proxy shall indicate in bold-face type that the shareholder may appoint a proxyholder other than any person designated in the form of proxy to attend and act on the shareholder's behalf at the meeting and shall contain instructions as to the manner in which the shareholder may do so.

(3) If a form of proxy shows a person as designated proxyholder, it shall provide a means for the shareholder to designate some other person as proxyholder.

(4) A form of proxy shall provide a means for the shareholder to specify that the shares registered in the shareholder's name shall be voted for or against each matter or group of related matters identified in the notice of meeting, a management information circular, a dissident's information circular or a proposal under section 99 of the Act, other than the appointment of an auditor, the remuneration of the auditor and the election of directors.

(5) A form of proxy may confer authority as to a matter for which a choice is not specified by the shareholder in accordance with subsection (4) if the form of proxy, the management information circular or the dissident's information circular states in bold-face type how the proxyholder will vote the shares in respect of each matter or group of related matters.

(6) A form of proxy shall provide a means for the shareholder to specify that the shares registered in the shareholder's name shall be voted or withheld from voting in respect of the appointment of an auditor, the remuneration of the auditor or the election of directors.

(7) A form of proxy, a management information circular or a dissident's information circular shall state that the shares represented by the proxy will be voted or withheld from voting in accordance with the instructions of the shareholder on any ballot that may be called for and that, if the shareholder specifies a choice with respect to any matter to be acted upon, the shares shall be voted accordingly.

(8) Subsections (2) to (7) apply only to forms of proxy required by section 111 and subsection 112(2) of the Act.

28. (1) Discretionary authority may be conferred by way of a form of proxy in respect of amendments or variations to matters identified in the notice of meeting or other matters that may properly come before the meeting where,

(a) the person by or on whose behalf the solicitation is made is not aware within a reasonable time before the solicitation that the amendments or other matters are to be presented for action at the meeting; and

(b) the form of proxy, the management information circular or the dissident's information circular states specifically that it confers such discretionary authority.

(2) Authority to vote shall not be conferred,

(a) in respect of the appointment of an auditor or the election of a director unless a good faith proposed nominee for the appointment or election is named in the form of proxy, a management information circular, a dissident's information circular or a proposal under section 99 of the Act; or

(b) at any meeting other than the meeting specified in the notice of meeting or any adjournment thereof.

(3) This section applies only to forms of proxy required by section 111 and subsection 112(2) of the Act.

29. A form of proxy, other than that required by section 111 and subsection 112(2) of the Act, shall indicate,

(a) the meeting at which it is to be used;

(b) whether the proxy is solicited by or on behalf of management of the corporation; and

(c) the powers granted under the proxy.

29.1 For the purposes of clause (i) of the definition of "solicit" and "solicitation" in section 109 of the Act, a prescribed public announcement is a public announcement that is made by,

(a) a speech in a public forum; or

(b) a press release, an opinion, a statement or an advertisement,

(i) provided through a broadcast medium or by a telephonic, electronic or other communication facility, or

(ii) appearing in a newspaper, a magazine or another publication generally available to the public.

O. Reg. 59/07, s. 4

29.2 (1) For the purposes of clause (j) of the definition of "solicit" and "solicitation" in section 109 of the Act, a communication made to shareholders of the corporation is not included in the meaning of "solicit" or "solicitation",

(a) in the situation where the person making the communication does not seek, directly or indirectly, the power to act as a proxy for a shareholder;

(b) in the set of circumstances set out in subsection (2); and

(c) in the set of circumstances set out in subsection (3).

(2) The following comprise the set of circumstances referred to in clause (1)(b):

1. The communication is,

i. a communication concerning the business and affairs, or the management of the business and affairs, of the corporation, an example of which would be a communication concerning proposals contained in a management proxy circular, or

ii. a communication concerning the organization of a dissident's proxy solicitation.

2. The communication is made by one or more shareholders of the corporation.

3. In the case of a communication referred to in subparagraph 1 i, the communication is not made by,

i. a shareholder who is an officer or director of the corporation, or who serves in a similar capacity, if the communication is financed directly or indirectly by the corporation,

ii. a shareholder who is a nominee, or who proposes a nominee, for election as a director, if the communication relates to the election of directors,

iii. a shareholder whose communication is in opposition to an amalgamation, arrangement, consolidation or other transaction recommended or approved by the board of directors of the corporation and who is proposing or intends to propose an alternative transaction to which the shareholder or an affiliate or associate of the shareholder is a party,

iv. a shareholder who, because of a material interest in the subject-matter to be voted on at a shareholders' meeting, is likely to receive a benefit from the approval or non-approval of the subject-matter, which benefit would not be shared rateably by all other holders of the same class of shares and does not arise from the shareholder's employment with the corporation, or

v. a person acting on behalf of a shareholder described in any of subparagraphs i to iv.

4. None of the shareholders making the communication nor a person acting on behalf of any of them sends a form of proxy to any of the shareholders to whom the communication is made.

(3) The following comprise the set of circumstances referred to in clause (1)(c):

1. The communication is made to shareholders of the corporation, as clients, by a person who gives financial, corporate governance or proxy voting advice in the ordinary course of business.

2. The communication concerns proxy voting advice.

3. The person making the communication discloses to the shareholders to whom the communication is made,

i. every significant relationship between the person and,

A. the corporation,

B. any of the affiliates of the corporation, or

C. a registered holder or beneficial owner of shares who has submitted a proposal pursuant to subsection 99(1) of the Act, and

ii. the material interest, if any, that the person has in relation to each matter on which the communication gives advice.

4. If the person making the communication receives any special commission or remuneration for giving the proxy voting advice, he or she receives it only from the shareholder or shareholders receiving the advice.

5. The proxy voting advice is not given on behalf of,

i. a person soliciting proxies, or

ii. a nominee for election as a director of the corporation.

O. Reg. 59/07, s. 4

29.3 The following circumstances are prescribed for the purposes of subsection 112(1.2) of the Act:

1. The solicitation conveyed by public broadcast, speech or publication contains the information described in paragraphs 1 to 6 and 8 of section 33.

2. Before making the solicitation, the person making it sends to the corporation the information described in paragraphs 1 to 6 and 8 of section 33 and a copy of all related written communications.

O. Reg. 59/07, s. 4

Management Information Circular

30. A management information circular shall contain the following information:

Revocability of Proxy

1. A statement of the right of the shareholder to revoke a proxy under subsection 110(4) of the Act and the method by which it may be exercised.

Persons Making the Solicitation

2. Where applicable, a statement that the execution or exercise of a proxy does not constitute a written objection for the purposes of subsection 185(6) of the Act.

3. A statement, in bold-face type, to the effect that the solicitation is made by or on behalf of the management of the corporation.

4. The name of every director of the corporation who has informed the management in writing that he or she intends to oppose any action intended to be taken by the management and the action that he or she intends to oppose.

5. The method of solicitation, if otherwise than by mail, and, if the solicitation is to be made by specially engaged employees or agents, the material features of any contract or arrangement and the cost or anticipated cost thereof.

6. The name of the person by whom the cost of the solicitation has been or will be borne, directly or indirectly.

Interest of Certain Persons in Matters to be Acted Upon

7. Details of every material interest, direct or indirect, of,

i. each person who was a director or officer of the corporation at any time since the beginning of its last completed financial year,

ii. each proposed management nominee for election as a director of the corporation, and

iii. each associate of every person referred to in subparagraphs i and ii,

in every matter to be acted upon at the meeting other than the election of directors or the appointment of an auditor.

Voting Securities and Principal Holders of Voting Securities

8. The number of shares of each class of shares of the corporation entitled to be voted at the meeting and the number of votes to which each share of each such class is entitled on each matter to be acted upon at the meeting.

9. The name of each person who, to the knowledge of the directors or officers of the corporation, beneficially owns or exercises control or direction over securities carrying more than 10 per cent of the voting rights attached to any class of outstanding voting securities of the corporation entitled to be voted at the meeting, the approximate number of the securities so owned, controlled or directed by each such person and the percentage of the class of outstanding voting securities of the corporation represented by the number of voting securities so owned, controlled or directed.

10. If a change in the effective control of the corporation has occurred since the beginning of its last financial year, the name of the person who, to the knowledge of the directors or officers of the corporation, acquired control, the date and description of the transaction in which control was acquired and the percentage of voting rights attached to all outstanding voting securities entitled to be voted at the meeting now owned, controlled or directed by the person.

11. The percentage of votes required for the approval of any matter to be submitted to a vote of shareholders that requires approval by more than a majority of the votes

cast on the matter at the meeting other than the election of directors or the appointment and remuneration of an auditor.

Election of Directors

12. If directors are to be elected, a statement of any right of any class of shareholders to elect a specified number of directors or to cumulate their votes and of any conditions precedent to the exercise thereof.

13. In tabular form, if directors are to be elected, so far as practicable, with respect to each person proposed by management for nomination for election as a director and each director whose term of office will continue after the meeting,

i. the name of each person, the time when his or her term of office or the term of office for which he or she is a proposed nominee expires and all other major positions and offices with the corporation or any of its significant affiliates currently held by the person, indicating which of the persons are proposed nominees for election as directors at the meeting,

ii. the present principal occupation or employment of each such person, the name and principal business of any body corporate or other organization in which the occupation or employment is carried on and similar information as to all principal occupations or employments of each such person within the five preceding years, unless the person is now a director and was elected to his or her present term of office by a vote of shareholders at a meeting the notice of which was accompanied by an information circular containing that information,

iii. if any such person is or has been a director of the corporation, the period or periods during which the person has so served,

iv. the number of securities of each class of voting securities of the corporation and of its holding body corporate beneficially owned, directly or indirectly, or over which control or direction is exercised by each such person, and

v. if more than 10 per cent of the votes attached to voting securities of any class of the corporation or of its holding body corporate are beneficially owned or subject to control or direction by any such person and the person's associates, the number of each class of voting securities so owned, controlled or directed by the associates and the name of each associate.

14. The details of any contract, arrangement or understanding between any proposed management nominee and any other person, except the directors and officers of the corporation acting solely in such capacity, pursuant to which the nominee is to be elected, including the name of the other person.

Directors' and Officers' Remuneration

15. A statement of executive compensation completed in accordance with Form 40 of Regulation 1015 of Revised Regulations of Ontario, 1990, under the *Securities Act* and for the purposes of this item a reference to an issuer in subitem I.1 and items II to VI of the said Form 40 shall be deemed to read as a reference to a corporation.

16. If indemnification under section 136 of the Act was paid or became payable in the last complete financial period,

i. the amount paid or payable,

ii. the name and title of the individual indemnified or to be indemnified, and

iii. the circumstances that gave rise to the indemnity.

17. If insurance referred to in subsection 136(4) of the Act was purchased during the last completed financial year,

i. the amount or, where there is a comprehensive liability policy, the approximate amount of premium paid by the corporation in respect of directors as a group and officers as a group,

ii. the aggregate amount of premium, if any, paid by the individuals in each such group,

iii. the total amount of insurance purchased for each such group, and

iv. a summary of any deductibility or co-insurance clause or other provision in the insurance contract that exposes the corporation to liability in addition to the payment of the premiums.

Indebtedness of Directors and Officers

18. A statement in respect of,

i. each director and senior officer of the corporation,

ii. each proposed management nominee for election as a director of the corporation, and

iii. each associate of any director, senior officer or proposed management nominee,

who is or has been indebted to the corporation or any of its subsidiaries at any time during the last completed financial year, of the largest aggregate amount of debt outstanding at any time since the beginning of the corporation's last completed financial year, the nature of the debt, details of the transaction in which it was incurred, the amount currently outstanding and the rate of interest paid or charged thereon, but no disclosure need be made of debts considered to be routine indebtedness in the circumstances or in repect of a person whose aggregate debt did not exceed $10,000 at any time during the period.

19. State the name and home address in full or, alternatively, solely the municipality of residence or postal address of each person or company whose indebtedness is described in paragraph 18, 21, 22 or 23.

20. If a corporation makes loans to employees generally, whether or not in the ordinary course of business, loans shall be considered to be routine indebtedness if made on terms, including those as to interest or collateral, no more favourable to the borrower than the terms on which loans are made by the issuer to employees generally, but the amount at any time remaining unpaid under such loans to any one director, senior officer or proposed management nominee together with his or her associates that are treated as routine indebtedness hereunder shall not exceed $25,000.

21. Whether or not the corporation makes loans in the ordinary course of business, a loan to a director or senior officer shall be considered to be routine indebtedness if,

i. the borrower is a full-time employee of the issuer,

ii. the loan is fully secured against the residence of the borrower, and

iii. the amount of the loan does not exceed the annual salary of the borrower.

22. Where a corporation makes loans in the ordinary course of business, a loan shall be considered to be routine indebtedness if it is made to a person or company, other than a full-time employee of the corporation, and if it,

i. is made on substantially the same terms, including those as to interest rate and collateral, as were available when the loan was made to other customers of the corporation with comparable credit ratings, and

ii. involves no more than usual risks of collectibility.

23. Indebtedness arising by reason of purchases made on usual trade terms or of ordinary travel or expense advances or for similar reasons shall be considered to be routine indebtedness if the repayment arrangements are in accord with usual commercial practice.

Interests of Insiders In Material Transactions

24. The details including, where practicable, the approximate amount of any material interest, direct or indirect, of,

i. a director or senior officer of the corporation,

ii. a proposed management nominee for election as a director of the corporation,

iii. a shareholder required to be named by paragraph 9, and

iv. an associate or affiliate of every person referred to in subparagraphs i, ii and iii,

in any transaction since the beginning of the corporation's last completed financial year or in any proposed transaction that has materially affected or will materially affect the corporation or any of its affiliates, but,

v. an interest arising from the ownership of securities of the corporation may be omitted unless the security holder receives a benefit or advantage not shared rateably by all holders of the same class of security or all holders of the same class of security who are resident in Canada,

and any transaction or interest may be omitted where,

vi. the rate or charges involved in the transaction are fixed by law or determined by competitive bids,

vii. the interest of the person in the transaction is solely that of a director of another body corporate that is a party to the transaction,

viii. the transaction involves services as a bank or other depository of funds, transfer agent, registrar, trustee under a trust indenture or other similar services, or;

ix. the transaction does not involve remuneration for services and,

A. the interest of the person results from the beneficial ownership of less than 10 per cent of any class of security of another body corporate that is a party to the transaction,

B. the transaction is in the ordinary course of business of the corporation or any of its affiliates, and

C. the amount of the transaction or series of transactions is less than 10 per cent of the total sales or purchases, as the case may be, of the corporation and its affiliates for the last completed financial year and details of transactions not omitted under subparagraphs v to ix that involve remuneration paid, directly or indirectly, to any of the persons referred to in this paragraph for services in any capacity shall be included, unless the interest of the person arises solely from the beneficial ownership of less than 10 per cent of any class of shares of another body corporate furnishing the services to the body corporation or its affiliates.

25. Details of each transaction referred to in paragraph 24, the name and address of each person whose interest in the transaction is disclosed and the nature of the relationship by reason of which the interest is required to be disclosed.

26. Where a transaction referred to in paragraph 24 involves the purchase or sale of assets by the corporation or any affiliate otherwise than in the ordinary course of business, the cost of the assets to the purchaser and the cost of the assets to the seller if acquired by the seller within the two years prior to the transaction.

27. Details of a material underwriting discount or commission with respect to the sale of securities by the corporation where any person referred to in paragraph 24 has contracted or will contract with the corporation in respect of an underwriting or is an associate or affiliate of a person that has so contracted or will so contract.

Appointment of Auditors

28. If a new auditor is proposed for appointment, the name of the proposed auditor, the name of each auditor appointed within the preceding five years and the date on which each auditor was first appointed.

Management Contracts

29. Where a person other than the directors or officers of the corporation or any of its affiliates manages the corporation or any of its subsidiaries,

i. details of the management agreement or arrangement including the name and address of every person who is a party to the agreement or arrangement or who is responsible to perform it,

ii. the names and addresses of the insiders of a body corporate with which the corporation or any of its subsidiaries has a management agreement or arrangement,

iii. the amounts paid or payable by the corporation and any of its subsidiaries to a person named under subparagraph i since the beginning of the corporation's last completed financial year,

iv. details of any debt owed to the corporation or any of its subsidiaries by a person referred to in subparagraphs i and ii and that person's associates and affiliates that was outstanding at any time since the beginning of the corporation's last completed financial year, and

v. details of any transaction or arrangement, other than one referred to in subparagraph i, with the corporation or any of its subsidiaries since the beginning of the corporation's last completed financial year in which a person referred to in subparagraph i or ii has a material interest that would be required to be disclosed by paragraph 24,

and for the purposes of this paragraph,

vi. "details" of debt include the largest aggregate amount of debt outstanding at any time during the period, the nature of the debt, the details of the transaction in which it was incurred, the amount currently outstanding and the rate of interest paid or charged thereon,

vii. an amount owing for purchases, subject to usual trade terms, for ordinary travel and expense advances and for other transactions in the ordinary course of business may be omitted in determining debt, and

viii. a matter that is not material may be omitted.

Particulars of Matters to be Acted Upon

30. A statement of the rights of a shareholder to dissent under section 185 of the Act with respect to any matter to be acted upon at the meeting and a brief summary of the procedure to be followed.

31. If action is to be taken with respect to any matter other than the approval of minutes of an earlier meeting or the approval of financial statements, the substance of each such matter or group of related matters, to the extent it has not been described under another provision in this section, in sufficient detail to permit shareholders to form a reasoned judgment concerning the matter.

32. For the purpose of paragraph 31, where a reorganization or similar restructuring is involved, reference should be made to a prospectus form or other appropriate form under the *Securities Act*, including requirements with respect to financial statements, for guidance as to what is material.

33. For the purposes of paragraphs 30 and 31, if any such matter is not required to be submitted to a vote of the shareholders the reasons for so submitting it and the action intended to be taken by management in the event of a negative vote by the shareholders.

General

34. If the proceeds of an issue of securities were used for a purpose other than that stated in the document under which the securities were issued, the date of the document, the amount and designation of the securities so issued and details of the use made during the financial period of the proceeds.

35. If the corporation has amended its articles for a purpose set out in section 42 of the Act to restrict the issue, transfer or ownership of its shares, the general nature of the restrictions.

36. Details of every action brought or taken under section 246 or 248 of the Act to which the corporation is a party.

37. Details of any financial assistance, in circumstances permitted by subsection 20(1) of the Act or referred to in clause 20(2)(e) of the Act, given by a corporation since the beginning of its last completed financial year,

i. to a shareholder of the corporation or any of its affiliates who is not a director, officer or employee thereof, or to an associate of any shareholder,

ii. to any group of employees other than directors or officers in connection with the purchase of shares issued or to be issued by the corporation, or

iii. to any other person in connection with a purchase of shares issued or to be issued by the corporation,

if the giving of the assistance was material to the corporation or any of its affiliates or to the recipient of the assistance.

38. A statement, signed by a director or officer of the corporation, that the contents and the sending of the circular have been approved by the directors.

31. A management information circular that is filed with the Commission pursuant to subsection 112(2) of the Act shall be accompanied by a statement signed by a director or officer that a copy of the circular has been sent to,

(a) each director;

(b) each shareholder entitled to notice of the meeting to which the circular relates; and

(c) the auditor of the corporation.

Dissident's Information Circular

32. For the purposes of section 33, **"dissident"** means any person, other than a person who is part of the management of the corporation or its affiliates and associates, by or on behalf of whom a solicitation is made, and includes a committee or group that solicits proxies, any members of the committee or group, and any person whether or not named as a member, who acting alone or with one or more other persons, directly or indirectly, engages in organizing, directing or financing any such committee or group, except,

(a) a person who contributes not more than $250 and who does not otherwise participate in the solicitation;

(b) a bank or other lending institution or a broker or dealer that, in the ordinary course of business, lends money or executes orders for the purchase or sale of shares and that does not otherwise participate in the solicitation;

(c) a person who is employed to solicit and whose activities are limited to the performance of duties in the course of such employment;

(d) a person who only sends soliciting material or performs other ministerial or clerical duties;

(e) a person employed in the capacity of lawyer, accountant, advertiser, public relations or financial adviser and whose activities are limited to the performance of duties in the course of such employment; and

(f) an officer or director of, or person employed by, a person by or on behalf of whom a solicitation is made if he or she does not directly participate in the solicitation.

Contents Of Dissident's Information Circular

33. A dissident's information circular shall contain the following information:

1. The name and address of the corporation to which the solicitation relates.

2. The information required by paragraphs 1, 2, 5 and 6 of section 30.

3. Details of the identity and background of each dissident, including,

i. the dissident's name and address,

ii. the dissident's present principal occupation or employment and the name, principal business and address of any body corporate or other person in which the occupation or employment is carried on,

iii. all material occupations, offices or employments during the preceding five years, with starting and ending dates of each and the name, principal business and address of the body corporate or other business organization in which each such occupation, office or employment was carried on, and

iv. whether the dissident is or has been a dissident within the preceding ten years and, if so, the body corporate involved, the principals and the dissident's relationship to them, the subject matter and the outcome of the solicitation.

4. The circumstances under which each dissident became involved in the solicitation and the nature and extent of activities as a dissident.

5. The information required by paragraphs 9, 10 and 11 of section 30, if known to a dissident.

6. Details of the interest of each dissident in the securities of the corporation to which the solicitation relates, including,

i. the number of securities of each class of voting securities of the corporation that the dissident owns beneficially, directly or indirectly, or over which the dissident exercises control or direction,

ii. the dates on which securities of the corporation were purchased or sold during the preceding two years, the amount purchased or sold on each date and the price at which they were purchased or sold,

iii. if any part of the purchase price or market value of any of the securities specified in subparagraph ii is represented by funds borrowed or otherwise obtained for the purpose of acquiring or holding the securities, the amount of the indebtedness as of the latest practicable date and a brief description of the transaction including the names of the parties, other than a bank, broker or dealer acting in the transaction in the ordinary course of business,

iv. whether the dissident is or was within the preceding year a party to a contract, arrangement or understanding with any person in respect of securities of the corporation, including joint ventures, loan or option arrangements, puts or calls, guarantees against loss or guarantees of profit, division of losses or profits or the giving or withholding of proxies and, if so, the names of the parties to, and the details of, the contract, arrangement or understanding,

v. the number of each class of securities of an affiliate of the corporation that the dissident owns beneficially, directly or indirectly, or over which the dissident exercises control or direction, and

vi. the number of securities of each class of securities of the corporation that each associate of the dissident beneficially, directly or indirectly, owns or exercises control or direction over and the name and address of each such associate.

7. If directors are to be elected, information required by paragraphs 7, 13, 14 and 24 of section 30, in respect of each proposed nominee for election as a director and his or her associates.

8. The information required by paragraphs 14 and 24 of section 30 in respect of each dissident and the dissident's associates.

9. Details of any contract, arrangement or understanding, including the names of the parties, between a dissident or the dissident's associates and any person with respect to,

i. future employment by the corporation or any of its affiliates, or

ii. future transactions to which the corporation or any of its affiliates will or may be a party.

34. If a dissident is a partnership, body corporate, association or other organization, the information required by paragraphs 3, 4, 6, 8 and 9 of section 33 to be included in a dissident's information circular shall be given in respect of each partner, officer and director and of each person who controls the dissident and who is not a dissident.

35. Information that is not known to a dissident and that cannot be reasonably ascertained by the dissident may be omitted from a dissident's information circular but the circumstances that render the information unavailable shall be disclosed therein.

36. (1) A dissident's information circular shall contain a statement, signed by a dissident or a person authorized by the dissident, that the contents and the sending of the circular have been approved by the dissident.

(2) A dissident's information circular that is filed with the Commission under subsection 112(2) of the Act shall be accompanied by a statement signed by the dissident or a person authorized by the dissident to the effect that,

(a) the circular complies with this Regulation; and

(b) a copy of the circular has been sent to each director, each shareholder entitled to notice of the meeting to which the circular relates, the auditor of the corporation and the corporation.

INFORMATION CIRCULARS — GENERAL

37. (1) The information in a management information circular or a dissident's information circular shall be given as of a specified date not more than thirty days prior to the date upon which the information circular is first sent to any of the shareholders of the corporation.

(2) The information contained in an information circular shall be clearly presented and the statements made therein shall be divided into groups according to subject matter and the various groups of statements shall be preceded by appropriate headings.

(3) The order of items set out in sections 30 and 33 need not be followed.

(4) Where practicable and appropriate, information required by sections 30 and 33 shall be presented in tabular form.

(5) All amounts required by sections 30 and 33 shall be stated in figures.

(6) Information required by more than one applicable item need not be repeated.

(7) No statement need be made in response to any item that is inapplicable and negative answers to any item may be omitted.

(8) There may be omitted from an information circular any information contained in any other information circular, notice of meeting or a form of proxy sent to the persons whose proxies were solicited in connection with the same meeting if reference is made to the particular document containing the information.

Financial Statements In Information Circular

38. (1) Where financial statements accompany or form part of an information circular, the statements shall be prepared in the manner prescribed for financial statements in Part XII of the Act.

(2) The financial statements referred to in subsection (1), if not reported upon by the auditor of the corporation, shall be accompanied by a report of the chief financial officer of the corporation stating that the financial statements have not been audited but have been prepared in accordance with Part XII of the Act.

Audit Exemption

39, 39.1 [Revoked O. Reg. 190/99, s. 3.]

Auditors and Financial Statements

40. (1) Subject to subsection (2), the financial statements referred to in Part XII of the Act shall be prepared in accordance with the standards, as they exist from time to time, set forth in the Handbook of the Canadian Institute of Chartered Accountants.

(2) An offering corporation may prepare the financial statements referred to in Part XII of the Act in accordance with such other standards as may be permitted in the rules made under section 143 of the *Securities Act*.

O. Reg. 246/05, s. 6; 648/05, s. 1

41. (1) Subject to subsection (2), the auditor's report referred to in Part XII of the Act shall be prepared in accordance with the standards, as they exist from time to time, set forth in the Handbook of the Canadian Institute of Chartered Accountants.

(2) The auditor's report of an offering corporation referred to in Part XII of the Act may be prepared in accordance with such other standards as may be permitted in the rules made under section 143 of the *Securities Act*.

O. Reg. 246/05, s. 6; 648/05, s. 2

42. (1) The financial statements referred to in clause 154(1)(a) of the Act shall include at least,

(a) a balance sheet;

(b) a statement of retained earnings;

(c) an income statement; and

(d) a statement of changes in financial position.

(2) Financial statements need not be designated by the names set out in subsection (1).

General

43. (0.1) For the purposes of subclause 177(1)(b)(ii) of the Act, articles of amalgamation may differ from the articles of the amalgamating holding corporation by providing for,

(a) a different name; or

(b) a different address where the registered office is to be located.

(1) For the purposes of subclause 177(2)(b)(ii) of the Act, articles of amalgamation may differ from the articles of the amalgamating subsidiary corporations by providing for,

(a) a different name;

(b) a different number or minimum and maximum number of directors;

(c) a different address where the registered office is to be located; or

(d) imposition, variation or elimination of any restrictions on the business that the amalgamated corporation may carry on or on the powers that the amalgamated corporation may exercise.

O. Reg. 190/99, s. 4

44. (1) Notice to the holders of affected securities under subsection 190(3) of the Act may be given by one publication a week for two consecutive weeks in a newspaper or newspapers having general circulation in the place where the corporation has,

(a) its registered office;

(b) its securities register;

(c) its register of transfers;

(d) any branch registers; and

(e) its principal place of business.

(2) The notice referred to in subsection (1) shall first be published not less than forty days prior to the date of the meeting and shall state,

(a) the date, time, place and purpose of the meeting;

(b) the place where the information circular and any other relevant material may be examined; and

(c) that the material will be sent to any holder of affected securities upon request.

Application To Court — Oppression Remedy

45. [Revoked O. Reg. 400/95, s. 5.]

Forms

46-54 [Revoked O. Reg. 288/00, s. 3.]

55. [Revoked O. Reg. 400/95, s. 5.]

56-62 [Revoked O. Reg. 288/00, s. 3.]

Fees

63-65.1 [Revoked O. Reg. 190/99, s. 5.]

REFUNDS

66. [Revoked O. Reg. 190/99, s. 5.]

SCHEDULE [REVOKED]

[Revoked O. Reg. 190/99, s. 6.]

Form 1–20 — [Revoked]

[Editor's Note: Forms 12 and 13 were revoked by O. Reg. 400/95. Form 20 was revoked by O. Reg. 190/99. All other forms in R.R.O. 1990, Reg. 62, were revoked by O. Reg. 288/00. See now O. Reg. 289/00, s. 2, and the forms under the heading "OBCA Forms", following.]

ONT. REG. 289/00 — FORMS

made under the *Business Corporations Act*

O. Reg. 289/00, as am. O. Reg. 441/02; 109/06; CTR 30 AU 10 - 1.

FORM OF DOCUMENTS

1. (1) All documents sent to the Director or filed in the office of the Director including all affidavits, applications, assurances, balance sheets, by-laws, consents, dissents, forms, notices and statements shall be printed, typewritten or reproduced legibly and, in the opinion of the Director, suitable for photographing on microfilm, upon one side of good quality white paper that is,

(a) 210 millimetres by 297 millimetres with a margin of 30 millimetres on the left-hand side; or

(b) 8 1/2 inches by 11 inches, with a margin of 1 1/4 inches on the left-hand side.

(2) A document consisting of two or more pages shall have no backing or binding, and be stapled in the upper left-hand corner and each page shall be numbered consecutively.

(3) A document that is sent to the Director shall be on good quality white paper of the size prescribed in subsection (1) that is capable of being endorsed by the Director without smudging.

(4) Articles, applications or statements filed with the Director requiring the signature of one or more persons shall be signed manually by each required person and not by an attorney.

FORMS

2. The following forms shall be in the form approved by the Minister:

1. Articles of incorporation.

2. A consent to act as first director, where required under subsection 5(2) of the Act.

3. A certificate of incorporation.

4. Articles of amendment made under section 171 of the Act.

5. Articles of amalgamation under section 178 of the Act.

6. Restated articles of incorporation under section 173 of the Act.

7. Articles of continuance under section 180 of the Act.

8. An application for authorization to continue in another jurisdiction under section 181 of the Act.

9. An application under section 181.1 of the Act for authorization to continue as a co-operative corporation under the *Co-operative Corporations Act*.

10. Articles of arrangement under section 183 of the Act.

11. Articles of reorganization under section 186 of the Act.

12. Articles of dissolution under subsection 238(1) of the Act.

13. Articles of dissolution under subsection 238(2) of the Act.

14. An application under subsection 144(4) of the Act rescinding an order made under subsection 144(3) of the Act to remove records from the registered office of the corporation.

15. Articles of revival under section 241 of the Act.

16. A notice concerning the winding up of a corporation under subsection 193(4) of the Act, a notice under subsection 205(2) of the Act or a notice under subsection 210(4) of the Act.

17. A statutory declaration under subsection 52(1) of the Act.

18. A statutory declaration under subsection 146(1) of the Act.

3. Articles of continuance under section 180 of the Act shall be accompanied by,

(a) a copy of the incorporating document of the body corporate, together with all amendments to the document, certified by the officer of the incorporating jurisdiction who is authorized to so certify;

(b) a letter of satisfaction, certificate of continuance or other document issued by the proper officer of the incorporating jurisdiction that indicates that the body corporate is authorized under the laws of the jurisdiction in which it was incorporated or continued to apply for articles of continuance; and

(c) except in the case of a body corporate incorporated or continued under the laws of another Canadian jurisdiction, a legal opinion to the effect that the laws of the jurisdiction to which the body corporate is subject authorize the body corporate to apply for articles of continuance.

4. An application for authorization to continue in another jurisdiction under section 181 of the Act shall be accompanied by,

(a) a consent from the Minister of Finance;

(b) if the corporation is an offering corporation, a consent from the Ontario Securities Commission; and

(c) except in the case of continuance under the laws of another Canadian jurisdiction, a legal opinion to the effect that the laws of the other jurisdiction meet the requirements set out in subsection 181(9) of the Act.

O. Reg. 109/06, s. 1

5. Articles of dissolution under subsection 238(1) or (2) of the Act shall be accompanied by a consent to the dissolution of the corporation, issued by the Minister of Finance.

O. Reg. 441/02, s. 1; 109/06, s. 2

6. (1) Articles of revival under section 241 of the Act shall be accompanied by,

(a) a consent to the revival of the corporation, issued by the Minister of Finance, if the corporation was dissolved by order under subsection 241(1) of the Act or a predecessor of that subsection;

(b) a consent to the revival of the corporation, issued by the Ontario Securities Commission, if the corporation was dissolved by order under subsection 241(2) of the Act or a predecessor of that subsection.

(2) If a corporation was dissolved by order under subsection 241(3) of the Act or a predecessor of that subsection, the Director may require that the articles of revival be accompanied by a consent to the revival of the corporation, issued by the Minister of Finance.

(3) If a corporation was dissolved by order under section 241 of the Act or a predecessor of that section, the Director may require that the articles of revival be accompanied by a statement in writing by the Public Guardian and Trustee that he or she has no objection to the revival of the corporation.

O. Reg. 109/06, s. 3; CTR 30 AU 10 - 1

7. A consent or undertaking given by a person pursuant to section 4, 8, 9, or 12 of Regulation 62 of the Revised Regulations of Ontario, 1990 may be in the form approved by the Minister.

ONT. REG. 665/05 — HEALTH PROFESSION CORPORATIONS

made under the *Business Corporations Act*

O. Reg. 665/05, as am. O. Reg. 263/14.

1. Definitions — In this Regulation,

"child", in relation to a shareholder of a health profession corporation, includes a person whom the shareholder has demonstrated a settled intention to treat as a child of his or her family, except under an arrangement where the child is placed for valuable consideration in a foster home by a person having lawful custody;

"family member" means, in relation to a shareholder of a health profession corporation, the shareholder's spouse, child or parent;

"dentist corporation" means a health profession corporation that holds a certificate of authorization issued by the Royal College of Dental Surgeons of Ontario under the *Regulated Health Professions Act, 1991* or under Schedule 2 to that Act;

"parent", in relation to a shareholder of a health profession corporation, includes a person who has demonstrated a settled intention to treat the shareholder as a child of his or her family, except under an arrangement where the child is placed for valuable consideration in a foster home by a person having lawful custody;

"physician corporation" means a health profession corporation that holds a certificate of authorization issued by the College of Physicians and Surgeons of Ontario under the *Regulated Health Professions Act, 1991* or under Schedule 2 to that Act;

"voting dentist shareholder" means, in relation to a dentist corporation, a member of the Royal College of Dental Surgeons of Ontario who owns voting shares of the corporation;

"voting physician shareholder" means, in relation to a physician corporation, a member of the College of Physicians and Surgeons of Ontario who owns voting shares of the corporation.

O. Reg. 263/14, s. 1

2. Physician corporations — **(1)** A physician corporation is exempt from the application of paragraph 1 of subsection 3.2(2) of the Act and, in lieu of that paragraph, the following rules apply:

1. Each issued and outstanding voting share of the corporation shall be legally and beneficially owned, directly or indirectly, by a member of the College of Physicians and Surgeons of Ontario.

2. Each issued and outstanding non-voting share of the corporation shall be owned in one of the following ways:

   i. It shall be legally and beneficially owned, directly or indirectly, by a member of the College of Physicians and Surgeons of Ontario.

ii. It shall be legally and beneficially owned, directly or indirectly, by a family member of a voting physician shareholder.

iii. It shall be owned legally by one or more individuals, as trustees, in trust for one or more children of a voting physician shareholder who are minors, as beneficiaries.

(2) A physician corporation and its directors and officers are exempt from the application of paragraph 2 of subsection 3.2(2) of the Act and, in lieu of that paragraph, the following rule applies:

1. All officers and directors of the corporation shall be shareholders of the corporation who are members of the College of Physicians and Surgeons of Ontario.

(3) A physician corporation is exempt from the application of subsection 3.2(4) of the Act and, in lieu of that subsection, the following rule applies:

1. An agreement or proxy that vests the right to vote the rights attached to a voting share of a physician corporation in a person other than a shareholder of the corporation who is a member of the College of Physicians and Surgeons of Ontario is void.

(4) A physician corporation and its shareholders are exempt from the application of subsection 3.2(5) of the Act and, in lieu of that subsection, the following rule applies:

1. A unanimous shareholder agreement in respect of a physician corporation is void unless each voting shareholder of the corporation is a member of the College of Physicians and Surgeons of Ontario and each non-voting shareholder of the corporation is,

   i. a member of the College of Physicians and Surgeons of Ontario,

   ii. a family member of a voting physician shareholder, or

   iii. a trustee under a trust described in subparagraph 2 iii of subsection 2(1).

(5) A non-voting shareholder of a physician corporation who is not a member of the College of Physicians and Surgeons of Ontario is exempt from the application of subsections 3.4(2), (4) and (6) of the Act.

(6) A physician corporation, its shareholders and its directors and officers are exempt from the application of subsection 108(5) of the Act and, in lieu of that subsection, the following rule applies:

1. A shareholder of a physician corporation who is a party to a unanimous shareholder agreement in respect of the corporation and who is a member of the College of Physicians and Surgeons of Ontario has all the rights, powers, duties and liabilities, whether arising under this Act or otherwise, of a director of the corporation to the extent that the agreement restricts the discretion or powers of the directors to manage or supervise the management of the business and affairs of the corporation, and the directors are thereby relieved of their duties and liabilities, including any liabilities under section 131 of the Act, to the same extent.

3. Dentist corporations — **(1)** A dentist corporation is exempt from the application of paragraph 1 of subsection 3.2(2) of the Act and, in lieu of that paragraph, the following rules apply:

1. Each issued and outstanding voting share of the corporation shall be legally and beneficially owned, directly or indirectly, by a member of Royal College of Dental Surgeons of Ontario.

2. Each issued and outstanding non-voting share of the corporation shall be owned in one of the following ways:

i. It shall be legally and beneficially owned, directly or indirectly, by a member of the Royal College of Dental Surgeons of Ontario.

ii. It shall be legally and beneficially owned, directly or indirectly, by a family member of a voting dentist shareholder.

iii. It shall be owned legally by one or more individuals, as trustees, in trust for one or more children of a voting dentist shareholder who are minors, as beneficiaries.

(2) A dentist corporation and its directors and officers are exempt from the application of paragraph 2 of subsection 3.2(2) of the Act and, in lieu of that paragraph, the following rule applies:

1. All officers and directors of the corporation shall be shareholders of the corporation who are members of the Royal College of Dental Surgeons of Ontario.

(3) A dentist corporation is exempt from the application of subsection 3.2(4) of the Act and, in lieu of that subsection, the following rule applies:

1. An agreement or proxy that vests the right to vote the rights attached to a voting share of a dentist corporation in a person other than a shareholder of the corporation who is a member of the Royal College of Dental Surgeons of Ontario is void.

(4) A dentist corporation and its shareholders are exempt from the application of subsection 3.2(5) of the Act and, in lieu of that subsection, the following rule applies:

1. A unanimous shareholder agreement in respect of a dentist corporation is void unless each voting shareholder of the corporation is a member of the Royal College of Dental Surgeons of Ontario and each non-voting shareholder of the corporation is,

i. a member of the Royal College of Dental Surgeons of Ontario,

ii. a family member of a voting dentist shareholder, or

iii. a trustee under a trust described in subparagraph 2 iii of subsection 3(1).

(5) A non-voting shareholder of a dentist corporation who is not a member of the Royal College of Dental Surgeons of Ontario is exempt from the application of subsections 3.4(2), (4) and (6) of the Act.

(6) A dentist corporation, its shareholders and its directors and officers are exempt from the application of subsection 108(5) of the Act and, in lieu of that subsection, the following rule applies:

1. A shareholder of a dentist corporation who is a party to a unanimous shareholder agreement in respect of the corporation and who is a member of the Royal College of Dental Surgeons of Ontario has all the rights, powers, duties and liabilities, whether arising under this Act or otherwise, of a director of the corporation to the extent that the agreement restricts the discretion or powers of the directors to manage or supervise the management of the business and affairs of the corporation, and the directors are thereby relieved of their duties and liabilities, including any liabilities under section 131 of the Act, to the same extent.

4. Commencement — This Regulation comes into force on January 1, 2006.

OBCA FORMS

Form 1 — Articles of Incorporation*

INSTRUCTIONS FOR COMPLETING

This form together with required supporting documents and fee, must be filed with the Ministry to incorporate an Ontario business corporation under the *Business Corporations Act*.

Articles in duplicate may be mailed to the Toronto address listed below. For over-the-counter service articles may be filed in person at the Toronto office or at some Land Registry/ServiceOntario offices in Ontario. For a list of locations see the "Offices That Endorse Articles Submitted Under the *Business Corporations Act*" information sheet or visit the Ministry's web site at: www.mgs.gov.on.ca. Choose your language preference, select "Services for Business" from the "Service Ontario" menu on the right hand side of the page, then choose "Company Information" from the services listed and scroll down to "Frequently Asked Questions".

Electronic Filing of Articles of Incorporation is available through Service Providers under contract with the Ministry of Government Services. For information about Service Providers visit the ServiceOntario website at: www.serviceontario.ca. Select "Gateway for Business" on the left-hand side of the page and then "Private-Sector Service Providers" from the "Other Resources" section on the right-hand side of the page.

FEE

$360.00 BY MAIL - Cheque or money order payable to the Minister of Finance.
IN PERSON – (at the Toronto office) – cash, cheque or money order payable to Minister of Finance, Visa, MasterCard, American Express or debit card. (If you are filing the documents at a Land Registry or ServiceOntario Office, call first to confirm whether credit or debit cards are acceptable).

There will be a service charge payable for any cheque returned as non-negotiable by a bank or financial institution.

SUPPORTING DOCUMENTS

NAME SEARCH

If you are incorporating under a name instead of a number name, you must obtain an Ontario-biased NUANS report for the proposed name. NUANS is a computerized search system that compares a proposed corporate name or trade-mark with databases of existing corporate bodies and trade-marks. This comparison determines the similarity that exists between the proposed name or mark and existing names in the database, and produces a listing of names that are found to be most similar. This search must be submitted together with the duplicate Articles of Incorporation within 90 days from production by the NUANS system. For example, articles submitted on November 28th could be accompanied by a NUANS name search report dated as early as August 30th, but not dated earlier.

The Companies and Personal Property Security Branch does not provide this search. Suppliers are listed in the Yellow Pages under the heading "Searchers of Records" or visit Industry Canada's NUANS site at, www.nuans.com for a list of registered search houses that can assist you with obtaining a NUANS search report and filing your corporate documents with the Ministry of Government Services. Please note the NUANS search **must be Ontario biased.**

It is the applicant's responsibility to check the search for similar/identical names and to obtain any consent that may be required. The Ministry will not grant a name that is identical to the current name or former name of another corporation operating in Ontario whether active or not, unless it has been more than ten years since the other corporation dissolved or changed its name. The only exception to this rule is when the corporation meets the requirements of Subsection 6(2) of Regulation 62 under the *Business Corporations Act*. In this case a legal opinion must accompany the articles being filed. The legal opinion must be on legal letterhead and must be signed by an individual lawyer (not a law clerk or law firm). It must also clearly indicate that the corporations involved comply with Subsection 6(2) by referring to each clause specifically.

07116E (06/2007)

BILINGUAL NAMES

When incorporating a corporation with an English and French form of the name a name search is required for each form of the name (English and French) unless the English and French forms of the name are identical and the legal element in the French form is the French version of the legal element in the English form (for example, INCORPOREE and INCORPORATED). There should be a forward slash (/) separating the two forms of the name.

NUMBER NAMES

You do not require a name search for a number name. In article one on the form, leave nine empty boxes, then type or print in block capital letters the word "ONTARIO" followed by one of the following legal elements: LIMITED, LIMITÉE, INCORPORATED, INCORPORÉE, CORPORATION or the corresponding abbreviation LTD., LTÉE, INC., or CORP. The Companies and Personal Property Security Branch will assign a number to the corporation.

COVERING LETTER

Enclose a covering letter setting out the name of a contact person, a return address and a telephone number. This will facilitate the processing of the articles should a question arise as to the content of the articles.

APPEARANCE OF DOCUMENTS

The Articles of Incorporation must be completed in duplicate on Form 1 as approved by the Minister. All documents must be legible and compatible with the microfilming process, with the information typed or hand printed in block capital letters, on one side of good quality white bond paper 8 ½" X 11".

The article headings are numbered 1 to 10 and must remain in that order. Do not leave out any of the headings. If a section does not apply type "nil" or "not applicable". When additional pages are required, due to lack of space, they should be the same size as all the other pages and should be inserted after the applicable heading with the same number as the heading page with the addition of alphabet characters to indicate sequence. For example, pages inserted after page 3 would be numbered 3A, 3B, etc.

ARTICLE 1 Set out the name of the corporation in block capital letters starting from the first box of the first line on the left with one letter per box and one empty box for a space. Punctuation marks are entered in separate boxes. Complete one line before starting in the first box of the next line. The name entered must be exactly the same as that on the name search report.

EAST SIDE INVESTMENT AND MANAG
EMENT LTD.

ARTICLE 2 The address (where multi-office building include room or suite number) of the registered office of the corporation must be set out in full including the street name, street number or R.R. #, municipality, province, country and the postal code. A post office box alone is not an acceptable address. If there is no street and number, set out the lot and concession or lot and plan numbers. The registered office must be in Ontario.

ARTICLE 3 Set out the number of directors. This can be a fixed number of directors (e.g.. 1) or a minimum and maximum number (e.g. minimum 1, maximum 10). Do not complete both.

ARTICLE 4 The name(s) (including first name, middle names and surname) and the address for service for each of the first directors must be set out. The address should include the street name, street number, suite (or R.R. #) municipality, province, country and postal code. Directors must be individuals, not corporations. State if the director(s) is/are Resident Canadian(s). At least 25 per cent of the directors must be resident Canadians (if 25% of the directors is not a whole number round up to the nearest whole number). Where a corporation has less than four directors, at least one must be a resident Canadian. The directors must be individuals, not corporations.

07116E (06/2007)

Form 2, Consent to Act as a First Director - A person listed as a director (article 4) who is not an incorporator (article 10) and therefore is not signing the form is required to complete a Form 2, Consent to Act as First Director. The completed and signed Form 2 must be available for inspection at the registered office of the corporation.

ARTICLE 5 Set out restrictions, if any, on the business the corporation may carry on or on the powers that the corporation may exercise. If none, state so.

ARTICLE 6 Set out the classes and any maximum number of shares that the corporation is authorized to issue. This item should be completed (e.g., unlimited common shares).

ARTICLE 7 Set out the rights, privileges, restrictions and conditions (if any) attached to each class of shares and directors authority with respect to any class of shares that may be issued in series.

ARTICLE 8 Set out restrictions on issue, transfer or ownership of shares (if any).

ARTICLE 9 Set out other provisions (if any).

ARTICLE 10 Set out name and address for service of each of the incorporators. If the incorporator is a corporation set out the address of the registered or head office. The address should include the street name, street number and suite (if applicable) or R.R. # and the municipality, province, country and postal code.

EXECUTION Both copies of the articles must be signed by each of the incorporators. Print the full name of the incorporator beside his/her signature or if the incorporator is a corporation print the name of the corporation and the name and office of the individual signing for the corporation (e.g., President).

Articles (in duplicate), original Ontario-biased NUANS name search report (if applicable), covering letter and filing fee should be mailed or delivered to:

COMPANIES AND PERSONAL PROPERTY SECURITY BRANCH
MINISTRY OF GOVERNMENT SERVICES
393 UNIVERSITY AVENUE, SUITE 200
TORONTO ON M5G 2M2
375 UNIVERSITY AVENUE, 2ND FLOOR (IN PERSON)

1

For Ministry Use Only
À l'usage exclusif du ministère

Ontario Corporation Number
Numéro de la société en Ontario

Form 1
Business Corporations Act

*Formule 1
Loi sur les sociétés par actions*

ARTICLES OF INCORPORATION
STATUTS CONSTITUTIFS

1. The name of the corporation is: (Set out in BLOCK CAPITAL LETTERS)
Dénomination sociale de la société : (Écrire en LETTRES MAJUSCULES SEULEMENT)

2. The address of the registered office is:
Adresse du siège social :

(Street & Number or R.R. Number & if Multi-Office Building give Room No.)
(Rue et numéro ou numéro de la R.R. et, s'il s'agit d'un édifice à bureaux, numéro du bureau)

ONTARIO

(Name of Municipality or Post Office)
(Nom de la municipalité ou du bureau de poste)

(Postal Code)
(Code postal)

3. Number of directors is/are:
Nombre d'administrateurs :

Fixed number
Nombre fixe

OR minimum and maximum
OU *minimum et maximum*

4. The first director(s) is/are:
Premier(s) administrateur(s) :

First name, middle names and surname *Prénom, autres Prénoms et nom de famille*	Address for service, giving Street & No. or R.R. No., Municipality, Province, Country and Postal Code *Domicile élu, y compris la rue et le numéro, le numéro de la R.R. ou le nom de la municipalité, la province, le pays et le code postal*	Resident Canadian? Yes or No *Résident canadien? Oui/Non*

07116E (06/2007)

5. Restrictions, if any, on business the corporation may carry on or on powers the corporation may exercise.
Limites, s'il y a lieu, imposées aux activités commerciales ou aux pouvoirs de la société.

6. The classes and any maximum number of shares that the corporation is authorized to issue:
Catégories et nombre maximal, s'il y a lieu, d'actions que la société est autorisée à émettre :

07116E (06/2007)

7. Rights, privileges, restrictions and conditions (if any) attaching to each class of shares and directors authority with respect to any class of shares which may be issued in series:
Droits, privilèges, restrictions et conditions, s'il y a lieu, rattachés à chaque catégorie d'actions et pouvoirs des administrateurs relatifs à chaque catégorie d'actions qui peut être émise en série :

07116E (06/2007)

8. The issue, transfer or ownership of shares is/is not restricted and the restrictions (if any) are as follows:
L'émission, le transfert ou la propriété d'actions est/n'est pas restreint. Les restrictions, s'il y a lieu, sont les suivantes :

9. Other provisions if any:
Autres dispositions, s'il y a lieu :

07116E (06/2007)

10. The names and addresses of the incorporators are: 6
Noms et adresses des fondateurs :

First name, middle names and surname or corporate name *Prénom, autres prénoms et nom de famille ou dénomination sociale*	Full address for service or if a corporation, the address of the registered or head office giving street & No. or R.R. No., municipality, province, country and postal code *Domicile élu au complet ou, dans le cas d'une société, adresse du siège social ou adresse de l'établissement principal, y compris la rue et le numéro ou le numéro de la R.R., la municipalité, la province, le pays et le code postal*

These articles are signed in duplicate.
Les présents statuts sont signés en double exemplaire.

Full name(s) and signature(s) of incorporator(s). In the case of a corporation set out the name of the corporation and the name and office of the person signing on behalf of the corporation
Nom(s) au complet et signature(s) du ou des fondateurs. Si le fondateur est une société, indiquer la dénomination sociale et le nom et le titre de la personne signant au nom de la société

Signature / signature

Name of incorporator (or corporation name & signatories name and office)
Nom du fondateur (ou dénomination sociale et nom et titre du signataire)

Signature / signature

Name of incorporator (or corporation name & signatories name and office)
Nom du fondateur (ou dénomination sociale et nom et titre du signataire)

Signature / signature

Name of incorporator (or corporation name & signatories name and office)
Nom du fondateur (ou dénomination sociale et nom et titre du signataire)

Signature / signature

Name of incorporator (or corporation name & signatories name and office)
Nom du fondateur (ou dénomination sociale et nom et titre du signataire)

07116E (06/2007)

Form 2 — Consent to Act as a First Director*

Form 2
Business Corporations Act

Formule 2
Loi sur les sociétés par actions

CONSENT TO ACT AS A FIRST DIRECTOR
CONSENTEMENT DU PREMIER ADMINISTRATEUR

I,/*Je soussigné(e),* ______________________________
(First name, middle names and surname)
(Prénom, autres Prénoms et nom de famille)

address for service
domicile élu

____
(Street & No. or R.R. No., Municipality, Province, Country & Postal Code)
(Rue et numéro, ou numéro de la R.R., nom de la municipalité, province, pays et code postal)

hereby consent to act as a first director of
accepte par la présente de devenir premier administrateur de

____
(Name of Corporation)
(Dénomination sociale de la société)

____
(Signature of the Consenting Person)
(Signature de l'acceptant)

07117 (06/01)

Form 3 — Articles of Amendment*

INSTRUCTIONS FOR COMPLETING

Articles in duplicate may be mailed to the Toronto address listed above. For over-the-counter service they may also be filed in person at the Toronto office or at some Land Registry/ServiceOntario offices in Ontario. For a list of locations see the "Offices That Endorse articles Submitted Under the *Business Corporations Act*" information sheet or visit the ServiceOntario web site at: www.ServiceOntario.ca

FEE

$150.00 **BY MAIL** - cheque or money order payable to the Minister of Finance.

IN PERSON (at the Toronto office) - cash, cheque or money order payable to the Minister of Finance, Visa, MasterCard, American Express or debit card. (If you are filing the documents at a Land Registry/ ServiceOntario office, call first to confirm whether credit or debit cards are acceptable).

There will be a service charge payable for any cheque returned as non-negotiable by a bank or financial institution.

SUPPORTING DOCUMENTS

NAME SEARCH (if you are changing the corporation name)

If you are changing the name of the corporation, you must obtain an original Ontario-biased NUANS name search report. NUANS stands for (Newly Upgraded Automated Name Search). It is a six-page computer-printed search report consisting of corporate names, business names and trademarks that have already been incorporated/ registered and are similar to the proposed corporate name. This search report must be submitted together with the duplicate Articles of Amendment and cannot be dated more than 90 days prior to the submission of the articles. For example, articles submitted on November 28th could be accompanied by a NUANS name search report dated as early as August 30th, but not dated earlier.

The NUANS name search report must be obtained from a private name search company. These companies are listed in the Yellow Pages under the heading "Searchers of Records". The Ministry does not provide this search. It is the applicant's responsibility to check the search report for similar/identical names and to obtain any consent that may be required.

The Ministry will not grant a name that is identical to the current name or former name of another corporation operating in Ontario whether active or not, unless it has been more than ten years since the other corporation dissolved or changed its name. The only exception to this rule is when the corporation meets the requirements of Subsection 6(2) of the Regulations, under the *Business Corporations Act*. In this case, Companies and Personal Property Security Branch policy requires that a legal opinion accompany the articles being filed. The legal opinion must be on legal letterhead and must be signed by an individual lawyer (not a law clerk). It must also clearly indicate that the corporations involved comply with Regulation 6(2) by referring to each clause specifically.

BILINGUAL NAMES

If you are changing the name to a name with an English and French version of the name (where the versions can be used separately), a name search is required for each version of the name (English and French). There should be a forward slash (/) separating the two versions of the name.

NUMBER NAMES

You do not require a name search for a number name. In Article two on the form, leave nine empty boxes, then type or print in block capital letters the word "ONTARIO" followed by one of the legal elements...LIMITED, LIMITÉE, INCORPORATED, INCORPOREE, CORPORATION or the corresponding abbreviation LTD., LTEE., INC., or CORP. The Director of Companies and Personal Property Security Branch will assign a number to the corporation.

APPEARANCE OF DOCUMENTS

The Articles of Amendment must be completed in duplicate on a Form 3 as approved by the Minister. All documents must be legible and compatible with the microfilming process, with the information typed or hand printed in block capital letters, on one side of good quality, white bond paper 8 1/2" X 11".

The Article headings are numbered 1 to 7 and should remain in that order. Do not leave out any of the headings. When additional pages are required, due to lack of space, they should be the same size as all the other pages and should be inserted after the applicable heading with the same number as the heading page with the addition of alphabet characters to indicate sequence. For example, pages inserted after page 1 would be numbered 1A, 1B, etc.

07119 (2011/05)

ARTICLE 1 Set out the current name of the corporation in block capital letters starting from the first box of the first line on the left with one letter per box and one empty box for a space. Punctuation marks are entered in separate boxes. Complete one line before starting in the first box of the next line. The name entered must be exactly the same as it appeared on the original Articles of Incorporation or Articles of Amalgamation. If there has been a name change, the name entered must be exactly the same as it appears on the most recent Articles of Amendment.

EAST SIDE INVESTMENT AND MANAG
EMENT LTD.

ARTICLE 2 If this is a name change; set out the new name in block capital letters starting from the first box of the first line on the left with one letter per box and one empty box for a space. Punctuation marks are entered in separate boxes. Complete one line before starting in the first box of the next line. The name entered must be exactly the same as that on the name search.

ARTICLE 3 Set out the date of incorporation or amalgamation.

ARTICLE 4 Complete only if there is a change in the "number" or "minimum and maximum" number of directors. Complete the "number" field if the corporation has a fixed number of directors **OR** the "minimum and maximum" field if the corporation has a minimum and maximum number of directors **(do not complete both)**.

ARTICLE 5 Set out an extract from the resolution to amend the articles listing the changes i.e., Resolved that:

(a) The name of the corporation is changed to ABC Holdings Inc.
(b) The authorized capital of the corporation is amended by...

If you require more space for Article 5 than is provided, please continue on page 1A, 1B etc. Page 2 should follow in sequence.

ARTICLE 6 The amendment must be authorized as required by sections 168 and 170 (as applicable) of the *Business Corporations Act*. This statement must be included in the Articles, and is already pre-printed on the form.

ARTICLE 7 Set out the date on which the resolution authorizing the amendment was approved by the shareholders/directors of the corporation.

EXECUTION The current name of the corporation from Article 1 should be printed above the signature. Both copies of the Articles must have original signature(s) of an officer or director of the corporation. Beside the signature set out the office of the person who is signing (e.g. President, Director, Secretary). If the corporation has a seal it should be affixed to the Articles next to the signature.

Articles (in duplicate), original Ontario-biased NUANS name search report (if applicable), covering letter and filing fee should be mailed or delivered to:

Ministry of Government Services
Companies and Personal Property Security Branch
393 University Avenue, Suite 200
Toronto ON M5G 2M2

375 University Avenue, 2nd Floor (In Person)

07119 (2011/05)

Statuts de modification
Formule 3
Loi sur les sociétés par actions

INSTRUCTIONS – COMMENT REMPLIR LE FORMULAIRE

On peut envoyer les *Statuts de modification* par courrier au bureau de Toronto à l'adresse susmentionnée. On peut aussi les remettre en personne au bureau de Toronto ou à l'un des bureaux désignés d'enregistrement immobilier / ServiceOntario de la province. Pour une liste des adresses de ces bureaux, voir le feuillet d'information « Bureaux habilités à apposer le certificat sur les statuts relevant de la *Loi sur les sociétés par actions* », ou consulter le site Web de ServiceOntario : www.ServiceOntario.ca.

DROITS

150 $ Envoi **PAR COURRIER** – Paiement par chèque ou mandat libellé à l'ordre du « Ministre des Finances ».
Dépôt **EN PERSONNE** (au bureau de Toronto) – Paiement en argent comptant; par chèque ou mandat libellé à l 'ordre du « Ministre des Finances »; ou par Visa, MasterCard, American Express ou carte de débit. (Si on dépose le document à un bureau d'enregistrement immobilier/bureau de ServiceOntario, appeler d'abord le bureau pour savoir s'il accepte les cartes de crédit ou de débit.)

Des frais d'administration seront facturés pour tout chèque refusé par la banque ou l'institution financière.

DOCUMENTS À L'APPUI

RAPPORT DE RECHERCHE NUANS (si on change la dénomination sociale)

Si on change la dénomination sociale de la société, il faut obtenir et soumettre l'original d'un rapport de recherche NUANS axé sur l'Ontario. C'est un rapport de 6 pages produit par ordinateur qui indique les noms de sociétés (constituées), les noms commerciaux (d'entreprises enregistrées) et les marques de commerce déjà existants qui sont similaires au nom proposé pour la société. Le rapport NUANS doit être déposé en même temps que les deux exemplaires des *Statuts de modification.* Le rapport ne peut pas porter une date antérieure de plus de 90 jours à la date du dépôt des statuts; par exemple, des statuts déposés le 28 novembre pourraient être accompagnés d'un rapport NUANS portant une date antérieure pouvant aller jusqu'au 30 août précédent seulement.

Le rapport doit être obtenu auprès d'une société de recherche de raisons sociales. On trouvera ces sociétés dans l'annuaire des *Pages jaunes* sous le titre « Titres et archives – Recherche » ou « Searchers of Records ». Le ministère n'offre pas ces services de recherche. Il incombe au demandeur de faire effectuer une recherche et d'obtenir toute autorisation qui pourrait être requise relativement à un nom similaire.

Le ministère n'acceptera pas une dénomination sociale identique à celle d'une autre société opérant en Ontario, que celle-ci soit en activité ou qu 'elle soit dissoute, sauf si cette société a été dissoute ou a changé de nom il y a plus de 10 ans. Cette règle ne s'applique pas dans le cas où la société remplit les conditions énoncées au paragraphe 6 (2) du règlement se rapportant à la *Loi sur les sociétés par actions.* Dans ce cas, la Direction des compagnies et des sûretés mobilières demande qu'une opinion juridique soit jointe aux statuts déposés. L'opinion juridique doit être présentée sur le papier à en-tête officiel de l'avocat et doit être signée par l'avocat (et non par son clerc). Elle doit aussi indiquer clairement que les sociétés concernées se conforment au paragraphe 6 (2) du règlement en reprenant chacun des alinéas du paragraphe.

DÉNOMINATION SOCIALE BILINGUE

Si on remplace la dénomination sociale par une dénomination anglaise et française (les deux versions pouvant être utilisées séparément), il faut obtenir et soumettre un rapport de recherche NUANS pour chacune des deux versions. Les noms anglais et français doivent être séparés par une ligne oblique (/).

DÉNOMINATION SOCIALE NUMÉRIQUE

Si on donne à la société une dénomination numérique, il n'est pas nécessaire de soumettre un rapport de recherche NUANS. Pour inscrire le nouveau nom numérique, dans la grille de la section 2, laisser 9 cases vides, puis inscrire tout en lettres majuscules, une lettre par case, le mot ONTARIO suivi d'un des éléments juridiques suivants : LIMITED, LIMITÉE, INCORPORATED, INCORPORÉE, CORPORATION, ou les abréviations correspondantes : LTD, LTÉE, INC. ou CORP. La directrice de la Direction des compagnies et des sûretés mobilières assignera ensuite un numéro à la société.

PRÉSENTATION DES DOCUMENTS

Les *Statuts de modification* doivent être soumis en double exemplaire, sur la Formule 3 approuvée par le ministre. Tous les documents soumis doivent être lisibles et se prêter à la photographie sur microfilm. L'information est soit dactylographiée, soit écrite en lettres majuscules au recto seulement d'un papier filigrané blanc de bonne qualité, de format 8 ½ po x 11 po.

Le formulaire des *Statuts de modification* comporte 7 sections numérotées de 1 à 7, qui doivent rester dans cet ordre. Ne retirer aucune page ou section. Si, par manque d'espace, on insère des pages supplémentaires, celles-ci doivent être du même format que les autres pages et porter le même numéro que la page originale suivi d'une lettre de l'alphabet pour en indiquer l'ordre. Par exemple, les pages insérées après la page 1 seront numérotées 1A, 1B, etc.

07119 (2011/05)

SECTION 1 Inscrire le nom actuel de la société en lettres majuscules, une lettre par case, en commençant à la première case de la première ligne. Pour chaque espace entre les mots, laisser une case vide. Chaque signe de ponctuation occupe aussi une case distincte. Il faut remplir chaque ligne jusqu'au bout avant de com mencer la suivante. Le nom entré doit être identique au nom indiqué sur les *Statuts constitutifs* ou les *Statuts de fusion*. S'il y a déjà eu un changement de nom, il faut entrer le nom exact qui figure sur les *Statuts de modification* les plus récents.

SOCIÉTÉ DE PLACEMENTS ET DE GE
STION DU PATRIMOINE INC.

SECTION 2 Si on change le nom de la société, inscrire ici le nouveau nom en lettres majuscules, une lettre par case, en commençant à la première case de la première ligne. Pour chaque espace entre les mots, laisser une case vide. Chaque signe de ponctuation occupe aussi une case distincte. Il faut remplir chaque ligne jusqu'au bout avant de commencer la suivante, même si un mot doit être coupé. Le nom entré doit être identique au nom indiqué sur le rapport de recherche NUANS.

SECTION 3 Indiquer la date de la constitution ou de la fusion, dans l'ordre indiqué.

SECTION 4 À remplir seulement si le nombre ou les nombres minimum et maximum d'administrateurs ont changé. Remplir la zone « Nombre » si la société a un nombre fixe d'administrateurs; **SINON**, remplir la zone « minimum et maximum » si la société prévoit un minimum et un maximum d'administrateurs. (**Ne pas remplir les deux**.)

SECTION 5 Énoncer ici la résolution votée par la société visant à modifier les statuts et indiquant les modifications apportées. Par exemple :
Résolution :
a) La dénomination sociale de la société est modifiée; la nouvelle dénomination est : Société ABC Inc.
b) Le capital autorisé de la société est réduit de ...

Si, pour la section 5, vous manquez d'espace, veuillez continuer sur d'autres pages à numéroter 1A, 1B, etc. Placez la page 2 à la suite.

SECTION 6 La modification doit être autorisée conformément aux articles 168 et 170 (selon le cas) de la *Loi sur les sociétés par actions*. Cet énoncé, qui est déjà imprimé sur le formulaire, doit être inclus dans les statuts.

SECTION 7 Inscrire, dans l'ordre indiqué, la date à laquelle les actionnaires ou les administrateurs de la société ont approuvé la résolution autorisant la modification.

SIGNATURE Au-dessus de la signature, indiquer la dénomination sociale actuelle de la société (celle inscrite à la section 1). Les deux exemplaires des *Statuts de modification* doivent porter la signature originale d'un dirigeant ou d'un administrateur de la société. Indiquer aussi la fonction du signataire (président, directeur, secrétaire, etc.). Si la société a un sceau, apposer le sceau près de la signature.

Envoyer ou remettre les* Statuts de modification *(en double exemplaire) accompagnés de la version originale du rapport de recherche NUANS (s'il y a lieu), d'une lettre d'introduction et des droits prescrits, à l'adresse suivante :

Ministère des Services gouvernementaux
Direction des compagnies et des sûretés mobilières
393, avenue University, bureau 200
Toronto ON M5G 2M2

375, avenue University, 2e étage (dépôt en personne)

07119 (2011/05)

For Ministry Use Only
À l'usage exclusif du ministère

Ontario Corporation Number
Numéro de la société en Ontario

Form 3
Business Corporations Act

Formule 3
Loi sur les sociétés par actions

ARTICLES OF AMENDMENT
STATUTS DE MODIFICATION

1. The name of the corporation is: (Set out in BLOCK CAPITAL LETTERS)
Dénomination sociale actuelle de la société (écrire en LETTRES MAJUSCULES SEULEMENT) :

2. The name of the corporation is changed to (if applicable): (Set out in BLOCK CAPITAL LETTERS)
Nouvelle dénomination sociale de la société (s'il y a lieu) (écrire en LETTRES MAJUSCULES SEULEMENT) :

3. Date of incorporation/amalgamation:
Date de la constitution ou de la fusion :

(Year, Month, Day)
(année, mois, jour)

4. **Complete only if there is a change in the number of directors or the minimum / maximum number of directors.**
Il faut remplir cette partie seulement si le nombre d'administrateurs ou si le nombre minimal ou maximal d'administrateurs a changé.

Number of directors is/are: <u>minimum and maximum</u> number of directors is/are:
Nombre d'administrateurs : nombres <u>minimum et maximum</u> d'administrateurs :

Number <u>minimum and maximum</u>
Nombre <u>minimum et maximum</u>

or
ou

5. The articles of the corporation are amended as follows:
Les statuts de la société sont modifiés de la façon suivante :

07119 (2011/05)

Page 1 of/de 2

6. The amendment has been duly authorized as required by sections 168 and 170 (as applicable) of the *Business Corporations Act*.
La modification a été dûment autorisée conformément aux articles 168 et 170 (selon le cas) de la *Loi sur les sociétés par actions*.

7. The resolution authorizing the amendment was approved by the shareholders/directors (as applicable) of the corporation on
Les actionnaires ou les administrateurs (selon le cas) de la société ont approuvé la résolution autorisant la modification le

____
(Year, Month, Day)
(année, mois, jour)

These articles are signed in duplicate.
Les présents statuts sont signés en double exemplaire.

____
(Print name of corporation from Article 1 on page 1)
(Veuillez écrir le nom de la société de l'article un à la page une).

By/
Par :

______________________________ ______________________________
(Signature) (Description of Office)
(Signature) (Fonction)

07119 (2011/05)

Page 2 of/de 2

1A

07119 (2008/06)

1B

07119 (2008/06)

1C

07119 (2008/06)

Form 4 — Articles of Amalgamation*

INSTRUCTIONS FOR COMPLETING

This form together with required supporting documents and fee, must be filed with the Ministry of Government Services to amalgamate two or more Ontario business corporations under the *Business Corporations Act*.

Articles in duplicate may be mailed to the Toronto address listed below. For over-the-counter service articles may be filed in person at the Toronto office or at some Land Registry/ServiceOntario offices in Ontario. For a list of locations see the "Offices That Endorse articles Submitted Under the *Business Corporations Act*" information sheet or visit the ServiceOntario web site at: www.ServiceOntario.ca.

FEE

$330.00 (10 or fewer amalgamating corporations)

$500.00 (11 or more amalgamating corporations)

BY MAIL – Cheque or money order payable to the Minister of Finance

IN PERSON – (at the Toronto office) – cash, cheque or money order payable to Minister of Finance, Visa, MasterCard, American Express or debit card. (If you are filing the documents at a Land Registry or ServiceOntario Office, call first to confirm whether credit or debit cards are acceptable).

There will be a service charge payable for any cheque returned as non-negotiable by a bank or financial institution.

EFFECTIVE DATE

Articles are effective on the date set out in the certificate endorsed on the articles by the Branch. The certificate is dated the day the Director receives the duplicate originals of the articles together with all other required documents executed in accordance with the Act and the required fee, if they are acceptable as per the Branch's endorsement as of right policy. An effective date of up to 30 days later than the earliest date the articles can be endorsed may be requested **in writing, in the covering letter, using bold or highlighted letters,** upon submission of the articles to the branch. If you are presenting your documents in person you must also verbally bring this request to the attention of the counter clerk.

SUPPORTING DOCUMENTS

NAME SEARCH

The name of a corporation formed by the amalgamation of two or more corporations may be identical to the name of one of its amalgamating corporations, if it is **not a number name.** In this case a name search is not required.

If you are amalgamating under a new name you must obtain an original Ontario-biased NUANS name search report. NUANS is a computerized search system that compares a proposed corporate name or trade-mark with databases of existing corporate bodies and trade-marks. This comparison determines the similarity that exists between the proposed name or mark and existing names in the database, and produces a listing of names that are found to be most similar. This search must be submitted together with the duplicate Articles of Amalgamation within 90 days from production by the NUANS system. For example, articles submitted on November 28th could be accompanied by a NUANS name search report dated as early as August 30th, but not dated earlier. The Companies and Personal Property Security Branch does not provide this search.

Suppliers are listed in the Yellow Pages under the heading "Searchers of Records" or visit Industry Canada's NUANS site at, **www.nuans.com** for a list of registered search houses that can assist you with obtaining a NUANS search report and filing your corporate documents with the Ministry of Government Services. Please note the NUANS search must be **Ontario biased.**

07121 (201105)

NAME SEARCH
CONTINUED

It is the applicant's responsibility to check the search for similar/identical names and to obtain any consent that may be required. The Ministry will not grant a name that is identical to the current name or former name of another corporation operating in Ontario whether active or not, unless it has been more than ten years since the other corporation dissolved or changed its name. The only exception to this rule is when the corporation meets the requirements of Subsection 6(2) of Regulation 62, under the *Business Corporations Act*. In this case a legal opinion must accompany the articles being filed. The legal opinion must be on legal letterhead and signed by an individual lawyer (not a law clerk or law firm). It must also clearly indicate that the corporations involved comply with Subsection 6(2) by referring to each clause specifically.

BILINGUAL NAMES

When amalgamating a corporation with an English and French form of the name a name search is required for each form of the name (English and French) unless the English and French forms of the name are identical and the legal element in the French form is the French version of the legal element in the English form (for example, INCORPOREE and INCORPORATED). There should be a forward slash (/) separating the two forms of the name.

NUMBER NAMES

You do not require a name search for a number name. In Article one on the form, leave nine empty boxes, then type or print in block capital letters the word "ONTARIO" followed by one of the legal elements...LIMITED, LIMITÉE, INCORPORATED, INCORPOREE, CORPORATION or the corresponding abbreviation LTD., LTEE.,INC., or CORP. The Director of the Companies and Personal Property Security Branch will assign a number to the corporation.

The amalgamated corporation cannot retain the number name of an amalgamating company. When two or more corporations amalgamate a new corporation is formed. The Director assigns a new corporation number and in the case of a number name, this new number becomes the number part of the name.

SCHEDULES

SCHEDULE A A statement of a director or an officer of each of the amalgamating corporations completed as required under subsection 178(2) of the *Business Corporations Act* must be attached to both copies of the articles.

SCHEDULE B (i) A copy of the amalgamation agreement adopted by the shareholders pursuant to subsection 176(4) of the *Business Corporations Act*

Or

(ii) The director's resolutions of each amalgamating corporation as required under Section 177 of the *Business Corporations Act*

must be attached to both copies of the articles.

Schedules A and B must contain a signature of the appropriate shareholder(s), officer(s) or director(s) of the corporation as required under the Act. Photocopied amalgamation schedules that do not contain the required signature(s) will not be accepted.

COVERING LETTER

Enclose a covering letter setting out the name of a contact person, a return address and a telephone number. This will facilitate the processing of the articles should a question arise as to the content of the Articles of Amalgamation.

APPEARANCE OF DOCUMENTS

The Articles of Amalgamation must be completed in duplicate on Form 4 as approved by the Minister. All documents must be legible and compatible with the microfilming process, with the information typed or hand printed in block capital letters, on one side of good quality white bond paper 8 ½" X 11".

The article headings are numbered 1 to 12 and should remain in that order. Do not leave out any of the headings. If a section does not apply, type "nil" or "not applicable". When additional pages are required, due to lack of space, they should be the same size as all the other pages and should be inserted after the applicable heading with the same number as the heading page, but with the addition of alphabet characters to indicate sequence. For example, pages inserted after page 4 would be numbered 4A, 4B, etc.

07121 (201105)

ARTICLE 1 Set out the name of the amalgamated corporation in block capital letters starting from the first box of the first line on the left with one letter per box and one empty box for a space. Punctuation marks are entered in separate boxes. Complete one line before starting in the first box of the next line. The name entered must be exactly the same as that on the name search report or the same as one of the amalgamating corporations (if not a number name). Where a "number name" is to be used, leave the first nine boxes blank and complete as follows: "........Ontario Inc." (see "number names)

EAST SIDE INVESTMENT AND MANAG
EMENT LTD.

ARTICLE 2 The address (if multi-office building, include room or suite number) of the registered office of the corporation must be set out in full, including the street name, street number and suite or R.R. #, the municipality, province, country and the postal code. A post office box alone is not an acceptable address. If there is no street and number, set out the lot and concession or lot and plan numbers. The registered office must be in Ontario.

ARTICLE 3 Set out the number of directors. This can be either a fixed number of directors (i.e. 1) or a minimum and maximum number (i.e. minimum 1, maximum 10). Do not complete both.

ARTICLE 4 The name(s) (including first name, middle names and surname) and the address for service for each of the first directors must be set out. The address should include the street name, street number, suite (or R.R. #) municipality, province, country and postal code. Directors must be individuals, not corporations. State if the director(s) is/are Resident Canadian(s). At least 25 per cent of the directors must be resident Canadians (if 25% of the directors is not a whole number, round up to the nearest whole number). Where a corporation has less than four directors, at least one must be a resident Canadian

ARTICLE 5 Check the appropriate box **(A)** or **(B)**:

Check box (A) Amalgamation Agreement *- if the amalgamation agreement has been adopted by the shareholders of each of the amalgamating corporations under Subsection 176(4) of the Business Corporations Act.* In this case Schedule "B" referred to in Article 12 on the form must be a copy of the amalgamation agreement containing the signatures of a director or authorized signing officer of each amalgamating corporation.

OR

Check box (B) Amalgamation of a holding corporation and one or more of its subsidiaries or amalgamation of subsidiaries *- if the amalgamation has been approved by the directors of each of the amalgamating corporations by a resolution as required by Section 177 of the Business Corporations Act.* In this case schedule "B" referred to in article 12 must be a copy of the director's resolutions (containing the required signatures) for each amalgamating corporation. If all the directors approved the resolution without a meeting being held, each director is required to sign the resolution. If the resolution was approved at a directors' meeting, its approval must be certified in writing with a signature by the Secretary (or other authorized officer) of the corporation. If (B) is checked, on the line provided, set out the name of the amalgamating corporation containing the same provisions in substance as the Articles of Amalgamation now being submitted.

Under the corresponding headings, set out the corporation name, Ontario corporation number and the date of adoption/approval of the amalgamation agreement or directors resolutions for each of the amalgamating corporations.

ARTICLE 6 Set out restrictions, if any, on the business the corporation may carry on or on the powers that the corporation may exercise. If none, state so.

ARTICLE 7 Set out the classes and any maximum number of shares that the corporation is authorized to issue. This item must be completed (e.g., unlimited common shares).

07121 (201105)

ARTICLE 8	Set out the rights, privileges, restrictions, and conditions etc. (if any) attached to each class of shares, and directors' authority with respect to any class of shares which may be issued in series.
ARTICLE 9	Set out restrictions on issue, transfer or ownership of shares (if any).
ARTICLE 10	Set out other provisions (if any).
ARTICLE 11	***The statements required by Subsection 178(2) of the Business Corporations Act are attached as Schedule "A"***. The statements (original or photocopy) must set out specific information as required under the Act and must contain the signature of a director or officer as evidence that the person signing has approved all of the contents of the statement This Item must be included in the articles and the required Schedule must be attached.
ARTICLE 12	***A copy of the amalgamation agreement or directors' resolutions (as the case may be) is/are attached as Schedule "B".*** This Item must be included in the articles and the required schedule must be attached.
EXECUTION	Both copies of the articles must have an **original** signature of an officer or director of each of the amalgamating corporations. Set out the name of the officer/director who is signing, the name of the corporation and the office held by the individual in the corporation (e.g., president, director, secretary).

Articles with schedules "A" and "B" (in duplicate), original Ontario-biased NUANS name search report (if applicable), covering letter and filing fee should be mailed or delivered to:

Ministry of Government Services
Companies and Personal Property Security Branch
393 University Avenue, Suite 200
Toronto ON M5G 2M2

375 University Avenue, 2nd Floor (In Person)

07121 (201105)

INSTRUCTIONS POUR REMPLIR LE FORMULAIRE

Pour fusionner des sociétés par actions de l'Ontario, il faut déposer ce formulaire accompagné des documents nécessaires et du paiement requis auprès du ministère des Services gouvernementaux.

On peut envoyer les statuts – en deux exemplaires – par courrier au bureau de Toronto à l'adresse mentionnée à la fin des instructions. On peut aussi les déposer en personne au bureau de Toronto ou à l'un des bureaux désignés d'enregistrement immobilier / ServiceOntario de la province. Pour une liste des adresses de ces bureaux, voir le feuillet d'information « Bureaux habilités à apposer le certificat sur les statuts relevant de *la Loi sur les sociétés par actions* », ou consulter le site Web de ServiceOntario : www.ServiceOntario.ca

DROITS

330 $ (pour la fusion de 2 à 10 sociétés)

500 $ (pour la fusion de plus de 10 sociétés)

Envoi **PAR COURRIER** – Paiement par chèque ou mandat libellé à l'ordre du « Ministre des Finances ».

Dépôt **EN PERSONNE** (au bureau de Toronto) – Paiement en argent comptant; par chèque ou mandat libellé à l'ordre du « Ministre des Finances »; ou par Visa, MasterCard, American Express ou carte de débit. (Si on dépose le document à un bureau d'enregistrement immobilier ou un bureau de ServiceOntario, appeler d'abord le bureau pour savoir s'il accepte les cartes de crédit ou de débit.)

Des frais d'administration seront perçus pour tout chèque refusé par l'établissement financier.

DATE D'ENTRÉE EN VIGUEUR

Les statuts entrent en vigueur à la date indiquée sur le certificat qui y est apposé. Si les statuts sont acceptables aux termes de la politique d'examen de la Direction des compagnies et des sûretés mobilières qui a le pouvoir de certifier les documents, le certificat porte la date du jour où la directrice reçoit les deux exemplaires originaux des statuts accompagnés des droits prescrits et de tous les documents requis aux termes de la *Loi*. Au moment du dépôt des statuts, le client peut demander que le certificat de fusion porte une date ultérieure, mais cette date doit être choisie parmi les 30 jours suivant la première date à laquelle les statuts peuvent être certifiés. **La demande d'une date ultérieure doit être présentée par écrit, en caractères gras ou surlignés.** Si l'on remet les statuts en personne, l'on doit adresser cette demande verbalement au préposé chargé d'apposer le certificat.

DOCUMENTS À L'APPUI

RAPPORT DE RECHERCHE NUANS

La dénomination sociale d'une société issue d'une fusion peut être identique à la dénomination de l'une des sociétés fusionnantes, à condition que ce **ne soit pas une dénomination sociale numérique.** Dans le cas où l'on conserve la dénomination d'une des sociétés fusionnantes, la soumission d'un rapport de recherche NUANS n'est pas requise.

Si, pour la société issue de la fusion, on adopte une nouvelle dénomination, il faut obtenir et soumettre l'original d'un rapport de recherche NUANS axé sur l'Ontario. NUANS est un système de recherche informatisée qui compare la dénomination ou la marque de commerce proposée pour votre société avec des bases de données de personnes morales et de marques de commerce existantes dans le but de déterminer si le nom proposé est identique ou semblable à des noms existants. Le système produit une liste des noms qui se rapprochent le plus du nom proposé. Le rapport NUANS doit être déposé en même temps que les *Statuts de fusion*; il doit être remis dans les 90 jours suivant la date de sa production. Par exemple, des statuts déposés le 28 novembre pourraient être accompagnés d'un rapport NUANS daté du 30 août précédent, mais non d'une date antérieure au 30 août. La Direction des compagnies et des sûretés mobilières ne fournit pas cette recherche.

07121 (201105)

Les fournisseurs de services de recherche sont indiqués dans les Pages jaunes de l'annuaire, sous « Titres et archives – Recherche » ou « Searchers of Records ». Le site NUANS d'Industrie Canada (**www.nuans.com**) fournit aussi une liste de maisons de recherche homologuées qui peuvent aider à obtenir le rapport NUANS et à remplir les statuts. Ne pas oublier que le rapport NUANS doit être axé sur l'Ontario.

Il incombe au demandeur de faire effectuer une recherche et d'obtenir toute autorisation qui pourrait être requise relativement à un nom similaire. Le ministère n'acceptera pas une dénomination sociale identique à celle, courante ou ancienne, d'une autre société opérant en Ontario, que celle-ci soit en activité ou non, sauf si cette société a été dissoute ou a changé de nom il y a plus de 10 ans. Cette règle ne s'applique pas dans le cas où la société remplit les conditions énoncées au paragraphe 6 (2) du règlement se rapportant à la *Loi sur les sociétés par actions*. Dans ce cas-ci une opinion légale doit accompagner les articles étant classés. L'opinion juridique doit être présentée sur le papier à lettre officiel à en-tête de l'avocat et doit être signée par l'avocat (et non par son clerc). Elle doit aussi indiquer clairement que les sociétés concernées se conforment au paragraphe 6 (2) du règlement en reprenant chacun des alinéas du paragraphe.

DÉNOMINATION SOCIALE BILINGUE

Si on donne à la société issue de la fusion une nouvelle dénomination sociale anglaise et française, il faut obtenir et soumettre un rapport de recherche NUANS pour chacune des deux versions, sauf si les versions anglaise et française sont identiques, l'élément juridique à la fin de la version française devant être la traduction de l'élément juridique de la version anglaise (p. ex. : INCORPORÉE pour INCORPORATED, ou LTÉE pour LTD). Les noms anglais et français doivent être séparés par une ligne oblique (/).

DÉNOMINATION SOCIALE NUMÉRIQUE

Si on donne à la société une dénomination numérique, il n'est pas nécessaire de soumettre un rapport de recherche NUANS. Pour inscrire le nouveau nom numérique, dans la grille de la section 1, laisser 9 cases vides, puis inscrire tout en lettres majuscules, une lettre par case, le mot ONTARIO suivi d'un des éléments juridiques suivants : LIMITED, LIMITÉE, INCORPORATED, INCORPORÉE, CORPORATION, ou les abréviations correspondantes : LTD, LTÉE, INC. ou CORP. La directrice de la Direction des compagnies et des sûretés mobilières assignera ensuite un numéro à la société.

La société issue de la fusion ne peut pas conserver la dénomination sociale numérique d'une des sociétés fusionnantes. Étant donné que la fusion donne naissance à une nouvelle société, la directrice lui assigne un nouveaunuméro matricule. Si l'on adopte une dénomination numérique, cette dénomination sera constituée du nouveau numéro assigné.

ANNEXES

ANNEXE A Une déclaration d'un administrateur ou d'un dirigeant de chaque société fusionnante, préparée conformément au paragraphe 178 (2) de la *Loi sur les sociétés par actions*, doit être jointe aux *Statuts de fusion*.

ANNEXE B L'un des documents suivants doit aussi être joint aux *Statuts de fusion* :

i) Un exemplaire de la convention de fusion adoptée par les actionnaires, conformément au paragraphe 176 (4) de la *Loi sur les sociétés par actions*.

ou

ii) Un exemplaire des résolutions des administrateurs des sociétés fusionnantes approuvant la fusion, conformément à l'article 177 de la *Loi*.

Conformément à la *Loi*, les annexes A et B doivent porter la signature du ou des actionnaires, dirigeants ou administrateurs appropriés de chaque société fusionnante. Les photocopies d'annexes qui ne portent pas les signatures requises ne seront pas acceptées.

LETTRE D'INTRODUCTION

Joindre une lettre d'introduction indiquant le nom de la personne à contacter, l'adresse de retour et le numéro de téléphone. Ceci facilitera le traitement des statuts au cas où l'on doive contacter la personne pour poser des questions sur le contenu des documents.

07121 (201105)

PRÉSENTATION DES DOCUMENTS

Les *Statuts de fusion* doivent être soumis en double exemplaire sur la Formule 4 approuvée par le ministre. Tous les documents soumis doivent être lisibles et se prêter à la photographie sur microfilm. L'information est soit dactylographiée, soit écrite en lettres majuscules au recto seulement d'un papier filigrané blanc de bonne qualité, de format 8 ½ po x 11 po.

La formule des *Statuts de fusion* comporte 12 sections numérotées de 1 à 12, qui doivent rester dans cet ordre. Ne retirer aucune page ou section. Si un article ne s'applique pas, ecrire « néant » ou « sans objet ». Si, par manque d'espace, on insère des pages supplémentaires, celles ci doivent être du même format que les autres pages et porter le même numéro que la page originale suivi d'une lettre de l'alphabet pour en indiquer l'ordre. Par exemple, les pages insérées après la page 4 seront numérotées 4A, 4B, etc.

SECTION 1

Inscrire en lettres majuscules le nom de la nouvelle société issue de la fusion; entrer une lettre par case, en commençant à la première case de la première ligne. Pour chaque espace entre les mots, laisser une case vide. Chaque signe de ponctuation occupe aussi une case distincte. Il faut remplir chaque ligne jusqu'au bout avant de commencer la suivante. Le nom entré doit être identique au nom indiqué sur le rapport de recherche NUANS ou au nom de la société fusionnante proposé pour la nouvelle société (si ce n'est pas une dénomination numérique). S'il s'agit d'une dénomination numérique, laisser les 9 premières cases vides et inscrire à la suite : Ontario Inc. (voir plus haut « Dénomination sociale numérique »).

SOCIÉTÉ DE PLACEMENTS ET DE GE
STION DU PATRIMOINE INC.

SECTION 2

Indiquer l'adresse complète du siège social : rue et numéro, bureau (dans le cas d'un immeuble à bureaux), municipalité, province, pays et code postal. Une adresse composée d'une case postale n'est pas acceptée. S'il n'y a ni rue ni numéro, indiquer les numéros de lot et de concession. Le siège social doit être situé en Ontario.

SECTION 3

Indiquer le nombre d'administrateurs dans la case appropriée. Ce peut être un nombre fixe (p. ex. : 1); sinon, indiquer les nombres minimal et maximal d'administrateurs (p. ex. : minimum : 1; maximum : 10). **Ne pas remplir les deux.**

SECTION 4

Inscrire le nom complet (prénom, autre prénom et nom de famille) et le domicile élu de chacun des premiers administrateurs. L'adresse doit être complète : rue et numéro, bureau, ou R.R., municipalité, province, pays et code postal. Les administrateurs doivent être des personnes physiques, non des personnes morales. Pour chaque administrateur, indiquer s'il est ou non résident canadien. Au moins 25 % des administrateurs doivent être résidents canadiens (si 25 % produit un nombre non entier, arrondir au chiffre entier le plus proche). Si la société a moins de quatre administrateurs, un au moins doit être résident canadien.

SECTION 5

Cocher la case appropriée : A ou B.

Cocher la case A : Convention de fusion, si les actionnaires de chaque société fusionnante ont adopté la convention de fusion conformément au paragraphe 176 (4) de la *Loi sur les sociétés par actions*. Dans ce cas, à la section 12 des statuts, l'annexe B qu'il faut joindre doit être une copie de la convention de fusion portant la signature d'un administrateur ou d'un signataire autorisé de chaque société fusionnante.

Ou

Cocher la case B : Fusion d'une société mère avec une ou plusieurs de ses filiales ou fusion de filiales, si les administrateurs de chaque société fusionnante ont approuvé la fusion par voie de résolution conformément à l'article 177 de la Loi.

SECTION 5 Dans ce cas, à la section 12 des statuts, l'annexe B qu'il faut joindre doit être une copie des résolutions (portant les signatures requises) des administrateurs de chaque société fusionnante. Si tous les administrateurs ont approuvé la résolution sans tenir une réunion, chaque administrateur doit signer la résolution. Si la résolution a été approuvée au cours d'une réunion du conseil d'administration, son approbation doit être attestée par écrit avec signature du secrétaire (ou d'un signataire autorisé) de la société. En cochant la case B, il faut indiquer, sur la ligne prévue à cet effet, le nom de la société fusionnante dont les dispositions des statuts constitutifs sont substantiellement reprises dans les *Statuts de fusion* que l'on soumet.

Ensuite, indiquer la dénomination sociale de chaque société fusionnante, son numéro matricule de l'Ontario et, pour chaque société, la date de l'adoption de la convention de fusion ou de l'approbation de la résolution des administrateurs.

SECTION 6 Indiquer ici, le cas échéant, les limites imposées aux activités ou aux pouvoirs que peut exercer la société. S'il n'y a pas de limites, l'énoncer.

SECTION 7 Indiquer les catégories et le nombre maximal d'actions, le cas échéant, que la société est autorisée à émettre. Quoi qu'il en soit, il faut donner une réponse à cette section (p. ex. : actions ordinaires illimitées).

SECTION 8 Énoncer les droits, les privilèges, les restrictions et les conditions, s'il y a lieu, rattachés à chaque catégorie d'actions et les pouvoirs des administrateurs relatifs à chaque catégorie d'actions qui peut être émise en série.

SECTION 9 Indiquer les restrictions, le cas échéant, concernant l'émission, le transfert ou la propriété d'actions.

SECTION 10 Énoncer d'autres dispositions, s'il y a lieu.

SECTION 11 **Les déclarations exigées aux termes du paragraphe 178 (2) de la *Loi sur les sociétés par actions* constituent l'annexe A.** Les déclarations (l'original ou une photocopie) des sociétés fusionnantes doivent chacune indiquer les renseignements spécifiques exigés par la *Loi* et doivent porter la signature d'un administrateur ou d'un dirigeant, la signature prouvant que le signataire a approuvé le contenu entier de la déclaration. Cette section fait partie intégrante des statuts; elle doit toujours figurer dans les statuts soumis, et l'annexe requise doit être jointe.

SECTION 12 ***Une copie de la convention de fusion ou les résolutions des administrateurs (selon le cas) constitu(ent) l'annexe B.*** Cette section fait partie intégrante des statuts; elle doit toujours figurer dans les statuts soumis, et l'annexe requise doit être jointe.

SIGNATURE Les deux exemplaires des statuts doivent porter la signature **originale** d'un dirigeant ou d'un administrateur de chaque société fusionnante. Sous la signature, indiquer en lettres moulées le nom du signataire, le nom de la société fusionnante, et la fonction du signataire (p. ex. : président, administrateur, secrétaire).

Envoyer ou remettre les statuts (en deux exemplaires) – avec les annexes A et B (en deux exemplaires), la copie originale du rapport NUANS (s'il y a lieu), une lettre d'introduction et les droits prescrits – à l'adresse suivante :

Ministère des Services gouvernementaux
Direction des compagnies et des sûretés mobilières
393, avenue University, bureau 200
Toronto ON M5G 2M2

375, avenue University, 2e étage (dépôt en personne)

07121 (201105)

For Ministry Use Only
À l'usage exclusif du ministère

Ontario Corporation Number
Numéro de la société en Ontario

Form 4
Business Corporations Act

Formule 4
Loi sur les sociétés par actions

ARTICLES OF AMALGAMATION
STATUTS DE FUSION

1. The name of the amalgamated corporation is: (Set out in BLOCK CAPITAL LETTERS)
Dénomination sociale de la société issue de la fusion: (Écrire en LETTRES MAJUSCULES SEULEMENT) :

2. The address of the registered office is:
Adresse du siège social :

Street & Number or R.R. Number & if Multi-Office Building give Room No. /
Rue et numéro ou numéro de la R.R. et, s'il s'agit d'un édifice à bureaux, numéro du bureau

ONTARIO

Name of Municipality or Post Office /
Nom de la municipalité ou du bureau de poste

Postal Code/Code postal

3. Number of directors is: Nombre d'administrateurs : Fixed number / Nombre fixe OR minimum and maximum / OU minimum et maximum

4. The director(s) is/are: / Administrateur(s) :

First name, middle names and surname Prénom, autres prénoms et nom de famille	Address for service, giving Street & No. or R.R. No., Municipality, Province, Country and Postal Code Domicile élu, y compris la rue et le numéro ou le numéro de la R.R., le nom de la municipalité, la province, le pays et le code postal	Resident Canadian State 'Yes' or 'No' Résident canadien Oui/Non

07121 (201105) Page 1 of/de 6

5. Method of amalgamation, check A or B
Méthode choisie pour la fusion – Cocher A ou B :

A - **Amalgamation Agreement / Convention de fusion :**

☐ The amalgamation agreement has been duly adopted by the shareholders of each of the amalgamating corporations as required by subsection 176 (4) of the *Business Corporations Act* on the date set out below.

Les actionnaires de chaque société qui fusionnne ont dûment adopté la convention de fusion conformément au paragraphe 176(4) de la *Loi sur les sociétés par actions* à la date mentionnée ci-dessous.

or
ou

B - **Amalgamation of a holding corporation and one or more of its subsidiaries or amalgamation of subsidiaries / Fusion d'une société mère avec une ou plusieurs de ses filiales ou fusion de filiales :**

☐ The amalgamation has been approved by the directors of each amalgamating corporation by a resolution as required by section 177 of the *Business Corporations Act* on the date set out below.

Les administrateurs de chaque société qui fusionne ont approuvé la fusion par voie de résolution conformément à l'article 177 de la *Loi sur les sociétés par actions* à la date mentionnée ci-dessous.

The articles of amalgamation in substance contain the provisions of the articles of incorporation of
Les statuts de fusion reprennent essentiellement les dispositions des statuts constitutifs de

____

and are more particularly set out in these articles.
et sont énoncés textuellement aux présents statuts.

Names of amalgamating corporations Dénomination sociale des sociétés qui fusionnent	Ontario Corporation Number Numéro de la société en Ontario	Date of Adoption/Approval Date d'adoption ou d'approbation Year / année — Month / mois — Day / jour

07121 (201105) Page 2 of/de 6

6. Restrictions, if any, on business the corporation may carry on or on powers the corporation may exercise.
Limites, s'il y a lieu, imposées aux activités commerciales ou aux pouvoirs de la société.

7. The classes and any maximum number of shares that the corporation is authorized to issue:
Catégories et nombre maximal, s'il y a lieu, d'actions que la société est autorisée à émettre :

8. Rights, privileges, restrictions and conditions (if any) attaching to each class of shares and directors authority with respect to any class of shares which may be issued in series:

   Droits, privilèges, restrictions et conditions, s'il y a lieu, rattachés à chaque catégorie d'actions et pouvoirs des administrateurs relatifs à chaque catégorie d'actions qui peut être émise en série :

9. The issue, transfer or ownership of shares is/is not restricted and the restrictions (if any) are as follows:
L'émission, le transfert ou la propriété d'actions est/n'est pas restreint. Les restrictions, s'il y a lieu, sont les suivantes :

10. Other provisions, (if any):
Autres dispositions, s'il y a lieu :

11. The statements required by subsection 178(2) of the *Business Corporations Act* are attached as Schedule "A".
Les déclarations exigées aux termes du paragraphe 178(2) de la *Loi sur les sociétés par actions* constituent l'annexe A.

12. A copy of the amalgamation agreement or directors' resolutions (as the case may be) is/are attached as Schedule "B".
Une copie de la convention de fusion ou les résolutions des administrateurs (selon le cas) constitue(nt) l'annexe B.

07121 (201105) Page 5 of/de 6

These articles are signed in duplicate.
Les présents statuts sont signés en double exemplaire.

Name and **original signature** of a director or authorized signing officer of each of the amalgamating corporations. Include the name of each corporation, the signatories name and description of office (e.g. president, secretary). **Only a director or authorized signing officer can sign on behalf of the corporation.** / Nom et **signature originale** d'un administrateur ou d'un signataire autorisé de chaque société qui fusionne. Indiquer la dénomination sociale de chaque société, le nom du signataire et sa fonction (p. ex. : président, secrétaire). **Seul un administrateur ou un dirigeant habilité peut signer au nom de la société.**

Names of Corporations / Dénomination sociale des sociétés
By / *Par*

Signature / Signature | Print name of signatory / Nom du signataire en lettres moulées | Description of Office / Fonction

Names of Corporations / Dénomination sociale des sociétés
By / *Par*

Signature / Signature | Print name of signatory / Nom du signataire en lettres moulées | Description of Office / Fonction

Names of Corporations / Dénomination sociale des sociétés
By / *Par*

Signature / Signature | Print name of signatory / Nom du signataire en lettres moulées | Description of Office / Fonction

Names of Corporations / Dénomination sociale des sociétés
By / Par

Signature / Signature | Print name of signatory / Nom du signataire en lettres moulées | Description of Office / Fonction

Names of Corporations / Dénomination sociale des sociétés
By / *Par*

Signature / *Signature* | Print name of signatory / Nom du signataire en lettres moulées | Description of Office / Fonction

07121 (201105) Page 6 of/de 6

Form 5 — Restated Articles of Incorporation*

INSTRUCTIONS FOR COMPLETING

This form is used to restate Articles of Incorporation as amended (i.e. to consolidate all amendments and the original articles into one set of articles). Restated articles supersede the original articles and all the amendments that have been made to them.

Articles in duplicate may be mailed to the Toronto address listed below. For over-the-counter service, articles may be filed in person at the Toronto office or at some Land Registry/ServiceOntario offices in Ontario. For a list of locations see the "Offices That Endorse Articles Submitted Under the *Business Corporations Act*" information sheet or visit the Ministry's web site at: www.mgs.gov.on.ca. Choose your language preference, select "Services for Business" from the "Service Ontario" menu on the right hand side of the page, then choose "Company Information" from the services listed and scroll down to "Frequently Asked Questions".

FEE

$ 150.00 BY MAIL – Cheque or money order payable to the Minister of Finance

IN PERSON – (at the Toronto office) – cash, cheque or money order payable to Minister of Finance, Visa, MasterCard, American Express or debit card. (If you are filing the documents at a Land Registry or ServiceOntario Office, call first to confirm whether credit or debit cards are acceptable).

There will be a service charge payable for any cheque returned as non-negotiable by a bank or financial institution.

COVERING LETTER

Enclose a covering letter setting out the name of a contact person, a return address and a telephone number. This will facilitate the processing of the articles should a question arise as to the content of the Restated Articles of Incorporation.

APPEARANCE OF DOCUMENTS

The Restated Articles of Incorporation must be completed in duplicate on Form 5 as approved by the Minister. All documents must be legible and compatible with the microfilming process, with the information typed or hand printed in block capital letters, on one side of good quality, white bond paper 8 ½" X 11".

The article headings are numbered 1 to 11 and must remain in that order. Do not leave out any of the headings. If a section does not apply type "nil" or "not applicable". When additional pages are required, due to lack of space, they should be the same size as all the other pages and should be inserted after the applicable heading with the same number as the heading page with the addition of alphabet characters to indicate sequence. For example, pages inserted after page 3 would be numbered 3A, 3B, etc.

ARTICLE 1 Set out the current name of the corporation in block capital letters starting from the first box on the left-hand side of the first line, with one letter per box and one empty box for a space. Punctuation marks are entered in separate boxes. Complete one line before starting in the first box of the next line. The name entered must be exactly the same as it appeared on the original Articles of Incorporation or Articles of Amalgamation, or if there has been a name change, the most recent Articles of Amendment changing the name.

EAST SIDE INVESTMENT AND MANAG
EMENT LTD.

07120E (2011/05)

ARTICLE 2	Set out the original date of incorporation/amalgamation of the corporationn.
ARTICLE 3	The address (where multi-office building include room or suite number) of the registered office of the corporation must be set out in full including the street name, street number or R.R. #, municipality, province, country and the postal code. A post office box alone is not an acceptable address. If there is no street and number, set out the lot and concession or lot and plan numbers. The registered office must be in Ontario.
ARTICLE 4	Set out the number of directors as appear on the articles as amended. This can be a fixed number of directors (i.e. 1) or a minimum and maximum number (i.e. minimum 1, maximum 10). Do not complete both.
ARTICLE 5	The name(s) (including first name, middle names and surname) and the address for service for each of the directors must be set out. The address should include the street name, street number, suite (or R.R. #) municipality, province, country and postal code. State if the director(s) is/are resident Canadian(s). At least 25 per cent of the directors must be resident Canadians (if 25% of the directors is not a whole number, round up to the nearest whole number). Where a corporation has less than four directors, at least one director must be a resident Canadian.
ARTICLE 6	Restrictions, if any, on the business the corporation may carry on or on the powers that the corporation may exercise, as set out in the articles as amended. If none, state so.
ARTICLE 7	The classes and any maximum number of shares that the corporation is authorized to issue as set out in the articles as amended.
ARTICLE 8	Set out the rights, privileges, restrictions and conditions (if any) attaching to each class of shares and directors authority with respect to any class of shares which may be issued in series, as set out in the articles as amended.
ARTICLE 9	Set out restrictions on issue, transfer or ownership of shares as set out in the articles as amended (if any).
ARTICLE 10	Other provisions as set out in the articles as amended (if any).
ARTICLE 11	*These restated articles of incorporation correctly set out the corresponding provisions of the articles of incorporation as amended and supersede the original articles of incorporation and all the amendments thereto.* This statement must be included in the articles.
EXECUTION	Both copies of the articles must contain the full name and original signature of an officer or director of the corporation. Set out the name of the corporation above the signature and in the spaces provided set out the applicant's full name and office (e.g., President, Director, Secretary).

Articles (in duplicate), covering letter and filing fee should be mailed or delivered to:

Ministry of Government Services
Central Production and Verification Services Branch
393 University Avenue, Suite 200
Toronto ON M5G 2M2

375 University Avenue, 2nd Floor (In Person)

07120E (2011/05)

INSTRUCTIONS POUR REMPLIR LE FORMULAIRE

On utilise ce formulaire pour mettre à jour les statuts constitutifs tels que modifiés (autrement dit pour réunir toutes les modifications et les statuts d'origine en un seul document). Les statuts mis à jour remplacent les statuts d'origine et toutes les modifications qui y ont été apportées.

On peut envoyer les statuts – en deux exemplaires – par courrier au bureau de Toronto à l'adresse mentionnée à la fin des instructions. On peut aussi les déposer en personne au bureau de Toronto ou à l'un des bureaux désignés d'enregistrement immobilier / ServiceOntario de la province. Pour une liste des adresses de ces bureaux, voir le feuillet d'information « Bureaux habilités à apposer le certificat sur les statuts relevant de *la Loi sur les sociétés par actions* », ou consulter le site Web du ministère : www.mgs.gov.on.ca. À la page d'accueil du site, choisir la langue et à la page suivante, dans la colonne de droite, sélectionner « Services aux entreprises », puis « Information sur les compagnies »; descendre au bas de l'écran pour trouver le feuillet d'information sous « Questions fréquentes ».

DROITS

150 $ Envoi PAR COURRIER – Paiement par chèque ou mandat libellé à l'ordre du « Ministre des Finances ».

Dépôt EN PERSONNE (au bureau de Toronto) – Paiement en argent comptant; par chèque ou mandat libellé à l'ordre du « Ministre des Finances »; ou par Visa, MasterCard, American Express ou carte de débit. (Si on dépose le document à un bureau d'enregistrement immobilier ou un bureau de ServiceOntario, appeler d'abord le bureau pour savoir s'il accepte les cartes de crédit ou de débit.)

Des frais de service seront perçus pour tout chèque refusé par l'établissement financier.

LETTRE D'INTRODUCTION

Joindre une lettre d'introduction indiquant le nom de la personne à contacter, l'adresse de retour et le numéro de téléphone. Ceci facilitera le traitement des statuts au cas où l'on doive contacter la personne pour poser des questions sur le contenu des documents.

PRÉSENTATION DES DOCUMENTS

Les *Statuts constitutifs mis à jour* doivent être soumis en double exemplaire sur la Formule 5 approuvée par le ministre. Tous les documents soumis doivent être lisibles et se prêter à la photographie sur microfilm. L'information est soit dactylographiée, soit écrite lisiblement en lettres majuscules au recto seulement d'un papier filigrané blanc de bonne qualité, de format 8 ½ po x 11 po (210 mm x 297 mm).

La formule 5 des *Statuts constitutifs mis à jour* comporte des sections numérotées de 1 à 11, qui doivent rester dans cet ordre. Ne retirer aucune page ou section. Si un article ne s'applique pas, inscrire « néant » ou « sans objet » sous le titre. Si, par manque d'espace, on insère des pages supplémentaires, celles ci doivent être du même format que les autres pages et porter le même numéro que la page originale suivi d'une lettre de l'alphabet pour en indiquer l'ordre. Par exemple, les pages insérées après la page 3 seront numérotées 3A, 3B, etc.

SECTION 1 Dans la grille, inscrire le nom courant de la société en lettres majuscules, une lettre par case, en commençant à la première case de la première ligne. Pour chaque espace entre les mots, laisser une case vide. Chaque signe de ponctuation occupe aussi une case distincte. Il faut remplir chaque ligne jusqu'au bout avant de commencer la suivante, même si un mot doit être coupé. Le nom entré doit être identique au nom indiqué sur les *Statuts constitutifs* d'origine ou les *Statuts de fusion*, ou s'il y a eu un changement de nom, au nom qui figure sur les *Statuts de modification* les plus récents.

SOCIÉTÉ DE PLACEMENTS ET DE GE
STION DU PATRIMOINE INC.

07120F (2011/05)

SECTION 2 Indiquer la date originale de la constitution ou de la fusion.

SECTION 3 Indiquer l'adresse du siège social au complet : rue et numéro, bureau (dans le cas d'un immeuble à bureaux), municipalité, province, pays et code postal. Une adresse composée d'une case postale n'est pas acceptée. S'il n'y a pas de rue ni de numéro, indiquer les numéros de lot et de concession. Le siège social doit être situé en Ontario.

SECTION 4 Indiquer le nombre d'administrateurs, tel qu'il figure aux statuts modifiés. Ce peut être un nombre fixe (p. ex. : 1); sinon, indiquer les nombres minimal et maximal d'administrateurs (p. ex. : minimum : 1; maximum : 10). Ne pas remplir les deux.

SECTION 5 Inscrire le nom complet (prénom, autre prénom et nom de famille) et le domicile élu de chacun des premiers administrateurs. L'adresse doit être complète : rue et numéro, bureau, ou R.R., municipalité, province, pays et code postal. Pour chaque administrateur, indiquer s'il est ou non résident canadien. Au moins 25 % des administrateurs doivent être résidents canadiens (si 25 % produit un nombre non entier, arrondir au chiffre entier le plus proche). Si la société a moins de quatre administrateurs, un au moins doit être résident canadien.

SECTION 6 Le cas échéant, indiquer les limites, telles qu'elles figurent aux statuts modifiés, qui sont imposées aux activités ou aux pouvoirs que peut exercer la société. S'il n'y a pas de limites, l'énoncer.

SECTION 7 Indiquer, tels que les renseignements figurent aux statuts modifiés, les catégories et le nombre maximal d'actions, le cas échéant, que la société est autorisée à émettre.

SECTION 8 Énoncer, tels qu'ils figurent aux statuts modifiés, les droits, les privilèges, les restrictions et les conditions, s'il y a lieu, rattachés à chaque catégorie d'actions et les pouvoirs des administrateurs relatifs à chaque catégorie d'actions qui peut être émise en série.

SECTION 9 Le cas échéant, indiquer, telles qu'elles figurent aux statuts modifiés, les restrictions concernant l'émission, le transfert ou la propriété d'actions.

SECTION 10 Énoncer d'autres dispositions, s'il y a lieu, telles qu'elles figurent aux statuts modifiés.

SECTION 11 *Les présents statuts constitutifs mis à jour énoncent correctement les dispositions correspondantes des statuts constitutifs telles qu'elles sont modifiées et remplacent les statuts constitutifs et les modifications qui y ont été apportées.* Cette section fait partie intégrante des statuts; elle doit toujours figurer dans les statuts soumis.

SIGNATURE Les deux exemplaires des statuts doivent indiquer le nom complet et porter la signature **originale** d'un dirigeant ou d'un administrateur. Dans les espaces prévus, indiquer en lettres moulées la dénomination sociale de la société, la fonction du signataire (p. ex. : président, administrateur, secrétaire), et son nom complet.

Envoyer ou remettre les statuts (en deux exemplaires) – avec une lettre d'introduction et les droits prescrits – à l'adresse suivante :

Ministère des Services gouvernementaux
Direction des services centraux de production et de vérification
393, avenue University, bureau 200
Toronto ON M5G 2M2

375, avenue University, 2e étage (dépôt en personne)

07120F (2011/05)

For Ministry Use Only
À l'usage exclusif du ministère

Ontario Corporation Number
Numéro de la société en Ontario

Form 5
Business Corporations Act

Formule 5
Loi sur les sociétés par action

RESTATED ARTICLES OF INCORPORATION
STATUTS CONSTITUTIFS MIS À JOUR

1. The name of the corporation is: (Set out in BLOCK CAPITAL LETTERS)
Dénomination sociale de la société : (Écrire en LETTRES MAJUSCULES SEULEMENT)

2. Date of incorporation/amalgamation:
Date de la constitutioon ou de la fusion

Year, Month, Day / *année, mois, jour*

3. The address of the registered office is:
Adresse du siège social

Street & Number or R.R. Number & if Multi-Office Building give Room No. /
Rue et numéro ou numéro de la R.R. et, s'il s'agit d'un édifice à bureaux, numéro du bureau

ONTARIO

Name of Municipality or Post Office /
Nom de la municipalité ou du bureau de poste

Postal Code/*Code postal*

4. Number of directors is: Fixed number **OR** minimum and maximum
Nombre d'administrateurs : *Nombre fixe* ***OU*** *minimum et maximum*

5. The director(s) is/are: / *Administrateur(s) :*

First name, middle names and surname *Prénom, autres prénoms et nom de famille*	Address for service, giving Street & No. or R.R. No., Municipality, Province, Country and Postal Code *Domicile élu, y compris la rue et le numéro ou le numéro de la R.R., le nom de la municipalité, la province, le pays et le code postal*	Resident Canadian State 'Yes' or 'No' *Résident canadien* *Oui/Non*

07120 (2011/05)

Page 1 of 5

6. Restrictions, if any, on business the corporation may carry on or on powers the corporation may exercise.
Limites, s'il y a lieu, imposées aux activités commerciales ou aux pourvoirs de la société.

7. The classes and any maximum number of shares that the corporation is authorized to issue:
Catégories et nombre maximal, s'il y a lieu, d'actions que la société est autorisée à émettre :

8. Rights, privileges, restrictions and conditions (if any) attaching to each class of shares and directors authority with respect to any class of shares which may be issued in series:

   Droits, privilèges, restrictions et conditions, s'il y a lieu, rattachés à chaque catégorie d'actions et pouvoirs des administrateurs relatifs à chaque catégorie d'actions qui peut être émise en série :

07120 (2011/05)

9. The issue, transfer or ownership of shares is/is not restricted and the restrictions (if any) are as follows:
L'émission, le transfert ou la propriété d'actions est/n'est pas restreint. Les restrictions, s'il y a lieu, sont les suivantes :

10. Other provisions (if any):
Autres dispositions, s'il y a lieu :

11. These restated articles of incorporation correctly set out the corresponding provisions of the articles of incorporation as amended and supersede the original articles of incorporation and all the amendments thereto.
Les présents statuts constitutifs mis à jour énoncent correctement les dispositions correspondantes des statuts constitutifs telles qu'elles sont modifiées et remplacent les statuts constitutifs et les modifications qui y ont été apportées.

These articles are signed in duplicate.
Les présents statuts sont signés en double exemplaire.

____
Name of Corporation / *Dénomination sociale de la société*

By/
Par

____
Signature / *Signature*

____
Print name of signatory / *Nom du signataire en lettres moulées*

____
Description of Office / *Fonction*

These articles **must** be signed by an officer or director of the corporation (e.g. president, secretary)
Ces statuts doivent être signés par un administrateur ou un dirigeant de la société (p. ex. : président, secrétaire).

Form 6 — Articles of Continuance*

INSTRUCTIONS FOR COMPLETING

This form together with the required supporting documents and fee, must be submitted to the Ministry of Government Services by a corporation that is incorporated under the laws of a jurisdiction outside Ontario to apply to continue into Ontario as an Ontario corporation subject to the Ontario *Business Corporations Act* (OBCA).

The Application completed in duplicate with original signatures on both copies may be delivered in person or mailed to the Toronto address listed below. Please note Articles of Continuance are not checked while you wait. The service time for applications filed over-the-counter is 48 hrs or 24 hrs if the expedite fee is paid.

FEES

$ 330.00 **BY MAIL** – cheque or money order payable to the Minister of Finance.
IN PERSON – minimum 48 hour service (at the Toronto office) – cash, cheque or money order payable to Minister of Finance, Visa, MasterCard, American Express or debit card.

$ 500.00 **IN PERSON – 24 hour, expedite service** - (at the Toronto office) – cash, cheque or money order payable to Minister of Finance, Visa, MasterCard, American Express or debit card.

There will be a service charge payable for any cheque returned as non-negotiable by a bank or financial institution.

EFFECTIVE DATE

Articles are effective on the date set out in the certificate endorsed on the articles by the Branch. The certificate is dated the day the Director receives the duplicate originals of the articles together with all other required documents executed in accordance with the Act and the required fee, if they are acceptable as per the Branch's endorsement as of right policy. An effective date of up to 30 days later than the earliest date the articles can be endorsed may be requested **in writing, in the covering letter, using bold or highlighted letters,** upon submission of the articles to the Branch. If you are presenting your documents in person you must also verbally bring this request to the attention of the counter clerk.

SUPPORTING DOCUMENTS

NAME SEARCH

An original Ontario-biased NUANS name search report is required for the name of the corporation or if it is continuing under a new name for the proposed name. A NUANS is not required if the corporation continues under an Ontario number name (see Number Names below). NUANS is a computerized search system that compares a proposed corporate name or trade-mark with databases of existing corporate bodies and trade-marks. This comparison determines the similarity that exists between the proposed name or mark and existing names in the database, and produces a listing of names that are found to be most similar. This search must be submitted together with the duplicate Articles of Continuance within 90 days from production by the NUANS system. For example, articles submitted on November 28th could be accompanied by a NUANS name search report dated as early as August 30th, but not dated earlier. The Companies and Personal Property Security Branch does not provide this search. Suppliers are listed in the Yellow Pages under the heading "Searchers of Records" or visit Industry Canada's NUANS site at, www.nuans.com for a list of registered search houses that can assist you with obtaining a NUANS search report and filing your corporate documents with the Ministry of Government Services. Please note the NUANS search must be **Ontario biased.**

It is the applicant's responsibility to check the search for similar/identical names and to obtain any consent that may be required. The Ministry will not grant a name that is identical to the current name or former name of another corporation operating in Ontario whether active or not, unless it has been more than ten years since the other corporation dissolved or changed its name. The only exception to this rule is when the corporation meets the requirements of Subsection 6(2) of Regulation 62, under the *Business Corporations Act*. In this case a legal opinion must accompany the articles being filed. The legal opinion must be on legal letterhead and must be signed by an individual lawyer (not a law clerk or law firm). It must also clearly indicate that the corporations involved comply with Subsection 6(2) by referring to each clause specifically.

07171 (2011/05)

BILINGUAL NAMES

When continuing a corporation with an English and French form of the name a name search is required for each form of the name (English and French) unless the English and French forms of the name are identical and the legal element in the French form is the French version of the legal element in the English form (for example, INCORPOREE and INCORPORATED). There should be a forward slash (/) separating the two forms of the name.

NUMBER NAMES

You do not require a name search for a number name. In Article 2 on the form, leave nine empty boxes, then type or print in block capital letters the word "ONTARIO" followed by one of the legal elements, LIMITED, LIMITÉE, INCORPORATED, INCORPORÉE, CORPORATION or the corresponding abbreviation LTD., LTÉE, INC., or CORP. The Director of the Companies and Personal Property Security Branch will assign a number to the corporation. Please note an extra-provincial number corporation cannot retain its number name. The corporation must continue under a new name or request an Ontario number name.

CERTIFIED COPY OF INCORPORATING DOCUMENT

Articles of Continuance must be accompanied by a copy of the incorporating document together with all amendments to the document certified by the officer of the incorporating jurisdiction who is authorized to so certify. If the corporation has continued into its current jurisdiction, a copy of the continuation documents and all amendments since continuation certified by an authorized officer of the jurisdiction is required. If the continuation documents do not contain the original date of incorporation a copy of the original incorporation document will also be required.

LETTER OF SATISFACTION / AUTHORIZATION TO CONTINUE

A letter of satisfaction or authorization to continue or other document issued by the proper officer of the jurisdiction in which the corporation is currently incorporated/continued, indicating that the corporation is authorized under the laws of the jurisdiction to apply for Articles of Continuance in Ontario.

LEGAL OPINION

The application must be accompanied by a legal opinion **except for a corporation incorporated under the laws of another Canadian jurisdiction**. The legal opinion must be from an individual lawyer (not a law clerk or law firm) authorized to practice in the jurisdiction and must be to the effect that the laws of the jurisdiction to which the corporation is subject authorize the corporation to apply for continuance.

COVERING LETTER

Enclose a covering letter setting out the name of a contact person, a return address and a telephone number. This will facilitate the processing of the articles should a question arise as to the content of the Articles of Continuance.

EXTRA-PROVINCIAL CORPORATIONS CARRYING ON BUSINESS IN ONTARIO

If prior to continuance the corporation has been carrying on business in Ontario, the Ontario corporation number assigned under the *Corporations Information Act* or the *Extra-Provincial Corporations Act* should be inserted in the box labelled "Ontario Corporation Number" on the first page of the form. The extra-provincial corporation must ensure filings under the *Corporations Information Act* and if applicable the *Extra-Provincial Corporations Act* are current including any corporation name change before filing Articles of Continuance. This is to ensure that information filed prior to continuance is linked with the continued corporation and that the corporation is not assigned duplicate Ontario corporation numbers. Please note that an extra-provincial corporation that is currently carrying on business in Ontario must obtain an original Ontario-biased NUANS name search report before it can continue unless it is continuing under an Ontario number name.

APPEARANCE OF DOCUMENTS

The Articles of Continuance must be completed in duplicate on Form 6 as approved by the Minister. All documents must be legible and compatible with the microfilming process, with the information typed or hand printed in block capital letters, on one side of good quality white bond paper 8 ½" X 11".

07171 (2011/05)

The article headings are numbered 1 to 15 and must remain in that order. Do not leave out any of the headings. If a section does not apply, type "nil" or "not applicable". When additional pages are required, due to lack of space, they should be the same size as all the other pages and should be inserted after the applicable heading with the same number as the heading page, but with the addition of alphabet characters to indicate sequence. For example, pages inserted after page 4 would be numbered 4A, 4B, etc.

ARTICLE 1 Set out the current name of the corporation in block capital letters starting from the first box of the first line on the left with one letter per box and one empty box for a space. Punctuation marks are entered in separate boxes. Complete one line before starting in the first box of the next line. The name entered must be exactly the same as it appeared on the original incorporation document or if there has been a name change, the most recent document changing the name. If the corporation is continuing under its current name the name must be the same as on the NUANS name search.

E	A	S	T		S	I	D	E		I	N	V	E	S	T	M	E	N	T		A	N	D		M	A	N	A	G
E	M	E	N	T		L	T	D	.																				

ARTICLE 2 If the corporation is to be continued in Ontario under a name different from its current corporation name, set out the new name in block capital letters starting from the first box of the first line on the left with one letter per box and one empty box for a space. Punctuation marks are entered in separate boxes. Complete one line before starting in the first box of the next line. The name must be the same as that on the NUANS name search report. If the corporation is continuing with an Ontario number name a NUANS is not required (see "Number Names" above).

ARTICLE 3 Set out the name of the jurisdiction where the corporation is currently incorporated or continued.

ARTICLE 4 Set out the original date of incorporation or amalgamation of the corporation. Do not set out a continuation date.

ARTICLE 5 The address (if multi-office building, include room or suite number) of the registered office of the corporation must be set out in full, including the street name, street number, suite or R.R. #, municipality, province, country and the postal code. A post office box alone is not an acceptable address. If there is no street and number, set out the lot and concession or lot and plan numbers. The registered office must be in Ontario.

ARTICLE 6 Set out the number of directors. This can be either a fixed number of directors (i.e. 1) or a minimum and maximum number (i.e. minimum 1, maximum 10). Do not complete both.

ARTICLE 7 The name(s) (including first name, middle names and surname) and the address for service for each of the directors must be set out. The address should include the street name and number or R.R. #, suite, municipality, province, country and postal code. State if the director(s) is/are Resident Canadian(s). At least 25 per cent of the directors must be resident Canadians (if 25% of the directors is not a whole number round up to the nearest whole number). Where a corporation has less than four directors, at least one must be a resident Canadian.

ARTICLE 8 Set out restrictions, if any, on the business the corporation may carry on or on the powers that the corporation may exercise. If none, state so.

ARTICLE 9 Set out the classes and any maximum number of shares that the corporation is authorized to issue. This item must be completed (e.g., unlimited common shares).

ARTICLE 10 Set out the rights, privileges, restrictions, and conditions etc. (if any) attached to each class of shares, and directors' authority with respect to any class of shares which may be issued in series.

ARTICLE 11 Set out restrictions on issue, transfer or ownership of shares (if any).

ARTICLE 12 Set out other provisions (if any).

07171 (2011/05)

ARTICLE 13 *The corporation has complied with subsection 180(3) of the Business Corporations Act.* This statement must be included in the form confirming that, pursuant to subsection 180(3) of the OBCA, the Articles of Continuance contain any amendment to the incorporating documents required to make the articles conform to the laws of Ontario.

ARTICLE 14 Set out the date the application to continue under the laws of Ontario, was authorized under the laws of the jurisdiction to which the corporation is subject,

ARTICLE 15 *The corporation is to be continued under the Business Corporations Act to the same extent as if it had been incorporated thereunder.* This statement must be included in the application.

EXECUTION Both copies of the articles must have an original signature of an officer or director of the corporation. Set out the name of the officer/director who is signing, the name of the corporation and the office held by the individual in the corporation (e.g., president, director, secretary).

Articles (in duplicate), original Ontario-biased NUANS name search report (if applicable), certified copies of incorporating documents, letter of satisfaction, legal opinion (if applicable), covering letter and filing fee should be mailed or delivered to:

Articles (in duplicate), original Ontario-biased NUANS name search report (if applicable), certified copies of incorporating documents, letter of satisfaction, legal opinion (if applicable), covering letter and filing fee should be mailed or delivered to:

Ministry of Government Services
Companies and Personal Property Security Branch
393 University Avenue, Suite 200
Toronto ON M5G 2M2

375 University Avenue, 2nd Floor (In Person)

07171 (2011/05)

INSTRUCTIONS POUR REMPLIR LE FORMULAIRE

Une société par actions qui n'est pas de l'Ontario et qui désire quitter sa province ou son pays d'origine pour être maintenue en Ontario en tant que société ontarienne doit déposer ce formulaire auprès du ministère des Services gouvernementaux.

Les statuts – en deux exemplaires portant chacun une signature originale – peuvent être déposés en personne ou envoyés à l'adresse appropriée mentionnée à la fin des instructions. Si on les soumet en personne, les Statuts de maintien ne peuvent pas être traités au moment du dépôt. Dans ce cas, le délai de traitement est de 48 heures (service ordinaire), ou de 24 heures (service accéléré facturé).

DROITS

330.00 $ Envoi **PAR COURRIER** – Paiement par chèque ou mandat libellé à l'ordre du « Ministre des Finances ». Dépôt **EN PERSONNE – Service minimum de 48 heures** (bureau de Toronto) – Paiement en argent comptant; par chèque ou mandat libellé à l'ordre du « Ministre des Finances »; ou par Visa, MasterCard, American Express ou carte de débit.

500.00 $ Dépôt **EN PERSONNE – Service accéléré de 24 heures** (bureau de Toronto) – Paiement en argent comptant; par chèque ou mandat libellé à l'ordre du « Ministre des Finances »; ou par Visa, MasterCard, American Express ou carte de débit.

Des frais de service seront perçus pour tout chèque refusé par l'établissement financier.

DATE D'ENTRÉE EN VIGUEUR

Les statuts entrent en vigueur à la date indiquée sur le certificat qui y est apposé. Si les statuts sont acceptables aux termes de la politique d'examen de la Direction des compagnies et des sûretés mobilières qui a le pouvoir de certifier les documents, le certificat porte la date du jour où la directrice reçoit les deux exemplaires originaux des statuts accompagnés des droits prescrits et de tous les documents requis aux termes de la Loi. Au moment du dépôt des statuts, le client peut demander que le certificat de fusion porte une date ultérieure, mais cette date doit être choisie parmi les 30 jours suivant la première date à laquelle les statuts peuvent être certifies. **La demande d'une date ultérieure doit être présentée par écrit, en caractères gras ou surlignés.** Si l'on remet les statuts en personne, l'on doit adresser cette demande verbalement au préposé chargé d'apposer le certificat.

DOCUMENTS À L'APPUI

RAPPORT DE RECHERCHE NUANS

Il faut obtenir l'original d'un rapport de recherche NUANS axé sur l'Ontario pour la dénomination sociale existante de la société ou pour la nouvelle dénomination proposée. Le rapport NUANS n'est pas exigé si la société est maintenue sous une dénomination numérique de l'Ontario (voir plus bas « Dénomination sociale numérique »). NUANS est un système de recherche informatisée qui compare la dénomination ou la marque de commerce proposée pour votre société avec des bases de données de personnes morales et de marques de commerce existantes dans le but de déterminer si le nom proposé est identique ou semblable à des noms existants. Le système produit une liste des noms qui se rapprochent le plus du nom proposé. Le rapport NUANS doit être déposé en même temps que les Statuts de maintien; il doit être remis dans les 90 jours suivant la date de sa production.

Par exemple, des statuts déposés le 28 novembre pourraient être accompagnés d'un rapport NUANS daté du 30 août précédent, mais non d'une date antérieure au 30 août. La Direction des compagnies et des sûretés mobilières ne fournit pas cette recherche.

Les fournisseurs de services de recherche sont indiqués dans les Pages jaunes de l'annuaire, sous « Titres et archives – Recherche » ou « Searchers of Records ». Le site NUANS d'Industrie Canada (www.nuans.com) fournit aussi une liste de maisons de recherche homologuées qui peuvent aider à obtenir le rapport NUANS et à remplir les statuts. Ne pas oublier que le rapport NUANS **doit être axé sur l'Ontario**.

Il incombe au demandeur de faire effectuer une recherche et d'obtenir toute autorisation qui pourrait être requise relativement à un nom similaire. Le ministère n'acceptera pas une dénomination sociale identique à celle, courante ou ancienne, d'une autre société opérant en Ontario, que celle ci soit en activité ou non, sauf si cette société a été dissoute ou a changé de nom il y a plus de 10 ans. Cette règle ne s'applique pas dans le cas où la société remplit les conditions énoncées au paragraphe 6 (2) du Règlement 62 de la *Loi sur les sociétés par actions.* Dans ce cas-ci une opinion légale doit accompagner les articles étant classés. L'opinion juridique doit être présentée sur le papier à lettre officiel à en tête de l'avocat et doit être signée par l'avocat (et non par son clerc). Elle doit aussi indiquer clairement que les sociétés concernées se conforment au paragraphe 6 (2) du règlement en reprenant chacun des alinéas du paragraphe.

07171 (2011/05)

DÉNOMINATION SOCIALE BILINGUE

Si on maintient la société une dénomination anglaise et française, il faut obtenir et soumettre un rapport de recherche NUANS pour chacune des deux versions, sauf si les versions anglaise et française sont identiques, l'élément juridique à la fin de la version française devant être la traduction de l'élément juridique de la version anglaise (p. ex. : INCORPORÉE pour INCORPORATED). Les noms anglais et français doivent être séparés par une ligne oblique (/).

DÉNOMINATION SOCIALE NUMÉRIQUE

Si on donne à la société une dénomination numérique, il n'est pas nécessaire de soumettre un rapport de recherche NUANS. Dans la grille de la section 2 du formulaire, pour inscrire le nouveau nom de la société, laisser 9 cases vides, puis inscrire tout en lettres majuscules, une lettre par case, le mot ONTARIO suivi d'un des éléments juridiques suivants : LIMITED, LIMITÉE, INCORPORATED, INCORPORÉE, CORPORATION, ou les abréviations correspondantes : LTD, LTÉE, INC. ou CORP. La Direction des compagnies et des sûretés mobilières assignera ensuite un numéro à la société. Il faut savoir qu'une société extraprovinciale à dénomination numérique ne peut pas conserver cette dénomination numérique. Pour être maintenue en Ontario, la société doit prendre une nouvelle dénomination ou demander une dénomination numérique de l'Ontario.

COPIE CERTIFIÉE DE L'ACTE CONSTITUTIF

Les Statuts de maintien doivent être accompagnés d'une copie de l'acte constitutif et de toutes les modifications s'y rapportant, ces documents devant être certifiés par le fonctionnaire compétent du territoire (p. ex. : province ou territoire canadien, État ou pays) où la société a été constituée. Si la société a fait l'objet d'un maintien dans la province ou le pays où elle opère présentement, il faut joindre une copie de l'acte de maintien et de toutes les modifications s'y rapportant, ces documents devant être certifiés par le fonctionnaire compétent du territoire courant. Si les actes de maintien ne portent pas la date de la constitution originale, une copie de l'acte constitutif original doit être également jointe.

LETTRE D'APPROBATION / AUTORISATION DE MAINTIEN

Il faut joindre une lettre d'approbation ou une autorisation de maintien ou tout autre document délivré par le fonctionnaire compétent du territoire (p. ex. : province ou territoire canadien, État ou pays) dont relève la société, qui indique que la société est autorisée, aux termes des lois de ce territoire, à demander des statuts de maintien pour l'Ontario.

AVIS JURIDIQUE

Dans le cas où la société a été constituée hors du Canada, il faut joindre un avis juridique d'un avocat individuel (et non de son clerc ni du cabinet d'avocats) autorisé à exercer dans le territoire d'origine, indiquant que les lois du territoire dont relève la société autorisent la société à demander des statuts de maintien.

LETTRE D'INTRODUCTION

Joindre une lettre d'introduction indiquant le nom de la personne à contacter, l'adresse de retour et le numéro de téléphone. Ceci facilitera le traitement des statuts au cas où l'on doive contacter la personne pour poser des questions sur le contenu des Statuts de maintien.

SOCIÉTÉS EXTRAPROVINCIALES MENANT DES ACTIVITÉS EN ONTARIO

Si la société mène déjà des activités en Ontario avant son maintien en Ontario, le numéro de la société en Ontario assigné aux termes de la *Loi sur les renseignements exigés des personnes morales* ou de la *Loi sur les personnes morales extraprovinciales* doit être indiqué dans la case prévue à cet effet en haut du formulaire. Avant de déposer les Statuts de maintien, la société doit s'assurer qu'elle a déposé tous les documents requis aux termes de la *Loi sur les renseignements exigés des personnes morales* et, s'il y a lieu, de la *Loi sur les personnes morales extraprovinciales*, y compris, le cas échéant, les statuts de modification de dénomination sociale. De cette manière, on s'assure que l'information déposée avant le maintien en Ontario est ensuite rattachée à la société une fois maintenue et que la société ne se retrouve pas avec deux numéros matricule pour l'Ontario. Veuillez noter que, pour être maintenue en Ontario, une société extraprovinciale qui mène déjà des activités en Ontario doit obtenir et fournir au préalable l'original d'un rapport de recherche NUANS axé sur l'Ontario, sauf si la société est maintenue sous une dénomination sociale numérique.

07171 (2011/05)

PRÉSENTATION DES DOCUMENTS

Les Statuts de maintien doivent être soumis en double exemplaire sur la Formule 6 approuvée par le ministre. Tous les documents soumis doivent être lisibles et se prêter à la photographie sur microfilm. L'information est soit dactylographiée, soit écrite lisiblement en lettres majuscules au recto seulement d'un papier filigrané blanc de bonne qualité, de format 8 ½ po x 11 po.

La formule des Statuts de maintien comporte 15 sections numérotées de 1 à 15, qui doivent rester dans cet ordre. Ne retirer aucune page ou section. Si un article ne s'applique pas, inscrire « néant » ou « sans objet » sous le titre. Si, par manque d'espace, on insère des pages supplémentaires, celles ci doivent être du même format que les autres pages et porter le même numéro que la page originale suivi d'une lettre de l'alphabet pour en indiquer l'ordre. Par exemple, les pages insérées après la page 4 seront numérotées 4A, 4B, etc.

SECTION 1 Dans la grille, inscrire le nom de la société en lettres majuscules, une lettre par case, en commençant à la première case de la première ligne. Pour chaque espace entre les mots, laisser une case vide. Chaque signe de ponctuation occupe aussi une case distincte. Il faut remplir chaque ligne jusqu'au bout avant de commencer la suivante, même si un mot doit être coupé. Le nom entré doit être identique au nom indiqué sur les Statuts constitutifs d'origine ou, s'il y a eu un changement de nom, au nom qui figure sur les Statuts de modification les plus récents. Si la société est maintenue sous son nom actuel, le nom doit être identique à celui qui figure sur le rapport de recherche NUANS.

S	O	C	I	É	T	É		D	E		P	L	A	C	E	M	E	N	T	S		E	T		D	E		G	E
S	T	I	O	N		D	U		P	A	T	R	I	M	O	I	N	E		I	N	C	.						

SECTION 2 Si la société doit être maintenue en Ontario sous une dénomination sociale différente de sa dénomination actuelle, inscrire le nouveau nom en lettres majuscules, une lettre par case, en commençant à la première case de la première ligne. Pour chaque espace entre les mots, laisser une case vide. Chaque signe de ponctuation occupe aussi une case distincte. Il faut remplir chaque ligne jusqu'au bout avant de commencer la suivante, même si un mot doit être coupé. Le nom doit être identique au nom qui figure sur le rapport de recherche NUANS. Si la société est maintenue sous une dénomination sociale numérique de l'Ontario, un rapport de recherche NUANS n'est pas requis (voir plus loin loin la rubrique « Dénomination sociale numérique »)

SECTION 3 Indiquer le nom du territoire de provenance (p. ex. : province ou territoire canadien, État ou pays) où la société a été constituée ou maintenue.

SECTION 4 Indiquer la date originale de la constitution ou la date de la fusion de la société. Ne pas indiquer ici la date du maintien.

SECTION 5 Indiquer l'adresse du siège social au complet : rue et numéro, bureau (dans le cas d'un immeuble à bureaux), municipalité, province, pays et code postal. Une adresse composée d'une case postale n'est pas acceptée. S'il n'y a pas de rue ni de numéro, indiquer les numéros de lot et de concession. Le siège social doit être situé en Ontario.

SECTION 6 Indiquer le nombre d'administrateurs dans la case appropriée. Ce peut être un nombre fixe (p. ex. : 1); <u>sinon</u>, indiquer les nombres minimal et maximal d'administrateurs (p. ex. : minimum : 1; maximum : 10). <u>Ne pas remplir les deux.</u>

SECTION 7 Inscrire le nom complet (prénom, autre prénom et nom de famille) et le domicile élu de chacun des premiers administrateurs. L'adresse doit être complète : rue et numéro, bureau, ou R.R., municipalité, province, pays et code postal. Les administrateurs doivent être des personnes physiques, non des personnes morales. Pour chaque administrateur, indiquer s'il est ou non résident canadien. Au moins 25 % des administrateurs doivent être résidents canadiens (si 25 % produit un nombre non entier, arrondir au chiffre entier le plus proche). Si la société a moins de quatre administrateurs, un au moins doit être résident canadien.

07171 (2011/05)

SECTION 8 Indiquer ici, le cas échéant, les limites imposées aux activités ou aux pouvoirs que peut exercer la société. S'il n'y a pas de limites, l'énoncer.

SECTION 9 Indiquer les catégories et le nombre maximal d'actions, le cas échéant, que la société est autorisée à émettre. Quoi qu'il en soit, il faut donner une réponse à cette section (p. ex. : actions ordinaires illimitées).

SECTION 10 Énoncer les droits, les privilèges, les restrictions et les conditions, (s'il y a lieu), rattachés à chaque catégorie d'actions et indiquer aussi les pouvoirs des administrateurs relatifs à chaque catégorie d'actions qui peut être émise en série.

SECTION 11 Indiquer les restrictions, le cas échéant, concernant l'émission, le transfert ou la propriété d'actions, (s'il y a lieu).

SECTION 12 Énoncer d'autres dispositions, (s'il y a lieu).

SECTION 13 *La société s'est conformée au paragraphe 180 (3) de la Loi sur les sociétés par actions.* Cette déclaration vise à confirmer que les Statuts de maintien renferment toute modification qu'il a fallu apporter aux statuts constitutifs pour rendre les statuts conformes aux lois de l'Ontario. Cette section fait partie intégrante des statuts; elle doit toujours figurer dans les statuts soumis.

SECTION 14 Indiquer la date à laquelle la demande pour être maintenue en Ontario a été autorisée par l'autorité législative du territoire dont relève actuellement la société.

SECTION 15 *Le maintien de la société en vertu de la Loi sur les sociétés par actions a le même effet que si la société avait été constituée en vertu de cette loi.* Cette section fait partie intégrante des statuts; elle doit toujours figurer dans les statuts soumis.

SIGNATURE Les deux exemplaires des statuts doivent porter la signature originale d'un dirigeant ou d'un administrateur. Dans les espaces prévus, indiquer en lettres moulées la dénomination sociale de la société, la fonction du signataire (p. ex. : président, administrateur, secrétaire), et son nom complet.

Envoyer ou remettre les statuts (en deux exemplaires) – avec l'original d'un rapport de recherche NUANS axé sur l'Ontario (s'il y a lieu), les copies certifiées de l'acte constitutif et des modifications, une lettre d'approbation, un avis juridique (s'il y a lieu), une lettre d'introduction et les droits prescrits – à l'adresse suivante:

Ministère des Services gouvernementaux
Direction des compagnies et des sûretés mobilières
393, avenue University, bureau 200
Toronto ON M5G 2M2

375, avenue University, 2e étage (dépôt en personne)

07171 (2011/05)

For Ministry Use Only
À l'usage exclusif du ministère

Ontario Corporation Number
Numéro de la société en Ontario

Form 6
Business Corporations Act

Formule 6
Loi sur les sociétés par actions

ARTICLES OF CONTINUANCE
STATUTS DE MAINTIEN

1. The name of the corporation is: (Set out in BLOCK CAPITAL LETTERS)
Dénomination sociale de la société : (Écrire en LETTRES MAJUSCULES SEULEMENT) :

2. The corporation is to be continued under the name (if different from 1):
Nouvelle dénomination sociale de la société (si elle différente de celle inscrite ci-dessus) :

3. Name of jurisdiction the corporation is leaving: / Nom du territoire (province ou territoire, État ou pays) que quitte la société :

Name of jurisdiction / Nom du territoire

4. Date of incorporation/amalgamation: / Date de la constitution ou de la fusion :

Year, Month, Day / année, mois, jour

5. The address of the registered office is: / Adresse du siège social en :

Street & Number or R.R. Number & if Multi-Office Building give Room No.
Rue et numéro ou numéro de la R.R. et, s'il s'agit d'un édifice à bureaux, numéro du bureau

ONTARIO

Name of Municipality or Post Office / Nom de la municipalité ou du bureau de poste

Postal Code/Code postal

07171 (2011/05)

Page 1 of/de 7

6. Number of directors is/are: Nombre d'administrateurs :

Fixed number / Nombre fixe		OR minimum and maximum / OU minimum et maximum		

7. The director(s) is/are: / Administrateur(s) :

First name, middle names and surname Prénom, autres prénoms et nom de famille	Address for service, giving Street & No. or R.R. No., Municipality, Province, Country and Postal Code Domicile élu, y compris la rue et le numéro ou le numéro de la R.R., le nom de la municipalité, la province, le pays et le code postal	Resident Canadian State 'Yes' or 'No' Résident canadien Oui/Non

8. Restrictions, if any, on business the corporation may carry on or on powers the corporation may exercise.
Limites, s'il y a lieu, imposées aux activités commerciales ou aux pouvoirs de la société.

07171 (2011/05)

Page 2 of/de 7

9. The classes and any maximum number of shares that the corporation is authorized to issue:
Catégories et nombre maximal, s'il y a lieu, d'actions que la société est autorisée à émettre :

07171 (2011/05) Page 3 of/de 7

10. Rights, privileges, restrictions and conditions (if any) attaching to each class of shares and directors authority with respect to any class of shares which may be issued in series:
Droits, privilèges, restrictions et conditions, s'il y a lieu, rattachés à chaque catégorie d'actions et pouvoirs des administrateurs relatifs à chaque catégorie d'actions qui peut être émise en série :

07171 (2011/05)

Page 4 of/de 7

11. The issue, transfer or ownership of shares is/is not restricted and the restrictions (if any) are as follows:
L'émission, le transfert ou la propriété d'actions est/n'est pas restreint. Les restrictions, s'il y a lieu, sont les suivantes :

12. Other provisions, (if any):
Autres dispositions s'il y a lieu :

07171 (2011/05)

13. The corporation has complied with subsection 180(3) of the *Business Corporations Act*.
La société s'est conformée au paragraphe 180(3) de la *Loi sur les sociétés par actions*.

14. The continuation of the corporation under the laws of the Province of Ontario has been properly authorized under the laws of the jurisdiction in which the corporation was incorporated/amalgamated or previously continued on
Le maintien de la société en vertu des lois de la province de l'Ontario a été dûment autorisé en vertu des lois de l'autorité législative sous le régime de laquelle la société a été constituée ou fusionnée ou antérieurement maintenue le

Year, Month, Day
année, mois, jour

15. The corporation is to be continued under the *Business Corporations Act* to the same extent as if it had been incorporated thereunder.
Le maintien de la société en vertu de la *Loi sur les sociétés par actions* a le même effet que si la société avait été constituée en vertu de cette loi.

These articles are signed in duplicate.
Les présents statuts sont signés en double exemplaire.

Name of Corporation / Dénomination sociale de la société

By / Par

Signature / Signature

Print name of signatory / Nom du signataire en lettres moulées

Description of Office / Fonction

These articles **must** be signed by a director or officer of the corporation (e.g. president, secretary)
Ces statuts doivent être signés par un administrateur ou un dirigeant de la société (p. ex. : président, secrétaire).

07171 (2011/05)

Page 7 of/de 7

Form 7 — Application for Authorization to Continue in Another Jurisdiction*

INSTRUCTIONS FOR COMPLETING

This form must be completed by a corporation incorporated under the *Business Corporations Act* for authorization by the Director to apply to continue in a jurisdiction outside Ontario (transfer out of Ontario).

The Application completed in duplicate with original signatures on both copies may be mailed to the Toronto address listed below or filed in person at the Toronto office for over-the-counter service.

FEE

$330.00 **BY MAIL**- cheque or money order payable to the Minister of Finance.

IN PERSON – (at the Toronto office) – cash, cheque or money order payable to Minister of Finance, Visa, MasterCard, American Express or debit card.

There will be a service charge payable for any cheque returned as non-negotiable by a bank or financial institution.

SUPPORTING DOCUMENTS

CONSENT FROM THE MINISTER OF REVENUE

The application must be accompanied by written consent from the Minister of Revenue to apply to continue outside Ontario, and must be submitted within 60 days after the Minister of Revenue provides consent. To obtain this consent, contact the Ministry of Revenue at:

Ministry of Revenue
Client Accounts and Services Branch
33 King Street West
PO Box 622
Oshawa ON L1H 8H5
Fax: 905 433-5418

Telephone Enquiries can be made to the Canada Revenue Agency at:
Service in English: 1 800 959-5525
Service in French: 1 800 959-7775
TTY : 1 800 665-0354

CONSENT OF THE ONTARIO SECURITIES COMMISSION

Where the corporation is offering securities to the public within the meaning of subsection 1(6) of the Ontario *Business Corporations Act* (OBCA), the application must be accompanied by written consent from the Ontario Securities Commission. You can contact the Ontario Securities Commission at:

By Telephone at: 416 593-8314 (local Toronto calling area)
or Toll-Free number (throughout Canada) at: 1 877 785-1555
TTY: 1 866 827-1295
By E-Mail at: inquiries@osc.gov.on.ca.
By regular mail: Ontario Securities Commission
20 Queen Street West, Suite 1903
Toronto ON M5H 3S8

07170 (2011/04)

LEGAL OPINION

If the corporation is applying to continue in a jurisdiction outside Canada, the application must be accompanied by a legal opinion from an individual lawyer (not a law clerk) authorized to practice in the other jurisdiction, to the effect that the laws of the jurisdiction to which the corporation is applying to continue, meet all the requirements set out in subsection 181(9) of the Ontario *Business Corporations Act.* The legal opinion must be on letterhead paper, and signed by an individual lawyer. The legal opinion must refer to each clause under subsection 181(9), specifically stating that the laws of the other jurisdiction provide in effect that:

a) the property of the corporation continues to be the property of the body corporate;
b) the body corporate continues to be liable for the obligations of the corporation;
c) an existing cause of action, claim or liability to prosecution is unaffected;
d) a civil, criminal or administrative action or proceeding pending by or against the corporation may be continued to be prosecuted by or against the body corporate; and
e) a conviction against the corporation may be enforced against the body corporate or a ruling, order or judgment in favour of or against the corporation may be enforced by or against the body corporate.

COVERING LETTER

A covering letter setting out the name of a contact person, a return address and a telephone number is required. This will facilitate the processing of the Application should a question arise as to the content of the Application.

APPEARANCE OF DOCUMENTS

The Application for Authorization to Continue in Another Jurisdiction must be completed in duplicate on Form 7 as approved by the Minister. All documents must be legible and compatible with the microfilming process, with the information typed or hand printed in block capital letters, on one side of good quality, white bond paper 81/2" by 11".

The headings on the form should be numbered 1 to 9 and should remain in that order. Do not leave out any of the headings.

APPLICATION

ITEM 1 Set out the current name of the corporation in block capital letters starting from the first box on the left-hand side of the first line, with one letter per box and one empty box for a space. Punctuation marks are entered in separate boxes. Complete one line before starting in the first box of the next line. The name entered must be exactly the same as it appeared on the original Articles of Incorporation or Articles of Amalgamation, or if there has been a name change, the most recent Articles of Amendment changing the name.

ITEM 2 Set out the original date of incorporation/amalgamation of the corporation.

ITEM 3 The corporation is not in default in filing notices and returns under the *Corporations Information Act* and all outstanding fees have been paid. ***This statement must be included on the application confirming all filings under the Corporations Information Act have been made and all outstanding fees paid.***

ITEM 4 On the line provided set out the name of the jurisdiction where the corporation is applying to continue. (e.g. Canada-federal, Alberta, Delaware, Germany)

ITEM 5 The Corporation must confirm that the laws of the jurisdiction where it is applying to continue meet the requirements set out in subsection 181(9) of the *Business Corporations Act* (paragraphs, 5(a) to 5(e) on the form).

07170 (2011/04)

ITEM 6 Indicate by checking the appropriate box whether the corporation is applying to continue in another Canadian jurisdiction or to a jurisdiction outside Canada. If the corporation is applying to continue outside Canada, a legal opinion to the effect that the laws of the other jurisdiction meet the requirements set out in 181(9) of the Act must accompany the application (see above, Legal Opinion).

ITEM 7 This application has been authorized by a special resolution. ***This statement must be included on the application confirming that the application for continuance has been authorized by a special resolution of the shareholders.***

ITEM 8 Consent from the Minister of Revenue to apply to continue the corporation in a jurisdiction outside Ontario must accompany the application (see above, Consent from the Minister of Revenue).

ITEM 9 Indicate by checking the appropriate box whether the corporation is offering securities to the public within the meaning of subsection 1(6) of the *Business Corporations Act*. If the corporation is an offering corporation, consent from the Ontario Securities Commission to apply to continue out of Ontario must accompany the application (see above, Consent of the Ontario Securities Commission).

EXECUTION

Both copies of the application must have original signatures of an officer or director of the corporation. Set out the name of the corporation above the signature and beside the signature set out the applicant's office (e.g., President, Director, Secretary).

PLEASE NOTE

The authorization of the Director to continue outside Ontario, if provided, expires six months after the effective date stamped on the application (subsection 181(6) of the *Business Corporations Act*), unless within the six-month period the corporation is continued under the laws of the other jurisdiction. If the corporation does not continue to the other jurisdiction within the six months, it remains an Ontario corporation. A new application would be required if the corporation still wishes to continue in another jurisdiction after the authorization expires.

The corporation is required to file with the Director a copy of the instrument of continuance issued to it by the other jurisdiction within sixty days after the date of issuance (subsection 181(7) of the *Business Corporations Act*). The corporation will appear on the public record as an Ontario corporation until the Companies and Personal Property Security Branch receives a copy of the instrument of continuance.

Applications (in duplicate), consent of the Minister of Revenue, consent of the Ontario Securities Commission (if applicable), any outstanding notices or returns, a covering letter, the filing fee and any outstanding Notice/Return fee should be mailed or delivered to:

Ministry of Government Services
Central Production and Verification Services Branch
393 University Avenue, Suite 200
Toronto ON M5G 2M2

375 University Avenue, 2nd Floor (In Person)

07170 (2011/04)

INSTRUCTIONS – COMMENT REMPLIR LE FORMULAIRE

Une société par actions constituée en société en vertu de la *Loi sur les sociétés par actions* doit remplir la présente formule dans le but de demander l'autorisation du directeur de présenter une demande d'autorisation de maintien sous le régime d'une autre autorité législative que l'Ontario (transfert à l'extérieur de l'Ontario).

On peut envoyer la demande d'autorisation remplie en double exemplaire et portant la signature d'origine par courrier au bureau de Toronto à l'adresse ci-dessous ou les remettre en personne au bureau de Toronto.

DROITS

330.00 $ **PAR COURRIER** – Paiement par chèque ou mandat libellé à l'ordre du « Ministre des Finances ».
EN PERSONNE (au bureau de Toronto) – Paiement en argent comptant; par chèque ou mandat libellé à l'ordre du « Ministre des Finances »; ou par Visa, MasterCard, American Express ou carte de débit.

Des frais d'administration seront perçus pour tout chèque refusé par une banque ou une institution financière.

DOCUMENTS À L'APPUI
CONSENTEMENT ÉMANANT DU MINISTRE DU REVENU

La demande doit être accompagnée d'un consentement écrit émanant du ministre du Revenu pour demander l'autorisation de présenter une demande de maintien à l'extérieur de l'Ontario, et elle doit être soumise dans les 60 jours suivant le consentement du ministre du Revenu. Pour obtenir un consentement, prière de communiquer avec le ministère du Revenu à l'adresse suivante :

Ministère du Revenu
Direction des services et des dossiers clients
33, rue King Ouest
CP 622 Oshawa ON L1H 8H5
Télélecopieur : 905 433-5418

Les demandes par téléphone peuvent être adressées à l'agence du Revenu du Canada aux numéros suivants :
Service en anglais : 1 800 959-5525
Service en français : 1 800 959-7775
ATS : 1 800 665-0354

CONSENTEMENT DE LA COMMISSION DES VALEURS MOBILIÈRES DE L'ONTARIO

S'il s'agit d'une société qui offre des valeurs mobilières au public au sens du paragraphe 1(6) de la *Loi sur les sociétés par actions* de l'Ontario, la demande doit être accompagnée du consentement écrit de la Commission des valeurs mobilières de l'Ontario. Prière de communiquer avec la Commission des valeurs mobilières de l'Ontario à l'adresse suivante :

Par téléphone : 416 593-8314 (numéro local à Toronto)
ou au numéro sans frais : 1 877 785-1555 (partout au Canada)
ATS (malentendants/malvoyants) : 1 866 827-1295
Par courriel : inquiries@osc.gov.on.ca.
Par la poste : Commission des valeurs mobilières de l'Ontario
20, rue Queen Ouest, bureau 1903
Toronto ON M5H 3S8

07170 (2011/04)

AVIS JURIDIQUE

Si la société présente une demande de maintien à l'extérieur du Canada, la demande doit être accompagnée d'un avis juridique d'un avocat (et non d'un stagiaire en droit) autorisé à pratiquer le droit dans l'autre autorité législative, stipulant que les lois de l'autorité législative dans laquelle la société veut être maintenue répondent à toutes les exigences énoncées au paragraphe 181(9) de la *Loi sur les sociétés par actions* de l'Ontario. L'opinion juridique doit être présentée sur papier à en-tête et signée par l'avocat. L'avis juridique doit faire référence à chacune des dispositions du paragraphe 181(9) et indiquer que les lois de l'autre autorité législative prévoient effectivement ce qui suit :

a) la personne morale devient propriétaire des biens de la société;
b) la personne morale est responsable des obligations de la société;
c) il n'est pas porté atteinte aux causes d'action, demandes ou responsabilités possibles existantes;
d) la personne morale remplace la société dans les poursuites civiles, pénales ou administratives intentées par ou contre celle-ci;
e) toute décision judiciaire ou quasi judiciaire rendue en faveur de la société ou contre elle est exécutoire à l'égard de la personne morale.

LETTRE D'INTRODUCTION

Il faut fournir une lettre d'introduction qui indique le nom de la personne à contacter, une adresse d'expéditeur et un numéro de téléphone. Cela permettra de traiter plus facilement la demande en cas de questions sur son contenu.

PRÉSENTATION DES DOCUMENTS

La Demande d'autorisation de maintien sous le régime d'une autre autorité législative doit être soumise en double exemplaire, sur la Formule 7 approuvée par arrêté ministériel. Tous les documents doivent être lisibles et se prêter à la photocopie sur microfilm. L'information est soit dactylographiée, soit écrite en lettres majuscules au recto seulement d'un papier filigrané blanc de bonne qualité, de format 8 ½ po x 11 po.

La formule comporte des sections numérotées de 1 à 9, qui doivent rester dans cet ordre. Ne retirer aucune section.

DEMANDE

SECTION 1 Dans la grille, inscrire le nom actuel de la société en lettres majuscules, une lettre par case, en commençant à la première case de la première ligne. Pour chaque espace entre les mots, laisser une case vide. Chaque signe de ponctuation occupe une case distincte. Il faut remplir chaque ligne jusqu'au bout avant de commencer la suivante, même si un mot doit être coupé. Le nom inscrit doit être le nom indiqué sur les Statuts constitutifs ou les Statuts de fusion. S'il y a eu un changement de nom, il faut inscrire le nom qui figure dans les Statuts de modification les plus récents.

SECTION 2 Indiquer la date initiale de la constitution ou de la fusion de la société.

SECTION 3 La société n'a pas omis de déposer les avis et déclarations exigés par la *Loi sur les renseignements exigés des personnes morales* et tous les droits ont été acquittés. **Cette déclaration doit être incluse dans la demande et confirmer que tous les rapports en vertu de la *Loi sur les renseignements exigés des personnes morales* ont été déposés, y compris l'acquittement de tous les droits.**

SECTION 4 Indiquer, sur la ligne prévue à cet effet, le nom de l'autorité législative dans laquelle la société veut être maintenue (p. ex., Canada-fédéral, Alberta, Delaware, Allemagne).

SECTION 5 La société doit confirmer que les lois de l'autorité législative dans laquelle elle veut être maintenue répondent à toutes les exigences énoncées au paragraphe 181(9) de la *Loi sur les sociétés par actions* (alinéas 5(a) à 5(e) de la formule).

07170 (2011/04)

SECTION 6 Indiquer, en cochant l'une des deux cases, si la société veut demander le maintien dans une autorité législative au Canada ou dans une autorité législative à l'extérieur du Canada. Si la société présente une demande de maintien à l'extérieur du Canada, la demande doit être accompagnée d'un avis juridique stipulant que les lois de l'autorité législative dans laquelle la société veut être maintenue répondent à toutes les exigences énoncées au paragraphe 181(9) de la Loi (veuillez consulter la section Avis juridique ci-haut).

SECTION 7 La présente demande a été autorisée par une résolution spéciale. ***Cette déclaration doit être incluse dans la demande et confirmer que la demande d'autorisation de maintien a été autorisée par une résolution spéciale des actionnaires.***

SECTION 8 La demande doit être accompagnée d'un consentement émanant du ministre du Revenu pour demander l'autorisation de présenter une demande de maintien à l'extérieur de l'Ontario (veuillez consulter la section Consentement émanant du ministre du Revenu ci-haut).

SECTION 9 Indiquer, en cochant l'une des deux cases, s'il s'agit d'une société qui offre des valeurs mobilières au public au sens du paragraphe 1(6) de la *Loi sur les sociétés par actions.* Si la société offre des valeurs mobilières au public, la demande doit être accompagnée du consentement de la Commission des valeurs mobilières de l'Ontario pour demander l'autorisation de présenter une demande de maintien à l'extérieur de l'Ontario (veuillez consulter la section Consentement de la Commission des valeurs mobilières de l'Ontario ci-haut).

SIGNATURE

Les deux exemplaires de la demande doivent porter la signature originale d'un dirigeant ou d'un administrateur de la société. Indiquer la dénomination sociale de la société au-dessus de la signature et indiquer le mandat de la personne qui signe les documents à côté de la signature (p. ex., président, administrateur, secrétaire).

NOTE

L'autorisation de la demande de maintien à l'extérieur de l'Ontario accordée par le directeur, le cas échéant, devient caduque six mois après la date de l'apposition de l'autorisation sur la demande (paragraphe 181(6) de la LSAO), sauf si, au cours de cette période, la société est maintenue en vertu des lois de l'autre compétence législative. Si la société n'est pas maintenue dans une autre autorité législative dans les six mois, elle demeure une société ontarienne. La société doit présenter une nouvelle demande si elle veut être maintenue dans une autre autorité législative après que l'autorisation soit devenue caduque.

Dans les soixante jours de la date d'émission, la société doit déposer auprès du directeur un exemplaire de l'acte de maintien émis par l'autre compétence législative (paragraphe 181(7) de la LSAO). La société demeurera inscrite au registre public des sociétés de l'Ontario jusqu'à ce que la Direction des compagnies et des sûretés mobilières reçoive un exemplaire de l'acte de maintien.

Envoyer ou remettre (en double exemplaire), le consentement émanant du ministre du Revenu, le consentement de la Commission des valeurs mobilières de l'Ontario (s'il y a lieu), tous les avis ou déclarations en circulation, une lettre d'introduction, les droits prescrits ainsi que les droits prescrits relatifs à tous les avis ou déclarations en circulation à l'adresse suivante :

Ministère des Services gouvernementaux
Direction des services centraux de production et de vérification
393, avenue University, bureau 200
Toronto ON M5G 2M2

375, avenue University, 2e étage (dépôt en personne)

07170 (2011/04)

For Ministry Use Only
À l'usage exclusif du ministère

Ontario Corporation Number
Numéro de la société en Ontario

Form 7
Business Corporations Act

Formule 7
Loi sur les sociétés par actions

APPLICATION FOR AUTHORIZATION TO CONTINUE IN ANOTHER JURISDICTION
DEMANDE D'AUTORISATION DE MAINTIEN SOUS LE RÉGIME D'UNE AUTRE AUTORITÉ LÉGISLATIVE

1. The name of the corporation is: (Set out in BLOCK CAPITAL letters)
Dénomination sociale de la société : (Écrire en LETTRES MAJUSCULES SEULEMENT)

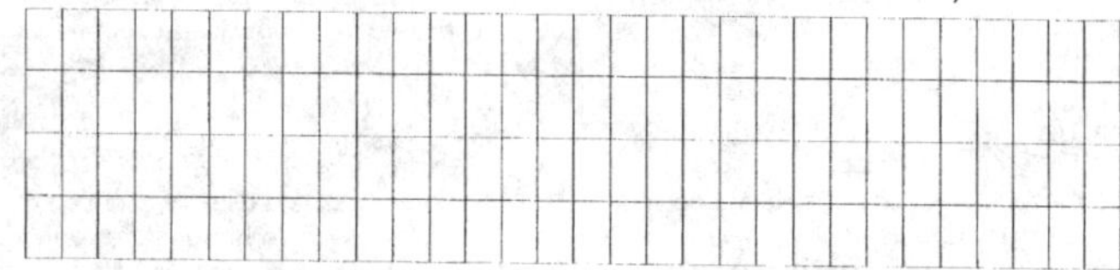

2. Date of incorporation/amalgamation:
Date de la constitution ou de la fusion :

Year, Month, Day / année, mois, jour

3. The corporation is not in default in filing notices and returns under the *Corporations Information Act* and all out standing fees have been paid.
La société n'a pas omis de déposer les avis et déclarations exigés par la *Loi sur les renseignements exigés des personnes morales* et tous les droits ont été acquittés.

4. It is requested that the corporation be authorized by the Director under section 181 of the *Business Corporations Act* to apply to the appropriate official or public body of the following jurisdiction requesting that the corporation be continued as if it had been incorporated under the laws of that jurisdiction :
La société demande l'autorisation du directeur aux termes de l'article 181 de la *Loi sur les sociétés par actions* de demander au fonctionnaire ou à l'organisme public compétents de l'autorité législative suivante que la société soit maintenue comme si elle avait été constituée en vertu des lois de cette autorité législative :

(Set out the name of the jurisdiction where the corporation is applying to continue)
(Indiquer le nom de l'autorité législative dans laquelle la société demande d'être maintenue)

5. The laws of the jurisdiction to which the corporation will apply for an instrument of continuance provide in effect that:
Les lois de l'autorité législative à laquelle la société va demander un acte de maintien prévoient effectivement ce qui suit :

a) the property of the corporation continues to be the property of the body corporate;
la personne morale devient propriétaire des biens de la société;

b) the body corporate continues to be liable for the obligations of the corporation;
la personne morale est responsable des obligations de la société;

c) an existing cause of action, claim or liability to prosecution is unaffected;
il n'est pas porté atteinte aux causes d'action, demandes ou responsabilités possibles existantes;

07170 (2011/04)

Page 1 of/de 2

d) a civil, criminal or administrative action or proceeding pending by or against the corporation may be continued to be prosecuted by or against the body corporate; and
la personne morale remplace la société dans les poursuites civiles, pénales ou administratives intentées par ou contre celle-ci;

e) a conviction against the corporation may be enforced against the body corporate or a ruling, order or judgement in favour of or against the corporation may be enforced by or against the body corporate.
toute décision judiciaire ou quasi judiciaire rendue en faveur de la société ou contre elle est exécutoire à l'égard de la personne morale.

6. Select the one button that applies:
Choisir le bouton qui s'applique:

☐ The corporation is applying to continue under the laws of another Canadian jurisdiction.
La société présente une demande de maintien en vertu des lois d'une autre autorité législative au Canada.

☐ The corporation is applying to continue under the laws of a jurisdiction outside Canada, and this application is accompanied by a legal opinion to the effect that the laws of the other jurisdiction meet the requirements set out in 181(9) of the Act.
La société présente une demande de maintien en vertu des lois d'une autorité législative à l'extérieur du Canada et la demande est accompagnée d'un avis juridique stipulant que les lois de l'autre autorité législative répondent à toutes les exigences énoncées au paragraphe 181(9) de la Loi.

7. This application has been authorized by a special resolution.
La présente demande a été autorisée par résolution spéciale.

8. This application is accompanied by consent from the Minister of Revenue.
La présente demande est accompagnée du consentement émanant du ministre du Revenu.

9. Select the one button that applies:
Choisir le bouton qui s'applique:

☐ The corporation is offering securities to the public within the meaning of subsection 1(6) of the *Business Corporations Act* and consent from the Ontario Securities Commission accompanies this application.
La société offre des valeurs mobilières au public au sens du paragraphe 1(6) de la *Loi sur les sociétés par actions* et la demande est accompagnée du consentement écrit de la Commission des valeurs mobilières de l'Ontario.

☐ The corporation is not offering securities to the public within the meaning of subsection 1(6) of the *Business Corporations Act*.
La société n'offre pas de valeurs mobilières au public au sens du paragraphe 1(6) de la *Loi sur les sociétés par actions*.

The authorization of the Director for an application for continuance, if provided, expires six months after the date of endorsement of the authorization unless, within the six-month period, the corporation is continued under the laws of the other jurisdiction.

L'autorisation de la demande de maintien à l'extérieur de l'Ontario accordée par le directeur, le cas échéant, devient caduque six mois après la date de l'apposition de l'autorisation sur la demande, sauf si, au cours de cette période, la société est maintenue en vertu des lois de l'autre compétence législative.

The corporation shall file with the Director a copy of the instrument of continuance issued to it by the other jurisdiction within sixty days after the date of issuance.

Dans les soixante jours de la date d'émission, la société doit déposer auprès du directeur un exemplaire de l'acte de maintien émis par l'autre compétence législative.

This application is signed in duplicate.
La présente demande est signée en double exemplaire.

Name of Corporation / Dénomination sociale de la société

By/Par: Signature / Signature — Description of Office / Fonction

07170 (2011/04) Page 2 of/de 2

Form 7.1 — Application for Authorization to Continue under the *Co-operative Corporations Act*[*]

INSTRUCTIONS FOR COMPLETING

This form must be completed by an Ontario business corporation for authorization by the Director under section 181.1 of the *Business Corporations Act* to apply to the Minister of Finance under the *Co-operative Corporations Act* to be continued as a co-operative corporation.

The Application completed in duplicate with original signatures on both copies may be mailed or delivered to the Toronto address listed below.

FEE

$ 330.00 BY MAIL – cheque or money order payable to the Minister of Finance.
IN PERSON – if you are delivering the application in person at the Toronto office – cash, cheque or money order payable to Minister of Finance, Visa, MasterCard, American Express or debit card. Please note these documents are not reviewed while you wait; they take a few weeks to process.

There will be a service charge payable for any cheque returned as non-negotiable by a bank or financial institution.

SUPPORTING DOCUMENTS

COVERING LETTER

A covering letter setting out the name of a contact person, a return address and a telephone number is required. This will facilitate the processing of the Application should a question arise as to the content of the Application.

APPEARANCE OF DOCUMENTS

The Application for Authorization to Continue Under the *Co-operative Corporations Act* must be completed in duplicate on Form 7.1 as approved by the Minister. All documents must be legible and compatible with the microfilming process, with the information typed or hand printed in block capital letters, on one side of good quality, white bond paper 81/2" X 11".

The headings on the form are numbered 1 to 5 and must remain in that order. Do not leave out any of the headings.

APPLICATION

ITEM 1 Set out the current name of the corporation in block capital letters starting from the first box on the left-hand side of the first line, with one letter per box and one empty box for a space. Punctuation marks are entered in separate boxes. Complete one line before starting in the first box of the next line. The name entered must be exactly the same as it appeared on the original Articles of Incorporation or Articles of Amalgamation, or if there has been a name change, the most recent Articles of Amendment changing the name.

ITEM 2 Set out the original date of incorporation/amalgamation of the corporation.

ITEM 3 The corporation is not in default in filing notices and returns under the *Corporations Information Act*. ***This statement must be included on the application confirming all filings under the Corporations Information Act have been made, including payment of any outstanding fees.***

ITEM 4 It is requested that the corporation be authorized by the Director under section 181.1 of the *Business Corporations Act*, to apply to the Minister of Finance for articles of continuance continuing the corporation as if it had been incorporated under the *Co-operative Corporations Act*. ***This statement must be included on the application.***

ITEM 5 The application has been authorized by a special resolution. ***This statement must be included on the application confirming the application for continuance was authorized by a special resolution of the shareholders.***

EXECUTION The application must be completed in duplicate, and both copies must have original signatures of an officer or director of the corporation (not photocopies). Set out the name of the corporation above the signature and the applicant's office (e.g., President, Director, Secretary) beside the signature.

PLEASE NOTE

The authorization of the Director for an application to continue as a co-operative corporation expires six months after the date of endorsement of the authorization unless, within the six-month period, the corporation is continued under the *Co-operative Corporations Act*. If the corporation does not continue under the *Co-operative Corporations Act* within the six months, it remains subject to the *Business Corporations Act*. A new application would be required if the corporation still wishes to continue under the *Co-operative Corporations Act* after the authorization expires.

After continuing, the corporation is required to file with the Director a copy of the certificate of continuance issued to it under the *Co-operative Corporations Act* within sixty days after the date of issuance (subsection 181.1(6) of the *Business Corporations Act*).

Applications (in duplicate), any outstanding notices or returns, covering letter, and the filing fee and any outstanding Notice/Return fee should be mailed or delivered to:

COMPANIES AND PERSONAL PROPERTY SECURITY BRANCH
MINISTRY OF GOVERNMENT SERVICES
393 UNIVERSITY AVENUE, SUITE 200
TORONTO ON M5G 2M2
375 UNIVERSITY AVENUE, 2ND FLOOR (in person)

07172 (03/2006)

INSTRUCTIONS – COMMENT REMPLIR LE FORMULAIRE

Une société par actions de l'Ontario doit remplir la présente formule dans le but de demander l'autorisation du directeur aux termes de la *Loi sur les sociétés par actions* de s'adresser au ministre des Finances pour obtenir des statuts assurant son maintien comme si elle avait été constituée en vertu de la *Loi sur les sociétés coopératives*

On peut envoyer les deux exemplaires de la demande d'autorisation remplie et portant la signature d'origine par courrier ou la remettre en personne au bureau de Toronto à l'adresse susmentionnée.

DROITS

330 $ PAR COURRIER – Paiement par chèque ou mandat libellé à l'ordre du « Ministre des Finances ».
EN PERSONNE – Si vous déposez la demande en personne au bureau de Toronto, vous pouvez payer en argent comptant; par chèque ou mandat libellé à l'ordre du « Ministre des Finances »; ou par Visa, MasterCard ou American Express ou carte de débit. Notez que ces documents ne sont pas examinés pendant que vous attendez. Il faut quelques semaines pour les traiter.

Des frais d'administration seront facturés pour tout chèque refusé par la banque ou l'institution financière.

DOCUMENTS À L'APPUI

LETTRE D'INTRODUCTION

Il faut fournir une lettre d'introduction qui indique le nom de la personne à contacter, une adresse d'expéditeur et un numéro de téléphone. Cela permettra de traiter plus facilement la demande en cas de questions sur son contenu.

PRÉSENTATION DES DOCUMENTS

La Demande d'autorisation d'un maintien présentée en vertu de la *Loi sur les sociétés coopératives* doit être soumise en double exemplaire, sur la Formule 7.1 approuvée par arrêté ministériel. Tous les documents doivent être lisibles et se prêter à la photocopie sur microfilm. L'information est soit dactylographiée, soit écrite en lettres majuscules au recto seulement d'un papier filigrané blanc de bonne qualité, de format 8 ½ po x 11 po.

La formule 7.1 comporte des sections qui sont numérotées de 1 à 5 et qui doivent rester dans cet ordre. Ne retirer aucun objet.

DEMANDE

OBJET 1 Dans la grille, inscrire le nom actuel de la société en lettres majuscules, une lettre par case, en commençant à la première case de la première ligne. Pour chaque espace entre les mots, laisser une case vide. Chaque signe de ponctuation occupe une case distincte. Il faut remplir chaque ligne jusqu'au bout avant de commencer la suivante, même si un mot doit être coupé. Le nom entré doit être le nom indiqué sur les Statuts constitutifs ou les Statuts de fusion. S'il y a eu déjà un changement de nom, il faut entrer le nom qui figure dans les Statuts de modification les plus récents.

OBJET 2 Indiquer la date initiale de la constitution ou de la fusion de la société, dans l'ordre indiqué.

OBJET 3 La société n'a pas omis de déposer les avis et déclarations exigés par la *Loi sur les renseignements exigés des personnes morales.* **Cette déclaration doit être incluse dans la demande et confirmer que tous les rapports en vertu de la *Loi sur les renseignements exigés des personnes morales* ont été déposés, y compris l'acquittement de tous les frais.**

OBJET 4 La société demande l'autorisation du directeur aux termes de l'article 181.1 de la *Loi sur les sociétés par actions* de s'adresser au ministre des Finances pour obtenir des statuts assurant son maintien comme si elle avait été constituée en vertu de la *Loi sur les sociétés coopératives.* **Cette déclaration doit être incluse dans la demande.**

OBJET 5 La présente demande a été autorisée par une résolution spéciale. **Cette déclaration doit être incluse dans la demande et confirmer que la demande d'autorisation de maintien a été autorisée par une résolution spéciale des actionnaires.**

SIGNATURE Les deux exemplaires de la Demande d'autorisation de maintien doivent porter la signature originale d'un dirigeant ou d'un administrateur de la société (pas de photocopies). Indiquer le nom de la société et le mandat de la personne qui signe les documents au-dessus de la signature, et le mandat de la personne qui fait la demande (p. ex. : président, administrateur, secrétaire) à côté de la signature.

NOTE

L'autorisation du directeur pour une demande de maintien à titre de société coopérative expire six mois après la date d'apposition de l'autorisation à moins que, dans les six mois, la société soit maintenue conformément à la *Loi sur les sociétés coopératives.* Si la société n'est pas maintenue en vertu de la *Loi sur les sociétés coopératives* dans les six mois, elle reste assujettie à la *Loi sur les sociétés par actions.* Si on veut maintenir la société en vertu de la *Loi sur les sociétés coopératives* après l'expiration de l'autorisation, il faudra présenter une nouvelle demande.

Après son maintien, la société dépose auprès du directeur un exemplaire du certificat de maintien qui lui a été délivré en vertu de la *Loi sur les sociétés coopératives* dans les six mois après la date de délivrance (paragraphe 181.1 (6) de la *Loi sur les sociétés par actions*).

Envoyer ou remettre (en double exemplaire) les demandes accompagnées de tous les avis ou déclarations, d'une lettre d'introduction et des droits prescrits ainsi que des droits prescrits relatifs à tous les avis ou déclarations en circulation à l'adresse suivante :

DIRECTION DES COMPAGNIES ET DES SÛRETÉS MOBILIÈRES
MINISTÈRE DES SERVICES GOUVERNEMENTAUX
393, AVENUE UNIVERSITY, BUREAU 200
TORONTO (ONTARIO) M5G 2M2
375, AVENUE UNIVERSITY, 2e ÉTAGE (EN PERSONNE)

07172 (03/2006)

For Ministry Use Only
À l'usage exclusif du ministère

Ontario Corporation Number
Numéro de la société en Ontario

Form 7.1
Business Corporations Act

Formule 7.1
Loi sur les sociétés par actions

APPLICATION FOR AUTHORIZATION TO CONTINUE UNDER THE *CO-OPERATIVE CORPORATIONS ACT*
DEMANDE D'AUTORISATION DE MAINTIEN EN VERTU DE LA LOI SUR LES SOCIÉTÉS COOPÉRATIVES

1. The name of the corporation is: (Set out in BLOCK CAPITAL LETTERS)
Dénomination sociale de la société : (Écrire en LETTRES MAJUSCULES SEULEMENT) :

2. Date of incorporation/amalgamation: / *Date de la constitution ou de la fusion :*

Year, Month, Day / *année, mois, jour*

3. The corporation is not in default in filing notices and returns under the *Corporations Information Act.*
La société n'a pas omis de déposer les avis et déclarations exigés par la Loi sur les renseignements exigés des personnes morales.

4. It is requested that the corporation be authorized by the Director under section 181.1 of the *Business Corporations Act* to apply to the Minister of Finance for articles of continuance continuing the corporation as if it had been incorporated under the *Co-operative Corporations Act.* / *La société demande l'autorisation du directeur aux termes de l'article 181.1 de la* Loi sur les sociétés par actions *de s'adresser au ministre des Finances pour obtenir des statuts assurant son maintien comme si elle avait été constituée en vertu de la Loi sur les sociétés coopératives.*

5. This application has been authorized by a special resolution. / *La présente demande a été autorisée par résolution spéciale.*

This application is signed in duplicate.
La présente demande est signée en double exemplaire.

Name of Corporation / *Dénomination sociale de la société*

By/
Par :

Signature / *Signature* Description of Office / *Fonction*

07172 (03/2006)

Form 8 — Articles of Arrangement*

INSTRUCTIONS FOR COMPLETING

FEES

$330 **BY MAIL** - Cheque or money order payable to the Minister of Finance.

APPEARANCE OF DOCUMENTS
The Articles of Arrangement must be completed in duplicate on a Form 8 as approved by the Minister. All documents must be legible and compatible with the microfilming process, with the information typed or hand printed in block capital letters, on one side of good quality, white bond paper 8 ½" X 11".

The Article headings are numbered 1 to 7 and should remain in that order. Do not leave out any of the headings. If a section does not apply type "nil" or "not applicable". When additional pages are required, due to lack of space, they should be the same size as all the other pages and should be inserted after the application heading with the same number as the heading page with the addition of alphabet characters to indicate sequence. For example, pages inserted after page 1 would be number 1A, 1B, etc.

ARTICLE 1 Set out the current name of the corporation in block capital letters.

ARTICLE 2 If the name of the corporation is changed by the arrangement insert "new" name of the corporation in block capital letters.

ARTICLE 3 Set out the date of incorporation/amalgamation.

ARTICLE 6 Set out the date on which the arrangement was approved by the court.

EXECUTION Articles must be signed in duplicate by an officer or director of the corporation and signatures on both copies must be original signatures and not photocopies. The name of the corporation must be set out and the office of the person who is signing the articles. If the corporation has a corporate seal it should be affixed to the articles next to the signature of the officer/director of the corporation.

Articles (in duplicate), original Ontario-biased NUANS name search report (if applicable), covering letter and filing fee should be mailed or delivered to:

Ministry of Government Services
Central Production and Verification Services Branch
393 University Avenue, Suite 200
Toronto ON M5G 2M2

375 University Avenue, 2nd Floor (In Person)

07163 (2011/07)

DIRECTIVES POUR REMPLIR LE FORMULAIRE

LES DROITS

330 $ **PAR COURRIER** – Un chèque ou un mandat à l'ordre du Ministre des Finances.

PRÉSENTATION DES DOCUMENTS
Les statuts d'arrangement doivent être remplis en double exemplaire sur le formulaire 8 tel qu'approuvé par le Ministre. Tous les documents doivent être lisibles et conformes au processus de microphotographie, et les renseignements doivent être dactylographiés ou écrits lisiblement en lettres majuscules, au recto d'un papier filigrané blanc de bonne qualité de format 8 ½ po x 11 po.

Les titres des statuts sont numérotés de 1 à 7 et doivent rester dans cet ordre. N'enlevez pas de titres. Si certaines sections ne concernent pas les requérants, indiquez « néant » ou « sans objet » (s/o). Si faute d'espace, il faut insérer des pages supplémentaires, elles devront être du même format que les autres et elles devraient être insérées à la suite du titre de la demande comportant le même numéro que la page titre avec l'ajout d'une lettre pour en indiquer la séquence. À titre d'exemple, les pages insérées après la page 1 seraient numérotées 1A, 1B, etc.

SECTION 1	Insérez la dénomination sociale de la société en lettres majuscules.
SECTION 2	Si le nom de la société est changé par l'arrangement, indiquez le « nouveau » nom de la société en lettres majuscules.
SECTION 3	Inscrire la date complète de constitution ou de fusion de la société.
SECTION 6	Indiquer la date complète où l'arrangement a été approuvé par la cour.
SIGNATURE	Un dirigeant ou un administrateur de la société doit signer en double exemplaire les statuts et les signatures sur les deux exemplaires doivent être de sa main et non pas des photocopies, et doivent toujours apparaître en dessous de la dénomination sociale de la société ainsi que le titre de la personne qui signe les articles. Si la société a un sceau, il doit être apposé aux articles près de la signature du dirigeant ou de l'administrateur de la société.

Les statuts (en double exemplaire), l'original d'un rapport de recherche NUANS axé sur l'Ontario (s'il y a lieu), une lettre d'accompagnement et les droits de dépôt doivent être envoyés par la poste ou livrés à :

Ministère des Services gouvernementaux
Direction des services centraux de production et de vérfication
393, avenue University, bureau 200
Toronto ON M5G 2M2

375, avenue University, 2e étage (dépôt en personne)

07163 (2011/07)

For Ministry Use Only
À l'usage exclusif du ministère

Ontario Corporation Number
Numéro de la société en Ontario

Form 8
Business Corporations Act

Formule 8
Loi sur les sociétés par actions

ARTICLES OF ARRANGEMENT
STATUTS D'ARRANGEMENT

1. The name of the corporation is: (Set out in BLOCK CAPITAL LETTERS)
   Dénomination sociale de la société : (Écrire en LETTRES MAJUSCULES SEULEMENT) :

2. The new name of the corporation if changed by the arrangement: (Set out in BLOCK CAPITAL LETTERS)
   Nouvelle dénomination sociale de la société si elle est modifiée par suite de l'arrangement :
   (Écrire en LETTRES MAJUSCULES SEULEMENT)

3. Date of incorporation/amalgamation: / Date de la constitution ou de la fusion :

   Year, Month, Day / année, mois, jour

4. The arrangement has been approved by the shareholders of the corporation in accordance with section 182 of the *Business Corporation Act*. / Les actionnaires de la société ont approuvé l'arrangement conformément à l'article 182 de la *Loi sur les sociétés par actions*.

5. A copy of the arrangement is attached to these articles as Exhibit "A" / Une copie de l'arrangement constitute l'annexe «A».

6. The arrangement was approved by the court on / La cour a approuvé l'arrangement le

   Year, Month, Day / année, mois, jour

   and a certified copy of the Order of the court is attached to these articles as Exhibit "B". / Une copie certifiée conforme de l'ordonnance de la cour constitue l'annexe «B».

7. The terms and conditions to which the scheme is made subject by the Order have been complied with.
   Les conditions que l'ordonnance impose au projet d'arrangement ont été respectées.

These articles are signed in duplicate. / Les présents statuts sont signés en double exemplaire.

Name of Corporation / Dénomination sociale de la société

By/
Par :

Signature / Signature

Description of Office / Fonctions

07163 (2011/07)

Form 9 — Articles of Reorganization*

INSTRUCTIONS FOR COMPLETING

FEES

$150 BY MAIL- Cheque or money order payable to the Minister of Finance.

APPEARANCE OF DOCUMENTS

The Articles of Reorganization must be completed in duplicate on a Form 9 as approved by the Minister. All documents must be legible and compatible with the microfilming process, with the information typed or hand printed in block capital letters, on one side of good quality, white bond paper 8 ½" X 11".

The Article headings are numbered 1 to 6 and should remain in that order. Do not leave out any of the headings. When additional pages are required, due to lack of space, they should be the same size as all the other pages and should be inserted after the application heading with the same number as the heading page with the addition of alphabet characters to indicate sequence. For example, pages inserted after page 1 would be number 1A, 1B, etc.

ARTICLE 1 Set out the current name of the corporation in block capital letters.

ARTICLE 2 Set out "new" name if changed by the reorganization in block capital letters.

ARTICLE 3 Set out the date of incorporation/amalgamation.

ARTICLE 4 Set out the date on which the reorganization was ordered by the court.

ARTICLE 5 Set out the amendments to the corporation's articles which have been ordered by the court. If you require more space for Article 5 than is provided, please continue on page 1A, 1B etc. Page 2 should follow in sequence.

EXECUTION Articles must be signed in duplicate by an officer or director of the corporation and signatures on both copies must be original signatures and not photocopies. The name of the corporation must be set out. Beside the signature set out the office of the person who is signing (e.g. President, Director, Secretary). If the corporation has a corporate seal it should be affixed to the articles next to the signature of the officer/director of the corporation.

Articles (in duplicate), original Ontario-biased NUANS name search report (if applicable), covering letter and filing fee should be mailed or delivered to:

COMPANIES AND PERSONAL PROPERTY SECURITY BRANCH
MINISTRY OF GOVERNMENT SERVICES
393 UNIVERSITY AVENUE, SUITE 200
TORONTO ONTARIO M5G 2M2

375 UNIVERSITY AVENUE, 2ND FLOOR (IN PERSON)

07114 (03/2006)

DIRECTIVES POUR REMPLIR LE FORMULAIRE

LES DROITS

150 $ PAR COURRIER – Un chèque ou un mandat à l'ordre du Ministre des Finances.

PRÉSENTATION DES DOCUMENTS

Les statuts de réorganisation doivent être remplis en double exemplaire sur le formulaire 9 tel qu'approuvé par le Ministre. Tous les documents doivent être lisibles et conformes au processus de microphotographie, et les renseignements doivent être dactylographiés ou écrits lisiblement en lettres majuscules, au recto d'un papier filigrané blanc de bonne qualité de format 8 ½ po x 11 po.

Les titres des statuts sont numérotés de 1 à 6 et doivent rester dans cet ordre. N'enlevez pas de titres. Si certaines sections ne concernent pas les requérants, indiquez « néant » ou « sans objet » (s/o). Si faute d'espace, il faut insérer des pages supplémentaires, elles devraient être du même format que les autres et elles devraient être insérées à la suite du titre de la demande comportant le même numéro que la page titre avec l'ajout d'une lettre pour en indiquer la séquence. À titre d'exemple, les pages insérées après la page 1 seraient numérotées 1A, 1B, etc.

SECTION 1 — Insérez la dénomination sociale de la société en lettres majuscules.

SECTION 2 — Indiquez le « nouveau » nom de la société en lettres majuscules, s'il est modifié par la réorganisation.

SECTION 3 — Inscrire la date complète de constitution ou de fusion de la société.

SECTION 4 — Indiquer la date complète où la cour a ordonné la réorganisation.

SECTION 5 — Inscrire les modifications apportées aux statuts de la société qui ont été ordonnées par la cour. Faute d'espace suffisant pour l'article 5, veuillez continuer sur la page 1A, 1B, etc. La page 2 devrait suivre par la suite.

SIGNATURE — Un dirigeant ou un administrateur de la société doit signer en double exemplaire les articles et les signatures sur les deux exemplaires doivent être de sa main et non pas des photocopies, et doivent toujours apparaître en dessous de la dénomination sociale de la société ainsi que le titre de la personne qui signe les statuts (par ex., président, directeur, secrétaire). Si la société a un sceau, il doit être apposé aux articles près de la signature du dirigeant ou de l'administrateur de la société.

Les statuts (en double exemplaire), le rapport original de recherche de dénominations sociales NUANS axé sur l'Ontario (s'il y a lieu), une lettre d'accompagnement et les droits de dépôt doivent être envoyés par la poste ou livrés à :

Direction des compagnies et des sûretés mobilières
Ministère des Services gouvernementaux
393, avenue University, bureau 200
Toronto (Ontario) M5G 2M2

375, avenue University, 2e étage (en personne)

07114 (03/2006)

1

For Ministry Use Only
À l'usage exclusif du ministère

Ontario Corporation Number
Numéro de la société en Ontario

Form 9
Business Corporations Act

Formule 9
Loi sur les sociétés par actions

ARTICLES OF REORGANIZATION
STATUTS DE RÉORGANISATION

1. The name of the corporation is: (Set out in BLOCK CAPITAL LETTERS)
Dénomination sociale de la société : (Écrire en LETTRES MAJUSCULES SEULEMENT) :

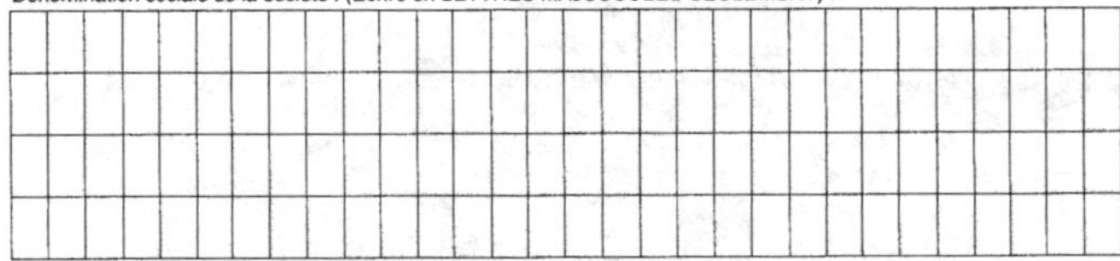

2. The new name of the corporation if changed by the reorganization: (Set out in BLOCK CAPITAL LETTERS)
Nouvelle dénomination sociale de la société si elle est modifiée par suite de la réorganisation : (Écrire en LETTRES MAJUSCULES SEULEMENT) :

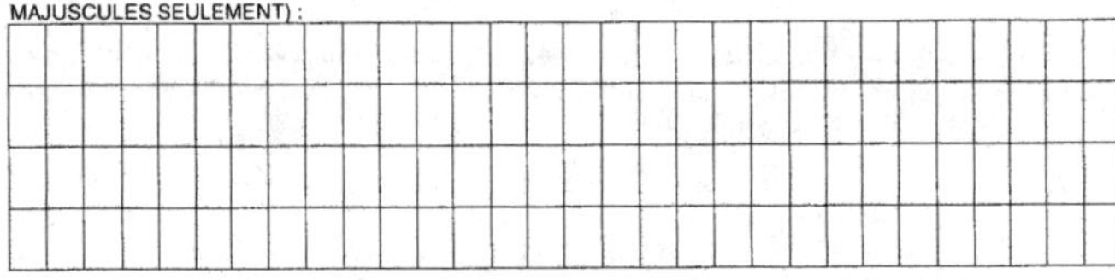

3. Date of incorporation/amalgamation: / *Date de la constitution ou de la fusion :*

Year, Month, Day / *année, mois, jour*

4. The reorganization was ordered by the court on / *La cour a ordonné la réorganisation le*

Year, Month, Day / *année, mois, jour*

and a certified copy of the Order of the court is attached to these articles as Exhibit "A". / *une copie certifiée conforme de l'ordonnance de la cour constitue l'annexe «A».*

5. In accordance with the Order for reorganization the articles of the corporation are amended as follows:
Conformément à l'ordonnance de réorganisation, les statuts de la société sont modifiés de la façon suivante :

07114 (03/2006)

2

6. The terms and conditions to which the reorganization is made subject by the Order have been complied with.
Les conditions que l'ordonnance impose à la réorganisation ont été respectées.

These articles are submitted under section 186 of the *Business Corporations Act* and are signed in duplicate.
Les présents statuts sont déposés en vertu de l'article 186 de la Loi sur les sociétés par actions. *Ils sont signés en double exemplaire.*

____
Name of Corporation / *Dénomination sociale de la société*

By/
Par :

______________________________ ______________________________
Signature / *Signature* Description of Office / *Fonction*

07114 (03/2006)

Form 10 — Articles of Dissolution*

INSTRUCTIONS FOR COMPLETING

This form is to be used for voluntary dissolution of a business corporation where the dissolution has been authorized by the shareholders of the corporation.

Articles in duplicate may be mailed to the Toronto address listed below. For over-the-counter service articles may be filed in person at the Toronto office or at some Land Registry/ServiceOntario offices in Ontario. For a list of locations see the "Offices That Endorse Articles Submitted Under the *Business Corporations Act*" information sheet or visit the ServiceOntario website at www.ServiceOntario.ca

FEE

$25.00 **BY MAIL** - cheque or money order payable to the Minister of Finance.
IN PERSON (at the Toronto office) - cash, cheque or money order payable to the Minister of Finance, Visa, MasterCard, American Express or debit card. If you are filing the documents at one of the Land Registry/ServiceOntario offices, call first to confirm whether credit or debit cards are acceptable.

There will be a service charge payable for any cheque returned as non-negotiable by a bank or financial institution.

SUPPORTING DOCUMENTS
CONSENT FROM THE MINISTER OF REVENUE

Articles must be accompanied by written consent to the dissolution from the Minister of Revenue, and must be submitted within 60 days after the Minister of Revenue provides consent. To obtain this consent, contact the Ministry of Revenue at the following address:

Ministry of Revenue
Client Accounts and Services Branch
33 King Street West
PO Box 622
Oshawa ON L1H 8H5
Fax: 905 433-5418

Telephone Enquiries can be made to the Canada Revenue Agency at:
Service in English: 1 800 959-5525
Service in French: 1 800 959-7775
TTY : 1 800 665-0354

07122 (2011/04)

APPEARANCE OF DOCUMENTS

The Articles of Dissolution must be completed in duplicate on a Form 10 as approved by the Minister. All documents must be legible and compatible with the microfilming process, with the information typed or hand printed in block capital letters, on one side of good quality, white bond paper 8 ½" X 11".

ARTICLES

ARTICLE 1 Set out the **current** name of the corporation in block capital letters starting from the first box on the left-hand side of the first line, with one letter per box and one empty box for a space. Punctuation marks are entered in separate boxes. Complete one line before starting in the first box of the next line. The name entered must be exactly the same as it appeared on the original Articles of Incorporation, Articles of Amalgamation or the most recent Articles of Amendment, if there has been a name change.

EAST SIDE INVESTMENT AND MANAG
EMENT LTD.

ARTICLE 2 Set out the date of incorporation or amalgamation.

ARTICLE 3 The dissolution must be authorized as required by section 237 (a) or (b) **(as applicable)** of the *Business Corporations Act*. **This statement must be included in the Articles.**

ARTICLE 4 Mark (X) in the box beside the one statement that applies.

ARTICLE 5 Mark (X) in the box beside the one statement that applies.

ARTICLE 6 There are no proceedings pending in any court against the corporation. **This statement must be included in the Articles.**

ARTICLE 7 The corporation has obtained consent from the Minister of Revenue to the dissolution and has filed all notices and returns required under the *Corporations Information Act*. **This statement must be included in the Articles. The requirement to file all notices and returns includes payment of any outstanding fees. A letter of consent issued by the Ministry of Revenue must accompany the application.**

EXECUTION **The current name of the corporation should be printed above the signature in BLOCK CAPITAL LETTERS.** Both copies of the Articles must have an original signature of an officer or director of the corporation. **Beside the signature set out the office of the person who is signing i.e. President, Director, Secretary....** If the corporation has a corporate seal it should be affixed to the articles next to the signature. An executor, accountant or lawyer cannot sign Articles of Dissolution only an officer or director.

Articles (in duplicate), consent letter from the Ministry of* Revenue *and filing fee should be mailed or delivered to:

Ministry of Government Services
Central Production and Verification Services Branch
393 University Avenue, Suite 200
Toronto ON M5G 2M2

375 University Avenue, 2nd Floor (In Person)

07122 (2011/04)

POUR REMPLIR LE FORMULAIRE

On doit utiliser ce formulaire pour la dissolution volontaire d'une société par actions lorsque la dissolution a été autorisée par les actionnaires de la société.

On peut envoyer les *Statuts de dissolution* par courrier au bureau de Toronto à l'adresse indiquée ci-dessous. On peut aussi les remettre en personne au bureau de Toronto ou à certains de nos bureaux d'enregistrement immobilier/ServiceOntario en Ontario. Consulter la liste des adresses qui se trouve sur le feuillet d'information « Bureaux acceptant les *Statuts de dissolution* soumis en vertu de la *Loi sur les sociétés par actions* » ou visiter le site Web de ServiceOntario : www.ServiceOntario.ca .

DROITS

25.00 $ **PAR COURRIER** – Paiement par chèque ou mandat libellé à l'ordre du « Ministre des Finances ». **EN PERSONNE** (au bureau de Toronto) – Paiement en argent comptant; par chèque ou mandat libellé à l'ordre du « Ministre des Finances »; ou paiement par Visa, MasterCard, American Express ou carte de débit. Si on dépose les documents à l'un des bureaux d'enregistrement immobilier/ServiceOntario, appeler d'abord le bureau pour savoir s'il accepte les cartes de crédit ou de débit.

Des frais d'administration seront perçus pour tout chèque refusé par l'établissement financier.

DOCUMENTS À L'APPUI
CONSENTEMENT DU MINISTRE DU REVENU

Les statuts doivent être accompagnés d'une lettre du ministre du Revenu indiquant son consentement et soumis dans les 60 jours qui suivent ce consentement. Pour obtenir un consentement, prière de contacter le ministère du Revenu à l'adresse suivante :

Ministère du Revenu
Direction des services et des dossiers clients
33, rue King Ouest
CP 622
Oshawa ON L1H 8H5
Télécopieur : 905 433-5418

Les demandes par téléphone peuvent être adressées à l'agence du Revenu du Canada aux numéros suivants :
Service en anglais : 1 800 959-5525
Service en français : 1 800 959-7775
ATS : 1 800 665-0354

07122 (2011/04)

PRÉSENTATION DES DOCUMENTS

Les *Statuts de dissolution* doivent être remplis en double exemplaire sur la Formule 10 approuvée par le ministre. Tous les documents doivent être lisibles et se prêter à la photographie sur microfilm. L'information est soit dactylographiée, soit écrite lisiblement en lettres majuscules au recto seulement d'un papier filigrané blanc de bonne qualité, de format 8 ½ po x 11 po.

SECTIONS DU FORMULAIRE

SECTION 1 Dans la grille, inscrire le nom **actuel** de la société en lettres majuscules, une lettre par case, en commençant à la première case de la première ligne. Pour chaque espace entre les mots, laisser une case vide. Chaque signe de ponctuation occupe aussi une case distincte. Il faut remplir chaque ligne jusqu'au bout avant de commencer la suivante, même si un mot doit être coupé (voir exemple ci-dessous). Le nom entré doit être le nom indiqué sur les *Statuts constitutifs* ou les *Statuts de fusion*. S'il y a déjà eu un changement de nom, il faut entrer le nom qui figure sur les *Statuts de modification* les plus récents.

S	O	C	I	É	T	É		D	E		P	L	A	C	E	M	E	N	T	S		E	T		D	E		G	E
S	T	I	O	N		D	U		P	A	T	R	I	M	O	I	N	E		I	N	C	.						

SECTION 2 Indiquer la date de la constitution ou de la fusion.

SECTION 3 La dissolution doit être autorisée conformément à l'alinéa 237 a) ou b) **(selon le cas)** de la *Loi sur les sociétés par actions*. ***L'énoncé confirmant l'autorisation, déjà imprimé sur le formulaire, doit toujours être inclus dans les statuts.***

SECTION 4 Cocher (X) la case correspondant à l'énoncé approprié.

SECTION 5 Cocher (X) la case correspondant à l'énoncé approprié.

SECTION 6 « Aucune instance n'est en cours contre la société ». ***Cet énoncé, déjà imprimé sur le formulaire, doit toujours être inclus dans les statuts.***

SECTION 7 Le ministre du Revenu a approuvé la dissolution de la société. La société a déposé tous les avis et rapports requis par la *Loi sur les renseignements exigés des personnes morales*. **Cet énoncé doit être inclus dans les statuts. L'obligation de déposer tous les avis et rapports inclut tout paiement en souffrance. Joindre la lettre de consentement du ministère du Revenu à la demande.**

SIGNATURE **Au-dessus de la signature, indiquer en LETTRES MAJUSCULES le nom actuel de la société.** Les deux exemplaires des *Statuts de dissolution* doivent porter la signature originale d'un dirigeant ou d'un administrateur. **Indiquer aussi la fonction du signataire (président, administrateur, secrétaire, etc.)** Si la société a un sceau, apposer le sceau près de la signature. Un exécuteur testamentaire, un comptable ou un avocat ne peut pas signer les *Statuts de dissolution*, seul un administrateur ou un directeur peut le faire.

Envoyer ou remettre les Statuts de dissolution (en double exemplaire), accompagnés de la lettre de consentement du ministère* du Revenu, *à l'adresse suivante :

Ministère des Services gouvernementaux
Direction des services centraux de production et de vérification
393, avenue University, bureau 200
Toronto ON M5G 2M2

375, avenue University, 2e étage (dépôt en personne)

07122 (2011/04)

For Ministry Use Only
À l'usage exclusif du ministère

Ontario Corporation Number
Numéro de la société en Ontario

Form 10
Business Corporations Act

Formule 10
Loi sur les sociétés par actions

ARTICLES OF DISSOLUTION
STATUTS DE DISSOLUTION

1. The name of the corporation is: (Set out in BLOCK CAPITAL LETTERS)
   Dénomination sociale de la société : (Écrire en LETTRES MAJUSCULES SEULEMENT)

2. Date of incorporation/amalgamation:
   Date de la constitution ou de la fusion :

   (Year, Month,Day)
   (année, mois, jour)

3. The dissolution has been duly authorized under clause 237 (a) or (b) (as applicable) of the *Business Corporations Act*.
   La dissolution de la société a été dûment approuvée aux termes de l'alinéa 237 a) ou b) (le cas échéant) de la *Loi sur les sociétés par actions.*

4. The corporation has, (Mark (X) in the box beside the one statement that applies.)
   La société, selon le cas : (cocher la case appropriée)

   ☐ (A) no debts, obligations or liabilities;
   (A) n'a ni dettes, ni obligations, ni passif;

   ☐ (B) duly provided for its debts, obligations or liabilities in accordance with subsection 238 (3) of the *Business Corporations Act;*
   (B) a pourvu à ses dettes, à ses obligations ou à son passif conformément au paragraphe 238(3) de la *Loi sur les sociétés par actions;*

   ☐ (C) obtained consent to its dissolution from its creditors or other persons having interests in its debts, obligations or liabilities.
   (C) a obtenu de ses créanciers ou des autres intéressés à ses dettes, à ses obligations ou à son passif, le consentement à sa dissolution.

5. After satisfying the interests of creditors in all its debts, obligations and liabilities, if any, the corporation has,
   (Mark (X) in the box beside the one statement that applies.)
   Après avoir désintéressé tous ses créanciers, s'il y a lieu, la société, selon le cas :
   (cocher la case appropriée)

   ☐ (A) no property to distribute among its shareholders; **or**
   (A) n'a plus de biens à répartir entre ses actionnaires; **ou**

   ☐ (B) distributed its remaining property rateably among its shareholders according to their rights and interests in the corporation or in accordance with subsection 238 (4) of the *Business Corporations* Act where applicable.
   (B) a réparti les biens qui lui restaient entre ses actionnaires au prorata de leurs droits dans la société ou conformément au paragraphe 238 (4) de la *Loi sur les sociétés par actions*, s'il y a lieu.

07122 (2011/04)

Page 1 of/de 2

6. There are no proceedings pending in any court against the corporation.
Aucune instance n'est en cours contre la société.

7. The corporation has obtained consent from the Minister of Revenue to the dissolution and has filed all notices and returns required under the *Corporations Information Act.*
Le ministre du Revenu a approuvé la dissolution de la société. La société a déposé tous les avis et rapports requis par la *Loi sur les renseignements exigés des personnes morales.*

These articles are signed in duplicate.
Les présents statuts sont signés en double exemplaire.

(Name of Corporation)
(Dénomination sociale de la société)

By
Par :

(Signature) (Signature)	**(Description of Office) (Fonction)**

07122 (2011/04)

Form 11 — Articles of Dissolution*

INSTRUCTIONS FOR COMPLETING

This form is to be used for voluntary dissolution of a business corporation only where the corporation has not issued any shares, has not commenced business, and the dissolution has been authorized by all its incorporators or their personal representatives.

Note: If the corporation has issued shares or commenced business, you cannot file this form but can instead file a form 10, Articles of Dissolution - and shareholder approval is required.

Articles in duplicate may be mailed to the Toronto address listed below. For over-the-counter service articles may be filed in person at the Toronto office or at some Land Registry /ServiceOntario offices in Ontario. For a list of locations see the "Offices That Endorse Articles Submitted Under the Business Corporations Act" information sheet or visit the ServiceOntario website at www.ServiceOntario.ca

FEE

$25.00 **BY MAIL** - cheque or money order payable to the Minister of Finance.

IN PERSON (at the Toronto office) - cash, cheque or money order payable to the Minister of Finance, Visa, MasterCard, American Express or debit card. (If you are filing the documents at one of the Land Registry/ServiceOntario offices, call first to confirm whether credit or debit cards are acceptable).

There will be a service charge payable for any cheque returned as non-negotiable by a bank or financial institution.

SUPPORTING DOCUMENTS

CONSENT FROM THE MINISTER OF REVENUE

Articles must be accompanied by written consent to the dissolution from the Minister of Revenue, and must be submitted within 60 days after the Minister of Revenue provides consent. To obtain this consent, contact the Ministry of Revenue at the following address:

Ministry of Revenue
Client Accounts and Services Branch
33 King Street West
PO Box 622
Oshawa ON L1H 8H5
Telephone Enquiries can be made to the Canada Revenue Agency at:
Service in English: 1 800 959-5525
Service in French: 1 800 959-7775
TTY : 1 800 665-0354

COVERING LETTER

Enclose a covering letter setting out the name of a contact person, a return address and a telephone number. This will facilitate the processing of the articles should a question arise as to the content of the articles.

APPEARANCE OF DOCUMENTS

The Articles of Dissolution must be completed in duplicate on Form 11 as approved by the Minister. All documents must be legible and compatible with the microfilming process, with the information typed or hand printed in block capital letters, on one side of good quality, white bond paper 81/2" by 11". The headings on the form must be numbered 1 to 9 and should remain in that order. Do not leave out any of the headings.

07123E (2011/04)

ARTICLE 1 Set out the current name of the corporation in block capital letters starting from the first box on the left-hand side of the first line, with one letter per box and one empty box for a space. Punctuation marks are entered in separate boxes. Complete one line before starting in the first box of the next line. The name entered must be exactly the same as it appeared on the original Articles of Incorporation or Articles of Amalgamation, or the most recent Articles of Amendment if there has been a name change.

EAST SIDE INVESTMENT AND MANAG
EMENT LTD.

ARTICLE 2 Set out the original date of incorporation or amalgamation of the corporation.

ARTICLE 3 **The corporation has not commenced business.** This statement must be included in the articles. If the corporation has started business this form cannot be used, instead complete Articles of Dissolution, **Form 10**.

ARTICLE 4 **None of the shares of the corporation has been issued.** This statement must be included in the articles. If the corporation has issued shares this form cannot be used, instead complete Articles of Dissolution **Form 10**.

ARTICLE 5 **The dissolution has been duly authorized under clause 237(c) of the *Business Corporations Act*.** This statement confirming the dissolution has been authorized by all of the incorporators of the corporation or their personal representatives pursuant to section 237(c) of the *Business Corporations Act* must be included in the articles.

ARTICLE 6 **The corporation has no debts, obligations or liabilities.** This statement confirming the corporation has no debts, obligations or liabilities must be included in the articles.

ARTICLE 7 Indicate by checking the appropriate box whether after satisfying the interests of creditors in all its debts, obligations and liabilities, if any, the corporation has no property to distribute or that it has distributed its remaining property to the persons entitled thereto.

ARTICLE 8 **There are no proceedings pending in any court against the corporation.** This statement must be included in the articles. If there are court proceedings against the corporation this form cannot be filed.

ARTICLE 9 **The corporation has obtained consent from the Minister of Revenue to the dissolution and has filed all notices and returns required under the *Corporations Information Act*.** This statement must be included on the articles. The requirement to file all notices and returns includes payment of any outstanding fees. A letter of consent issued by the Ministry of Revenue must accompany the application.

EXECUTION Both copies of the articles must have original signatures of all of the incorporators of the corporation or their personal representatives. Set out the incorporators' name or if the articles are signed by a personal representative, set out the representative's name, the capacity in which he/she is signing (e.g. executor, trustee) and the name of the incorporator he/she is representing.

Articles (in duplicate), consent letter from the Minister of Revenue and filing fee should be mailed or delivered to:

Ministry of Government Services
Central Production and Verification Services Branch
393 University Avenue, Suite 200
Toronto ON M5G 2M2

375 University Avenue, 2nd Floor (In Person)

07123E (2011/04)

POUR REMPLIR LE FORMULAIRE

On doit utiliser ce formulaire pour la dissolution volontaire d'une société par actions uniquement lorsque la société n'a pas émis d'actions, qu'elle n'a pas encore commencé ses activités et que la dissolution a été autorisée par tous ses fondateurs ou leurs représentants personnels.

Remarque : Si la société a émis des actions ou a commencé ses activités, on ne peut pas déposer le présent formulaire, mais plutôt la Formule 10 Statuts de dissolution et, dans ce cas, l'approbation des actionnaires est requise.

On peut envoyer les Statuts de dissolution en double exemplaire par la poste au bureau de Toronto à l'adresse indiquée ci-dessous. On peut aussi les remettre en personne au bureau de Toronto ou à l'un des bureaux désignés d'enregistrement immobilier / ServiceOntario en Ontario. Consulter la liste des adresses qui se trouve sur le feuillet d'information « Bureau acceptant les Statuts de dissolution soumis en vertu de la *Loi sur les sociétés par actions* » ou visiter le site Web de ServiceOntario à l'adresse www.ServiceOntario.ca

DROITS

25.00 $ **PAR LA POSTE** – Paiement par chèque ou mandat libellé à l'ordre du ministre des Finances.

EN PERSONNE (au bureau de Toronto) – Paiement en espèces, par chèque ou mandat à l'ordre du ministre des Finances ou paiement par carte Visa, MasterCard, American Express ou carte de débit (Si l'on dépose les documents à l'un des bureaux d'enregistrement immobilier / ServiceOntario, appelerd'abord le bureau pour savoir s'il accepte les cartes de crédit et de débit.)

Des frais d'administration sont perçus pour tout chèque refusé par la banque ou l'établissement financier.

DOCUMENTS À L'APPUI

CONSENTEMENT DU MINISTRE DU REVENU

Les statuts doivent être accompagnés d'une lettre du ministre du Revenu indiquant son consentement et soumis dans les 60 jours qui suivent ce consentement. Pour obtenir un consentement, prière de contacter le ministère du Revenu à l'adresse suivante :

Ministère du Revenu
Direction des services et des dossiers clients
33, rue King Ouest
CP 622
Oshawa ON L1H 8H5
Les demandes par téléphone peuvent être adressées à l'agence du Revenu du Canada aux numéros suivants :
Service en anglais : 1 800 959-5525
Service en français : 1 800 959-7775
ATS : 1 800 665-0354

LETTRE D'ENVOI

Joindre une lettre d'envoi indiquant le nom de la personne à contacter, l'adresse de retour et le numéro de téléphone. Cela facilitera le traitement des statuts au cas où l'on aurait des questions à poser sur le contenu des documents.

PRÉSENTATION DES DOCUMENTS

Les Statuts de dissolution doivent être remplis en double exemplaire sur la Formule 11 approuvée par le ministre. Tous les documents doivent être lisibles et se prêter à la photographie sur microfilm. L'information est soit dactylographiée, soit écrite lisiblement en lettres majuscules au recto seulement d'un papier bond blanc de bonne qualité, de format 8 1/2 x 11 po. Le formulaire compte 9 sections numérotées de 1 à 9, qui doivent rester dans cet ordre. On ne doit omettre aucune section.

07123F (2011/04)

SECTION 1 Dans la grille, inscrire le nom actuel de la société en lettres majuscules, une lettre par case, en commençant à la première case de la première ligne; laisser une case vierge pour chaque espace. Chaque signe de ponctuation occupe une case distincte. Il faut remplir chaque ligne jusqu'au bout avant de passer à la suivante. Le nom entré doit être identique au nom indiqué dans les Statuts constitutifs d'origine ou les Statuts de fusion, ou, s'il y a eu un changement de nom, à celui qui figure dans les Statuts de modification les plus récents.

SOCIETE DE PLACEMENTS ET DE GE
STION DU PATRIMOINE INC

SECTION 2 Indiquer la date originale de constitution ou la date de fusion de la société.

SECTION 3 **La société n'a pas encore commencé ses opérations.** Cette déclaration doit faire partie des statuts. Si la société a commencé ses activités, on ne peut pas utiliser le présent formulaire, mais plutôt la **Formule 10** Statuts de dissolution.

SECTION 4 **La société n'a émis aucune action.** Cette déclaration doit faire partie des statuts. Si la société a émis des actions, on ne peut pas utiliser le présent formulaire, mais plutôt la **Formule 10** Statuts de dissolution.

SECTION 5 **La dissolution de la société a été dûment approuvée aux termes de l'alinéa 237 c) de la** *Loi sur les sociétés par actions.* Cette déclaration confirmant que la dissolution a été autorisée par tous les fondateurs de la société ou leurs représentants personnels, conformément à l'alinéa 237 c) de la *Loi sur les sociétés* par actions doit faire partie intégrante des statuts.

SECTION 6 **La société n'a ni dettes, ni obligations, ni passif.** Cette déclaration confirmant que la société n'a ni dettes, ni obligations, ni passif doit faire partie intégrante des statuts.

SECTION 7 Cocher la case appropriée pour indiquer si, après avoir désintéressé tous ses créanciers, s'il y a lieu, la société n'a plus de biens à répartir ou qu'elle a réparti les biens qui lui restaient entre les personnes qui y ont droit.

SECTION 8 **Aucune instance n'est en cours contre la société.** Cette déclaration doit faire partie des statuts. On ne peut pas déposer ce formulaire s'il y a des instances judiciaires en cours contre la société.

SECTION 9 **Le ministère du Revenu a approuvé la dissolution de la société. La société a déposé tous les avis et rapports requis par la** *Loi sur les renseignements exigés des personnes morales.* Cette déclaration doit faire partie des statuts. L'obligation de déposer tous les avis et rapports inclut le paiement des droits en souffrance. Joindre la lettre de consentement du ministère du Revenu à la demande.

SIGNATURE Les deux exemplaires des statuts doivent porter la signature originale de tous les fondateurs de la société ou de leurs représentants personnels. Sous la signature de chaque fondateur, indiquer son nom en lettres moulées. Si les statuts sont signés par un représentant personnel, indiquer le nom du représentant, la qualité en laquelle il signe (p. ex., exécuteur, fiduciaire) et le nom du fondateur qu'il représente.

Envoyer ou remettre les statuts (en deux exemplaires), la lettre de consentement du ministre du Revenu et les droits de dépôt à l'adresse suivante :

Ministère des Services gouvernementaux
Direction des services centraux de production et de vérification
393, avenue University, bureau 200
Toronto ON M5G 2M2

375, avenue University, 2e étage (en personne)

07123F (2011/04)

For Ministry Use Only
À l'usage exclusif du ministère

Ontario Corporation Number
Numéro de la société en Ontario

Form 11
Business Corporations Act

Formule 11
Loi sur les sociétés par actions

ARTICLES OF DISSOLUTION
STATUTS DE DISSOLUTION

1. The name of the corporation is: (Set out in BLOCK CAPITAL LETTERS)
Dénomination sociale de la société : (Écrire en LETTRES MAJUSCULES SEULEMENT) :

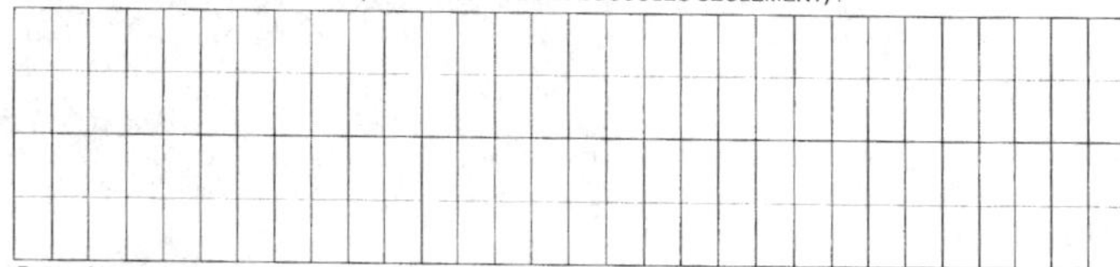

2. Date of incorporation/amalgamation:
Date de la constitution ou de la fusion :

(Year, Month, Day)
(année, mois, jour)

3. The corporation has not commenced business.
La société n'a pas encore commencé ses opérations.

4. None of the shares of the corporation has been issued.
La société n'a émis aucune action.

5. The dissolution has been duly authorized under clause 237 (c) of the *Business Corporations* Act.
La dissolution de la société a été dûment approuvée aux termes de l'alinéa 237 c) de la *Loi sur les sociétés par actions*.

6. The corporation has no debts, obligations or liabilities.
La société n'a ni dettes, ni obligations, ni passif.

7. After satisfying the interests of creditors, in all its debts, obligations and liabilities, if any, the corporation: (mark (x) in the box beside **the one statement that applies**):
Après avoir désintéressé tous ses créanciers, s'il y a lieu, la société, selon le cas (cocher la **case appropriée**) :

☐ (a) has no property to distribute; **or**
(a) n'a plus de biens à répartir; **ou**

☐ (b) has distributed its remaining property to the persons entitled thereto.
(b) a réparti les biens qui lui restaient entre les personnes qui y ont droit.

8. There are no proceedings pending in any court against the corporation.
Aucune instance n'est en cours contre la société.

9. The corporation has obtained consent from the Minister of Revenue to the dissolution and has filed all notices and returns required under the *Corporations Information Act*.

Le ministre du Revenu a approuvé la dissolution de la société. La société a déposé tous les avis et rapports requis par la *Loi sur les renseignements exigés des personnes morales*.

07123 (2011/04)

Page 1 of/de 2

These articles are signed in duplicate.
Les présents statuts sont signés en double exemplaire.

Signature and names of all the incorporators or their personal representatives
Signature et nom de tous les fondateurs ou de leurs représentants

Signature / signature

Incorporators' name or the personal representatives name and the capacity in which he/she is signing (e.g. executor, trustee) and the name of the incorporator he/she is representing
Nom du fondateur ou, le cas échéant, le nom du représentant, la qualité en laquelle celui-ci signe (p. ex. : exécuteur, fiduciaire) et le nom du fondateur qu'il représente

Signature / signature

Incorporators' name or the personal representatives name and the capacity in which he/she is signing (e.g. executor, trustee) and the name of the incorporator he/she is representing
Nom du fondateur ou, le cas échéant, le nom du représentant, la qualité en laquelle celui-ci signe (p. ex. : exécuteur, fiduciaire) et le nom du fondateur qu'il représente

Signature / signature

Incorporators' name or the personal representatives name and the capacity in which he/she is signing (e.g. executor, trustee) and the name of the incorporator he/she is representing
Nom du fondateur ou, le cas échéant, le nom du représentant, la qualité en laquelle celui-ci signe (p. ex. : exécuteur, fiduciaire) et le nom du fondateur qu'il représente

Signature / signature

Incorporators' name or the personal representatives name and the capacity in which he/she is signing (e.g. executor, trustee) and the name of the incorporator he/she is representing
Nom du fondateur ou, le cas échéant, le nom du représentant, la qualité en laquelle celui-ci signe (p. ex. : exécuteur, fiduciaire) et le nom du fondateur qu'il représente

07123 (2011/04)

Forms 12, 13 — [Revoked]

[Revoked O. Reg. 400/95, s. 6.]

Form 14 — [Revoked]

[Revoked O. Reg. 288/00, s. 4.]

Form 15 — Articles of Revival*

INSTRUCTIONS FOR COMPLETING

This form is to be used to revive a corporation where the Director has by order cancelled the certificate of incorporation under Section 241 of the *Business Corporations Act* and it is less than twenty years after the date of dissolution.

Articles in duplicate with original signatures on both copies must be mailed to the Toronto address listed below or for over the counter service, they may also be filed in person at the Toronto address.

FEE

$330.00 **BY MAIL** - cheque or money order payable to the Minister of Revenue.

IN PERSON (at the Toronto office) - cash, cheque or money order payable to the Minister of Revenue, Visa, MasterCard, American Express or debit card.

There will be a service charge payable for any cheque returned as non-negotiable by a bank or financial institution.

SUPPORTING DOCUMENTS

SPECIAL NOTICE/ANNUAL RETURN FILINGS AND FEES

All outstanding notices and returns required to be filed by the corporation under the *Corporations Information Act* must be attached except for any outstanding current annual return, which the corporation must file with the Ministry of Revenue or electronically immediately upon revival. Any outstanding Special Notice/Annual Return filings for the period 1992 to 1995 must be attached together with outstanding fees ($50.00 for each year not paid). If you have questions contact the Companies Helpline, at 416 314 8880 or toll-free in Ontario at 1 800 361-3223.

NAME SEARCH

An original Ontario-biased NUANS name search report is required only if the Articles of Revival are submitted more than ten years from the date the corporation was cancelled or for a proposed new name if the corporate name is to be changed on revival.

NUANS is a computerized search system that compares a proposed corporate name or trade-mark with databases of existing corporate bodies and trade-marks. This comparison determines the similarity that exists between the proposed name or mark and existing names in the database, and produces a listing of names that are found to be most similar. This search must be submitted together with the duplicate Articles of Revival within 90 days from production by the NUANS system. For example, articles submitted on November 28th could be accompanied by a NUANS name search report dated as early as August 30th, but not dated earlier. The Central Production and Verification Services Branch does not provide this search.

Suppliers are listed in the Yellow Pages under the heading "Searchers of Records" or visit Industry Canada's NUANS site at, www.nuans.com for a list of registered search houses that can assist you with obtaining a NUANS search report and filing your corporate documents with the Ministry of Government Services. Please note the NUANS search must be Ontario biased.

07127E (2011/05)

CONSENT FROM THE MINISTER OF REVENUE

If the corporation was dissolved for failure to comply with the provisions of the *Corporations Tax Act, Employer Health Tax Act, Fuel Tax Act, Gasoline Tax Act, Land Transfer Tax Act, Retail Sales Tax Act or the Tobacco Tax Act* a letter consenting to the revival from the Ministry of Finance must accompany the Articles of Revival.

Ministry of Revenue
Client Accounts and Services Branch
33 King Street West
PO Box 622
Oshawa ON L1H 8H6
Fax: 905 433-5418
Telephone Enquiries can be made to the Canada Revenue Agency at
English: 1 800 959-5525
En Francais : 1 800 959-7725
TTY: 1 800 665-0354

CONSENT FROM THE OFFICE OF THE PUBLIC GUARDIAN AND TRUSTEE
A statement in writing from the Office of the Public Guardian and Trustee (OPGT) that it has no objection to the revival is generally not required unless the OPGT is currently dealing with assets formerly owned by the dissolved corporation. For further information, please contact the OPGT at 416 326-1963 or toll free in Ontario 1 800 366-0335.

CONSENT OF THE ONTARIO SECURITIES COMMISSION
Consent to the revival from the Ontario Securities Commission is required only if the corporation was dissolved for failure to comply with sections 77 & 78 of the *Securities Act.*

COVERING LETTER
Enclose a covering letter setting out the name of a contact person, a return address and a telephone number. This will facilitate the processing of the articles should a question arise as to the content of the Articles of Revival.

APPEARANCE OF DOCUMENTS
The Articles of Revival must be completed in duplicate on Form 15 as approved by the Minister. All documents must be legible and compatible with the microfilming process, with the information typed or hand printed in block capital letters, on one side of good quality, white bond paper 8 ½" by 11".

The Article headings are numbered 1 to 7 and should remain in that order. Do not leave out any of the headings.

ARTICLES

ARTICLE 1 Set out the name of the corporation at the time of cancellation in block capital letters starting from the first box of the first line on the left with one letter per box and one empty box for a space. Punctuation marks are entered in separate boxes. Complete one line before starting in the first box of the next line. The name entered must be exactly the same as it appeared on the original Articles of Incorporation or Articles of Amalgamation. If there has been a name change, the name entered must be exactly the same as it appears on the most recent Articles of Amendment.

EAST SIDE INVESTMENT AND MANAG
EMENT LTD.

ARTICLE 2 If the corporation is to be revived under a name other than the name at the time of cancellation, the new name must be set out in block capital letters starting from the first box of the first line on the left with one letter per box and one empty box for a space. Punctuation marks are entered in separate boxes. Complete one line before starting in the first box of the next line. Unless the name is to be a number name a name search for the new name must be submitted with the Articles of Revival. The name entered must be exactly the same as that on the name search.

07127E (2011/05)

ARTICLE 3 Set out original date of incorporation/amalgamation of the corporation.

ARTICLE 4 Set out the date of dissolution of the corporation. If the corporation has been dissolved for 10 to 20 years, the articles must be accompanied by a name search report. Articles of Revival cannot be filed if it is more than twenty years after the date of dissolution.

ARTICLE 5 The address (where multi-office building include room or suite number) of the registered office of the corporation must be set out in full including the street name, street number or R.R. #, municipality, province, country and the postal code. A post office box alone is not an acceptable address. If there is no street and number or R.R. #, set out the Lot and Concession numbers. The registered office must be in Ontario.

ARTICLE 6 The following terms and conditions have been complied with:

a) all outstanding notices and returns required to be filed by the corporation under the *Corporations Information Act* are attached except for any current outstanding annual return, which the corporation will file immediately upon revival.

b) all documents required to be filed by the corporation under Ontario tax statutes have been filed and all defaults of the corporation under the tax statutes have been remedied.

c) consent from the Minister of Revenue to the requested revival (if applicable) is attached.

d) the consent of the Public Guardian & Trustee to the requested revival (if applicable) is attached.

e) the consent of the Ontario Securities Commission to the requested revival (if applicable) is attached.

f) all other defaults of the corporation to the date of dissolution have been remedied and it is not more than 20 years after the date of dissolution.

Article 6 showing the above statements must be included in the articles. The applicant must also file any applicable consents or notices or returns. Any current outstanding annual return must be filed immediately upon revival.

ARTICLE 7 The applicant's interest in the corporation (for example, director, officer, shareholder, creditor, estate trustee of shareholder) must be set out in the space provided.

EXECUTION Both copies of the articles must be signed manually by the applicant. In the spaces provided set out the first name, middle names and surname of the applicant together with the applicant's address for service.

Articles (in duplicate), original Ontario-biased NUANS name search report (if applicable), any applicable consents, any outstanding notices or returns, a covering letter, the filing fee and any outstanding Notice/ Return fee should be mailed or delivered to:

Ministry of Government Services
Central Production and Verification Services Branch
393 University Avenue, Suite 200
Toronto ON M5G 2M2

375 University Avenue, 2nd Floor (In Person)

07127E (2009/11)

INSTRUCTIONS POUR REMPLIR LE FORMULAIRE

On utilise ce formulaire pour reconstituer une société qui a été dissoute sur un ordre du directeur ayant annulé le certificat de constitution en vertu de l'article 241 de la *Loi sur les sociétés par actions*, à condition que la reconstitution ait lieu moins de 20 ans après la dissolution.

Le formulaire doit être rempli en deux exemplaires, chaque exemplaire portant une signature originale. On doit l'envoyer par courrier à l'adresse à Toronto qui est indiquée ci-dessous ou le remettre en personne à cette même adresse.

DROITS

330 $ Envoi **PAR COURRIER** – Paiement par chèque ou mandat libellé à l'ordre du « Ministre du Revenu ».

Dépôt **EN PERSONNE** (au bureau de Toronto) – Paiement en argent comptant; par chèque ou mandat libellé à l'ordre du « Ministre du Revenu »; ou par Visa, MasterCard, American Express ou carte de débit.

Des frais de service seront perçus pour tout chèque refusé par l'établissement financier.

DOCUMENTS À L'APPUI

AVIS SPÉCIAL OU RAPPORT ANNUEL EN SOUFFRANCE

Joindre tout avis ou rapport en souffrance que la société doit déposer aux termes de la *Loi sur les renseignements exigés des personnes morales*, à l'exclusion de tout rapport annuel courant éventuellement en souffrance que la société doit déposer immédiatement après la reconstitution auprès du ministère du Revenu ou par voie électronique. Les avis spéciaux ou les rapports annuels en souffrance des années 1992 à 1995 doivent être joints ensemble, accompagnés des droits requis (50 $ pour chaque année omise). Pour toutes questions à ce sujet, veuillez contacter le Service de renseignement des compagnies au 416 314-8880, ou sans frais en Ontario, au 1 800 361-3223.

RAPPORT DE RECHERCHE NUANS

Joindre l'original d'un rapport de recherche NUANS axé sur l'Ontario seulement si la reconstitution est effectuée plus de 10 ans après la dissolution ou si la société change sa dénomination sociale lors de la reconstitution.

NUANS est un système de recherche informatisée qui compare la dénomination ou la marque de commerce proposée pour votre société avec des bases de données de personnes morales et de marques de commerce existantes dans le but de déterminer si le nom proposé est identique ou semblable à des noms existants. Le système produit une liste des noms qui se rapprochent le plus du nom proposé. Le rapport NUANS doit être déposé en même temps que les *Statuts de reconstitution*; il doit être remis dans les 90 jours suivant la date de sa production. Par exemple, des statuts déposés le 28 novembre pourraient être accompagnés d'un rapport NUANS daté du 30 août précédent, mais non d'une date antérieure au 30 août. La Direction des services centraux de production et de vérification ne fournit pas cette recherche.

Les fournisseurs de services de recherche sont indiqués dans les Pages jaunes de l'annuaire, sous « Titres et archives – Recherche » ou « Searchers of Records ». Le site NUANS d'Industrie Canada (www.nuans.com) fournit aussi une liste de maisons de recherche homologuées qui peuvent aider à obtenir le rapport NUANS et à remplir les statuts. Ne pas oublier que le rapport NUANS doit être axé sur l'Ontario.

07127F (2011/05)

CONSENTEMENT DU MINISTÈRE DU REVENU

Si la société a été dissoute pour manque de se conformer aux dispositions de la *Loi sur l'imposition des sociétés*, la *Loi sur l'impôt-santé des employeurs*, la *Loi de la taxe sur les carburants*, la *Loi de la taxe sur l'essence*, la *Loi sur les droits de cession immobilière*, la *Loi sur la taxe de vente au détail* ou la *Loi de la taxe sur le tabac*, il faut joindre une lettre du ministère des Finances indiquant son consentement aux *Statuts de reconstitution*.

Ministère du Revenu
Direction des services et des dossiers clients
33 rue King Ouest
CP 622
Oshawa ON L1H 8H6
Télécopieur : 905 433-5418
Pour des renseignements par téléphone, appelez l'Agence du revenu du Canada :
En anglais : 1 800 959-5525

En français : 1 800 959-7725
ATS (malentendants/malvoyants) : 1 800 665-0354

CONSENTEMENT DU BUREAU DU TUTEUR ET CURATEUR PUBLIC

Le consentement à la reconstitution du Bureau du Tuteur et curateur public est requis seulement si le Bureau est couramment responsable d'actifs ayant appartenu à la société dissoute. Pour des renseignements à ce sujet, veuillez contacter le Bureau au 416 326-1963, ou sans frais en Ontario, au 1 800 366-0335.

CONSENTEMENT DE LA COMMISSION DES VALEURS MOBILIÈRES DE L'ONTARIO

Le consentement de la Commission des valeurs mobilières de l'Ontario est requis seulement si la société a été dissoute pour défaut de se conformer aux articles 77 et 78 de la *Loi sur les valeurs mobilières*.

LETTRE D'INTRODUCTION

Joindre une lettre indiquant le nom d'un contact, son adresse et son numéro de téléphone. Cette information nous sera utile si nous avons des questions concernant les renseignements fournis.

PRÉSENTATION DES DOCUMENTS

Les *Statuts de reconstitution* doivent être soumis en double exemplaire, sur la Formule 15 approuvée par le ministre. Tous les documents soumis doivent être lisibles et se prêter au microfilmage. L'information est soit dactylographiée, soit écrite lisiblement en lettres majuscules au recto seulement d'un papier filigrané blanc de bonne qualité, de format 8 ½ po x 11 po.

Le formulaire des *Statuts de reconstitution* comporte 7 sections numérotées de 1 à 7, qui doivent rester dans cet ordre. Ne retirer aucune page ou section.

SECTIONS À REMPLIR

SECTION 1 Inscrire le nom de la société dissoute en lettres majuscules, une lettre par case, en commençant à la première case de la première ligne. Pour chaque espace entre les mots, laisser une case vide. Chaque signe de ponctuation occupe aussi une case distincte. Remplir chaque ligne jusqu'au bout avant de commencer la suivante. Le nom entré doit être identique au nom indiqué sur les *Statuts constitutifs* ou les *Statuts de fusion* de la société dissoute. S'il y avait déjà eu un ou plusieurs changements de nom avant la dissolution, il faut entrer le nom exact figurant sur les *Statuts de modification* déposés en dernier.

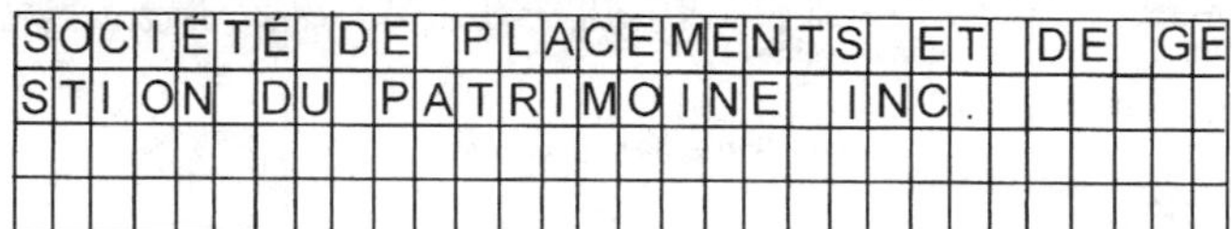
SOCIÉTÉ DE PLACEMENTS ET DE GE
STION DU PATRIMOINE INC.

07127F (2011/05)

SECTION 2 Si la société est reconstituée sous une dénomination sociale autre que celle existant à la dissolution, indiquer le nouveau nom en lettres majuscules, une lettre par case, en commençant à la première case de la première ligne. Pour chaque espace entre les mots, laisser une case vide. Chaque signe de ponctuation occupe aussi une case distincte. Remplir chaque ligne jusqu'au bout avant de commencer la suivante. Sauf si le nom est une dénomination numérique, il faut joindre un rapport de recherche NUANS, et le nom entré ici doit être identique au nom figurant sur le rapport NUANS.

SECTION 3 Indiquer la date de la constitution ou de la fusion de la société dissoute.

SECTION 4 Indiquer la date de la dissolution de la société. Rappel : Si la société est dissoute depuis 10 à 20 ans, joindre aux statuts un rapport de recherche NUANS. On ne peut pas déposer des *Statuts de reconstitution* plus de 20 ans après la dissolution.

SECTION 5 Indiquer l'adresse du siège social au complet : rue et numéro, bureau (dans le cas d'un immeuble à bureaux), municipalité, province, pays et code postal. Une adresse composée d'une case postale n'est pas acceptée. S'il n'y a pas de rue ni de numéro, indiquer les numéros de lot et de concession. Le siège social doit être situé en Ontario.

SECTION 6 Cette section énumère les conditions auxquelles l'auteur de la demande doit se conformer pour la reconstitution de la société. Ces conditions, telles qu'énoncées ci-dessous, doivent être incluses dans les statuts déposés.

a) Tous les avis et rapports en souffrance que la société doit déposer aux termes de la *Loi sur les renseignements exigés des personnes morales* sont joints aux statuts, sauf les rapports annuels courants éventuellement en souffrance, que la société déposera immédiatement après la reconstitution.

b) Tous les documents exigés par les lois d'imposition de l'Ontario ont été déposés et toutes les omissions commises par la société à l'égard de ces lois ont été corrigées.

c) Le ministre du Revenue a approuvé (le cas échéant) la reconstitution. Son consentement est annexe.

d) Le Tuteur et curateur public a approuvé (le cas échéant) la reconstitution. Son consentement est annexé.

e) La Commission des valeurs mobilières de l'Ontario a approuvé (le cas échéant) la reconstitution. Son consentement est annexé.

f) Toutes les omissions commises par la société avant la dissolution ont été corrigées, et la reconstitution a lieu moins de 20 ans après la date de dissolution.

L'article 6 en entier doit figurer ou être reproduit tel quel sur les statuts. L'auteur de la demande doit aussi déposer tous les consentements, avis ou rapports applicables. Tout rapport annuel couramment en souffrance doit être déposé immédiatement après la reconstitution.

SECTION 7 Indiquer l'intérêt de l'auteur de la demande dans la société (p. ex. : administrateur, dirigeant, actionnaire, créancier, exécuteur testamentaire d'un actionnaire, etc.)

SIGNATURE Les deux exemplaires des statuts doivent porter la signature originale de l'auteur de la demande. Dans les espaces prévus, indiquer en lettres moulées le nom complet de celui ci et l'adresse de son domicile élu aux fins de signification.

Envoyer ou remettre les *Statuts de reconstitution* en double exemplaire, accompagnés des droits prescrits et de tout document éventuellement requis (l'original d'un rapport de recherche NUANS axé sur l'Ontario, consentements applicables, avis et rapports en souffrance, y compris les droits de dépôt s'y rapportant, et lettre d'introduction) à l'adresse suivante :

Ministère des Services gouvernementaux
Direction des services centraux de production et de vérification
393, avenue University, bureau 200
Toronto ON M5G 2M2

375, avenue University, 2e étage (dépôt en personne)

07127F (2011/05)

For Ministry Use Only
À l'usage exclusif du ministère

Ontario Corporation Number
Numéro de la société en Ontario

Form 15
Business Corporations Act

Formule 15
Loi sur les sociétés par actions

ARTICLES OF REVIVAL
STATUTS DE RECONSTITUTION

1. Name of dissolved corporation: (Set out in BLOCK CAPITAL LETTERS)
Dénomination sociale de la société dissoute (écrire en LETTRES MAJUSCULES SEULEMENT) :

2. The name under which the corporation is to be revived if other than name at dissolution:
(Set out in BLOCK CAPITAL LETTERS)
Dénomination sociale après la reconstitution si elle est différente de celle de la société lors de la dissolution (écrire en LETTRES MAJUSCULES SEULEMENT) :

3. Date of incorporation/amalgamation:
Date de la constitution ou de la fusion :

Year année | Month mois | Day jour

4. Date of dissolution:
Date de la dissolution :

Year année | Month mois | Day jour

5. The address of the registered office is:
Adresse du siège social :

(Street & Number or R.R. Number or Lot and Concession & if Multi-Office Building give Room No. - Post Office Box not acceptable)
(Rue et numéro ou numéro de la R.R. ou de lot et concession et, s'il s'agit d'un édifice à bureaux, numéro du bureau – Case postale non acceptée)

ONTARIO

(Name of Municipality or Post Office)
(Nom de la municipalité ou du bureau de poste)

Postal Code/
Code postal

07127 (2011/05)

Page 1 of/de 2

6. The following terms and conditions have been complied with:
Les conditions suivantes ont été respectées :

a) all outstanding notices and returns required to be filed by the corporation under the *Corporations Information Act* are attached except for any current outstanding annual return, which the corporation will file immediately upon revival.

a) Tous les avis et rapports en souffrance que la société doit déposer aux termes de la *Loi sur les renseignements exigés des personnes morales* sont joints aux statuts, sauf les rapports annuels courants éventuellement en souffrance, que la société déposera immédiatement après la reconstitution.

b) all documents required to be filed by the corporation under Ontario tax statutes have been filed and all defaults of the corporation under the tax statutes have been remedied.

b) Tous les documents exigés par les lois d'imposition de l'Ontario ont été déposés et toutes les omissions commises par la société à l'égard de ces lois ont été corrigées.

c) the consent from the Minister of Revenue to the requested revival (if applicable) is attached.

c) Le ministre du Revenue a approuvé (le cas échéant) la reconstitution. Son consentement est annexé.

d) the consent of the Public Guardian & Trustee to the requested revival (if applicable) is attached.

d) Le Tuteur et curateur public a approuvé (le cas échéant) la reconstitution. Son consentement est annexé.

e) the consent of the Ontario Securities Commission to the requested revival (if applicable) is attached.

e) La Commission des valeurs mobilières de l'Ontario a approuvé (le cas échéant) la reconstitution. Son consentement est annexé.

f) all other defaults of the corporation to the date of dissolution have been remedied and it is not more than twenty years from the date of dissolution.

f) Toutes les omissions commises par la société avant la dissolution ont été corrigées, et la reconstitution a lieu moins de 20 ans après la date de la dissolution.

7. The interest of the applicant in the corporation is: (for example, director, officer, shareholder, creditor, estate trustee of shareholder)
Indiquer l'intérêt de l'auteur de la demande dans la société (p. ex. : administrateur, dirigeant, actionnaire, créancier, exécuteur testamentaire d'un actionnaire, etc.) :

____

These articles are signed in duplicate.
Les présents statuts sont signés en double exemplaire.

____
Signature of applicant / Signature de l'auteur de la demande

____
Print applicant's first name, middle names and surname / Prénom, autre prénom, nom de famille de l'auteur de la demande (en lettres moulées)

____
Applicant's address for service - street & number or RR# & suite / Domicile élu de l'auteur de la demande – rue et numéro, bureau, ou R.R.

____
Municipality, province, country & postal code / Municipalité, province, pays et code postal

07127 (2011/05)

Page 2 of/de 2

Forms 16–19 — [Revoked]

[Revoked O. Reg. 288/00, s. 4.]

Form 20 — [Revoked]

[Revoked O. Reg. 190/99, s. 7.]

Information Sheets — Ministry of Government Services, Companies and Personal Property Security Branch

[BC-1] — Amalgamation (Business Corporations)*

Date: **November 30, 2007**

Companies and Personal Property Security Branch Requirements

In order to amalgamate two or more active Ontario business corporations, the following documentation must be submitted to the Companies and Personal Property Security Branch (CPPSB):

1. *Articles of Amalgamation* (Form 4 approved by the Minister under the Regulations to the *Business Corporations Act*) completed in duplicate, bearing original signatures on both copies.
2. *Schedule A*
   - A signed statement of a director or officer of each of the amalgamating corporations, as required under subsection 178(2) of the *Business Corporations Act.*
3. *Schedule B*
   - Long-Form Amalgamation requires a copy (in duplicate) of the amalgamation agreement as adopted by a special resolution under S. 176 of the *Business Corporations Act.*
   - Short-Form Amalgamation requires a copy (in duplicate) of the directors' resolutions (one from each amalgamating corporation) approved under S. 177 of the *Business Corporations Act.*
4. *Fee of $330.00* if 10 or fewer amalgamating corporations, or

   Fee of $500.00 if more than 10 amalgamating corporations.
5. *Ontario-biased NUANS* name search report; if the name of the amalgamated corporation will be different from the names of any of its amalgamating corporations and is not a number name.
6. *Covering letter* giving a contact name, return address and telephone number.

Forms

Articles of Amalgamation Form 4, are available on the ServiceOntario website at www.ServiceOntario.ca. They may also be purchased from most legal stationers or name search houses. Legal stationers and name search houses are listed in the Yellow Pages under "Legal Forms" and "Searchers of Records" respectively.

Name Search

NUANS is a computerized search system that compares a proposed corporate name or trade-mark with databases of existing corporate bodies and trade-marks. This comparison determines the similarity that exists between the proposed name or mark and existing names in the database, and produces a listing of names that are found to be most similar.

An Ontario-biased NUANS name search report, if required, must be obtained from a private name search company and cannot be dated more than 90 days prior to the submission of the articles. For example, article submitted on November 28th could be accompanied by a NUANS name search report dated as early as August 30th, but not dated earlier.

Suppliers are listed in the Yellow Pages under the heading "Searchers of Records" or visit Industry Canada's NUANS website at www.nuans.com for a list of registered search houses that can assist you with obtaining a NUANS search report and filing your corporate documents with the Ministry of Government and Consumer Services. The Companies and Personal Property Security Branch does not provide this search.

General Information

Please be advised that the Branch *CANNOT GIVE LEGAL ADVICE.* This information is intended as a general guide only. For further assistance or legal information, please consult private legal counsel.

If you need a lawyer, you may wish to contact the Lawyer Referral Service of the Law Society of Upper Canada. You will be referred to a lawyer for up to a half-hour free legal consultation, either in person or over the phone. Please note that this is a toll service and phoning the Lawyer Referral Service line will automatically generate a $6.00 charge on your phone bill, in the month following your call. You must be 18 years of age to access this service. The number is 1-900-565-4577 (1-900-565-4LRS).

Please refer to Sections 174 through 179 of the *Business Corporations Act* for details regarding the amalgamation of Ontario business corporations. The *Business Corporations Act* is available on the Internet at *www.e-laws.gov.on.ca* or can be purchased through Publications Ontario at (416) 326-5200 or toll-free at 1-800-668-9938. The website for Publications Ontario is *www.publications.gov.on.ca.*

Unauthorized Back to Back Amalgamation — Refers to the filing of two sets of Articles of Amalgamation with both amalgamations coming into effect on a future date (i.e. both coming into existence on a future date no more than 30 days from the date of filing). The amalgamated corporation arising from the first amalgamation is one of the corporations that would be amalgamating to form the second corporation. (e.g. Articles of Amalgamation submitted on September 13th to amalgamate corporations A & B with a requested effective date of September 30th, to form corporation C. On September 13th (or any date prior to September 30th) a second application for Articles of Amalgamation is submitted to amalgamate corporations C & D to form corporation E).

Only the first set of post-dated Articles is acceptable for filing with the Companies and Personal Property Security Branch. This is because the first amalgamated corporation must be in existence to authorize the second amalgamation. Articles of Amalgamation must be approved in accordance with the Act's requirements to be valid, and the Act clearly requires the approval of the directors (S. 177) or shareholders (S. 176) of each amalgamating corporation. If one of the amalgamating corporations does not yet exist, it is impossible for the necessary approval to be obtained to form a new amalgamation. However, it may be possible to obtain a court-ordered arrangement under section 182 of the Act in these circumstances. Please see the Arrangement (Business Corporations) information sheet.

Long-Form Amalgamation — Refers to the amalgamation of two or more Ontario business corporations. Each amalgamating corporation must enter into an agreement setting out the terms and means of effecting amalgamation. The agreement must comply with S. 175 and must also be adopted as per S. 176 before submission to the Companies and Personal Security Branch.

Short-Form Amalgamation — Refers to the amalgamation of a holding corporation and one or more of its subsidiary corporations where all of the issued shares of each amalgamating subsidiary corporation are held by one or more of the other amalgamating corporations, or the amalgamation of two or more wholly-owned subsidiary corporations of the same holding corporation.

An amalgamation between a holding corporation and its subsidiary or subsidiaries is subject to S. 177(1) of the *Business Corporations Act* and is sometimes referred to as a *"vertical"* amalgamation.

An amalgamation between subsidiaries is subject to S. 177(2) of the *Business Corporations Act* and is sometimes referred to as a *"horizontal"* amalgamation.

In each case, the amalgamation must be approved by a resolution of the directors of each amalgamating corporation and the directors' resolutions must comply with S. 177(1) or S. 177(2), as applicable, of the *Business Corporations Act.*

NOTE: Section 177 can only be used when amalgamating a holding corporation and its subsidiary/subsidiaries or when amalgamating subsidiaries of the same holding corporation.

"As prescribed" — Subsections 177(1)(b)(ii) and 177(2)(b)(ii) refer to that which may be prescribed in the Regulations. Section 43 of Ontario Regulation 62 specifies changes that may be included in the Articles of Amalgamation in the case of a Short Form Amalgamation. Except for these prescribed differences, the articles of amalgamation must be the same as the articles of the amalgamating holding corporation (S. 177(1)(b)(ii)) or the same as the articles of the amalgamating subsidiary corporation whose shares are not cancelled (S. 177(2)(b)(ii))

Corporate Name — The name of the amalgamated corporation may be identical to the name of one of its amalgamating corporations, if the name is not a number name (S. 10 of Regulation 62 under the *Business Corporations Act*).

In the case where the name of the amalgamated corporation will be identical to the name of one of its amalgamating corporations, a NUANS name search report is not required to accompany the Articles of Amalgamation.

When the name of the amalgamated corporation is to be a number name, the newly assigned Ontario Corporation Number shall be used in the name. The Ontario corporation number is assigned by the Companies and Personal Property Security Branch and will not be the same Ontario corporation number as any of the amalgamating corporations.

Effective Date — Articles are dated as of the day the duplicate originals of the Articles together with all other required documents are received by CPPSB or an effective date of up to 30 days later can be requested in *writing using bold or highlighted letters*, upon submission of the Articles to the Companies and Personal Property Security Branch. If you are presenting your documents in person at the public counter, as well a requesting a future date in your letter, *you must also verbally bring this request to the attention of the counter clerk* who endorses your Articles, as required under subsection 273(2) of the *Business Corporations Act.* Articles are effective on the date shown on the certificate.

The dates of adoption appearing on page 2 of the Articles of Amalgamation, the dates appearing on the Schedule A directors' statements, the date the agreement was made (if set out) and the date on the directors' resolutions (if any) must not be future dates.

Corrections — Any minor changes or corrections to documents prior to submission to the Companies and Personal Property Security Branch may be crossed out and/or added bearing the initials of the appropriate officer of the corporation authorized to make changes. However, no visible corrections are permitted on page 1 of the articles. Liquid paper corrections are not acceptable, but pages corrected with liquid paper that do not bear original signatures can be photocopied.

Documents must be clearly legible at all times.

Please note it is the responsibility of the applicant in consultation with their legal counsel to ensure that articles filed under the Business Corporations Act conform to law.

[BC-2] — Amendment (Business Corporations)*

Date: November 30, 2007

Companies and Personal Property Security Branch Requirements

A corporation may amend, add, change or remove provisions set out in its Articles by filing the following with the Companies and Personal Property Security Branch:

1. *Articles of Amendment* (Form 3 approved by the Minister under the Regulations to the *Business Corporations Act*), completed in duplicate, bearing original signatures on both copies;
2. *Ontario-biased NUANS name search report* if there is a change of name (not required if the new name is a number name);
3. *Fee of $150.00*;
4. *Covering letter* giving a contact name, return address and telephone number.

Forms

Articles of Amendment, Form 3 is available on the ServiceOntario website at www.ServiceOntario.ca. Articles of Amendment may also be purchased from most legal stationers or name search companies. Legal stationers and name search companies are listed in the Yellow Pages under "Legal Forms" and "Searchers of Records" respectively.

Name Search

NUANS is a computerized search system that compares a proposed corporate name or trade-mark with databases of existing corporate bodies and trade-marks. This comparison determines the similarity that exists between the proposed name or mark and existing names in the database, and produces a listing of names that are found to be most similar. A NUANS search is not required if incorporating a number company.

An original Ontario-biased NUANS name search report must be obtained from a private name search company and cannot be dated more than 90 days prior to the submission of the articles. For example, articles submitted on November 28th could be accompanied by a NUANS name search report dated as early as August 30th, but not dated earlier. Suppliers are listed in the Yellow Pages under the heading "Searchers of Records" or visit Industry Canada's NUANS website at www.nuans.com for a list of registered search houses that can assist you with obtaining a NUANS search report and filing your corporate documents with the Ministry of Government and Consumer Services. The Companies and Personal Property Security Branch does not provide this search.

General Information

Please be advised that the Branch *CANNOT GIVE LEGAL ADVICE*. This information is intended as a general guide only. For further assistance or legal information, please consult private legal counsel.

If you need a lawyer, you may wish to contact the Lawyer Referral Service of the Law Society of Upper Canada. You will be referred to a lawyer for up to a half-hour free legal consultation, either in person or over the phone. Please note that this is a toll service and phoning the Lawyer Referral Service line will automatically generate a $6.00 charge on your phone bill, in the month following your call. You must be 18 years of age to access this service. The number is 1-900-565-4577 (1-900-565-4LRS).

Changes to Information

Corporation Name — Articles of Amendment must be accompanied by a NUANS name search report for the proposed new name (not required if the name is changing to a number name).

Registered Office Address — A corporation may by resolution of its directors change the location of its registered office within a municipality or geographic township (S. 14(3) of the *Business Corporations Act*).

A corporation may by special resolution change the municipality or geographic township in which its registered office is located to another place in Ontario (S. 14(4) of the *Business Corporations Act*).

Whenever a corporation changes its office address, an Initial Return/Notice of Change, Form 1 under the *Corporations Information Act* must be completed and filed with the Companies and Personal Property Security Branch within 15 days of the change (S. 4(1) of the *Corporations Information Act*).

Directors — A corporation may increase or decrease the number, or the minimum or maximum number of its directors as set out in the Articles of Incorporation (S. 125(1) of the *Business Corporations Act*).

Where a minimum and maximum number of directors of a corporation is provided for in its Articles, the number of directors of the corporation shall be determined from time to time by special resolution, or if the special resolution empowers the directors to determine the number, by resolution of the directors (S. 125(3) of the *Business Corporations Act*).

Whenever the number of directors changes within the minimum and maximum number provided for in the Articles, an Initial Return/Notice of Change, Form 1 under the *Corporations Information Act* must be filed within 15 days after the change.

Any change to the board of directors of a corporation must be set out in an Initial Return/Notice of Change, Form 1 under the *Corporations Information Act* and filed with the Companies and Personal Property Security Branch within 15 days after the change (S. 4(1) of the *Corporations Information Act*).

NOTE: The above resolutions and special resolutions are no longer filed with the Branch nor is notice of these changes published in the Ontario Gazette or newspaper.

Shares — Any change to clauses relating to shares, as set out in the Articles of Incorporation, must be clearly set out in Articles of Amendment.

Other Related Information Sheets

Corrected Certificate (Business Corporations)

Initial Return/Notice of change Making Changes to Corporate Information

[BC-3] — Arrangement (Business Corporations)*

Date: **November 30, 2007**

Companies and Personal Property Security Branch Requirements

To file Articles of Arrangement in Ontario, the following documentation must be submitted to the Companies and Personal Property Security Branch:

1. *Articles of Arrangement* (Form 8 approved by the Minister under the Regulations to the *Business Corporations Act*), completed in duplicate, bearing original signatures on both copies;
2. *Exhibit A* to the Articles — a copy of the Plan of Arrangement;
3. *Exhibit B* to the Articles — a copy of the court order, certified by the court. Only one original certified copy is required. The certified copy submitted with the second set of Articles may be a photocopy;
4. *Summary of those changes made by the Arrangement* that will affect records at the Companies and Personal Property Security Branch, including the page numbers of the Arrangement where the following information is located: the kind of action being taken (e.g. name change, amalgamation, etc.); the names of the affected corporations; their Ontario Corporation Numbers; the new corporate names, if any; the names and addresses for service of the first directors, the minimum and maximum number of directors and registered office of any resulting corporation(s);
5. *Ontario-biased NUANS* name search report for each new corporate name, if the Arrangement includes a change of corporate name. This does not apply if the new name is a number name, or, in the case of an amalgamation, if the name is identical to the name of one of the amalgamating corporations;
6. *Fee of $330.00* (for standard service in person — 48 hours minimum or 2–4 weeks by mail) or *fee of $500* (for expedited service — 24-hour service when submitted in person.) For 24-and 48-hour service, the Branch requires notification with a draft copy of the Plan of Arrangement, at least 7 working days in advance of the filing date.
7. *Covering letter* giving a contact name, return address and telephone number.

 For the most recent version of this form, please visit: http://www.gov.on.ca/ontprodconsume/groups/content/@onca/@bundles/@cppsb/documents/document/stel02_168093.pdf

Forms

Articles of Arrangement, Form 8, is available on the ServiceOntario website at www.ServiceOntario.ca. Articles of Arrangement may be purchased from most legal stationers or name search houses. Legal stationers and name search houses are listed in the Yellow Pages under "Legal Forms" and "Searchers of Records" respectively.

Name Search

NUANS is a computerized search system that compares a proposed corporate name or trade-mark with databases of existing corporate bodies and trade-marks. This comparison determines the similarity that exists between the proposed name or mark and existing names in the database, and produces a listing of names that are found to be most similar.

An original Ontario-biased NUANS name search report must be obtained from a private name search company and be submitted with the Articles of Incorporation. The NUANS report cannot be dated more than 90 days prior to the submission of the articles. For example, articles submitted on November 28th could be accompanied by a NUANS name search report dated as early as August 30th, but not dated earlier. The Companies and Personal Property Security Branch does not provide this search.

Suppliers are listed in the Yellow Pages under the heading "Searchers of Records" or visit Industry Canada's NUANS site at www.nuans.com for a list of registered search houses that can assist you with obtaining a NUANS search report and filing your corporate documents with the Ministry of Government and Consumer Services.

[BC-4] — Authorization to Continue in Another Jurisdiction (Business Corporations)*

Date: **November 30, 2007**

Companies and Personal Property Security Branch Requirements

An Ontario business corporation that wishes to obtain authorization from the Director to apply to continue the corporation in a jurisdiction outside Ontario, (e.g. within Canada — federal, Alberta or; outside Canada — Delaware-USA, Germany) must submit the following documentation to the Companies and Personal Property Security Branch:

1. *Application for Authorization to Continue in Another Jurisdiction* (Form 7 approved by the Minister as provided for in the Regulations under the *Business Corporations Act*), completed in duplicate, bearing original signatures on both copies;
2. *Consent letter* from the Minister of Finance;
3. *Consent letter* from the Ontario Securities Commission, *only if the corporation is an offering corporation*;
4. *Legal opinion (except in the case of continuance under the laws of another Canadian jurisdiction, including federal)*, to the effect that the laws of the other jurisdiction meet the requirements set out in s. 181(9) of the *Business Corporations Act*;
5. *Fee of $330.00.*

 For the most recent version of this form, please visit: http://www.gov.on.ca/ontprodconsume/groups/content/@onca/@bundles/@cppsb/documents/document/stel02_168095.pdf

6. *Covering letter* giving a contact name, return address and telephone number;

Forms

The Application For Authorization to Continue in Another Jurisdiction, Form 7 is available on the ServiceOntario website at www.ServiceOntario.ca. The forms may also be purchased from most legal stationary stores and search houses. Legal stationers and name search houses are listed in the Yellow Pages under "Legal forms" and "Searchers of Records" respectively.

Consent of the Minister Of Finance

The Application for Authorization to Continue in Another Jurisdiction must be accompanied by written consent to apply to continue outside Ontario from the Minister of Finance, and must be submitted within 60 days after the Minister of Finance provides consent. To obtain consent, contact the Ministry of Finance at the following address:

Ministry of Finance

Corporations Tax

33 King Street West, 4th Floor

P.O. Box 622

Oshawa ON L1H 8H5

TELEPHONE: 1-800-263-7965

Consent of the Ontario Securities Commission

If the corporation is offering securities to the public within the meaning of subsection 1(6) of the Ontario *Business Corporations Act*, the Application for Authorization to Continue in Another Jurisdiction must be accompanied by written consent from the Ontario Securities Commission. The Commission can be contacted at:

Telephone: 416-593-8314 (local Toronto calling area)

1-877-785-1555 (toll free in Canada).

E-Mail: inquiries@osc.gov.on.ca.

Regular mail: Ontario Securities Commission

20 Queen Street West, Suite 1903

Toronto ON M5H 3S8

Legal Opinion

If the corporation is applying to continue in a jurisdiction outside Canada the application for authorization must be accompanied by a legal opinion from an individual lawyer (not a law clerk) who is authorized to practice in the other jurisdiction, to the effect that the laws of the jurisdiction to which the corporation is applying to continue meet the requirements set out in subsection 181(9) of the Ontario *Business Corporations Act*. The legal opinion must be on letterhead paper, signed by an individual lawyer. The legal opinion must refer to each clause under subsection 181(9), specifically stating that the laws of the other jurisdiction provide in effect that:

a) the property of the corporation continues to be the property of the body corporate;

b) the body corporate continues to be liable for the obligations of the corporation;

c) an existing cause of action, claim or liability to prosecution is unaffected;

d) a civil, criminal or administrative action or proceeding pending by or against the corporation may be continued to be prosecuted by or against the body corporate; and

e) a conviction against the corporation may be enforced against the body corporate or a ruling, order or judgment in favour of or against the corporation may be enforced by or against the body corporate.

General Information

Please be advised that the *COMPANIES AND PERSONAL PROPERTY SECURITY BRANCH CANNOT GIVE LEGAL ADVICE.* This information is intended as a general guide only. For further assistance or legal advice, please consult your lawyer.

If you need a lawyer, you may wish to contact the Lawyer Referral Service of the Law Society of Upper Canada. You will be referred to a lawyer for up to a half-hour free legal consultation, either in person or over the phone. Please note that this is a toll service and phoning the Lawyer Referral Service line will automatically generate a $6.00 charge on your phone bill, in the month following your call. You must be 18 years of age to access this service. The number is 1-900-565-4577 (1-900-565-4LRS).

Please refer to *section 181 of the Business Corporations Act* for details on the requirements to obtain authorization by the Director to apply to continue in a jurisdiction outside Ontario as if the corporation had been incorporated under the laws of that other jurisdiction.

Authorization by Shareholders

Before applying to the appropriate official of another jurisdiction requesting that the corporation be continued under the laws of that jurisdiction, the corporation must obtain authorization from its shareholders and the Director (section 181). The application for continuance becomes authorized by the shareholders when the shareholders have approved of the continuance by a special resolution in accordance with the Act.

Expiry

The authorization of the Director to continue outside Ontario expires six months after the effective date stamped on the application (subsection 181(6) of the OBCA), unless within the 6- month period, the corporation is continued under the laws of the other jurisdiction. If the corporation does not continue to the other jurisdiction within the six months, it remains an Ontario corporation. A new application would be required if the corporation still wishes to continue in another jurisdiction after the authorization expires.

Effective date

The *Business Corporations Act* ceases to apply to the corporation on the date upon which the corporation is continued under the laws of the other jurisdiction.

Requirements After Continuation

The corporation is required to file with the Director a copy of the instrument of continuance issued to it by the other jurisdiction, within sixty days after the date of issuance (subsection 181(7) of the OBCA). The corporation will appear on the public record as an Ontario corporation until the Companies and Personal Property Security Branch receives a copy of the instrument of continuance. Upon receiving a copy of the continuance, the Ontario Business Information System (ONBIS) will be updated to show the new jurisdiction of the corporation and the status of the corporation will be changed to inactive.

The copy of the instrument of continuance should be mailed to:

Corporate Returns
Companies and Personal Property Security Branch
Ministry of Government and Consumer Services
393 University Ave, Suite 200
Toronto ON M5G 2M2

Corporations from other Canadian Jurisdictions Operating in Ontario

If, after continuing under the laws of another *Canadian* jurisdiction, the corporation still wishes to carry on business in Ontario, it must file a Form 2 under the *Corporations Information Act* (CIA) along with a copy of the instrument of continuance issued by the other jurisdiction and any amendments to the corporation name since continuation. This form and more information is available on the ServiceOntario website. (see above — FORMS)

Foreign Extra-Provincial Corporations Operating in Ontario

If, after continuing under the laws of a jurisdiction *outside Canada*, the corporation still wishes to carry on business in Ontario, it must obtain a licence under the *Extra-Provincial Corporations Act*. Forms and information on how to obtain an Extra-Provincial Licence are available on the ServiceOntario website (see above — FORMS)

Ontario Corporation Operating In Another Jurisdiction

An Ontario corporation that wishes to operate in another jurisdiction but remain subject to the Ontario *Business Corporations Act* and keep its head office in Ontario should not complete a Form 7. In this case the corporation should contact the other jurisdiction to acquire a licence to operate in the jurisdiction while remaining an Ontario-based corporation subject to Ontario legislation.

[BC-5] — Continuance (*Business Corporations Act*)*

Date: November 30, 2007

Companies and Personal Property Security Branch Requirements

In order to continue a business corporation from another jurisdiction into Ontario (transfer out of the original jurisdiction), the following documentation must be submitted to the Companies and Personal Property Security Branch.

1. *Articles of Continuance* (Form 6 approved by the Minister under the Regulations to the *Business Corporations Act*), completed in duplicate, bearing original signatures on both copies;

2. *Copy of the incorporating document*, together with all amendments made, certified by the appropriate official of the incorporating jurisdiction;

---

*© Queen's Printer for Ontario, 2007. Reproduced with permission. For the most recent version of this form, please visit: http://www.gov.on.ca/ontprodconsume/groups/content/@onca/@bundles/@cppsb/documents/document/stel02_168101.pdf

3. *Letter of satisfaction, certificate of discontinuance or other document* issued by the appropriate officer of the incorporating jurisdiction that indicates that the corporation is authorized under the laws of that jurisdiction to apply for Articles of Continuance;

4. *Legal opinion* to the effect that the laws of the jurisdiction to which the corporation is subject, authorize the corporation to apply for continuance, if the corporation is incorporated outside of Canada;

5. *NUANS* name search report (not required if continuing as a number company);

6. *Fee of $330.00* (standard service 48 hours or 2–4 weeks by mail) or *Fee of $500.00* (expedited service 24 hours if delivered in person);

7. *Covering letter* giving a contact name, return address and telephone number.

NOTE: These requirements do not apply to a corporation that merely wishes to operate in Ontario, as opposed to continuing/transferring out of its home jurisdiction. If the corporation is incorporated within Canada and wishes to operate in Ontario, the corporation must file an Initial Return, Form 2, under the *Corporations Information Act* and it will be issued an Ontario Corporation Number. A corporation incorporated outside of Canada must apply for an Extra-Provincial Licence.

Forms

Articles of Continuance, Form 6 is available on the ServiceOntario website at www.ServiceOntario.ca. The form may be purchased from most legal stationers or name search houses. Legal stationers and name search houses are listed in the Yellow Pages under "Legal Forms" and "Searchers of Records" respectively.

Name Search

NUANS is a computerized search system that compares a proposed corporate name or trade-mark with databases of existing corporate bodies and trade-marks. This comparison determines the similarity that exists between the proposed name or mark and existing names in the database, and produces a listing of names that are found to be most similar.

An original Ontario-biased NUANS name search report must be obtained from a private name search company and cannot be dated more than 90 days prior to the submission of the articles. For example, articles submitted on November 28th could be accompanied by a NUANS name search report dated as early as August 30th, but not dated earlier.

Suppliers are listed in the Yellow Pages under the heading "Searchers of Records" or visit Industry Canada's NUANS website at www.nuans.com for a list of registered search houses that can assist you with obtaining a NUANS search report and filing your corporate documents with the Ministry of Government and Consumer Services. The Companies and Personal Property Security Branch does not provide this search.

[BC-6] — Corrected Certificate (Business Corporations)*

Date: **November 30, 2007**

Companies and Personal Property Security Branch Requirements

An application for a Corrected Certificate for a document filed under *the Business Corporations Act* must be submitted to the Companies and Personal Property Security Branch and must include the following:

1) *Corrected articles* or other document in duplicate bearing original signatures on both copies. There is no special form for a corrected certificate. You must complete new articles in duplicate the same as were originally filed but without the error;

2) *Certified copy of a resolution* of the directors confirmed by the shareholders, authorizing the application for the Corrected Certificate.

The resolution must state that the corporation waives any right to be heard by the Director under *Section 275 of the Business Corporations Act.*

The resolution must be on 8 ½" by 11" size paper pursuant to the Regulations;

3) *Surrender of the original articles* or other documents as issued by the Companies and Personal Property Security Branch, bearing the original effective date;

4) *Fee of $500.00* made payable to the Minister of Finance;

5) Covering letter giving a contact name, return address and telephone number and clearly outlining the nature of the error to be corrected.

(6) *Any supporting documents* requested by the Ministry (e.g. affidavits).

Forms

Forms prescribed under the *Business Corporations Act* may be purchased from most legal stationers or name search houses. Legal stationers and name search houses are listed in the Yellow Pages under "Legal Forms" and "Searchers of Records" respectively.

Selected forms under the *Business Corporations Act* are available at no cost on the ServiceOntario website at www.ServiceOntario.ca.

General Information

Please be advised that the Branch *CANNOT GIVE LEGAL ADVICE.* This information is intended as a general guide only. For further assistance or legal information, please consult private legal counsel.

If you need a lawyer, you may wish to contact the Lawyer Referral Service of the Law Society of Upper Canada. You will be referred to a lawyer for up to a half-hour free legal consultation, either in person or over the phone. Please note that this is a toll service and phoning the Lawyer Referral Service line will automatically generate a $6.00 charge on your phone bill, in the month following your call. You must be 18 years of age to access this service. The number is 1-900-565-4577 (1-900-565-4LRS).

Please refer to *Section 275 of the Business Corporations Act* on application for a Corrected Certificate.

Errors

Application for corrected certificate under S. 275 of the *Business Corporations Act* may be made for an error contained in any document filed under the Act. In order to qualify for correction, the error must be on the face of the document, be a clerical error or provisions in the articles that do not conform to the Act. Errors must be clearly explained in writing and each application is dealt with on an individual basis. In some cases, affidavits or supporting documentation such as evidence that there was an error at the time the articles were filed may be required.

Examples of Circumstances Which May Warrant A Corrected Certificate

- An error in the name of the corporation (does not correspond to the NUANS report, legal ending omitted, missing a word, etc.);
- Incorrect Ontario corporation number (number misquoted on the Articles of Amendment, on page 2 of the Articles of Amalgamation, on Restated Articles, etc.);
- Typographical errors, obvious spelling errors, words which were clearly omitted from a sentence;
- Missing pages or clauses (where it is apparent they are missing);
- Anything that was clearly intended to be done at the time of the original application (as evidenced by the original resolution).

Examples of Circumstances For Which A Corrected Certificate Would NOT Be Granted

- Things that were not intended to be done at the time of the original application;
- Change in effective date (if no specific date had been requested);
- Change from a long-form to a short-form amalgamation;
- Where the error invalidates the certificate (e.g. no shareholder approval).

[BC-7] — Directors' Liability (*Business Corporations Act*)*

Date: November 30, 2007

General Information

Please be advised that the Branch *CANNOT GIVE LEGAL ADVICE.* This information is intended as a general guide only. For further assistance or legal information, please consult private counsel.

Please refer to *Sections 130 and 131 of the Business Corporations Act* for details on directors' liability and Sections 136 and 138 for information on indemnification of directors and insider liability.

Directors of a corporation are jointly and severally liable to the employees of the corporation for all debts not exceeding six months' wages and up to 12 months' vacation pay (S. 131).

Every director must act honestly and in good faith with the best interests of the corporation in mind when exercising powers and discharging duties (S. 134(1)).

Every director and officer of an Ontario business corporation must comply with the *Business Corporations Act*, the Regulations to the *Business Corporations Act*, the Articles and bylaws of the corporation and any unanimous shareholder agreement (S. 134(2)).

Other Potential Liability

There may also be potential liability under Federal and other provincial statutes (e.g. *Income Tax Act*, *Employment Standards Act* and environmental statutes). If you have any questions about your potential liability as a director or officer, please contact your lawyer.

[BC-8] — Articles of Incorporation — Incorporating a Business Corporation*

Date: November 30, 2007

Articles of Incorporation, Form 1 under the Ontario *Business Corporations Act* (OBCA) must be completed and filed to incorporate a business corporation in Ontario.

Methods of Incorporation

There are three service delivery choices available to clients who wish to incorporate a business corporation in Ontario:

1) File Articles of Incorporation electronically via the Internet through one of the Service Providers under contract with the Ministry of Government and Consumer Services.

2) For over-the-counter service, articles may be filed in person at the Toronto office or at some Land Registry/ServiceOntario offices in Ontario (See the "Offices That Endorse Articles Submitted Under the *Business Corporations Act*" information sheet). The information sheet is available on the SeviceOntario website at: www.ServiceOntario.ca.

3) Submit Articles of Incorporation by mail to the Companies and Personal Property Security Branch, 393 University Ave., Suite 200, Toronto ON M5G 2M2.

Electronic Incorporation

Electronic filing of Articles of Incorporation, OBCA Form 1, is available through Service Providers under contract with the Ministry of Government and Consumer Services. The Ministry's fee to file Articles of Incorporation electronically is $300. The Service Providers

---

*© Queen's Printer for Ontario, 2007. Reproduced with permission. For the most recent version of this form, please visit: http://www.gov.on.ca/ontprodconsume/groups/content/@onca/@bundles/@cppsb/documents/document/stel02_168137.pdf

charge an additional fee for the immediate online service they provide. For information about Service Providers visit the ServiceOntario website at www.ServiceOntario.ca

Incorporation in Person or by Mail

To incorporate a business corporation in Ontario, the following documentation must be submitted:

1. *Articles of Incorporation* (Form 1 approved by the Minister under the Regulations to the *Business Corporations Act*), completed in duplicate and bearing original signatures on both copies.

2. *Ontario-biased NUANS* (for a proposed name). NUANS is a computerized search system that compares a proposed corporate name or trade-mark with databases of 2 existing corporate bodies and trade-marks. This comparison determines the similarity that exists between the proposed name or mark and existing names in the database, and produces a listing of names that are found to be most similar. A NUANS search is not required if incorporating a number company.

3. *Fee* of $360. Make cheque payable to the Minister of Finance.

4. *Covering letter* giving a contact name, return address and telephone number. If a future date of incorporation (up to 30 days ahead) is required it must be set out in the covering letter.

5. *Other support documents*, if required (e.g. legal opinion). Please note: Consent to Act as First Director is no longer required to be filed with the Branch but it must be kept at the corporation's registered office.

Forms

Articles of Incorporation, Form 1, and Consent to Act as First Director, Form 2 are available on the ServiceOntario website at www.ServiceOntario.ca. The forms may also be purchased from most legal stationers or name search houses. Legal stationers and name search houses are listed in the Yellow Pages under "Legal Forms" and "Searchers of Records" respectively.

Name Search

Unless the corporation will have a number name, an original Ontario-biased NUANS name search report must be obtained from a private name search company and be submitted with the Articles of Incorporation. The NUANS report cannot be dated more than 90 days prior to the submission of the articles. For example, articles submitted on November 28th could be accompanied by a NUANS name search report dated as early as August 30th, but not dated earlier. The Companies and Personal Property Security Branch does not provide this search.

Suppliers are listed in the Yellow Pages under the heading "Searchers of Records" or visit Industry Canada's NUANS site at, www.nuans.com for a list of registered search houses that can assist you with obtaining a NUANS search report and filing your corporate documents with the Ministry of Government and Consumer Services.

General Information

Please be advised that the Branch *CANNOT GIVE LEGAL ADVICE.* This information is intended as a general guide only. For further assistance or legal information, please consult private legal counsel.

If you need a lawyer, you may wish to contact the Lawyer Referral Service of the Law Society of Upper Canada. You will be referred to a lawyer for up to a half-hour free legal consultation, either in person or over the phone. Please note that this is a toll service and phoning the Lawyer Referral Service line will automatically generate a $6.00 charge on your phone bill, in the month following your call. You must be 18 years of age to access this service. The number is 1-900-565-4577 (1-900-565-4LRS).

Please refer to the *Business Corporations Act* for details governing business corporations in Ontario. The *Business Corporations Act* is available on the Internet at www.e-laws.gov.on.ca or can be purchased through Publications Ontario at (416) 326-5300 or toll-free at 1-800-668-9938. The website for Publications Ontario is www.publications.gov.on.ca.

Corporation Name

It is the responsibility of the incorporators to ensure the name for an Ontario business corporation complies with the *Business Corporations Act* and its Regulations.

Legal Element

The word "Limited", "Limitée", "Incorporated", "Incorporée" or "Corporation" or the corresponding abbreviations "Ltd.", "Ltée", "Inc." or "Corp." shall be part of the name of every corporation, but a corporation may be legally designated by either the full or the abbreviated form (S. 10(1)).

English/French Versions

The name of a corporation may be in an English form only, a French form only, an English and a French form combined, or an English form and a French form which are equivalent but used separately (S. 10(2)).

When incorporating a corporation with an English and French form of the name a name search is required for each form of the name (English and French) unless the English and French forms of the name are identical and the legal element in the French form is the French version of the legal element in the English form (for example, INCORPOREE and INCORPORATED). There should be a forward slash (/) separating the two forms of the name.

Versions in Languages Other Than English

A corporation may have in its articles, a special provision permitting it to set out its name in any language and the corporation may be legally designated by that name (S. 10(4)). This would allow the corporation to legally use a foreign version of its corporate name for the purposes of conducting business. However, the foreign version would not be entered into the Branch's electronic database (ONBIS) and, therefore, would not appear on a Certificate of Status produced in respect of the corporation name. Despite subsection (4), a corporation shall set out its name in legible characters in all contracts, invoices, negotiable instruments and orders for goods or services issued or made by or on behalf of the corporation and in all documents sent to the Director under this Act (S. 10(5)).

Identical Names

A corporation may only acquire a name identical to that of another corporation if it meets the requirements of Sections 6(1) or 6(2) of Regulation 62 under the *Business Corporations Act*.

Subsection 6(1)

Except as provided in subsection (2) and section 10, no corporation may acquire a name identical to the name of former name of another body corporate, whether in existence or not unless, (a) the body corporate was incorporated under the laws of a jurisdiction outside Ontario and has never carried on any activities or identified itself in Ontario; or (b) at least ten years have elapsed since the body corporate was dissolved or changed its name.

Please note that although a Federal corporation with an identical name to a proposed Ontario corporate name may not be currently operating or active in Ontario it is entitled to commence activities in Ontario at any time in the future. Incorporators who incorporate with the same or similar name are therefore assuming the risk of an objection to their corporate name, which may result in a name hearing under section 12 of the *Business Corporations Act.*

Subsection 6(2)

Before the name can be duplicated under Subsection 6(2), Companies and Personal Property Security Branch requires that a legal opinion accompany the articles being filed. The legal opinion must be on legal letterhead and must be signed by an individual lawyer *(not a law clerk or law firm).* It must also clearly indicate that the corporations involved comply with Section 6(2) by referring to each clause specifically.

Section 10

Under Section 10 of the Regulations the name of a corporation formed by the amalgamation of two or more corporations may be identical to the name of one of its amalgamating corporations, if the name is not a number name.

Requirement for a Name that is not Identical

Corporation names can be duplicated only if the name is not a number name and only in the case of an amalgamation, or where the corporations comply with S. 6(1) or S. 6(2) of Regulation 62. All other instances prohibit the use of a name for a corporation that is identical to the name or former name of another corporation, whether the corporation is active or not (S. 6(1) of Regulation 62).

In order to acquire a name that is not identical, the name may be varied by the addition or deletion of words, numerals, or initials, or by substituting one of the other required legal elements or their corresponding abbreviations.

The addition or deletion of punctuation marks or other symbols is not sufficient to make the name different for the purposes of the Act (S. 7 of Regulation 62).

Please note that under the *Business Corporations Act*, incorporators are responsible for ensuring that Articles conform to law. Under the policy of Endorsement as of Right, the Branch does not review proposed corporation names for similarity to any other name. It is the applicant's responsibility to ensure the corporation name is not confusingly similar to that of another corporation, business name or trademark. A corporation that acquires a name similar to that of another corporation may be subject to a names hearing under Section 12 of the *Business Corporations Act* or a lawsuit.

Number Company

If an applicant wishes to incorporate with a number name, a name search is not required. The Companies and Personal Property Security Branch will assign a number. When completing the forms leave 9 empty boxes (for the number) and then the word "ONTARIO" followed by a legal element (see above).

Other Business Names

A corporation may carry on its business activities under a name other than its corporate name, provided that the name is registered under the *Business Names Act*. For more information about registering the operating name see the "Registering Your Business Name in Ontario" information sheet.

Directors

The directors shall manage or supervise the management of the business and affairs of the corporation. The board of directors of a corporation must consist of at least one individual, and in the case of an offering corporation, not fewer than three individuals (S. 115(2)).

The Articles of Incorporation may set out a fixed number of directors or a minimum and maximum number of directors (floating board), but each director must be at least 18 years of age (S. 118(1)).

At least 25 per cent of the directors must be resident Canadians (if 25% of the directors is not a whole number round up to the nearest whole number). Where a corporation has less than four directors, at least one must be a resident Canadian (S. 118(3))

Shareholders

Please note that all business corporations must be authorized to issue shares. Therefore, Article 6, "The classes and any maximum number of shares that the corporation is authorized to issue," of the Articles of Incorporation form must be completed (e.g. "unlimited common shares").

Effective Date

When Articles are filed with the Companies and Personal Property Security Branch they are endorsed with a certificate and are effective on the date set out in the certificate. Articles cannot be endorsed until all requirements under the *Business Corporations Act* have been met under the policy of Endorsement as of Right.

An effective date of up to 30 days later than the earliest date the Articles can be endorsed may be requested in *writing on a cover letter using bold or highlighted letters*, upon submission of the Articles to the Branch. If you are presenting your Articles in person and require a future effective date, *you must verbally bring this request to the attention of the counter clerk who endorses your Articles.*

Ontario Corporation Number (OCN)

Upon incorporation, the Branch assigns every corporation a number, which is unique to that corporation. It cannot be transferred to another corporation, nor can a corporation ever change its corporation number. When corporations amalgamate, the amalgamated corporation is assigned a new number.

Corrections to Documents

Any changes or corrections made to documents prior to submission to the Companies and Personal Property Security Branch may be crossed out and/or added bearing the initials of the appropriate officer of the corporation authorized to make changes. However, no visible corrections are permitted on page 1 of the Articles. Liquid paper corrections are not acceptable; however, corrected pages can be photocopied as long as they bear original signatures. Documents must be clearly legible at all times.

Professional Corporations

The proclamation of the professional incorporation provisions allowing a number of regulated professionals to incorporate their practices in Ontario occurred on November 1, 2001.

The *Business Corporations Act* allows a number of regulated professionals to incorporate their practices. The following professions are eligible to operate a professional corporation:

- Chartered accountants
- Certified general accountants
- Lawyers
- Health professionals regulated under the *Regulated Health Professions Act*
- Social workers and social service workers
- Veterinarians

Although framework legislation is in effect, the ability to practice by means of a professional corporation will depend on whether the profession in question has had the necessary regulations and by-laws enacted. It is important that regulated professionals who wish to incorporate their practices consult with their governing body for conditions of incorporation specific to their profession and timing of implementation.

Regulated professionals who wish to incorporate their practices have the same service delivery options listed above and must also meet the requirements outlined above. Professionals should contact their governing body for conditions of incorporation specific to their profession.

Under subsection 3.2(2.1) of the *Business Corporations Act* a professional corporation that has a name that includes the words "société professionnelle" is not required to include any additional legal element under subsection 10(1) of the *Business Corporations Act.*

Ontario Regulation 665/05 under the *Ontario Business Corporations Act* (OBCA) relating to health profession corporations came into force on January 1, 2006 along with the amendments to the *Business Corporations Act* contained in Bill 197, *Budget Measures Act, 2005.*

This regulation allows family members to become non-voting shareholders of a dentist or physician corporation. A "family member" is a spouse, child or parent of a voting shareholder who is a member of the profession. Non-voting shares may be held in trust for a minor child who is a family member. Persons who wish to acquire shares in these types of corporations should seek legal and/or financial advice from a lawyer or an accountant to determine whether they qualify under the new regulation.

For further information about professional corporations, please view the Information Bulletin available on the ServiceOntario website at www.ServiceOntario.ca.

Director's Liability under the *Business Corporations Act*

Registering your Business Name in Ontario

Offices That Endorse Articles Submitted Under the *Business Corporations Act*

[BC-9] — Request for the Companies and Personal Property Security Branch to Cancel Invalid Certificates (Business Corporations)*

Date: **November 30, 2007**

Companies and Personal Property Security Branch Requirements

A request to cancel invalid Certificate(s) must be in writing, addressed to the Director of the Companies and Personal Property Security Branch and must include the following:

1. *Reasons* why invalid Certificate(s) should be cancelled;
2. *Documentation to support reasons* why the Certificate(s) should be cancelled;
3. *Consent to the Order and Waiver of Hearing* by the corporation, if the request is made by the corporation. *Please note: an officer or director must sign the Consent and Waiver on behalf of the corporation.*

OR

If the request is made by someone other than an officer or director of the corporation, a Consent for the Companies and Personal Property Security Branch to send a copy of the cancellation request to the corporation for its written response.

PLEASE NOTE: While some errors in corporate Articles make the documents invalid, other errors may be corrected by filing a *Corrected Certificate*. For further information, please refer to the Information Sheet "Corrected Certificate (Business Corporations)".

The above procedures should not be confused with *Voluntary Dissolution* of a corporation. To voluntarily dissolve a corporation, please see the Information Sheet "Voluntary Dissolution (Business Corporations)".

[BC-10] — Revival (Business Corporations)*

Date: **January 1, 2009**

Companies and Personal Property Security Branch Requirements

To revive a business corporation where the Director has by order cancelled the certificate of incorporation under section 241 of the *Business Corporations Act (see below — When Articles of Revival Can be Filed)*, the following documentation must be submitted to the Companies and Personal Property Security Branch not more than 20 years after the date of dissolution:

1. **Articles of Revival** (Form 15 approved by the Minister under the Regulations to the *Business Corporations Act*) completed in duplicate, bearing original signatures on both copies.

2. **All outstanding notices and returns required to be filed by the corporation under the *Corporations Information Act* except for** *Corporations Information Act* Annual Returns, with no fees outstanding.

3. **All Outstanding Special Notice/*Corporations Information Act* Annual Return filings for the period of 1992 to 1995** must be attached together with the outstanding fees ($50.00 for each year not paid).

4. **Fee of $330.00**.

5. **Ontario-biased NUANS name search report** (required if the corporation is reviving under a name other than the name at dissolution or if more than ten years but fewer than 20 years have elapsed since the corporation was dissolved). A NUANS search is not required if reviving a number company.

6. **Consent** from the Minister of Revenue, the Office of the Public Guardian and Trustee or the Ontario Securities Commission, if applicable. (see below — Consents).

7. **Covering letter** giving a contact name, return address and telephone number.

Forms

Articles of Revival, Form 15, is available at: *www.Ontario.ca*. The forms may also be purchased from most legal stationers or name search houses. Legal stationers and name search houses are listed in the Yellow Pages under "Legal Forms" and "Searchers of Records" respectively.

Outstanding Filings Under the *Corporations Information Act*

To find out if the corporation has outstanding Special Notice/*Corporations Information Act* Annual Return filings and/or fees, contact the Companies Helpline for a revival package. The package includes a special notice/Annual Return form (setting out any outstanding fees) and the Articles of Revival, Form 15. The package is available without charge from:

Ministry of Government and Consumer Services
Companies and Personal Property Security Branch
393 University Avenue, Suite 200
Toronto ON M5G 2M2
Telephone: (416) 314-8880 or toll free in Ontario 1-800-361-3223
TTY: 416-325-3408
TTY Toll Free: 1-800-268-7095

PLEASE NOTE: With all requests, please include the following:

- Ontario corporation number and corporate name
- Date of incorporation/amalgamation
- Contact person's name, address and telephone number

Name Search

NUANS is a federal government computerized search system that compares a proposed corporate name or trademark with databases of existing corporate bodies and trademarks. This comparison determines the similarity that exists between the proposed name or mark and existing names in the database, and produces a listing of names that are found to be most similar.

An original Ontario-biased NUANS name search report must be obtained from a private name search company and cannot be dated more than 90 days prior to the submission of the articles. For example, articles submitted on November 28th could be accompanied by a NUANS name search report dated as early as August 30th, but not dated earlier.

Suppliers are listed in the Yellow Pages under the heading "Searchers of Records". For a list of registered search houses that can assist you with obtaining a NUANS search report and filing your corporate documents with the Ministry of Government Services, visit Industry Canada's NUANS website at: www.nuans.com. The Companies and Personal Property Security Branch does not provide this search.

Consents

Minister of Revenue

IIf the corporation was dissolved for failure to comply with the provisions of the *Corporations Tax Act, Employer Health Tax Act, Fuel Tax Act, Gasoline Tax Act, Land Transfer Tax Act, Retail Sales Tax Act or the Tobacco Tax Act*, consent to the revival from the Minister of Revenue, **MUST** accompany the Articles of Revival.

To request a consent letter contact:

Ministry of Revenue

Client Accounts and Services Branch

P.O. Box 622

33 King Street West
Oshawa ON L1H 8H6

Fax: 905-433-5418

Telephone Enquires can be made to the Canada Revenue Agency at:

Service in English: 1-800-959-5525
Service in French: 1-800-959-7775
TTY: 1-800-665-0354

Office of the Public Guardian and Trustee

Consent to the revival from the Office of the Public Guardian and Trustee (OPGT) is generally not required unless the OPGT is currently dealing with assets formerly owned by the dissolved corporation. For further information, please contact the OPGT at (416) 327-6683 or toll free in Ontario at 1-800-366-0335.

Ontario Securities Commission

If the corporation was dissolved for failure to comply with the provisions of the *Securities Act* consent from the Ontario Securities Commission must accompany the Articles of Revival. Contact:

Ontario Securities Commission

Telephone: at 416-593-8314 or

Toll-Free number (throughout Canada) at 1-877-785-1555

Methods of Filing Articles of Revival

1. Over the counter, in person at the Companies and Personal Property Security Branch Public Office in Toronto.

2. By mail to the Companies and Personal Property Security Branch, 393 University Ave., Suite 200, Toronto ON M5G 2M2.

General Information

Please be advised that the **COMPANIES AND PERSONAL PROPERTY SECURITY BRANCH CANNOT GIVE LEGAL ADVICE**. This information is intended as a general guide only. For further assistance or legal advice, please consult your lawyer.

If you need a lawyer, you may wish to contact the Lawyer Referral Service of the Law Society of Upper Canada. You will be referred to a lawyer for up to a half-hour free legal consultation, either in person or over the phone. Please note that this is a toll service and phoning the Lawyer Referral Service line will automatically generate a $6.00 charge on your phone bill, in the month following your call. You must be 18 years of age to access this service. The number is 1-900-565-4577 (1-900-565-4LRS).

Please refer to **section 241** of the ***Business Corporations Act*** for details on reviving an Ontario business corporation.

Who Can File Articles of Revival

Any "interested person" (for example, an officer, director, shareholder, creditor, or estate trustee of a shareholder) may at any time apply to revive a corporation that has been cancelled under section 241(4) of the *Business Corporations Act*.

When Articles of Revival Can be Filed

The *Business Corporations Act* allows for the revival of a corporation, not more than 20 years from the date of dissolution under subsection 241(4) for default in compliance with a notice given pursuant to:

- the *Corporations Tax Act, Employer Health Tax Act, Fuel Tax Act, Gasoline Tax Act, Land Transfer Tax Act, Retail Sales Tax Act OR the Tobacco Tax Act*;
- sections 77 and 78 of the Ontario *Securities Act*;
- a filing requirement under the *Corporations Information Act* or failure to pay a fee under the *Business Corporations Act*.

When Articles Of Revival Cannot be Filed

If the corporation voluntarily dissolved by filing Articles of Dissolution or was cancelled by the Companies and Personal Property Security Branch for cause (e.g. not having the required number of directors), or if it is more than 20 years after the date of dissolution, the corporation may only be revived by a ***special act*** of the Legislature (Private Act).

For information contact:

Clerk of the Standing Committee on Regulations and Private Bills

Legislative Assembly of Ontario

Telephone: 416-325-3515

Website at: www.ontla.on.ca

After Revival

Upon revival, the corporation subject to the rights, if any, acquired by any person during the period of dissolution, shall be deemed for all purposes to never have been dissolved (s. 241 (5)).

TThe corporation must ensure it complies with the requirements of the *Corporations Information Act*, by filing *Corporations Information Act* Annual Returns and notices of change to the corporation's registered office address, mailing address, the directors or the five most senior officers.

Related Information Sheets

Filing of *Corporations Information Act* Annual Returns

Initial Return/Notice of Change Making Changes to Corporate Information

[BC-11] — Involuntary Dissolution (Business Corporations)*

Date: **November 30, 2007**

A corporation may be involuntarily dissolved (cancelled) by order of the Director of the Companies and Personal Property Security Branch (CPPSB) under the *Business Corporations Act* (BCA) for reasons set out in sections 240 and 241 of the BCA.

General Information

Please be advised that the *COMPANIES AND PERSONAL PROPERTY SECURITY BRANCH CANNOT GIVE LEGAL ADVICE*. This information is intended as a general guide only. For further assistance or legal advice, please consult your lawyer.

If you need a lawyer, you may wish to contact the Lawyer Referral Service of the Law Society of Upper Canada. You will be referred to a lawyer for up to a half-hour free legal consultation, either in person or over the phone. Please note that this is a toll service and phoning the Lawyer Referral Service line will automatically generate a $6.00 charge on your phone bill, in the month following your call. You must be 18 years of age to access this service. The number is 1-900-565-4577 (1-900-565-4LRS).

Cancellation for Cause under Section 240 of the *Business Corporations Act*

Section 240 of the BCA provides that where sufficient cause is shown, the Director may, after giving the corporation an opportunity to be heard, by order cancel a certificate issued or endorsed under the BCA, and,

(a) in the case of the cancellation of a certificate of incorporation, the corporation is dissolved on the date fixed in the order; and

(b) in the case of the cancellation of any other certificate, the matter that became effective upon the issuance of the certificate ceases to be in effect from the date fixed in the order.

With respect to cancellation of a certificate "sufficient cause" includes:

- The corporation has not maintained the required number of directors; or
- The corporation has not maintained the required number (at least 25 per cent) of resident Canadian directors; or
- The corporation has been convicted of an offence under the *Criminal Code* of Canada or any federal statute or an offence as defined in the *Provincial Offences Act*, and cancellation of the certificate is in the public interest; or
- The corporation has engaged in conduct described in s. 248(2) ("motifs suffisants").

Revival by Private Act Only

Corporations cancelled for cause pursuant to section 240 of the BCA, *CANNOT* apply for revival. The only way to revive the corporation is by way of a special act of the Legislature (Private Act). For information on obtaining a special act contact:

Clerk of the Standing Committee on Regulations and Private Bills

Committees Branch

Telephone: 416/325-3515

Website at: www.ontla.on.ca

Involuntary Dissolution under Section 241 of the *Business Corporation Act*

Section 241 of the BCA provides that the Director may by order cancel a certificate of incorporation and the corporation is dissolved on the date fixed in the order, for default in compliance with notice that:

- the corporation is in default in complying with any of the following Ministry of Finance statutes: *Corporations Tax Act, Employer Health Tax Act, Fuel Tax Act, Gasoline Tax Act, Land Transfer Tax Act, Retail Sales Tax Act or the Tobacco Tax Act; or*
- the corporation has not complied with sections 77 and 78 of the *Securities Act*; or
- The corporation has failed to comply with a filing requirement under the *Corporations Information Act* or has failed to pay a fee required under the BCA. (Prior to March 1, 1999 corporations cancelled for failure to file a fee were cancelled for cause under section 240.)

Revival

Corporations cancelled pursuant to section 241(4) of the *Business Corporations Act* for any of the reasons listed above may be revived, on the application of any interested person (for example, an officer, director, shareholder, creditor, or estate trustee of a shareholder) *if not more than twenty years from the date of dissolution*. For information on filing Articles of Revival see the information sheet "Revival (Business Corporations)".

Upon revival, the corporation, subject to the rights, if any, acquired by any person during the period of dissolution, shall be deemed for all purposes to have never been dissolved (s. 241(5)).

Notification

Compliance letters and notices are sent to the corporation's registered office address shown on the public record to give the corporation an opportunity to remedy its default(s) and avoid cancellation for cause under section 240. In the case of section 241, a notice of default may be published in *The Ontario Gazette*, followed by cancellation if the corporation fails to come into compliance. It is therefore important to ensure that the corporation remains in compliance with all applicable legislation, and that information on the public record concerning the corporation and its registered office address is up to date. The *Corporations Information Act* requires that corporations file a Form 1, Initial Notice/Notice of Change, within 15 days after a change takes place in information previously filed. (For details see the information sheets "Initial Return/Notice of Change, Making Changes to Corporate Information" and "Checklist for Completing Form 1, Initial Return/Notice of Change").

Continuing Business Activity After Dissolution

Upon dissolution, the corporation ceases to exist. If the activities of the business continue, the business is then operating without corporate status. Consult with your lawyer regarding the personal liability of the owners and operators of a business that is operating without the limited liability shelter of a corporation.

Property After Dissolution

Upon dissolution, any property of a corporation that has not been disposed of at the date of dissolution immediately becomes the property of the Crown (s. 244(1)), legally it "forfeits to the Crown". However, such property is available to satisfy any judgment, order or other decision made in connection with a proceeding brought against the corporation, as set out in sections 242–244.

In Ontario the Office of the Public Guardian and Trustee represents the Crown. For information concerning property of a corporation that has been involuntarily dissolved please contact the Office of the Public Guardian and Trustee at:

Office of the Public Guardian and Trustee

595 Bay Street, Suite 800

Toronto, ON M5G 2M6

Tel: (416) 326-1963 or in Ontario toll free at 1-800-366-0335

Actions After Dissolution

Despite dissolution of a corporation under the *Business Corporations Act*, a civil, criminal or administrative action or proceeding commenced by or against the corporation *before* its dissolution may be continued as if the corporation had not been dissolved (s. 242(1)).

A civil, criminal or administrative action or proceeding may be brought against a corporation *after* its dissolution as if the corporation had not been dissolved.

Notice Of Action

A person who commences an action, suit or other proceeding against a corporation after its dissolution must provide notice to the Office of the Public Guardian and Trustee that such proceeding has commenced (s. 242(3)).

Please refer to *sections 242 through 244 of the Business Corporations Act* for further details on actions, liability and property after dissolution.

Other Related Information Sheets

Revival (Business Corporations)

Initial Return/Notice of Change Making Changes to Corporate Information
Filing of Annual Returns

[BC-12] — Voluntary Dissolution (Business Corporations)*

Date: January 1, 2009

Companies and Personal Property Security Branch Requirements

To voluntarily dissolve, a corporation must file Articles of Dissolution Form 10 or Form 11 as follows:

Form 10 — Articles of Dissolution

This form is to be used for voluntary dissolution of a business corporation where the dissolution has been authorized by the shareholders of the corporation.

The following documents must be submitted to the Companies and Personal Property Security Branch:

1. **Articles of Dissolution** (Form 10 approved by the Minister as provided for in the Regulations made under the *Business Corporations Act*) in duplicate, bearing original signatures on both copies.
2. **A letter consenting to the dissolution from the Minister of Revenue**.
3. **Covering letter** giving a contact name, return address and telephone number.
4. **Fee of $25.00**.

Form 11 — Articles of Dissolution

Form 11 may be used for voluntary dissolution **only where** the corporation meets all of the following conditions:

- the corporation has not issued any shares.
- the corporation has not commenced business; and
- all of the incorporators or their personal representatives have authorized the dissolution.

Note: *If the corporation has issued shares or commenced business, you cannot file this form but must instead file a Form 10, Articles of Dissolution. Shareholder approval is required.*

The following documents must be submitted to dissolve a corporation that has not commenced business and meets all the conditions set out above:

1. **Articles of Dissolution** (Form 11 approved by the Minister as provided for in the Regulations made under the *Business Corporations Act*) in duplicate bearing original signatures on both copies and signed by all incorporators or their personal representatives.
2. **A letter consenting to the dissolution from the Minister of Revenue**.
3. **Covering letter** giving a contact name, return address and telephone number.

---

4. **Fee of $25.00**.

Forms

Articles of Dissolution, Form 10 and Form 11, are available on the Internet at: *www.Ontario.ca*. The forms may also be purchased from most legal stationers or name search houses. Legal stationers and name search houses are listed in the Yellow Pages under "Legal Forms" and "Searchers of Records" respectively.

Consent of the Minister of Revenue

Articles of Dissolution must be accompanied by written consent to the dissolution from the Minister of Revenue, and must be submitted within 60 days after the Minister of Revenue provides consent. To obtain consent, contact the Ministry of Revenue as follows:

Ministry of Revenue

Client Accounts and Services Branch

33 King Street West

Oshawa ON L1H 8H6

Fax: 905-433-5418

Telephone Enquires can be made to the Canada Revenue Agency at:

Service in English: 1-800-959-5525
Service in French: 1-800-959-7775
TTY: 1-800-665-0354

NOTE: There is no requirement to publish notification of the corporation's intention to dissolve in the newspaper or in the Ontario Gazette.

Methods of Filing Articles of Dissolution

1. For over-the-counter service, articles may be filed in person at the Toronto office or at some Land Registry/ServiceOntario offices in Ontario (See the "Offices That Endorse Articles Submitted Under the Business Corporations Act" information sheet). The information sheet is available on the Internet at: *www.Ontario.ca*.

2. By mail to the Companies and Personal Property Security Branch, 393 University Avenue, Suite 200, Toronto ON M5G 2M2.

General Information

Please be advised that the **COMPANIES AND PERSONAL PROPERTY SECURITY BRANCH CANNOT GIVE LEGAL ADVICE**. This information is intended as a general guide only. For further assistance or legal information, please consult private legal counsel.

Please refer to **Sections 237 through 239 of the *Business Corporations Act*** for details on voluntary dissolution of an Ontario business corporation.

Voluntary Dissolution — Form 10

An Ontario business corporation may be voluntarily dissolved if authorized by a special resolution passed at a meeting of the shareholders in accordance with s. 237(a) or with the consent in writing of all the shareholders entitled to vote at such meeting (s. 237(b)). In this case, Form 10 under the *Business Corporations Act* must be completed.

Who signs Articles of Dissolution, Form 10?

A director or an officer of the corporation must sign Form 10, Articles of Dissolution (s. 273). An executor, lawyer or accountant cannot sign this form.

Voluntary Dissolution — Form 11

An Ontario Business Corporation may also be voluntarily dissolved where the corporation has not issued any shares, has not commenced business, and all of its incorporators or their personal representatives have authorized the dissolution (s. 237(c)). In this case, Form 11 should be filed with the Companies and Personal Property Security Branch.

Who signs Articles of Dissolution, Form 11?

All the incorporators of the corporation or their personal representatives must sign Form 11, Articles of Dissolution. Some examples of personal representatives are, executor, estate trustee, administrator, guardian or trustee.

Information For Executors

Under section 115 of the Ontario *Business Corporations Act*, a corporation's business and affairs are managed by the directors. Directors are elected by, and accountable to, the corporation's owners (the shareholders). Directors may in turn appoint officers and delegate management powers to them. **Articles of Dissolution (Form 10) therefore require the signature of a director or officer under section 273**.

A corporation may not dissolve unless it has satisfied the Act's requirements with respect to satisfying the interests of creditors, and distributing any remaining property in accordance with the Act. The corporation's shareholders must authorize the filing of Articles of Dissolution in accordance with the requirements of the Act.

Ministry staff cannot give advice on the management of the business and affairs of a corporation, or on the course of action that an executor should take.

Executors are, therefore, advised to consult a lawyer to determine whether it is appropriate to replace directors and/or authorize the corporation's dissolution. If so, the executor should ask the lawyer whether it is advisable (i) to elect themselves or other person(s) to replace existing directors, and (ii) sign a resolution authorizing the dissolution of the corporation..

If, after obtaining such advice, you are able to pass the necessary resolutions and wish to dissolve the corporation, please refer to "Companies and Personal Property Security Branch Requirements" on page 1.

Also, please note that when a corporation changes its directors, a Notice of Change, Form 1, *Corporations Information Act*, must be completed in full and filed with the Ministry.

Lawyer Referral Service

If you need a lawyer, you may wish to contact the Lawyer Referral Service of the Law Society of Upper Canada. You will be referred to a lawyer for up to a half-hour free legal consultation, either in person or over the phone. Please note that this is a toll service and phoning the Lawyer Referral Service line will automatically generate a $6.00 charge on your phone bill, in the month following your call. You must be 18 years of age to access this service. The number is 1-900-565-4577 (1-900-565-4LRS).

Actions after Dissolution

Despite dissolution of a corporation under the Act, a civil, criminal or administrative action or proceeding commenced by or against the corporation *before* its dissolution may be continued as if the corporation had not been dissolved (s. 242(1)(a)).

Please refer to Section 242 of the *Business Corporations Act* for further details on actions after dissolution and Section 243 for details on shareholder liability after dissolution.

Revival

There is no provision under the *Business Corporations Act* to file Articles of Revival to revive a corporation that voluntarily dissolved (i.e. filed Articles of Dissolution). In this case, the only way to revive the corporation would be by a **Special Act** of the Legislature.

Other Related Information Sheets

Revival (Business Corporations)

Offices That Endorse Articles Submitted Under the *Business Corporations Act*

[BC-13] — Initial Return / Notice of Change Making Changes to Corporate Information*

Date: November 30, 2007

An Ontario business or not-for-profit corporation must file a Form 1, Initial Return/Notice of Change under the *Corporations Information Act* to report any change to the following corporate information contained on the Companies and Personal Property Security Branch Public Record:

- Registered or head office address
- Mailing address
- Language of preference
- Director/officer information (e.g. address for service, date elected/appointed, date ceased to hold office, officer title, etc.)

Companies and Personal Property Security Branch Requirements

Form 1, Initial Return/Notice of Change

All Ontario business and not-for-profit corporations are required to file a Form 1, Initial Return setting out the prescribed information within 60 days after the date of incorporation, amalgamation or continuation into Ontario of the corporation (S. 2(1) & (2) of the *Corporations Information Act*).

After filing a Form 1, Initial Return, business and not-for-profit corporations are required to file a Form 1, Notice of Change for any change in the information previously filed within 15

*© Queen's Printer for Ontario, 2007. Reproduced with permission. For the most recent version of this form, please visit: http://www.gov.on.ca/ontprodconsume/groups/content/@onca/@bundles/@cppsb/documents/document/stel02_168138.pdf

days after any change takes place (e.g., when a corporation changes its address or any information concerning its directors or officers, S. 4(1) of the *Corporations Information Act*).

Fee

There is no Ministry fee to file an Initial Return/Notice of Change.

Forms

The Form 1, Initial Return/Notice of Change is available on the ServiceOntario website at www.ServiceOntario.ca.

Forms may also be picked up at the Companies and Personal Property Security Branch Public Office at the above address.

Completing the Form 1, Initial Return/Notice of Change

To help clients complete the Form 1, Initial Return/Notice of Change correctly, the Branch has created an information sheet entitled "Checklist for Completing Form 1, Initial Return/Notice of Change, under the *Corporations Information Act.*"

Clients may obtain the information sheet from the ServiceOntario website at www.ServiceOntario.ca.

The completed forms can be dropped off or mailed to the above address. Due to the large number of filings it takes several weeks until the updated information is recorded on the public record. Clients should wait 25 business days if they wish to order a Corporation Profile Report with the updated information.

Electronic Filing of Form 1, Initial Return/Notice of Change

Clients who wish to have the corporation's updated information reflected on the Public Record immediately may file the Initial Return/Notice of Change electronically through Service Providers under contract with the Ministry of Government and Consumer Services.

Clients may order an electronic data extraction report (data extract) to facilitate the electronic filing process. The data extract allows clients to review existing corporate information on the Public Record, temporarily store and edit this information, prior to filing the changes electronically.

For information about visit Service Providers under contract with the Ministry of Government and Consumer Services visit the ServiceOntario website at: www.ServiceOntario.ca.

General Information

Please be advised that the *COMPANIES AND PERSONAL PROPERTY SECURITY BRANCH CANNOT GIVE LEGAL ADVICE.* This information is intended as a general guide only. For further assistance or legal information, please consult private legal counsel. If you need a lawyer, you may wish to contact the Lawyer Referral Service of the Law Society of Upper Canada. You will be referred to a lawyer for up to a half-hour free legal consultation, either in person or over the phone. Please note that this is a toll service and phoning the Lawyer Referral Service line will automatically generate a $6.00 charge on your phone bill, in the month following your call. You must be 18 years of age to access this service. The number is 1-900-565-4577 (1-900-565-4LRS).

For details governing the information filing requirements for corporations in Ontario, please refer to the *Corporations Information Act*. The *Corporations Information Act* is available on the Internet at www.e-laws.gov.on.ca or can be purchased through Publications Ontario at (416) 326-5300 or toll-free at 1-800-668-9938. The website for Publications Ontario is www.publications.gov.on.ca.

Registered or Head Office Address

Whenever a business or not-for-profit corporation changes its registered/head office address, a Form 1, Notice of Change, under the *Corporations Information Act* must be completed and filed with the Companies and Personal Property Security Branch within 15 days after the change takes place (S. 4(1) of the *Corporations Information Act*).

Directors

An Initial Return listing the names of all the directors of the corporation, their address for service and date they were elected/appointed or ceased to be a director, must be filed within 60 days from the date of incorporation, amalgamation or continuation into Ontario. If any of the information changes a Notice of Change must be filed setting out all the current information within 15 days after the change takes place.

Corporations are no longer required to file a copy of a resolution or special resolution concerning changes to director or officer information or the registered/head office address. However, this information must be kept at the registered or head office of the corporation.

Officers

Only the five most senior officer positions must be recorded on the Initial Return/Notice of Change. If one individual is both the president and secretary of the corporation it counts as two positions (i.e. 2 separate officer positions must be reported on the form). If the information concerning the five most senior officers changes, a Notice of Change must be filed within 15 days after the change. Information concerning any officers other than the five most senior officers reported on the form must be kept at the registered/head office address.

Related Information Sheets

- Checklist for completing Form 1, Initial Return/Notice of Change under the *Corporations Information Act*

[BC-14] — Offices That Endorse Articles Submitted Under the *Business Corporations Act**

Date: December 31, 2007

The following forms under the Ontario *Business Corporations Act* can be filed *in person* at the offices listed below. Forms are reviewed while you wait; do not mail applications to these offices:

- *Articles of Incorporation, Form 1*
- *Articles of Amendment, Form 3*

- *Articles of Amalgamation, Form 4*
- *Restated Articles of Incorporation, Form 5*
- *Articles of Dissolution, Form 10*
- *Articles of Dissolution, Form 11*

Barrie

Barrie Land Registry Office
Court House
114 Worsley Street
Tel: (705) 725-7232

Hamilton

Hamilton Land Registry Office
Ontario Government Building
119 King Street West, 4th floor
Tel: (905) 521-7561

Kanata

Government Service Centre in Kanata
580 Terry Fox Drive
Tel: 1 800 268-8758

Kingston

Kingston Land Registry Office
1 Court Street
Tel: (613) 548-6767

Kitchener

Kitchener Land Registry Office
30 Duke Street West, 2nd Floor
Tel: (519) 571-6043

London

London ServiceOntario Centre
100 Dundas Street
Tel: 1 800 267-8097

Ottawa

Government Service Centre in Ottawa
Ottawa City Hall
110 Laurier Avenue West
Tel: 1 800 268-8758

Peterborough

Peterborough Land Registry Office
300 Water Street, 2nd Floor

Robinson Place South Tower
Tel: (705) 755-1342

Sarnia

Sarnia Land Registry Office
Court House
700 North Christina Street, Suite 102
Tel: (519) 337-2393

Sault Ste. Marie

Sault Ste. Marie Land Registry Office
420 Queen Street East
Tel: (705) 253-8887

St. Catharines

St. Catharines Land Registry Office
59 Church Street
Tel: (905) 684-6351

Sudbury

Sudbury Government Service Centre
199 Larch Street, Suite 301
Tel: (705) 564-4300

Thunder Bay

Thunder Bay Land Registry Office
189 Red River Road, Suite 201
Tel: (807) 343-7436

Toronto

Toronto — Companies and Personal Property
Security Branch (Public Office)
375 University Avenue, 2nd Floor
Tel: (416) 314-8880
Toll Free: 1-(800) 361-3223
Downtown Toronto ServiceOntario Centre
777 Bay St
Market Level, Suite M 212
1-(800) 268 -8758

Whitby

Whitby ServiceOntario Centre
590 Rossland Road East
Tel: 1 800 267-8097

Windsor

Windsor Land Registry Office

949 McDougall Street, Suite 100

Tel: (519) 971-9980

In addition, the following Forms may also be filed in person at the Companies and Personal Property Security Branch Public Office in Toronto:

- *Articles of Revival, Form 15* — (reviewed while you wait)
- *Application for Authorization to Continue in Another Jurisdiction, Form 7* — (reviewed while you wait)
- *Articles of Continuance, Form 6* — (not issued immediately. If documents are filed in person the service times are 48 hours — fee $330 or 24 hours — fee $500)

For processing by mail:

Forms should be mailed to the following address in Toronto:

Ministry of Government and Consumer Services

Companies and Personal Property Security Branch

393 University Ave., Suite 200

Toronto ON M5G 2M2

(Allow 4–6 weeks for processing by mail)

Forms and information on incorporation and making changes to your corporation are available from the ServiceOntario website at www.ServiceOntario.ca.

[NFP-1] — Corrected Letters Patent (Not-For-Profit Corporations)*

Date: November 30, 2007

Companies and Personal Property Security Branch Requirements:

An application for a Corrected Letters Patent for a document filed under the *Corporations Act* must be submitted to the Companies and Personal Property Security Branch and must include the following:

1. Corrected Letters Patent or Supplementary Letters Patent in duplicate and bearing original signatures on both copies;

2. A certified copy of a resolution of the directors confirmed by the members, authorizing the application for the Corrected Letters Patent;

(The resolution must be on 8 1/2" by 11" size paper pursuant to the Regulations.)

3. The surrender of the original Letters Patent or Supplementary Letters Patent as issued by the Companies and Personal Property Security Branch bearing the original effective date;

4. The fee of $155.00 made payable to the Minister of Finance;

5. A covering letter giving a contact name, return address and telephone number and clearly outlining the nature of the original error.

Forms:

Applications for Incorporation of a Corporation without Share Capital are available on the ServiceOntario website at www.ServiceOntario.ca.

Forms prescribed under the *Corporations Act* may be obtained, at no charge, from:

Companies and Personal Property Security Branch

Ministry of Government and Consumer Services

393 University Avenue, Suite 200

Toronto ON M5G 2M2

Tel: (416) 314-8880 or toll-free in Ontario 1-800-361-3223

TTY: (416) 212-1476

Please be advised that the Branch *CANNOT GIVE LEGAL ADVICE.* This information is intended as a general guide only. For further assistance or legal information, please consult private legal counsel.

Please refer to the *Corporations Act* for details governing not-for-profit corporations in Ontario. The *Corporations Act* is available on the Internet at www.e-laws.gov.on.ca or can be purchased through Publications Ontario at (416) 326-5200 or toll-free at 1-800-668-9938. The website for Publications Ontario is www.publications.gov.on.ca.

General Information:

Please refer to Section 16 of the *Corporations Act* for details on application for a Corrected Letters Patent.

Errors — Application for a Corrected Letters Patent under S. 16 of the *Corporations Act* may be made for an error contained in Letters Patent or Supplementary Letters Patent filed under the Act.

In order to qualify for correction, the error must be on the face of the document, a clerical error or provisions in the application which do not conform to the Act. Errors must be clearly explained in writing. Each application is dealt with on an individual basis. In many cases, supporting documentation such as original resolutions is required.

Date — Corrected Letters Patent or Supplementary Letters Patent may bear the date of the Letters Patent or Supplementary Letters Patent which are being replaced.

Examples of circumstances which may warrant application for Corrected Letters Patent:

- an error in the name of the corporation (does not correspond to the NUANS report, missing a word, etc.)
- incorrect Ontario Corporation Number (# misquoted on Application for Supplementary Letters Patent, etc.)
- typographical errors, obvious spelling errors, words which have clearly been omitted from a sentence
- missing pages or clauses (where it is apparent that they are missing)
- anything that was *clearly intended* to be done at the time of the original application (as evidenced by the original resolution)

Examples of circumstances under which Corrected Letters Patent would NOT be granted:

- things that *were not intended* to be done at the time of the original application

- change in effective date (unless the specific date had originally been requested)
- where the error invalidates the document (e.g. no confirmation by members)

[NFP-2] — Directors' Liability under the *Corporations Act* (Not-For-Profit Corporations)*

Date: November 30, 2007

General Information

Please be advised that the *COMPANIES AND PERSONAL PROPERTY SECURITY BRANCH CANNOT GIVE LEGAL ADVICE.* This information is intended as a general guide only. For further assistance or legal information, please consult private legal counsel.

Please refer to the *Corporations Act* for details on directors' liability with respect to a not-for-profit corporation.

A director's duty is to the corporation and its members. As such, directors must act honestly and in good faith with the best interests of the corporation in mind when exercising powers and discharging duties.

Directors of a not-for-profit corporation must comply with the *Corporations Act*, Letters Patent, bylaws and other instruments governing the affairs of the corporation.

Directors of a not-for-profit corporation are jointly and serverally liable to the employees of the corporation for debts not exceeding six months' wages and up to 12 months' vacation pay (S. 81(1)).

Please note: As of March 1, 1999, not-for-profit, *NON CHARITABLE* corporations are permitted to indemnify officers as well as directors for all costs incurred for legal proceeding related to the performance of their duties. Charitable corporations are able to purchase liability insurance if they meet the requirements of the *Corporations Act* as well as the *Charities Accounting Act*.

Directors may be responsible for statutory penalties for failure to make appropriate filings and to keep proper records for the corporation (S. 231(2), S. 277(5), S. 285(3), S. 296(9), S. 303 and S. 304(4)).

Other Potential Liability

There may also be potential liability under Federal and other provincial statutes. If you have any questions about your potential liability as a director or officer, please contact your lawyer.

 For the most recent version of this form, please visit: http://www.gov.on.ca/ontprodconsume/groups/content/@onca/@bundles/@cppsb/documents/document/stel02_168414.pdf

[NFP-3] — Incorporation (Not-for-Profit Corporations)*

Date: December 31, 2007

Companies and Personal Property Security Branch Requirements

In order to incorporate a not-for-profit corporation in Ontario, the following documentation must be submitted to the Companies and Personal Property Security Branch. If you are incorporating a *charity*, see *CHARITABLE ORGANIZATIONS* below regarding filing options.

1. *Application for Incorporation of a Corporation without Share Capital* (Form 2 prescribed under the Regulations to the *Corporations Act*), completed in duplicate and bearing original signatures on both copies;
2. *Ontario-biased NUANS* Name Search Report;
3. *Fee of $155* (standard service — processing time 6–8 weeks) or a *fee of $255* (expedited service — processing time 7 business days);
4. *Covering letter* giving a contact name, return address and telephone number.

Forms

Applications for Incorporation of a Corporation without Share Capital are available on the ServiceOntario website at www.ServiceOntario.ca.

Forms are also available in person at no cost from:

Ministry of Government and Consumer Services

Companies and Personal Property Security Branch

393 University Avenue, Suite 200

Toronto ON M5G 2M2

Name Search

NUANS is a computerized search system that compares a proposed corporate name or trade-mark with databases of existing corporate bodies and trade-marks. This comparison determines the similarity that exists between the proposed name or mark and existing names in the database, and produces a listing of names that are found to be most similar. A NUANS search is not required if incorporating a number company.

An original Ontario-biased NUANS name search report must be obtained from a private name search company and cannot be dated more than 90 days prior to the submission of the articles. For example, articles submitted on November 28th could be accompanied by a NUANS name search report dated as early as August 30th, but not dated earlier.

Suppliers are listed in the Yellow Pages under the heading "Searchers of Records" or visit Industry Canada's NUANS website at www.nuans.com for a list of registered search houses that can assist you with obtaining a NUANS search report and filing your corporate documents with the Ministry of Government and Consumer Services. The Companies and Personal Property Security Branch does not provide this search.

Charitable Organizations

Effective October 1, 1999, charities have two options for incorporating.

1) — Incorporate using pre-approved standard objects and provisions (filed with the Companies and Personal Property Security Branch)

Applicable objects and provisions must be used word for word. As there is no requirement to obtain approval from the Office of the Public Guardian and Trustee (OPGT), there is no OPGT fee. The Companies and Personal Property Security Branch fee is $155 for standard service and $255 for expedited service. You may obtain a copy of the preapproved standard objects and provisions from the Companies and Personal Property Security Branch or from the OPGT website. (see below).

2) — Incorporate using non-standard objects and provisions (filed with the Office of the Public Guardian and Trustee)

If you do not use the preapproved standard objects and provisions, you must submit your application to the OPGT for review and approval. The OPGT fee of $150, plus the applicable Companies and Personal Property Security Branch fee of $155 or $255 must be included. (*Note: Expedited service applies only to the service provided by the Companies and Personal Property Security Branch after OPGT approval.*) Once approved, the OPGT will forward the documents to the Companies and Personal Property Security Branch. The proposed objects for a not-for-profit charitable corporation must meet the criteria set out by the Charitable Property Program of the Office of the Public Guardian and Trustee.

Ministry of the Attorney General

Office of the Public Guardian and Trustee

Charitable Property Program

595 Bay Street, Suite 800

Toronto ON M5G 2M6

Telephone: (416) 326-1963 or toll free in Ontario 1-800-366-0335

Website: http://www.attorneygeneral.jus.gov.on.ca/english/family/pgt/

General Information

Please be advised that the Branch *CANNOT GIVE LEGAL ADVICE.* This information is intended as a general guide only. For further assistance or legal information, please consult private legal counsel.

If you need a lawyer, you may wish to contact the Lawyer Referral Service of the Law Society of Upper Canada. You will be referred to a lawyer for up to a half-hour free legal consultation, either in person or over the phone. Please note that this is a toll service and phoning the Lawyer Referral Service line will automatically generate a $6.00 charge on your phone bill, in the month following your call. You must be 18 years of age to access this service. The number is 1-900-565-4577 (1-900-565-4LRS).

Please refer to the *Corporations Act* for details governing not-for-profit corporations in Ontario. The *Corporations Act* is available on the Internet at www.e-laws.gov.on.ca or can be purchased through Publications Ontario at (416) 326-5200 or toll-free at 1-800-668-9938. The website for Publications Ontario is www.publications.gov.on.ca.

Corporation Name

General — The proposed name for a not-for-profit corporation in Ontario must meet specific criteria before it can be granted. A name that is identical to the name of another corporation, or that contravenes the *Corporations Act* or Regulations, will not be approved for use. If the proposed name is confusingly similar to an existing corporate name, or the name contains the name of an individual, the consent of the existing corporation or the individual may be required before the name can be approved.

The proposed name must reflect the objects of the corporation and must not infer that it could be a business corporation.

Legal Ending — The name of a not-for-profit corporation may have the word "Incorporated", "Incorporée", "Corporation" or the corresponding abbreviation as a legal ending, but a legal ending is not necessary. A not-for-profit corporation *CANNOT* have the word "Limited", "Limitée" or the corresponding abbreviations as part of its corporate name.

Foreign Words in the Name — Names containing foreign words may be granted to not-for-profit corporations, provided that only letters from the alphabet of the English language are used in the name (S. 8(1) of the Regulations).

Corporations wishing to separately use a foreign version of an approved corporation name, may do so by including in the Application for Incorporation (or, after incorporation, in an Application for Supplementary Letters Patent), a provision for the use of the name in such form and in such language (S. 22).

For more detailed information on the requirements for the name of a not-for-profit corporation in Ontario, please refer to the Not-For-Profit Incorporator's Handbook. (For sale at Publications Ontario at (416) 326-5300 or toll-free in Ontario 1-800-668-9938. The website for Publications Ontario is www.publications.gov.on.ca. The cost is $8.00 + G.S.T.)

Directors

A board of directors manages the affairs of a not-for-profit corporation. The board must consist of a fixed number of directors, not fewer than three and each director must be at least eighteen years of age (S. 283(1), S. 283(2), S. 286(4)).

Election of Directors — The directors are elected by the members and each director must also be a member of the corporation (S. 286(1), S. 287(1)).

By-Laws

The by-laws of a not-for-profit corporation are passed by the directors and govern the conduct of affairs of the corporation (e.g. the qualification and the conditions of membership, the time for and the manner of elections, the procedures involved in the holding of meetings, etc. (S. 129, S. 130)).

The by-laws are considered to be an internal document and should not be included in the application for incorporation of a not-for-profit corporation.

Social Clubs

As of March 1, 1995, a corporation with objects that are in whole or in part of a social nature is no longer required to include ten applicants in their application for incorporation.

Amalgamation

Two or more active Ontario not-for-profit corporations having the same or similar objects may amalgamate and continue as one corporation (S. 113). In this case, an Application for Letters Patent of Amalgamation, Form 11 prescribed under the Regulations to the *Corporations Act*, must be completed and filed with the Companies and Personal Property Security Branch. Where two or more corporations amalgamate, the name of the amalgamated corporation may be the same as the name of one of the amalgamating corporations (S. 4 of the Regulations).

Precedents

Precedents for by-laws and amalgamation clauses may be found in the Ontario Corporations Manual.

Reporting Requirements for Charitable Corporations

Upon incorporation, not-for-profit charitable corporations are regulated by the Office of the Public Guardian and Trustee as well as by the Companies and Personal Property Security Branch. As such, they are subject to certain reporting requirements with both.

Effective Date

A not-for-profit corporation comes into existence on the date of the letters patent incorporating it (S. 12(1)). The Letters Patent take effect on the date set forth therein (S. 12(2)) and are dated when all the required documents are received and complete.

Corrections to Documents

Any minor changes or corrections made to documents prior to submission to the Companies and Personal Property Security Branch may be crossed out and/or added bearing the initials of the appropriate officer of the corporation authorized to do so. However, no visible corrections are permitted on page 1 of the application. Liquid paper corrections are not acceptable; however, corrected pages can be photocopied as long as they bear original signatures.

Documents must be clearly legible at all times.

[NFP-4] — Revival (Non-Profit Corporations)*

Date: **November 30, 2007**

Companies and Personal Property Security Branch Requirements:

In order to revive a non-profit corporation (a corporation without share capital), the following documentation must be submitted to the Branch;

1. *Application for Revival* (Form 10 as prescribed under the Regulations to the *Corporations Act*) in duplicate and bearing original signatures on both copies.
2. Any outstanding *Special Notice/Annual Return filings and fees* for the period of 1992–1995 ($25.00 for each year not paid).
3. *Revival Fee of $100.00.* (Revival fee was reinstated September 1, 1996.)

 For the most recent version of this form, please visit: http://www.gov.on.ca/ontprodconsume/groups/content/@onca/@bundles/@cppsb/documents/document/stel02_168103.pdf

4. Ontario-biased *NUANS name search report*. (Required if the corporation is reviving under a name other than the name at dissolution.)

5. A *covering letter* giving a contact name, return address and telephone number.

Forms:

A revival package including the necessary forms to be completed is available at no charge from:

Ministry of Government and Consumer Services

Companies and Personal Property Security Branch

393 University Avenue, Suite 200

Toronto ON M5G 2M2

Tel: (416) 314-8880 or toll-free 1-800-361-3223

In all requests, please include the following information:

- Ontario corporation number and corporate name
- Date of incorporation/amalgamation
- Contact person's name, address and telephone number

Name Search:

NUANS is a computerized search system that compares a proposed corporate name or trade-mark with databases of existing corporate bodies and trade-marks. This comparison determines the similarity that exists between the proposed name or mark and existing names in the database, and produces a listing of names that are found to be most similar. A NUANS search is not required if reviving a number company.

An original Ontario-biased NUANS name search report must be obtained from a private name search company and cannot be dated more than 90 days prior to the submission of the articles. For example, articles submitted on November 28th could be accompanied by a NUANS name search report dated as early as August 30th, but not dated earlier.

Suppliers are listed in the Yellow Pages under the heading "Searchers of Records" or visit Industry Canada's NUANS website for a list of registered search houses that can assist you with obtaining a NUANS search report and filing your corporate documents with the Ministry of Government and Consumer Services. The Companies and Personal Property Security Branch does not provide this search.

General Information:

Please be advised that the *COMPANIES AND PERSONAL PROPERTY SECURITY BRANCH CANNOT GIVE LEGAL ADVICE*. This information is intended as a general guide only. For further assistance or legal information, please consult private legal counsel. If you need a lawyer, you may wish to contact the Lawyer Referral Service of the Law Society of Upper Canada. You will be referred to a lawyer for up to a half-hour free legal consultation, either in person or over the phone. Please note that this is a toll service and phoning the Lawyer Referral Service line will automatically generate a $6.00 charge on your phone bill, in the month following your call. You must be 18 years of age to access this service. The number is 1-900-565-4577 (1-900-565-4LRS).

Please refer to Section 317 of the *Corporations Act* for details on revival of a corporation without share capital.

The *Corporations Act* allows for the revival of a corporation without share capital, which has been dissolved for failure to comply with a filing requirement under the *Corporations Information Act*.

The corporation may be revived, at any time, by any "interested person" (e.g. former director, officer, member, or creditor). Upon revival, the corporation is restored to its legal position, including all its property, rights and privileges, and is subject to all its liabilities, contracts and debts, as of the date of its dissolution, in the same manner as if it had not been dissolved (S. 317(10)).

Consent:

A consent to the revival from the Office of the Public Guardian and Trustee is generally not required. If, however, that office is currently dealing with assets formerly owned by the dissolved corporation, such a consent will be necessary. For further information, please call the Office of the Public Guardian and Trustee at *416-327-6683 or toll free in Ontario at 1-800-366-0335*.

Charitable:

If a charitable non-profit corporation is to be revived, the Charitable Property Division of the Office of the Public Guardian and Trustee should be contacted at (416) 326-1965.

[EPC-1] — Extra-Provincial Corporations from Within Canada (Domestic)*

Date: **November 30, 2007**

Companies and Personal Property Security Branch Requirements

A corporation incorporated or continued federally, or under the laws of *any other Canadian jurisdiction* outside of Ontario, *NEED NOT* obtain an Extra-Provincial Licence in order to operate in Ontario. It must, however, file the following information with the Companies and Personal Property Security Branch:

1. An Initial Return/Notice of Change, Form 2 under the *Corporations Information Act*, within 60 days after the date the corporation begins to carry on business in Ontario.

   Please note: Effective July 27, 2000, branch policy requires that the following accompany an Initial Return:

   - A photocopy of the page or pages of the most recent Articles (e.g. incorporation/amalgamation/amendment) or other constating documents, containing the correct name and incorporation/amalgamation date, and the names of the amalgamating corporations, filed with the jurisdiction to which the corporation is subject.

   - Where an amendment has been filed, pages 1 and 2 of the Articles of Amendment showing both the former and amended corporation names, are to accompany Form 2.

 For the most recent version of this form, please visit: http://www.gov.on.ca/ontprodconsume/groups/content/@onca/@bundles/@cppsb/documents/document/stel02_168164.pdf

2. An Initial Return/Notice of Change, Form 2 under the *Corporations Information Act*, within 15 days after the change to information previously filed takes place.

Forms

The Initial Return/Notice of Change, Form 2 under the *Corporations Information Act*, is available at no cost from:

Ministry of Government and Consumer Services
Companies and Personal Property Security Branch
393 University Avenue, Suite 200
Toronto ON M5G 2M2

The Initial Return/Notice of Change, Form 2 is also available on the ServiceOntario website at www.ServiceOntario.ca.

Note: The Companies and Personal Property Security Branch does not require these corporations to appoint an agent for service in Ontario. It may, however, be a requirement of other legislation, so the branch will accept an appointment of agent for service in Ontario form submitted with an Initial Return/Notice of Change, Form 2.

Ceasing to carry on business in Ontario

If the corporation decides to cease carrying on business within the province of Ontario, the corporation must file an Initial Return/Notice of Change, Form 2, under the *Corporations Information Act* with the Companies and Personal Property Security Branch. This form must be completed with the appropriate information and must include the "Date Commenced" business activity in Ontario and the "Date Ceased" carrying on business activity in Ontario (item numbers 9 and 10 on the form).

[EPC-2] — Extra-Provincial Licence (Corporations From Outside Canada)*

Date: **January 1, 2009**

Companies and Personal Property Security Branch Requirements

To obtain an Extra-Provincial Licence for a business corporation incorporated or continued under the laws of a jurisdiction outside of Canada and wishing to operate in Ontario, the following documentation must be submitted to the Companies and Personal Property Security Branch:

1. **Application for Extra-Provincial Licence** (Form 1 prescribed under the Regulations to the *Extra-Provincial Corporations Act*) completed in duplicate and bearing original signatures on both copies;

2. **Appointment of Agent for Service** (Form 2 prescribed under the Regulations to the *Extra-Provincial Corporations Act*) completed in duplicate and bearing original signatures on both copies;

3. **Ontario-biased NUANS** name search report;

 For the most recent version of this form, please visit: http://www.gov.on.ca/ontprodconsume/groups/content/@onca/@bundles/@cppsb/documents/document/stel02_168169.pdf

4. An original **Certificate of Status** issued by the government of the home jurisdiction, and signed by an official of the governing jurisdiction authorized to do so, setting out:

(i) the name of the corporation,

(ii) the date of incorporation or amalgamation,

(iii) the jurisdiction to which the corporation is subject,

(iv) that the corporation is a valid and subsisting corporation;

Note: If the home jurisdiction will not issue an original Certificate of Status with the above information, a legal opinion from a lawyer authorized to practise in that jurisdiction is required, setting out all the above information.

5. **Fee of $330.00**;

6. **Covering letter** giving a contact name, return address and telephone number.

There are other filing requirements after the corporation has obtained its Extra-Provincial Licence (please see page 3 for more information).

Forms

Application for Extra-Provincial Licence, Form 1 and Appointment for Agent for Service, Form 2, are available at no charge from:

Ministry of Government Services
Companies and Personal Property Security Branch
393 University Avenue, Suite 200
Toronto ON M5G 2M2
Telephone: (416) 314-8880 or toll free in Ontario 1-800-361-3223
TTY: 416-325-3408
TTY Toll Free: 1-800-268-7095

The Application for Extra-Provincial Licence, Form 1 and Appointment for Agent for Service, Form 2 are also available at no cost on the Internet at: *www.Ontario.ca*

Name Search

NUANS is a computerized search system that compares a proposed corporate name or trade-mark with databases of existing corporate bodies and trade-marks. This comparison determines the similarity that exists between the proposed name or mark and existing names in the database, and produces a listing of names that are found to be most similar.

An original Ontario-biased NUANS name search report must be obtained from a private name search company and cannot be dated more than 90 days prior to the submission of the application. For example, an application submitted on November 28th could be accompanied by a NUANS name search report dated as early as August 30th, but not dated earlier.

Suppliers are listed in the Yellow Pages under the heading "Searchers of Records" or visit Industry Canada's NUANS website at: www.nuans.com for a list of registered search houses that can assist you with obtaining a NUANS search report and filing your corporate documents with the Ministry of Government Services. The Companies and Personal Property Security Branch does not provide this search.

General Information

Please be advised that the **COMPANIES AND PERSONAL PROPERTY SECURITY BRANCH CANNOT GIVE LEGAL ADVICE**. This information is intended as a general guide only. For further assistance or legal information, please consult private legal counsel.

Please refer to the *Extra-Provincial Corporations Act* for details on the requirements of foreign corporations operating in Ontario.

If you need a lawyer, you may wish to contact the Lawyer Referral Service of the Law Society of Upper Canada. You will be referred to a lawyer for up to a half-hour free legal consultation, either in person or over the phone. Please note that this is a toll service and phoning the Lawyer Referral Service line will automatically generate a $6.00 charge on your phone bill, in the month following your call. You must be 18 years of age to access this service. The number is 1-900-565-4577 (1-900-565-4LRS).

Extra-Provincial Licence — Corporations incorporated or continued under the laws of a jurisdiction outside of Canada must obtain an Extra-Provincial Licence in order to conduct their business activities in Ontario (S.4 (2)).

Extra-Provincial Corporation Name — An Extra-Provincial Licence will not be issued to a foreign corporation with a name that is identical to a corporate name already in use in Ontario. In the case where the identical name is no longer in use, a licence will only be issued if at least ten years have elapsed since the other body corporate was dissolved or changed its name.

Agent for Service — These foreign corporations must also appoint an Agent for Service in Ontario. An Agent of Service may be an individual, 18 years of age or older who is resident in Ontario, or a corporation having its registered office in Ontario. The foreign corporation must ensure the continuing appointment of an Agent and report any changes to the Agent's name, address, etc. (S.19).

Other Business Names — PLEASE NOTE: Effective March 27, 2000, foreign corporations can only be licensed under their corporate name. Licences are no longer issued with a business name. A corporation which has obtained an Extra-Provincial Licence in Ontario may carry on its business activities under a name other than its corporate name, provided that the name is registered under the *Business Names Act*. (S.9).

Penalties — A foreign corporation operating in Ontario without having obtained a licence or without an appointed Agent for Service, may face possible prosecution under S.20 of the *Extra-Provincial Corporations Act*, and is not capable of maintaining an action or other proceeding in an Ontario court (S.21 (1)).

Filing Requirements After an Extra-Provincial Licence is Obtained

Initial Return/Notice of Change

A corporation that has obtained an Extra-Provincial licence to carry on business in Ontario, must file an Initial Return/Notice of Change, Form 2, under the *Corporations Information Act* within 60 days after the date the corporation begins to carry on business in Ontario. If the information filed changes, the corporation must file another Initial Return/Notice of Change, Form 2 within 15 days after the change takes place.

Corporations Information Act Annual Return (CIA AR)

For tax years ending **AFTER** December 31, 2008, foreign business corporations licensed under the *Extra-Provincial Corporations Act* to carry on business in Ontario, are required to file a Schedule 548, *Corporations Information Act* Annual Return for Foreign Business Corporations, together with their T2 return to the Canada Revenue Agency. This schedule must be filed within six months after the end of each tax year.

For all tax years ending ***BEFORE*** January 1, 2009, corporations are required to file their CIA AR with the Ontario Ministry of Revenue.

The information collected on the Initial Return/Notice of Change and the CIA AR is used to update the public record maintained by the Ontario Ministry of Government Services.

Not-for-Profit Corporations — A not-for-profit corporation incorporated or continued under the laws of a jurisdiction outside of Canada, NEED NOT obtain an Extra-Provincial Licence to operate in Ontario. It must, however, file an Initial Return/Notice of Change, Form 2 under the *Corporations Information Act*, together with a photocopy of its incorporating documents with the Companies and Personal Property Security Branch within 60 days after the date the corporation begins to carry on business in Ontario.

It must also file an Initial Return/Notice of Change, Form 2 under the *Corporations Information Act* with the Branch, within 15 days after the change to information previously filed takes place.

The Initial Return/Notice of Change, Form 2 under the *Corporations Information Act*, is available at no cost from:

Ministry of Government Services
Companies and Personal Property Security Branch
393 University Avenue, Suite 200
Toronto ON M5G 2M2
Telephone: (416) 314-8880 or toll free in Ontario 1-800-361-3223
TTY: 416-325-3408
TTY Toll Free: 1-800-268-7095

The Initial Return/Notice of Change, Form 2 is also available on the Internet at: *www.Ontario.ca*

These corporations are NOT REQUIRED to appoint an Agent for Service in Ontario.

Changes to Information on an Extra-Provincial Licence

Name of Jurisdiction — A change to the name of the corporation in its home jurisdiction or a change of home jurisdiction due to a continuance, requires that an Application for Amendment to Extra-Provincial Licence, Form 3 under the *Extra-Provincial Corporations Act*, be completed and filed in duplicate with the Companies and Personal Property Security Branch, along with a Certificate of Status and an Ontario-biased NUANS name search (if the corporation has changed its name). The fee for filing an Application for Amendment to Extra-Provincial Licence is $150.00.

The Application for Amendment to Extra-Provincial Licence, Form 3 is available at no cost from:

Ministry of Government Services
Companies and Personal Property Security Branch
393 University Avenue, Suite 200
Toronto ON M5G 2M2
Telephone: (416) 314-8880 or toll free in Ontario 1-800-361-3223
TTY: 416-325-3408
TTY Toll Free: 1-800-268-7095

The Application for Amendment to Extra-Provincial Licence, Form 3 is also available at no cost on the Internet at: *www.Ontario.ca*

Agent for Service — A change of Agent for Service requires the following to be completed and filed with the Companies and Personal Property Security Branch:

- Revised Appointment of Agent for Service, Form 2 under the *Extra-Provincial Corporations Act*; and
- Initial Return/Notice of Change, Form 2 under the *Corporations Information Act*.

Head or Registered Office Address — A change of Head or Registered Office Address requires that an Initial Return/Notice of Change, Form 2 under the *Corporations Information Act*, be completed and filed with the Companies and Personal Property Security Branch within 15 days after the change of Head or Registered Office address takes place.

Ceasing to Carry on Business in Ontario

If a corporation with an Extra-Provincial Licence decides to cease carrying on business within the province of Ontario, the corporation must complete and submit in duplicate, Application for Termination of Extra-Provincial Licence, Form 4 under the *Extra-Provincial Corporations Act* to the Companies and Personal Property Security Branch.

In addition, the corporation must submit an Initial Return/Notice of Change, Form 2, under the *Corporations Information Act* to the Companies and Personal Property Security Branch with the Application for Termination of Extra-Provincial Licence, Form 4. This form must be completed with the appropriate information and must include the "Date Commenced" business activity in Ontario and the "Date Ceased" carrying on business activity in Ontario (item numbers 9 and 10 on the form).

Not-for-profit corporations must submit only an Initial Return/Notice of Change, Form 2, under the *Corporations Information Act* to the Companies and Personal Property Security Branch. This form must be completed with the appropriate information and must include the "Date Commenced" business activity in Ontario and the "Date Ceased" carrying on business activity in Ontario (item numbers 9 and 10 on the form).

Cancelled Extra-Provincial Licence

The *Extra-Provincial Corporations Act* does not contain any provision for "revival" of a cancelled licence. A person aggrieved by a decision of the Director appointed under the Act to cancel a licence may appeal to the Divisional Court. If no appeal is made to the Divisional Court, the Director may, at any time, review an order to cancel a licence and may affirm, revoke, or vary any such order, if in the Director's opinion, it is appropriate to do so. Otherwise, once a licence has been cancelled for cause, a foreign corporation must apply for a new licence if it wishes to resume carrying on business in Ontario.

[EPC-3] — Important Information for Extra-Provincial Domestic Corporations and Unincorporated Businesses Wanting to do Business in Ontario*

Date: November 30, 2007

To determine which form the Ministry of Government and Consumer Services, Companies and Personal Property Security Branch requires an extra-provincial domestic corporation or unincorporated business to file in order to carry on business in the province of Ontario, please identify the situation that applies to you. The information that applies to you will outline which Companies and Personal Property Security Branch form must be completed, where the form can be submitted, how long it will take to process the form and the filing fee.

---

*© Queen's Printer for Ontario, 2007. Reproduced with permission. For the most recent version of this form, please visit: http://www.gov.on.ca/ontprodconsume/groups/content/@onca/@bundles/@cppsb/documents/document/stel02_168146.pdf

Situation #1

✓ *An extra-provincial domestic corporation (e.g. Quebec) without an Ontario Corporation Number wishes to operate in Ontario*

If an extra-provincial domestic corporation wishes to operate in Ontario, the corporation must file an Initial Return/Notice of Change, Form 2 under the *Corporations Information Act* with the Companies and Personal Property Security Branch, Ministry of Government and Consumer Services. You must include a photocopy of the page or pages of the most recent Articles (e.g. incorporation/ amalgamation/ amendment) or other constating documents, containing the correct name and incorporation/amalgamation date, and the names of the amalgamating corporations, filed with the jurisdiction to which the corporation is subject. Where an amendment has been filed, pages 1 and 2 of the Articles of Amendment showing both the former and amended corporation names are to accompany the Form 2.

If the Initial Return/Notice of Change, Form 2 is submitted by mail, the processing time is 25 business days. If the Initial Return/Notice of Change, Form 2 is submitted to the Information Desk in the Public Office, the Branch will process it within 48 hours provided that a cover letter is attached that outlines in detail the circumstances that require expedited service. Requests for 48-hour service and the Form 2 must be submitted and picked-up at the Public Office in Toronto.

There is no fee for filing the Initial Return/Notice of Change, Form 2.

This service is not available at ServiceOntario workstations or through the private-sector Service Providers under contract with the Ministry of Government and Consumer Services, by fax, or via the Internet.

Situation #2

✓ *An extra-provincial domestic corporation (e.g. Quebec) with an assigned Ontario Corporation Number wishes to register an operating or style name in Ontario*

✓ *The principal place of business for the operating/style name is located in Ontario*

The corporation may complete a registration for an operating or style name at a ServiceOntario workstation; via the Internet at the ServiceOntario website; through private-sector Service Providers under contract with the Ministry of Government and Consumer Services or through the Canada Revenue Agency's Business Registration Online (BRO), provided that the principal place of business for the operating name is in Ontario. The fee for registering an operating or style name is $60.00. Private-sector Service Providers charge an additional fee for the services they provide.

If a Form 2 registration under the *Business Names Act* is submitted to the Companies and Personal Property Security Branch by mail, the registration fee is $80.00 and the Branch will process it within 6 to 8 weeks. The Form 2 can also be submitted in person at the Companies and Personal Property Security Branch Public Office. The registration fee is $80.00 and processing of the registration is immediate.

Situation #3

✓ An extra-provincial domestic corporation (e.g. Quebec) with an assigned Ontario Corporation Number wishes to register an operating or style name in Ontario

✓ The principal place of business for the operating/style name is not located in Ontario

The corporation must submit a Business Name Registration, Form 2 to the Companies and Personal Property Security Branch (by mail or at the Public Office). The client must enter "Not Applicable" in the "Principal Place of Business" field. The processing fee for registrations received by mail and in person at the Companies and Personal Property Security Branch Public Office is $80.00. The processing time for registrations received by mail is six to eight weeks and those done in person are processed immediately.

Situation #4

✓ An unincorporated business from another province (e.g. Quebec) wishes to operate in Ontario

✓ The principal place of business is located in Ontario

If an unincorporated business wishes to operate in Ontario, the business may complete a registration at a ServiceOntario workstation, through private-sector Service Providers (SPs) under contract with the Ministry of Government and Consumer Services, via the Internet at the ServiceOntario website or through Canada Revenue Agency's Business Registration Online (BRO) provided that the principal place of business for the operating name is in Ontario. The fee for registering a business name is $60.00. Private sector Service Providers charge an additional fee for the services they provide.

If a Form 1 under the *Business Names Act* is submitted to the Companies and Personal Property Security Branch by mail, the registration fee is $80.00 and the Branch will process it within 6 to 8 weeks. The Form 1 can also be submitted in person at the Companies and Personal Property Security Branch Public Office. The registration fee is $80.00 and processing of the registration is immediate.

Situation #5

✓ An unincorporated business from another province (e.g. Quebec) wishes to operate in Ontario

✓ The principal place of business is not located in Ontario

If the unincorporated business wishes to operate in Ontario but the principal place of business for the operating name is not in Ontario, the client must submit a Business Name Registration, Form 1 to the Companies and Personal Property Security Branch (by mail or at the Public Office). The client must enter "Not Applicable" in the "Principal Place of Business" field. The processing fee for registrations received by mail and in person at the Companies and Personal Property Security Branch Public Office is $80.00. The processing time for registrations received by mail is six to eight weeks and those done in person are processed immediately.

List of Definitions

To assist you in determining the situation that applies to you, we have included the following list of definitions.

Registered Office: According to the Ontario *Business Corporations Act*, "registered office" means the office of a corporation located at the address specified in its articles or in the notice most recently filed with the Companies and Personal Property Security Branch by the corporation. The corporation's registered office must be located in Ontario at all times. What was previously referred to as the corporation's "head office" is now referred to as the corporation's "registered office."

Business Address in Ontario: The business address field is found on the Form 2, under the *Business Names Act*. It refers to the physical address of the business and therefore, a post office box is not an acceptable address. If the business address is not located in Ontario, the words "Not Applicable" can be entered in the "Business Address in Ontario" field.

Address of Principal Place of Business in Ontario: The principal place of business field is found on the Form 1, under the *Business Names Act*. It refers to the physical address of the business and therefore, a post office box is not an acceptable address. If there is more than one place of business in Ontario, one must be chosen and entered into this field. If the business address is not located in Ontario, the words "Not Applicable" can be entered in the "Principal Place of Business in Ontario" field.

Forms:

Business Name Registration Forms 1 and 2, under the *Business Names Act* (BNA) and Form 2, Initial Return/Notice of Change, under the *Corporations Information Act (CIA)* are available at no cost from:

Ministry of Government and Consumer Services

Companies and Personal Property Security Branch

393 University Avenue, Suite 200

Toronto ON M5G 2M2

These forms are also available on the ServiceOntario website at www.ServiceOntario.ca.

[SP-1] — Search Products: Business Names & Limited Partnerships (BNLP)*

Date: November 30, 2007

Search Products: Description/Guide

Electronic Search Products

A. — Business Names Report

This report displays current information on the public record for business names registered or renewed within the past 5 years, including information filed on amendments and cancellations.

---

*© Queen's Printer for Ontario, 2007. Reproduced with permission. For the most recent version of this form, please visit: http://www.gov.on.ca/ontprodconsume/groups/content/@onca/@bundles/@cppsb/documents/document/stel02_168104.pdf

B. — Limited Partnerships Report

This report displays current information on the public record for limited partnerships registered or renewed within the past 5 years, including information filed for changes, dissolutions and withdrawals. Former limited partnership names will only be displayed for Declarations registered on or after April 1, 1994.

C. — Document Replica

An electronic replica of any one specific BNLP document (e.g., new, renewal, amendment/change and cancellation/dissolution/withdrawal) filed in the last 5 years for a business name or limited partnership.

D. — BNLP Document List

The BNLP Document List is available for sole proprietorships, general partnerships, corporation business names, limited partnerships, limited liability partnerships and partnership business names registered on or after April 1, 1994. This report sets out all documents that have been filed in relation to the business name or limited partnership registered, including the filing date for each document.

E. — Partnership Business Names List

The Partnership Business Names List sets out all additional business names registered or renewed by the firm since July 15, 1996.

F. — Certificate of Non-Registration

This certificate states that there is no record of the registration under the *Business Names Act* or a declaration under the *Limited Partnerships Act* in the subject name or BIN (Business Identification Number).

G. — Statement of No Match Found

This statement indicates that there is no record of the registration under the *Business Names Act* or a declaration under the *Limited Partnerships Act* in the subject name or BIN (Business Identification Number).

Non-Electronic Search Products

H. — Expired Search

This search covers a 15-year period of expired records. Records which have been expired for more than 15 years are stored in the Archives of Ontario. This new retention policy commences with records with a 1992 registration date.

BNLP refers to an unincorporated business name or limited partnership registered under either the Business Names Act or the Limited Partnerships Act.

[SP-2] — Search Products: Corporations*

Date: **November 30, 2007**

Search Products: Description/Guide

A. — Corporation Point-In-Time Report

This report displays information on the public record for the subject corporation as of a specific date since June 27, 1992. All active directors and officers are listed. Some historical information such as amalgamating corporations, where the subject corporation is an amalgamation, and name history are included in the report. In addition, directors and officers reported as ceased on document(s) filed on the "as of date" will be listed as inactive.

B. — Corporation Profile Report

This report displays current information on the public record for the subject corporation. All active directors and officers are listed. Some historical information, such as amalgamating corporations, where the subject corporation is an amalgamation, and name history is included in the report.

C. — Corporation Document List

This report identifies all documents filed by the corporation since June 27, 1992 forward. Where the information has been recorded in ONBIS, the report also identifies the name of the person authorizing the filing of a document filed under the *Corporations Information Act*.

D. — List of Business Names Registered by a Corporation

This report provides a list of business names, including registration dates, (new/renewal) filed by the corporation within the previous 5 years. If you require more information on a business name, please request an Unincorporated Business Names Search.

E. — Certificate of Status

This certificate provides the current status of the corporation.

F. — Certificate of No Record

This certificate is issued if there is no record of the corporation in the Ontario Business Information System (ONBIS).

G. — Certificate of Non-Filing

This certificate is issued based on information recorded in the Ontario Business Information System (ONBIS) on or after June 27, 1992 when a corporation has not filed under the *Corporations Information Act*. Additional historical information may exist on the Companies and Personal Property Security Branch corporate microfiche.

 For the most recent version of this form, please visit: http://www.gov.on.ca/ontprodconsume/groups/content/@onca/@bundles/@cppsb/documents/document/stel02_168105.pdf

H. — Copy of Document/Notice

This is available only if a Corporation Profile Report is not available.

I. — TC Files

i) TC or RC paper files are inactive files stored off-site. They are made available 10 working days from date of ordering.

ii) Persons viewing paper files must leave their driver's licence or other acceptable identification as a security deposit.

iii) Paper files must not be removed from the public office or taken apart.

iv) Clearly identify the certified/non-certified copies required.

J. — Corporate Microfiche

This is part of the official public record and provides incorporating and amending documents. It does not provide a complete and current record. The following documents will not appear on the microfiche record.

i) Initial Notices/Initial Returns for Ontario corporations filed after December 31, 1994.

ii) All Notices of Change filed after December 31, 1994.

iii) 1994/95 Special Notices (Year 3).

iv) Notices of Intention to Dissolve/Notices of Opportunity to be Heard and Cancellation Orders for Failure to file a Special Notice or Annual Return.

v) 1995 Annual Returns and forward.

[SP-3] — Searching the Public Record*

Date: November 30, 2007

Clients can verify whether their proposed name has been registered or incorporated and obtain information regarding business entities and not-for-profit organizations operating in Ontario by conducting corporate name and unincorporated business name and limited partnership (BNLP) searches of the Ontario public record.

Note: The Companies and Personal Property Security Branch (CPPSB) does not provide information about trademarks. Clients should contact the Canadian Intellectual Property Office (CIPO) at 1-866-997-1936, TTY: 1-866-442-2476 or visit CIPO's website at http://strategis.ic.gc.ca/sc_mrksv/cipo/ for information about trademarks or to conduct a trademark search.

Clients may also wish to search the NUANS database, a Canada-wide corporate, business name and trademark registry. A NUANS search report will display corporations, business names and trademarks, which are similar to your proposed name. A NUANS report may be obtained from the NUANS website at www.nuans.com or through private search houses listed in the Yellow Pages of your local phone book under "Searchers of Records".

For information on corporations and business entities operating in other jurisdictions, please contact that jurisdiction directly.

Corporate Names

CPPSB records the name and Ontario Corporation Number (OCN) of *Ontario* corporate entities that are incorporated, continued or amalgamated in Ontario as well as extra-provincial corporations carrying on business within Ontario and corporations enacted by Special Acts. The public record is comprised of corporations, which conduct business for profit as well as notfor- profit organizations such as charities (local and extra-provincial).

Unincorporated Business Names and Limited Partnerships (BNLP)

CPPSB records the business name, Business Identification Number (BIN) and registrant information of businesses operating in Ontario. The record is comprised of sole proprietorships, general partnerships, limited partnerships, Ontario limited liability partnerships, and extraprovincial limited liability partnerships and extra-provincial limited liability companies that carry on business in Ontario. The public record also contains business name(s) registered by a corporation. (A corporation using a name other than its corporate name must register the operating name under the *Business Names Act*).

Enhanced Business Name Search for Unincorporated Businesses

This new type of search provides several improvements over the exact name search. Among these are:

- The ability to select a name from a list of up to 120 business names matching or similar to the business name searched;
- The ability to search words in a business name and have a list of business names returned with the word appearing *anywhere* within the business name;
- The specific street number and name are included in the business address.

The Enhanced Business Name Search significantly improves the clients' ability to obtain a Business Names Report for a specific business name when more than one exact or similar business name is registered in Ontario.

The Enhanced Business Name Search is available on the Internet through ServiceOntario's website or through Service Providers under contract with the Ministry of Government and Consumer Services or at the CPPSB's Toronto Public Office.

Searching Corporation names via the Internet

Corporate record searches may be conducted via the Internet through Service Providers under contract with the Ministry of Government and Consumer Services. Results are received almost immediately and reports can be printed from the convenience of your home or office.

The Service Providers provide access to the Electronic Corporate Index (ECI) prior to requesting a corporate search. The Electronic Corporate Index is a computerized alphabetical listing of corporations, which are, or have been, active in Ontario. It provides fundamental information on Ontario corporations and extra-provincial corporations carrying on business in Ontario and can be searched by the corporate name, corporate number or by keyword. The Electronic Corporate Index displays the following information: corporation name, Ontario Corporation Number, incorporation date, jurisdiction, status and establishment type.

Please see the Companies Service Standards and Fees document or call the CPPSB Helpline (see below) for a list of products and their corresponding fees and processing times. The Service Providers charge a fee in addition to the Ministry's fee for the immediate online services they provide.

Searching the Public Record in Person or by Mail

A search may be done in person at the Companies and Personal Property Security Branch Public Office in Toronto between 8:30 a.m. and 5:00 p.m., Monday to Friday (excluding statutory holidays). Search results are immediate and you will receive a report to take home with you. Clients also have access to the Electronic Corporate Index (ECI) referenced above.

A search request can also be mailed to CPPSB. Allow 4 — 6 weeks for processing. Please print clearly the company names to be searched and enclose a cheque or money order payable to the Minister of Finance. If you are searching for a business located in a specific area, please indicate the city/town in your letter. This will enable staff to provide the appropriate report if the search shows more than one business under the name searched.

If a search request is mailed in with a business name registration form, please include separate cheques or money orders for the registration and search fees. Please indicate whether you still want to register the name if our search reveals another business is already using it.

Please see the Companies Service Standards and Fees document or call the CPPSB Helpline (see below) for a list of products and their corresponding fees and processing times.

Requirements to Conduct a Search of the Public Record

In order to complete a corporate or Business Name/Enhanced Business Name Search request, clients should know the following information:

- Ontario Corporation Number (OCN) or Business Identification Number (BIN);
- Accurate spelling of the corporation's name, the business name, limited partnership or the corporation's operating name.

CPPSB recommends that clients conduct both corporate and BNLP/Enhanced Business Name Searches when they are uncertain as to whether the name belongs to a corporation or an unincorporated business.

For detailed product descriptions, please refer to the "Corporate Search Products" and "Business Name and Limited Partnership Search Products" information sheets.

For more information. . .

Companies Helpline

Telephone: (416) 314-8880

Toll free in Ontario: 1-800-361-3223

TTY: 416-325-3408

TTY Toll Free: 1-800-268-7095

Internet: www.ServiceOntario.ca

Service Providers

For information about Service Providers under contract with the Ministry of Government and Consumer Services visit the ServiceOntario website at: www.ServiceOntario.ca.

[G-1] — Registering your Business Name in Ontario*

Date: November 30, 2007

Business names are registered with the Companies and Personal Property Security Branch (CPPSB) of the Ministry of Government and Consumer Services (MGCS) and are placed on the Public Record maintained by CPPSB for public disclosure. Anyone may search business name information contained on the Public Record for a fee to find the owners or principals behind a business name.

Who Must Register Under the *Business Names Act*?

The Ontario *Business Names Act* administered by the Companies and Personal Property Security Branch applies to:

- sole proprietorships (one owner) carrying on business under a name other than the individual's full name;
- partnerships carrying on business under a firm name other than the full names of the partners;
- corporations carrying on business under a name other than their corporate name;
- an existing general partnership or limited partnership registering a business name different from the registered firm name;
- limited liability partnerships;
- extra-provincial limited liability partnerships; and
- extra-provincial limited liability companies

Where can I register a business name and obtain a Master Business Licence?

ServiceOntario

ServiceOntario's website provides access to the government's electronic services that simplify and streamline registration, renewal and reporting processes for Ontario businesses. New entrepreneurs and existing corporations can electronically complete the most important applications to register their business at one location, including applications for Business Name Registration, Retail Sales Tax Vendor Permit, Employer Health Tax and Workplace Safety and Insurance Board. When registering via Business Registration Online (a partnership between Canada Revenue Agency (CRA) and some provincial governments including Ontario), you may apply for the above programs as well as for a Federal Business Number (BN) and other CRA programs.

Business names can be searched and registered through ServiceOntario via the following channels:

- ServiceOntario's website at www.ServiceOntario.ca.
- Self-help workstations located at ServiceOntario service locations across the province

 For the most recent version of this form, please visit: http://www.gov.on.ca/ontprodconsume/groups/content/@onca/@bundles/@cppsb/documents/document/stel02_168153.pdf

- Business Registration Online (BRO) at www.businessregistration.gc.ca.
- Mail: ServiceOntario, P.O. Box 1028 STN B, Toronto ON M5T 3H3

Please note that you must enter the business information yourself when using BRO, the ServiceOntario website and self-help workstations. For more information about workstation service locations, fees and processing times or to obtain ServiceOntario applications, please visit the ServiceOntario website or call:

Local: (416) 314-9151

Toll-Free in Ontario: 1-800-565-1921

TTY: (416) 325-3408 or toll free: 1-800-268-7095

Website: www.ServiceOntario.ca

Service Providers

Electronic business name searches and registrations are also available through Service Providers under contract with the Ministry of Government and Consumer Services. For information about Service Providers visit the ServiceOntario website at www.ServiceOntario.ca.

Companies and Personal Property Security Branch

Business names may be searched and registered *in person* from 8:30 a.m. to 5:00 p.m. on regular business days at:

Companies and Personal Property Security Branch

Ministry of Government and Consumer Services

Second floor, 375 University Ave.

Toronto ON M5G 2M2

To reach the Companies and Personal Property Security Branch Public Office, take the *escalator* from the lobby of 375 University Avenue to the second floor.

Registrations submitted to the Branch *by mail* should be addressed to:

Companies and Personal Property Security Branch

Ministry of Government and Consumer Services

393 University Ave., Suite 200

Toronto ON M5G 2M2

Ministry Fee for Registration

The Ministry fee for registering a business name:

- Through ServiceOntario, electronically $60; by mail $80.
- Through the Service Providers $60; however the Service Providers charge a separate service fee. Please contact the Service Providers directly for information about the fees they charge for the immediate online service they provide.
- In person at the Branch (service time is immediate) or by mail (service time is 6–8 weeks) is $80.

Business Identification Number (BIN) and Business Number (BN)

The Companies and Personal Property Security Branch assigns a Business Identification Number (BIN) when a business name is registered in Ontario. It should not be confused with the federal Business Number (BN) assigned by the Canada Revenue Agency (CRA) for federal programs, including Goods and Services Tax/Harmonized Sales Tax (GST/HST), Import/Export Accounts, Payroll Deductions and Corporate Income Tax.

Business Name Registration Forms

If you are registering a business name under the *Business Names Act* directly with the Companies and Personal Property Security Branch, the following forms must be submitted to the Branch:

Form 1 — Registration of a Sole Proprietorship/General Partnership

Used to register a business name for a sole proprietorship (one owner), or the firm name of a general partnership (more than one owner).

Form 2 — Registration of a Business Name for a Corporation

Used when a corporation wishes to carry on business under a name different from the corporation's name. Not-for-profit corporations must also complete this form to publicly use a name other than their corporation name.

Form 5 — Registration of a Business Name for a Partnership/Limited Partnership (Must be filed in person or by mail to the Companies and Personal Security Branch)

Used when a registered general partnership or existing limited partnership wishes to carry on business under a name different from the firm name of the partnership or limited partnership.

Form 6 — Ontario Limited Liability Partnership, Extra-Provincial Limited Liability Partnership, Extra-Provincial Limited Liability Company (Must be filed in person or by mail to the Companies and Personal Security Branch)

- *Limited Liability Partnerships* must register the firm name and can carry on business in Ontario only under the registered firm name. An LLP is a partnership with special characteristics related to liability, and may be formed only by professionals whose governing legislation permits LLP's to practice the profession. Currently in Ontario, only lawyers, chartered accountants and certified general accountants may form a Limited Liability Partnership. The words "limited liability partnership" or "société à responsabilité limitée" or the abbreviations "LLP", "L.L.P." or "s.r.l." must appear in the name of a limited liability partnership.

- *Extra-Provincial Limited Liability Partnership* must register the firm name to carry on business in Ontario, and can carry on business only under the registered firm name. An Extra-Provincial LLP may carry on business in Ontario only if it practices a profession that Ontario LLP's are authorized to practice.

- *Extra-Provincial Limited Liability Companies* must register the company name to carry on business in Ontario. A limited liability company is an unincorporated association, other than a partnership, formed under the laws of another jurisdiction that grants its members limited liability. There is no statute to establish an Ontario LLC.

Availability of Forms

The forms are available on the ServiceOntario website at www.ServiceOntario.ca.

The forms may also be picked up at the Companies and Personal Property Security Branch Public Office during regular business hours (8:30 a.m. to 5:00 p.m., Monday to Friday).

Master Business Licence (MBL)

When registering a business name, you will be issued an MBL, which shows the registration and expiry dates as well as the Business Identification Number (BIN). The MBL can be used as one of the proofs of business name registration at financial institutions and to facilitate any other business-related registration with the Ontario government.

When registering your business name through any of the self-help workstations located at ServiceOntario service locations across the province, the ServiceOntario website (between 8:30 a.m. and 6:00 p.m., Monday to Friday), Business Registration Online (BRO), Service Providers or at the Companies and Personal Property Security Branch, you will receive a Master Business Licence (MBL) immediately following registration. If registering after hours through the ServiceOntario website or BRO, you will receive your MBL by mail, within two weeks of registration.

Please note a Master Business Licence is not issued for registration of a business name for a Partnership/Limited Partnership (Form 5) or for an Ontario Limited Liability Partnership, Extra-Provincial Limited Liability Partnership or Extra-Provincial Limited Liability Company (Form 6). You will receive a copy of the application with a validation showing the Business Identification Number, date of registration and the expiry date.

Checking to see if Another Business is Already Using the Business Name

Before making a final decision on your business name and ordering business cards or stationery you will want to know if someone else is already using the name. A search of the Companies and Personal Property Security Branch records will determine whether another *Ontario* business is using the name you have selected and where that business is located.

For detailed information about searching a business name and product descriptions, and for information on corporate name searches as well as NUANS and trademark searches, please refer to the "Searching the Public Record" information sheet available on the ServiceOntario website at www.ServiceOntario.ca.

Registration Expiry/Renewal

A business name registration is effective for five years. To continue using the name it must be renewed before the expiry date set out on the registration, and a renewal fee must be paid. It is the registrant's responsibility to keep the information on the registration up to date and to renew the registration on time. *The Branch does not issue reminders.* An updated Master Business Licence (MBL) will be issued immediately if renewed in person or mailed within two weeks after a successful online renewal.

Amending or Cancelling a Registration

To ensure the Public Record is accurate, you must notify the Companies and Personal Property Security Branch when the information in your registration has changed. Changes in address, business activity or partners (as long as one of the original partners remains the same), must be filed on the Ministry form within 15 days after the change. There is no filing fee. However, changing the name of your business registration is considered a new registration and the relevant fee applies. Changing the type of registration, e.g. a partnership registration to a sole proprietorship, or changing all the partners in a partnership, is also considered a new registration.

If the business ceases to operate, you should cancel your business name registration. There is no filing fee for the cancellation of a business name.

The amended or cancelled registration can be submitted to the Branch by mail or in person at the Public Office in Toronto. Alternatively, the registrant can amend or cancel a business name registration online through the ServiceOntario website at www.ServiceOntario.ca. The registrant will receive confirmation of the changes by mail in approximately three weeks.

Does Registration Protect my Business Name?

The *Business Names Act* does not protect the exclusivity of a registered name. You may be able to protect your business name by registering a trademark under the *Trade-Marks Act* (federal legislation). It may be useful to talk to your lawyer or contact the Canada Ontario Business Service Centre for more information on trademarks.

The *Business Names Act* does not prohibit registration of identical names, but if you decide to use a name that is the same as or confusingly similar to that of an existing business, it could result in a lawsuit. The person registering the name also assumes full responsibility for any risk of confusion with an existing corporation, business name or trademark.

You may also wish to do some research to see if incorporating is a better alternative for your business. Identical corporation names cannot be incorporated in Ontario. If you incorporate and carry on business under the corporate name set out in the Articles of Incorporation, there is no requirement to register under the *Business Names Act*. However, if the corporation is operating with a name that is different from its corporate name, the operating name must be registered under the *Business Names Act*.

Liability

The registrant of a business name who has suffered damages because someone else has registered the same name or one that is deceptively similar can take legal action through the courts. The *Business Names Act* entitles you to recover compensation for damages suffered and provides for a court order cancelling the registration that was the cause of the action.

Companies and Personal Property Security Branch staff cannot provide specific advice on name selection. If you are not sure about the use of a name, you should consult a lawyer.

If you need a lawyer, you may wish to contact the Lawyer Referral Service of the Law Society of Upper Canada. You will be referred to a lawyer for up to a half-hour free legal consultation, either in person or over the phone. Please note that this is a toll service and phoning the Lawyer Referral Service line will automatically generate a $6.00 charge on your phone bill, in the month following your call. You must be 18 years of age to access this service. The number is 1-900-565-4577 (1-900-565-4LRS).

Penalties for not Registering

Under the *Business Names Act*, fines of up to $2,000 can be levied against individuals and up to $25,000 for corporations for failure to register or for registering false or misleading information.

Help Choosing a Business Name

Choosing the right name for your new business is an important decision. You want a name that will draw potential customers, help clients identify your company and build your business image. A name that is easy to remember and provides information about the products or services you offer is always a good choice. Choose a distinctive name to stand out from your competitors. Make sure the name is not misleading or confusing in its description of the goods or services you will provide.

Restrictions on Business Names

When choosing your business name, remember that certain words or expressions cannot be used.

- Words or expressions, in any language, that are obscene or objectionable in nature.
- Words that imply the business is a different type of organization. For example, you may not imply that a sole proprietorship is a partnership. You may not use numbers or words that imply the business name is a corporate number name. Also the registered name of a business carried on for profit should not contain words that imply it is a not-for-profit organization.
- The words "college," "institute," or "university" cannot be used, if it would suggest the registrant is a post-secondary educational institution, without the written consent of the Ministry of Training, Colleges and Universities. To obtain consent in writing from this ministry, please contact:

  Ministry of Training, Colleges and Universities

  Postsecondary Accountability Branch

  General Inquiries: (416) 325-1816

  Advise the ministry that you are registering under the *Business Names Act*.
- You may not use the words "Limited", "Limitée", "Incorporated", "Incorporée", "Corporation", or the corresponding abbreviations "Ltd.", "Ltée", "Inc." or "Corp.", unless the word "limited" is used in the name of a limited liability partnership, extra-provincial limited liability company or in the name of a limited partnership formed under the *Limited Partnerships Act*.
- You may not use the words "Limited Liability Partnership" or the abbreviation "LLP" in the business name unless you are registering an Ontario limited liability partnership or an extra-provincial limited liability partnership.
- You may not use the words "Limited Liability Company" or the abbreviation "LLC" in the business name unless you are registering an extra-provincial limited liability company.
- Words that are prohibited under federal or Ontario laws or words that are restricted unless the restriction is satisfied.
- Words that imply the business is connected with the Crown, the Government of Canada, of a province or of a territory, a municipality, or an agency of the Crown, government or municipality, without written consent of the appropriate authority.
- Names of individuals may not be used unless they have or had a material interest in the business activity and have given their written permission. If the individual is deceased

and his or her name is used within 30 years of the date of death, the written consent of the estate or the estate trustee (i.e. the executor or administrator) must be obtained.

It's your responsibility to make sure your business name does not contain any of the above words or expressions unless proper consent has been obtained. If you register a name that is contrary to the Act or regulations, the name is subject to cancellation at any time.

Business names must be registered in the Roman alphabet (English, French, Spanish, Italian, Latin, etc.) and may contain numerals. Business names composed of characters from other alphabets must be translated and registered in a language using the Roman alphabet. A business name in a language other than one using the Roman alphabet may be used in advertising and signs, but the business name must also be displayed in a language using the Roman alphabet. For example, a business that registers its name in English may have letterhead or signs in Chinese characters as long as the English name is also displayed at the place of business.

The following marks may also be included in the name, but may not be used as the first character:

@ ! “ # $ % & ’ ( ) * + , - . / : ; > = < ? [ ] \ ^ ‘ ’ .

Where can I Find More Help and Information?

Ministry of Economic Development and Trade

The Ministry of Economic Development and Trade operates enterprise centres and business self-help offices across the province to assist anyone wanting to start a new business. They provide information, access to resource material and advice on preparing a business plan, managing a new business and governmental assistance available to entrepreneurs.

Ministry of Economic Development and Trade and Ministry of Small Business and Entrepreneurship

General Inquiries

8th Floor, Hearst Block

900 Bay St.

Toronto ON M7A 2E1

Toll-free: 1-866-668-4249 or 1-866-ONT4BIZ

In Toronto: (416) 325-6666

Email:info@edt.gov.on.ca

Website: www.ontariocanada.com

The Canada-Ontario Business Service Centre

The Canada-Ontario Business Service Centre (COBSC) provides access to accurate, timely and relevant information on federal and provincial business-related programs, services and regulations. The COBSC is jointly managed by Industry Canada and the Ontario Ministry of Government Services. The COBSC has a contact centre staffed by knowledgeable Information Officers who can respond to business-related enquiries in both official languages between 8:30 a.m. and 6:00 p.m., Monday to Friday (every Government business day).

For more information, call *1-800-567-2345* or visit the Canada-Ontario Business Service Centre website at www.cbsc.org/ontario.

Other Related Information Sheets

Searching the Public Record

Business Name and Limited Partnership Search Products

[G-2] — Business Information Guide*

Date: November 30, 2007

- A *business name registration* refers to a registration under the *Business Names Act.* It expires after 5 years and must be renewed. The Ministry of Government and Consumer Services (MGCS), Companies and Personal Property Security Branch, maintains a registry of business names of sole proprietorships, general partnerships, Ontario limited liability partnerships, extra-provincial limited liability partnerships, extra-provincial limited liability companies and business names registered for a corporation operating with a name other than its corporate name. A business name registration should not be confused with an incorporation (see corporation) or a business licence (see business licence).

  A Corporation may operate under a name other than its legal corporate name by filing a Form 2 under the *Business Names Act.* The operating name cannot have the legal endings of Incorporated, Inc., Corporation, Corp., Limited or Ltd.

- A *business identification number (BIN)* is the number assigned by the Companies and Personal Property Security Branch, Ontario Business Information System (ONBIS) to your business name registration. This is not your federal business number issued by the Canada Revenue Agency.

- A *business number (BN)* is a federal numbering system that replaces the multiple numbers businesses require to deal with government. The business number includes Goods and Services Tax (GST), payroll deductions and/or corporate income tax.

- A *Business Licence* is required by particular businesses in order to operate in Ontario. This is *in addition* to the business name registration. For example, "Joe's Garage" is required to register its business name with the Companies and Personal Property Security Branch and obtain a licence in order to operate as a garage. To determine if your business will be affected by local regulations, licences, municipal business tax or zoning requirements contact the clerk of the city, town, village or rural municipality where your business will be located. These numbers can be found in the Blue Pages of the Telephone Directory under the appropriate heading (e.g. Licences and Permits).

- A *Master Business Licence* (MBL) is issued when a business name is registered under the *Business Names Act.* The Master Business Licence can be used as proof of business name registration at financial institutions and to facilitate any other business-related registration with the Ontario government.

- *Sole Proprietorship* refers to an unincorporated business with one (sole) owner. The owner must be an individual. It is NOT a corporation. The business name of a sole proprietorship is registered by filing a Form 1 under the *Business Names Act.*

 For the most recent version of this form, please visit: http://www.gov.on.ca/ontprodconsume/groups/content/@onca/@bundles/@cppsb/documents/document/stel02_168099.pdf

- *General Partnership* refers to an unincorporated business with 2 or more owners. The general partnership may consist of individuals, corporations or other unincorporated businesses. This is not the same as a limited partnership. The business name of a general partnership is registered by filing a Form 1 under the *Business Names Act.*

- A *Limited Partnership* is a special type of partnership that consists of at least one general partner and one or more limited partners. It is not incorporated. Generally speaking, subject to the *Limited Partnerships Act*, general partners have unlimited liability, while limited partners have limited liability up to the amount that they contribute or agree to contribute to the limited partnership. Filing a Declaration, Form 3, with the Registrar under the *Limited Partnerships Act* forms a limited partnership. Extra-provincial limited partnerships must also file a declaration with the Ministry of Government and Consumer Services to carry on business in Ontario.

- A *Limited Liability Partnership* is a partnership, other than a Limited Partnership, that is formed or is continued as a Limited Liability Partnership in Ontario under *Section 44.1* of the *Partnerships Act.*

- An *Extra-Provincial Limited Liability Partnership* is defined in *subsection 1.(1)* of the *Partnerships Act* as a limited liability partnership formed under the laws of another jurisdiction but does not include an extra-provincial limited partnership within the meaning of the *Limited Partnerships Act.* The law under which an EP LLP is formed determines how it is governed and the personal liability of its partners as per *subsection 44.4(4)* of the *Partnerships Act.*

- An *Extra-Provincial Limited Liability Company* is defined in *subsection 2.1(1)* of the *Business Names Act* as an unincorporated association, other than a partnership, formed under the laws of another jurisdiction that grants to each of its members limited liability with respect to the liabilities of the association. For more information regarding interpretation, consult a lawyer.

  If you need a lawyer, you may wish to contact the Lawyer Referral Service of the Law Society of Upper Canada. You will be referred to a lawyer for up to a half-hour free legal consultation, either in person or over the phone. Please note that this is a toll service and phoning the Lawyer Referral Service line will automatically generate a $6.00 charge on your phone bill, in the month following your call. You must be 18 years of age to access this service. The number is 1-900-565-4577 (1-900-565-4LRS).

- A *Corporation* is an incorporated entity with its own rights and responsibilities as a distinct person under the law. A business corporation is owned by the shareholders and managed by directors chosen by the shareholders. The owners of a corporation are not personally responsible for the debts of the corporation. The corporation is responsible for its debts. A corporation should not be confused with an unincorporated business name registered under the *Business Names Act.*

- A *Business Corporation* is a business entity incorporated under the Ontario *Business Corporations Act.* The purpose of a business corporation is to make a profit for its owners. A business corporation is distinguished by the use of the following legal endings within the corporate name: Incorporated, Inc., Corporation, Corp., Limited, Ltd.

- A *Not-For-Profit Corporation* carries on its activities without the purpose of gain for its members. It is incorporated under the *Corporations Act* as a corporation that does not issue shares. It must have not-for-profit purposes, and use any profits to promote those purposes. The most common types are: charitable (including religious organizations), social clubs, service clubs, sporting and athletic organizations, professional and trade associations, ratepayers' associations, and other community organizations. A not-for-profit corporation may have Incorporated, Inc., Corporation or Corp. as a legal ending but it is not a requirement.

[G-3] — Checklist for Completing Form 1, Initial Return/Notice of Change, under the *Corporations Information Act*[*]

Date: November 30, 2007

To help you complete your Initial Return/Notice of Change correctly, we have identified the most common deficiencies and developed a checklist to which you may refer when completing your Initial Return/Notice of Change. It is recommended that you order a Corporation Profile Report to obtain a list of the corporation's current administrators to use as reference when completing the Schedule A portion of your Initial Return/Notice of Change.

Before mailing your Initial Return/Notice of Change, review the following checklist to ensure it is completed correctly.

- *Corporation name and number are correct throughout all pages of the form.* For confirmation of the name and Ontario Corporation Number, please check your Certificate of Incorporation, Articles of Incorporation, Continuation, Amalgamation, Amendment, Letters Patent or Supplementary Letters Patent (whichever is the most current applicable document), or your Corporation Profile Report. Ensure that the corporation name is set out *exactly* as it appears on the most recently filed document listed above, including proper spelling, spacing and punctuation.

- *Date of Incorporation/Amalgamation is correct* as per the original Certificate of Incorporation/Amalgamation or Letters Patent. The date must be completed in full (year, month, day). For example, December 31st 2001 should be set out as 2001/12/31.

- *The Registered/Head Office address is completed in full* and includes street number and name, city or town, and postal code. Ontario and Canada are pre-printed on the form. A post office box alone is not acceptable; include Rural Route or Lot and Concession.

- *Return all pages of the Initial Return/Notice of Change.* The Initial Return/Notice of Change consists of two parts: Form 1 (page 1) and Schedule A.

Administrator (Director/Officer) data is completed in full.

- *The appropriate number of directors and officers is completed on Schedule A.* To report any change (e.g. head office address) the entire form must be completed in full including Schedule A with all current director /officer information.

---

[*] For the most recent version of this form, please visit: http://www.gov.on.ca/ontprodconsume/groups/content/@onca/@bundles/@cppsb/documents/document/stel02_168100.pdf

Please Note: Corporations must report all directors but not more than five senior officers, two of whom must be a president and a secretary, where mandatory.

Corporation Type	**Requirement**
Business corporation — not offering shares	Minimum of 1 director
Business corporation — offering shares	Minimum of 3 directors
Not-for-Profit corporation	Minimum of 3 directors, *only* 1 president and 1 secretary

- The administrator's first and last names are provided.
- The address is completed in full and includes street number and name, city or town, Rural Route, Lot and Concession (if applicable) and postal code.
- Director and officer names are completed exactly as shown on previous filings (i.e. John Michael Doe and not John M. Doe). If there are variations in the name, the intended change will not be reflected against the existing administrator record, but instead will result in the creation of an additional record for the same individual. For example, John D. Smith on a previous filing cannot be matched with John Doe Smith on a current filing. If you need to change the director/officer's name, cease the incorrect individual name and add the correct name, address and date elected/appointed.
- Indicate whether or not the director is a Canadian resident by checking the appropriate box. (Please note that at least 25% of the directors of a business corporation must be Canadian residents)
- Date Elected is completed in full (year/month/day) and is not a date prior to the date of incorporation or amalgamation or a date in the future.
- Date Ceased (if applicable) is completed in full (year/month/day) and is not a date in the future.
- When ceasing a director/officer, ensure that both the date elected/appointed and the date ceased are completed in full (year/month/day).
- When the date under "Other Titles" is completed ensure that the appropriate "other" title is checked off from the checklist provided above the date box.
- Previously reported generic "Other" positions have been ceased if an officer is to be assigned a specific position under "Other Titles". For example, on the former CIA Form 1, which did not display specific "Other" positions, John D. Smith, vice president, was previously reported generically as "Other". He should now be ceased as "Other" and in the next "Director/Officer Information" section of the same filing, be reported as vicepresident under "Other Titles". (Note: if you do not first cease John D. Smith properly under "Other", this officer will appear under both "Other" and "vice-president". See details below).

Other Titles

In January 1999, a list of titles under "Other Titles" was introduced on the CIA Form 1 replacing "Other", previously used to report all untitled officer positions other than president, secretary, treasurer and general manager. Officers previously reported generically as "Other" (e.g. chair, chair person, vice-chair, vice-president) can now be reflected with specific titles on the Public Record under "Other Titles".

As corporations can report only the five most senior officers, it is important to cease officers who are in excess of the filing requirement.

Officers previously reported as "Other" who fall under specific positions listed under "Other Titles" (e.g. vice-president), should be amended to reflect the specific title. As well, officers previously reported as "Other" whose status has now changed to president, secretary, treasurer or general manager, should be ceased as "Other" and then reported under one or more of these four titles.

To change a position previously reported as "Other" to a new position from "Other Titles" (for example, you now wish "Other" to be identified as "vice president"), you must first cease the old position of "Other" as follows:

Complete the "Director/Officer Information" portion on Schedule A (name, address, postal code).

Then, under "Officer Information" within the same section on Schedule A:

- Place an "X" in the "Other Untitled" box located under "Other Titles".
- Complete the date elected and the date ceased.

Go to the next new "Director/Officer Information" portion on Schedule A and complete this portion (name, address, postal code).

Then, under "Officer Information" within the same section on Schedule A:

- Select the position you wish to report from the "Other Titles" (e.g. vice president) and place an "X" in that box.
- Complete the date appointed.

Where a change is made to the filing and an officer previously reported as "Other" remains as "Other" (because the appropriate title is not identified on the form):

Complete the "Director/Officer Information" portion on Schedule A (name, address, postal code).

Then under "Officer Information" within the same section on Schedule A:

- Place an X in the "Other" untitled box under "Other Titles".
- Complete the date appointed.

If the officer holds more than one "Other-Untitled" position with different appointment dates, a separate "Director/Officer Information" section must be completed for each.

REMEMBER: You must set out information for all Directors and the five most senior officer positions whether or not changes have occurred to the information. Where changes have occurred, you must show the changes on the Notice of Change. The completed first page of CIA Form 1 must always accompany a Schedule A.

Electronic Filing

Form 1, Initial Return/Notice of Change may be filed electronically through Service Providers under contract with the Ministry of Government and Consumer Services.

You will be able to complete Form 1 Initial Return/Notice of Change, submit it to the Companies and Personal Property Security Branch for filing and within minutes receive confirmation once the information has been updated to the Public Record, all from the convenience of your home or office.

Prior to filing, you will also have the opportunity to order an electronic data extraction report commonly referred to as a data extract. When you order a data extract, the most current information on file with the Branch will be automatically inserted into the form. All you have to do is add new information or make changes to the existing information.

The online software will guide you through the completion of the form and the edits and validations will help to ensure that your filing complies with the *Corporations Information Act* and will be accepted by the Companies and Personal Property Security Branch.

There is no government fee for filing the Form 1 Initial Return/Notice of Change but there is an $8 fee for the data extract.

For information about Service Providers visit the ServiceOntario website at www.ServiceOntario.ca.

Other Related Information Sheets

Initial Return/Notice Of Change Making Changes To Corporate Information

Filing of Annual Returns

[G-6] — *Corporations Information Act* Annual Return Filing Requirements*

Date: April 1, 2010

Effective January 1, 2009, changes have been made to the filing requirements for the *Corporations Information Act* Annual Return (CIA AR), resulting from the Single Administration of Ontario Corporate Tax initiative.

Below are the new CIA AR filing requirements for tax years ending **AFTER** December 31, 2008.

CIA AR Filing Options for Tax Years Ending After December 31, 2008

Ontario corporations and foreign business corporations licensed to carry on business in Ontario are required to file their CIA AR with the Canada Revenue Agency within six months after the end of each tax year as follows:

- Corporations subject to the *Ontario Business Corporations Act* are required to file a Schedule 546, *Corporations Information Act* Annual Return for Ontario Corporations, together with their T2 return.
- Foreign business corporations licensed under the Ontario *Extra-Provincial Corporations Act* to carry on business in Ontario are required to file a Schedule 548, *Corpora-*

 For the most recent version of this form, please visit: http://www.gov.on.ca/ontprodconsume/groups/content/@onca/@bundles/@cppsb/documents/document/stel02_168168.pdf

tions Information Act Annual Return for Foreign Business Corporations, together with their T2 return.

- Non-profit corporations subject to the Ontario *Corporations Act* that *ARE* Registered Charities under the federal *Income Tax Act* (ITA) are required to file their *Corporations Information Act* Annual Return using either:
  - Charities RC232WS — Director/Officer Worksheet and Ontario *Corporations Information Act* Annual Return, or
  - Charities RC232 — Ontario *Corporations Information Act* Annual Return Worksheet in combination with the T1235, Director/Trustees and Like Officials Worksheet.

  The appropriate worksheet(s) must be submitted along with the T3010 Registered Charity Information Return.
- Non-profit corporations subject to the Ontario *Corporations Act* that are *NOT* Registered Charities under the federal ITA are required to file a Schedule 546, *Corporations Information Act* Annual Return for Ontario Corporations, together with their T2 return.

Ontario corporations, non-profit corporations and Extra-Provincial Foreign corporations have the option of filing their CIA AR electronically with the Service Providers under contract with the Ontario government, instead of with the Canada Revenue Agency.

Note: During a 'transition period' from January 1, 2009 until September 30, 2009, the Ontario Ministry of Revenue (MOR) continues to process the integrated Corporations Information Act Annual Return for corporations with tax years ending before January 1, 2009. ***In order to be processed by the Ontario Ministry of Revenue, your Corporations Information Act Annual Return must be received at the Ontario Ministry of Revenue by September 30, 2009.*** As of October 1, 2009, it will no longer be possible to file the *Corporations Information Act* Annual Return with MOR. Ontario business and notfor- profit corporations may file a standalone Corporations Information Act Annual Return with the Ontario government Service Providers.

CIA AR Filing Dates

Ontario business and foreign corporations are required to file their CIA AR within six months after the end of their tax year-end.

Ontario non-profit corporations are required to file their CIA AR within six (6) months after the end of their tax/fiscal year-end. Previously, (for tax year ends prior to January 1, 2009), the CIA AR was filed within 60 days of the anniversary of incorporation or amalgamation.

CIA AR Forms

The CIA AR schedules and worksheets are available through the Canada Revenue Agency at: *www.cra-arc.gc.ca*, under Forms and Publications.

CIA AR Enquiry Telephone Number Changes

The CRA handles general enquiries about the CIA AR, including those related to tax years ending on or before December 31, 2008. Following are the CIA AR enquiry telephone numbers:

Type of Enquiry	Telephone Number
Enquiries for T2/CIA AR, including prior year CIA AR filings	1-800-959-5525 (English) 1-800-959-7775 (French) 1-800-665-0354 (TTY)
Charities enquiries including the CIA AR	1-800-267-2384 (English) 1-888-892-5667 (French) 1-800-665-0354 (TTY)

More information about the Single Administration initiative is available at:

Canada Revenue Agency *www.cra-arc.gc.ca*
Ontario Ministry of Revenue *www.ontario.ca/revenue*
ServiceOntario *www.Ontario.ca*

[G-7] — *Corporations Information Act* Annual Return Questions & Answers*

Date: April 1, 2010

Q1: Why is a corporation required to file a *Corporations Information Act* Annual Return?

A1: The *Corporations Information Act* Annual Return is a mandatory filing requirement that helps to ensure the corporation's information is up to date on the corporate Public Record.

Q2. What types of Corporations are required to file a *Corporations Information Act* Annual Return?

A2. Per Subsection 6(2) of *Ontario Regulation 182* made under the *Corporations Information Act*, the following types of corporations are required to file a *Corporations Information Act* Annual Return:

1. Corporations subject to the *Business Corporations Act* (BCA)
2. Corporations subject to the *Corporations Act* (CA)
3. Foreign corporations with a licence endorsed under the *Extra-Provincial Corporations Act* (EPCA)

Q3. Is there a fee for filing a *Corporations Information Act* Annual Return?

A3. No, there is currently no fee for filing a *Corporations Information Act* Annual Return.

Q4. What are the filing requirements for Ontario business corporations?

A4. For tax years ending **after December 31, 2008,** you are required to file a Schedule 546, *Corporations Information Act* Annual Return for Ontario Corporations, with the Canada Revenue Agency, together with your T2 Corporation Income Tax return. This return must be filed within six months after the end of each tax year.

 For the most recent version of this form, please visit: http://www.gov.on.ca/ontprodconsume/groups/content/@onca/@bundles/@cppsb/documents/document/stel02_168012.pdf

You continue to have the option of filing a standalone *Corporations Information Act* Annual Return electronically with the Service Providers under contract with the Ontario government.

Q5. What are the filing requirements for non-profit corporations?

A5. Non-registered Charities (federal *Income Tax Act*) — If you have a not-for-profit corporation which ***is not*** a charity registered under the federal *Income Tax Act*, for tax years ending after December 31, 2008, you are required to file a Schedule 546, *Corporations Information Act* Annual Return for Ontario Corporations, with the Canada Revenue Agency, together with your T2 Corporation Income Tax return. This return must be filed within six months after the end of each tax year.

Registered Charities (federal *Income Tax Act*) — If you have a not-for-profit corporation which *is* a charity registered under the federal *Income Tax Act*, for tax years ending after December 31, 2008, you are required to file a *Corporations Information Act* Annual Return using either the Charities RC232WS — Director/Officer Worksheet and Ontario *Corporations Information Act* Annual Return, or the Charities RC232 — Ontario *Corporations Information Act* Annual Return Worksheet in combination with the T1235, Director/Trustees and Like Officials Worksheet. The appropriate worksheet(s) must be submitted along with the T3010 Registered Charity Information Return.

This return must be filed within six months after the end of each tax year. In the past, for anniversary dates prior to January 1, 2009, *Corporations Information Act* Annual Returns for all not-for-profit corporations were filed within 60 days of the anniversary of the incorporation or amalgamation.

You continue to have the option to file a standalone *Corporations Information Act* Annual Return electronically with the Service Providers under contract with the Ontario government.

Q6. I didn't receive a turnaround document from the Canada Revenue Agency. How do I file?

A6. If you are a not-for-profit corporation but **not** a charity registered under the federal *Income Tax Act*, there is no longer a turnaround document provided to you. You are required to file Schedule 546. For details, refer to **A5**. above.

If you **are** a charity registered under the federal *Income Tax Act* and you didn't receive a turnaround document, you are required to file the RC232, in combination with the T1235 worksheet. For details, refer to **A5**. above).

Q7. What are the filing requirements for Extra-Provincial Foreign corporations?

A7. For tax years ending **after December 31, 2008,** you are required to file a Schedule 548, *Corporations Information Act* Annual Return for Foreign Business Corporations, with the Canada Revenue Agency, together with the T2 Corporation Income Tax return. This return must be filed within six months after the end of each tax year.

Q8. For what date should I report my information on my *Corporations Information Act* Annual Return?

A8. The information on your *Corporations Information Act* Annual Return must always be the current information as of the date of delivery to the Minister responsible for the administration of the *Corporations Information Act* or the Canada Revenue Agency, in accordance with the regulations under the *Corporations Information Act*.

Q9. What if after January 1, 2009, my corporation has to file a *Corporations Information Act* Annual Return for a year prior to 2009?

A9. Ontario business corporations are required to file their Corporations Information Act Annual Return electronically with the Service Providers under contract with the Ontario government ***for tax years ending before January 1, 2009***.

Ontario not-for-profit corporations are required to file their Corporations Information Act Annual Return electronically with the Service Providers under contract with the Ontario government ***for incorporation or amalgamation anniversary dates before January 1, 2009***.

Note: Ontario business and not-for-profit corporations may file a standalone Corporations Information Act Annual Return with the Ontario government Service Providers.

Q10. My corporation does not have taxable income in Ontario. Am I still required to file a *Corporations Information Act* Annual Return?

A10. Yes. In the absence of Ontario taxable income, a corporation must file a *Corporations Information Act* Annual Return each year as required under the *Corporations Information Act*. The information on the *Corporations Information Act* Annual Return is required to be filed under the Act, regardless of any requirements under federal and Ontario corporate income tax acts.

For tax years ending AFTER December 31, 2008: Business corporations are required to file their *Corporations Information Act* Annual Return with the Canada Revenue Agency, together with their T2 Corporation Income Tax return for each tax year, whether or not the corporation has taxable income in Ontario. Ontario business and not-for-profit corporations have the option to file a standalone *Corporations Information Act* Annual Return through the Service Providers under contract with the Ontario government.

Q11. If my corporation is dissolved, am I required to file a *Corporations Information Act* Annual Return?

A11. No. If a corporation is dissolved or has been cancelled, filing transactions updating the corporate record cannot be accepted.

Q12. Are there any fines or penalties associated with non-compliance of the *Corporations Information Act* Annual Return?

A12. Corporations that fail to file a *Corporations Information Act* Annual Return are subject to cancellation. Also, a corporation that is in default of a requirement to file a return or notice under the Act is not capable of maintaining a proceeding in an Ontario court in respect of the corporation's business except with leave of the court.

Q13. How is the term senior officer defined?

A13. The term senior officer is defined in the *BCA* as (a) the chair of the board of the directors, a vice-chair of the board of directors, the president, a vice-president, the secretary, the treasurer or the general manager of a corporation or any other individual who performs functions for a corporation similar to those normally performed by an individual occupying any such office, and (b) each of the five highest paid employees of the corporation including any individual referred to in clause (a).

Q14. My corporation has amalgamated. Am I still required to file a *Corporations Information Act* Annual Return for the pre-amalgamated corporations?

A14. The original amalgamating corporations that have since amalgamated and continued as one amalgamated corporation are **NOT** required to file a *Corporations Information Act* Annual Return. Filing transactions updating the corporate record cannot be accepted for these corporations. The corporation resulting from the amalgamation is required to file a *Corporations Information Act* Annual Return at the appropriate time.

Q15. If my corporation is in receivership, am I still required to file the *Corporations Information Act* Annual Return?

A15. A corporation in receivership remains subject to the legal requirement to file a *Corporations Information Act* Annual Return. However, if it is a court-ordered receiver, the Central Production and Verification Services Branch should be provided with a copy of the court order to determine whether it 4 of 6 contains provisions that could affect the initiation of enforcement proceedings by the Central Production and Verification Services Branch.

Q16. My corporation has just declared bankruptcy. Do I need to file the *Corporations Information Act* Annual Return?

A16. The Central Production and Verification Services Branch should be notified if a corporation is subject to the federal *Bankruptcy and Insolvency Act*. While a corporation in bankruptcy remains subject to the legal requirement to file a *Corporations Information Act* Annual Return, the Central Production and Verification Services Branch refrains from initiating enforcement proceedings involving the corporation until the bankruptcy is discharged or a court orders otherwise.

Q17. How can I obtain a current list of current administrators on file for my corporation?

A17. You can obtain a list of current administrators by purchasing a *Corporation Profile Report*. A Corporation Profile Report displays current information on the Public Record for a corporation. All active directors and officers are listed. Some historical information, such as amalgamating corporations, where the corporation is an amalgamation, and name history, is also included in the report. The Corporation Profile Report can be obtained electronically, in person, or by mail as described below.

Electronic Service

A Corporation Profile Report can be ordered via one of the three Service Providers under contract with the Ontario government. **Note:** The Service Providers levy a service charge for the online services they provide. As their rates are competitive, clients should check with each one before choosing a Service Provider. Once a report has been ordered via a Service Provider, the results are immediate. For a list of Service Providers, visit: *www.Ontario.ca*.

Staff Assisted

In Person at the Public Office

A Corporation Profile Report may be ordered in person at the ServiceOntario Public Office in Toronto between 8:30 a.m. and 5:00 p.m., Monday to Friday (excluding statutory and government holidays). The Public Office is located at: 375 University Avenue on the second floor. Search results are immediate.

By Mail

A Corporation Profile Report can also be ordered via mail from ServiceOntario at 393 University Avenue, Suite 200, Toronto, Ontario M5G 2M2. Allow four to six weeks for processing.

Cost of the Corporation Profile Report

For information on the cost of the Corporation Profile Report, please refer to the Companies Service Standards and Fees document at: *www.Ontario.ca.*

Q18. My *Corporations Information Act* Annual Return Correction Request shows duplications in officers/directors and some administrators who should not be there. How do I remove these duplications or administrators who should not be there?

A18. You may remove any duplicated and additional administrators once you have determined that they should not be shown on the Public Record or that they were erroneously reported.

You can remove each administrator that was either duplicated or erroneously reported by indicating a **Date Ceased** equal to the **Date Appointed/Elected** for each administrator you have determined should not be displayed on the Public Record. This in effect cancels out the administrator and the positions held by that administrator. However, previous records for that corporation will still reflect the administrators that were ceased.

Q19. I have an Ontario corporation. Can I file my *Corporations Information Act* Annual Return and make corrections to it electronically?

A19. Yes. Ontario business and non-profit corporations, will continue to be able to file and make corrections to the *Corporations Information Act* Annual Return electronically through the Service Providers under contract with the Ontario government.

Q20. How do I obtain a replacement *Corporations Information Act* Annual Return?

A20. For tax years ending **after December 31, 2008**, corporations can file an integrated federal/provincial tax return and *Corporations Information Act* Annual Return with the Canada Revenue Agency. These forms are available from the Canada Revenue Agency.

Ontario corporations can also file a standalone *Corporations Information Act* Annual Return electronically through one of the Service Providers under contract with the Ontario government. For a list of Service Providers, visit: *www.Ontario.ca.*

Q21. Can an Extra-Provincial Foreign corporation file a *Corporations Information Act* Annual Return electronically through one of the Service Providers?

A21. Yes. Effective March 31, 2010, the Service Providers under contract with the Ontario government began offering electronic filing of the Corporations Information Act Annual Return Form 2, which provides for Extra-Provincial Foreign Corporations with the same service option provided to Ontario corporations.

Q22. Can I file a standalone *Corporations Information Act* Annual Return with the Canada Revenue Agency?

A22. No. The *Corporations Information Act* Annual Return must be filed with the Canada Revenue Agency, together with your T2 Corporation Income Tax Return or your T3010 Registered Charity Information Return. The Canada Revenue Agency will not accept a standalone *Corporations Information Act* Annual Return.

If you have an Ontario business or non-profit corporation, you can file a standalone *Corporations Information Act* Annual Return through the Service Providers under contract with the Ontario government and pay the applicable service charge.

Q23. Who do I contact if I have any questions regarding the completion of the *Corporations Information Act* Annual Return?

A23. The Canada Revenue Agency handles all general enquiries, those pertaining to filings for tax year-ends before January 1, 2009.

The Canada Revenue Agency helpline numbers are:

Type of Enquiry	Telephone Number
Enquiries for T2/CIA AR, including prior year CIA AR filings	1-800-959-5525 (English) 1-800-959-7775 (French) 1-800-665-0354 (TTY)
Charities enquiries including the CIA AR	1-800-267-2384 (English) 1-888-892-5667 (French) 1-800-665-0354 (TTY)

[G-8] — Guide to the Corporation Document List*

Date: **April 1, 2010**

General Information

The Corporation Document List identifies all documents filed since June 27, 1992, by an Ontario corporation or an Extra-provincial corporation carrying on business in Ontario. It is based on information that has been filed by the corporation and stored in ONBIS (Ontario Business Information System), Ontario's Public Record of corporate information. The Corporation Document List displays documents recorded on the Public Record for the subject corporation as of the date the report was ordered.

Please note that with the exception of documents filed under the *Corporations Information Act*, which are effective when they are entered in the Public Record, documents are effective as of the date of receipt of the required documents by the Central Production and Verification Services Branch (CPVSB). For example, Articles of Amendment received in the CPVSB mailroom on July 3rd and later reviewed and found to be complete, will be recorded with an effective date of July 3rd but may not be entered on the Public Record until July 8th. Therefore, it is possible to obtain a document list on July 7th and another on July 8th for the same corporation, where the July 8th document list displays an amendment effective July 3rd that was not displayed on the July 7th document list.

Fields on the Corporation Document List

Date Report Produced (located at the top right-hand corner of each page):

year/month/day

The date the report was printed.

Time Report Produced:

hour:minute:second

The time the report was printed.

Page:

Number of the page in the report.

Ontario Corporation Number:

The unique number the Central Production and Verification Services Branch assigned to the corporation.

Corporation Name:

The name of the corporation on the date the report was produced.

"ACT/CODE", "DESCRIPTION", "FORM" AND "DATE":

All of the documents that have been filed for the corporation will be listed under the headings, for example:

ACT/CODE	DESCRIPTION	FORM	DATE	
CIA	ANNUAL RETURN 2005 PAF: ROBERT SMITH	1C	2005/08/11	
BCA	ARTICLES OF AMENDMENT	3	2005/01/25	
CIA	ANNUAL RETURN 2004 PAF: SALLY SMITH	1C	2004/08/01	
CIA	INITIAL RETURN PAF: SALLY SMITH	1	2003/04/02	
BCA	ARTICLES OF INCORPORATION	1	2003/03/20	(ELECTRONIC FILING)

Act/Code:

An acronym representing the name of the Act or code under which the document was filed. For example:

BCA	*Business Corporations Act*
CA	*Corporations Act*
CIA	*Corporations Information Act*
CB	Companies and Personal Property Security Branch — appears beside a memo to file (correction/update) a court order or an electronic update.
CTA	*Corporations Tax Act*
EPCA	*Extra Provincial Corporations Act*

Description:

This field shows the name of the form or provides a brief description of the document filed with the Companies and Personal Property Security Branch.

Form:

The number of the form referred to in the description field.

Date (YY/MM/DD):

The date (year/month/day) the described document was *received* by the Central Production and Verification Services Branch. Documents filed under the *Corporations Information Act* show the date the document was recorded in the ONBIS system.

Corporations Information Act Annual Returns/Person Authorizing the Filing (PAF)

For *Corporations Information Act* Annual Returns filed through the Canada Revenue Agency or the Service Providers under contract with the Ontario government on or after February 5, 2005, the return year is displayed after the words "Annual Return". The name of the Person Authorizing the Filing (PAF) will be displayed beneath the name of the specific document for all documents filed on or after June 27, 1992, under the *Corporations Information Act*.

For example:

ACT/CODE	DESCRIPTION	FORM	DATE
CIA	ANNUAL RETURN 2005 PAF: ROBERT SMITH	1C	2005/08/11

Electronic Filings

If the document was filed through an electronic process the words "(ELECTRONIC FILING)" will appear after the document date.

For example:

ACT/CODE	DESCRIPTION	FORM	DATE	
BCA	ARTICLES OF INCORPORATION	1	2006/1/20	(ELECTRONIC FILING)

Administrative updates

Federal corporations

A joint project designed to improve the accuracy of the Public Record, was initiated April 16, 2005 whereby CPPSB receives electronic updates from Industry Canada, Corporations Canada (ICCC) of dissolved/cancelled Federal corporations. Where the corporation information on the Ontario database matches that of a Federal corporation with a Head Office in Ontario, but shows the wrong status, the dissolution/cancellation information is updated electronically. The following description appears where the status for a dissolved/cancelled Federal Extra-Provincial corporation has been updated electronically:

ACT/CODE	DESCRIPTION	FORM	DATE	
CB	CERT. OF DISS. (EPD)	461RE	2006/01/23	(ELECTRONIC FILING)

New document descriptions for defaults and cancellations (Ministry of Revenue — formerly Ministry of Finance)

On May 1, 2006, the *Business Corporations Act* (BCA) was amended to allow for the dissolution of corporations that are in default of compliance under the *Employer Health Tax Act, Fuel Tax Act, Gasoline Tax Act, Land Transfer Tax Act, Retail Sales Tax Act, Tobacco Tax Act* in addition to the *Corporations Tax Act*.

If a corporation is in default of one of these statutes, the document list will display the name of the applicable Act and the date of default. The corporation has 90 days to comply with the applicable statute. If after 90 days the Ministry of Revenue (formerly Ministry of Finance) advises CPPSB that the corporation still has not complied, CPPSB will cancel the corporation under Subsection 241(4) of the *Business Corporations Act.*

The following are examples of the entries that would appear on the document list for a default and cancellation for failure to comply with the *Gasoline Tax Act.*

ACT/CODE	DESCRIPTION	FORM	DATE
GTA	DEF. GASOLINE TAX ACT	GT	2006/02/07
BCAC	CANCELLED REQUEST GT	241/4	2006/05/20

[G-9] — Guide to the Corporation Profile Report*

Date: January 1, 2009

General Information

The Corporation Profile Report (CPR) contains information on Ontario corporations or Extra-Provincial corporations carrying on business in Ontario. It is based on information that has been filed by the corporation and stored on the Ontario Business Information System (ONBIS). The Corporation Profile Report displays information on the Public Record for the subject corporation as of the date the report was ordered. For Ontario corporations, all active directors and officers of the subject corporation are listed. Some historical information such as amalgamating corporations, where the subject corporation is the result of an amalgamation, and name history are included in the Corporation Profile Report. Extra-provincial corporations are only required to file fundamental information such as the head/registered office of the corporation. If your require information about the officers and directors of an Extra-Provincial corporation, you must contact the jurisdiction where the corporation is incorporated.

Explanation of "Not Applicable" and "Not Available"

Please note that there is a distinction between fields that are "Not Applicable" and those for which information is "Not Available".

"Not Applicable" is used when:

- A field does not apply because of corporation type.

"Not Available" is used when:

- The corporation has failed to report the required information since June 27, 1992.
- The data may have been reported prior to June 27, 1992, and exists on the corporation's microfiche record, but it has not been converted to ONBIS.
- For Mailing Address, corporation has selected the 'Show no mailing address on the public record' box when filing their *Corporations Information Act* Annual Return.
- For Address of Principal Office in Ontario, corporation has selected the 'Show no address of principal office on the public record' box when filing their *Corporations Information Act* Annual Return.

Fields on the Corporation Profile Report

Date Report Produced (located at the top right-hand corner of each page):

year/month/day

The date the report was printed.

Time Report Produced:

hour:minute:second

The time the report was printed.

Page:

Number of the page in the report.

Ontario Corp Number:

The unique number the Companies and Personal Property Security Branch assigned to the corporation.

Corporation Name:

The current name of the corporation.

The Ontario Corp Number and Name are repeated at the top of each page of the report.

Corporation Type:

The different corporation types are:

Ontario

Description on Corporation Profile Report

- ONTARIO BUSINESS CORP.
- ONTARIO CORP NON-SHARE
- CREDIT UNION
- INSURER
- SOCIAL CLUB WITH SHARE
- SOCIAL CLUB NON-SHARE
- CO-OP NON-SHARE
- CO-OP WITH SHARE
- LOAN AND TRUST CORP

Extra-Provincial (E.P.)

Description on Corporation Profile Report

- EP FOREIGN WITH SHARE
- EP FOREIGN NON-SHARE
- FEDERAL CORP WITH SHARE
- FEDERAL CORP NON-SHARE

- EP DOMESTIC NON-SHARE
- EP DOMESTIC WITH SHARE
- EP FOREIGN INSURER

Other (Exempt from filing under the* Corporations Information Act*)

Description on Corporation Profile Report

CONDOMINIUM CORPORATION

AGENCIES, BOARDS, COMMS

NON-FILERS

- *The Corporation Profile Report is available for these corporation types. Please note Extra-Provincial corporations are only required to file fundamental information with the Companies and Personal Property Security Branch. For detailed information, contact the incorporating jurisdiction.*

Corporation Status:

The different status descriptions are:

Active

Description on Corporation Profile Report	**Particulars**
ACTIVE	Active
CANCELLATION PROCESS — O.S.C.	In default — *Securities Act*
CANCELLATION PROCESS — C.T.	In default — *Corporations Tax Act*
CANCELLATION PROCESS — C. B.	In default — *Corporations Information Act*
DEFAULT PROCESS — MOF	In default — Ministry of Revenue (formerly Ministry of Finance) — tax statute
CONTINUED IN ONTARIO	Transferred to Ontario from another jurisdiction

Inactive

Description on Corporation Profile Report	**Particulars**
CANC BY O.S.C.	Cancelled for failure to comply with the Ontario *Securities Act*
CANC. BY C.T.	Cancelled for failure to comply with the *Corporations Tax Act*
CANC. BY COMPANIES BRANCH	Cancelled for default — *s. 241 BCA or s. 317(9) CA*
VOLUNTARY DISSOLUTION	Corporation was voluntarily dissolved
TERMINATION OF EPL	Extra-Provincial — No longer operating in Ontario
AMALGAMATED	Amalgamated with one or more corporations

Description on Corporation Profile Report	Particulars
EP DOM CORP CEASED	EP Domestic — no longer operating in Ontario
DISSOLVING CO-OP	Corp. dissolved — *Co-operative Corporations Act*
CANC FOR CAUSE	Canc. — *s. 240 BCA or 317(1) CA* need special act to revive
CANC. BY MOF	Failure to comply with MOR (formerly MOF) tax statute
VOLUNTARY WINDING UP	Winding up (liquidator)
DISSOLVING CREDIT UNIONS	Dissolved — *Credit Unions and Caisses Populaires Act*
FINAL REMOVAL *NOT ONTARIO	Extra-Provincial Corp. — has dissolved

Abbreviation Legend

BCA	— *Business Corporations Act*
O.S.C.	— Ontario Securities Commission
CA	— *Corporations Act*
CIA	— *Corporations Information Act*
C.T.	— Corporations Tax Branch
C.B. or CPPSB	— Companies and Personal Property Security Branch
E.P.	— Extra-provincial
MOF	— Ministry of Finance (now Ministry of Revenue)

EP Domestic, Federal and EP Foreign corporations will show "Refer to Jurisdiction" in this field. Co-operatives, Loan and Trust companies and Credit Unions will show "Refer to the Ministry of Finance".

Head Office/Registered Office Address:

Physical address of the corporation's Head Office/Registered Office.

Mailing Address:

The corporation's mailing address, or for Extra-Provincial corporations, the Principal Place of Business in Ontario.

Activity Classification:

This description identifies the type of business being carried on (e.g. Fishing/Trapping Industries, Manufacturing Industries, etc.). A corporation may have more than one description. Effective January 1, 1999, the Companies and Personal Property Security Branch no longer requires corporations to submit this information so it is likely that "Not Available" will show in this field.

Incorporation Date/Amalgamation Date:

year/month/day

The date the corporation came into existence. If the corporation came into existence as the result of an amalgamation of two or more other corporations, the field "Incorporation Date" will be replaced with "Amalgamation Date".

Jurisdiction:

The current jurisdiction governing the operation of the corporation.

Former Jurisdiction:

This field sets out the former jurisdiction governing the operation of the corporation.

Date Amalgamated:

year/month/day

If a corporation is no longer active because it amalgamated with another corporation or corporations, the date amalgamated will appear in this field and the Corporation Status field will read "Amalgamated".

Amalgamation Ind.:

If the corporation came into existence as a result of the amalgamation of two or more other corporations, "A" will appear in this field.

New Amal. Number:

If the status of the subject corporation is "Amalgamated" the Ontario Corporation Number of the new corporation formed by the amalgamation will appear under this field.

Notice Date:

year/month/day

A date in this field indicates the publication date in the Ontario Gazette of a Notice of Default, Notice of Intention to Dissolve, or Notice of Opportunity to be Heard, issued by the Companies and Personal Property Security Branch for failure to file a Special Notice or *Corporations Information Act* Annual Return (1992-1995).

Letter Date:

year/month/day

A date in this field indicates that compliance activity is in process by the Ministry of Revenue (formerly Ministry of Finance), which may result in the cancellation of the corporation. The date refers to the publication date in the Ontario Gazette of a Notice of Default in complying with the *Corporations Tax Act, Employer Health Tax Act, Fuel Tax Act, Gasoline Tax Act, Land Transfer Tax Act, Retail Sales Tax Act or Tobacco Tax Act*. If the corporation complies or if the status of the corporation changes to active or cancelled, the letter date will no longer be displayed.

Revival Date:

year/month/day

The corporation was inactive and has been revived on this date.

Continuation Date:

year/month/day

The date a corporation continued under the laws of Ontario, having transferred from another jurisdiction.

Transferred Out Date:

year/month/day

The date a corporation ceased to be subject to the laws of Ontario, and became subject to the laws of another jurisdiction.

Cancel/Inactive Date:

year/month/day

The date the corporation became inactive. Please refer to "Corporation Status" for further information.

EP Licence Eff. Date:

year/month/day

The date the Ontario extra-provincial licence became effective. Refers to an EP corporation originating in a jurisdiction outside Canada.

EP Licence Term. Date:

year/month/day

The date the Ontario Extra-Provincial licence was terminated. Refers to an EP corporation originating in a jurisdiction outside Canada.

Number of Directors (Minimum/Maximum):

The minimum and maximum number of directors the corporation may have. This field displays for Ontario business corporations only. If there is no data on ONBIS as to the minimum or maximum number of directors, the fields will display "Unknown".

Date Commenced in Ontario:

year/month/day

The date an Extra-Provincial corporation commenced carrying on business in Ontario.

Date Ceased in Ontario:

year/month/day

TThe date an Extra-Provincial corporation ceased carrying on business in Ontario.

Corporate Name History:

This field displays all the former names of the subject corporation, as well as the current corporation name for Ontario corporations only. If the corporation is an Extra-Provincial corporation, a message "Refer to Jurisdiction" will be displayed.

Effective Date:

year/month/day

The date that the corresponding name, of the subject corporation, in the Corporation Name History field became effective. This field will display for Ontario corporations only. If the effective date of the name change was prior to June 27, 1992, or in cases where the effective date has not yet been recorded to ONBIS, the words "Refer to Microfiche" will be displayed.

Current Business Name(s) Exist:

yes/no

This field will indicate whether any business name(s) registered in the past five years exist for the subject corporation. If current business name(s) exist, a message "Yes" will be displayed. To obtain more information, a business name search is required.

Expired Business Name(s) Exist:

This field will indicate whether any expired business name(s) exist for the subject corporation. If expired business name(s) exist, a message "YES — Search Required for details" will be displayed. To obtain an expired business name search, contact the Companies and Personal Property Security Branch.

Amalgamating Corporations:

This section will only display if the corporation came into existence as a result of an amalgamation. If amalgamation details are "Not Available", the Companies and Personal Property Security Branch corporate microfiche records will contain amalgamation information for Ontario business and non-profit corporations as well as insurers and social clubs. For other corporation types, clients should contact either the Ontario Ministry of Revenue (formerly Ministry of Finance) or the home jurisdiction.

Corporation Name: **Corporation Number**:

The name and corporate number of the corporations that amalgamated to form the subject corporation of the Corporation Profile Report.

Current Administrator Information:

If a corporation has not reported any administrators since June 27, 1992 or has ceased all administrators, this section of the Corporation Profile Report will not display.

Administrator Name (Individual/Corporation):

If the administrator is an individual, then his/her name (First Name, Middle Name or Initials, Surname) is set out. If the administrator is a corporation, then the full corporation name is set out.

Address:

If an individual, the full address for service is set out. If a corporation, the registered or head office address is set out.

Date Began:

year/month/day

The date on which the individual became a director or an officer.

First Director:

First Directors are the initial directors of a corporation. These individuals have special legislated responsibilities with respect to their participation on the Board of Directors of a corporation. An indicator (Yes) will identify those administrators who are first directors. This field will be "not applicable" if the corporation has filed a notice or return setting out changes to the directors.

Designation:

The designation of the administrator as an officer, director, agent for service or an officer/manager in Ontario.

Officer Type:

If an individual is an officer of the corporation, then the specific title is set out. This title will be one of the following: President, Secretary, Treasurer, General Manager, Chair, Chair Person, Chairman, Chairwoman, Vice-Chair, Vice-President, Assistant Secretary, Assistant Treasurer, Chief Manager, Executive Director, Managing Director, Chief Executive Officer, Chief Financial Officer, Chief Information Officer, Chief Operating Officer, Chief Administrative Officer, Comptroller, Authorized Signing Officer, or Other (untitled).

Agent for Service — Corporation Number:

This field will display when a corporation has been designated as an Agent for Service. That corporation's Ontario Corporation Number will show in this field.

Resident Canadian:

A 'Y' in this field indicates that the individual is a Resident Canadian. This field only applies to Ontario business corporations.

Last Document Recorded:

The name of the last document recorded on ONBIS (generally filed by the corporation) in the same format as that used in the Corporation Document List. (i.e. from left to right — Act/Code, Description, Form, Date (year/month/day)).

- Electronic Filing — If a document was filed electronically, the words "Electronic Filing" will be displayed beside the date.
- Administrative Update — Effective April 23, 2005, CPPSB receives electronic updates from Industry Canada, Corporations Canada of dissolved/cancelled federal corporations and compares the update to Federal corporations recorded on the Ontario public record with a head/registered office in Ontario. If the Ontario database shows an active status for a Federal corporation that has been dissolved/cancelled the status is updated electronically. In this case the last document for a Federal Extra-Provincial corporation would have the description, "Cert. Of Diss. (EPD)" and the words "(Admin. Update)" would be set out after the date of entry.
- *Corporations Information Act* Annual Return — For *Corporations Information Act* Annual Returns filed through the Canada Revenue Agency, the Ontario Ministry of Revenue (formerly Ministry of Finance), or through the Service Providers on or after February 5, 2005, the return year is displayed after the words, "Annual Return".
- Changes to the *Business Corporations Act* (BCA) effective May 1, 2006, provide for the dissolution of corporations that are in default of compliance under six Ontario Ministry of Revenue (formerly Ministry of Finance) tax statutes in addition to the *Corporations Tax Act*. These statutes are the *Employer Health Tax Act, Fuel Tax Act, Gasoline Tax Act, Land Transfer Tax Act, Retail Sales Tax Act and Tobacco Tax Act*. As a result of these changes, there are six new default document descriptions and six new cancellation document descriptions. The default descriptions will set out "default" and then the Act (i.e. Default *Fuel Tax Act*) and the cancellation description would have the words "Cancelled Request" and the initials of the applicable Act. For example, if cancelled under the *Fuel Tax Act*, the description would be "Cancelled Request FT".

Explanatory Note Re: Amalgamation

In an amalgamation, two or more corporations (A & B) amalgamate to create another corporation (C).

Corporations A & B will have entries in several fields of its Corporation Profile Report as follows:

i) **Date Amalgamated**:

This is the date that the two or more corporations (A & B) were amalgamated to create corporation (C). This date will be set out in the Corporation Profile Report of both A & B corporations, and their Cancel/Inactive Dates will display "Not Applicable". The

Date Amalgamated field will be "Not Applicable" on corporation C's Corporation Profile Report.

ii) **Corporation Status**:

This field in the Corporation Profile Reports of both A & B corporations will show "Amalgamated" as their status.

iii) **New Amal. Number**:

This is the new Ontario Corporation Number of corporation C, into which corporations A & B amalgamated, and will show on the Corporation Profile Reports for both A & B.

iv) **Incorporation Date**:

The date of incorporation of corporations A & B will be set out on the Corporation Profile Reports unless either one or both came into existence as a result of amalgamation in which case the date of amalgamation will be set out and the field name will change to "Amalgamation Date".

Corporation C will have entries in several fields of its Corporation Profile Report as follows:

i) **Amalgamation Date**:

The date that corporation C was created by amalgamation. In this case, the "Amalgamation Date" replaces "Incorporation Date" on the Corporation Profile Report for corporation C.

ii) **Corporation Status**:

The corporation status of corporation C will be "Active".

iii) **Amalgamation Ind.**:

Since corporation C came about as the result of the amalgamation of two or more corporations, the indicator "A" for amalgamation will appear in this field.

Explanatory Note Re: Extra Provincial Corporations

Corporations incorporated under the laws of a jurisdiction other than Ontario are referred to as "Extra-Provincial" (E.P.) corporations.

There are two kinds of Extra-Provincial (E.P.) corporations:

Domestic: A corporation incorporated or continued federally, or under the laws of any other Canadian jurisdiction outside of Ontario. "Date Commenced in Ontario" and "Date Ceased in Ontario" fields apply.

Foreign: A corporation incorporated or continued under the laws of a jurisdiction outside of Canada. The "EP Licence Eff. Date" and "EP Licence Term. Date" fields apply to foreign business corporations. For foreign not-for-profit and business corporations the "Date Commenced In Ontario" and "Date Ceased In Ontario" fields will be displayed if the corporation reported that information on any filing under the *Corporations Information Act*.

[G-10] — Guide to the Corporation Point-In-Time Report*

Date: **January 1, 2009**

General Information

The Corporation Point-in-Time Report is only available for Ontario corporations. It displays information on the Public Record for the subject corporation as of a specific date requested by the applicant ("As of Date"). It is based on information filed by the corporation and recorded in the Ontario Business Information System (ONBIS), since June 27, 1992 when the system was established. All active directors and officers on the "As of Date" will be listed. In addition if the "As of Date" is the same as the filing date of a notice or return it will display information concerning any director or officer that was reported as ceased on that particular notice or return.

To find out which document reported that a director or officer had ceased in a particular position, the applicant should first order a "Document List". The Document List sets out all the documents the corporation has filed since June 27, 1992 and the date of filing. The Applicant should request an "As of Date" the same as the filing date of the document they wish to view. All active directors and officers as of the date specified will be listed and any directors and officers reported as ceased on document(s) filed on the "As of Date".

The ONBIS system will carry forward information concerning a director or officer unless that position is ceased. That means that a director reported on a return filed February 1, 1999 but not included on returns filed in 2000 and 2001, will still appear as an active director on a Corporation Point-in-Time report issued in 2002.

Basic Rules

1. A Corporation Point-in-Time Report is available for a corporation whose jurisdiction was Ontario as of the date of the Corporation Point-In-Time Report.

2. Corporation Point-in-Time Reports cannot be produced against a corporation with an "As of Date" prior to ONBIS' corporate conversion date of June 27, 1992. If a client requests a Corporation Point-in-Time Report with an "As of Date" prior to the conversion date, ONBIS will automatically reset the "As of Date" to June 27, 1992.

3. Corporation Point-in-Time Reports cannot be produced against a corporation with an "As of Date" prior to the effective date of the first document filed for the corporation. If a client requests a Corporation Point-in-Time Report with an "As of Date" prior to the date of the first document filed for the corporation, a Statement of No Record will be generated instead of a Corporation Point-in-Time Report.

4. Corporation Point-in-Time Reports cannot be produced against a corporation with an "As of Date" greater than the current date.

5. Where there are multiple filings on the same date, the Corporation Point-in-Time Report as of that date will be a composite of the multiple filings and the existing information on ONBIS for the corporation.

6. If the "As of Date" requested matches the date on which a *Corporations Information Act* Annual Return, Initial Return or Notice of Change (Notice) was filed, the Corporation Point-in-Time Report will display all of the active administrators, as well as the administrators

---

 For the most recent version of this form, please visit: http://www.gov.on.ca/ontprodconsume/groups/content/@onca/@bundles/@cppsb/documents/document/stel02_168170.pdf

who were reported as ceased on the *Corporations Information Act* Annual Return, Initial Return or Notice filed on the "As of Date" of the Corporation Point-in-Time Report. But when the "As of Date" is not the same as the date on which a Return or Notice was filed, the Corporation Point-in-Time Report will display only the active administrators.

Format

The Corporation Point-in-Time Report follows the same format as the Corporation Profile Report with some modifications, the explanations for which are bolded and italicized in this guide.

Explanation of "Not Applicable" and "Not Available"

Please note that there is a distinction between fields that are "Not Applicable" and those for which information is "Not Available".

"Not Applicable" is used when:

- A field does not apply because of corporation type or because there has been no change to the information since June 27, 1992 (date of conversion to ONBIS).

"Not Available" is used when:

- The corporation has failed to report the required information since June 27, 1992.
- The data was reported prior to June 27, 1992, and exists on the corporation's microfiche record, but it has not been converted to ONBIS.
- For Mailing Address, corporation has selected the 'Show no mailing address on the public record' box when filing their *Corporations Information Act* Annual Return.
- For Address of Principal Office in Ontario, corporation has selected the 'Show no address of principal office on the public record' box when filing their *Corporations Information Act* Annual Return.

Fields on the Corporation Point-in-Time Report

Date Report Produced (located at the top right-hand corner of each page):

year/month/day

The date the report was printed.

Time Report Produced:

hour:minute:second

The time the report was printed.

Page:

Number of the page in the report.

As of Date:

The "As of Date" field is positioned to the right side of the report, on the same line as the title. The information set out on the Corporation Point-in-Time Report reflects information about the corporation as of the date displayed in this field. The "As of Date" is repeated at the top of each page of the report.

Ontario Corp Number:

The number the Companies and Personal Property Security Branch assigned to the corporation.

Corporation Name:

The current name of the corporation.

The Ontario Corp Number and Name are repeated at the top of each page of the report.

Corporation Type:

Describes the types of corporations. The various corporation descriptions are set out below:

Ontario

Description on Point-in-Time Report

- ONTARIO BUSINESS CORP.
- ONTARIO CORP. NON-SHARE
- CREDIT UNION
- INSURER
- SOCIAL CLUB WITH SHARE
- SOCIAL CLUB NON-SHARE
- CO-OP NON-SHARE
- CO-OP WITH SHARE
- LOAN AND TRUST CORP

Extra-Provincial (E.P.)

Description on Point-in-Time Report

EP FOREIGN WITH SHARE
EP FOREIGN NON-SHARE
FEDERAL CORP WITH SHARE
FEDERAL CORP NON-SHARE
EP DOMESTIC NON-SHARE
EP DOMESTIC WITH SHARE
EP FOREIGN INSURER

Other (Exempt from filing under the Corporations Information Act*)*

Description on Point-in-Time Report

CONDOMINIUM CORPORATION
AGENCIES, BOARDS, COMMS
NON-FILERS

- **Corporation Point-in-Time Report available for these Ontario corporation types**.

Corporation Status:

The different corporation status descriptions are:

Active

Description on Corporation Point-in-Time Report	Particulars
ACTIVE	Active
CANCELLATION PROCESS — O.S.C.	In default — *Securities Act*
CANCELLATION PROCESS — C.T.	In default — *Corporations Tax Act*
CANCELLATION PROCESS — C. B.	In default — *Corporations Information Act*
DEFAULT PROCESS — MOF	In default — Ministry of Revenue (formerly Ministry of Finance) — tax statute
CONTINUED IN ONTARIO	Transferred to Ontario from another jurisdiction

Inactive

Description on Corporation Point-in-Time Report	Particulars
CANC BY O.S.C.	Cancelled for failure to comply with the *Ontario Securities Act*
CANC. BY C.T.	Cancelled for failure to comply with the *Corporations Tax Act*
CANC.BY COMPANIES BRANCH	Cancelled for default — *s. 241 BCA or s. 317(9) CA*
VOLUNTARY DISSOLUTION	Corporation has voluntarily dissolved
TERMINATION OF EPL	Extra-Provincial — No longer operating in Ontario
AMALGAMATED	Amalgamated with one or more corporations
EP DOM CORP CEASED	EP Domestic — no longer operating in Ont.
DISSOLVING CO-OP	Corp. dissolved — *Co-operative Corporations Act*
CANC FOR CAUSE	Cancelled — *s. 240 BCA or 317(1) CA* — need special act to revive
CANC. BY MOF	Cancelled for failure to comply with MOR (formerly MOF) tax statute
VOLUNTARY WINDING UP	Winding up (liquidator)
DISSOLVING CREDIT UNIONS	Dissolved. — *Credit Unions and Caisses Populaires Act*
FINAL REMOVAL *NOT ONTARIO	Extra-Provincial Corp — has dissolved

Abbreviation Legend

BCA	— *Business Corporations Act*
O.S.C.	— Ontario Securities Commission
CA	— *Corporations Act*
CIA	— *Corporations Information Act*
C.T.	— Corporations Tax Branch
C.B. or CPPSB	— Companies and Personal Property Security Branch
E.P.	— Extra-provincial
MOF	— Ministry of Finance (now Ministry of Revenue)

Head Office/Registered Office Address:

Physical address of the corporation's Head Office/Registered Office.

Mailing Address:

The corporation's mailing address.

Activity Classification:

This description identifies the type of business being carried on (e.g. Fishing/Trapping Industries, Manufacturing Industries etc.) A corporation may have more than one description. Effective January 1, 1999, the Companies and Personal Property Security Branch no longer requires corporations to submit this information so it is likely that "Not Available" will show in this field.

Incorporation Date/Amalgamation Date:

year/month/day

The date the corporation came into existence. If the corporation came into existence as the result of an amalgamation of two or more other corporations, the field "Incorporation Date" will be replaced with "Amalgamation Date".

Jurisdiction:

Ontario — Corporation Point-in-Time reports are only available for Ontario corporations.

Former Jurisdiction:

This field sets out the former jurisdiction governing the operations of the corporation.

Date Amalgamated:

year/month/day

If a corporation is no longer active as it amalgamated with another corporation or corporations, the date it amalgamated will appear in this field and the Corporation Status field will read "Amalgamated".

Amalgamation Ind.:

If the corporation came into existence as a result of the amalgamation of two or more corporations, the letter "A" will appear in this field.

New Amal. Number:

This is the Ontario Corporation Number of the new corporation formed by the amalgamation.

Notice Date:

year/month/day

A date in this field indicates the publication date in the Ontario Gazette of a Notice of Default, Notice of Intention to Dissolve, or Notice of Opportunity to be Heard, issued by the Companies and Personal Property Security Branch for failure to file a Special Notice or *Corporations Information Act* Annual Return (1992–1995).

Letter Date:

year/month/day

A date in this field indicates that compliance activity is in process by the Ministry of Revenue (formerly Ministry of Finance), which may result in the cancellation of the corporation. The date refers to the publication date in the Ontario Gazette of a Notice of Default in complying with the *Corporations Tax Act, Employer Health Tax Act, Fuel Tax Act, Gasoline Tax Act, Land Transfer Tax Act, Retail Sales Tax Act or the Tobacco Tax Act.* If the corporation complies or if the status of the corporation changes to active or cancelled, the letter date will no longer be displayed.

Revival Date:

year/month/day

The corporation was inactive and has been revived on this date.

Continuation Date:

year/month/day

The date a corporation continued under the laws of Ontario, having transferred from another jurisdiction.

Transferred Out Date:

year/month/day

The date a corporation ceased to be subject to the laws of Ontario and became subject to the laws of another jurisdiction. This will be "not applicable" as the Corporation Point-in-Time Report is only available for Ontario corporations.

Cancel/Inactive Date:

year/month/day

The date the corporation became inactive. Please refer to "Corporation Status" for further information.

EP Licence Eff. Date:

year/month/day

The date the Ontario Extra-Provincial licence became effective. Refers to an EP corporation originating in a jurisdiction outside Canada. The Corporation Point-in-Time Report is available for Ontario corporations only, therefore, this field will always display "Not Applicable".

EP Licence Term. Date:

year/month/day

The date the Ontario Extra-Provincial licence was terminated. Refers to an EP corporation originating in a jurisdiction outside Canada. The Corporation Point-in-Time Report is available for Ontario corporations only, therefore, this field will always display "Not Applicable".

Number of Directors (Minimum/Maximum):

The minimum and maximum number of directors the corporation may have. This field displays for Ontario Business Corporations only. If there is no data on ONBIS as to the minimum or maximum number of directors, the fields will display "Unknown".

Date Commenced in Ontario:

year/month/day

The date an Extra-Provincial corporation commenced carrying on business in Ontario. Refers to an EP corporation originating in a jurisdiction inside of Canada or a Federal corporation. The Corporation Point-in-Time Report is available for Ontario corporations only, therefore, this field will always display "Not Applicable".

Date Ceased in Ontario:

year/month/day

The date an Extra-Provincial corporation ceased carrying on business in Ontario. Refers to an EP corporation originating in a jurisdiction inside of Canada or a Federal corporation. The Corporation Point-in-Time Report is available for Ontario corporations only, therefore, this field will always display "Not Applicable".

Corporate Name History:

This field contains all the former names of the subject corporation as well as the corporation name as of the date of the Corporation Point-in-Time Report.

Effective Date:

year/month/day

The date that the corresponding name of the subject corporation, in the Corporate Name History field, became effective. If the effective date of the name change, or in some cases where the effective date has not yet been recorded to ONBIS, was prior to June 27, 1992, the words "Refer to Microfiche" will be displayed.

Current Business Name(s) Exist:

yes/no

This field will indicate whether any business name(s) was registered/renewed for the subject corporation within five years prior to or on the "As of Date" of the Corporation Point-in-Time Report. If business name(s) did exist, a message "Yes" will be displayed. To obtain more information, a business name search is required.

Expired Business Name(s) Exist:

This field will indicate whether any expired business name(s) exist for the subject corporation. If expired business name(s) exist, a message "YES — Search Required for details" will be displayed. To obtain an expired business name search, contact the Companies and Personal Property Security Branch.

Amalgamating Corporations

This section will only display if the corporation came into existence as the result of an amalgamation. If amalgamation details are "Not Available", the Companies and Personal Property Security Branch corporate microfiche records will contain amalgamation information for Ontario business and non-profit corporations, as well as insurers and social clubs. For other corporation types, the reader should contact the Ontario Ministry of Revenue (formerly Ministry of Finance).

Corporation Name: **Corporation Number**:

The name and corporation number of each of the corporations that amalgamated to form the corporation that is the subject of the Corporation Point-in-Time Report.

Administrator Information

All directors and officers recorded as active up to and including the "As of Date" will be listed on the Corporation Point-in-Time Report. The word "Active" will appear before each occurrence of the word "Administrator" for all current administrators.

Directors and officers reported as ceased on document(s) filed on the "As of Date" of the Corporation Point-in-Time Report will be listed as inactive. The printing of inactive administrators (specific to the Corporation Point-in-Time Report) will immediately follow the active administrators. The word "Inactive" will appear before each occurrence of the word "Administrator" for inactive administrators.

Administrator Name (Individual/Corporation):

The administrator's full name is set out (First Name, Middle Name or Initials, Surname).

Address:

The full address for service of the administrator is set out.

Date Began:

year/month/day

The date on which the individual became a director or an officer.

Date Ceased:

year/month/day

This field indicates the date on which an individual ceased being a director or officer.

First Director:

First Directors are the initial directors of a corporation. These individuals have special legislated responsibilities with respect to their participation on the Board of Directors of a corporation. An indicator (Yes) will identify those administrators who are first directors. This field will display "not applicable" if the corporation has filed a notice or return setting out changes to the directors.

Designation:

The designation of the administrator as either an officer or director.

Officer Type:

If an individual is an officer of the corporation, then the specific title is set out. This title will include one of the following: President, Secretary, Treasurer, General Manager, Chair, Chair Person, Chairman, Chairwoman, Vice-Chair, Vice-President, Assistant Secretary, Assistant Treasurer, Chief Manager, Executive Director, Managing Director, Chief Executive Officer, Chief Financial Officer, Chief Information Officer, Chief Operating Officer, Chief Administrative Officer, Comptroller, Authorized Signing Officer or Other (untitled).

Resident Canadian:

A 'Y' in this field indicates that the individual is a Resident Canadian. This field only applies to Ontario business corporations.

Last Document Recorded:

The name of the last document recorded as of the date of the report, on ONBIS (generally filed by the corporation) in the same format as that used in the Corporation Document List. (i.e. from left to right — Act/Code, Description, Form, Date (year/month/day)).

- Electronic Filing — If a document was filed electronically, the words "Electronic Filing" will be displayed beside the date.
- *Corporations Information Act* Annual Returns (CIA AR) — For *Corporations Information Act* Annual Returns filed through the Canada Revenue Agency, the Ministry of Revenue (formerly the Ministry of Finance) or the Service Providers on or after February 5, 2005, the return year is displayed after the words "Annual Return".
- Changes to the *Business Corporations Act* (BCA) effective May 1, 2006, provide for the dissolution of corporations that are in default of compliance under six Ministry of Revenue (formerly Ministry of Finance) tax statutes in addition to the *Corporations Tax Act*. These statutes are the *Employer Health Tax Act, Fuel Tax Act, Gasoline Tax Act, Land Transfer Tax Act, Retail Sales Tax Act and Tobacco Tax Act*. As a result of these changes, there are six new default document descriptions and six new cancellation document descriptions. The default descriptions will set out "default" and then the Act (i.e. *Default Fuel Tax Act*) and the cancellation description would have the words "Cancelled Request" and the initials of the applicable Act. For example, if cancelled under the *Fuel Tax Act* the description would be "Cancelled Request FT".

Explanatory Note Re: Amalgamation

In an amalgamation, two or more corporations (A & B) amalgamate to create another corporation (C).

Corporations A & B will have entries in several fields of its Corporation Point-in-Time Report as follows:

i) Date Amalgamated:

This is the date that the two or more corporations (A & B) were amalgamated to create corporation (C). This date will be set out in the Corporation Point-in-Time Report of both A & B corporations, and their Cancel/Inactive Dates will display "Not Applicable". The Date Amalgamated field will be "Not Applicable" on corporation C's Corporation Point-in-Time Report.

ii) Corporation Status:

This field in the Corporation Point-in-Time Reports of both A & B corporations will show "Amalgamated" as their status.

iii) New Amal. Number:

TThis is the new Ontario Corporation Number of the corporation C, into which corporations A & B amalgamated.

iv) Incorporation Date:

The date of incorporation of corporations A & B will be set out on the Corporation Profile Reports unless either one or both came into existence as a result of amalgamation in which case the date of amalgamation will be set out.

Corporation C will have entries in several fields of its Corporation Point-in-Time Report as follows:

i) Amalgamation Date:

The date that corporation C was created by amalgamation. In this case the "Amalgamation Date" replaces "Incorporation Date" on the Corporation Point-in-Time Report for corporation C.

ii) Corporation Status:

The corporation status of corporation C will be "Active".

iii) Amalgamation Ind.:

Since corporation C came about as the result of the amalgamation of two or more corporations, the indicator "A" will appear in this field.

Modifications Made to the Statement of No Record as a Result of the Corporation Point-in-Time Report

The Statement of No Record will be modified to include an "As of Date" in the lower half of the report. The words "as of:" will be added to the end of the following paragraph: "After entering the information exactly as it is printed above, a record could not be found for the above corporation name and/or the above Ontario corporation number."

When a Statement of No Record is substituted for a Corporation Profile Report, the "As of Date" will be the same as the date on which the report was produced. However, when a Statement of No Record is substituted for a Corporation Point-in-Time Report, the "As of Date" will reflect the "As of Date" requested for the Corporation Point-in-Time Report and not the date on which the report was produced. This allows clients who order a Corporation Point-in-Time Report to receive a historical Statement of No Record that indicates that a corporation did not exist on the ONBIS database at a particular point in time.

BUSINESS NAMES ACT

R.S.O. 1990, c. B.17, as am. S.O. 1994, c. 27, s. 72; 1998, c. 2, s. 9; 1998, c. 18, Sched. E, ss. 33–39; 2001, c. 9, Sched. D, s. 13; 2004, c. 19, s. 4; 2006, c. 35, Sched. C, s. 9; 2010, c. 16, Sched. 5, s. 2, Sched. 8, s. 2 [Sched. 5, s. 2 not in force at date of publication.]; 2011, c. 1, Sched. 5, s. 2.

1. Definitions — In this Act,

"business" includes every trade, occupation, profession, service or venture carried on with a view to profit;

"corporation" means a corporation wherever or however incorporated;

"Minister" means the Minister of Consumer and Business Services;

"Ministry" means the Ministry of the Minister;

"person" includes an individual, sole proprietorship, partnership, limited partnership, unincorporated association, unincorporated syndicate, unincorporated organization, trust, body corporate, and an individual in his or her capacity as trustee, executor, administrator or other legal representative;

"prescribed" means prescribed by the regulations;

"Registrar" means the Registrar appointed under section 3;

"registered" means registered under this Act;

"regulations" means the regulations made under this Act.

1994, c. 27, s. 72(1); 2001, c. 9, Sched. D, s. 13

2. (1) Registering name — No corporation shall carry on business or identify itself to the public under a name other than its corporate name unless the name is registered by that corporation.

(2) Idem — No individual shall carry on business or identify his or her business to the public under a name other than his or her own name unless the name is registered by that individual.

(3) Same — No persons associated in partnership shall carry on business or identify themselves to the public unless the firm name of the partnership is registered by all of the partners.

(3.1) Same — No persons associated in partnership shall carry on business or identify themselves to the public under a name other than a firm name registered under subsection (3) unless the name is registered by all of the partners.

(3.2) Non-application — Subsection (1) does not apply to prohibit a corporation from carrying on business or identifying itself to the public by a name other than its corporate name if the name is set out in a partnership registration under subsection 4(1) or a declaration under the *Limited Partnerships Act*.

(3.3) Same — Subsection (3) does not apply to prohibit persons associated in a limited partnership from carrying on business under the firm name in accordance with the *Limited Partnership Act.*

(4) Exception — Subsection (3) does not apply to prohibit persons associated in partnership from carrying on business or identifying themselves to the public under a name that is composed of the names of the partners.

(5) Idem — This section does not apply to prohibit the use of a name that contains characters from an alphabet other than the Roman alphabet if the name is used in conjunction with the registered name.

(6) Name to be set out — A corporation and such other persons as are prescribed carrying on business under a registered name or, in the case of a corporation, identifying itself to the public under a registered name, shall set out both the registered name and the person's name in all contracts, invoices, negotiable instruments and orders involving goods or services issued or made by the person.

1994, c. 27, s. 72(2)

2.1 (1) Extra-provincial limited liability company — In this section,

"extra-provincial limited liability company" means an unincorporated association, other than a partnership, formed under the laws of another jurisdiction that grants to each of its members limited liability with respect to the liabilities of the association.

(2) Registration — No extra-provincial limited liability company shall carry on business in Ontario unless it has registered its company name.

(2.1) Use of "Limited" — Despite any other Act, the word "Limited" or any abbreviation of that word or any version of it in another language may be used in the registered company name of an extra-provincial limited liability company.

(3) Use of registered name only — No extra-provincial limited liability company shall carry on business in Ontario under a name other than its registered company name.

(3.1) Exception — Despite subsections (2) and (3), an extra-provincial limited liability company may carry on business or identify itself to the public under a name other than its company name, if the name is set out in a partnership registration under subsection 4(1) or a declaration under the *Limited Partnerships Act.*

(4) Laws of other jurisdictions — The laws of the jurisdiction under which an extra-provincial limited liability company is formed shall govern its organization and internal affairs and the liability of its managers and members.

(5) Service — A person may serve a notice or document on an extra-provincial limited liability company at its Ontario place of business, if any, or its address required to be maintained under the laws of the jurisdiction of formation or its principal office address.

1998, c. 18, Sched. E, s. 33; 2010, c. 16, Sched. 8, s. 2

3. (1) Registrar — The Minister shall appoint a public servant in the Ministry as the Registrar.

(2) Delegation of powers — The Registrar may delegate any of the duties or powers of the Registrar to any public servant employed under Part III of the *Public Service of Ontario Act, 2006.*

(3) Records — The Registrar shall maintain a record of every registration made under this Act or filed under the *Limited Partnerships Act.*

(4) Available to the public — Any person is entitled to examine, during normal business hours, the records maintained by the Registrar.

1994, c. 27, s. 72(3); 2006, c. 35, Sched. C, s. 9

4. (1) Registration — Upon payment of the required fee, any person may register a name for the purpose of complying with section 2 or section 2.1 or section 44.3 or 44.4 of the *Partnerships Act.*

(1.1) Period — The registration is effective for five years from the date that it is accepted for registration by the Registrar.

(2) Idem — The Registrar shall not accept for registration a name that does not comply with the prescribed requirements.

(3) Idem — Only letters from the Roman alphabet, Arabic numerals or a combination of letters from the Roman alphabet and Arabic numerals together with punctuation marks and such other marks as are prescribed may form part of a registered name.

(4) Changes — If there is a change in information set out in a registration, the registrant shall register, in the prescribed form within fifteen days after the change, an amended registration showing the change.

(5) Correcting information — If the Registrar has grounds to believe that information registered is not correct or current, he or she may give notice to the registrant requiring that the information be corrected or updated within the time specified in the notice.

(6) Idem — A registrant receiving a notice under subsection (5) shall comply with the request in the notice or provide evidence to the Registrar that the information registered is correct or current, as the case may be.

(7) Cancelling registration — The Registrar shall cancel a registration,

(a) if a name was accepted for registration that does not comply with the prescribed requirements;

(a.1) if the registrant fails to pay a fee required by the Minister under section 10.1; or

(b) if the registrant requests the cancellation.

(8) Idem — The Registrar may cancel a registration if the registrant is given a notice under subsection (5) and does not comply with subsection (6).

(9) Entering cancellation — The Registrar shall indicate, on the record, every cancellation under subsection (7) or (8).

(10) Notice of cancellation — Before cancelling a registration other than on the request of the registrant or pursuant to a Court order, the Registrar shall give the registrant twenty-one days notice of the intention to cancel.

(11) Appeal — A person whose application to register a name is refused may appeal to the Divisional Court within twenty-one days after the day of the refusal.

(12) Idem — A registrant who receives a notice under subsection (10) may appeal to the Divisional Court within twenty-one days after receipt of the notice.

(13) Idem — If a notice under subsection (10) is under appeal, the Registrar shall not cancel the registration unless a final determination is made upholding the Registrar's decision.

1994, c. 27, s. 72(4); 1998, c. 2, s. 9; 1998, c. 18, Sched. E, s. 34; 2004, c. 19, s. 4

5. (1) Renewal of registration — A registrant is entitled to renew a registration before it expires upon paying the required fee.

(2) Late renewal — A registrant is entitled to renew a registration within sixty days after it expires upon paying the required fee for late renewal.

(3) Effective date — A renewal made under subsection (1) and (2) is effective on the day immediately following the expiration day of the registration being renewed.

1998, c. 18, Sched. E, s. 35

6. (1) Liability for damages — A person who suffers damages by reason of the registration of a name that is the same as or deceptively similar to another person's registered name is entitled to recover compensation from the registrant for damages suffered because of the registration.

Proposed Amendment — 6(1)

(1) Liability for damages — A person is entitled to recover compensation from a registrant for damages the person suffered by reason of the registration by the registrant of a name that is the same as or deceptively similar to,

(a) a name registered by the person; or

(b) the person's name, even though the person is not required to register that name under this Act.

2010, c. 16, Sched. 5, s. 2(1) [Not in force at date of publication.]

(2) Idem — For the purposes of subsection (1), the compensation is limited to the greater of $500 and the actual amount of damages incurred.

Proposed Amendment — 6(2)

(2) Same — The compensation under each of clauses (1)(a) and (b) is limited to the greater of $500 and the actual amount of damages incurred.

2010, c. 16, Sched. 5, s. 2(2) [Not in force at date of publication.]

(3) Cancelling registration — In giving a judgment for a plaintiff in an action brought under subsection (1), the court shall order the Registrar to cancel the registration that was the cause of the action.

7. (1) Ability to sue — A person carrying on business in contravention of subsection 2(1), (2) or (3) or subsection 4(4) or (6) is not capable of maintaining a proceeding in a court in Ontario in connection with that business except with leave of the court.

(2) Idem — The court shall grant leave if the person seeking to maintain the proceeding satisfies the court that,

(a) the failure to register was inadvertent;

(b) there is no evidence that the public has been deceived or misled; and

(c) at the time of the application to the court, the person is not in contravention of this Act or the regulations.

(3) **Contracts valid** — No contract is void or voidable by reason only that it was entered into by a person who was in contravention of this Act or the regulations at the time the contract was made.

8. (1) **Certified copies** — Upon the payment of the required fee, the Registrar shall issue to any person applying for it,

(a) a certifed copy of the record with respect to any name registered; or

(b) if a name is not registered, a certificate so stating.

(2) **Idem** — A certified copy or a certificate issued under this section is admissible in evidence in all courts as proof, in the absence of evidence to the contrary, of the contents of the document or of the non-registration of a name, as the case may be, without proof of the appointment or signature of the Registrar.

(3) **Idem** — For the purpose of this section, the signature of the Registrar may be printed or otherwise mechanically or electronically reproduced.

1998, c. 18, Sched. E, s. 36

9. (1) **Form of records** — Records prepared and maintained by the Registrar may be in bound or loose-leaf or electronic form or in a photgraphic film form or may be entered or recorded by any system of mechanical or electronic data processing or by any other information storage device that is capable of reproducing any required information in an accurate and intelligible form within a reasonable time.

(2) **Idem** — If records maintained by the Registrar are prepared and maintained otherwise than in written or other form, the Registrar shall furnish any copy required to be furnished in intelligible written form.

(3) **Idem** — A report reproduced from records prepared and maintained otherwise than in written form that purports to be certified by the Registrar is, without proof of the Registrar's office or signature, admissible in evidence.

(4) **Copies** — The Registrar is not required to produce the original of a document if a copy is furnished in compliance with subsection (2).

(5) **Idem** — For the purpose of this section, a document is a copy of an original if it contains all the information contained in the original.

1994, c. 27, s. 72(5)–(7)

9.1 (1) **Delivery of notices, etc.** — A notice or other document that is required or permitted by this Act to be sent by the Registrar may be sent by ordinary mail or by any other method, including registered mail, certified mail or prepaid courier, if there is a record by the person who has delivered it that the notice or document has been sent.

(2) **Same** — A notice or other document referred to in subsection (1) may be sent by telephone transmission of a facsimile of the notice or other document or by another form of electronic transmission where there is a record that the notice or other document has been sent.

(3) **Deemed delivery** — A notice or other document sent by mail by the Registrar shall be deemed to have been received by the intended recipient on the earlier of,

(a) the day the intended recipient actually receives it; or

(b) the fifth business day after it is mailed.

(4) Same — A notice or other document sent by the Registrar by a method referred to in subsection (2) shall be deemed to be received by the intended recipient on the earlier of,

(a) the day the intended recipient actually receives it; or

(b) the first business day after the day the transmission is sent by the Registrar.

(5) Fax delivery — Subject to the regulations, a registration may be sent in duplicate to the Registrar by telephone transmission of a facsimile.

1994, c. 27, s. 72(8)

10. (1) Offence — Every person who, without reasonable cause, contravenes section 2 or 2.1 or subsection 4(4) or (6) or submits a statement in an application for a registration under this Act that is false or misleading with respect to any material fact is guilty of an offence and on conviction is liable to a fine of not more than $2,000 or, if the person is a corporation, to a fine of not more than $25,000

(2) Idem — If a corporation is guilty of an offence under subsection (1), every director or officer of the corporation and every person acting as its representative in Ontario who authorized, permitted or acquiesced in such an offence is also guilty of an offence and on conviction is liable to a fine of not more than $2,000.

1998, c. 18, Sched. E, s. 37

10.1 Powers of Minister — (0.1) Minister's regulations — The Minister may make regulations,

(a) governing the registration of forms in electronic format, including the manner of acceptance of forms and the determination of the date of receipt;

(b) governing the registration of forms sent by telephone transmission of a facsimile;

(c) governing the custody and destruction of registrations and certificates.

(1) Fees — The Minister may by order require the payment of fees for registrations, late renewals, search reports, or copies of documents or information, or other services under this Act and may approve the amounts of those fees.

1998, c. 18, Sched. E, s. 38; 2011, c. 1, Sched. 5, s. 2(1)

10.2 Registrar's regulations — The Registrar may make regulations prescribing forms and providing for their use.

2011, c. 1, Sched. 5, s. 2(2)

11. Regulations — The Lieutenant Governor in Council may make regulations,

(a) prescribing information to be contained in a registration;

(b) prescribing the duties of the Registrar;

(c) [Repealed 1998, c. 18, Sched. E, s. 39(1).]

(d) [Repealed 2011, c. 1, Sched. 5, s. 2(3).]

(d.1) [Repealed 2011, c. 1, Sched. 5, s. 2(3).]

(d.2) [Repealed 2011, c. 1, Sched. 5, s. 2(3).]

(d.3) authorizing the Registrar to enter into an agreement with any person respecting the use, disclosure, sale or licensing of records maintained under this Act and prescribing terms and conditions for any such agreement;

(e) exempting any class of person or business from the application of section 2, or any provision in the regulation, and prescribing conditions for any such exemption;

(f) prescribing and prohibiting the use of connotations, suggestions, words, expressions or phrases in a name shown in a registration;

(g) [Repealed 2011, c. 1, Sched. 5, s. 2(3).]

(h) [Repealed 1998, c. 18, Sched. E, s. 39(1).]

(i) prescribing any matter required or permitted by this Act to be prescribed for which a specific power is not otherwise provided.

1994, c. 27, s. 72(9); 1998, c. 18, Sched. E, s. 39; 2011, c. 1, Sched. 5, s. 2(3), (4)

12. (1) Transition — A name or designation that is stated in a declaration or a renewal thereof filed under section 1 or 9 of the *Partnerships Registration Act*, being chapter 371 of the Revised Statutes of Ontario, 1980, shall be deemed to be registered under and in accordance with this Act and the regulations.

(2) Idem — A registration of a name or style or a renewal thereof that is filed under section 2 of the *Corporations Information Act*, being chapter 96 of the Revised Statutes of Ontario, 1980, shall be deemed to be a registration under and in accordance with this Act and the regulations.

ONT. REG. 121/91 — GENERAL

made under the *Business Names Act*

O. Reg. 121/91, as am. O. Reg. 579/91; 334/92; 595/92; 624/93; 175/94; 401/95; 441/95; 256/96; 309/96; 562/98; 191/99; 26/01; 57/07.

REGISTRATION FOR AN INDIVIDUAL

1. (1) To register a name under the Act or to amend, renew or cancel the registration of a name under the Act, an individual shall set out the following information on a form approved by the Registrar:

1. The name to which the form relates.

2. An indication whether the form is for a new registration or a renewal, amendment or cancellation of a registration.

3. If the individual has a place of business in Ontario,

   i. the mailing address of the individual, and

   ii. the address of the principal place of business of the individual in Ontario, including the municipality, the street and number, if any, and the postal code.

4. If the individual does not have a place of a business in Ontario, the address of the principal place of business of the individual outside Ontario, including the municipality, the street and number, if any, and the postal code.

5. A description of the activity being carried out under the name to which the form relates, which description shall not exceed 40 characters, including punctuation marks and spaces.

6. An indication whether the individual is carrying out the activity in sole proprietorship.

7. The name of the individual including the first given name, the initial of the second given name, if any, and the surname.

8. The address of the individual, including the municipality, the street and number, if any, and the postal code.

9. If the individual has not authorized an attorney to submit the form, the name of the individual.

10. If the individual has authorized an attorney to submit the form, the name of the attorney.

(2) A form mentioned in subsection (1) can be submitted by an attorney acting under a power of attorney that authorizes the attorney to submit the form on behalf of the individual.

(3) An individual who amends, renews or cancels a registration shall set out on the form,

(a) the business identification number assigned by the Registrar to the first renewal of the registration made on or after April 1, 1994, if the registration was made before that date; or

(b) the business identification number assigned by the Registrar to the registration, if the registration was made on or after April 1, 1994.

O. Reg. 334/92, s. 1; 175/94, s. 1; 441/95, s. 1

REGISTRATION FOR A PARTNERSHIP

2. (1) To register the firm name of a partnership or to amend, renew or cancel the registration of the firm name of a partnership, the persons associated in the partnership shall set out the following information on a form approved by the Registrar:

1. The firm name followed by,

   i. if the partnership is a limited liability partnership as defined in the *Partnerships Act* formed under the laws of Ontario, the words "limited liability partnership" or "société à responsabilité limitée" or the abbreviations "LLP", "L.L.P." or "s.r.l." as required by subsection 44.3(3) of that Act, or

   ii. if the partnership is an extra-provincial limited liability partnership as defined in the *Partnerships Act*, the words or abbreviations, if any, that identify the partnership as a limited liability partnership and that are required by the laws of the jurisdiction under which the partnership is formed.

2. An indication whether the form is for a new registration or a renewal, amendment or cancellation of a registration.

3. If the partnership has a place of business in Ontario,

   i. the mailing address of the partnership, and

   ii. the address of the principal place of business of the partnership in Ontario, including the municipality, the street and number, if any, and the postal code.

4. If the partnership does not have a place of business in Ontario, the address of the principal place of business of the partnership outside Ontario, including the municipality, the street and number, if any, and the postal code.

5. A description of the activity being carried out under the firm name, which description shall not exceed 40 characters, including punctuation marks and spaces.

6. The name of each partner.

7. The address of each partner that is an individual, including the municipality, the street and number, if any, and the postal code.

8. The address for service of each partner that is not an individual, including the municipality, the street and number, if any, and the postal code.

9. The name of the person submitting the form on behalf of the partnership.

10. In the case of a limited liability partnership as defined in the *Partnerships Act*,

   i. an indication as to whether it is a limited liability partnership formed under the laws of Ontario or an extra-provincial limited liability partnership as defined in that Act, and

   ii. the jurisdiction under whose laws the partnership is formed.

(2) A form mentioned in subsection (1) can be submitted on behalf of the partnership by,

(a) one of the partners; or

(b) an attorney acting under a power of attorney that authorizes the attorney to submit the form on behalf of the partnership.

(2.1) For the purpose of paragraph 1 of subsection (1), if a registration sets out an English form and a French form for the firm name of a limited liability partnership, the "/" mark shall separate the two forms of the firm name.

(3) For the purpose of paragraph 6 of subsection (1), the name of a partner shall include,

(a) the first given name, the initial of the second given name, if any, and the surname, if the partner is an individual; and

(b) the Ontario corporation number, if the partner is a corporation.

(4) Persons associated in a partnership who amend, renew or cancel a registration shall set out on the form,

(a) the business identification number assigned by the Registrar to the first renewal of the registration made on or after April 1, 1994, if the registration was made before that date; or

(b) the business identification number assigned by the Registrar to the registration, if the registration was made on or after April 1, 1994.

O. Reg. 334/92, s. 2; 175/94, s. 2; 441/95, s. 1; 26/01, s. 1; 57/07, s. 1

2.1 (1) To register a name other than the firm name of a partnership or to amend, renew or cancel the registration of the name, the persons associated in the partnership shall set out the following information on a form approved by the Registrar:

1. The name to which the form relates.

2. An indication whether the form is for a new registration or a renewal, amendment or cancellation of a registration.

3. If the partnership has a place of business in Ontario where it uses the name,

   i. the mailing address of the partnership, and

   ii. the address of a place of business that the partnership has in Ontario where it uses the name, including the municipality, the street and number, if any, and the postal code.

4. If the partnership does not have a place of business in Ontario where it uses the name, the address of a place of business that the partnership has outside Ontario, including the municipality, the street and number, if any, and the postal code.

5. A description of the activity being carried out under the name, which description shall not exceed 40 characters, including punctuation marks and spaces.

6. An indication as to the type of partnership.

7. The firm name.

8. The business identification number, if any, assigned by the Registrar to,

   i. the first renewal of the registration of the firm name made on or after April 1, 1994, if the registration was made before that date, or

   ii. the registration of the firm name, if the registration was made on or after April 1, 1994.

9. The name of the person submitting the form on behalf of the partnership.

(2) A form mentioned in subsection (1) can be submitted on behalf of the partnership by,

(a) one of the partners, other than a limited partner in a limited partnership; or

(b) an attorney acting under a power of attorney that authorizes the attorney to submit the form on behalf of the partnership.

O. Reg. 256/96, s. 1

3. (1) A partner who submits a form mentioned in subsection 2(1) on behalf of a partnership shall be known as a designated partner if more than 10 persons are associated in the partnership and the partnership has a principal place of business in Ontario.

(2) A designated partner may omit from the form the information required by paragraphs 6, 7 and 8 of subsection 2(1) for persons who are associated in the partnership other than the designated partner if the requirements of subsections (3) to (7) are met.

(3) A designated partner shall maintain at the principal place of business in Ontario,

(a) a record showing,

i. the persons associated in the partnership who carry out the business of the partnership in Ontario,

ii. the information required by paragraphs 6, 7 and 8 of subsection 2(1) respecting each of them, and

iii. the date on which each of them became associated in the partnership; and

(b) a record showing,

i. the persons who were associated in the partnership on or after May 1, 1991, who carried out the business of the partnership in Ontario and who subsequently left the partnership, and

ii. the period during which each person was associated in the partnership.

(4) A designated partner may delete from the records information concerning a person who has left the partnership once six years have elapsed after the departure.

(5) Upon request and without charge, any partner shall permit a person to inspect the records during the normal business hours of the partnership and to make copies or take extracts from them.

(6) Upon request and without charge, any partner shall provide a person with a copy of the records.

(7) Upon delivery of a written notice from the Registrar, any partner shall provide a copy of the records, within the time stated in the notice, to the Registrar or to such other person as the notice specifies.

O. Reg. 441/95, s. 1

REGISTRATION FOR A CORPORATION

4. (1) To register a name under the Act or to amend, renew or cancel the registration of a name under the Act, a corporation shall set out the following information on a form approved by the Registrar:

1. The name to which the form relates.

2. An indication whether the form is for a new registration or a renewal, amendment or cancellation of a registration.

3. If the corporation has a place of business in Ontario,

   i. the mailing address of the corporation, and

   ii. the address of the principal place of business of the corporation in Ontario, including the municipality, the street and number, if any, and the postal code.

4. If the corporation does not have a place of business in Ontario, the address of the registered or head office of the corporation, including the municipality, the street and number, if any, and the postal code.

5. A description of the activity being carried out under the name to which the form relates, which description shall not exceed 40 characters, including punctuation marks and spaces.

6. The name of the corporation.

7. The Ontario corporation number, if any, except if the corporation is an extra-provincial corporation to which the *Corporations Information Act* and the *Extra-Provincial Corporations Act* do not apply.

8. The jurisdiction in which the corporation was incorporated.

9. The name of the person submitting the form on behalf of the corporation.

(2) A form mentioned in subsection (1) can be submitted on behalf of the corporation by,

(a) an officer or director of the corporation; or

(b) an attorny acting under a power of attorney that authorizes the attorney to submit the form on behalf of the corporation.

(3) A corporation that amends, renews or cancels a registration shall set out on the form,

(a) the business identification number assigned by the Registrar to the first renewal of the registration made on or after April 1, 1994, if the registration was made before that date; or

(b) the business identification number assigned by the Registrar to the registration, if the registration was made on or after April 1, 1994.

O. Reg. 441/95, s. 1

EXTRA-PROVINCIAL LIMITED LIABILITY COMPANY

5. (1) To register its company name under the Act or to amend, renew or cancel the registration of the name, an extra-provincial limited liability company as defined in subsection 2.1(1) of the Act shall set out the following information on a form approved by the Registrar:

1. The name of the company, including the words or abbreviations identifying the company as a limited liability company as required under the laws of the jurisdiction under which the company is formed.

2. An indication whether the form is for a new registration or a renewal, amendment or cancellation of a registration.

3. If the company has a place of business in Ontario,

   i. the mailing address of the company, and

   ii. the address of the principal place of business of the company in Ontario, including the municipality, the street and number, if any, and the postal code.

4. If the company does not have a place of business in Ontario, the address of the principal place of business of the company outside Ontario, including the municipality, the street and number, if any, and the postal code.

5. A description of the activity being carried on under the company name, which description shall not exceed 40 characters, including punctuation marks and spaces.

6. An indication that the company is an extra-provincial limited liability company.

7. The jurisdiction under whose laws the company is formed.

8. The name of the person submitting the form on behalf of the company.

(2) A form mentioned in subsection (1) can be submitted on behalf of the company by,

(a) a general manager or representative of the company; or

(b) an attorney acting under a power of attorney that authorizes the attorney to submit the form on behalf of the company.

(3) A company that amends, renews or cancels a registration shall set out on the form the business identification number assigned by the Registrar to the registration.

O. Reg. 334/92, s. 3; 175/94, s. 3; 441/95, s. 1; 26/01, s. 2

DUTIES OF THE REGISTRAR

6. (1) Upon payment of the applicable fee and receipt of the applicable form, the Registrar shall register a name.

(2) Upon payment of the applicable fee, if any, and receipt of the applicable form, the Registrar shall amend, renew or cancel the registration of a name.

6.1 (1) A form to register a name under the Act or to amend, renew or cancel the registration of a name under the Act may be submitted in electronic format, if,

(a) the person submitting the form satisfies the technical requirements established by the Registrar;

(b) the Registrar has approved the electronic format of the form; and

(c) the form is sent to the Registrar during business hours approved by the Registrar.

(2) A registration made under subsection(1) is effective on the date assigned by the computer system that the Registrar has established for registrations.

O. Reg. 441/95, s. 2

7. (1) Upon payment of the applicable fee, the Registrar shall issue to any person who makes a request a certificate stating that a name is not registered.

(2) Upon payment of the applicable fee, the Registrar shall issue to any person who makes a request a copy, or a certified copy, of the record with respect to any name registered.

CUSTODY AND DESTRUCTION OF RECORDS

8. Sections 9 and 10 apply with respect to records maintained under the Act and records maintained by the Registrar for declarations filed under the *Limited Partnerships Act.*

9. The Registrar may authorize the destruction of documents that form the record with respect to a name registered if the Registrar has microfilmed the documents or has entered the registration information in the computer system that the Register has established for registrations.

O. Reg. 441/95, s. 3

10. (1) The Registrar may segregate the record with respect to any name registered when the registration expires or is cancelled. The Registrar may authorize the destruction of the record when five years have elapsed after the expiry or cancellation.

(2) When a registration is renewed, the Registrar may segregate the record with respect to the registration as it existed before the renewal. The Registrar may authorize the destruction of the segregated portion of the record when five years have elapsed after the renewal.

(3) For the purposes of subsection 8(1) of the Act and section 7, a record that has been segregated shall be deemed not to exist.

FEES

11. [Revoked O. Reg. 191/99, s. 1.]

11.1 [Revoked O. Reg. 191/99, s. 1.]

EXEMPTIONS FROM SECTION 2 OF THE ACT

12. (1) Subsection 2(6) of the Act does not apply with respect to corporations carrying on business in Ontario, or identifying themselves to the public in Ontario, in any form of partnership or business association,

(a) if the partnership or association consists of at least two corporations;

(b) if the name of the partnership or association is registered under the Act; and

(c) if the partnership or association complies with subsection (2).

(2) The name of the partnership or business association, together with the words "Registered Name", "nom enregistré", "Reg'd Name" or "nom enr." must be set out in all contracts, invoices, negotiable instruments and orders involving goods or services issued or made by the association or partnership.

TRANSITIONAL PROVISIONS

13. [Revoked O. Reg. 121/91, s. 13(3).]

14. [Revoked O. Reg. 121/91, s. 14(3).]

15. [Revoked O. Reg. 121/91, s. 15(3).]

COMMENCEMENT

16. This Regulation comes into force on the 1st day of May, 1991.

Forms 1, 2

[Revoked O. Reg. 441/95, s. 5.]

ONT. REG. 122/91 — RESTRICTIONS RESPECTING NAMES

made under the *Business Names Act*

O. Reg. 122/91, as am. O. Reg. 247/05.

GENERAL

1. The first character of a name shown in a registration must be a letter of the Roman alphabet or an Arabic numeral.

2. (1) For the purposes of subsection 4(3) of the Act, the following are prescribed as the punctuation marks and other marks that may form part of a registered name:

“ # $ % & ‘ ( ) * + , . / : ; lesser than angle bracket = < ? [ ] /, ^ ‘ @

(2) A name shown in a registration must not consist only or primarily of a combination of punctuation marks and other marks.

(3) A name shall be set out in a registration with only one space between each word.

O. Reg. 247/05, s. 1

3. If the name contains characters from an alphabet other than the Roman alphabet, the name shown in the registration must consist of a translation of the name into a language which contains only letters from the Roman alphabet.

PROHIBITED USAGE

4. (1) A name shown in a registration must not include, in any language, a word or expression that is contrary to public policy, including a word that is scandalous, obscene or immoral.

(2) A name shown in a registration must not use a word or expression that would suggest that the registrant is engaged in an activity that is contrary to public policy.

5. A name shown in a registration must not include a word, an expression or an abbreviation the use of which is prohibited under a federal Act or an Ontario Act.

6. A name shown in a registration must not use Arabic numerals or a word or expression that would suggest that the name is a corporate number name.

7. A name shown in a registration must not use a word or expression that would suggest that the registrant is a form of organization that the registrant is not.

RESTRICTIONS

8. (1) A name shown in a registration must not include the name of a specific individual,

(a) unless, at any time before or during the period of the registration of the name, the individual has or had a material interest in the business or activity carried on by the registrant; and

(b) unless the individual consents in writing to the use of his or her name.

(2) For the purpose of clause (1)(b), if the individual is deceased and his or her death occurred within thirty years before the name is registered, the heir, executor or administrator of the individual may consent in writing to the use of the individual's name.

(3) This section does not apply if the individual is deceased and his or her death occurred thirty years or more before the name is registered.

9. A name shown in a registration must not include a word, expression or abbreviation the use of which is restricted under a federal Act or an Ontario Act unless the registrant satisfies the restriction.

10. (1) Subject to subsection (2), a name shown in a registration must not include a word or expression that suggests that the business or activity of the registrant is connected with,

(a) the Crown in right of Canada or in right of a province;

(b) the Government of Canada, of a territory or of a province;

(c) a municipality; or

(d) an agency of the Crown, government or municipality.

(2) If the registrant obtains the written consent of the applicable Crown, government, municipality or agency, a name shown in a registration may include a word or expression described in subsection (1).

11. A name shown in a registration must not include in any language the word "college", "institute" or "university", if the use of the word would suggest that the registrant is a post-secondary educational institution, unless the Minister of Colleges and Universities gives written consent to the use of the word.

EXCEPTIONS

12. (1) Sections 1, 2, 3, 6, 7, 8, 10 and 11 do not apply with respect to a name shown in a registration if, on the 30th day of April, 1991,

(a) the registrant was using the name; and

(b) the registrant was not required to file a declaration under the *Partnerships Registration Act* (R.S.O. 1980, c. 371) respecting the name.

(2) Sections 1, 2, 3, 6, 7, 8, 10 and 11 do not apply with respect to a name shown in a registration,

(a) if the registrant was using the name on the 30th day of April, 1991; and

(b) if the registrant was required, on the 30th day of April, 1991, to file a declaration under the *Partnerships Registration Act* (R.S.O. 1980, c. 371) respecting the name before the 1st of July, 1991.

COMMENCEMENT

13. This Regulation comes into force on the 1st day of May, 1991.

ONT. REG. 18/07 — REFUND OF FEE FOR ELECTRONIC APPLICATION FOR NEW REGISTRATION

made under the *Business Names Act*

O. Reg. 18/07

1. Definitions — In this Regulation,

"application" means an electronic application for a new registration of a name for the purposes of complying with subsection 2(1), (2) or (3) of the Act; *("demande")*

"business day" means Monday to Friday, and excludes a holiday; *("jour ouvrable")*

"calendar day" means any one of the seven days in a week; *("jour civil")*

"Master Business Licence" means a confirmation of a new registration of a name under the Act, provided by the Ministry where the application for registration was submitted electronically using the Integrated Business Services Application on the internet website maintained by the Ministry. *("permis principal d'entreprise")*

2. Holiday — **(1)** This section sets out the meaning of "holiday" for the purposes of this Regulation.

(2) The following days are holidays:

1. New Year's Day.
2. Good Friday.
3. Easter Monday.
4. Victoria Day.
5. Canada Day.
6. Civic Holiday.
7. Labour Day.
8. Thanksgiving Day.
9. Remembrance Day.
10. Christmas Day.
11. Boxing Day.
12. Any special holiday proclaimed by the Governor General or Lieutenant Governor.

(3) If New Year's Day, Canada Day or Remembrance Day falls on a Saturday or Sunday, the following Monday is a holiday.

(4) If Christmas Day falls on a Saturday or Sunday, the following Monday and Tuesday are holidays.

(5) If Christmas Day falls on a Friday, the following Monday is a holiday.

3. Deemed receipt — For the purposes of this Regulation, an application received by the Ministry on a Saturday, Sunday, holiday or after 8 p.m. on a business day shall be deemed to have been received on the next business day.

4. Fee refund — **(1)** Subject to subsections (2) and (3), the fee paid in respect of an application shall be refunded to the applicant if,

(a) within two business days after the day the Ministry receives the application, a Master Business Licence is not sent by the Ministry by e-mail to the e-mail address provided by the applicant; and

(b) all of the additional conditions set out in section 5 are met.

(2) No fee is refundable under subsection (1) if any of the following circumstances impaired the Ministry's ability to electronically produce the Master Business Licence, or to send it by e-mail to the e-mail address provided by the applicant, within the time period specified in clause (1)(a):

1. Lack of power supply.
2. Major failure in a technological system.
3. Labour disruption.
4. Natural disaster.
5. Any other factor beyond the reasonable control of the Government of Ontario.

(3) If, within the time period specified in clause (1)(a), the Ministry sent the Master Business Licence by e-mail to the e-mail address provided by the applicant, no fee is refundable under subsection (1) regardless of whether or when the applicant actually received the Master Business Licence by e-mail.

(4) Nothing in this section affects the authority of the Registrar to cancel a registration at any time in accordance with the Act, and this section does not apply if a registration has been cancelled.

5. Additional conditions for refund — The following are the additional conditions referred to in clause 4(1)(b):

1. The application was submitted electronically using the Integrated Business Services Application on the internet website maintained by the Ministry.
2. In the application, the applicant provided a valid e-mail address for the purpose of receiving an electronic copy of the Master Business Licence by e-mail.
3. The application appears to meet the requirements set out in the Act and the regulations.
4. The required fee was paid to the Ministry when the application was submitted.
5. The name the applicant applied to register appears to comply with the Act and the regulations.
6. No earlier than three business days, and no later than 30 calendar days, after the day the Ministry received the application, the applicant requested a refund of the fee paid in respect of the application by submitting a refund request electronically on the internet website maintained by the Ministry.
7. The refund request is complete and accurate.

6. Response to refund request — **(1)** On receiving a refund request submitted in accordance with paragraph 6 of section 5, the Ministry shall, within a reasonable period of time, determine whether the applicant meets all of the conditions for the refund, as set out in sections 4 and 5, and,

(a) if the applicant meets those conditions, make the refund to the applicant; or

(b) if the applicant does not meet those conditions, notify the applicant that the applicant does not meet the conditions for the refund.

(2) The determination made under subsection (1) is final and binding.

BNA Forms

Form 1 — Registration (Sole Proprietorship/Partnership)*

Print clearly in CAPITAL LETTERS / Écrivez clairement en LETTRES MAJUSCULES

1. Registration Type / Type d'enregistrement

Page_____ of / de_____

If B, C, or D enter "Business Identification Number" / En cas de B, C ou D, inscrivez le n° d'identification de l'entreprise.

A ☐ New / Nouvel B ☐ Renewal / Renouvellement C ☐ Amendment / Modification D ☐ Cancellation / Révocation

BIN Business Identification No./ NIE le n° d'identification de l'entreprise

2. Business Name / Nom commercial

3. Mailing Address of Registrant/ L'Adresse postale de Registrant

Street No / N° de rue Suite No. / Bureau n° Street Name / Nom de la rue

City / Town / Ville Province / Province Postal Code / Code postal

Country / Pays

4. Address of principal place of business in Ontario *(PO Box not acceptable)* / **Adresse de l'établissement principal en Ontario** *(Case postale non acceptée)* ☐ Same as above / comme ci-dessus

Street No. / N° de rue Street Name / Nom de la rue Suite No. / Bureau n° City / Town / Ville

Province / Province Country / Pays Postal Code / Code postal

5. Give a brief description of the ACTIVITY being carried out under the business name./ Résumez brièvement le genre d'ACTIVITÉ exercée sous le nom commercial.

6. Type of Registrant / Type de personne enregistrée A ☐ Sole proprietorship / Entreprise personnelle B ☐ Partnership / Société en nom collectif ☐ More than 10 Partners records at business address / Plus de 10 associés dossiers à l'adresse d'affaires

7. Registrant Information / Renseignements sur la personne enregistrée

Last Name / Nom de famille First Name / Prénom Middle Initial / initiale 2e prénom

8. Street No. / N° de rue Street Name / Nom de la rue Suite No. / Bureau n° City / Town / Ville

Province / Province Country / Pays Postal Code / Code postal

Additional Information. Only complete if the registrant is not an individual. See instructions 7/8 on the form. / **Renseignements supplémentaires.** À remplir uniquement si la personne enregistrée n'est pas un particulier. Voir les instructions 7 et 8 sur le formulaire.

Ont. Corporation No. / *(For Corporate Partners Only)* N° matricule de la personne morale en Ontario *Pour les personnes morales associées seulement*

7. Last Name / Nom de famille First Name / Prénom Middle Initial / initiale 2e prénom

8. Street No. / N° de rue Street Name / Nom de la rue Suite No. / Bureau n° City / Town / Ville

Province / Province Country / Pays Postal Code / Code postal

Additional Information. Only complete if the registrant is not an individual. See instructions 7/8 on the form. / **Renseignements supplémentaires.** À remplir uniquement si la personne enregistrée n'est pas un particulier. Voir les instructions 7 et 8 sur le formulaire.

Ont. Corporation No. / *(For Corporate Partners Only)* N° matricule de la personne morale en Ontario *Pour les personnes morales associées seulement*

9. Print name of person authorizing this registration / *(either the sole proprietor, a partner or a person acting under a power of attorney)* If the person is a corporation, complete **additional information** below only. / **Indiquez en lettres majuscules le nom de la personne autorisant l'enregistrement** / *(propriétaire unique, associé, ou personne habilitée en vertu d'une procuration).* (Si c'est une personne morale qui autorise l'enregistrement, compléter les **renseignements supplémentaires** ci-dessous).

Last Name / Nom de famille First Name / Prénom Middle Initial / initiale 2e prénom

If person authorizing the registration is not an individual (eg. corporation, trust, syndicate), print name below and do not complete last, first and middle names above. / Si la personne qui autorise l'enregistrement n'est pas un individu (c'est-à-dire une personne morale, un trust ou syndicat) ne pas remlir le nom de famille, prénom et 2e prénom.

Additional Information / Renseignements supplémentaires

MINISTRY USE ONLY - RÉSERVÉ AU MINISTÈRE

It is the responsibility of the applicant(s) to ensure the accuracy of the information submitted. It is an offence under section 10 of the *Business Names Act* to submit false or misleading information. / Il incombe aux demandeurs de veiller à l'exactitude des renseignements présentés. Le demandeur qui fait une déclaration fausse ou trompeuse commet une infraction en vertu de l'article 10 de la *Loi sur les noms commerciaux*.

07219 (2014/11)

INSTRUCTIONS **It is important to read these notes before completing the attached form.**

Print all information clearly in CAPITAL LETTERS using black ink.

It is the responsibility of the applicant(s) to ensure that information submitted under the *Business Names Act* is accurate and complete. It is an offence under section 10 of the Act if a person, without reasonable cause, submits a statement in an application for a registration under this Act that is false or misleading with respect to any material fact. On conviction, a person guilty of an offence is liable to a fine of not more than $2,000 or, if the person is a corporation, to a fine of not more than $25,000. If a corporation is guilty of an offence, every director or officer of the corporation and every person acting as its representative in Ontario who authorized, permitted or acquiesced in such an offence is also guilty of an offence and on conviction is liable to a fine of not more than $2,000.

Complete all sections of the form. Incomplete forms will be returned.

Fees:
- there is a fee payable for new registrations and renewals;
- fees may be paid in cash, money order or cheque;
- payable to the **Ontario Minister of Finance;**
- do not send cash in the mail;
- a handling fee will be charged for a non-negotiable cheque.

Please forward both copies of the enclosed form to the Ministry of Government and Consumer Services. The Client copy will no longer be certified consistent with Ontario Regulation 175 / 94 Section 4. The Client copy will be **returned**, with a validation in the bottom right-hand corner.

Return completed forms to:

Ministry of Government and Consumer Services
Central Production and
Verification Services Branch
393 University Ave, Suite 200
Toronto ON M5G 2M2

Please do not separate the form.

Refer to these notes while completing form.

1. Registration Type - Check the appropriate box:
   New (Fee payable)
   - a new registration is the first filing of the business name
   - a change of business name, sole proprietor, or a complete change of partners, is considered a new registration

   Renewal (Fee payable)
   - a registration expires in five years and must be renewed

   Amendment (No fee payable)
   - an amendment should be filed whenever there is a change in address or change of activity

   Cancellation (No fee payable)
   - a cancellation should be submitted if you stop using the business name

   BIN
   For renewal, amendment or cancellation, enter "Business Identification No.".

2. Business Name - Please print the business name. This is the name you are registering. The business name must be set out in Block Capital Letters in the squares provided and must commence on the first line of the 'grid' in the first square. Each square of the grid represents a letter of the alphabet, a punctuation mark, or a space. If there is not sufficient space on the grid for the name, please use additional form(s). Please complete all items on additional form(s) and note the number of each additional page in the top right-hand corner of each form.

3. Mailing Address of Registrant - Include street number, name, municipality and postal code. Your copy of the registration will be mailed to this address.

4. Address of Principal Place of Business in Ontario - Include street, number, name, municipality and postal code. A post office box is not acceptable in a business address. If there is more than one place of business, select one as the principal place.

   Where the business address is outside Ontario, set out the words "Not Applicable" in item 4. If this is the case, please ensure that Item 3, the mailing address, includes the street address of the principal place of busness outside of Ontario, as a post office box is not acceptable.

5. Activity - Include a brief description of the activity being performed.

6. Type of Registrant - Check the appropriate box. If you are registering a partnership with more than 10 partners, you may set out the name and address of a designated partner(s), and check the box marked "More than 10 Partners". Information on all partners carrying on business in Ontario must be kept and made available to the public at the partnership business address.

7/8. Registrant Information - include the full name and residential address or address for service of the sole proprietor, each partner, or designated partner(s). A post office box is not acceptable. For partnerships with more than two partners, please fill out and attach another form(s) with the additional names and addresses.

   Additional Information - If the registrant is **not** an individual, enter the name of the business or corporation in "Additional Information". Also enter the address of the business or corporation in item 8. If the registrant is a corporation, enter the corporation number in the space titled "Ontario Corporation No.".

9. Print the name of the person authorizing this registration, (either a sole proprietor, or a partner, or a person acting under a power of attorney).

   Additional Information: If the person authorizing the registration is not an individual, (e.g. corporation, trust, syndicate) set out the name in "Additional Information" and do not complete the boxes for the last, first and middle names.

07219 (2014/11)

INSTRUCTIONS **Il est important de lire ces remarques avant de remplir la formule ci-jointe.**

Inscrivez les renseignements clairement en LETTRES MAJUSCULES à l'encre noire.

Il est de la responsabilité du demandeur de veiller à ce que les renseignements fournis en vertu de la *Loi sur les noms commerciaux* sont exacts et complets. Quiconque fait, sans motifs raisonnables, dans une demande d'enregistrement en vertu de cette loi, une déclaration fausse ou trompeuse sur un fait important est coupable d'une infraction en vertu de l'article 10 de la loi. Cette personne est passible, sur déclaration de culpabilité, d'une amende d'au plus de 2 000 $ ou, si cette personne est une personne morale, d'une amende d'au plus 25 000 $. Si la personne morale est coupable d'une infraction, ses administrateurs ou dirigeants, ainsi que les personnes agissant en qualité de mandataires en Ontario qui ont autorisé ou permis cette infraction, ou qui y ont acquiescé, sont aussi coupables d'une infraction et passibles, sur déclaration de culpabilité, d'une amende d'au plus 2 000 $.

Remplissez toutes les sections de la formule. Les formules incomplètes seront retournées.

Droits :
- il faut payer des droits pour les nouveaux enregistrements et les renouvellements;
- les droits peuvent être réglés en espèces, par mandat ou par chèque;
- payables à l'ordre du **ministre des Finances de l'Ontario**;
- n'envoyez aucun argent en espèces par la poste;
- des frais administratifs seront facturés pour tout chèque non négociable.

Veuillez envoyer les deux copies de la formule ci-jointe au ministère des Services gouvernementaux et des Services aux consommateurs .
La copie du Client ne sera plus certifiée conformément à l'article 4 du Règlement 175 / 94 de l'Ontario.
La copie du client sera validée dans le coin inférieur droit et vous sera **retournée**.

Retournez les formules remplies à : **Ministère des Services gouvernementaux et des Services aux consommateurs**
Direction des services
centraux de production et de vérification
393, av University, bureau 200
Toronto ON M5G 2M2

Ne séparez pas les pages de la formule.

Consultez ces remarques lorsque vous remplissez la formule.

1. Type d'enregistrement - Cochez la case appropriée :
   Nouvel (Droits à payer)
   - un nouvel enregistrement est le premier enregistrement du nom commercial;
   - une modification apportée au nom commercial, de l'entreprise personnelle ou une modification complète des associés, sont considérées comme un nouvel enregistrement.

   Renouvellement (Droits à payer)
   - un enregistrement expire au bout de cinq ans; il doit être renouvelé.

   Modification (Aucuns droits à payer)
   - une modification devrait être déposée chaque fois qu'il y a un changement d'adresse ou d'activité.

   Révocation (Aucuns droits à payer)
   - il convient de soumettre une révocation si vous n'utilisez plus le nom commercial.

   NIE
   Pour un renouvellement, une modification ou une révocation, indiquez le numéro d'identification de l'entreprise.

2. Nom commercial - Inscrivez en majuscules le nom commercial que vous enregistrez, une lettre par case, en commençant à la première case de la première ligne Utilisez aussi un espace pour chaque signe de ponctuation et pour chaque espace entre les mots. Si vous manquez d'espace, prenez d'autres formules, au besoin. Sur chaque formule supplémentaire,remplissez toutes les rubiques et numérotez les pages dans le coin supérieur droit.

3. L'Adresse postale de Registrant - Inscrivez le numéro et le nom de la rue, le nom de la ville et le code postal. Votre copie de l'enregistrement sera expédiée à cette adresse.

4. Adresse de l'establissement principal en Ontario - L'adresse doit comprendre le numéro et le nom de la rue, la ville et le code postal. Une case postale n'est pas acceptée comme adresse d'affaires. S'il existe plus d'u établissement, choisissez-en un comme établissement principal. Lorsque l'établissement principal est situé à l'extérieur de l'Ontario, inscrivez «Sans objet» à la section 4. Dans ce cas, à la section 3, l'adresse postale doit être l'adresse complète de l'établissement principal situé hors de l'Ontario, une case postale n'étant pas acceptée.

5. Activité - Donnez une brève description de l'activité exercée.

6. Type de personne enregistrée - Cochez la case appropriée. Si vous enregistrez une société à responsabilité limitée (de l'Ontario ou extraprovinciale) comprenant plus de 10 associés, vous pouvez indiquer le nom et l'adresse de l'associé ou des associés désignés; cochez aussi la case « Plus de 10 associés : dossiers à l'adresse d'affaires». Les renseignements relatifs à tous les associés menant à une activité commerciale en Ontario doivent être conservés et mis à la disposition du public à l'adresse d'affaires ontarienne de la société.

7/8. Renseignements sur la personne enregistrée - Comprend le nom complet et l'adre de l'entreprise personnelle, de chaque associé ou de l'associé désigné. Les cases postales ne sont pas acceptées. Pour les sociétés en nom collectif possédant plus de deux associés, veuillez remplir et joindre d'autres formules portant les noms et les adresses supplémentaires.

   Renseignements supplémentaires - Si la personne enregistrée n'est **pas** un particulier, indiquez le nom de l'entreprise ou de la personne morale sous «Renseignements supplémentaires». Indiquez également l'adresse de l'entreprise ou de la personne morale à la rubrique 8. Si la personne enregistrée est une personne morale, indiquez le numéro de la personne morale dans l'espace désigné «Numéro matricule de la personne morale en Ontario».

9. Indiquez en lettres majuscules le nom de la personne autorisant l'enregistrement (propriétaire, unique, associé ou personne, ou personne habilitée en vertu d'une procuration).

   Renseignements supplémentaires : Si la personne autorisant l'enregistrement n'est pas un particulier (p. ex : personne morale, société de fiducie, consortium), indiquez dans cette section le nom de la société et n'inscrivez rien à la case «Nom de famille, Prénom, 2e prénom».

07219 (2014/11)

Form 2 — Registration (Corporations)*

Print clearly in CAPITAL LETTERS / Écrivez clairement en LETTRES MAJUSCULES

1. Registration Type / Type d'enregistrement
If B, C, or D enter Business Identification Number. / En cas de B, C ou D, inscrivez le nº d'identification de l'entreprise.

Page____of / de____

A ☐ New / Nouvel B ☐ Renewal / Renouvellement C ☐ Amendment / Modification D ☐ Cancellation / Révocation

BIN Business Identification No. / NIE le nº d'identification de l'entreprise

2. Business or Identification Name / Nom commercial ou d'identification

3. Mailing Address of Registrant / L'Adresse postale de Registrant

Street No. / Nº de rue Street Name / Nom de la rue Suite No. / Bureau nº
City / Town / Ville Province / Province Postal Code / Code postal
Country / Pays

For mailing purposes, the address information you key into #3 beside will automatically shift to the left.

Pour faciliter l'envoi par courrier, les éléments de l'adresse postale tapés à côté de (section 3) se déplaceront automatiquement vers la gauche.

4. Address of principal place of business in Ontario / Adresse de l'établissement principal en Ontario *(P.O. Box not acceptable / Case postale non acceptée)*

☐ Same as above / comme ci-dessus

Street No. / Nº de rue Street Name / Nom de la rue Suite No. / Bureau nº
City / Town / Ville Province Postal Code / Code postal
Country / Pays

5. Give a brief description of the **ACTIVITY** being carried out under the business/identification name. / Résumez brièvement le genre **d'ACTIVITÉ** exercée sous le nom commercial ou d'identification.

6. Corporation Name / Personne morale

7. Ontario Corporation Number / Numéro matricule de la personne morale en Ontario

8. Jurisdiction in which the corporation was incorporated / Le territoire de compétence où la personne morale a été constituée

9. Address of Head or Registered Office of the corporation *(P.O. Box not acceptable)* / Adresse du siège social ou du bureau enregistré de la personne morale *(Case postale non acceptée)*

Street No. / Nº de rue Street Name / Nom de la rue Suite No. / Bureau nº
City / Town / Ville Province Postal Code / Code postal
Country / Pays

10. Print name of person authorizing this registration *(either an officer, or a director, or a person acting under a power of attorney)*. / Indiquez en lettres majuscules le nom de la personne autorisant l'enregistrement *(dirigeant, administrateur, ou personne habilitée en vertu d'une procuration)*.

Last Name / Nom de famille First Name / Prénom Middle Initial / initiale 2e prénom

If person authorizing the registration is not an individual (eg. corporation, trust, syndicate), print name below and do not complete last, first and middle names above. / Si la personne qui autorise l'enregistrement n'est pas un individu (c'est-à-dire une personne morale, un trust ou syndicat) ne pas remlir le nom de famille, prénom et 2e prénom.

Additional Information / Renseignements supplémentaires

MINISTRY USE ONLY / RÉSERVÉ AU MINISTÈRE

It is the responsibility of the applicant(s) to ensure the accuracy of the information submitted. It is an offence under section 10 of the *Business Names Act* to submit false or misleading information. / Il incombe aux demandeurs de veiller à l'exactitude des renseignements présentés. Le demandeur qui fait une déclaration fausse ou trompeuse commet une infraction en vertu de l'article 10 de la *Loi sur les noms commerciaux*.

07197 (2009/11)

INSTRUCTIONS **It is important to read these notes before completing the attached form.**

Print all information clearly in CAPITAL LETTERS using black ink.

It is the responsibility of the applicant(s) to ensure that information submitted under the *Business Names Act* is accurate and complete. It is an offence under section 10 of the Act if a person, without reasonable cause, submits a statement in an application for a registration under this Act that is false or misleading with respect to any material fact. On conviction, a person guilty of an offence is liable to a fine of not more than $2,000 or, if the person is a corporation, to a fine of not more than $25,000. If a corporation is guilty of an offence, every director or officer of the corporation and every person acting as its representative in Ontario who authorized, permitted or acquiesced in such an offence is also guilty of an offence and on conviction is liable to a fine of not more than $2,000.

Complete all sections of the form. Incomplete forms will be returned.

Fees:
- there is a fee payable for new registrations and renewals;
- fees may be paid in cash, money order or cheque;
- payable to the **Ontario Minister of Finance**;
- do not send cash in the mail;
- a handling fee will be charged for a non-negotiable cheque.

Please forward both copies of the enclosed form to the Ministry of Government Services.
The Client copy will no longer be certified consistent with Ontario Regulation 175 / 94 Section 4.
The Client copy will be **returned**, with a validation in the bottom right-hand corner.

Return completed forms to: **Ministry of Government Services**
Central Production and Verification Services Branch
393 University Avenue, Suite 200
Toronto ON M5G 2M2

Please do not separate the form.

Refer to these notes while completing form.

1. Registration Type - Check the appropriate box:

   New (Fee payable)
   - a new registration is the first filing of the business name;
   - a change of business name/identification name is considered a new registration.

   Renewal (Fee payable)
   - a registration expires in five years and must be renewed.

   Amendment (No fee payable)
   - an amendment should be filed whenever there is a change in address, activity or corporation name.

   Cancellation (No fee payable)
   - a cancellation should be submitted if you stop using the business name.

   BIN

   For renewal, amendment or cancellation, enter "Business Identification No." (BIN).

2. Business or Identification Name - Please print the business name. This is the name you are registering. The business name must be set out in Block Capital Letters in the squares provided and must commence on the first line of the 'grid' in the first square. Each square of the grid represents a letter of the alphabet, a punctuation mark, or a space. If there is not sufficient space on the grid for the name, please use additional form(s). Please complete all items on additional form(s) and note the number of each additional page in the top right-hand corner of each form.

3. Mailing Address of Registrant - Include street number, name, municipality and postal code. Your copy of the registration will be mailed to this address.

4. Business Address (Address of Principal Place of Business) in Ontario - Include street number, name, municipality and postal code.

   A post office box is not acceptable in a business address. If there is more than one place of business, select one as the principal place. Where the business address is outside Ontario, set out the words "Not Applicable" in item 4. If this is the case, please ensure that Item 3, the mailing address, includes the street address of the principal place of business outside of Ontario, as a post office box is not acceptable.

5. Activity - Include a brief description of the activity being performed.

6. Corporation Name - the name of the corporation that is registering the business name.

7. Ontario Corporation Number - the number assigned to the corporation named in item 6.

8. Jurisdiction - the name of the jurisdiction in which the corporation was incorporated. Please do not use abbreviations.

9. Address of the Head or Registered Office of the corporation - include the number, street, municipality and postal code of the head or registered office address. **A post office box is not acceptable.**

10. Print the name of the person authorizing the registration, (either an officer, or a director, or a person acting under a power of attorney).

    Additional Information: If the person authorizing the registration is not an individual e.g. corporation, trust, syndicate set out the name in "Additional Information" and do not complete the boxes for the last, first and middle names.

07197 (2009/11)

Form 5 — Registration (Partnership/Limited Partnership)*

Print clearly in CAPITAL LETTERS
Écrivez clairement en LETTRES MAJUSCULES

1. Registration Type
Type d'enregistrement

Page____ of / de____

If B, C, or D enter "Business Identification Number"
En cas de B, C ou D, inscrivez le nº d'identification de l'entreprise.

A ☐ New / Nouveau B ☐ Renewal / Renouvellement C ☐ Amendment / Modification D ☐ Cancellation / Révocation

BIN Business Identification No.
NIE Nº d'identification de l'entreprise

2. Partnership Business Name / Nom commercial

3. Mailing Address of Registrant / Adresse postale de Registrant

Street No./ Nº de rue Street Name / Nom de la rue Suite No. / Bureau nº
City / Town / Ville Province / Province Postal Code / Code postal
Country / Pays

4. Address of principal place of business in Ontario *(P.O. Box not acceptable)*
Adresse de l'établissement principal en Ontario *(Case postale non acceptée)*

☐ Same as above / *comme ci-dessus*

Street No. / Nº de rue Street Name / Nom de la rue Suite No. / Bureau nº City / Town / Ville
Province / Province Postal Code / Code postal Country / Pays

5. Give a brief description of the ACTIVITY being carried out under the business name.
Résumez brièvement le genre d'ACTIVITÉ exercée sous le nom commercial.

6. Type of Registrant
Type d'entité enregistrée

A ☐ General Partnership / Société en nom collectif B ☐ Limited Partnership / Société en commandite

7. Firm Name
Raison sociale de la société

8. BIN Business Identification No. for Firm Name *(refer to #7)*
NIE de la société désignée en 7

9. Print name of person authorizing this registration *(either a general partner or a person acting under a power of attorney).*
Indiquez en lettres majuscules le nom de la personne autorisant l'enregistrement *(associé, commandité ou personne habilitée en vertu d'une procuration).*

Last Name / Nom de famille First Name / Prénom Middle Initial / Initiale 2ᵉ prénom

Additional Information: If the person authorizing the registration is not an individual, (e.g. corporation, trust, syndicate), **set out the name, together with the name of the individual authorized to sign on that person's behalf,** in "Additional Information", and do not complete the space above **(see Instructions, number 9). / Renseignements supplémentaires :** Si l'enregistrement est autorisé par une entreprise (personne morale, société de fiducie, consortium, etc.), **indiquez ci-dessous la raison sociale de l'entité et le nom de la personne habilitée à signer (voir Instructions, art. 9).**

Additional Information ***(name)*** **/ Renseignements supplémentaires** ***(raison sociale)***

Authorized to Sign / Signataire autorisé
Last Name / Nom de famille First Name / Prénom

MINISTRY USE ONLY - RÉSERVÉ AU MINISTÈRE

It is the responsibility of the applicant(s) to ensure the accuracy of the information submitted. It is an offence under section 10 of the *Business Names Act* to submit false or misleading information.
Il incombe aux demandeurs de veiller à l'exactitude des renseignements présentés. Le demandeur qui fait une déclaration fausse ou trompeuse commet une infractionen vertu de l'article 10 de la *Loi sur les noms commerciaux.*

07215 (2008/05)

INSTRUCTIONS **It is important to read these notes before completing the attached form.**

Print all information clearly in CAPITAL LETTERS using black ink.

It is the responsibility of the applicant(s) to ensure that information submitted under the *Business Names Act* is accurate and complete. It is an offence under section 10 of the Act if a person, without reasonable cause, submits a statement in an application for a registration under this Act that is false or misleading with respect to any material fact. On conviction, a person guilty of an offence is liable to a fine of not more than $2,000 or, if the person is a corporation, to a fine of not more than $25,000. If a corporation is guilty of an offence, every director or officer of the corporation and every person acting as its representative in Ontario who authorized, permitted or acquiesced in such an offence is also guilty of an offence and on conviction is liable to a fine of not more than $2,000.

Complete all sections of the form. Incomplete forms will be returned.

Fees:
- there is a fee payable for new registrations and renewals;
- fees may be paid in cash, money order or cheque;
- payable to the **Ontario Minister of Finance;**
- do not send cash in the mail;
- a handling fee will be charged for a non-negotiable cheque.

Please forward both copies of the form to the Ministry of Government Services.
The Client copy will no longer be certified consistent with Ontario Regulation 175 / 94 Section 4.
The Client copy will be **returned,** with a validation in the bottom right-hand corner.

Return completed forms to: **Ministry of**
Government Services
Companies and Personal Property Security Branch
393 University Avenue, Suite 200
Toronto ON M5G 2M2

Please do not separate the form.

Refer to these notes while completing form.

1. **Registration Type** - Check the appropriate box:

   New *(Fee payable)*
   - a new registration is the first filing of the partnership business name
   - a change of partnership business name is considered a new registration

   Renewal *(Fee payable)*
   - a registration expires in five years and must be renewed

   Amendment *(No fee payable)*
   - an amendment should be filed whenever there is a change in address or change of activity

   Cancellation *(No fee payable)*
   - a cancellation should be submitted if you stop using the partnership business name

   BIN
   For renewal, amendment or cancellation, enter "Business Identification No.".

2. **Partnership Business Name** - Please print the partnership business name. This is the name you are registering. The partnership business name must be set out in Block Capital Letters in the squares provided and must commence on the first line of the 'grid' in the first square. Each square of the grid represents a letter of the alphabet, a punctuation mark, or a space. If there is not sufficient space on the grid for the name, please use additional form(s). Please complete all items on additional form(s) and note the number of each additional page in the top right-hand corner of each form.

3. **Mailing Address of Registrant** - Include street number, name, municipality and postal code. Your copy of the registration will be mailed to this address.

4. **Address of Principal Place of Business in Ontario** - Include street, number, name, municipality and postal code. A post office box is not acceptable in a business address. If there is more than one place of business, select one as the principal place. Where the business address is outside Ontario, set out the words "Not Applicable" in item 4. If this is the case, please ensure that Item 3, the mailing address, includes the street address of the principal place of business outside of Ontario, as a post office box is not acceptable.

5. **Activity** - Include a brief description of the activity being performed.

6. **Type of Registrant** - Check the appropriate box for either a General Partnership or a Limited Partnership.

7. **Firm Name** - set out the exact name previously registered by the partnership.

8. **Firm's BIN** - set out the corresponding Business Identification Number for the firm.

9. **Print the name of the person authorizing the registration** *(either a general partner or a person acting under a power of attorney).*

   Additional Information: If the person authorizing the registration is not an individual, *(e.g. corporation, trust, syndicate)*, **set out the name, together with the name of the individual authorized to sign on that person's behalf**, in "Additional Information", and do not complete the space above. Eg:

   xxxx Limited
   Authorized to Sign: Last and First Name

07215 (2008/05)

INSTRUCTIONS **Il est important de lire ces remarques avant de remplir le formulaire.**

Inscrivez les renseignements clairement en LETTRES MAJUSCULES, au stylo noir.

Il est de la responsabilité du demandeur de veiller à ce que les renseignements fournis en vertu de la *Loi sur les noms commerciaux* sont exacts et complets. Quiconque fait, sans motifs raisonnables, dans une demande d'enregistrement en vertu de cette loi, une déclaration fausse ou trompeuse sur un fait important est coupable d'une infraction en vertu de l'article 10 de la loi. Cette personne est passible, sur déclaration de culpabilité, d'une amende d'au plus de 2 000 $ ou, si cette personne est une personne morale, d'une amende d'au plus 25 000 $. Si la personne morale est coupable d'une infraction, ses administrateurs ou dirigeants, ainsi que les personnes agissant en qualité de mandataires en Ontario qui ont autorisé ou permis cette infraction, ou qui y ont acquiescé, sont aussi coupables d'une infraction et passibles, sur déclaration de culpabilité, d'une amende d'au plus 2 000 $.

Remplissez toutes les sections. Les formulaires incomplets seront retournés.

Droits :
- Perçus pour les nouveaux enregistrements et les renouvellements;
- Payables en espèces, par mandat ou par chèque;
- À l'ordre du **ministre des Finances de l'Ontario**;
- N'envoyez pas d'argent en espèces par la poste;
- Des frais administratifs seront facturés pour tout chèque non négociable.

Envoyez les DEUX COPIES du formulaire au ministère des Services gouvernementaux. La copie du Client ne sera plus certifiée, conformément à l'article 4 du Règlement de l'Ontario 175 / 94. La copie du Client sera validée et vous sera **retournée.**

Retournez le formulaire rempli au : **Ministère des Services gouvernementaux**
Direction des compagnies et des sûretés mobilières
393, avenue University, bureau 200
Toronto ON M5G 2M2

Ne séparez pas les pages du formulaire.

Consultez ces remarques lorsque vous remplissez le formulaire.

1. **Type d'enregistrement** - Cochez la case appropriée :

   Nouveau *(Droits à payer)*
   - le premier enregistrement du nom commercial constitue un nouvel enregistrement;
   - une modification apportée au nom commercial est considérée comme un nouvel enregistrement.

   Renouvellement *(Droits à payer)*
   - un enregistrement expire au bout de cinq ans; il doit être renouvelé.

   Modification *(Aucuns droits à payer)*
   - une modification devrait être déposée chaque fois qu'il y a un changement d'adresse ou d'activité.

   Révocation *(Aucuns droits à payer)*
   - il convient de soumettre une révocation si vous n'utilisez plus le nom commercial.

   NIE
   Pour un renouvellement, une modification ou une révocation, indiquez le numéro d'identification de l'entreprise.

2. **Nom commercial** – Inscrivez en majuscules le nom commercial que vous enregistrez, une lettre par case, en commençant à la première case de la première ligne. Utilisez aussi un espace pour chaque signe de ponctuation et pour chaque espace entre les mots. Si vous manquez d'espace, prenez d'autres formulaires, au besoin. Sur chaque formulaire supplémentaire, remplissez toutes les rubriques et numérotez les pages dans le coin supérieur droit.

3. **Adresse postale de Registrant** – Inscrivez le numéro et le nom de la rue, le nom de la ville et le code postal. Votre copie de l'enregistrement sera expédiée à cette adresse.

4. **Adresse de l'établissement principal en Ontario** – L'adresse doit comprendre le numéro et le nom de la rue, la ville et le code postal. Une case postale n'est pas acceptée comme adresse d'affaires. S'il existe plus d'un établissement, choisissez-en un comme établissement principal. Lorsque l'établissement principal est situé à l'extérieur de l'Ontario, inscrivez «Sans objet» à la section 4. Dans ce cas, à la section 3, l'adresse postale doit être l'adresse complète de l'établissement principal situé hors de l'Ontario, une case postale n'étant pas acceptée.

5. **Activité** – Donnez une brève description de l'activité exercée.

6. **Type d'entité enregistrée** – Cochez la case appropriée : société en nom collectif ou société en commandite.

7. **Raison sociale de la société** – Indiquez la raison sociale exacte sous laquelle opère actuellement la société.

8. **NIE de la société désignée en 7** – Indiquez le numéro d'identification de la société (NIE) correspondant à la raison sociale existante.

9. **Personne autorisant l'enregistrement** – Indiquez son nom, prénom, initiale en majuscules (associé, commandité ou personne habilitée en vertu d'une procuration).

Renseignements supplémentaires - Si l'enregistrement est autorisé par une entreprise (personne morale, société de fiducie, consortium, etc.), **indiquez dans cette case la raison sociale de l'entité et le nom de la personne habilitée à signer en son nom** – p. ex. :

xxxx Ltée
Signataire autorisé : Nom de famille et prénom

07215 (2008/05)

Form 6 — Registration (Ontario Limited Liability Partnership, Extra-Provincial Limited Liability Partnership and Extra-Provincial Limited Liability Company)*

Print clearly in CAPITAL LETTERS
Écrivez clairement en LETTRES MAJUSCULES

1. Registration Type / Type d'enregistrement
If B, C, or D enter "Business Identification Number"
En cas de B, C ou D, inscrivez le nº d'identification de l'entreprise.
Page_____ of / de_____

A ☐ New / Nouveau B ☐ Renewal / Renouvellement C ☐ Amendment / Modification D ☐ Cancellation / Révocation
BIN Business Identification No.
NIE Nº d'identification de l'entreprise

2. Business Name / Nom commercial

3. Mailing Address of Registrant / Adresse postale de Registrant
Street No./ Nº de rue Street Name / Nom de la rue Suite No. / Bureau nº
City / Town / Ville Province / Province Postal Code / Code postal
Country / Pays

4. Address of principal place of business in Ontario *(P.O. Box not acceptable)*
Adresse de l'établissement principal en Ontario *(Case postale non acceptée)*
☐ Same as above / comme ci-dessus
Street No. / Nº de rue Street Name / Nom de la rue Suite No. / Bureau nº City / Town / Ville
Province / Province Postal Code / Code postal Country / Pays

5. Give a brief description of the ACTIVITY being carried out under the business name.
Résumez brièvement le genre d'ACTIVITÉ exercée sous le nom commercial.

6. Type of Registrant / Type d'entité enregistrée
☐ More than 10 Partners: records at business address / Plus de 10 associés : dossiers à l'adresse d'affaires
A ☐ Ontario Limited LiabilityPartnership / Société à responsabilité limitée de l'Ontario OR / OU B ☐ Extra-ProvincialLimited Liability Partnership / Société à responsabilité limitée extraprovinciale OR / OU C ☐ Extra-Provincial Limited Liability Company / Société de capitaux extraprovinciale

7. Jurisdiction of Formation / Territoire d'origine

8. Registrant Information *(P.O. Box not acceptable)*
Renseignements sur la personne enregistrée *(Case postale non acceptée)*
Last Name / Nom de famille First Name / Prénom Middle Initial / Initiale 2ᵉ prénom

9. Street No. / Nº de rue Street Name / Nom de la rue Suite No. / Bureau nº City / Town / Ville
Province / Province Postal Code / Code postal Country / Pays

Additional Information. Only complete if the registrant is not an individual. See instructions 8/9 on the form.
Renseignements supplémentaires. À remplir uniquement si la personne enregistrée n'est pas un particulier.
(Voir instructions, art. 8 /9)
Ont. Corporation No.
Nº matricule de la personne morale en Ontario

8. Last Name / Nom de famille First Name / Prénom Middle Initial / Initiale 2ᵉ prénom

9. Street No. / Nº de rue Street Name / Nom de la rue Suite No. / Bureau nº City / Town / Ville
Province / Province Postal Code / Code postal Country / Pays

Additional Information. Only complete if the registrant is not an individual. See instructions 8/9 on the form.
Renseignements supplémentaires. À remplir uniquement si la personne enregistrée n'est pas un particulier.
(Voir instructions, art. 8 /9)
Ont. Corporation No.
Nº matricule de la personne morale en Ontario

10. Print name of person authorizing this registration *(either a partner (for LLP), a general manager/representative (for LLC) or a person acting under power of attorney).*
Indiquez en lettres majuscules le nom de la personne autorisant l'enregistrement *(associé (s.r.l.), directeur général / représentant (s.c.), ou personne habilitée en vertu d'une procuration).*
Last Name / Nom de famille First Name / Prénom Middle Initial / Initiale 2ᵉ prénom

Additional Information: If the person authorizing the registration is not an individual, (e.g. corporation, trust, syndicate), **set out the name, together with the name of the individual authorized to sign on that person's behalf**, in "Additional Information", and do not complete the space above **(see Instructions, number 10). / Renseignements supplémentaires :** Si l'enregistrement est autorisé par une entreprise (personne morale, société de fiducie, consortium, etc.), **indiquez ci-dessous la raison sociale de l'entité et le nom de la personne habilitée à signer (voir instructions, art. 10).**

Additional Information ***(name)*** **/ Renseignements supplémentaires** ***(raison sociale)***

Authorized to Sign / Signataire autorisé
Last Name / Nom de famille First Name / Prénom

MINISTRY USE ONLY - *RÉSERVÉ AU MINISTÈRE*

It is the responsibility of the applicant(s) to ensure the accuracy of the information submitted. It is an offence under section 10 of the *Business Names Act* to submit false or misleading information. / Il incombe aux demandeurs de veiller à l'exactitude des renseignements présentés. Le demandeur qui fait une déclaration fausse ou trompeuse commet une infractionen vertu de l'article 10 de la *Loi sur les noms commerciaux*.
07193 (2008/05)

INSTRUCTIONS It is important to read these notes before completing the attached form.

Print all information clearly in CAPITAL LETTERS using black ink.

It is the responsibility of the applicant(s) to ensure that information submitted under the *Business Names Act* is accurate and complete. It is an offence under section 10 of the Act if a person, without reasonable cause, submits a statement in an application for a registration under this Act that is false or misleading with respect to any material fact. On conviction, a person guilty of an offence is liable to a fine of not more than $2,000 or, if the person is a corporation, to a fine of not more than $25,000. If a corporation is guilty of an offence, every director or officer of the corporation and every person acting as its representative in Ontario who authorized, permitted or acquiesced in such an offence is also guilty of an offence and on conviction is liable to a fine of not more than $2,000.

Complete all sections of the form. Incomplete forms will be returned.

Fees:
- there is a fee payable for new registrations and renewals;
- fees may be paid in cash, money order or cheque;
- payable to the **Ontario Minister of Finance;**
- do not send cash in the mail;
- a handling fee will be charged for a non-negotiable cheque.

Please forward both copies of the form to the Ministry of Government Services.
The Client copy will no longer be certified consistent with Ontario Regulation 175 / 94 Section 4.
The Client copy will be **returned**, with a validation in the bottom right-hand corner.

Return completed forms to: **Ministry of
Government Services**
Companies and Personal Property Security Branch
393 University Avenue, Suite 200
Toronto ON M5G 2M2

Please do not separate the form.

Refer to these notes while completing form.

1. **Registration Type** - Check the appropriate box:

   New *(Fee payable)*
   - a new registration is the first filing of the business name
   - a change of business name, or a complete change of partners is considered a new registration

   Renewal *(Fee payable)*
   - a registration expires in five years and must be renewed

   Amendment (No fee payable)
   - an amendment should be filed whenever there is a change in address or change of activity

   Cancellation *(No fee payable)*
   - a cancellation should be submitted if you stop using the business name

   BIN
   For renewal, amendment or cancellation, enter "Business Identification No.".

2. **Business Name** - The name must contain the legal element which identifies the entity, for example; Limited Liability Partnership, LLP, Limited Liability Company, LLC or the equivalent French or other similar terms required under the law where the entity was formed. Please print the business name in Block Capital Letters in the squares provided, commencing on the first line of the "grid" in the first square. Each square of the grid represents a letter of the alphabet, a punctuation mark or a space. If there is not sufficient space on the grid for the name, please use additional form(s) and write the number of each additional page in the top right-hand corner of each form.

3. **Mailing Address of Registrant** - Include street number, name, municipality and postal code. Your copy of the registration will be mailed to this address.

4. **Address of Principal Place of Business in Ontario** - Include street, number, name, municipality and postal code. A post office box is not acceptable in a business address. If there is more than one place of business, select one as the principal place. For an Extra-Provincial Limited Liability Partnership or an Extra-Provincial Limited Liability Company where the business address may be outside of Ontario, set out the words "Not Applicable" in item 4. If this is the case, please ensure that item 3, the mailing address, includes the street address of the principal place of business outside of Ontario, as a post office is not acceptable.

5. **Activity** - Include a brief description of the activity being performed.

6. **Type of Registrant** - Check the appropriate box. If you are registering an Ontario Limited Liability Partnership or an Extra-Provincial Limited Liability Partnership with more than 10 partners, you may set out the name and address of a designated partner(s) and check the box marked "More than 10 Partners". Information on all partners carrying on business in Ontario must be kept and made available to the public at the Limited Liability Partnership's business address in Ontario.

7. **Jurisdiction of Formation** - Enter the name of the jurisdiction in which the Ontario Limited Liability Partnership, the Extra-Provincial Limited Liability Partnership or the Extra-Provincial Limited Liability Company was formed. Please do not use abbreviations.

8/9. **Registrant Information** - This item applies only to an Ontario Limited Liability Partnership or to an Extra-Provincial Limited Liability Partnership (*it is not required for an Extra-Provincial Limited Liability Company*). Include the full name and residential address or address for service of each partner or designated partner(s). A post office box is not acceptable. If there are more than two partners, please fill out and attach another form(s) with the additional names and addresses.

Additional Information - If the registrant is **not** an individual, enter the name of the business or corporation in "Additional Information". Also enter the address of the business or corporation in item 9. If the registrant is a corporation, enter the Ontario Corporation No.

10. **Print the name of the person authorizing this registration,** *(either a partner for a Limited Liability Partnership, a general manager/representative for a Limited Liability Company or a person acting under power of attorney).*

    Additional Information: If the person authorizing the registration is not an individual, *(e.g. corporation, trust, syndicate)*, **set out the name, together with the name of the individual authorized to sign on that person's behalf,** in "Additional Information", and do not complete the space above. Eg:

    xxxx Limited
    Authorized to Sign: Last and First Name

07193 (2008/05)

INSTRUCTIONS **Il est important de lire ces remarques avant de remplir le formulaire.**

Inscrivez les renseignements clairement en LETTRES MAJUSCULES, au stylo noir.

Il est de la responsabilité du demandeur de veiller à ce que les renseignements fournis en vertu de la *Loi sur les noms commerciaux* sont exacts et complets. Quiconque fait, sans motifs raisonnables, dans une demande d'enregistrement en vertu de cette loi, une déclaration fausse ou trompeuse sur un fait important est coupable d'une infraction en vertu de l'article 10 de la loi. Cette personne est passible, sur déclaration de culpabilité, d'une amende d'au plus de 2 000 $ ou, si cette personne est une personne morale, d'une amende d'au plus 25 000 $. Si la personne morale est coupable d'une infraction, ses administrateurs ou dirigeants, ainsi que les personnes agissant en qualité de mandataires en Ontario qui ont autorisé ou permis cette infraction, ou qui y ont acquiescé, sont aussi coupables d'une infraction et passibles, sur déclaration de culpabilité, d'une amende d'au plus 2 000 $.

Remplissez toutes les sections. Les formulaires incomplets seront retournés.

Droits :
- Perçus pour les nouveaux enregistrements et les renouvellements;
- Payables en espèces, par mandat ou par chèque;
- À l'ordre du **ministre des Finances de l'Ontario;**
- N'envoyez pas d'argent en espèces par la poste;
- Des frais administratifs seront facturés pour tout chèque non négociable.

Envoyez les DEUX COPIES du formulaire au ministère des Services gouvernementaux. La copie du Client ne sera plus certifiée, conformément à l'article 4 du Règlement de l'Ontario 175 / 94. La copie du Client sera validée et vous sera **retournée.**

Retournez le formulaire rempli au : **Ministère des**
Services gouvernementaux
Direction des compagnies et des sûretés mobilières
393, avenue University, bureau 200
Toronto ON M5G 2M2

Ne séparez pas les pages du formulaire.

Consultez ces remarques lorsque vous remplissez le formulaire.

1. **Type d'enregistrement** - Cochez la case appropriée :

   Nouveau *(Droits à payer)*
   - le premier enregistrement du nom commercial constitue un nouvel enregistrement;
   - une modification apportée au nom commercial ou un changement de tous les associés constitue un nouvel enregistrement.

   Renouvellement *(Droits à payer)*
   - un enregistrement expire au bout de cinq ans; il doit être renouvelé.

   Modification *(Aucuns droits à payer)*
   - une modification devrait être déposée chaque fois qu'il y a un changement d'adresse ou d'activité.

   Révocation *(Aucuns droits à payer)*
   - il convient de soumettre une révocation si vous n'utilisez plus le nom commercial.

   NIE
   Pour un renouvellement, une modification ou une révocation, indiquez le numéro d'identification de l'entreprise.

2. **Nom commercial** – Le nom doit comprendre l'élément légal qui identifie l'entité; p. ex. : société à responsabilité limitée, s.r.l., société de capitaux, s.c., ou l'équivalent anglais, ou d'autres termes semblables requis par les lois du territoire où a été formée la société. Inscrivez en majuscules le nom commercial que vous enregistrez, une lettre par case, en commençant à la première case de la première ligne. Utilisez aussi un espace pour chaque signe de ponctuation et pour chaque espace entre les mots. Si vous manquez d'espace, prenez d'autres formulaires, remplissez toutes les rubriques sur chaque formulaire et numérotez les pages dans le coin supérieur droit.

3. **Adresse postale de registrant** – Inscrivez le numéro et le nom de la rue, le nom de la ville et le code postal. Votre copie de l'enregistrement sera expédiée à cette adresse.

4. **Adresse de l'établissement principal en Ontario** – L'adresse doit comprendre le numéro et le nom de la rue, la ville et le code postal. Une case postale n'est pas acceptée comme adresse d'affaires. S'il existe plus d'un établissement, choisissez-en un comme établissement principal. Pour une société à responsabilité limitée extraprovinciale ou une société de capitaux extraprovinciale dont l'établissement principal est situé hors de l'Ontario, inscrivez «Sans objet» à la section 4. Dans ce cas, à la section 3, l'adresse postale doit être l'adresse complète de l'établissement principal situé hors de l'Ontario, une case postale n'étant pas acceptée.

5. **Activité** – Donnez une brève description de l'activité exercée.

6. **Type d'entité enregistrée** – Cochez la case appropriée. Si vous enregistrez une société à responsabilité limitée (de l'Ontario ou extraprovinciale) comprenant plus de 10 associés, cochez aussi la case « Plus de 10 associés », puis, à la section 8, indiquez le nom et l'adresse d'un associé ou des associés désignés. Les renseignements relatifs à tous les associés menant des activités en Ontario doivent être conservés et mis à la disposition du public à l'adresse d'affaires ontarienne de la société.

7. **Territoire d'origine** – Indiquez au complet le territoire de compétence où la société à responsabilité limitée ou la société de capitaux a été formée. N'utilisez pas d'abréviations.

8/9. **Renseignements sur la personne enregistrée** – Cette section doit être remplie uniquement dans le cas d'une société à responsabilité limitée (de l'Ontario ou extra-provinciale). Indiquez le nom complet et l'adresse personnelle ou le domicile élu de chaque associé ou des associés désignés. Une case postale n'est pas acceptée. Si la société compte plus de deux associés, veuillez remplir et joindre d'autres formulaires portant les noms et adresses supplémentaires.

   Renseignements supplémentaires – Si la personne enregistrée **n'est pas** un particulier, inscrivez dans cette case le nom de l'entreprise ou de la personne morale, et indiquez son adresse à la section 9. Dans le cas d'une personne morale, indiquez aussi son numéro matricule de l'Ontario dans l'espace prévu à cet effet.

10. **Personne autorisant l'enregistrement** – Indiquez son nom, prénom et initiale en majuscules (ce peut être un associé pour une s.r.l.; un directeur général ou représentant pour une s.c.; ou une personne habilitée en vertu d'une procuration).

   Renseignements supplémentaires – Si l'enregistrement est autorisé par une entreprise (personne morale, société de fiducie, consortium, etc.), **indiquez dans cette case la raison sociale de l'entité et le nom de la personne habilitée à signer en son nom – p. ex. :**

   xxxx Ltée
   Signataire autorisé : Nom de famille et prénom

07193 (2008/05)

Business Records Protection Act

R.S.O. 1990, c. B.19, as am. S.O. 2006, c. 19, Sched. C, s. 1(1).

1. Business records not to be taken from Ontario — No person shall, under or under the authority of or in a manner that would be consistent with compliance with any requirement, order, direction or summons of any legislative, administrative or judicial authority in any jurisdiction outside Ontario, take or cause to be taken, send or cause to be sent or remove or cause to be removed from a point in Ontario to a point outside Ontario, any account, balance sheet, profit and loss statement or inventory or any resume or digest thereof or any other record, statement, report, or material in any way relating to any business carried on in Ontario, unless such taking, sending or removal,

(a) is consistent with and forms part of a regular practice of furnishing to a head office or parent company or organization outside Ontario material relating to a branch or subsidiary company or organization carrying on business in Ontario;

(b) is done by or on behalf of a company or person as defined in the *Securities Act*, carrying on business in Ontario and as to a jurisdiction outside Ontario in which the securities of the company or person have been qualified for sale with the consent of the company or person;

(c) is done by or on behalf of a company or person as defined in the *Securities Act*, carrying on business in Ontario as a dealer or salesperson as defined in the *Securities Act*, and as to a jurisdiction outside Ontario in which the company or person has been registered or is otherwise qualified to carry on business as a dealer or salesperson, as the case may be; or

(d) is provided for by or under any law of Ontario or of the Parliament of Canada.

2. (1) Undertaking and recognizance — Where the Attorney General or any person having an interest in a business as mentioned in section 1 has reason to believe that a requirement, order, direction or summons as mentioned in section 1 has been or is likely to be made, issued or given in relation to such business, the Attorney General or that person, as the case may be, may apply to the Superior Court of Justice for an order requiring any person, whether or not that person is named in the requirement, order, direction or subpoena, to furnish an undertaking and recognizance for the purpose of ensuring that the person will not contravene section 1 and the court may make such order as the court considers proper.

(2) Contempt of Court — Every person who, having received notice of an application under this section, contravenes this Act shall be deemed to be in contempt of court and is liable to one year's imprisonment.

(3) Idem — Every person required to furnish an undertaking or recognizance who contravenes this Act is in contempt of court and in addition to any penalty provided by the recognizance is liable to one year's imprisonment.

2006, c. 19, Sched. C, s. 1(1)

BUSINESS REGULATION REFORM ACT, 1994

An Act to reform the Law regulating Business

S.O. 1994, c. 32, as am. S.O. 2006, c. 21, Sched. F, s. 136(1), Table 1; 2006, c. 33, Sched. C; 2006, c. 35, Sched. C, s. 10; 2007, c. 7, Sched. 7, s. 182; 2012, c. 8, Sched. 5.

Her Majesty, by and with the advice and consent of the Legislative Assembly of the Province of Ontario, enacts as follows:

1. Purpose — The purpose of this Act is to assist the formation and operation of businesses in Ontario by simplifying government regulatory requirements, eliminating duplication in procedures and improving government organizational arrangements.

2. Definitions — In this Act,

"business" means a person within the meaning of the *Business Names Act* authorized or entitled to carry on business in Ontario;

"business information" means,

(a) the business identifier, if any, assigned to a business by the system of business identifiers established under section 8 or by a system of business identifiers established by the Government of Canada or an agent of the Government of Canada or by a municipality, local board or other municipal entity,

(b) the name of the business and any operating names or other business names used by it,

(c) the legal structure of the business,

(d) the mailing and email addresses, of the business,

(e) the telephone and fax numbers, if any, of the business,

(f) if the business is a corporation,

(i) the date of its incorporation,

(ii) the jurisdiction under whose laws it is incorporated and its incorporation number in that jurisdiction,

(iii) for a business incorporated in a jurisdiction other than Ontario, a copy of its licence under the *Extra-Provincial Corporations Act*, if required to carry on any of its business in Ontario,

(iv) the names of its directors,

(g) if the business is a partnership, the names of the partners,

(h) if the business is an unincorporated organization other than a partnership, the name of at least one individual who alone or together with others is responsible for the management of the business or affairs of the organization, and

(i) any other prescribed information;

"file" means to file, to register, to submit, to deposit, to make an application or to otherwise make available.

"local board" has the same meaning as in the *Municipal Act, 2001*;

"municipality" has the same meaning as in the *Municipal Act, 2001*;

"municipal entity" means any authority, board, commission, corporation, office or organization of persons some or all of whose members, directors or officers are appointed or chosen by or under the authority of a municipality in Ontario, but does not include a local board.

2012, c. 8, Sched. 5, s. 1

3. Designation of Acts — The Lieutenant Governor in Council may designate any Act for the purpose of this Act.

4. (1) Minister's recommendation — The Lieutenant Governor in Council shall not make a regulation or an order in council or approve a form under this Act that affects the administration of a designated Act except on the recommendation of the Minister responsible for the administration of the designated Act.

(2) Same — A Minister shall not make a regulation, approve a form or enter into an agreement under this Act that affects the administration of a designated Act except on the recommendation of the Minister responsible for the administration of the designated Act.

5. (1) Conflict — A provision of this Act or the regulations or orders in council made under this Act that is mandatory and that conflicts with a provision of a designated Act or the regulations made under that Act prevails if it expressly mentions the provision over which it prevails.

(2) Same, non-mandatory provision — If a provision of this Act or the regulations or orders in council made under this Act conflicts with a provision of a designated Act or the regulations or orders in council made under that Act but is not mandatory, a person may elect under which provision to proceed.

6. (1) Unified requirements — The Lieutenant Governor in Council may make regulations,

(a) unifying procedures for business to file information under designated Acts;

(b) unifying financial and statistical reporting requirements and procedures for businesses under designated Acts;

(c) prescribing common dates or time periods for businesses to file information or to pay fees, taxes or other charges under designated Acts;

(d) prescribing methods for allocating a payment made by a business of less than the full amount of its liability under the designated Acts in respect of which the payment was made.

(2) Other requirements — In a regulation made under subsection (1), the Lieutenant Governor in Council may prescribe all requirements that are necessary in the circumstances to achieve the objective of the regulation, including adjusting the amount of fees that businesses are required to pay under designated Acts.

(3) Funds — Nothing in this section affects a provision in a designated Act with respect to the maintenance of separate funds or the priority of entitlement to funds under the designated Act.

7. (1) Forms — The Lieutenant Governor in Council may approve forms that have the same effect as forms prescribed or approved by the Lieutenant Governor in Council under designated Acts.

(2) Same, Minister — The Minister responsible for the administration of this section may approve forms that have the same effect as forms prescribed or approved by a Minister, board or agency under designated Acts.

(3) Variations — Despite subsections (1) and (2), the Minister responsible for the administration of this section may combine forms prescribed or approved under either of those subsections into a single form and may adapt the form as is necessary in the circumstances for the purposes of a designated Act.

(4) Use of forms — The Lieutenant Governor in Council may make regulations providing for the use of forms that are prescribed or approved under this section.

8. (1) Business identifiers — The Lieutenant Governor in Council may by order in council establish a system of business identifiers.

(2) Agreements with Canada — The Minister responsible for the administration of this section may enter into agreements with the Government of Canada or an agent of the Government of Canada for the purpose of integrating a system of business identifiers established under this section with any system of business identifiers established by the Government of Canada or an agent of the Government of Canada.

(2.1) Agreements with municipalities — The Minister responsible for the administration of this section may, with the approval of the Government of Canada or an agent of the Government of Canada who has entered into an agreement under subsection (2), enter into agreements with a municipality, local board or other municipal entity in Ontario for the purpose of integrating a system of business identifiers established under this section with any system of business identifiers established by the municipality, local board or municipal entity.

(3) Agreements re use of business identifiers — The Minister responsible for the administration of this section may enter into agreements with a Minister of another Ministry of the Government of Ontario or with an agency, board or commission established under an Act of Ontario respecting whether the Ministry, agency, board or commission must,

(a) assign business identifiers to businesses in accordance with the system of business identifiers established under this section; and

(b) use the system of business identifiers for any other purpose.

(3.1) Same, municipalities — The Minister responsible for the administration of this section may enter into agreements with a municipality, local board or other municipal entity respecting whether the municipality, local board or municipal entity may,

(a) assign business identifiers to businesses in accordance with the system of business identifiers established under this section; and

(b) use the system of business identifiers for any other purpose.

(4) Regulations — The Lieutenant Governor in Council may make regulations providing for the use that businesses are required to make of the system of business identifiers established under this section.

(5) General or particular — A regulation made under subsection (4) may be general or particular.

2006, c. 33, Sched. C, s. 1; 2012, c. 8, Sched. 5, s. 2

8.1 Business information — (1) Minister may require business information — If an agreement mentioned in subsection 8(3) is entered into in relation to any Act, the Minister responsible for the administration of that Act may require that a person subject to that Act provide prescribed business information to him or her.

(2) Disclosure of business information — Business information received under subsection (1),

(a) shall be disclosed to the Minister responsible for the administration of this section, for the purposes of this Act; and

(b) may be disclosed to the Government of Canada or an agent of the Government of Canada.

(3) Same — After an agreement referred to in subsection (1) is entered into in relation to an Act, subsection (2) applies to all business information received by the Minister responsible for that Act, regardless of whether the business information was received before or after the agreement referred to in subsection (1) was entered into.

(4) Minister may require business information, municipalities — If an agreement mentioned in subsection 8(3.1) is entered into with a municipality, local board or other municipal entity, the Minister responsible for the administration of this section,

(a) may require that the municipality, local board or municipal entity provide prescribed business information to the Minister; and

(b) may receive business information from the municipality, local board or municipal entity.

(5) Disclosure of business information, municipalities — Business information received under subsection (4) may be disclosed,

(a) to a municipality, local board or other municipal entity; and

(b) to the Government of Canada or an agent of the Government of Canada.

(6) Same — After an agreement referred to in subsection (4) is entered into, subsection (5) applies to all business information received by the Minister responsible for this section, regardless of whether the business information was received before or after the agreement referred to in subsection (4) was entered into.

(7) Regulations — The Lieutenant Governor in Council may make regulations,

(a) prescribing business information for the purposes of subsections (1) and (4);

(b) authorizing, for specified purposes, the collection, use and disclosure, by specified persons and entities, of specified business information received under any Act or from any municipality, local board or other municipal entity;

(c) authorizing, for specified purposes, the collection, use and disclosure, by municipalities, local boards or other municipal entities, of specified business information received by the Minister,

(i) under any Act, or

(ii) from any municipality, local board or other municipal entity.

(8) Confidentiality provisions do not apply — Any requirement or authority under this section, or under a regulation made under clause (7)(b) or (c), to disclose business information applies despite any confidentiality provision in another Act.

(9) Same — Unless it is expressly provided in any other Act that its provisions and regulations, rules or by-laws made under it apply despite subsection (8), subsection (8) prevails over the provisions of such other Act and over regulations, rules or by-laws made under such other Act which conflict with it.

2006, c. 33, Sched. C, s. 1; 2012, c. 8, Sched. 5, s. 3

9. (1) Use of agents — Information that businesses are required to file or are authorized to access under a designated Act may be filed or accessed, as the case may be, by a person who is authorized to do so by the Minister responsible for the administration of this section or by a person who is a member of a class of persons that is authorized to do so.

(2) Conditions — The Minister responsible for the administration of this section may attach conditions to an authorization given under subsection (1).

10. (1) Method of filing — The Lieutenant Governor in Council may make regulations,

(a) authorizing or requiring information, that businesses are required to file under this Act or a designated Act, to be filed and maintained in an electronic or other prescribed format;

(b) authorizing or requiring information, that businesses are required to file under this Act or a designated Act, to be filed by direct electronic transmission to an electronic database;

(c) authorizing or requiring forms, that businesses are required to file under this Act or a designated Act, to be signed by electronic signature or by signature copied or reproduced in the prescribed manner;

(d) authorizing or requiring forms, that businesses are required to file under this Act or a designated Act, to be filed without signatures;

(e) prescribing fees for filing information or forms that businesses are required to file under this Act;

(f) prescribing fees for filing information or forms that businesses are required to file under a designated Act to replace the filing fees prescribed under the designated Act.

(2) Time of filing — If information is filed by direct electronic transmission, the time or date of filing shall be the time or date assigned in the manner prescribed under this Act.

(3) Effect of electronic form — A form filed in electronic form has the same effect for all purposes as if it had been in writing.

(4) Effect of unsigned form — A form filed under clause (1)(d) has the same effect for all purposes as if it had been signed by the party or parties that would have been required to sign it, but for a regulation made under that clause.

11. (1) Deduction from payment — A financial institution described in subsection (2) that receives a payment of fees, taxes, interest, penalties or other charges under this Act or a designated Act on behalf of a Minister by the credit card of the institution, may deduct from the payment the amount of compensation that the Minister of Finance and the institution agree may be deducted.

(2) Financial institutions — A financial institution referred to in subsection (1) is,

(a) a bank or authorized foreign bank within the meaning of section 2 of the *Bank Act* (Canada);

(b) a corporation registered under the *Loan and Trust Corporations Act*;

(c) a credit union within the meaning of the *Credit Unions and Caisses Populaires Act, 1994*;

(d) a retail association as defined under the *Cooperative Credit Associations Act* (Canada); or

(e) any other financial institution prescribed under this Act.

2007, c. 7, Sched. 7, s. 182

12. (1) Provision of services — The Lieutenant Governor in Council may by order in council,

(a) establish an organization in any Ministry or an agency or a corporation to provide any service under this Act or a designated Act and provide for all matters necessary to fund, staff and operate the organization, agency or corporation;

(b) if the Lieutenant Governor in Council has made a regulation under subsection 6(1) unifying procedures for businesses to apply for licences and permits under designated Acts, establish a service to be known in English as Ontario Business Registration Access and in French as Accès à l'enregistrement des entreprises de l'Ontario or by such other name as the Lieutenant Governor in Council assigns to receive the applications and to issue the licences and permits;

(c) enter into agreements with the Government of Canada or any province or municipality to provide a service under this Act or a designated Act in co-operation with that government;

(d) enter into agreements with Government of Canada or any province or municipality to operate a business regulation service on behalf of that government for the purpose of this Act.

(2) Powers of Minister — The Minister responsible for the administration of this section may,

(a) appoint a public servant employed under Part III of the *Public Service of Ontario Act, 2006* to perform any function or service under a designated Act for the purpose of this Act; or

(b) enter into an agreement with any other person to perform any function or service under a designated Act for the purpose of this Act.

(3) Powers of person — A person who, under subsection (2), is appointed or required by an agreement to perform a function or service has the power to perform the function or service mentioned in the appointment or the agreement, as the case may be.

(4) Not an employee of the Crown — A person who, by an agreement mentioned in clause (2)(b), is required to perform a function or service is not and shall not be deemed to be an employee of the Crown for the purposes of the function or service.

2006, c. 35, Sched. C, s. 10(1), (2)

13. Databases — The Lieutenant Governor in Council may by order in council,

(a) establish a unified database to be known in English as the Business Access Registry and in French as Registre d'accès aux entreprises or by such other name as the Lieutenant Governor in Council assigns for information required to be maintained under designated Acts;

(b) set conditions governing the creation of, maintenance of, access to and use of the database mentioned in clause (a);

(c) enter into agreements with the Government of Canada or any province or municipality to adopt common forms, reporting and filing processes with that government or to share databases with that government.

14. Standards — The Lieutenant governor in Council may make regulations prescribing standards that persons are required to comply with, for the purpose of this Act, in the definition, collection, transmission and presentation of information under this Act or in the provision of services under designated Acts.

15. (1) Disclosure of personal information — The Minister responsible for the administration of this section who receives personal information under this Act or a designated Act may disclose it,

(a) to a Minister for the purpose of the administration of a designated Act, including the updating of a record or database;

(b) to the Government of Canada or any province or municipality in accordance with an agreement between that government and the Government of Ontario; or

(c) to a person,

(i) whom the Minister responsible for the administration of this section has authorized to access the information in the prescribed manner, or

(ii) with whom the Minister responsible for the administration of this section has entered into an agreement regarding the use of the information.

(2) Limitation — Despite subsection (1), a Minister shall not disclose personal information under that subsection unless the disclosure,

(a) is authorized by the Minister responsible for the administration of the Act under which the information was collected;

(b) complies with the regulations made under this Act; and

(c) complies with the agreement mentioned in clause (1)(b) or (c), if an agreement has been made under that clause.

(3) Personal information received — Personal information provided by the Government of Canada or any province or municipality under an agreement mentioned in clause (1)(b) shall not be used or disclosed to any person except in accordance with the terms of that agreement.

16. (1) Compensation — Subject to subsection (5) and the regulations made under this Act, a person is entitled to compensation from the Crown for any monetary loss that the person suffers that is directly attributable to an error or omission of a public servant employed under Part III of the *Public Service of Ontario Act, 2006* who performs a duty or provides a service under this Act or a designated Act for the purpose of this Act.

(2) Protection from liability — No action or other proceeding for damages shall be instituted against the Crown for any monetary loss that a person suffers as a result of,

(a) an error or omission of a person who is not a public servant referred to in subsection (1) and who performs a duty or provides a service under this Act or a designated Act for the purpose of this Act; or

(b) any inaccuracy or incompleteness in a record maintained under this Act or a designated Act for the purpose of this Act.

(3) No personal liability — No action or other proceeding for damages shall be instituted against a public servant referred to in subsection (1) for an act done in good faith in the execution or intended execution of a duty or service under this Act or a designated Act for the purpose of this Act or for an alleged neglect or default in the execution in good faith of the duty or service.

(4) Crown liability — Despite subsections 5(2) and (4) of the *Proceedings against the Crown Act*, subsection (3) does not relieve the Crown of liability in respect of a tort committed by a public servant referred to in subsection (1) to which it would otherwise be subject.

(5) Exception — Subsections (1) to (4) do not apply to a claim for compensation that relates to the administration of a designated Act if the designated Act contains provisions on the right to compensation and the amount of compensation that is payable to a person who suffers a monetary loss.

(6) Regulations — The Lieutenant Governor in Council may make regulations,

(a) attaching conditions to the right to receive compensation under this section, including specifying cases in which no compensation is payable;

(b) establishing a compensation fund for the purpose of subsection (1) or a designated Act;

(c) governing the right to receive compensation out of the fund and the amount of compensation payable out of the fund for a claim or a class of claims;

(d) governing procedures for making claims against the fund;

(e) providing for the appointment of persons to hear claims against the fund and governing the conditions for hearings.

(7) Compensation fund — If the regulations made under this Act have established a compensation fund, a claim for compensation under this Act or a designated Act shall be made to the fund.

(8) Protection from liability — No action or other proceeding for damages shall be instituted against the Crown with respect to any matter in relation to which a claim against a compensation fund established under this Act may be filed.

(9) Agreements with Canada — Despite clause (2)(a) or any provision in a designated Act, the Minister responsible for the administration of this section may enter into agreements with the Government of Canada or any province or municipality to pay compensation where records are maintained or duties are performed in co-operation with that government.

(10) Payment out of fund — If the Minister responsible for the administration of this section is required to pay compensation under an agreement mentioned in subsection (9) and the regulations made under this Act have established a compensation fund, the payment may be made from the compensation fund.

2006, c. 35, Sched. C, s. 10(3), (4)

17. Not regulations — An order in council made under this Act shall not be deemed to be a regulation within the meaning of Part III (Regulations) of the *Legislation Act, 2006*.

2006, c. 21, Sched. F, s. 136(1), Table 1

18. General regulations — The Lieutenant Governor in Council may make regulations,

(a) prescribing any matter mentioned in this Act as prescribed;

(b) respecting any matter necessary or advisable to carry out effectively the intent and purpose of this Act;

(c) prescribing information for the purpose of clause (i) of the definition of "business information" in section 2.

2012, c. 8, Sched. 5, s. 4

19. Commencement — This Act comes into force on a day to be named by proclamation of the Lieutenant Governor.

20. Short title — The short title of this Act is the *Business Regulation Reform Act, 1994*.

Ont. Reg. 442/95 — General

made under the *Business Regulation Reform Act, 1994*

O. Reg. 442/95, as am. O. Reg. 25/03; 185/05; 276/07; 240/09; 260/10; 124/11; 364/11; 431/12, ss. 1–3, 4 (Fr.); 195/13; 196/13; 257/13.

Designation of Acts

1. The following Acts are designated for the purpose of the Act:

0.1 The *Accessibility for Ontarians with Disabilities Act, 2005.*

0.2 The *Aggregate Resources Act.*

1. The *Alcohol and Gaming Regulation and Public Protection Act, 1996.*

1.1 The *Business Corporations Act.*

2. The *Business Names Act.*

2.0.1-2.0.3 [Repealed O. Reg. 260/10, s. 1.]

2.1 The *City of Ottawa Act, 1999.*

3. The *Clean Water Act, 2006.*

3.1 The *Corporations Act.*

3.2 The *Corporations Information Act.*

4. The *Corporations Tax Act.*

4.1 The *Crown Forest Sustainability Act, 1994.*

5. The *Electricity Act, 1998.*

6. The *Employer Health Tax Act.*

7. The *Employment Standards Act, 2000.*

7.1 The *Endangered Species Act, 2007.*

8. The *Environmental Assessment Act.*

9. The *Environmental Bill of Rights, 1993.*

10. The *Environmental Protection Act.*

10.1 The *Extra-Provincial Corporations Act.*

10.2 The *Fish and Wildlife Conservation Act, 1997.*

10.3 The *Highway Traffic Act.*

11. The *Labour Relations Act, 1995.*

11.0.1 The *Lakes and Rivers Improvement Act.*

11.1 The *Limited Partnerships Act.*

11.2 The *Ministry of Natural Resources Act.*

12. The *Nutrient Management Act, 2002.*

13. The *Occupational Health and Safety Act.*

13.1 The *Oil, Gas and Salt Resources Act.*

14. The *Ontario Water Resources Act.*

14.1 The *Partnerships Act.*

15. The *Pesticides Act.*

16. The *Private Career Colleges Act, 2005.*

16.1 The *Private Security and Investigative Services Act, 2005.*

16.2 The *Provincial Parks and Conservation Reserves Act, 2006.*

16.3 The *Public Lands Act.*

17. The *Retail Sales Tax Act.*

18. The *Safe Drinking Water Act, 2002.*

19. The *Workplace Safety and Insurance Act, 1997.*

O. Reg. 25/03, s. 1; 185/05, s. 1; 240/09, s. 1; 260/10, s. 1; 124/11, s. 1; 364/11, s. 1; 431/12, s. 1; 195/13, s. 1; 196/13, s. 1; 257/13, s. 1

UNIFIED FORM

2. (1) In accordance with this Regulation, a business may file a unified form with the Minister responsible for the administration of section 7 of the Act to,

(a) register a name or an amendment or cancellation of a registration under the *Business Names Act*;

(b) respond to a request for information made by the Minister of Finance under section 40 of the *Employer Health Tax Act*;

(c) apply under the *Retail Sales Tax Act* for a permit to transact business in Ontario as a vendor;

(d) comply with the requirements of section 75 of the *Workplace Safety and Insurance Act, 1997*; or

(e) record a change in information that is required to be filed under the *Corporations Tax Act*, the *Employer Health Tax Act*, or the *Retail Sales Tax Act*.

(2) Subject to subsections (3) and (4), a business that files a unified form in accordance with this Regulation is not required to,

(a) complete a form to register a name or an amendment or cancellation of a registration under the *Business Names Act*;

(b) complete an application to register with the Minister of Finance as a taxpayer liable to pay tax under the *Employer Health Tax Act*;

(c) complete an application under the *Retail Sales Tax Act* for a permit to transact business in Ontario as a vendor;

(d) comply with the requirements of section 75 of the *Workplace Safety and Insurance Act, 1997*; or

(e) complete a form to record a change in information filed under the *Corporations Tax Act*, the *Employer Health Tax Act*, or the *Retail Sales Tax Act*.

(3) The Minister responsible for a designated Act other than the *Workplace Safety and Insurance Act, 1997* may require a business that files a unified form in accordance with this Regulation to provide such additional information that the Minister requires for the purpose of filing under the designated Act.

(4) The Workplace Safety and Insurance Board may require a business that files a unified form in accordance with this Regulation to provide such additional information that the Board requires for the purposes of the *Workplace Safety and Insurance Act, 1997*.

(5) A business that files a unified form to file under a designated Act shall include in the form,

(a) all information that the Minister responsible for the administration of section 7 of the Act specifies for the purpose of determining the designated Acts under which the filing is made; and

(b) the following information if it is required under the designated Act:

1. The legal name of the business and the name of the person, if any, filing on behalf of the business.

2. The name under which the business operates, if it is not the legal name of the business.

3. An indication whether the business is a sole proprietorship, general partnership, corporation or other type of ownership.

4. The name, home address and home telephone number of,

i. the sole proprietor, if the business is a sole proprietorship,

ii. the partners who are individuals, if the business is a partnership, and

iii. an officer, if the business is a corporation.

5. An indication whether the business has more than one business location.

6. The address of the principal place of business, the address of the head office and the mailing address of the business.

7. The telephone and fax number for the principal place of business of the business.

8. If the business is a corporation, its Ontario corporation number and the jurisdiction where it was incorporated.

9. The business number assigned to the business for the purpose of the *Income Tax Act* (Canada) and the *Excise Tax Act* (Canada).

10. The date on which the business started operating.

11. If the business has purchased another business before filing, the name under which the other business operated.

12. If the business is seasonal, the periods during which it operates.

13. The employer account number assigned to the business by the Minister of National Revenue (Canada).

14. The dates on which the employees and contractors of the business started work, the estimated annual gross payroll of the business and if the business is seasonal, the payroll periods.

15. An indication whether the business is an employer that,

i. does not ordinarily maintain a permanent establishment in Ontario but will establish a permanent establishment in Ontario for a period not exceeding 24 months, or

ii. contracts or does business with an employer described in subparagraph i.

16. If there has been a change in ownership of the business before the filing, the nature of the change.

17. If the business has an annual income of more than $40,000 and is a sole proprietorship or a general partnership,

i. the social insurance number of the sole proprietor or a partner, if any, who is an individual,

ii. the employer health tax number of the business if it has been assigned, and

iii. the primary source of income of the business.

18. The business activity, including a description of the products and services to be sold and whether the business will be operated on a full-time or part-time basis.

19. The business identification number assigned to the registration for the purposes of the *Business Names Act*.

(6) A business that files a unified form to file under a designated Act is responsible for the accuracy and completeness of the information contained in the form.

(7) If a business files a unified form but is not required to file under a designated Act,

(a) the business is not required to set out the information related to the designated Act; and

(b) the Minister responsible for the administration of section 7 of the Act may omit the information related to the designated Act from any document or report or copy of them concerning the filing.

(8) Despite subsection (5), the Minister responsible for the administration of section 7 of the Act may accept for filing a form that does not comply with the requirements of that subsection, but the business shall be deemed not to have complied with that subsection until all of the requirements are satisfied.

O. Reg. 25/03, s. 2

FILING UNDER THE PRIVATE CAREER COLLEGES ACT, 2005

[Heading added O. Reg. 185/05, s. 2. Amended O. Reg. 431/12, s. 2(1).]

2.1 (1) In accordance with this Regulation, a business may file the following forms and information with the Minister responsible for the administration of section 7 of the Act for the purposes of the *Private Career Colleges Act, 2005*:

1. Initial application for registration to operate a private career college.
2. Application for registration to operate a private career college.
3. Application to renew a registration to operate a private career college.
4. Notification of change of college location.
5. Application for approval to provide a new vocational program.
6. Application to renew an approval of a vocational program.

(2) An initial application for registration to operate a private career college shall include the following information:

1. The name of the legal entity applying to be registered as a proposed private career college.

2. The name under which the proposed private career college will carry on business.

3. The business identification number assigned to the proposed private career college's name, if the name is registered under the *Business Names Act*.

4. An indication as to whether the proposed private career college will be a branch or franchise of an existing registered private career college.

5. An indication as to whether the legal entity applying to be registered as a proposed private career college is a sole proprietorship, a partnership or a corporation.

6. If the legal entity applying to be registered as a proposed private career college is a corporation,

i. the Ontario corporation number assigned to it by the Ministry of Government Services,

ii. the federal corporation number assigned to it by the Canada Revenue Agency,

iii. an indication as to whether the corporation is entitled to offer its shares to the public, and

iv. an indication as to whether any of its shares are held for the benefit of another person.

7. A list of the vocational programs for which the proposed private career college intends to apply for approval.

8. The names of all applicants, including,

i. in the case of a sole proprietorship, the name of the sole proprietor,

ii. in the case of a partnership, the names of all partners in the partnership, and

iii. in the case of a corporation, the names of all officers and directors of the corporation.

9. The name, address, telephone number, e-mail address, and fax number, if any, of a contact person.

(3) An application for registration to operate a private career college shall include the following information:

1. The name of the private career college, including the name under which the college will be carrying on business as well as,

i. in the case of a sole proprietorship, the name of the sole proprietor,

ii. in the case of a partnership, the firm name and the names of all of the partners, and

iii. in the case of a corporation, the incorporated name.

2. The full street address, telephone number, e-mail address, and fax number and website address, if any, of the private career college.

3. The mailing address of the private career college, if different from the full street address required by paragraph 2.

4. Information on each registered location of the private career college, including ownership of the premises.

5. The name, telephone, and cell phone and pager numbers, if any, of the campus director for each registered location of the private career college.

6. A list of the vocational programs for which the private career college intends to apply for approval.

7. Financial information regarding the private career college, including information on the college's financial security, such as projected gross tuition revenues, the amount of financial security required to be deposited with the Superintendent of private career colleges appointed under the *Private Career Colleges Act, 2005*, the type and amount of a financial bond and, where applicable, the name of the surety company.

8. An indication that the applicant or a person authorized by the applicant certifies that all information provided in the application and any attachments is accurate.

(4) The following information shall be filed for the purposes of a renewal of a registration to operate a private career college:

1. The total student enrolment in each vocational program and the enrolment of international students in each vocational program during the private career college's fiscal year immediately prior to its application for renewal.

2. Current financial information regarding the private career college, including information on tuition revenue for bonding purposes and a statement of revenue and expenditure.

3. Any other changes to information previously filed, including an indication as to whether any listed courses or programs are not intended to be offered in the current year.

4. An indication that the applicant or a person authorized by the applicant certifies that all filed information is current, including information filed for the purposes of renewal of a registration.

(5) A notification of change for college location shall include the following information:

1. The name of the private career college.

2. The name and telephone number of a contact person.

3. The full street address of the private career college's new location.

4. The date on which the private career college is scheduled to move to the new location.

(6) An application for approval to provide a new vocational program shall include the following information:

1. The name and full street address of the private career college.

2. The name, position and telephone number of the person responsible for the program's development.

3. The title of the program.

4. The occupation or occupations to which the program is directed and the occupational classification code for each occupation.

5. The language of instruction for the program.

6. The main method or methods of program delivery.

7. The format of the program.

8. The length of the program.

9. Enrolment information for the program.

10. Admission requirements for the program.

11. Fees for the program.

(7) An application to renew an approval of a vocational program shall include the following information:

1. The name of the private career college and, if applicable, the branch or campus at which the program is being delivered.

2. The name, position and telephone number of a contact person.

3. The current title of the program.

4. An indication as to whether there is a change in,

   i. the title of the program and, if applicable, a proposed new title and reason for the change, or

   ii. the length of a program and, if applicable, the current and proposed new lengths and reason for the change.

5. Fees for the program.

(8) The Superintendent of private career colleges appointed under section 2 of the *Private Career Colleges Act, 2005* may require a business that files a form or information under the *Private Career Colleges Act, 2005* in accordance with this Regulation to provide such additional information that the Superintendent requires for the purposes of filing under that Act.

O. Reg. 185/05, s. 2; 431/12, s. 2

Filing Format

3. (1) A business may file a unified form or a form or information under section 2.1 in an electronic format to file under a designated Act if,

(a) the Minister responsible for the administration of section 10 of the Act has approved the electronic format of the form; and

(b) the business enters the form by direct electronic transmission into a system and at a place approved by the Minister.

(2) A business that files a unified form or a form or information under section 2.1 in an electronic format under subsection (1) is not required to sign the form by electronic signature or by signature copied or reproduced in any other manner.

(3) The Minister responsible for the administration of section 10 of the Act may authorize the discontinuance or destruction of any paper, microfilm or other copies of information that a business has filed under the Act or a designated Act if the Minister or the Minister responsible for the administration of a designated Act who is authorized to receive the information has created an electronic record of it.

O. Reg. 185/05, s. 3

Business Identifier

4. (1) The Minister responsible for the administration of section 8 of the Act may require a business to use the business number assigned to it by the Minister of National Revenue

(Canada) for the purpose of the *Income Tax Act* (Canada) and the *Excise Tax Act* (Canada) if the business,

(a) files a form to file under a designated Act; or

(b) inquires about a record of a filing under a designated Act.

(2) If a business does not have a business number required by subsection (1) when it files a form to file under a designated Act, the Minister responsible for the administration of section 8 of the Act shall,

(a) request a number from the Minister of National Revenue (Canada); or

(b) if authorized to do so by the Minister of National Revenue (Canada), assign a number in the manner prescribed by the Minister of National Revenue (Canada).

(3) If a business has a business number under this section and files a form to file under a designated Act other than the *Workplace Safety and Insurance Act, 1997*, the Minister responsible for the designated Act may discontinue any other system of business identification for the filing of the business under a designated Act other than the *Workplace Safety and Insurance Act, 1997*.

(4) If a business has a business number under this section and files a form to file under the *Workplace Safety and Insurance Act, 1997*, the Workplace Safety and Insurance Board may discontinue any other system of business identification for the filing of the business under that Act.

O. Reg. 25/03, s. 3

Disclosure of Tax Information

5. (1) The Minister responsible for the administration of section 7 of the Act who receives tax information in respect of a business that files a unified form to file under a designated Act shall not disclose the information to any person other than the Minister of Finance, the Minister of National Revenue (Canada) or the business.

(2) In subsection (1),

"tax information" means information in respect of a business that is required solely for the purpose of the *Corporations Tax Act*, the *Employer Health Tax Act*, the *Retail Sales Tax Act* or all of them.

O. Reg. 25/03, s. 4

Compensation

6. No compensation is payable under section 16 of the Act in respect of any matter pertaining to the *Workplace Safety and Insurance Act, 1997*.

O. Reg. 25/03, s. 5

Business Information

[Heading amended O. Reg. 276/07, s. 1.]

7. The following information is prescribed for the purposes of clause (i) of the definition of "business information" in section 2 of the Act:

1. The address of the head office of the business, if different from the mailing address of the business, and if applicable, the address of every other location at which the business operates.
2. The name, phone number and mailing address of the person or persons designated by the business for the purpose of receiving communications and correspondence on behalf of the business, and whether the preferred language of communication is English or French.
3. A description of the business activities of the business, including a description of any products or services sold.
4. Any business identifier assigned to the business under a system of business identification established under an Act referred to in section 1.

O. Reg. 276/07, s. 1; 431/12, s. 3; 257/13, s. 2

8. (0.1) All business information, including business information prescribed under section 7, is prescribed for the purposes of subsection 8.1(1) of the Act.

(1) The following persons and entities may, upon request of the Minister responsible for the administration of section 8.1 of the Act, apply in writing to the Minister to collect business information received by the Minister under clause 8.1(2)(a) of the Act:

1. A Minister of another Ministry of the Government of Ontario, or his or her delegate.
2. The chair or chief executive officer of an agency, board or commission established under an Act of Ontario.
3. The Public Guardian and Trustee.
4. The chair or chief executive officer of an administrative authority designated under subsection 3(2) of the *Safety and Consumer Statutes Administration Act, 1996*.
5. A municipality, local board or other municipal entity.

(2) The Minister responsible for the administration of section 8.1 of the Act may disclose the business information to the following persons and entities if the Minister is satisfied that the collection and use of the information by those persons or entities is necessary for the following purposes, and those persons or entities may collect and use the information for the same purposes:

1. In the case of an application under paragraph 1 of subsection (1), to the Minister of the other Ministry, his or her delegate, or a person employed in the Ministry, for the administration of a statute or program for which the Minister is responsible.
2. In the case of an application under paragraph 2 of subsection (1), to the chair or chief executive officer of the agency, board or commission, or a person employed in the agency, board or commission, for the administration of,
    i. a statute that the agency, board or commission is authorized to administer, or
    ii. a program or service provided by the agency, board or commission.
3. In the case of an application under paragraph 3 of subsection (1), to the Public Guardian and Trustee, or a person employed in the Office of the Public Guardian and

Trustee, for the administration of a program or service provided by the Public Guardian and Trustee.

4. In the case of an application under paragraph 4 of subsection (1), to the chair or chief executive officer of the administrative authority, or a person employed in the administrative authority, for the administration of a statute for which the administrative authority is designated.

5. In the case of an application under paragraph 5 of subsection (1), to the municipality, local board or other municipal entity, for the administration of a municipal by-law or a service or program provided by a municipality.

(3) The Minister responsible for the administration of section 8.1 of the Act may, in writing, delegate any of his or her powers or duties under this section to the chief executive officer of ServiceOntario, subject to the limitations and conditions set out in the delegation.

(4) An authorization to collect, use or disclose information, under this section and section 8.1 of the Act, that existed immediately before the day section 3 of Schedule 5 to the *Strong Action for Ontario Act (Budget Measures), 2012* came into force, continues on and after that date.

O. Reg. 240/09, s. 2; 257/13, s. 3

CORPORATIONS ACT

R.S.O. 1990, c. C.38 [s. 5(2) not in force at date of publication. Repealed 2006, c. 21, Sched. F, s. 10.1(1).], as am. S.O. 1992, c. 32, s. 6; 1993, c. 16, s. 3; 1993, c. 27, Sched.; 1994, c. 11, s. 384; 1994, c. 17, s. 31; 1994, c. 27, s. 78; 1997, c. 19, s. 31; 1997, c. 28, ss. 50, 51; 1998, c. 18, Sched. E, ss. 59–82; 1999, c. 6, s. 16; 1999, c. 12, Sched. F, ss. 21, 22; 2000, c. 26, Sched. B, s. 9; 2001, c. 9, Sched. D, s. 5; 2002, c. 17, Sched. F, s. 1; 2002, c. 24, Sched. B, ss. 25, item 4, 31; 2004, c. 19, s. 10; 2004, c. 31, Sched. 38, s. 1; 2005, c. 5, s. 16; 2006, c. 21, Sched. F, s. 10.1(1); 2006, c. 33, Sched. O, ss. 17–27; 2006, c. 34, s. 10; 2007, c. 7, Sched. 7, s. 183; 2009, c. 18, Sched. 8; CTS 30 AU 10 – 1; 2010, c. 15, s. 211 [Not in force at date of publication.].

1. Definitions — In this Act,

"books" includes loose-leaf books where reasonable precautions are taken against the misuse of them;

"Commission" means the Ontario Securities Commission;

"company" means a corporation with share capital;

"corporation" means a corporation with or without share capital, but in Part III "corporation" means a corporation without share capital;

"court" means the Superior Court of Justice;

"Minister" means the member of the Executive Council to whom the administration of this Act is assigned by the Lieutenant Governor in Council;

"officer" means president, chair of the board of directors, vice-president, secretary, assistant secretary, treasurer, assistant treasurer, manager or any other person designated an officer by by-law of the corporation;

"private company" means a company as to which by its special Act, letters patent or supplementary letters patent,

(a) the right to transfer its shares is restricted,

(b) the number of its shareholders, exclusive of persons who are in the employment of the company, is limited to fifty, two or more persons holding one or more shares jointly being counted as a single shareholder, and

(c) any invitation to the public to subscribe for its shares or securities is prohibited;

"public company" means a company that is not a private company;

"registers" includes loose-leaf registers where reasonable precautions are taken against the misuse of them;

"securities" means the bonds, debentures, debenture stock or other like liabilities of a corporation whether constituting a charge on its property or not;

"special resolution" means a resolution passed by the directors and confirmed with or without variation by at least two-thirds of the votes cast at a general meeting of the shareholders or members of the corporation duly called for that purpose, or, in lieu of such confirmation, by the consent in writing of all the shareholders or members entitled to vote at such meeting.

2001, c. 9, Sched. D, s. 5(1)

2. Application — This Act does not apply to a company to which the *Business Corporations Act* or the *Co-operative Corporations Act* applies.

Proposed Amendment — 2

2. (1) Application of Act — This Act, except where it is otherwise expressly provided, applies to,

(a) a company that has objects in whole or in part of a social nature;

Proposed Repeal — 2(1)(a)

(a) [Repealed 2010, c. 15, s. 211(2). Not in force at date of publication.]

(b) an application to incorporate an insurer, within the meaning of the *Insurance Act*, that intends to undertake contracts of insurance in Ontario;

(c) an insurer, within the meaning of the *Insurance Act*, that undertakes contracts of insurance in Ontario and was incorporated under this Act; and

(d) an insurer, within the meaning of the *Insurance Act*, incorporated before April 30, 1954 under the laws of Ontario.

(2) Non-application of Act — This Act does not apply to a body corporate to which the *Business Corporations Act*, the *Co-operative Corporations Act* or the *Not-for-Profit Corporations Act, 2010* applies.

2010, c. 15, s. 211(1) [Not in force at date of publication.]

Proposed Addition — 2.1

2.1 (1) Continuance of share capital social clubs under other Acts — A corporation with share capital that has objects in whole or in part of a social nature shall, no later than the fifth anniversary of the day this section comes into force, apply, pursuant to a special resolution, to be continued,

(a) as a corporation without share capital under the *Not-for-Profit Corporations Act, 2010*;

(b) as a co-operative corporation under the *Co-operative Corporations Act*; or

(c) as a corporation under the *Business Corporations Act*.

(2) Minister's consent not required — Despite any requirement of any other Act, the Minister's authorization or consent is not required for a corporation described in subsection (1) to be continued as provided under that subsection.

(3) Letters patent not to be amended for purpose of continuance — A corporation shall not file supplementary letters patent under this Act to amend its letters patent in order to bring them into compliance with the Act under which the corporation applies to be continued under subsection (1).

(4) Application to court to waive shareholder approval — If a corporation is unable to obtain a quorum to approve a special resolution under subsection (1), the corporation may apply to the court for an order waiving the requirement for a special resolution.

(5) Same — The court may issue an order referred to in subsection (4) on the terms and conditions that the court considers appropriate in the circumstances if the court is satisfied that the corporation has made reasonable efforts to locate shareholders and serve them with a notice of meeting.

(6) Certificate to be filed — A corporation that is continued under another Act as described in subsection (1) shall file with the Minister a copy of its certificate of continuance within 60 days after that certificate has been issued to it.

(7) Dissolution of corporation if not continued — If a corporation that is required by subsection (1) to be continued under another Act is not so continued by the fifth anniversary of the day this section comes into force, the corporation is hereby dissolved as of the day after the fifth anniversary of the day this section comes into force.

(8) Saving — Despite subsection (7), a corporation is deemed to exist after its dissolution under that subsection for the following purposes:

1. To hold a meeting of the members in order to pass the special resolution referred to in subsection (1).
2. To apply to court under subsection (4).
3. To file articles of continuance under one of the Acts listed in subsection (1).

(9) Revival of dissolved corporation — A corporation dissolved under subsection (7) is revived on the date that a certificate of continuance is issued under one of the Acts listed in subsection (1) and upon revival, the corporation is deemed for all purposes to have never been dissolved, subject to any terms and conditions imposed by the Director appointed under the Act under which the corporation is continued, and the rights, if any, acquired by any person during the period of dissolution.

(10) Act ceases to apply — This Act, except for subsections (6) and (9) of this section, ceases to apply to a corporation described in subsection (1) upon its being continued under another Act.

2010, c. 15, s. 211(3) [Not in force at date of publication.]

PART I — CORPORATIONS, INCORPORATION AND NAME

3. Application — This Part, except where it is otherwise expressly provided, applies,

(a) to every corporation incorporated by or under a general or special Act of the Parliament of the late Province of Upper Canada;

(b) to every corporation incorporated by or under a general or special Act of the Parliament of the late Province of Canada that has its head office and carries on business in Ontario and that was incorporated with objects to which the authority of the Legislature extends; and

(c) to every corporation incorporated by or under a general or special Act of the Legislature, but this Part does not apply to a corporation incorporated for the construction and working of a railway, an incline railway or a street railway, or to a corporation within the meaning of the *Loan and Trust Corporations Act* except as provided by that Act.

Proposed Repeal — 3

3. [Repealed 2010, c. 15, s. 211(4). Not in force at date of publication.]

4. (1) Incorporation by letters patent — The Lieutenant Governor may in his or her discretion, by letters patent, issue a charter to any number of persons, not fewer than three, of eighteen or more years of age, who apply therefor, constituting them and any others who become shareholders or members of the corporation thereby created a corporation for any of the objects to which the authority of the Legislature extends, except those of railway and incline railway and street railway corporations and corporations within the meaning of the *Loan and Trust Corporations Act.*

(2) [Repealed 1994, c. 27, s. 78(1).]

(3) Incorporation of private company with limited objects — Despite subsection (1), a private company may be incorporated under this Act with power to lend and invest money on mortgage of real estate or otherwise, or with power to accept and execute the office of liquidator, receiver, assignee, trustee in bankruptcy or trustee for the benefit of creditors and to accept the duty of and to act generally in the winding up of corporations, partnerships and estates, other than estates of deceased persons, and shall not by reason thereof be deemed to be a corporation within the meaning of the *Loan and Trust Corporations Act*, but the number of its shareholders, exclusive of persons who are in employment of the company, shall be limited by its letters patent or supplementary letters patent to five, two or more persons holding one or more shares jointly being counted as a single shareholder, and no such company shall issue securities except to its shareholders, or borrow money on the security of its property except from its shareholders, or receive money on deposit.

1994, c. 27, s. 78(1)

5. (1) Supplementary letters patent — The Lieutenant Governor may in his or her discretion issue supplementary letters patent to any corporation that applies therefor amending or otherwise altering or modifying its letters patent or prior supplementary letters patent.

(2) [Repealed without coming into force 2006, c. 21, Sched. F, s. 10.1(1).]

(3) Subsection (2) comes into force on a day to be named by proclamation of the Lieutenant Governor.

6. Powers of Minister — The Minister may in his or her discretion and under the seal of his or her office have, use, exercise and enjoy any power, right or authority conferred by this Act on the Lieutenant Governor, but not those conferred on the Lieutenant Governor in Council.

7. Sufficiency of material to be established — An applicant under this Act shall establish to the satisfaction of the Minister the sufficiency of the application and all documents filed therewith and shall furnish such evidence regarding the application as the Minister considers proper.

8. Proof under oath — The Minister or any person in his or her ministry to whom an application is referred may take evidence under oath with respect thereto.

9. Variation of terms of application — On an application for letters patent, supplementary letters patent or an order, the Lieutenant Governor may give the corporation a name different from its proposed or existing name, may vary the objects or other provisions of the application and may impose such conditions as he or she considers proper.

10. Defects in form not to invalidate letters patent — The provisions of this Act relating to matters preliminary to the issue of letters patent or supplementary letters patent or an order are directory only, and no letters patent or supplementary letters patent or order are void or voidable on account of any irregularity or insufficiency in any matter preliminary to the issue thereof.

11. [Repealed 1994, c. 27, s. 78(2).]

12. (1) Commencement of existence — A corporation comes into existence on the date of the letters patent incorporating it.

(2) Effective date of letters patent, etc. — Letters patent of incorporation, letters patent of continuation, letters patent of amalgamation and supplementary letters patent, issued under this Act or any predecessor thereof, take effect on the date set forth therein.

13. (1) Corporate name — A corporation shall not be given a name,

(a) that is the same as or similar to the name of a known corporation, association, partnership, individual or business if its use would be likely to deceive, except where the corporation, association, partnership, individual or person consents in writing that its, his or her name in whole or in part be granted, and, if required by the Minister,

(i) in the case of a corporation, undertakes to dissolve or change its name within six months after the incorporation of the new corporation, or

(ii) in the case of an association, partnership or individual, undertakes to cease to carry on its, his or her business or activities, or change its, his or her name, within six months after the incorporation of the new corporation;

(b) that suggests or implies a connection with the Crown or any member of the Royal Family or the Government of Canada or the government of any province of Canada or any department, branch, bureau, service, agency or activity of any such government without the consent in writing of the appropriate authority;

(c) that, when the objects applied for are of a political nature, suggests or implies a connection with a political party or a leader of a political party;

(d) that is objectionable on any public grounds.

(2) Change of name — If a corporation, through inadvertence or otherwise, has acquired a name that is objectionable, the Minister may, after giving the corporation an opportunity to be heard, issue supplementary letters patent changing the name of the corporation to the name specified in the supplementary letters patent.

(2.1) Written hearing — A hearing under subsection (2) shall be in writing in accordance with rules made by the Minister under the *Statutory Powers Procedure Act*.

(3) Reference to court — A person who feels aggrieved as a result of the giving of a name under subsection (1) or the changing or refusing to change a name under subsection (2) may, upon at least seven days' notice to the Minister and to such other persons as the court directs, apply to the court for a review of the matter, and the court may make an order changing the name of the corporation to such name as it considers proper or may dismiss the application.

(4) Filing — A copy of an order made under subsection (3), certified under the seal of the court, shall be filed with the Minister by the corporation within ten days after it is made.

(5) Offence — A corporation that fails to comply with subsection (4) is guilty of an offence and on conviction is liable to a fine of not more than $200, and every director or officer of the corporation who authorizes, permits or acquiesces in any such failure is guilty of an offence and on conviction is liable to a like fine.

1998, c. 18, Sched. E, s. 59

14. Change not to affect rights, etc. — A change in the name of a corporation does not affect its rights or obligations.

15. Unauthorized use of "Limited", etc. — A person, partnership or association that trades or carries on a business or undertaking under a name in which "Limited", "Limitée", "Incorporated", "Incorporée", or "Corporation" or any abbreviation thereof is used, unless incorporated, is guilty of an offence and on conviction is liable to a fine of not more than $200.

16. (1) Corrected letters patent — If letters patent or supplementary letters patent issued under this Act or a predecessor of this Act contain an error, the directors or members of the corporation may apply to the Minister for corrected letters patent or corrected supplementary letters patent.

(2) Same — The Minister, on his or her own initiative or on an application under subsection (1), may issue corrected letters patent or corrected supplementary letters patent.

(3) Surrender of documents — The corporation shall surrender the letters patent or supplementary letters patent which are being corrected,

(a) at the time of making an application under subsection (1); or

(b) forthwith upon the request of the Minister if he or she is issuing the correcting documents on his or her own initiative.

(4) Conditions — The Minister may issue the corrected letters patent or supplementary letters patent subject to such conditions as he or she may impose.

(5) Date of corrections — Corrected letters patent or supplementary letters patent may bear the date of the letters patent or supplementary letters patent which are being replaced.

1994, c. 27, s. 78(3)

PART II — COMPANIES

17. Application — Subject to section 2 and except where it is otherwise expressly provided, this Part applies,

(a) to every company incorporated by or under a general or special Act of the Parliament of the late Province of Upper Canada;

(b) to every company incorporated by or under a general or special Act of the Parliament of the late Province of Canada that has its head office and carries on business in Ontario and that was incorporated with objects to which the authority of the Legislature extends; and

(c) to every company incorporated by or under a general or special Act of the Legislature,

but this Part does not apply to a company, incorporated for the construction and working of a railway, an incline railway or a street railway, or to a corporation within the meaning of the *Loan and Trust Corporations Act* except as provided by that Act.

Proposed Repeal — 17

17. [Repealed 2010, c. 15, s. 211(4). Not in force at date of publication.]

18. (1) Application for incorporation — The applicants for incorporation of a company shall file with the Lieutenant Governor an application showing:

1. The names in full and the address for service of each of the applicants.

2. The name of the company to be incorporated.

3. The objects for which the company is to be incorporated.

4. The place in Ontario where the head office of the company is to be situate.

5. The authorized capital, the classes of shares, if any, into which it is to be divided, the number of shares of each class, and the par value of each share, or, where the shares are to be without par value, the consideration, if any, exceeding which each share or the aggregate consideration, if any, exceeding which all the shares of each class may not be issued.

6. Where there are to be preference shares, the preferences, rights, conditions, restrictions, limitations or prohibitions attaching to them or each class of them.

7. Where the company is to be a private company, a statement to that effect and the restrictions to be placed on the transfer of its shares.

8. The names of the applicants who are to be the first directors of the company.

9. The class and number of shares to be taken by each applicant and the amount to be paid therefor.

10. Any other matters that the applicants desire to have included in the letters patent.

(2) Idem — The applicants may ask to have included in the letters patent any provision that could be the subject of a by-law of the company.

2001, c. 9, Sched. D, s. 5(2)

19. Original shareholders — Upon incorporation of a company, each applicant becomes a shareholder holding the class and number of shares stated in the application to be taken by the applicant and is liable to the company for the amount to be paid therefor.

20. (1) Use of word "Limited" — The name of a company shall have the word "Limited" or "Limitée" as the last word thereof, but a company may use the abbreviation "Ltd." or "Ltée" for "Limited" and may be referred to in the same manner.

(2) Not applicable to insurers — This section does not apply to insurers incorporated under Part V.

21. (1) Use of name — Where a company or a director, officer or employee thereof uses the name of the company, the word "Limited" or "Limitée", or the abbreviation "Ltd." or "Ltée", shall appear as the last word thereof.

(2) Exception — Stamping, writing, printing or otherwise marking on goods, wares and merchandise of the company or upon packages containing the same shall not be deemed a use of the name within the meaning of subsection (1).

(3) Idem — A private company shall have the words "private company" or the words "compagnie fermée" on its seal if it has a seal.

(4) Offence — A company that contravenes any requirement of this section and every director, officer or employee of the company who authorizes, permits or acquiesces in any such contravention is guilty of an offence and on conviction is liable to a fine of not more than $200.

1993, c. 27, Sched.; 1998, c. 18, Sched. E, s. 60

22. Use of name — Despite subsection 20(1) and section 21, a company may use its name in such form and in such language as the letters patent or supplementary letters patent provide.

23. (1) Incidental powers — A company possesses, as incidental and ancillary to the objects set out in the letters patent or supplementary letters patent, power,

(a) to carry on any other business capable of being conveniently carried on in connection with its business or likely to enhance the value of or make profitable any of its property or rights;

(b) to acquire or undertake the whole or any part of the business, property and liabilities of any person carrying on any business that the company is authorized to carry on;

(c) to apply for, register, purchase, lease, acquire, hold, use, control, license, sell, assign or dispose of patents, patent rights, copyrights, trade marks, formulae, licences, inventions, processes, distinctive marks and similar rights;

(d) to enter into partnership or into any arrangement for sharing of profits, union of interests, co-operation, joint adventure, reciprocal concession or otherwise with any person or company carrying on or engaged in or about to carry on or engage in any business or transaction that the company is authorized to carry on or engage in or any business or transaction capable of being conducted so as to benefit the company, and to lend money to, guarantee the contracts of, or otherwise assist any such person or company, and to take or otherwise acquire shares and securities of any such company, and to sell, hold, reissue, with or without guarantee, or otherwise deal with the same;

(e) to take or otherwise acquire and hold shares in any other company having objects altogether or in part similar to those of the company or carrying on any business capable of being conducted so as to benefit the company;

(f) to enter into arrangements with any public authority that seem conducive to the company's objects and obtain from any such authority any rights, privileges or concessions;

(g) to establish and support or aid in the establishment and support of associations, institutions, funds or trusts for the benefit of employees or former employees of the company or its predecessors, or the dependants or connections of such employees or former employees, and grant pensions and allowances, and make payments towards insurance or for any object similar to those set forth in this clause, and subscribe or guarantee money for charitable, benevolent, educational or religious objects or for any exhibition or for any public, general or useful objects;

(h) to promote any company for the purpose of acquiring or taking over any of the property and liabilities of the company, or for any other purpose that may benefit the company;

(i) to purchase, lease or take in exchange. hire or otherwise acquire any personal property and any rights or privileges that the company may think necessary or convenient for the purposes of its business;

(j) to construct, improve, maintain, work, manage, carry out or control any roads, ways, tramways, branches, sidings, bridges, reservoirs, watercourses, wharves, factories, warehouses, electric works, shops, stores and other works and conveniences that may advance the company's interests, and to contribute to, subsidize or otherwise assist or take part in the construction, improvement, maintenance, working, management, carrying out or control thereof;

(k) to raise and assist in raising money for, and to aid by way of bonus, loan, promise, endorsement, guarantee or otherwise, any person or company with whom the company may have business relations or any of whose shares, securities or other obligations are held by the company and to guarantee the performance or fulfilment of any contracts or obligations or any such person or company, and in particular to guarantee the payment of the principal of and interest on securities, mortgages and liabilities of any such person or company;

(l) to draw, make, accept, endorse, discount, execute and issue bills of exchange, promissory notes, bills of lading, warrants and other negotiable or transferable instruments;

(m) to sell, lease, exchange or dispose of the undertaking of the company or any part thereof as an entirety or substantially as an entirety for such consideration as the company thinks fit, and in particular for shares or securities of any other company having objects altogether or in part similar to those of the company, if authorized so to do by a special resolution;

(n) to sell, improve, manage, develop, exchange, lease, dispose of, turn to account or otherwise deal with the property of the company in the ordinary course of its business;

(o) to adopt such means of making known the products of the company as seems expedient, and in particular by advertising in the press, by circulars, by purchase and exhibition of works of art or interest, by publication of books and periodicals or by granting prizes and rewards or making donations;

(p) to cause the company to be registered and recognized in any foreign country or province or territory of Canada, and to designate persons therein according to the laws of such foreign country or province or territory to represent the company and to accept service for and on behalf of the company of any process or suit;

(q) to allot and issue fully-paid shares of the company in payment or part payment of any property purchased or otherwise acquired by the company or for any past services rendered to the company;

(r) to distribute among the shareholders of the company in money, kind, specie or otherwise as may be resolved, by way of dividend, bonus or in any other manner considered advisable, any property of the company, but no such distribution shall decrease the capital of the company unless made in accordance with this Act;

(s) to pay all costs and expenses of or incidental to the incorporation and organization of the company;

(t) to invest and deal with the money of the company not immediately required for its objects in such manner as may be determined;

(u) to do any of the above things and all things authorized by the letters patent or supplementary letters patent as principals, agents, contractors, trustees or otherwise, and either alone or in conjunction with others;

(v) to do all such other things as are incidental or conducive to the attainment of the above objects and of the objects set out in the letters patent and supplementary letters patent.

(2) Powers may be withheld — Any of the powers set out in subsection (1) may be withheld or limited by the letters patent or supplementary letters patent.

24. (1) Loans to shareholders and directors — Except as provided in subsection (2), a company shall not make loans to any of its shareholders or directors or give, directly or indirectly, by means of a loan, guarantee, the provision of security or otherwise, any financial assistance for the purpose of, or in connection with, a purchase made or to be made by any person of any shares of the company.

(2) Exceptions — A company may,

(a) make loans to any of its shareholders or directors in the ordinary course of its business where the making of loans is part of the ordinary business of the company; or

(b) make loans to full-time employees of the company whether or not they are shareholders or directors, with a view of enabling them to purchase or erect dwelling houses for their own occupation, and may take from such employees mortgages or other securities for the repayment of such loans; or

(c) provide, in accordance with a scheme for the time being in force, money by way of loan for the purchase by trustees of fully-paid shares of the company, to be held by or for the benefit of employees of the company, whether or not they are shareholders or directors;

(d) make loans to employees of the company, other than directors, whether or not they are shareholders, with a view to enabling them to purchase fully-paid shares of the company to be held by them by way of beneficial ownership; or

(e) if it is a private company, make loans to any of its shareholders or directors with a view to enabling them to purchase issued shares of the company.

(3) By by-law only — The power mentioned in clause (2)(b), (c), (d) or (e) may be exercised only under the authority of a by-law passed by the directors and confirmed by at least two-thirds of the votes cast at a general meeting of the shareholders duly called for considering the by-law.

(4) Liability of directors — Every director and officer of a company making or assenting to a loan in contravention of this section is, until repayment of the loan, jointly and severally liable to the company and to its creditors for the debts of the company then existing or thereafter contracted to the amount of the loan with interest at the rate of 5 per cent per year.

25. (1) Authorized capita — The authorized capital of a company shall be divided into shares with par value or without par value or both and may consist of shares of more than one class.

(2) Par shares — Where the shares of a company are with par value, its authorized capital shall be expressed in dollars, pounds, francs or other currency in the letters patent or supplementary letters patent and is an amount equal to the total of the products of the number of shares of each class multiplied by the par value thereof.

(3) No par or par and no par shares — Where the shares of a company are without par value or where part of its shares are with par value and part are without par value, its authorized capital shall be expressed as a specified number of shares in the letters patent or supplementary letters patent.

(4) Consideration for no par shares — Where the shares of a company are without par value or where part of its shares are with par value and part are without par value, the letters patent or supplementary letters patent may provide that each share without par value or the shares of each class of shares without par value are not to be issued for a consideration exceeding in amount or value a stated amount in dollars, pounds, francs or other currency, and the letters patent or supplementary letters patent may provide, in addition, that such share or shares may be issued for such greater amount as the board of directors of the company considers expedient.

1994, c. 27, s. 78(4)

26. Nature of shares — Each share of a class shall be the same in all respects as every other share of that class.

27. (1) More than one class of shares — If a company has more than one class of shares, one class shall be common shares designated as such and the other class shall be preference shares howsoever designated.

(2) Application — Subsection (1) does not apply to shares authorized before the 30th day of April, 1954.

28. (1) Preference shares — If a company has more than one class of shares, the letters patent or supplementary letters patent shall provide that the preference shares of a class confer upon the holders thereof a preference or right over the holders of shares of another class, either preference or common, and such preference or right, without limiting the nature thereof, may be in respect of dividends, repayment of capital, the right to elect part of the board of directors or the right to convert such shares into shares of another class or other classes of shares or into securities.

(2) Conditions, etc. — The letters patent or supplementary letters patent of a company may provide that the preference shares of a class may have attached thereto conditions, restrictions, limitations or prohibitions including, but without limiting the nature thereof, the right of the company to purchase for cancellation or at its option to redeem all or part of the shares of that class or conditions, restrictions, limitations or prohibitions on the right to vote.

(3) **Redemption by shareholders** — If the letters patent or supplementary letters patent so provide or if a by-law creating preference shares passed and confirmed before the 30th day of April, 1954, so provides, any preference shares of a class may be redeemed by the company at the request of a holder or of a number or proportion of such holders.

(4) **No par preference shares not to be redeemed** — Preference shares without par value do not have a preference in respect of the repayment of capital and are not subject to redemption or purchase for cancellation.

(5) **Redemption of par value preference shares** — Where preference shares with par value are to be redeemed, they shall be redeemed at the amount paid up thereon, but, if the letters patent or supplementary letters patent so provide or if a by-law creating preference shares passed and confirmed before the 30th day of April, 1954, so provides, a premium, unpaid dividends or other stated amount may be paid.

(6) **Redemption at actual value** — Notwithstanding subsection (5), if the letters patent or supplementary letters patent so provide, the preference shares of a class may be redeemed out of money set aside in a fund for such purpose at a price as near as may be to the actual value thereof, and the method of determining such actual value shall be set out in the letters patent or supplementary letters patent.

(7) **Redemption of part** — Where the preference shares of a class are made redeemable by the letters patent or supplementary letters patent and where at any time some but not all of such shares are to be redeemed, the shares to be redeemed shall, except as provided in subsections (8) and (9), be selected by lot in such manner as the board of directors determines or as nearly as may be in proportion to the number of shares registered in the name of each shareholder.

(8) **Redemption of all or part** — Where at least 95 per cent of the holders of the preference shares of a class holding at least 95 per cent of the issued shares of such class consent in writing and where, after twenty-one days notice has been given by sending the notice to each of the holders of shares of such class to the holder's last address as shown on the books of the company, none of the holders of shares of such class dissents in writing to the company, the company may redeem all or any of such shares in such manner as the board of directors determines.

(9) **Redemption of preference shares of private company** — Where a holder of preference shares of a private company dies or leaves its employment, it may within one year of such event redeem all or any of the preference shares held by the deceased shareholder or former employee.

(10) **Power to withhold** — The letters patent or supplementary letters patent of a company may withhold any of the powers set out in subsection (7), (8) or (9).

(11) **Purchase of preference shares by company** — Where the letters patent or supplementary letters patent provide that the preference shares may be purchased for cancellation by the company, the company may purchase some or all of such shares at the lowest price at which, in the opinion of the directors, such shares are obtainable, but not exceeding the amount paid up thereon; but, if the letters patent or supplementary letters patent so provide, a premium, unpaid dividends or other stated amount may be paid.

(12) **Insolvency** — Preference shares shall not be redeemed or purchased for cancellation by the company if the company is insolvent or if the redemption or purchase would render the company insolvent.

(13) **Effect of redemption** — Where preference shares are redeemed or purchased for cancellation by the company, they shall be thereby cancelled, and the authorized and the issued capital of the company shall be thereby decreased.

(14) **Conversion of preference shares** — Where preference shares are converted into the same or another number of shares of another class or classes, whether preference or common, the shares converted thereupon become the same in all respects as the shares of the class or classes respectively into which they are converted and the number of shares of each class affected by the conversion is changed accordingly.

(15) **Issued capital unchanged on conversion** — Where preference shares are converted into another class or other classes of shares, the issued capital of the company shall not be increased or decreased by the conversion.

(16) **Application** — Subsections (1), (4), (7), (8), (9) and (11) do not apply to shares authorized before the 30th day of April, 1954.

29. (1) **Preference shares in series** — The letters patent or supplementary letters patent of a company may authorize the issue from time to time in one or more series of the preference shares of a class and may authorize the directors to fix from time to time before such issue the designation, preferences, rights, conditions, restrictions, limitations or prohibitions attaching to the shares of each series of such class.

(2) **Voting rights** — The shares of all series of the same class of preference shares shall carry the same voting rights or the same restrictions, conditions, limitations or prohibitions on the right to vote.

(3) **Dividends** — Where any dividends or amounts payable on a repayment of capital are not paid in full, the shares of all series of the same class of preference shall participate rateably in respect of such dividends, including accumulations, if any, in accordance with the sums that would be payable on such shares if all such dividends were declared and paid in full, and on any repayment of capital in accordance with the sums that would be payable on such repayment of capital if all sums so payable were paid in full.

(4) **Conditions precedent to issue** — No shares of any series of a class of preference shares shall be issued until supplementary letters patent have been issued setting forth the designation, preferences, rights, conditions, restrictions, limitations or prohibitions attaching to the shares of such series except in the case of the first series if such designation, preferences, rights, conditions, restrictions, limitations or prohibitions have been set forth in the letters patent or prior supplementary letters patent.

(5) **Issue of supplementary letters patent** — The Lieutenant Governor may issue such supplementary letters patent on the application of the company authorized by a resolution of the directors fixing the designation, preferences, rights, conditions, restrictions, limitations or prohibitions attaching to the shares of such series and the filing with the Minister of evidence of the due compliance with the conditions, if any, contained in the letters patent or in any prior supplementary letters patent, precedent to the creation and issue of the shares of such series.

30. (1) Voting rights — Subject to subsection 28(2) every holder of a preference share or a common share is entitled to one vote for each preference share or each common share held by him at all meetings of the shareholders of the company, but this subsection does not apply to shares authorized before the 30th day of April, 1954.

(2) Votes — The letters patent or supplementary letters patent may provide for a greater number of votes for each share of a class or classes at all times or on the happening of a stated event.

31. (1) Issued capital, par value shares — Where the shares of a company are with par value, its issued capital shall be expressed in dollars, pounds, francs or other currency and is an amount equal to the total of the products of the number of issued shares of each class multiplied by the par value thereof.

(2) No par value shares, etc. — Where the shares of a company are without par value or where part of its shares are with par value and part are without par value, its issued capital shall be expressed in dollars, pounds, francs or other currency and is an amount equal to the total of the products of the number of issued shares of each class with par value multiplied by the par value thereof, together with the amount of the consideration for which the shares without par value from time to time outstanding were issued and together with such amounts as from time to time by by-law of the company may be transferred thereto.

(3) Idem — Nothing in subsection (2) affects the capital of a company in respect of shares without par value issued before the 30th day of April, 1954, if the letters patent or the supplementary letters patent of the company provide that the capital is to be at least equal to the sum of the aggregatepar value of all issued shares having par value plus a sum in dollars, pounds, francs or other currency in respect of every issued share without par value plus such amounts as from time to time by by-law of the company may be transferred thereto.

(4) Idem — Where before the 30th day of April, 1954, a company has set aside part of the consideration received upon the allotment and issue of shares without par value as distributable surplus, the amount of such distributable surplus does not form part of its issued capital.

32. (1) Issue of shares — In the absence of a provision to the contrary in the letters patent, supplementary letters patent or by-laws of the company, shares may be allotted and issued at such times and in such manner and to such persons or class of persons as the directors determine.

(2) Consideration, par value shares — Shares with par value shall not be allotted and issued as fully paid except for a consideration payable in cash at least equal to the product of the number of shares allotted and issued multiplied by the par value thereof or for a consideration payable directly or indirectly in property or past services which the directors in good faith determine by express resolution to be in all circumstances of the transaction the fair equivalent of such cash consideration.

(3) Consideration, no par shares — Shares without par value may be allotted and issued for such consideration as is fixed by the directors acting in good faith and in the best interests of the company.

(4) Idem — Shares without par value shall not be allotted and issued as fully paid except for the consideration fixed by the directors as aforesaid payable in cash to the total amount of the consideration so fixed or for a consideration payable directly or indirectly in property or past services which the directors in good faith determine by express resolution to be in all circumstances of the transaction the fair equivalent of such cash consideration.

(5) Holders not liable to creditors, etc. — Shares allotted and issued in accordance with this section shall be fully paid and non-assessable upon receipt by the company of the consideration for the allotment and issue thereof, and upon such receipt the holders of such shares are not liable to the company or to its creditors in respect thereof.

33. (1) Commission on sale of shares — The directors may pass by-laws for the payment of commissions to persons in consideration of their subscribing or agreeing to subscribe, whether absolutely or conditionally, for shares in the company, or procuring or agreeing to procure subscriptions, whether absolute or conditional for such shares, but no such commission shall exceed 25 per cent of the amount of the subscription.

(2) Commission by-laws to be confirmed — No by-law passed under subsection (1) is effective until it is confirmed by at least two-thirds of the votes cast at a general meeting of shareholders duly called for considering it.

(3) No authorized commissions — Except as provided in subsection (1), no company shall apply any of its shares or capital, either directly or indirectly, in payment of any commission, discount or allowance to any person in consideration of the person's subscribing or agreeing to subscribe, whether absolutely or conditionally, for shares of the company or procuring or agreeing to procure subscriptions, whether absolute or conditional, for such shares, whether the shares or capital is so applied by being added to the purchase money of any property acquired by the company or to the contract price of any work to be executed for the company, or is paid out of the nominal purchase money or contract price or otherwise.

34. (1) Supplementary letters patent — A company may apply to the Lieutenant Governor for the issue of supplementary letters patent,

(a) extending, limiting or otherwise varying its objects;

(b) changing its name;

(c) increasing its authorized capital;

(d) decreasing,

(i) its authorized capital by cancelling issued or unissued shares with or without par value or by reducing the par value of issued or unissued shares, or

(ii) its issued capital, if it has shares without par value,

and, where it has more capital than it requires, authorizing the repayment of capital to the shareholders to the extent that the issued capital is decreased in any way under this clause;

(e) redividing its authorized capital into shares of lesser or greater par value;

(f) consolidating or subdividing any of its shares without par value;

(g) changing any of its shares with par value into shares without par value;

(h) changing any of its shares without par value into shares with par value;

(i) reclassifying any shares with or without par value into shares of a different class;

(j) varying any provision in its letters patent or prior supplementary letters patent;

(k) providing for any other matter or thing in respect of which provision may be made in letters patent under this Act;

(l) converting it into a public company;

(m) making it subject to Part IV;

Proposed Repeal — 34(1)(m)

(m) [Repealed 2010, c. 15, s. 211(4). Not in force at date of publication.]

(n) making it not subject to Part IV;

Proposed Repeal — 34(1)(n)

(n) [Repealed 2010, c. 15, s. 211(4). Not in force at date of publication.]

(o) converting it into a private company;

(p) converting it into a corporation without share capital;

(q) converting it into a corporation, with or without share capital.

(2) Authorization — An application under subsection (1) shall be authorized by a special resolution.

(3) [Repealed 2001, c. 9, Sched. D, s. 5(3).]

(4) Additional authorization for variation of rights of preference shareholders — If the application is to delete or vary a preference, right, condition, restriction, limitation or prohibition attaching to a class of preference shares or to create preference shares ranking in priority to or on a parity with an existing class of preference shares, then, subject to subsection (5) and, in addition to the authorization required by subscription (2), the application shall not be made until the application has been authorized in writing,

(a) by 100 per cent of the holders of the shares of such class or classes or shares; or

(b) by at least 95 per cent of the holders of the shares of such class or classes of shares holding at least 95 per cent of the issued shares of such class or classes,

but, in the case of authorization under clause (b), the application shall not be made until twenty-one days notice of the application has been given by sending the notice to each of the holders of shares of such class or classes to the holder's last address as shown on the books of the company and only if at the expiration of twenty-one days none of the holders of such class or classes has dissented in writing to the company.

(5) Idem — If the letters patent or supplementary letters patent so provide, the authorization required by subsection (4) may be given by at least two-thirds of the votes cast at a meeting of the holders of such class or classes of shares duly called for that purpose.

(6) Exception — If the letters patent or supplementary letters patent issued before the 30th day of April, 1954, provide for an authorization for an application for supplementary letters patent to delete or vary a preference, right, condition, restriction, limitation or prohibition attaching to preference shares or to create preference shares ranking in priority to or on a parity with an existing class of preference shares, such authorization is effective, and subsections (4) and (5) do not apply.

(7) [Repealed 1998, c. 18, Sched. E, s. 61.]

(8) Exception — Subsection (4) does not apply to an arrangement under section 112.

(9) **Special Act corporations excepted** — This section does not apply to a company incorporated by special Act, except that a company incorporated by special Act may apply under this section for the issue of supplementary letters patent changing its name.

1998, c. 18, Sched. E, s. 61; 2001, c. 9, Sched. D, s. 5(3)

35. Reduction of capital — On an application for supplementary letters patent decreasing authorized or issued capital, the company shall establish to the satisfaction of the Minister that after the decrease the company will be solvent and, if required by the Minister, shall establish to his or her satisfaction that there are no creditors who object to the application.

36. Decrease of issued capital — Where issued shares without par value are cancelled, the issued capital is thereby decreased by an amount equal to the total of the products of the average consideration for which the shares of each such class were issued multiplied by the number of shares cancelled of each such class, respectively.

37. (1) Liability on decrease of issued capital — On a decrease of the issued capital of a company by supplementary letters patent, each person who was a shareholder on the date of the supplementary letters patent is individually liable to the creditors of the company for the debts due on that date to an amount not exceeding the amount of the repayment to the person or reduction of the person's liability, or both, as the case may be.

(2) **Limitation of liability** — A person is not liable under subsection (1),

(a) unless the company has been sued for the debt within six months after the date of the supplementary letters patent and execution has been returned unsatisfied in whole or in part; and

(b) unless the person is sued for the debt within two years from the date of the supplementary letters patent.

(3) **Idem** — After execution has been so returned, the amount due on the execution, not exceeding the amount of the repayment to the person or the reduction of the person's liability, is the amount recoverable against the person.

(4) **Class actions** — Where it is made to appear that there are numerous shareholders who may be liable under this section, the court may permit an action to be brought against one or more of them as representatives of the class and, if the plaintiff establishes the plaintiff's claim as creditor, may make an order of reference and add as parties on the reference all such shareholders as may be found, and the referee shall determine the amount that each should contribute towards the plaintiff's claim and may direct payment of the sums so determined.

(5) **Shareholder holding shares in fiduciary capacity** — No person holding shares as executor, administrator, guardian or trustee, who is registered on the books of the company as a shareholder and therein described as representing in any such capacity a named estate, person or trust, is personally liable under this section, but the estate, person or trust is subject to all liabilities imposed by this section.

1992, c. 32, s. 6(1)

38. (1) Fractional shares — A person entitled to a fraction of a share is not entitled to be registered on the books of the company in respect thereof or to receive a share certificate therefor, but the person is entitled to receive a bearer fractional certificate in respect of such fraction and, on presentation at the head office of the company, or at a place designated by the company, of bearer fractional certificates for fractions that together represent a whole share, a share certificate for a whole share shall be issued in exchange therefor and the person in whose name such certificate is issued shall be registered on the books of the company as the holder of such share.

(2) **Transfer** — Such a bearer fractional certificate is transferable by delivery.

(3) **Purchase by company** — For the purpose of consolidating fractions of shares into whole shares, a company may purchase fractions of shares and, if it does so, it shall sell forthwith the whole shares resulting from the consolidation.

39. Shares deemed personal estate — The shares of a company shall be deemed to be personal estate.

40. (1) **Transfer of shares** — The shares of a company are transferable on the books of the company subject to such conditions and restrictions as this Act, the special Act, the letters patent or supplementary letters patent prescribe.

(2) **Transfer by-laws** — Subject to subsection (3), no by-law shall be passed that in any way restricts the right of a holder of fully-paid shares to transfer them, but by-laws may be passed regulating the method of their transfer.

(3) **Where shareholder indebted to company** — Except in the case of shares listed on a recognized stock exchange, where the letters patent, supplementary letters patent or by-laws so provide, the directors may refuse to permit the registration of a transfer of fully-paid shares registered in the name of a shareholder who is indebted to the company.

41. Register of transfers — Every company shall cause to be kept a register of transfers in which all transfers of shares and the date and other particulars of each transfer shall be set out.

42. Transfer agents — A company may appoint a transfer agent to keep the register of shareholders and the register of transfers and may also appoint one or more branch transfer agents to keep branch registers of shareholders and branch registers of transfers.

43. (1) **Where registers to be kept** — The register of shareholders and the register of transfers shall be kept at the head office of the company or at such other office or place in Ontario as is appointed by resolution of the directors, and the branch register or registers of shareholders and the branch register or registers of transfers may be kept at such office or offices of the company or other place or places, either in or outside Ontario, as are appointed by resolution of the directors.

(2) **Valid registration** — Registration of the transfer of a share of the company in the register of transfers or a branch register of transfers is a complete and valid registration for all purposes.

(3) **Entry in branch transfer register** — In each branch register of transfers shall be recorded only the particulars of the transfers of shares registered in that branch register of transfers.

(4) **Entry in register of transfers** — Particulars of every transfer of shares registered in every branch register of transfers shall be recorded in the register of transfers.

(5) Closing of register of transfers — The directors of a company may by resolution close the register of transfers and the branch register or registers of transfers, if any, for a period of time not exceeding forty-eight hours, exclusive of Saturdays and holidays, immediately preceding any meeting of the shareholders, and notice of every such closing shall be given in a newspaper published in the place where the register of transfers is kept and in a newspaper published in each place in which a branch register of transfers is kept.

44. (1) Share certificates — Every shareholder is entitled to a share certificate in respect of the shares held by the shareholder, signed by the proper officers in accordance with the company's by-laws in that regard, but the company is not bound to issue more than one share certificate in respect of a share or shares held jointly by several persons and delivery of a share certificate to one of several joint shareholders is sufficient delivery to all.

(2) Title — A share certificate is proof, in the absence of evidence to the contrary, of the title of the shareholder to the shares represented thereby.

(3) Fee — A company may charge a fee of not more than 50 cents for every share certificate issued, except that, in the case of the allotment and issue of shares, no fee shall be charged.

45. Lost certificates — Where a share certificate is defaced, destroyed or lost, a new certificate may be issued in its place on payment of such fee, if any, not exceeding $1 and on such terms, if any, as to evidence and indemnity as the directors determine.

46. (1) Contents of share certificates — Every share certificate,

(a) shall bear upon its face the name of the company, a statement in English or in French that the company is incorporated in the Province of Ontario and a statement of its authorized capital; and

(b) shall state the number and class of shares represented thereby and whether the shares are with par value or without par value and, if partly paid, the amount paid up thereon or that the shares are fully paid, as the case may be; and

(c) if it represents preference shares, shall state thereon in legible characters the preferences, rights, conditions, restrictions, limitations or prohibitions attaching to the class of preference shares to which it belongs; and

(d) if it represents shares of a private company, shall bear upon its face the words "Private Company" or the words "compagnie fermée".

(2) Exception — Where some but not all of the preference shares of a class are converted, redeemed or purchased for cancellation, it is unnecessary for the company to change the statement of its authorized capital on its share certificates.

47. Signing of share certificates — A share certificate shall be signed manually by at least one officer of the company or by or on behalf of a transfer agent or branch transfer agent of the company, and, the company may by by-law provide that any additional signatures required on share certificates may be printed, engraved, lithographed or otherwise mechanically reproduced thereon, and in such event share certificates so signed are as valid as if they had been signed manually.

48. (1) Trusts — A company is not bound to see to the execution of any trust, whether express, implied or constructive, in respect of any share.

(2) **Discharge** — The receipt of the shareholder in whose name the share is registered on the books of the company is a valid and binding discharge to the company for any payment made in respect of such share whether notice of such trust has been given to the company or not.

(3) **Application of money paid** — The company is not bound to see to the application of the money paid upon such receipt.

(4) **Authority to transfer** — The written authorization of an executor, administrator, guardian or trustee who is registered on the books of the company as holding shares in any such capacity is sufficient justification for the company to register a transfer of such shares, including a transfer into the name of such executor, administrator, guardian or trustee absolutely.

1992, c. 32, s. 6(2)

49. (1) **Share warrants** — A public company, if so authorized by its letters patent or supplementary letters patent and subject to the provisions respecting share warrants therein contained, may, with respect to any fully-paid shares, issue under the seal of the company a share warrant stating that the bearer of it is entitled to the share or shares therein specified, and may provide, by coupons or otherwise, for the payment of future dividends on the shares specified in the share warrant.

(2) **Entry of share warrant in company books** — On the issue of a share warrant, the company shall remove from its books the name of the shareholder then entered thereon as holding such share or shares as if the person had ceased to be a shareholder and shall enter in such books the following particulars:

1. The fact of the issue of the share warrant.
2. A statement of the shares specified in the share warrant.
3. The date of the issue of the share warrant.

(3) **Transfer** — A share warrant entitles the bearer thereof to the shares therein specified and the shares may be transferred by delivery of the warrant.

(4) **Bearer of share warrant deemed shareholder** — The bearer of a share warrant shall be deemed to be a shareholder of the company, except that the bearer is not entitled to receive notice of meetings or a copy of any financial statement or auditor's report and is not qualified in respect of shares specified in the share warrant to be a director of the company.

(5) **Voting rights** — Upon presentation of a share warrant at a meeting of shareholders, its bearer is entitled to attend the meeting and vote the shares specified in it.

(6) **Definition** — For the purpose of subsection (5), the expression **"share warrant"** includes a certificate or other document satisfactory to the company to the effect that its bearer is the holder of a share warrant in respect of the shares specified in the certificate or other document.

(7) **Exchange of warrant for registration as shareholder** — The bearer of a share warrant is, subject to the provisions respecting share warrants contained in the letters patent or supplementary letters patent, entitled, on surrendering it for cancellation, to have the shares specified in it registered in the bearers name on the books of the company, and the company is responsible for any loss incurred by any person by reason of the company entering on its books the name of the bearer of a share warrant in respect of the shares specified in it without the warrant being surrendered and cancelled.

(8) Surrender of share warrant — Upon the surrender of a share warrant for cancellation, the date of the surrender shall be entered in the books of the company.

50. (1) Transfers valid only after registration — No transfer of shares, unless made by sale under an execution or under a decree, order or judgment of a court of competent jurisdiction, is valid for any purpose whatsoever until registration thereof has been duly made in the register of transfers or in a branch register of transfers of the company, save only as exhibiting the rights of the parties thereto towards each other and, if absolute, of rendering any transferee jointly and severally liable with the transferor to the company and to its creditors.

(2) Exception — Despite subsection (1), where fully-paid shares are listed on a recognized stock exchange at the time of the delivery of a certificate for such shares with a duly executed instrument of transfer endorsed thereon or accompanying it, such delivery constitutes a valid transfer of the shares represented by such certificate, but, until registration of such transfer is duly made in the register of transfers or in a branch register of transfers of the company, the company may treat the person in whose name the shares represented by such certificate are registered on the books of the company as being solely entitled to receive notice of and vote at meetings of shareholders and receive any payments in respect of such shares whether by way of dividends or otherwise.

(3) Power of attorney not revoked by death — A power of attorney contained in a duly executed instrument of transfer endorsed on or accompanying a share certificate delivered for value before the death of the transferor is not revoked by the death of the transferor but is valid and effectual subject to the conditions or restrictions, if any, contained therein.

51. (1) Notice to owner — The directors may refuse to permit the registration of a transfer of shares on the books of the company for the purpose of notifying the person registered thereon as owner of such shares of the application for such registration, and in that event the company shall forthwith give notice to such person of such application.

(2) Owner may lodge caveat — The owner may within seven days after the giving of such notice lodge a caveat against the registration of the transfer and thereupon the registration of the transfer shall not be made for a period of forty-eight hours.

(3) Transfer may be registered if no order served — If within one week after the giving of such notice or the expiration of such period of forty-eight hours, whichever last expires, no order of a competent court enjoining the registration of the transfer has been served upon the company, the transfer may be registered.

(4) Liability of company — Where a transfer of shares is registered after the proceedings mentioned in this section, the company is not liable in respect of such shares to a person whose rights are purported to be transferred, but nothing in this subsection prejudices any claim the transferor may have against the transferee.

52. (1) Where consent of directors to transfer required — No registration of a transfer of shares that are not fully paid shall be made without the consent of the directors and of the transferee and, subject to subsection (4), where such registration is made with the consent of the directors, the transferor is not liable to the company or to its creditors for the amount unpaid on such shares.

(2) **Directors' liability** — Subject to subsection (3), where registration is made with the consent of the directors of a transfer of shares that are not fully paid to a person whom the directors have reason to believe is not of sufficient means to pay fully for such shares, the directors are jointly and severally liable to the company and to its creditors in the same manner and to the same extent as the transferor would have been liable if the registration had not been made.

(3) **Relief from liability** — If a director, present when such consent to registration is given, forthwith, or, if a director then absent, within seven days after he or she becomes aware of such consent, delivers to an officer of the company his written protest against such consent and, within seven days after delivery of such protest, sends a copy of such protest by registered mail to the Minister, such director thereby and not otherwise exonerates himself or herself from liability under subsection (2).

(4) **Liability where call remains unpaid** — Where the transfer of a share upon which a call is unpaid is registered with the consent of the directors and of the transferee, the transferee is liable for the call to the same extent and with the same liability to forfeiture of the share, if the call remains unpaid, as if the transferee had been the holder when the call was made, and the transferor also remains liable for the call until it is paid.

53. **Transmission of deceased shareholder's shares** — Where upon the death of a holder of any shares or securities of a company a transmission thereof takes place to or title to or control thereof vests or is claimed to vest in any person, herein called "the successor", the company is justified in permitting or consenting to the registration thereof in the name of the successor on the company's books or in paying the principal amount thereof or any dividend or interest thereon to the successor,

(a) if the successor claims by virtue of a grant of probate or letters of administration or other instrument issued or purporting to be issued by a court or other judicial authority in any jurisdiction, upon production of the same or an authenticated copy thereof or extract therefrom or a certificate of such grant under the seal of such court or other authority without any proof of the authenticity of such seal or other proof whatever and deposit of a copy thereof; or

(b) if the successor claims by virtue of the laws of any jurisdiction in which any such transmission or vesting of title or control takes place without a grant of probate or letters of administration or other court or judicial action, upon production and deposit of proof thereof in accordance with the laws of such jurisdiction and reasonable evidence of such laws; or

(c) if the net value of the estate of the deceased holder is less than $1,500 or if the market value of the shares or securities is less than $300, upon proof thereof to the reasonable satisfaction of the company,

together with, in any such event, production and deposit by the successor of a sworn statement showing the nature of the transmission or vesting of title or control, as the case may be.

54. (1) **Calls on shares** — The directors may by resolution call in and by notice thereof in writing demand from the shareholders the whole or any part of the amount unpaid on shares held by them at such times and places and in such payments or instalments as this Act, the special Act, the letters patent, the supplementary letters patent, the by-laws or the terms of allotment and issue of such shares require or allow.

(2) **Demand to state liability to forfeiture** — The demand shall state that, in the event of the call not being paid in accordance with the demand, the shares in respect of which the call was made will be liable to be forfeited.

(3) **Liability for interest** — If a shareholder fails to pay a call due by the shareholder on or before the day appointed for the payment thereof, the shareholder is liable to pay interest on the amount thereof at the rate of 5 per cent per annum from the day appointed for payment to the time of payment.

(4) **Forfeiture of shares** — In the event of the call not being paid in accordance with the demand, the directors may forfeit any shares on which the call is not paid.

(5) **Sale of forfeited shares** — Any forfeited shares become the property of the company upon the forfeiture, and, subject to its by-laws, may be sold.

(6) **Continuing liability** — Notwithstanding such forfeiture, the holder of such shares at the time of forfeiture continues liable to the company and to its creditors for the full amount unpaid on such shares at the time of forfeiture, less any sums that are subsequently received by the company in respect thereof.

(7) **Refund of excess on sale** — Where the company receives on the sale of forfeited shares an amount in excess of the amount then unpaid on such shares, the excess amount shall be paid to the person whose shares were forfeited.

(8) **Recovery of calls by suit** — The directors may, instead of forfeiting any shares, enforce payment of all calls and interest thereon by action in a court of competent jurisdiction.

55. **Right to receive uncalled money** — The directors may receive at any time from a shareholder all or any part of the money uncalled and unpaid upon shares held by him.

56. (1) **Shareholder's liability limited** — A shareholder shall not, as such, be held answerable or responsible for any act, default, obligation or liability of the company, or for any engagement, claim, payment, loss, injury, transaction, matter or thing relating to or connected with the company beyond the amount unpaid on the shareholder's shares.

(2) **Shareholder's liability** — A shareholder, until the whole amount has been paid up on the shareholder shares, is liable to the creditors of the company to an amount equal to that unpaid thereon, but the shareholder is not liable to an action therefor by a creditor until an execution at the suit of the creditor against the company has been returned unsatisfied in whole or in part.

(3) **Amount recoverable** — The amount due on such execution, not exceeding the amount unpaid on the shareholder's shares, is the amount recoverable from such shareholder and, when so recovered, shall be considered as paid on those shares.

(4) **Set-off** — A shareholder may plead by way of defence, in whole or in part, to any such action by a creditor any set-off that the shareholder could set up against the company except a claim for unpaid dividends or a salary or allowance as a director or officer of the company.

57. (1) **Trustees, etc., not personally liable** — No executor, administrator, guardian or trustee who is registered on the books of the company as a shareholder and therein described as representing in any such capacity a named estate, person or trust is personally liable in respect of the shares that he, she or it so represents.

(2) Liability of estate, etc. — The estate, person or trust so represented is liable as if the testator, intestate, mentally incapable person, ward or beneficiary were registered on the books of the company as the holder of the shares.

(3) Where trustee, etc., liable — If the testator, intestate, mentally incapable person, ward or beneficiary so represented is not named on the books of the company, the executor, administrator, committee, guardian or trustee is personally liable in respect of such shares as if he, she or it held them in his, her or its own name as owner thereof.

1992, c. 32, s. 6(4), (5)

58. (1) Definition — The word **"mortgagee"**, as used in subsection (2), includes a trustee for holders of securities.

(2) Mortgagee not personally liable — No mortgagee of a share of a company and no person holding such a share as collateral security who is registered on the books of the company as the holder of such share and therein described as representing in either of such capacities a named mortgagor or person giving such collateral security is personally liable in respect of such share that he or she or it so represents, but the mortgagor or other person giving such collateral security is liable as if the mortgagor or other person were registered on the books of the company as the holder of such share.

59. (1) Borrowing powers — The directors may pass by-laws,

(a) for borrowing money on the credit of the company; or

(b) for issuing, selling or pledging securities of the company; or

(c) for charging, mortgaging, hypothecating or pledging all or any of the property of the company, including book debts and unpaid calls, rights, powers, franchises and undertaking, to secure any securities or any money borrowed, or other debt, or any obligation or liability of the company.

(2) Definition — The expression **"property of the company"** in subsection (1) and in every predecessor thereof includes and has included always both present and future property of the company.

(3) Borrowing by-laws to be confirmed — No by-law passed under subsection (1) is effective until it has been confirmed by at least two-thirds of the votes cast at a general meeting of shareholders duly called for considering it.

60. Irredeemable securities — A condition contained in a security or in a deed for securing a security is not invalid by reason only that the security is thereby made irredeemable or redeemable only on the happening of a contingency, however remote, or on the expiration of a period, however long.

61. (1) Duplicate to be filed — A duplicate original, or a copy certified under the seal of the company, of any charge, mortgage or other instrument of hypothecation or pledge made by the company to secure its securities shall be filed forthwith in the office of the Minister.

(2) Exception — Subsection 1 does not apply to a charge or mortgage filed with the Minister under any other Act.

62. (1) Power to declare dividends — Subject to the special Act, letters patent or supplementary letters patent of the company, the directors may declare and the company may pay dividends on the issued shares of the company.

(2) Manner of payment — A dividend may be paid in money or in specie or in kind not exceeding in value the amount of the dividend.

(3) When dividend not to be declared — The directors shall not declare and the company shall not pay any dividend or bonus when the company is insolvent, or any dividend or bonus the payment of which renders the company insolvent or that diminishes its capital, and if any dividend or bonus is declared and paid contrary to this subsection, the directors are jointly and severally liable to the company for the amount of the dividend so declared and paid or such part thereof as renders the company insolvent or diminishes its capital.

(4) Relief from liability — If a director, present when any such dividend or bonus is declared, forthwith, or, if a director then absent, within seven days after he or she becomes aware of such declaration, delivers to an officer of the company a written protest against such declaration and, within seven days after delivery of such protest, sends a copy of such protest by registered mail to the Minister, such director thereby and not otherwise exonerates himself or herself from liability under subsection (3).

(5) Companies with wasting assets — Nothing in this section prevents a mining company or a company whose assets are of a wasting character, or a company incorporated for the object of acquiring and administering the assets or a substantial part of the assets of another corporation, either from such corporation or from the assign of such corporation, for the purpose of converting such assets into money and distributing the money among the shareholders of the company, from declaring and paying dividends out of funds derived from the operations of the company.

(6) Extent of impairment of capital — The powers conferred by subsection (5) may be exercised despite the fact that the value of the net assets of the company may be thereby reduced to less than the issued capital of the company if the payment of the dividends does not reduce the value of its remaining assets to an amount insufficient to meet all the liabilities of the company exclusive of its issued capital.

(7) Where confirmed by-law required — Subject to subsection (8), the powers conferred by subsection (5) may be exercised only under the authority of a by-law passed by the directors and confirmed by at least two-thirds of the votes cast at a general meeting of the shareholders duly called for considering it.

(8) Idem — Where dividends have been paid by a company in any of the cases mentioned in subsection (5) without the authority of a by-law, the payment thereof is nevertheless valid if a by-law adopting and approving the payment is passed by the directors and confirmed by the shareholders in the manner mentioned in subsection (7).

63. Stock dividends — For the amount of any dividend that the directors may declare payable in money, they may declare a stock dividend and issue therefor shares of the company as fully paid or may credit the amount of such dividend on shares of the company already issued but not fully paid, and the liability of the holders of such shares shall be reduced by the amount of such dividend.

64. Closing transfer registers — The directors, upon declaring a dividend, may direct that no transfer of shares shall be registered on the books of the company for a stated period, not exceeding two weeks, immediately preceding the payment of the dividend, and payment thereof shall be made to the shareholders of record on the date of closing the books.

65. Cumulative voting for directors — The letters patent, supplementary letters patent or by-laws of a company may provide that every shareholder entitled to vote at an election of directors has the right to cast thereat a number of votes equal to the number of votes attached to the shares held by him multiplied by the number of directors to be elected, and the shareholder may cast all such votes in favour of one candidate or distribute them among the candidates in such manner as the shareholder sees fit, and that, where a shareholder has voted for more than one candidate without specifying the distributon of the votes among such candidates the shareholder be deemed to have divided the votes equally among the candidates for whom the shareholder voted.

66. Removal of directors — Where the letters patent, supplementary letters patent or by-laws of a company provide for the election of directors by cumulative voting under section 65, the letters patent, supplementary letters patent or by-laws may provide that the shareholders may, by a resolution passed by at least two-thirds of the votes cast at a general meeting of which notice specifying the intention to pass such resolution has been given, remove any director before the expiration of his or her term of office, and may, by a majority of the votes cast at that meeting, elect any person in his or her stead for the remainder of the term, but that no director shall be removed where the votes cast against the resolution for his or her removal would, if cumulatively voted at an election of the full board of directors, be sufficient to elect one or more directors.

67. (1) Idem — Where the letters patent, supplementary letters patent or by-laws of a company do not provide for cumulative voting under section 65, the letters patent, supplementary letters patent or by-laws may provide that the shareholders may, by a resolution passed by at least two-thirds of the votes cast at a general meeting of which notice specifying the intention to pass such resolution has been given, remove any director before the expiration of his or her term of office, and may, by a majority of the votes cast at that meeting, elect any person in his or her stead for the remainder of the term.

(2) Exception — Subsection (1) does not affect the operation of any provision respecting the removal of directors in the letters patent or supplementary letters patent of a company issued before the 30th day of April, 1954.

68. (1) By-laws — The directors may pass by-laws not contrary to this Act or to the letters patent or supplementary letters patent to regulate,

(a) the allotment and issue of shares, the making of calls thereon, the payment thereof, the issue of share certificates, the forfeiture of shares for non-payment, the sale of forfeited shares, the transfer and the registration of transfers of shares;

(b) the declaration and payment of dividends;

(c) the qualification and remuneration of the directors;

(d) the time for and the manner of election of directors;

(e) the appointment, remuneration, functions, duties and removal of agents, officers and employees of the company and the security, if any, to be given by them to it;

(f) the time and place and the notice to be given for the holding of meetings of the shareholders and of the board of directors, the quorum at meetings of shareholders, the requirements as to proxies, and the procedure in all things at shareholders' meetings and at meetings of the board of directors;

(g) the conduct in all other particulars of the affairs of the company.

(2) **Confirmation** — A by-law passed under subsection (1) and a repeal, amendment or re-enactment thereof, unless in the meantime confirmed at a general meeting of the shareholders duly called for that purpose, is effective only until the next annual meeting of the shareholders unless confirmed thereat and, in default of confirmation thereat, ceases to have effect at and from that time, and in that case no new by-law of the same or like substance has any effect until confirmed at ageneral meeting of the shareholders.

(3) **Rejection, etc.** — The shareholders may at the general meeting or the annual meeting mentioned in subsection (2) confirm, reject, amend or otherwise deal with any by-law passed by the directors and submitted to the meeting for confirmation, but no act done or right acquired under any such by-law shall be prejudicially affected by any such rejection, amendment or other dealing.

69. **Payment of president and directors** — No by-law for the payment of the president as president or of any director as a director is effective until it has been confirmed at a general meeting of the shareholders duly called for that purpose.

70. (1) **Executive committee** — Where the number of directors on the board of directors of a company is more than six, the directors may pass a by-law authorizing them to elect from among their number an executive committee consisting of not fewer than three and to delegate to the executive committee any powers of the board, subject to the restrictions, if any, contained in the by-law or imposed from time to time by the directors.

(2) **Confirmation** — The by-law is not effective until it has been confirmed by at least two-thirds of the votes cast at a general meeting of the shareholders duly called for that purpose.

(3) **Quorum** — An executive committee may fix its quorum at not less than a majority of its members.

71. (1) **Disclosure by directors of interests in contracts** — Every director of a company who is in any way directly or indirectly interested in a proposed contract or a contract with the company shall declare his or her interest at a meeting of the directors of the company.

(2) **Time of declaration** — In the case of a proposed contract, the declaration required by this section shall be made at the meeting of the directors at which the question of entering into the contract is first taken into consideration or, if the director is not at the date of that meeting interested in the proposed contract, at the next meeting of the directors held after he or she becomes so interested, and, in a case where the director becomes interested in a contract after it is made, the declaration shall be made at the first meeting of the directors held after he or she becomes so interested.

(3) **General notice** — For the purposes of this section, a general notice given to the directors of a company by a director to the effect that he or she is a shareholder of or otherwise interested in any other company, or is a member of a specified firm and is to be regarded as interested in any contract made with such other company or firm, shall be deemed to be a sufficient declaration of interest in relation to a contract so made, but no such notice is effec-

tive unless it is given at a meeting of the directors or the director takes reasonable steps to ensure that it is brought up and read at the next meeting of the directors after it is given.

(4) **Effect of declaration** — If a director has made a declaration of his or her interest in a proposed contract or contract in compliance with this section and has not voted in respect of the contract, the director is not accountable to the company or to any of its shareholders or creditors for any profit realized from the contract, and the contract is not voidable by reason only of the director holding that office or of the fiduciary relationship established thereby.

(5) **Confirmation by shareholders** — Notwithstanding anything in this section, a director is not accountable to the company or to any of its shareholders or creditors for any profit realized from such contract and the contract is not by reason only of the director's interest therein voidable if it is confirmed by a majority of the votes cast at a general meeting of the shareholders duly called for that purpose and if the director's interest in the contract is declared in the notice calling the meeting.

(6) **Offence** — If a director is liable in respect of profit realized from any such contract and the contract is by reason only of his or her interest therein voidable, the director is guilty of an offence and on conviction is liable to a fine of not more than $200.

72. (1) **Definitions** — In this section and in sections 73 to 78,

"affiliate" means an affiliated company within the meaning of subsection 106(3);

"associate", where used to indicate a relationship with any person, means,

(a) any company of which such person beneficially owns directly or indirectly equity shares carrying more than 10 per cent of the voting rights attached to all equity shares of the company for the time being outstanding,

(b) any trust or estate in which such person has a substantial beneficial interest or as to which such person serves as trustee or in a similar capacity,

(c) any person to whom the person is married or with whom the person is living in a conjugal relationship outside marriage, or

(d) any relative of the person or of a person mentioned in clause (c) who, in any such case, has the same home as the person;

"capital security" means any share of any class of shares of a company or any bond, debenture, note or other obligation of a company, whether secured or unsecured;

"equity share" means any share of any class of shares of a company carrying voting rights under all circumstances and any share of any class of shares carrying voting rights by reason of the occurrence of any contingency that has occurred and is continuing;

"insider" or **"insider of a company"** means,

(a) any director or senior officer of a public company that has fifteen or more shareholders, two or more persons who are the joint registered owners of one or more shares being counted as one shareholder,

(b) any person who beneficially owns, directly or indirectly, equity shares of such a company carrying more than 10 per cent of the voting rights attached to all equity shares of the company for the time being outstanding, provided that in computing the percentage of voting rights attached to equity shares owned by an underwriter there shall be excluded any equity shares that have been acquired by the underwriter as underwriter in the course of distribution to the public of such shares, but such exclusion ceases to have effect on completion or cessation of the distribution to the public by the underwriter, or

(c) any person who exercises control or direction over the equity shares of such a company carrying more than 10 per cent of the voting rights attached to all equity shares of the company for the time being outstanding;

"senior officer" means,

(a) the chair or any vice-chair of the board of directors, the president, any vice-president, the secretary, the treasurer or the general manager of a company or any other individual who performs functions for the company similar to those normally performed by an individual occupying any such office, and

(b) each of the five highest paid employees of a company, including any individual referred to in subclause (i);

"underwriter" has the same meaning as in the *Securities Act*.

(2) **Interpretation** — For the purposes of this section and sections 73 to 78,

(a) every director or senior officer of a company that is itself an insider of another company shall be deemed to be an insider of such other company;

(b) an individual shall be deemed to own beneficially capital securities beneficially owned by a company controlled by him or her or by an affiliate of such company;

(c) a company shall be deemed to own beneficially capital securities beneficially owned by its affiliates; and

(d) the acquisition or disposition by an insider of a put, call or other transferable option with respect to a capital security shall be deemed a change in the beneficial ownership of the capital security to which such transferable option relates.

1999, c. 6, s. 16; 2005, c. 5, s. 16(1)

73. (1) Report — A person who becomes an insider of a company shall, within ten days after the end of the month in which the person becomes an insider, file with the Commission a report, as of the day on which the person became an insider, of the person's direct or indirect beneficial ownership of or control or direction over capital securities of the company.

(2) Idem — If a person who is an insider of a company, but has no direct or indirect beneficial ownership of or control or direction over capital securities of the company, acquires direct or indirect beneficial ownership of or control or direction over any such securities, the person shall, within ten days after the end of the month in which the person acquired such direct or indirect beneficial ownership or such control or direction, file with the Commission a report, as of the date of such acquisition, of the person's direct or indirect beneficial ownership of or control or direction over capital securities of the company.

(3) Report of subsequent changes — A person who has filed or is required to file a report under this section or any predecessor thereof and whose direct or indirect beneficial ownership of or control or direction over capital securities of the company changes from that shown or required to be shown in such report or in the last report filed by the person under this subsection shall, within ten days following the end of the month in which such change takes place, provided that the person was an insider of the company at any time during such month, file with the Commission a report of the person's direct or indirect beneficial ownership of or control or direction over capital securities of the company at the end of such month and the change or changes therein that occurred during the month, and giving such details of each transaction as may be required by the regulations made under section 78.

74. (1) Reports may be inspected — All reports filed with the Commission under section 73 or any predecessor thereof shall be open to public inspection at the offices of the Commission during normal business hours of the Commission, and any person may make extracts from such reports.

(2) Publication of information contained in reports — The Commission shall summarize in or as part of a monthly periodical for distribution to the public on payment of a reasonable fee therefor the information contained in the reports so filed.

75. (1) Offence — Every person who is required to file a report under section 73 or any predecessor thereof and who fails so to do is guilty of an offence and on conviction is liable to a fine of not more than $1,000, and, where such person is a company, every director or officer of such company who authorized, permitted or acquiesced in such failure is also guilty of an offence and on conviction is liable to a like fine.

(2) Idem — Every person who files a report under section 73 or any predecessor thereof that is false or misleading by reason of the misstatement or omission of a material fact is guilty of an offence and on conviction is liable to a fine of not more than $1,000, and, where such person is a company, every director or officer of such company who authorized, permitted or acquiesced in the filing of such false or misleading report is also guilty of an offence and on conviction is liable to a like fine.

(3) Saving — No person is guilty of an offence under subsection (2) if the person did not know and in the exercise of reasonable diligence could not have known that the report was false or misleading by reason of the misstatement or omission of a material fact.

(4) Consent to prosecute — No prosecution shall be brought under subsection (1) or (2) without the consent of the Commission.

76. (1) Liability of insiders — Every insider of a company or associate or affiliate of such insider, who, in connection with a transaction relating to the capital securities of the company, makes use of any specific confidential information for his, her or its own benefit or advantage that, if generally known, might reasonably be expected to affect materially the value of such securities, is liable to compensate any person for any direct loss suffered by such person as a result of such transaction, unless such information was known or ought reasonably to have been known to such person at the time of such transaction, and is also accountable to the company for any direct benefit or advantage received or receivable by such insider, associate or affiliate, as the case may be, as a result of such transaction.

(2) [Repealed 2002, c. 24, Sched. B, s. 25, item 4.]

2002, c. 24, Sched. B, s. 25, item 4

77. (1) Order to commence action — Upon application by any person who was at the time of a transaction referred to in subsection 76(1) or is at the time of the application an owner of capital securities of the company, the court may, if satisfied that,

(a) such person has reasonable grounds for believing that the company has a cause of action under section 76; and

(b) either,

(i) the company has refused or failed to commence an action under section 76 within sixty days after receipt of a written request from such person so to do, or

(ii) the company has failed to prosecute diligently an action commenced by it under section 76,

make an order, upon such terms as to security for costs and otherwise as to the judge seems fit, requiring the Commission to commence or continue an action in the name of and on behalf of the company to enforce the liability created by section 76.

(2) **Notice to company and O.S.C.** — The company and the Commission shall be given notice of any application under subsection (1) and shall have the right to appear and be heard thereon.

(3) **Order to require company to co-operate** — Every order made under subsection (1) shall provide that the company shall co-operate fully with the Commission in the institution and prosecution of such action and shall make available to the Commission all books, records, documents and other material or information known to the company or reasonably ascertainable by the company relevant to such action.

(4) **Appeal** — An appeal lies to the Divisional Court from an order made under subsection (1).

78. Regulations — The Lieutenant Governor in Council may make regulations,

(a) prescribing the form and content of the reports required to be filed under section 73;

(b) respecting any other matter necessary or advisable to carry out effectively the intent and purpose of sections 72 to 77.

79. (1) **Exception** — Upon the application of any interested person, the Commission may, if satisfied upon the circumstances of the particular case that there is adequate justification for so doing, make an order upon such terms and conditions as seem to the Commission to be expedient exempting in whole or in part any person from the requirements of section 73.

(2) **Hearing of Commission** — The provisions of the *Securities Act* respecting hearings by the Commission apply, so far as possible, to hearings of the Commission under this section.

(3) **Appeal from Commission** — Any person who feels aggrieved by a decision of the Commission under this section may appeal the decision to the Divisional Court, and subsections 9(2) to (6) of the *Securities Act* apply to the appeal.

80. Director [and officer] indemnified in suits respecting execution of office — Every director and officer of a company, and his or her heirs, executors and administrators, and estate and effects, respectively, may, with the consent of the company, given at any meeting of the shareholders, from time to time and at all times, be indemnified and saved harmless out of the funds of the company, from and against,

(a) all costs, charges and expenses whatsoever that he, she or it sustains or incurs in or about any action, suit or proceeding that is brought, commenced or prosecuted against him, her or it, for or in respect of any act, deed, matter or thing whatsoever, made, done or permitted by him, her or it, in or about the execution of the duties of his, her or its office; and

(b) all other costs, charges and expenses that he, she or it sustains or incurs in or about or in relation to the affairs thereof, except such costs, charges or expenses as are occasioned by his, her or its own wilful neglect or default.

1998, c. 18, Sched. E, s. 62

81. (1) Liability of directors for wages — The directors of a company are jointly and severally liable to the employees, apprentices and other wage earners thereof for all debts due while they are directors for services performed for the company, not exceeding six months wages, and for the vacation pay accrued for not more than twelve months under the *Employment Standards Act* or any predecessor thereof and the regulations thereunder or under any collective agreement made by the company.

(2) Limitation of liability — A director is liable under subsection (1) only if,

(a) the corporation is sued in the action against the director and execution against the corporation is returned unsatisfied in whole or in part; or

(b) before or after the action is commenced, the corporation goes into liquidation, is ordered to be wound up or makes an authorized assignment under the *Bankruptcy and Insolvency Act* (Canada), or a receiving order under that Act is made against it, and, in any such case, the claim for the debt has been proved.

(3) Idem — After execution has been so returned against the company, the amount recoverable against the director is the amount remaining unsatisfied on the execution.

(4) Rights of director who pays the debt — If the claim for the debt has been proved in liquidation or winding-up proceedings or under the *Bankruptcy Act* (Canada), a director who pays the debt is entitled to any preference that the creditor paid would have been entitled to or, if a judgment has been recovered for the debt, the director is entitled to an assignment of the judgement.

(5) Director holding shares in fiduciary capacity — No director holding shares as executor, administrator, guardian or trustee who is registered on the books of the company as a shareholder and therein described as representing in any such capacity a named estate, person or trust is personally liable under this section, but the estate, person or trust is subject to all the liabilities imposed by this section.

1992, c. 32, s. 6(6); 2002, c. 24, Sched. B, s. 31(1)

82. (1) Place of meetings — Subject to subsections (2) and (3), the meetings of the shareholders, the board of directors and the executive committee shall be held at the place where the head office of the company is situate.

(2) Exception — Where the by-laws of the company so provide, the meetings of the board of directors and of the executive committee may be held at any place in or outside Ontario and the meetings of the shareholders may be held at any place in Ontario.

(3) Exception — Where the letters patent or supplementary letters patent of the company so provide, the meetings of the shareholders may be held at one or more places outside Ontario designated therein.

(4) Where section not to apply — This section does not affect the operation of any provision in the letters patent or supplementary letters patent of a company issued before the 30th day of April, 1954, respecting the holdings of the meetings of the shareholders at any place outside Ontario.

83. Definitions — In this section and in sections 84 to 90,

"form of proxy" means a written or printed form that, upon completion and execution by or on behalf of a shareholder, becomes a proxy;

"information circular" means the circular referred to in subsection 86(1);

"proxy" means a completed and executed form of proxy by means of which a shareholder has appointed a person as the shareholder's nominee to attend and act for the shareholder and on the shareholder's behalf at a meeting of shareholders;

"solicit" and **"solicitation"** include,

(a) any request for a proxy whether or not accompanied by or included in a form of proxy,

(b) any request to execute or not to execute a form of proxy or to revoke a proxy,

(c) the sending or delivery of a form of proxy or other communication to a shareholder under circumstances reasonably calculated to result in the procurement, withholding or revocation of a proxy, and

(d) the sending or delivery of a form of proxy to a shareholder pursuant to section 85,

but do not include,

(e) the sending or delivery of a form of proxy to a shareholder in response to an unsolicited request made by the shareholder or on the shareholder's behalf, or

(f) the performance by any person of ministerial acts or professional services on behalf of a person soliciting a proxy.

84. (1) Proxies — Every shareholder, including a shareholder that is a corporation, entitled to vote at a meeting of shareholders may by means of a proxy appoint a person, who need not be a shareholder, as the shareholder's nominee to attend and act at the meeting in the manner, to the extent and with the power conferred by the proxy.

(2) Execution and termination — A proxy shall be executed by the shareholder or the shareholder's attorney authorized in writing or, if the shareholder is a corporation, under its corporate seal or by an officer or attorney thereof duly authorized, and ceases to be valid one year from its date.

(3) Contents — In addition to the requirements, where applicable, of section 88, a proxy shall contain the date thereof and the appointment and name of the nominee and may contain a revocation of a former proxy and restrictions, limitations or instructions as to the manner in which the shares in respect of which the proxy is given are to be voted or that may be necessary to comply with the laws of any jurisdiction in which the shares of the company are listed on a stock exchange or a restriction or limitation as to the number of shares in respect of which the proxy is given.

(4) Revocation — In addition to revocation in any other manner permitted by law, a proxy may be revoked by instrument in writing executed by the shareholder or by the shareholder's attorney authorized in writing or, if the shareholder is a corporation, under its corporate seal or by an officer or attorney thereof duly authorized, and deposited either at the head office of the company at any time up to and including the last business day preceding the day of the meeting, or any adjournment thereof, at which the proxy is to be used or with the chair of such meeting on the day of the meeting, or adjournment thereof, and upon either of such deposits the proxy is revoked.

(5) Time limit for deposit — The directors may by resolution fix a time not exceeding forty-eight hours, excluding Saturdays and holidays, preceding any meeting or adjourned meeting of shareholders before which time proxies to be used at that meeting must be deposited with the company or an agent thereof, and any period of time so fixed shall be specified in the notice calling the meeting or in the information circular relating thereto.

85. (1) Mandatory solicitation of proxies — Subject to section 87, the management of a company shall, concurrently with or prior to giving notice of a meeting of shareholders of the company, send by prepaid mail to each shareholder who is entitled to vote at such meeting at the shareholder's last address as shown on the books of the company a form of proxy for use at such meeting that complies with section 88.

(2) Offence — If the management of a company fails to comply with subsection (1), the company is guilty of an offence and on conviction is liable to a fine of not more than $1,000, and every director or officer of the company who authorized, permitted or acquiesced in such failure is also guilty of an offence and on conviction is liable to a like fine.

86. (1) Information circular — Subject to subsection (2) and section 87, no person shall solicit proxies unless,

(a) in the case of a solicitation by or on behalf of the management of a company, an information circular, either as an appendix to or as a separate document accompanying the notice of the meeting, is sent by prepaid mail to each shareholder of the company whose proxy is solicited at his last address as shown on the books of the company; or

(b) in the case of any other solicitation, the person making the solicitation, concurrently with or prior thereto, delivers or sends an information circular to each shareholder of the company whose proxy is solicited.

(2) Where subs. (1) does not apply — Subsection (1) does not apply to,

(a) any solicitation, otherwise than by or on behalf of the management of the company, where the total number of shareholders whose proxies are solicited is not more than fifteen, two or more persons who are the joint registered owners of one or more shares being counted as one shareholder;

(b) any solicitation by a person made under section 49 of the *Securities Act*; and

(c) any solicitation by a person in respect of shares of which the person is the beneficial owner.

(3) Offence — A person who fails to comply with subsection (1) is guilty of an offence and on conviction is liable to a fine of not more than $1,000, and, where such person is a company, every director or officer of such company who authorized, permitted or acquiesced in such failure is also guilty of an offence and on conviction is liable to a like fine.

(4) Idem — A person who effects a solicitation that is subject to this section by means of a form of proxy, information circular or other communication that contains an untrue statement of a material fact or omits to state a material fact necessary in order to make any statement contained therein not misleading in the light of the circumstances in which it was made is guilty of an offence and on conviction is liable to a fine of not more than $1,000, and, where such person is a company, every director or officer of such company who authorized, perm itted or acquiesced in such offence is also guilty of an offence and on conviction is liable to a like fine.

(5) Saving — No person is guilty of an offence under subsection (4) in respect of any untrue statement of a material fact or omission to state a material fact in a form of proxy or information circular, if the untruth of such statement or the fact of such omission was not known to the person who effected the solicitation and in the exercise of reasonable diligence could not have been known to such person.

87. (1) Where ss. 85, 86(1) do not apply — Section 85 and subsection 86(1) do not apply to a private company or to a public company that has fewer than fifteen shareholders, two or more persons who are the joint registered owners of one or more shares being counted as one shareholder.

(2) Exemption orders — Upon the application of any interested person, the Commission may, if satisfied that in the circumstances of the particular case there is adequate justification for so doing, make an order, on such terms and conditions as seem to the Commission to be just and expedient, exempting any person from the requirements, in whole or in part, of section 85 or of subsection 86(1).

(3) Hearing of Commission — The provisions of the *Securities Act* respecting hearings by the Commissionapply, so far as possible, to hearings of the Commission under this section.

(4) Appeal from Commission — Any person who feels aggrieved by a decision of the Commission under this section may appeal the decision to the Divisional Court, and subsections 9(2) to (6) of the *Securities Act* apply to the appeal.

88. Special form of proxy — Where section 85 or 86 is applicable to a solicitation of proxies,

(a) the form of proxy sent to a shareholder by a person soliciting proxies,

(i) shall indicate in bold-face type whether or not the proxy is solicited by or on behalf of the management of the company, and

(ii) shall provide a specifically designated blank space for dating the form of proxy;

(b) the form of proxy shall provide means whereby the person whose proxy is solicited is afforded an opportunity to specify that the shares registered in the person's name shall be voted by the nominee in favour of or against, in accordance with such person's choice, each matter or group of related matters identified therein or in the information circular as intended to be acted upon, other than the election of directors and the appointment of auditors, provided that a proxy may confer discretionary authority with respect to matters as to which a choice is not so specified by such means if the form of proxy or the information circular states in bold-face type how it is intended to vote the shares represented by the proxy in each such case;

(c) a proxy may confer discretionary authority with respect to,

(i) amendments or variations to matters identified in the notice of meeting, or

(ii) other matters which may properly come before the meeting, provided that,

(iii) the person by whom or on whose behalf the solicitation is made is not aware a reasonable time prior to the time the solicitation is made that any such amendments, variations or other matters are to be presented for action at the meeting, and

(iv) a specific statement is made in the information circular or in the form of proxy that the proxy is conferring such discretionary authority;

(d) no proxy shall confer authority,

(i) to vote for election of any person as a director of the company unless a nominee proposed in good faith for such election is named in the information circular, or

(ii) to vote at any meeting other than the meeting specified in the notice of meeting or any adjournment thereof.

(e) the information circular or form of proxy shall state that the shares represented by the proxy will be voted and that, where the person whose proxy is solicited specifies a choice with respect to any matter to be acted upon pursuant to clause (b), the shares shall, subject to section 89, be voted in accordance with the specifications so made;

(f) the information circular or form of proxy shall indicate in bold-face type that the shareholder has the right to appoint a person to attend and act for the shareholder and on the shareholder's behalf at the meeting other than the person, if any, designated in the form of proxy, and shall contain instructions as to the manner in which the shareholder may exercise such right; and

(g) if the form of proxy contains a designation of a named person as nominee, means shall be provided whereby the shareholder may designate in a form of proxy some other person as the shareholder's nominee for the purpose of subsection 84(1).

89. Where vote by ballot not required — If the aggregate number of shares represented at a meeting by proxies required to be voted for or against a particular matter or group of matters carries, to the knowledge of the chair of the meeting, less than 5 per cent of the voting rights attached to the shares entitled to vote and represented at the meeting, the chair of the meeting has the right not to conduct a vote by way of ballot on any such matter or group of matters unless a poll is demanded at the meeting.

90. Regulations re contents of information circular — The Lieutenant Governor in Council may make such regulations respecting the form and content of an information circular as the Lieutenant Governor in Council considers necessary or appropriate in the public interest.

91. Trustees, etc., may vote — An executor, administrator, guardian or trustee, and, where a corporation is such executor, administrator, guardian or trustee of a testator, intestate, mentally incapable person, ward or beneficiary, any person duly appointed a proxy for such corporation, shall represent the shares in his, her or its hands at all meetings of the shareholders of the company and may vote accordingly as a shareholder, and every person who mortgages or hypothecates his, her or its shares may nevertheless represent the shares at all such meetings and may vote accordingly as a shareholder unless in the instrument creating the mortgage or hypothec the person has expressly empowered the holder of such mortgage or hypothec to vote thereon, in which case only such holder or the person's proxy may vote in respect of such shares.

1992, c. 32, s. 6(7)

92. Joint holders of stock — If shares are held jointly by two or more persons, any one of them present at a meeting of the shareholders of the company may, in the absence of the other or others, vote thereon, but, if more than one of them are present or represented by proxy, they shall vote together on the shares jointly held.

93. (1) Shareholders' meetings — Subject to subsection (2) and in the absence of other provisions in that behalf in the by-laws of the company,

(a) notice of the time and place for holding a meeting of the shareholders shall, unless all the shareholders entitled to notice of the meeting have waived in writing the notice, be given by sending it to each shareholder entitled to notice of the meeting by prepaid mail ten days or more before the date of the meeting to the shareholder's last address as shown on the books of the company;

(b) no shareholder in arrears in respect of any call is entitled to vote at a meeting;

(c) all questions proposed for the consideration of the shareholders at a meeting of shareholders shall be determined by the majority of the votes cast and the chair presiding at the meeting has a second or casting vote in case of an equality of votes;

(d) the chair presiding at a meeting of shareholders may, with the consent of the meeting and subject to such conditions as the meeting decides, adjourn the meeting from time to time and from place to place;

(e) the president or, in his or her absence, a vice-president who is a director shall preside as chair at a meeting of shareholders, but, if there is no president or such a vice-president or if at a meeting neither of them is present within fifteen minutes after the time appointed for the holding of the meeting, the shareholders present shall choose a person from their number to be the chair;

(f) unless a poll is demanded, an entry in the minutes of a meeting of shareholders to the effect that the chair declared a motion to be carried is admissible in evidence as proof of the fact, in the absence of evidence to the contrary, without proof of the number or proportion of votes recorded in favour of or against the motion.

(2) Notice — The by-laws of the company shall not provide for fewer than ten days notice of meetings of shareholders and shall not provide that notice may be given otherwise than individually.

(3) Poll — If a poll is demanded, it shall be taken in such manner as the by-laws prescribe, and, if the by-laws make no provision therefor, then as the chair directs.

94. (1) Auditors — The shareholders of a company at their first general meeting shall appoint one or more auditors to hold office until the first annual meeting and, if the shareholders fail to do so, the directors shall forthwith make such appointment or appointments.

(2) Idem — The shareholders shall at each annual meeting appoint one or more auditors to hold office until the next annual meeting and, if an appointment is not so made, the auditor in office shall continue in office until a successor is appointed.

(3) Casual vacancy — The directors may fill any casual vacancy in the office of auditor, but, while such vacancy continues, the surviving or continuing auditor, if any, may act.

(4) Removal — The shareholders may, by resolution passed by at least two-thirds of the votes cast at a general meeting of which notice of intention to pass the resolution has been given, remove any auditor before the expiration of the auditor's term of office, and shall by a majority of the votes cast at that meeting appoint another auditor in the auditor's stead for the remainder of the term.

(5) Remuneration — The remuneration of an auditor appointed by the shareholders shall be fixed by the shareholders, or by the directors if they are authorized so to do by the shareholders, and the remuneration of an auditor appointed by the directors shall be fixed by the directors.

(6) Appointment by Minister — If for any reason no auditor is appointed, the Minister may, on the application of any shareholder, appoint one or more auditors for that year and fix the remuneration to be paid by the company for the services of the auditor or auditors.

(7) Notice — Notice of the appointment of an auditor shall be given in writing to the auditor forthwith after the appointment is made.

95. (1) Qualification of auditor — Except as provided in subsection (2), no person shall be appointed as auditor of a company who is a director, officer or employee of that company or an affiliated company or who is a partner, employer or employee of any such director, officer or employee.

(2) Private companies — Upon the unanimous vote of the shareholders of a private company present or represented at the meeting at which the auditor is appointed, a director, officer or employee of that company or an affiliated company, or a partner, employer or employee of such director, officer or employee may be appointed as auditor of that company, if it is not a subsidiary company of a company incorporated by any legislative jurisdiction in Canada which is not a private company within the meaning of this Act.

(3) Notice — A person appointed as auditor under subsection (2) shall indicate in the person's report to the shareholders on the annual financial statement of the company that the person is a director, officer or employee of the company or a partner, employer or employee of such director, officer or employee.

96. (1) Annual audit — The auditor shall make such examination as will enable the auditor to report to the shareholders as required under subsection (2).

(2) Auditor's report — The auditor shall make a report to the shareholders on the financial statement, other than the part thereof that relates to the period referred to in subclause 97(1)(b)(ii), to be laid before the company at any annual meeting during the auditor's term of office and shall state in the report whether in the auditor's opinion the financial statement referred to therein presents fairly the financial position of the company and the results of its operations for the period under review in accordance with generally accepted accounting principles applied on a basis consistent with that of the preceding period.

(3) Idem — If the financial statement contains a statement of source and application of funds or a statement of changes in net assets, the auditor shall include in the auditor's report a statement whether in the auditor's opinion, in effect, the statement of source and application of funds or the statement of changes in net assets presents fairly the information shown therein.

(4) Idem — The auditor in the auditor's report shall make such statements as the auditor considers necessary,

(a) if the company's financial statement is not in agreement with its accounting records;

(b) if the company's financial statement is not in accordance with the requirements of this Act;

(c) if the auditor has not received all the information and explanations that the auditor has required; or

(d) if proper accounting records have not been kept, so far as appears from the auditor's examination.

(5) **Right of access, etc.** — The auditor of a company has right of access at all times to all records, documents, books, accounts and vouchers of the company and is entitled to require from the directors and officers of the company such information and explanations as in the auditor's opinion are necessary to enable the auditor to report as required by subsection (2).

(6) **Auditor may attend shareholders' meetings** — The auditor of a company is entitled to attend any meeting of shareholders of the company and to receive all notices and other communications relating to any such meeting that any shareholder is entitled to receive and to be heard at any such meeting that the auditor attends on any part of the business of the meeting that concerns the auditor as auditor.

96.1 **Exemption from annual audit** — In respect of a financial year of a company, the company is exempt from the requirements of this Part regarding the appointment and duties of an auditor, if

(a) the company is not a public company;

(b) the annual income of the company is less than $100,000; and

(c) all of the shareholders consent, in writing, to the exemption in respect of the year.

1998, c. 18, Sched. E, s. 63; 2006, c. 34, s. 10(1)

97. (1) **Information to be laid before annual meeting** — The directors shall lay before each annual meeting of shareholders,

(a) in the case of a private company, a financial statement for the period that commenced on the date of incorporation and ended not more than six months before such annual meeting or, if the company has completed a financial year, that commenced immediately after the end of the last completed financial year and ended not more than six months before such annual meeting, as the case may be, made up of,

(i) a statement of profit and loss for such period,

(ii) a statement of surplus for such period, and

(iii) a balance sheet as at the end of such period;

(b) in the case of a public company, a comparative financial statement relating separately to,

(i) the period that commenced on the date of incorporation and ended not more than six months before such annual meeting or, if the company has completed a financial year, that commenced immediately after the end of the last completed financial year and ended not more than six months before such annual meeting, as the case may be, and

(ii) the period covered by the financial year next preceding such latest completed financial year, if any,

made up of,

(iii) a statement of profit and loss for each period,

(iv) a statement of surplus for each period,

(v) a statement of source and application of funds for each period, and

(vi) a balance sheet as at the end of each period;

(c) the report of the auditor to the shareholders;

(d) such further information respecting the financial position of the company as the letters patent, supplementary letters patent or by-laws of the company require.

(2) **Designation of statements** — It is not necessary to designate the statements referred to in subsection (1) as the statement of profit and loss, statement of surplus, statement of source and application of funds and balance sheet.

(3) **Auditor's report to be read** — The report of the auditor to the shareholders shall be read at the annual meeting and shall be open to inspection by any shareholder.

(4) **Omission of comparative statement** — Notwithstanding clause (1)(b), the financial statement referred to in such clause may relate only to the period that ended not more than six months before the annual meeting if the reason for the omission of the statement in respect of the period covered by the previous financial statement is set out in the financial statement to be laid before such meeting or by way of note thereto.

(5) **Omission of source and application statement** — Despite subclause (1)(b)(v), the statement of source and application of funds may be omitted if the reason for such omission is set out in the financial statement or by way of note thereto.

98. (1) **Statement of profit and loss** — The statement of profit and loss to be laid before an annual meeting shall be drawn up so as to present fairly the results of the operations of the company for the period covered by the statement and so as to distinguish severally at least,

(a) in the case of a public company, sales or gross operating revenue;

(b) the operating profit or loss before including or providing for other items of income or expense that are required to be shown separately;

(c) income from investments in subsidiaries whose financial statements are not consolidated with those of the company;

(d) income from investments in affiliated companies other than subsidiaries;

(e) income from other investments;

(f) non-recurring profits and losses of significant amount including profits or losses on the disposal of capital assets and other items of a special nature to the extent that they are not shown separately in the statement of earned surplus;

(g) provision for depreciation or obsolescence or depletion;

(h) amounts written off for goodwill or amortization of any other intangible assets to the extent that they are not shown separately in the statement of earned surplus;

(i) interest on indebtedness initially incurred for a term of more than one year, including amortization of debt discount or premium and expense;

(j) taxes on income imposed by any taxing authority,

and shall show the net profit or loss for the financial period.

(2) **Notes** — Despite subsection (1), items of the natures described in clauses (1)(g) and (h) may be shown by way of note to the statement of profit and loss.

(3) **Order for omission of sales or gross operating revenue** — A public company may apply to the Commission for an order permitting sales or gross operating revenue re-

ferred to in clause (1)(a) of this section or subclause 110(1)(b)(i) to be omitted from the statement of profit and loss or the interim financial statement, as the case may be, and the Commission may, on such terms and conditions as it may impose, permit such omission where it is satisfied that in the circumstances the disclosure of such information would be unduly detrimental to the interests of the company.

(4) **Hearing of Commission** — The provisions of the *Securities Act* respecting hearings by the Commission apply, so far as possible, to hearings of the Commission under this section.

(5) **Appeal from Commission** — Any person who feels aggrieved by a decision of the Commission under this section may appeal the decision to the Divisional Court, and subsections 9(2) to (6) of the *Securities Act* apply to the appeal.

99. (1) **Statement of surplus** — The statement of surplus shall be drawn up so as to present fairly the transactions reflected in the statement and shall show separately a statement of contributed surplus and a statement of earned surplus.

(2) **Contributed surplus** — The statement of contributed surplus shall be drawn up so as to include and distinguish the following items:

1. The balance of such surplus at the end of the preceding financial period.

2. The additions to and deductions from such surplus during the financial period including,

   (a) the amount of surplus arising from the issue of shares or the reorganization of the company's issued capital, including,

      (i) the amount of premiums received on the issue of shares at a premium,

      (ii) the amount of surplus realized on the purchase for cancellation of shares; and

   (b) donations of cash or other property by shareholders.

3. The balance of such surplus at the end of the financial period.

(3) **Earned surplus** — The statement of earned surplus shall be drawn up so as to distinguish at least the following items:

1. The balance of such surplus at the end of the preceding financial period.

2. The additions to and deductions from such surplus during the financial period and without restricting the generality of the foregoing at least the following:

   i. The amount of the net profit or loss for the financial period.

   ii. The amount of dividends declared on each class of shares.

   iii. The amount transferred to or from reserves.

3. the balance of such surplus at the end of the financial period.

100. Statement of source and application of funds — The statement of source and application of funds referred to in subclause 97(1)(b)(v) and clause 110(1)(a) shall be drawn up so as to present fairly the information shown therein for the period, and shall show separately at least,

(a) funds derived from,

   (i) current operations,

(ii) sale of non-current assets, segregating investments, fixed assets and intangible assets,

(iii) issue of securities or other indebtedness maturing more than one year after issue, and

(iv) issue of shares; and

(b) funds applied to,

(i) purchase of non-current assets, segregating investments, fixed assets and intangible assets,

(ii) redemption or other retirement of securities or repayment of other indebtedness maturing more than one year after issue,

(iii) redemption or other retirement of shares, and

(iv) payment of dividends.

101. Balance sheet — The balance sheet to be laid before an annual meeting shall be drawn up so as to present fairly the financial position of the company as at the date to which it is made up and so as to distinguish severally at least the following:

1. Cash.

2. Debts owing to the company from its directors, officers or shareholders, except debts of reasonable amount arising in the ordinary course of its business that are not overdue having regard to its ordinary terms of credit.

3. Debts owing to the company, whether on account of a loan or otherwise, from subsidiaries whose financial statements are not consolidated with those of the company.

4. Debts owing to the company, whether on account of a loan or otherwise, from affiliated companies other than subsidiaries.

5. Other debts owing to the company, segregating those that arose otherwise than in the ordinary course of its business.

6. Inventory, stating the basis of valuation.

7. Shares, bonds, debentures and other investments owned by the company, except those referred to in items 8 and 9, stating their nature and the basis of their valuation and showing separately those that are marketable with a notation of their market value.

8. Shares or securities of subsidiaries whose financial statements are not consolidated with those of the company, stating the basis of valuation.

9. Shares or securities of affiliated companies other than subsidiaries, stating the basis of valuation.

10. Lands, buildings, and plant and equipment, stating the basis of valuation, whether cost or otherwise, and, if valued on the basis of an appraisal, the date of appraisal, the name of the appraiser, the basis of the appraisal value and, if such appraisal took place within five years preceding the date to which the balance sheet is made up, the disposition in the accounts of the company of any amounts added to or deducted from such assets on appraisal and also the amount of amounts accumulated in respect of depreciation, obsolescence and depletion.

11. There shall be stated under separate headings, in so far as they are not written off, (i) expenditures on account of future business; (ii) any expense incurred in connection with any issue of shares; (iii) any expense incurred in connection with any issue of securities, including any discount thereon; and (iv) any one or more of the following: goodwill, franchises, patents, copyrights, trade marks and other intangible assets and the amount, if any, by which the value of any such assets has been written up after the 30th day of April, 1954.

12. The aggregate amount of any outstanding loans under clauses 24(2)(c), (d) and (e).

13. Bank loans and overdrafts.

14. Debts owing by the company on loans from its directors, officers or shareholders.

15. Debts owing by the company to subsidiaries whose financial statements are not consolidated with those of the company, whether on account of a loan or otherwise.

16. Debts owing by the company to affiliated companies other than subsidiaries whether on account of a loan or otherwise.

17. Other debts owing by the company, segregating those that arose otherwise than in the ordinary course of its business.

18. Liability for taxes, including the estimated liability for taxes in respect of the income of the period covered by the statement of profit and loss.

19. Dividends declared but not paid.

20. Deferred income.

21. Securities issued by the company, stating the interest rate, the maturity date, the amount outstanding and the existence of sinking fund, redemption requirements and conversion rights, if any.

22. The authorized capital, giving the number of each class of shares and a brief description of each such class, and indicating therein any class of shares that is redeemable and the redemption price thereof.

23. The issued capital, giving the number of shares of each class issued and outstanding and the amount received therefor that is attributable to capital, and showing,

(a) the number of shares of each class issued since the date of the last balance sheet and the value attributed thereto, distinguishing shares issued for cash, shares issued for services and shares issued for other consideration; and

(b) where any shares have not been fully paid,

(i) the number of shares in respect of which calls have not been made and the aggregate amount that has not been called, and

(ii) the number of shares in respect of which calls have been made and not paid and the aggregate amount that has been called and not paid.

24. Contributed surplus.

25. Earned surplus.

26. Reserves, showing the amounts added thereto and the amounts deducted therefrom during the financial period.

102. Notes to balance sheet — Explanatory information or particulars of any item mentioned in section 101 may be shown by way of note to the balance sheet.

103. (1) Notes to financial statement — There shall be stated by way of note to the financial statement particulars of any change in accounting principle or practice or in the method of applying any accounting principle or practice made during the period covered that affects the comparability of any of the statements with any of those for the preceding period, and the effect, if material, of any such change upon the profit or loss for the period.

(2) Change in accounting practice — For the purpose of subsection (1), a change in accounting principle or practice or in the method of applying any accounting principle or practice affects the comparability of a statement with that for the preceding period, even though it did not have a material effect upon the profit or loss for the period.

(3) Idem — Where applicable, the following matters shall be referred to in the financial statement of by way of note thereto:

1. The basis of conversion of amounts from currencies other than the currency in which the financial statement is expressed.

2. Foreign currency restrictions that affect the assets of the company.

3. Contractual obligations that will require abnormal expenditures in relation to the company's normal business requirements or financial position or that are likely to involve losses not provided for in the accounts.

4. Material contractual obligations in respect of long-term leases, including, in the year in which the transaction was effected, the principal details of any sale and lease transaction.

5. Contingent liabilities, stating their nature and, where practicable, the approximate amounts involved.

6. Any liability secured otherwise than by operation of law on any asset of the company, stating the liability so secured.

7. Any default of the company in principal, interest, sinking fund or redemption provisions with respect to any issue of its securities or credit agreements.

8. The gross amount of arrears of dividends on any class of shares and the date to which such dividends were last paid.

9. Where a company has contracted to issue shares or has given an option to purchase shares, the class and number of shares affected, the price and the date for issue of the shares or exercise of the option.

10. The aggregate direct remuneration paid or payable by the company and its subsidiaries whose financial statements are consolidated with those of the company to the directors, and the senior officers as defined by clause 72(1), of the company and, as a separate amount, the aggregate direct remuneration paid or payable to such directors and senior officers by the subsidiaries of the company whose financial statements are not consolidated with those of the company.

11. In the case of a holding company, the aggregate of any shares in, and the aggregate of any securities of, the holding company held by subsidiary companies whose financial statements are not consolidated with that of the holding company.

12. The amount of any loans by the company, or by a subsidiary company, otherwise than in the ordinary course of business, during the company's financial period, to the directors or officers of the company.

13. Any restriction by the letters patent, supplementary letters patent or by-laws of the company or by contract on the payment of dividends that is significant in the light of the company's financial position.

14. Any event or transaction, other than one in the normal course of business operations, between the date to which the financial statement is made up and the date of the auditor's report thereon that materially affects the financial statement.

15. In the case of a public company, the amount of any obligation for pension benefits arising from service prior to the date of the balance sheet, whether or not such obligation has been provided for in the accounts of the company, the manner in which the company proposes to satisfy such obligation and the basis on which it has charged or proposes to charge the related costs against operations.

(4) Idem — A note to a financial statement is a part of it.

104. Insignificant circumstances — Despite sections 98 to 103, it is not necessary to state in a financial statement any matter that in all the circumstances is of relative insignificance.

105. (1) Consolidated financial statement — A company, in this section referred to as "the holding company", may include in the financial statement to be submitted at an annual meeting the assets and liabilities and income and expense of any one or more of its subsidiaries, making due provision for minority interests, if any, and indicating in such financial statement that it is presented in consolidated form.

(2) Idem — Where the assets and liabilities and income and expense of any one or more subsidiaries of the holding company are not so included in the financial statement of the holding company,

(a) the financial statement of the holding company shall include a statement setting forth,

(i) the reason why the assets and liabilities and income and expense of such subsidiary or subsidiaries are not included in the financial statement of the holding company,

(ii) if there is only one such subsidiary, the amount of the holding company's proportion of the profit or loss of such subsidiary for the financial period coinciding with or ending in the financial period of the holding company, or, if there is more than one such subsidiary, the amount of the holding company's proportion of the aggregate profits less losses, or losses less profits, of all such subsidiaries for the respective financial periods coinciding with or ending in the financial period of the holding company,

(iii) The amount included as income from such subsidiary or subsidiaries in the statement of profit and loss of the holding company and the amount included therein as a provision for the loss or losses of such subsidiary or subsidiaries,

(iv) if there is only one such subsidiary, the amount of the holding company's proportion of the undistributed profits of such subsidiary earned since the acquisition of the shares of such subsidiary by the holding company to the extent that such amount has not been taken into the accounts of the holding company, or, if there is more than one such subsidiary, the amount of the holding company's proportion of the aggregate undistributed profits of all such subsidiaries earned since the acquisition of their shares by the holding company less its proportion of the losses, if any, suffered by any such subsidiary since the acquisition of its shares to the extent that such amount has not been taken into the accounts of the holding company,

(v) any qualifications contained in the report of the auditor of any such subsidiary on its financial statement for the financial period ending as aforesaid, and any note or reference contained in that financial statement to call attention to a matter that, apart from the note or reference, would properly have been referred to in such a qualification, in so far as the matter that is the subject of the qualification or note is not provided for by the company's own financial statement and is material from the point of view of its shareholders;

(b) if for any reason the directors of the holding company are unable to obtain such information as is necessary for the preparation of the statement that is to be included in the financial statement of the holding company, the directors who sign the financial statement shall so report in writing and their report shall be included in the financial statement in lieu of the statement;

(c) true copies of the latest financial statement of such subsidiary or subsidiaries shall be kept on hand by the holding company at its head office and shall be open to inspection by the shareholders of the holding company on request during the normal business hours of the holding company, but the directors of the holding company may by resolution refuse the right of such inspection if such inspection is not in the public interest or would prejudice the holding company or such subsidiary or subsidiaries, which resolution may, on the application of any such shareholder to the court, be set aside by the court;

(d) if, in the opinion of the auditor of the holding company, adequate provision has not been made in the financial statement of the holding company for the holding company's proportion,

(i) where there is only one such subsidiary, of the loss of such subsidiary suffered since acquisition of its shares by the holding company, or

(ii) where there is more than one such subsidiary, of the aggregate losses suffered by such subsidiaries since acquisition of their shares by the holding company in excess of its proportion of the undistributed profits, if any, earned by any of such subsidiaries since such acquisition,

the auditor shall state in the auditor's report the additional amount that in the auditor's opinion is necessary to make full provision therefor.

106. (1) Definitions: subsidiary company — For the purposes of this Act, a company shall be deemed to be a subsidiary of another company if, but only if,

(a) it is controlled by,

(i) that other, or

(ii) that other and one or more companies each of which is controlled by that other, or

(iii) two or more companies each of which is controlled by that other; or

(b) it is a subsidiary of a company that is that other's subsidiary.

(2) Holding company — For the purposes of this Act, a company shall be deemed to be another's holding company if, but only if, that other is its subsidiary.

(3) Affiliated company — For the purposes of this Act, one company shall be deemed to be affiliated with another company if, but only if, one of them is the subsidiary of the other or both are subsidiaries of the same company or each of them is controlled by the same person.

(4) Control — For the purposes of this Act, a company shall be deemed to be controlled by another company or person or by two or more companies if, but only

(a) shares of the first-mentioned company carrying more than 50 per cent of the votes for the election of directors are held, otherwise than by way of security only, by or for the benefit of such other company or person or by or for the benefit of such other companies; and

(b) the votes carried by such shares are sufficient, if exercised, to elect a majority of the board of directors of the first-mentioned company.

107. Reserves — In a financial statement, the term **"reserve"** shall be used to describe only,

(a) amounts appropriated from earned surplus at the discretion of management for some purpose other than to meet a liability or contingency known or admitted or a commitment made as at the statement date or a decline in value of an asset that has already occurred;

(b) amounts appropriated from earned surplus pursuant to the instrument of incorporation, instrument amending the instrument of incorporation or by-laws of the company for some purpose other than to meet a liability or contingency known or admitted or a commitment made as at the statement date or a decline in value of an asset that has already occurred; and

(c) amounts appropriated from earned surplus in accordance with the terms of a contract and that can be restored to the earned surplus when the conditions of the contract are fulfilled.

108. Approval of financial statement — The financial statement shall be approved by the board of directors, such approval to be evidenced by the signature at the foot of the balance sheet by two of the directors duly authorized to sign, and the auditor's report shall be attached to the financial statement or there shall be inserted at the foot of the balance sheet a reference to the report.

109. (1) Mailing of financial statement to shareholders — A public company shall, ten days or more before the date of the annual meeting, send by prepaid mail to each shareholder at the auditor's last address as shown on the books of the company a copy of the financial statement and a copy of the auditor's report.

(2) Financial statement, private companies — A shareholder of a private company is entitled to be furnished by the company on demand with a copy of the documents mentioned in subsection (1).

(3) Offence — A company that fails to comply with subsection (1) or (2) is guilty of an offence and on conviction is liable to a fine of not more than $200, and every director or officer of the company who authorizes, permits or acquiesces in any such failure is guilty of an offence and on conviction is liable to a like fine.

110. (1) Comparative interim financial statement — A public company shall send to each shareholder a copy of a comparative interim financial statement for the six-month period that commenced on the date of incorporation or, if the company has completed a financial year, for the six-month period that commenced immediately after the end of the last completed financial year and for the comparable six-month period, if any, in the twelve months immediately preceding the commencement of the six-month period in respect of which such interim financial statement is issued, made up of,

(a) a statement of source and application of funds for each period that complies with section 100; and

(b) sufficient relevant financial information in summary form to present fairly the results of the operations of the company for each period, including,

(i) a statement of sales or gross operating revenue,

(ii) extraordinary items of income or expense,

(iii) net income before taxes on income imposed by any taxing authority,

(iv) taxes on income imposed by any taxing authority, and

(v) net profit and loss.

(2) Idem — The interim financial statement required by subsection (1) may omit either or both of,

(a) the information relating to the comparable period; and

(b) the statement of source and application of funds,

if the reason for the omission or omissions, as the case may be, is set out in the interim financial statement or by way of note thereto.

(3) Idem — There shall be stated by way of note to the interim financial statement required by subsection (1) particulars of any change in accounting principle or practice or in the method of applying any accounting principle or practice made during the period covered that affects the comparability of such statement with the statement for the preceding period or with the interim financial statement for a part of the preceding period, and the effect, if material, of any such change upon the profit or loss for the period covered by the interim financial statement.

(4) Idem — For the purpose of subsection (3), a change in accounting principle or practice or in the method of applying any accounting principle or practice affects the comparability of a statement with that for the preceding period or part thereof, even though it did not have a material effect upon the profit or loss for the period covered by the interim financial statement.

(5) Idem — The interim financial statement required by subsection (1) shall be sent by prepaid mail to each shareholder, within sixty days of the date to which it is made up, at the shareholder's last address as shown on the books of the company.

(6) Offence — A company that fails to comply with this section is guilty of an offence and on conviction is liable to a fine of not more than $1,000, and every director or officer of the company who authorized, permitted or acquiesced in any such failure is guilty of an offence and on conviction is liable to a like fine.

111. (1) Subsidiaries not to hold shares of holding companies — Except in the cases mentioned in this section, a company shall not be a shareholder of a company that is its holding company, and any allotment or transfer or shares of a company to its subsidiary company is void.

(2) **Application** — This section does not apply to a subsidiary holding shares as executor, administrator, guardian or trustee unless the holding company or a subsidiary thereof is beneficially interested under the trust and is not so interested only by way of security for the purposes of a transaction entered into by it in the ordinary course of a business that includes the lending of money.

(3) **Exception** — This section does not prevent a subsidiary that on the 30th day of April, 1954, held shares of its holding company from continuing to hold such shares, but, subject to subsection (2), the subsidiary has no right to vote at meetings of shareholders of the holding company or at meetings of any class of shareholders thereof.

(4) **Nominees** — Subject to subsection (2), subsections (1) and (3) apply in relation to a nominee for a company that is a subsidiary as if the references in subsections (1) and (3) to such a company included references to a nominee for it.

1992, c. 32, s. 6(8)

112. (1) **Definition** — In this section, **"arrangement"** includes a reorganization of the authorized capital of a company and includes, without limiting the generality of the foregoing, the consolidation of shares of different classes, the reclassification of shares of a class into shares of another class and the variation of the terms, preferences, rights, conditions, restrictions, limitations or prohibitions attaching to shares of any class, and includes a reconstruction under which a company transfers or sells or proposes to transfer or to sell to another company the whole or a substantial part of its undertaking for a consideration consisting in whole or in part of shares or securities of the other company and in which it proposes to distribute a part of such consideration among its shareholders of any class or to cease carrying on its undertaking or the part of its undertaking so transferred or sold or so proposed to be transferred or sold.

(2) **Arrangements** — Where an arrangement is proposed between a company and its shareholders or a class or classes of them affecting the rights of such shareholders or class or classes under the company's letters patent or supplementary letters patent or by-laws, the court may, on application of the company or of a shareholder, order a meeting of the shareholders of the company or of the class or classes affected, as the case may be, to be held on twenty-one days notice, or such shorter time as the courts directs, served in such manner as the court directs.

(3) **Contents of notice calling meeting** — Where a meeting of the shareholders or of any class or classes of shareholders is called under subsection (2), the notice calling the meeting shall contain a statement explaining the effect of the arrangement and in particular stating any interest of the directors of the company, whether as directors or as shareholders of the company or otherwise, and the effect thereon of the arrangement, in so far as it is different from the effect on the like interest of other persons.

(4) **Sanction by court** — If the shareholders of the company or of the class or classes affected, as the case may be, present in person or by proxy at the meeting, agree by at least three-fourths of the shares of each class represented to the arrangement either as proposed or as varied at the meeting, the arrangement may be sanctioned by the court and, if so sanctioned, the arrangement and any decrease or increase in the authorized capital and any provisions for the allotment or disposition thereof by sale or otherwise as therein set forth may be

confirmed by supplementary letters patent and thereupon is binding on the company and on the shareholders of the company or on the class or classes of shareholders affected.

(5) **Notice to dissenters** — If dissenting votes are cast at the meeting and, despite such dissenting votes, the arrangement is agreed to by the shareholders or the class or classes represented in accordance with subsection (4) and unless the court in its discretion otherwise orders, the company shall notify each dissenting shareholder in such manner as the court directs of the time and place when application will be made to it for the sanction of the arrangement.

113. (1) **Amalgamation** — Any two or more companies, including a holding and subsidiary company, having the same or similar objects may amalgamate and continue as one company.

(2) **Agreement** — The companies proposing to amalgamate may enter into an agreement for the amalgamation prescribing the terms and conditions of the amalgamation, the mode of carrying the amalgamation into effect and stating the name of the amalgamated company, the names and address for service of each of the first directors of the company and how and when the subsequent directors are to be elected with such other details as may be necessary to perfect the amalgamation and to provide for the subsequent management and working of the amalgamated company, the authorized capital of the amalgamated company and the manner of converting the authorized capital of each of the companies into that of the amalgamated company.

(3) **Adoption by shareholders** — The agreement shall be submitted to the shareholders of each of the amalgamating companies at general meetings thereof called for the purpose of considering the agreement, and, if two-thirds of the votes cast at each such meeting are in favour of the adoption of the agreement, that fact shall be certified upon the agreement by the secretary of each of the amalgamating companies.

(4) **Joint application for letters patent** — If the agreement is adopted in accordance with subsection (3), the amalgamating companies may apply jointly to the Lieutenant Governor for letters patent confirming the agreement and amalgamating the companies so applying, and on and from the date of the letters patent such companies are amalgamated and are continued as one company by the name in the letters patent provided, and the amalgamated company possesses all the property, rights, privileges and franchises and is subject to all liabilities, contracts, disabilities and debts of each of the amalgamating companies.

1998, c. 18, Sched. E, s. 64; 2001, c. 9, Sched. D, s. 5(4)

114. (1) **Distribution of assets where winding up protracted** — Where a company has ceased to carry on business except for the purpose of winding up its affairs and has no debts or obligations that have not been provided for or protected, the directors may pass by-laws for distributing in money, kind, specie or otherwise the property of the company or any part of it rateably among the shareholders according to their rights and interests in the company.

(2) **Confirmation** — The by-law is not effective until it has been confirmed by two-thirds of the votes cast at a meeting of the shareholders duly called for considering the by-law nor until it has been confirmed by the Lieutenant Governor in Council.

115. (1) **Private companies contravening privileges, etc.** — If a private company contravenes any of the provisions of its special Act, letters patent or supplementary letters

patent respecting the restriction on the right to transfer its shares, the limitation on the number of its shareholders or the prohibition on invitations to the public to subscribe for its shares or securities, it ceases to be entitled to the privileges and exemptions conferred on private companies under this Act and thereupon this Act applies to the company as if it were not a private company.

(2) **Relief** — The court, on being satisfied that any such contravention was accidental or due to inadvertence or to some other sufficient cause, or that on other grounds it is just and equitable to grant relief, may, on the application of the company or any other person interested and on such terms and conditions as the court considers proper, order that the company be relieved from the consequences mentioned in subsection (1).

(3) **Offence** — In addition to the consequences mentioned in subsection (1), every company that contravenes any of the provisions of its special Act, letters patent or supplementary letters patent respecting the restriction on the right to transfer its shares, the limitation on the number of its shareholders or the prohibition on invitations to the public to subscribe for its shares or securities, and every director or officer of the company who authorizes, permits or acquiesces in any such contravention, is guilty of an offence and on conviction is liable to a fine of not more than $200.

116. (1) **Private company, rights of dissenting shareholders** — If, in the case of a private company, at a meeting of shareholders,

(a) a resolution passed by the directors authorizing the sale or disposition of the undertaking of the company or any part thereof as an entirety or substantially as an entirety is confirmed with or without variation by the shareholders; or

(b) a resolution passed by the directors authorizing an application for the issue of supplementary letters patent providing for the conversion of the company into a public company is confirmed with or without variation by the shareholders; or

(c) an agreement for the amalgamation of the company with one or more other companies, whether public or private, is confirmed by the shareholders,

any shareholder who has voted against the confirmation of such resolution or agreement, as the case may be, may within two days after the date of the meeting give notice in writing to the company requiring it to purchase the shareholder's shares.

(2) **Company bound to purchase shares** — Within ninety days from the date of the completion of the sale or disposition or the issue of the supplementary letters patent or the letters patent, as the case may be, the company shall purchase the shares of every shareholder who has given notice under subsection (1).

(3) **Saving** — The company shall not purchase any shares under subsection (2) if it is insolvent or if such purchase would render the company insolvent.

(4) **Price of shares** — The price and terms of the purchase of such shares shall be as may as agreed upon by the company and the dissenting shareholder, but, if they fail to agree, the price and terms shall be as determined by the court on the application of the dissenting shareholder.

(5) **Sale of shares** — Any shares purchased under subsection (2) shall not be cancelled by reason only of such purchase, and may be sold by the company at such price and on such terms as the directors determine.

(6) Where sale not completed — If the sale or disposition is not completed or the supplementary letters patent or letters patent are not issued, the rights of the dissenting shareholder under this section cease and the company shall not purchase the shares of such shareholder under this section.

PART III — CORPORATIONS WITHOUT SHARE CAPITAL

117. Application — This Part, except where it is otherwise expressly provided, applies,

(a) to every corporation incorporated by or under a general or special Act of the Parliament of the late Province of Upper Canada;

(b) to every corporation incorporated by or under a general or special Act of the Parliament of the late Province of Canada that has its head office and carries on business in Ontario and that was incorporated with objects to which the authority of the Legislature extends; and

(c) to every corporation incorporated by or under a general or special Act of the Legislature,

but this Part does not apply to a corporation incorporated for the construction and working of a railway, incline railway or a street railway.

Proposed Repeal — 117

117. [Repealed 2010, c. 15, s. 211(4). Not in force at date of publication.]

118. Incorporation — A corporation may be incorporated to which Part V applies or that has objects that are within the jurisdiction of the Province of Ontario.

Proposed Amendment — 118

118. Incorporation — A corporation may be incorporated to which Part V applies.

2010, c. 15, s. 211(5) [Not in force at date of publication.]

1994, c. 27, s. 78(5)

119. (1) Application for incorporation — The applicants for the incorporation of a corporation shall file with the Lieutenant Governor an application showing:

1. The names in full and the address for service of each of the applicants.
2. The name of the corporation to be incorporated.
3. The objects for which the corporation is to be incorporated.
4. The place within Ontario where the head office of the corporation is to be situate.
5. The names of the applicants who are to be the first directors of the corporation.
6. Any other matters that the applicants desire to have embodied in the letters patent.

(2) Idem — The applicants may ask to have embodied in the letters patent any provision that may be made the subject of a by-law of the corporation.

(3) Exception — Subsection (2) does not apply to a provision providing for the election and retirement of directors in accordance with subsection 287(2) or (5).

1998, c. 18, Sched. E, s. 65; 2001, c. 9, Sched. D, s. 5(5)

120. Classes of membership — The letters patent, supplementary letters patent or by-laws of a corporation may provide for more than one class of membership and in that case shall set forth the designation of and the terms and conditions attaching to each class.

121. Applicants become members — Upon incorporation of a corporation, each applicant becomes a member thereof.

122. Members not liable — A member shall not, as such, be held answerable or responsible for any act, default, obligation or liability of the corporation or for any engagement, claim, payment, loss, injury, transaction, matter or thing relating to or connected with the corporation.

123. Number of members — Unless the letters patent, supplementary letters patent or by-laws of a corporation otherwise provide, there is no limit on the number of members of the corporation.

124. (1) Admission to membership — Subject to subsection (2), a person or unincorporated association may be admitted to membership in a corporation by resolution of the board of directors, but the letters patent, supplementary letters patent or by-laws may provide that such resolution is not effective until it has been confirmed by the members in general meeting.

(2) Idem — The letters patent, supplementary letters patent or by-laws of a corporation may provide for the admission of members by virtue of their office.

1994, c. 27, s. 78(6)

125. Voting powers of members — Each member of each class of members of a corporation has one vote, unless the letters patent, supplementary letters patent or by-laws of the corporation provide that each such member has more than one vote or has no vote.

126. (1) Not to be carried on for gain — A corporation, except a corporation to which Part V applies, shall be carried on without the purpose of gain for its members and any profits or other accretions to the corporation shall be used in promoting its objects and the letters patent shall so provide, and, where a company is converted into a corporation, the supplementary letters patent shall so provide.

(2) Exception — Nothing in subsection (1) prohibits a director from receiving reasonable remuneration and expenses for his or her services to the corporation as a director or prohibits a director or member from receiving reasonable remuneration and expenses for his or her services to the corporation in any other capacity, unless the letters patent, supplementary letters patent or by-laws otherwise provide.

Proposed Repeal — 126

126. [Repealed 2010, c. 15, s. 211(6). Not in force at date of publication.]

127. Directors by virtue of their office — Subject to section 286, the letters patent, supplementary letters patent or by-laws of a corporation may provide for persons becoming directors by virtue of their office in lieu of election.

128. (1) Memberships not transferable, termination — Unless the letters patent or supplementary letters patent otherwise provide, the interest of a member in a corporation is not transferable and lapses and ceases to exist upon the member's death or when the member ceases to be a member by resignation or otherwise in accordance with the by-laws of the corporation.

(2) Where transferable — Where the letters patent or supplementary letters patent provide that the interest of a member in the corporation is transferable, the by-laws shall not restrict the transfer of such interest.

129. (1) By-laws — The directors of a corporation may pass by-laws not contrary to this Act or to the letters patent or supplementary letters patent to regulate,

(a) the admission of persons and unincorporated associations as members and as members by virtue of their office and the qualification of and the conditions of membership;

(b) the fees and dues of members;

(c) the issue of membership cards and certificates;

(d) the suspension and termination of memberships by the corporation and by the member;

(e) the transfer of memberships;

(f) the qualification of and the remuneration of the directors and the directors by virtue of their office, if any;

(g) the time for and the manner of election of directors;

(h) the appointment, remuneration, functions, duties and removal of agents, officers and employees of the corporation and the security, if any, to be given by them to it;

(i) the time and place and the notice to be given for the holding of meetings of the members and of the board of directors, the quorum at meetings of members, the requirement as to proxies, and the procedure in all things at members' meetings and at meetings of the board of directors;

(j) the conduct in all other particulars of the affairs of the corporation.

(2) Confirmation — A by-law passed under subsection (1) and a repeal, amendment or re-enactment thereof, unless in the meantime confirmed at a general meeting of the members duly called for that purpose, is effective only until the next annual meeting of the members unless confirmed thereat, and, in default of confirmation thereat, ceases to have effect at and from that time, and in that case no new by-law of the same or like substance has any effect until confirmed at a general meeting of the members.

(3) Rejection — The members may at the general meeting or the annual meeting mentioned in subsection (2) confirm, reject, amend or otherwise deal with any by-law passed by the directors and submitted to the meeting for confirmation, but no act done or right acquired under any such by-law is prejudicially affected by any such rejection, amendment or other dealing.

130. (1) By-laws respecting delegates — The directors of a corporation may pass by-laws providing for,

(a) the division of its members into groups that are composed of territorial groups, common interest groups or both territorial and common interest groups;

(b) the election of some or all of its directors,

(i) by such groups on the basis of the number of members in each group, or

(ii) for the groups in a defined geographical area, by the delegates of such groups meeting together;

(c) the election of delegates and alternative delegates to represent each group on the basis of the number of members in each group;

(d) the number and method of electing delegates;

(e) the holding of meetings of delegates;

(f) the authority of delegates at meetings or providing that a meeting of delegates shall for all purposes be deemed to be and to have all the powers of a meeting of the members;

(g) the holding of meetings of members or delegates territorially or on the basis of common interest.

(2) **Confirmation** — No by-law passed under subsection (1) is effective until it has been confirmed by at least two-thirds of the votes cast at a general meeting of the members duly called for considering the by-law.

(3) **Voting** — A delegate has only one vote and shall not vote by proxy.

(4) **Qualification of delegates** — No person shall be elected a delegate who is not a member of the corporation.

(5) **Saving** — No such by-law shall prohibit members from attending meetings of delegates and participating in the discussions at such meetings.

1998, c. 18, Sched. E, s. 66

131. (1) **Supplementary letters patent** — A corporation may apply to the Lieutenant Governor for the issue of supplementary letters patent,

(a) extending, limiting or otherwise varying its objects;

(b) changing its name;

(c) varying any provision in its letters patent or prior supplementary letters patent;

(d) providing for any matter or thing in respect of which provision may be made in letters patent under this Act;

(e) converting it into a company;

(f) converting it into a corporation, with or without share capital.

(2) **Authorization** — An application under subsection (1) shall be authorized by a special resolution.

(3) [Repealed 1999, c. 12, Sched. F, s. 21.]

(4) **Contents of application for conversion into company** — If the application is under clause (1)(e) or (f) and the corporation is to become a company, the application shall set forth the authorized capital, the classes of shares, if any, into which it is to be divided, the number of shares of each class, the par value of each share or, where the shares are to be without par value, the consideration, if any, exceeding which each share or the aggregate consideration, if any, exceeding which all the shares of each class may not be issued, and, where there are to be preference shares, the preferences, rights, conditions, restrictions, limi-

tations or prohibitions attaching to them or each class of them, and the terms and conditions on which the members will become shareholders.

(5) [Repealed 1998, c. 18, s. 67.]

(6) Special Act corporations excepted — This section does not apply to a corporation incorporated by special Act, except that a corporation incorporated by special Act may apply under this section for the issue of supplementary letters patent changing its name.

Proposed Repeal — 131(6)

(6) [Repealed 2010, c. 15, s. 211(6). Not in force at date of publication.]

1998, c. 18, Sched. E, s. 67; 1999, c. 12, Sched. F, s. 21

132. (1) Disposition of property on dissolution — A corporation may pass by-laws providing that, upon its dissolution and after payment of all of its debts and liabilities, its remaining property or a part of that property shall be distributed or disposed of to the Crown in right of Ontario or its agents, the Crown in right of Canada or its agents, municipal corporations, charitable organizations or organizations whose objects are beneficial to the community.

(2) Confirmation — Such a by-law is not effective until it has been confirmed by two-thirds of the votes cast at a general meeting of the members duly called for that purpose.

(3) [Repealed 1998, c. 18, Sched. E, s. 68.]

(4) [Repealed 1998, c. 18, Sched. E, s. 68.]

(5) Where no by-law — In the absence of such by-law and upon the dissolution of the corporation, the whole of its remaining property shall be distributed equally among the members or, if the letters patent, supplementary letters patent or by-laws so provide, among the members of a class or classes of members.

1998, c. 18, Sched. E, s. 68; 2004, c. 19, s. 10(1)

133. (1) Application of Part II provisions to Part III corporations — Section 22, clauses 23(1)(a) to (p), and (s) to (v), subsection 23(2), sections 59 to 61, 67, 69 to 71, 80 to 82, 84, 93 and 94, subsection 95(1), sections 96 and 96.1, clauses 97(1)(a), (c) and (d), subsection 97(3) and section 113 apply with necessary modifications to corporations to which this Part applies, and in so applying them the words **"company"** and **"private company"** mean **"corporation"** and the word **"shareholder"** means **"member"**.

(2) Charitable corporation — Despite subsection (1), in the case of a corporation to which this Part applies, the objects of which are exclusively for charitable purposes, it is sufficient notice of any meeting of the members of the corporation if notice is given by publication at least once a week for two consecutive weeks next preceding the meeting in a newspaper or newspapers circulated in the municipality or municipalities in which the majority of the members of the corporation reside as shown by their addresses on the books of the corporation.

Proposed Repeal — 133(2)

(2) [Repealed 2010, c. 15, s. 211(6). Not in force at date of publication.]

(2.1) [Repealed 2006, c. 34, s. 10(2).]

(2.2) Conditions for indemnification — Despite subsection (1), a corporation referred to in subsection 1(2) of the *Charities Accounting Act* cannot provide the indemnification referred to in section 80 unless,

(a) the corporation complies with the *Charities Accounting Act* or a regulation made under that Act that permits the provision of an indemnification; or

(b) the corporation or a director or officer of the corporation obtains a court order authorizing the indemnification.

Proposed Repeal — 133(2.2)

(2.2) [Repealed 2010, c. 15, s. 211(6). Not in force at date of publication.]

(3) Insurers — Clauses 97(1)(a) and (d), subsections 97(2) and (3), subsection 98(1), except clause (a) thereof, subsection 98(2), sections 99, 101, 102, 107 and 108 and subsections 109(1) and (3) apply with necessary modifications to corporations to which Part V applies, and so applying them the words **"company"** and **"private company"** mean **"corporation"** and the word **"shareholder"** means **"member"**.

1994, c. 27, s. 78(7); 1998, c. 18, Sched. E, s. 69; 2000, c. 26, Sched. B, s. 9; 2006, c. 34, s. 10(2)

PART IV — MINING COMPANIES

[Heading repealed 2010, c. 15, s. 211(7). Not in force at date of publication.]

134. Definition — In this Part, **"company"** means a company to which this Part applies.

Proposed Repeal — 134

134. [Repealed 2010, c. 15, s. 211(7). Not in force at date of publication.]

135. Application — This Part applies,

(a) to every mining company incorporated before the 1st day of July, 1907;

(b) to every mining company that was made subject to a predecessor of this Part by its letters patent or supplementary letters patent where the subjection has not been removed by supplementary letters patent; and

(c) to every mining company made subject to this Part by its letters patent or supplementary letters patent where the subjection has not been removed by supplementary letters patent.

Proposed Repeal — 135

135. [Repealed 2010, c. 15, s. 211(7). Not in force at date of publication.]

136. (1) Par value shares only — The shares of a company shall be with par value.

(2) Exception — Subsection (1) does not apply to shares authorized before the 30th day of April, 1954.

Proposed Repeal — 136

136. [Repealed 2010, c. 15, s. 211(7). Not in force at date of publication.]

137. (1) Issue of shares at discount — Unless the letters patent, supplementary letters patent or by-laws otherwise provide, a company may issue its shares at a discount.

(2) At par — Despite subsection (1), preference shares shall not be issued at a discount.

(3) Rate of discount — Where shares are to be issued at a discount, the rate of discount shall be specified in the resolution of the directors allotting such shares.

Proposed Repeal — 137

137. [Repealed 2010, c. 15, s. 211(7). Not in force at date of publication.]

138. Shareholders' liability — No shareholder of a company who holds shares that were validly issued at a discount before the 30th day of April, 1954, or that are validly issued at a discount on or after the 30th day of April, 1954, is personally liable for non-payment of any calls made upon the shareholder's shares beyond the amount agreed to be paid therefor.

Proposed Repeal — 138

138. [Repealed 2010, c. 15, s. 211(7). Not in force at date of publication.]

139. Share certificates — A company shall have upon every share certificate issued by it distinctly written or printed in red ink, where such certificates are issued with respect to shares subject to call, the words "SUBJECT TO CALL" or "NON LIBÉRÉES", or, where issued with respect to shares not subject to call, the words "NOT SUBJECT TO CALL" or "ENTIÈREMENT LIBÉRÉES".

Proposed Repeal — 139

139. [Repealed 2010, c. 15, s. 211(7). Not in force at date of publication.]

PART V — INSURANCE CORPORATIONS

140. (1) *Insurance Act* definitions — In this Part, unless the context otherwise requires, words and expressions defined under section 1 or 43 of the *Insurance Act* have the same meaning as in that Act.

(2) Definition — In this Part,

"county" means an upper-tier municipality and a single-tier municipality that is not within a territorial district or within an upper-tier municipality;

"spouse" means,

(a) a spouse as defined in section 1 of the *Family Law Act*, or

(b) either of two persons who live together in a conjugal relationship outside marriage.

(3) Meaning of "affiliated" — For the purposes of this Part, an individual is affiliated with an insurer if he or she is affiliated with the insurer for the purposes of Part II.2 of the *Insurance Act*.

2002, c. 17, Sched. F, s. 1; 2004, c. 31, Sched. 38, s. 1; 2005, c. 5, s. 16(2); 2006, c. 33, Sched. O, s. 17

141. (1) Application of Part — This Part applies to all applications for incorporation of insurers intending to undertake contracts of insurance in Ontario, and to such insurers when incorporated, and to all insurers incorporated before the 30th day of April, 1954, under the laws of Ontario.

(2) Application of Act — Except as otherwise provided in this Part, the provisions of this Act that are not inconsistent with this Part apply to all insurers to which this Part applies.

(2.1) Exception, s. 24 — Section 24 does not apply to an insurer.

(3) Exception — Sections 97 to 107 and 110 do not apply to insurers undertaking and transacting life insurance.

(4) Syndicates excluded — Corporations incorporated for the sole purpose of participating in or constituting a syndicate operating on The Canadian Insurance Exchange are not insurers within the meaning of subsection (1).

(5) Networking — An insurer incorporated under this Act may,

(a) act as an agent for any person in respect of the provision of a service that is provided by,

(i) a financial institution,

(ii) an entity that is a permitted entity with respect to the insurer for the purposes of Part XVII of the *Insurance Act*, or

(iii) another entity if regulations have been made under the *Insurance Act* that will apply to the networking arrangements between the insurer and that entity;

(b) enter into an arrangement with any person in respect of the provision of that service; and

(c) refer any other person to a person referred to in clause (a) or (b).

1994, c. 11, s. 384; 2006, c. 33, Sched. O, s. 18

141.1 (1) Application of ss. 141.2 to 141.4 — Except as otherwise provided by this section, sections 141.2, 141.3 and 141.4 apply to all insurers to which this Part applies.

(2) Pension funds and employees' mutual benefit societies — For the purposes of subsection (1), pension funds and employees' mutual benefit societies incorporated under section 185 are not considered to be insurers.

(3) Exemptions — Subsections 141.2(2) to (9) do not apply to,

(a) an insurer who is a reporting issuer under the *Securities Act*;

(b) an insurer who is exempt from section 121.24 of the *Insurance Act*.

2006, c. 33, Sched. O, s. 19

141.2 Board of directors of insurer — (1) Number of directors — Despite subsection 283(2) and subject to subsection 165(1) and subsection 210(2), the board of directors of an insurer shall be composed of at least six persons.

(2) Limit on affiliated directors — Not more than two-thirds of the directors of an insurer shall be affiliated with the insurer.

(3) Determination of whether a person is affiliated — The determination of whether an individual is affiliated with an insurer,

(a) shall be made annually, as of the day the notice of the annual general meeting of the insurer is sent to the members, participating policyholders or shareholders of the insurer; and

(b) shall apply for the period commencing on the day of that annual general meeting and ending on the day before the next following annual general meeting of the insurer, irrespective of whether the individual would have otherwise become affiliated or ceased to be affiliated with the insurer during that period.

(4) If person deemed affiliated under *Insurance Act* — Despite subsection (3), if the Superintendent makes a determination under section 121.23 of the *Insurance Act* that an individual is affiliated with an insurer, the individual continues to be affiliated with the insurer for the period determined under that section.

(5) Quorum must include non-affiliated director — Despite subsection 70(3), section 173 and subsection 288(1), a quorum of the board of directors of an insurer must include at least one director who is not affiliated with the insurer.

(6) Exception — Up to four employees of an insurer or a subsidiary of the insurer may be directors of the insurer, but any such directors must not constitute a majority of the board.

(7) Rules when second election required — Despite subsection 288(2), if there is a failure to elect a board of directors that complies with the requirements of this Part, the following rules apply:

1. The directors holding office immediately before the election shall continue in office until their successors are elected.

2. The directors then in office shall, without delay, call a special meeting of the members, participating policyholders or shareholders, as the case may be, to fill the vacancy or vacancies, and if they fail to call a meeting or if there are no directors then in office, any member, participating policyholder or shareholder, as the case may be, may call the special meeting.

3. Despite clause (3)(b), the determination of whether an individual is affiliated shall apply commencing on the day of that special meeting and ending on the day before the next following annual general meeting of the insurer, irrespective of whether the individual would have otherwise become affiliated or ceased to be affiliated with the insurer during that period.

(8) Vacancy — Despite subsection 288(2), a vacancy occurring in the board of directors must be filled for the remainder of the term by the directors then in office as soon as practicable after the vacancy occurs if the vacancy results in more than two-thirds of the directors of the insurer being affiliated with the insurer.

(9) Determination of whether new director is affiliated — The determination of whether an individual who fills a vacancy occurring in the board of directors is affiliated with an insurer shall be made as of the day the individual fills the vacancy and shall apply until the day before the next following annual general meeting of the insurer, irrespective of whether the individual would have otherwise become affiliated or ceased to be affiliated with the insurer during that period.

2006, c. 33, Sched. O, s. 19

141.3 Committees — The directors of an insurer shall establish such committees of the directors as may be required under the *Insurance Act* or under the regulations made under that Act.

2006, c. 33, Sched. O, s. 19

141.4 Validity of decisions — No decision of the board of directors or executive committee of an insurer is invalid by reason of any failure to comply with any requirement in section 141.2 or 141.3.

2006, c. 33, Sched. O, s. 19

142. (1) Incorporation of joint stock insurance companies — A joint stock insurance company may be incorporated for the purpose of undertaking and transacting any class of insurance for which a joint stock insurance company may be licensed under the *Insurance Act*.

(2) Notice — Applicants for incorporation shall, immediately before the application is made, publish in at least four consecutive issues of *The Ontario Gazette* notice of their intention to apply, and shall also, if so required by the Minister, publish elsewhere notice of such intention.

(3) Notice to Superintendent — Applicants for incorporation shall also give at least one month's notice to the Superintendent of their intention to apply for incorporation.

143. (1) Definition — In this section, **"money received on account of shares"** includes money received as premium on shares.

(2) Authorized capital — The authorized capital of a company shall be not less than $500,000.

(3) Exception — A company whose authorized capital immediately before the 13th day of June, 1968 was less than $500,000 shall not decrease its authorized capital, and subsection (2) does not apply to the corporation until its authorized capital is increased to $500,000 or more.

(4) Par value of shares — The authorized capital shall be divided into shares of $100 each, but, where not less than $200,000 of the authorized capital has been paid in cash, the shares or any class of shares may be redivided into shares having a par value of $1 or a multiple thereof, or an additional class or classes of shares having a par value of $1 or a multiple thereof may be created.

(5) Application of money received on account of shares — All money received on account of shares shall be paid into a trust account in a financial institution described in subsection (5.1) in trust for the proposed company and no money paid on account of shares before the first general meeting of the company has been organized shall be withdrawn or paid over to the company until after such meeting has been organized and an election of directors held thereat.

(5.1) Financial institutions — A financial institution referred to in subsection (5) is,

(a) a bank or authorized foreign bank within the meaning of section 2 of the *Bank Act* (Canada);

(b) a corporation registered under the *Loan and Trust Corporations Act*;

(c) a credit union within the meaning of the *Credit Unions and Caisses Populaires Act, 1994*; or

(d) a retail association as defined under the *Cooperative Credit Associations Act* (Canada).

(6) Return of subscriptions on failure to secure licence — A subscription for shares made before the granting of a licence under the *Insurance Act* shall contain the stipulation that all money received on account of shares will be returned to the subscribers without any deduction for promotion, organization or other expenses, in case the insurer fails to procure such a licence.

(7) Limit of percentage of subscriptions for charges — A subscription for shares shall contain the stipulation that no sum will be used or paid, before or after incorporation, for commission, promotion or organization expenses in excess of a percentage, not exceeding 15, of the amount of money received on account of shares.

2007, c. 7, Sched. 7, s. 183(1)

144. (1) Definition — In subsection (2), **"surplus to policyholders"** means surplus of assets over liabilities excluding issued capital shown in the annual financial statement of the company at the end of the next preceding calendar year as filed with and approved by the Superintendent.

(2) Reduction of capital life insurance companies — Where a company undertaking life insurance has insurance in force of less than $25,000,000 and has a surplus to policyholders of more than $500,000, the directors may pass a by-law authorizing an application to the Lieutenant Governor for the issue of supplementary letters patent decreasing its authorized, subscribed and paid-in capital by not more than 50 per cent.

(3) New par value to be declared — The by-law and the supplementary letters patent shall declare the new par value of the shares and the liability of the shareholders on partially paid-in shares.

(4) Application, when to be made — The application shall not be made until the by-law has been confirmed by a vote of the shareholders present or represented by proxy at a general meeting duly called for considering it and holding not less than two-thirds of the votes cast at such meeting.

(5) Surplus not to be decreased by dividends to shareholders — The supplementary letters patent shall contain a provision that any surplus created by reason of such decreaseof capital will not be decreased by dividends subsequently declared to shareholders.

145. Sections 165(2)–(4), 167, 168 applicable to company undertaking life insurance — A company undertaking life insurance may, by resolution passed at a special general meeting called for such purpose, provide that subsections 165(2), (3) and (4) and sections 167 and 168 apply to such company.

146. Amalgamation — Subject to the approval of the agreement of amalgamation under the *Insurance Act,* section 113 of this Act applies to the amalgamation of two or more joint stock insurance companies.

147. (1) Amalgamation etc., of mutual corporation and joint stock corporation — Subject to the *Insurance Act,* a mutual corporation incorporated under the laws of

Ontario transacting life insurance may amalgamate with or transfer its contracts to or reinsure such contracts with any licensed insurer transacting life insurance and may enter into all agreements necessary to such amalgamation, transfer or reinsurance.

(2) **Confirmation of agreement** — Despite anything in its Act or instrument of incorporation or in its constitution and by-laws, the board of directors may enter into any such agreement on behalf of the mutual corporation through its president and secretary, but no such agreement is binding or effective unless evidence satisfactory to the Superintendent is produced showing that the agreement has been confirmed by a vote of the majority of the members present or duly represented by proxy at a general or special general meeting of the mutual corporation and unless the agreement has been approved by the Lieutenant Governor in Council under the *Insurance Act*.

(3) **Agreement binding on all members of mutual corporation** — Despite anything contained in its Act or instrument of incorporation or in its constitution and by-laws, or in any policy or certificate or other document evidencing a contract issued by a mutual corporation, or in the constitution or laws of or certificates issued by any fraternal society whose contracts have been assumed by the mutual corporation or for which the mutual corporation has become responsible, the terms of any such agreement so confirmed and approved are valid and binding as of the date stipulated in the agreement upon all the members of the mutual corporation and upon their beneficiaries and legal representatives and upon all persons deriving legal rights from any such member or beneficiary so long as they do not involve any new or increased rates of contribution or premium, and the claims of all persons under any such contract of insurance shall be restricted to such benefits only as are continued inaccordance with the terms of such agreement, and such contracts shall be deemed to be amended accordingly.

(4) **Standards of valuations** — Upon the coming into force of any such agreement, the reinsurer, in complying with the requirements of the *Insurance Act* in respect of the valuation of contracts so reinsured or transferred, is entitled to base its valuation upon such tables of mortality and upon such rates of interest as would have been authorized by law for such mutual corporation if no such agreement had been made.

148. (1) **Incorporation of mutual and cash-mutual insurance corporations** — A mutual or cash-mutual corporation may be incorporated for the purpose of undertaking and transacting any class of insurance for which a mutual or cash-mutual insurance corporation may be licensed under the *Insurance Act*.

(2) **Idem** — A mutual insurance corporation may be incorporated for the purpose of undertaking contracts of fire insurance on the premium note plan upon agricultural property, weather insurance or livestock insurance.

(3) **Corporation for reinsurance** — A mutual insurance corporation, all the members of which are mutual or cash-mutual corporations, may be incorporated for the purpose of reinsuring contracts of insurance and such a corporation may enter into contracts of reinsurance for the purpose of retroceding all or part of reinsurance contracts entered into by it.

149. (1) **Incorporation of mutual fire insurance corporation** — Ten residents in any county or district may call a meeting of the residents thereof to consider whether it is expedient to establish therein a mutual fire insurance corporation to undertake contracts of fire insurance on the premium note plan upon agricultural property.

(2) Advertisements calling meeting — The meeting shall be called by advertisement, stating the time, place and object of the meeting and the advertisement shall be published once in *The Ontario Gazette* and at least once a week for three consecutive weeks in a newspaper published in the county or district.

(3) Subscription book — If thirty residents are present at the meeting and a majority of them determine that it is expedient to establish a mutual fire insurance corporation, they may elect from among themselves three persons to open and keep a subscription book in which owners of real or personal property in Ontario may sign their names and enter the sum for which they respectively bind themselves to effect insurance in the corporation.

(4) When meeting may be called — When 100 or more of such owners have signed their names in the subscription book and bound themselves to effect insurance in the corporation amounting in the aggregate to $250,000 or more, a meeting shall be called as hereinafter provided.

(5) How meeting to be called — When the subscription has been completed, any ten of the subscribers may call the first meeting of the proposed corporation at such time and place in the county or district as they determine by sending a printed notice by mail, addressed to each subscriber at the subscriber's post office address, at least ten days before the day of the meeting, and by advertisement in a newspaper having general circulation in the county or district.

(6) Contents of notice — The notice and advertisement shall state the object of the meeting and the time and place at which it is to be held.

(7) Election of directors — At such meeting, or at any adjournment of it, the name and style of the company, which shall include the work "mutual" or the word "mutuelle", shall be adopted, an acting secretary appointed, a board of directors elected as hereinafter provided and a central and generally accessible place in the county or district at which the head office of the company is to be located.

(8) Quorum of meeting — The presence of at least twenty-five of the subscribers is necessary to constitute a valid meeting.

(9) First meeting of directors — As soon as convenient after the meeting, the acting secretary shall call a meeting of the directors for the election from among themselves of a president or the appointment of a person as president who is not a director, for the appointment of a secretary and a treasurer or a secretary-treasurer and for the transaction of such other business as may be brought before the meeting.

(10) Certain documents to be delivered — With the application for incorporation, the applicants shall produce to the Minister, certified as correct under the hands of the chairman and secretary,

(a) a copy of the minutes of the meeting, including all resolutions respecting the objects of the proposed corporation, its name and the location of its head office;

(b) a copy of the subscription book;

(c) a list showing the names and addresses of the directors elected and of the officers appointed; and

(d) such further information as the Minister may require.

(11) Production of originals — There shall also, for verification, be produced to the Minister, if requested, the originals of such documents.

(12) Minister to ascertain correctness of proceedings — The Minister shall ascertain and determine whether the proceedings for the incorporation have been taken in accordance with the section and whether the subscriptions are genuine and by persons possessing property to insure.

(13) Powers deemed in letters patent — A mutual insurance corporation incorporated for the purpose of undertaking contracts of fire insurance on the premium note plan or under a contract to which the Fire Mutual Guarantee Fund is applicable in accordance with section 166 of the *Insurance Act*, has the power, and its letters patent shall be deemed to include the power, to undertake all classes of insurance for which a joint stock insurance company may be licensed under the *Insurance Act*.

2006, c. 33, Sched. O, s. 20

150. (1) Incorporation of mutual livestock insurance corporation — Ten owners of livestock in any county or district may call a meeting of the owners of livestock to consider whether it is expedient to establish a livestock insurance corporation upon the mutual plan.

(2) Organization — The mode of calling such meeting and the proceedings for the formation of the corporation shall be the same with necessary modifications as in the case of the formation of a mutual fire insurance corporation, except that the determination that it is expedient to establish the corporation shall be by thirty residents of the county or district, being owners of livestock in Ontario, and that the meeting for the organization of the corporation shall not be held unless fifty owners of livestock in Ontario have signed their names to the subscription book and bound themselves to effect insurance in the corporation that in the aggregate amounts to $50,000 or more.

(3) Powers — The letters patent or supplementary letters patent shall limit the powers of a mutual livestock insurance corporation incorporated under this section to undertaking contracts of insurance on the premium note plan against loss of livestock by fire, lightning, accident, disease or any other means, except that of design on the part of the insured or by the invasion of an enemy or by insurrection.

151. (1) Incorporation of mutual weather insurance corporation — Ten owners of agricultural property in any county or district may call a meeting of the owners of agricultural property to consider whether it is expedient to establish therein a weather insurance corporation upon the mutual plan.

(2) Organization — The mode of calling such meeting and the proceedings for the formation of the corporation shall be the same with necessary modifications as in the case of the formation of a mutual fire insurance corporation, except that the determination that it is expedient to establish the corporation shall be by thirty residents of the county or district, being owners of agricultural property in Ontario, and that the meeting for the organization of the corporation shall not be held unless fifty owners of agricultural property in Ontario have signed their names to the subscription book andbound themselves to effect insurance in the corporation that in the aggregate amounts to $50,000 or more.

(3) Powers — The letter patent or supplementary letters patent shall limit the powers of a mutual weather insurance corporation incorporated under this section to undertaking contracts of insurance on the premium note plan on any kind of agricultural property or property that is not mercantile or manufacturing against loss or injury arising from such atmospheric disturbances, discharges or conditions as the contract of insurance specifies.

152. (1) Incorporation of cash-mutual insurance corporations — Ten residents of any county or district may call a meeting of other residents thereof to consider whether it is expedient to establish a cash-mutual insurance corporation for the purpose of undertaking any class of insurance for which a cash-mutual corporation may be licensed under the *Insurance Act*.

(2) Organization — The mode of calling such meeting and the proceedings for the formation of the corporation shall be the same with necessary modifications as in the case of a mutual fire insurance corporation undertaking contracts of fire insurance under the premium note plan, except that the determination that it is expedient to establish the corporation shall be by thirty residents of the county or district, and that the meeting for the organization of the corporation shall not be held unless fifty residents have signed the subscription book and bound themselves to effect insurance in the corporation that in the aggregate amounts to $250,000 or more.

153. (1) When mutual company writing on the premium note plan may become a cash-mutual corporation — A mutual insurance corporation incorporated for the purposes of undertaking contracts of insurance on the premium note plan that has a net surplus of assets over all liabilities of not less than $500,000, may apply to the Lieutenant Governor in Council for the issue of supplementary letters patent converting it into a cash-mutual corporation in the manner provided in this Act.

(2) Approval of members — The application shall be authorized by a resolution of three-fourths in number of the directors of the corporation and confirmed by the members of the corporation by vote representing at least 90 per cent of the members present at a special general meeting duly called for that purpose, but the application shall not be made until twenty-one days notice of the application has been given by sending the notice to each member at the member's latest address as shown on the books of the corporation.

(3) Notice of application — Notice of intention to make the application and of the confirmation by the members of the corporation shall be published in at least four consecutive issues of *The Ontario Gazette* and in a newspaper having general circulation in the county or district in which the head office of the corporation is situate at least once a week for four consecutive weeks.

(4) Certain documents to be delivered — With the application for supplementary letters patent, submitted under this section, the applicants shall produce to the Minister certified as correct under the hands of the chair and secretary,

(a) a copy of the notice of the special meeting of the members of the corporation and the notices published in *The Ontario Gazette* and the newspaper;

(b) a copy of the minutes of the special meeting of the members, including all resolutions respecting the objects of the proposed corporation, its name and the location of its head office;

(c) a copy of the corporation's audited financial statement made up to a date not more than seven months prior to the date of the application;

(d) a list of the proposed officers and directors of the cash-mutual corporation;

(e) such further information as the Minister may require.

(5) Report by Superintendent — The Superintendent shall report to the Minister whether the proceedings for supplementary letters patent are in accordance with the provisions of this section and the requirements of the *Insurance Act*.

154. (1) When cash-mutual company may become a joint stock company — A mutual or a cash-mutual corporation that has surplus assets, not including premiums notes, sufficient to reinsure all its outstanding risks may apply to the Lieutenant Governor for the issue of supplementary letters patent converting it into a joint stock insurance corporation in the manner provided in this Act.

(2) Approval of members — The application shall be authorized by a resolution of three-fourths in number of the directors of the corporation and confirmed by the members of the corporation by vote representing at least 90 per cent of the members present at a special general meeting duly called for that purpose, but the application shall not be made until twenty-one days notice of the application has been given by sending the notice to each member at the member's latest address as shown on the books of the corporation.

(3) Notice of application — Notice of intention to make the application and of the confirmation by the members of the corporation shall be published in at least four consecutive issues of *The Ontario Gazette* and in a newspaper having general circulation in the county or district in which the head office of the corporation is situate at least once a week for four consecutive weeks.

(4) Priority of members in subscribing stock — A person who is a member of the corporation on the day of the meeting is entitled to priority in subscribing to the capital stock of the corporation for one month after the opening of the books of subscription in the ratio that the insurance held by the person bears to the aggregate of the unexpired risks then in force.

(5) Certain documents to be delivered — With the application for supplementary letters patent, submitted under this section, the applicants shall produce to the Minister certified as correct under the hands of the chair and secretary,

(a) a copy of the notice of the special meeting of the members of the corporation and the notices published in *The Ontario Gazette* and the newspaper;

(b) a copy of the minutes of the special general meeting of members, including all resolutions respecting the objects of the proposed corporation, its name and the location of its head office;

(c) a copy of the corporation's audited financial statement made up to a date not more than seven months prior to the date of the application;

(d) a list of the proposed officers and directors of the cash-mutual corporation;

(e) such further information as the Minister may require.

(6) Report of Superintendent — The Superintendent shall report to the Minister whether the application for supplementary letters patent is in accordance with this section and the requirements of the *Insurance Act*.

155. Vesting of assets and preservation of liabilities — A corporation formed under section 153 or 154 is answerable for all liabilities of the corporation from which it has been formed and may sue and be sued under its new corporate name, and the assets and property of the old corporation are vested in the new corporation from the date of its formation.

156. When distribution of assets among members permitted — No mutual or cash-mutual insurance corporation that has ceased to do new business shall divide among its members any part of its assets, except income from investments, until it has performed or cancelled its policy obligations and upon proof to the Superintendent that such policy obligations have been performed or cancelled.

157. Application of ss. 158–173 — Sections 158 to 173 apply only to mutual and cash-mutual insurance

158. (1) Insured deemed member — A person insured under a policy issued by a corporation shall, from the date uponwhich the insurance becomes effective, be deemed a member of such corporation.

(2) Member's liability — No member is liable in respect of any claim or demand against the corporation beyond the amount unpaid on the member's premium note.

(3) Member withdrawing — A member may, with the consent of the directors, withdraw from the corporation on such terms as the directors may lawfully prescribe, subject to the *Insurance Act*.

159. (1) Annual meeting — A meeting of the shareholders and members for the election of directors shall be held within the first three months of every year at such time and place as the by-laws of the corporation prescribe.

(2) Annual statement — Before the election, the annual statement for the year ending on the previous 31st day of December shall be presented and read.

1998, c. 18, Sched. E, s. 70

160. Failure to elect directors — If an election of directors is not made on the day on which it ought to have been made, the corporation shall not for that cause be dissolved, but the election may be held on a subsequent day at a meeting tobe called by the directors or as otherwise provided by the by-laws of the corporation, and in such case the directors then in office continue to hold office until their successors are elected.

161. Notice of meetings — (1) Annual general meeting — Notice of every annual general meeting of the corporation must be,

(a) sent by mail to every shareholder or member of the corporation at least 21 days before the day of the meeting; or

(b) published at least 21 days before the day of the meeting in a newspaper published at or near the place where the head office of the corporation is located.

(2) Making annual statement available to shareholders or members — The directors shall make available to shareholders or members the annual statement for the year ending on the previous December 31 by doing one or more of the following at least 21 days before the day of the annual general meeting at which the annual statement will be considered:

1. Sending a copy of the annual statement to the shareholders or members by mail.

2. Publishing the annual statement in a newspaper published at or near the place where the corporation's head office is located.

3. Publishing the annual statement on the corporation's website.

(3) Same — If the corporation publishes its annual statement on its website, the notice of the annual general meeting must state that the annual statement is available on the corporation's website and that a shareholder or member may obtain a copy by sending a written request to the corporation's head office at least 14 days before the meeting.

(4) **Same** — The corporation shall mail a copy of the annual statement to a shareholder or member who makes a written request under subsection (3).

(5) **Requirements of annual statement** — The annual statement must be certified by the corporation's auditors and prepared in accordance with the *Insurance Act* and the regulations made under that Act.

(6) **Power of directors to call special general meetings** — The directors may call a special general meeting of the corporation at any time.

(7) **Notice of special general meeting** — Notice of every special general meeting of the corporation must be,

(a) sent by mail to every shareholder or member of the corporation at least seven days before the day of the meeting; or

(b) published at least seven days before the day of the meeting in a newspaper published at or near the place where the corporation's head office is located.

1998, c. 18, Sched. E, s. 71; 2009, c. 18, Sched. 8, s. 1

162. (1) **Voting of members of mutual or cash-mutual insurance corporations** — A member of a mutual or cash-mutual insurance corporation who is not in arrear for any assessment orcash payment due by the member to the corporation is entitled at all meetings of the corporation to one vote if the amount of premium paid by the member annually is in excess of $25 and no member is entitled to more than one vote.

(2) **Where policy made to two or more persons** — Where a policy on the premium note plan is made to two or more persons, one only is entitled to vote, and the right of voting belongs to the one first named on the register of policyholders if the person is present or, if not present, to the one who stands second, and so on.

(3) **Where property insured by trustee board** — Where property is insured by a trustee board, any member of the board or its secretary-treasurer duly appointed in writing pursuant to its resolution may vote on its behalf.

163. **Right of mere applicants** — No applicant for insurance is competent to vote or otherwise take part in the corporation's proceedings until the applicant's application has been accepted by the directors.

164. (1) [Repealed 2006, c. 33, Sched. O, s. 21.]

(2) **Where corporation has a share capital** — Where the corporation has a share capital, not less than two-thirds of the directors shall also be holders of shares, each to an amount not less than $1,000, upon which all calls have been paid.

(3) **Representation of corporations** — The president or director of a member corporation that has the qualifications that would qualify an individual to be a director is eligible to be a director of the corporation.

(4) Representation of partnerships — Where a partnership has the qualifications that would qualify an individual to be a director of the corporation, one member of the partnership is eligible to be a director of the corporation.

2006, c. 33, Sched. O, s. 21

165. (1) Number of directors — The board shall consist of six, nine, twelve or fifteen directors, to be determined by resolution passed at the meeting held under subsection 149(5).

(2) Increase or decrease in number — The number of directors may from time to time be increased or decreased if so determined at a special general meeting of the corporation called for the purpose, or at an annual general meeting, if notice in writing of the intention to propose a by-law for that purpose at such annual meeting is given to the secretary of the corporation at least one month before the holding of the meeting, but the increased or decreased number of directors shall in any such case be six, nine, twelve or fifteen.

(3) Notice of proposed change — Where such a notice has been given to the secretary, that fact shall be stated in the notice of the annual general meeting.

(4) Copy of resolution and list of directors to be filed — With the copy of the by-law filed with the Superintendent there shall be filed a list of the directors elected thereunder certified under the hands of the chair and secretary of the meeting.

166. Filing by-laws for remuneration of directors — At any annual general meeting of the shareholders or members of a corporation, or at any special general meeting thereof, if such purpose was clearly expressed in the notice of the special general meeting, it is lawful to pass by-laws for the remuneration of the directors, and a certified copy of every such by-law shall, within seven days after its passing, be filed with the Superintendent.

167. Retirement of directors in rotation — One-third of the directors shall retire annually, in rotation, and, at the first meeting of the directors or as soon thereafter as possible, it shall be determined by lot which of them shall hold office for one, two or three years respectively, and the determination shall be entered on the minutes of the meeting.

168. Annual election to fill vacancies — At every annual general meeting thereafter, one-third of the total number of directors shall be elected for a period of three years to fill the places of the retiring directors, who are eligible for re-election.

169. Manager may be a director and be paid salary — The manager or president of the corporation may be a director of the corporation and may be paid an annual salary under a by-law passed in accordance with section 166.

2006, c. 33, Sched. O, s. 22

170. Certain persons not eligible as directors — No agent or paid officer, or officer of the bankers of the corporation, or person in the employment of the corporation, other than the manager or president, is eligible to be elected as a director or shall interfere in the election of directors.

2006, c. 33, Sched. O, s. 23

171. (1) Election of directors — The election of directors shall be held and made by such shareholders and members as attend for that purpose in person, or in the case of a corporation or partnership by a director, officer or member authorized in writing to represent it.

(2) **Ballot** — The election shall be by ballot.

(3) **Case of a tie at an election** — If two or more members have an equal number of votes so that less than the whole number to be elected appear to have been chosen directors by a majority of votes, the members present shall proceed to ballot until it is determined which of the persons so having an equal number of votes shall be the director or directors.

(4) **President** — At the first meeting after each election of directors, the directors shall elect or appoint a president of the corporation.

(5) **Same** — A person who is not a director may be appointed as the president or the directors may elect a president from among themselves.

(6) **Same** — If the directors elect a president from among themselves, the election shall be by ballot and the secretary shall preside at the election.

(7) **Manager** — The president of the corporation may also be given the title of manager.

2006, c. 33, Sched. O, s. 24

172. **Interim vacancies** — If a vacancy occurs among the directors, during the term for which they have been elected, by death, resignation, ceasing to have the prescribed qualification, insolvency or by absence without previous leave of the directors from three successive regular meetings, which shall by reason of that fact create such vacancy, the vacancy, in the case of a board limited to six directors, shall be filled and, in the case of a board limited to a number of directors exceeding six, may be filled until the next annual general meeting by any person duly qualified chosen by a majority of the remaining directors as soon as may be after the vacancy occurs, and at the next annual general meeting the vacancy shall be filled for the portion of the term still unexpired.

173. (1) **Quorum of directors** — A majority of the directors constitutes a quorum for the transaction of business, and, in the case of an equality of votes at any meeting, the question passes in the negative.

(2) **Recording dissent** — A director disagreeing with the majority at a meeting may have his or her dissent recorded with the reasons therefor.

174. (1) **Security of accountants** — Every officer or person appointed or elected to any office concerning the receipt or proper application of money shall furnish security for the just and faithful execution of the duties of the person's office according to the by-laws or rules of the corporation, and any person entrusted with the performance of any other service may be required to furnish similar security, and security so furnished and then subsisting shall be produced to the auditors at the annual audit.

(2) **Minimum security** — The security given by the treasurer or other officer having charge of the money of the corporation shall not be less than $5,000 or such greater amount as may be required by the by-laws of the corporation or by the Superintendent.

175. **Amalgamation** — Subject to the approval of the agreement of amalgamation under the *Insurance Act,* section 113 applies with necessary modifications to the amalgamation of two or more mutual or cash-mutual insurance corporations.

176. (1) **Incorporation of fraternal societies** — The Lieutenant Governor may in his or her discretion, by letters patent, issue a charter to any number of persons, not fewer than

seventy-five, of eighteen or more years of age, five of whom apply therefor, constituting such persons and any others who have signed the membership book, and persons who thereafter become members in the fraternal society thereby created, a corporation for the purposes of undertaking any class of insurance for which a fraternal society may be licensed under the *Insurance Act*.

(2) Notice — The applicants for incorporation, immediately before the application, shall publish in at least four consecutive issues of The Ontario Gazette notice of their intention to apply and shall also, if so required, publish elsewhere notice of such intention.

(3) Particulars of application — The application for the incorporation of a fraternal society shall show,

(a) its proposed name;

(b) the place in Ontario where its head office is to be situate;

(c) the name in full and the place of residence of each of the applicants who are to be its first trustees or managing officers;

(d) such other information as the Minister requires.

(4) Other documents — The application shall be accompanied by the original membership book or list containing the signatures duly certified of at least seventy-five persons who thereby agree to become members of the fraternal society if and when incorporated, by a copy of the proposed by-laws of the fraternal society and by evidence that the approval of the Superintendent to the proposed by-laws and rules has been obtained.

2004, c. 19, s. 10(2)

177. Organization meeting — Within thirty days after the issue of the letters patent and upon due notice to all members of the society, an organization meeting of the society shall be held at which the by-laws shall be adopted and the officers of the society elected.

178. (1) Incorporation of foreign fraternal society — Where a fraternal society licensed under the *Insurance Act* has its head office elsewhere than in Ontario, the grand or other provincial body of the lodges or a majority of the lodges in Ontario may apply to the Lieutenant Governor for the issue of a charter and, from the time of the issue of the letters patent, the applicants become a corporation for the purpose of undertaking any class of insurance for which a fraternal society may be licensed under the *Insurance Act*.

(2) Application of s. 176(1) — Subsection 176(1) applies to an incorporation under this section.

(3) Approval of Superintendent — Before the issue of the letters patent, evidence shall be produced to the Minister that the approval of the Superintendent to the application has been secured.

179. Incorporation of local branch — An auxiliary or local subordinate body or branch of a licensed fraternal society may be separately incorporated by like proceedings.

180. (1) Amalgamation or reinsurance by fraternal society — Subject to the *Insurance Act*, any fraternal society may amalgamate with any other fraternal society or transfer all or any portion of its contracts to or reinsure them with any insurer licensed for the transaction of life insurance and may enter into all agreements necessary to such amalgamation, transfer or reinsurance.

(2) Agreement for amalgamation, etc — Notwithstanding anything in its Act for instrument of incorporation or in its constitution and by-laws, the governing executive authority may enter into any such agreement on behalf of the society through its principal officer and secretary, but no such agreement is binding or effective unless evidence satisfactory to the Superintendent is produced showing that the principle of amalgamation, transfer or reinsurance has been approved and that the agreement has been confirmed by a vote of the majority of the members present or duly represented at a general or special meeting of the supreme legislative or governing body of the society duly called.

181. Confirmation of amalgamation — Subsection 113(4) applies with necessary modifications to the amalgamation of two or more fraternal societies.

182. [Repealed 1997, c. 19, s. 31(1).]

183. Application of ss. 184–195 — Sections 184–195 apply to pension fund and employees' mutual benefit societies incorporated under this Part.

184. Definitions — In this section and sections 185 to 195,

(a) **"parent corporation"** means a corporation any of whose officers establish a pension fund or employees' mutual benefit society under this Part;

(b) **"society"** means a pension fund or employees' mutual benefit society incorporated under this Part;

(c) **"subsidiary corporation"** means a corporation, wherever incorporated, at least 75 per cent of whose issued common shares are owned by a parent corporation.

185. (1) Charter by letters patent — The Lieutenant Governor may in his or her discretion, by letters patent, issue a charter to any number of persons, not fewer than five, of eighteen or more years of age, two of whom are officers of a corporation legally transacting business in Ontario who apply therefor, constituting such persons and the employees of such corporation and of its subsidiary corporations who join the society and those who replace them from time to time a pension fund or employees' mutual benefit society corporation.

(2) Contents of application — The application for the incorporation of a pension fund or employees' mutual benefit society shall show,

(a) its proposed name;

(b) the name of its parent corporation;

(c) the place in Ontario where its head office is to be situate;

(d) the name in full and the place of residence of each of the applicants; and

(e) the names, not fewer than five, of those who are to be its first directors.

(3) Notice — Notice of the application for incorporation of a society shall be published in at least four consecutive issues of *The Ontario Gazette* and the notice shall state,

(a) its proposed name;

(b) the place in Ontario where its head office is to be situate; and

(c) the name of its secretary.

2004, c. 19, s. 10(3)

186. First meeting — The first directors have power to call the first meeting of the society and at such meeting directors may be elected and by-laws may be passed under this Act, and a copy of such by-laws shall be filed with the Minister within two weeks after the passing thereof, and copies of subsequent by-laws in amendment thereof, in addition thereto or diminution therefrom, shall also be filed with the Minister within two weeks after the passing thereof.

187. (1) Directors — The affairs of the society shall be administered by a board of directors who shall be appointed or elected in such manner, in such number, with such qualifications and for such period as are determined by the by-laws, but at the first meeting of the society five directors shall be elected, subject to addition to such number if so sanctioned by the by-laws, and other officers may be appointed in such manner with such remuneration and under such provisions touching their powers and duties as are established by the by-laws.

(2) Management of fund by trust corporation — The board of directors may by by-law entrust the whole or a part of the fund of the society to a trust corporation licensed under the law of Ontario and may delegate to such trust corporation all or any of its powers and discretions relating to the custody and management of the fund.

188. (1) Definition — In this section,

"dependants" means the spouses, and children under eighteen years of age, including adopted children, of officers or employees within the meaning of this section.

(2) Powers and objects of society — After its incorporation, every pension fund and employees' mutual benefit society has the power, by means of voluntary contribution or otherwise as its by-laws provide, to form a fund or funds and may invest, hold and administer the same and may therefrom,

(a) provide for the support and payment of pensions and other benefits to officers and employees of the parent corporation and its subsidiary corporations who have retired or who cease to be employed by the parent corporation or one of its subsidiary corporations;

(b) provide, in such manner as the by-laws specify, for the payment of pensions, annuities, gratuities or other benefits to the surviving spouses and children or other surviving relatives or legal representatives of officers and employees or retired officers and employees of the parent corporation and its subsidiary corporations who have died;

(c) provide for the payment of benefits to officers and employees of the parent corporation or one of its subsidiary corporations by reason of illness, accident or disability;

(d) provide for the payment of benefits by reason of illness, accident or disability to former officers and employees of the parent corporation and its subsidiary corporations who are retired;

(e) provide for the payment of benefits to officers and employees or retired officers and employees of the parent corporation or one of its subsidiary corporations in respect of illness, accident or disability affecting dependents of such officers or employees; and

(f) upon the death of such officers or employees, pay a funeral benefit in such manner as the by-laws specify.

2005, c. 5, s. 16(3), (4)

189. (1) Power to pass by-laws — A pension fund and employees' mutual benefit society has all corporate powers necessary for its purposes and may pass by-laws not contrary to law defining and regulating in the premises, and prescribing the mode of enforcement of, all the rights, powers and duties of,

(a) the society;

(b) its individual members;

(c) the officers and employees of the parent corporation and its subsidiary corporations;

(d) the surviving spouses and children or other surviving relatives, or the personal representatives of such officers and employees; and

(e) the parent corporation.

(2) **Additional by-laws** — Every such society may also make by-laws as aforesaid for,

(a) the formation and maintenance of the fund;

(b) the management and distribution of the fund;

(c) the enforcement of any penalty or forfeiture in the premises; and

(d) the government and ordering of all business and affairs of the society.

(3) **Sanction of parent corporation** — No such by-law is effective unless it has been sanctioned by the board of directors of the parent corporation.

2005, c. 5, s. 16(5)

190. **By-laws defining rights and remedies of beneficiaries, etc.** — All the powers, authority, rights, penalties and forfeitures whatever of the society or of its members, officers or employees, or of such surviving spouses and children or other surviving relatives or legal representatives, or of the parent corporation shall be such and such only and may be enforced in such mode and in such mode only, as by such by-laws are defined and limited.

2005, c. 5, s. 16(6)

191. **Revenue** — All the revenue of the society, from whatever source derived, shall be devoted exclusively to the maintenance of the society and the furtherance of the objects of the fund and to no other purpose.

192. **Contribution by parent corporation** — The parent corporation may contribute annually or otherwise to the funds of the society by a vote of its directors or its shareholders.

193. **Prohibition against member assigning interest** — The interest of a member in the funds of the society is not transferable or assignable by way of pledge, hypothecation, sale, security or otherwise.

194. (1) **Special audit** — Where it is shown to the satisfaction of the Minister that the accounts of a society have been materially or wilfully falsified, or where there is filed in the office of the Minister a requisition for audit bearing the signatures and addresses of at least 25 per cent of the members of the society and alleging in a sufficiently particular manner to the satisfaction of the Minister specific fraudulent or illegal acts, or the repudiation of obligations or insolvency, the Minister may appoint one or more accountants or actuaries who shall, under the Minister's direction, make a special audit of the books and accounts and report thereon in writing verified upon oath to the Minister.

(2) **Security for costs** — Where an audit is requested, the persons requesting it shall, with their requisition, deposit with the Minister security for the costs of the audit in such sum as

the Minister fixes, and, where the facts alleged in the requisition appear to the Minister to have been partly or wholly disproved by the audit, he or she may pay the costs thereof partly or wholly out of the deposit.

(3) Duty to facilitate special audit — The society, its officers and servants shall facilitate the making of such special audit so far as it is in their power and shall produce for inspection and examination by the person so appointed such books, securities and documents as the person may require.

(4) Expense of special audit — Subject to subsection (2), the expense of such special audit shall be borne by the society, and the auditor's account, when approved in writing by the Minister shall be paid by the society forthwith.

2004, c. 19, s. 10(4)

195. Return to Minister — A society formed under this Act shall at all times when thereunto required by the Minister make a full return of its assets and liabilities and of its receipts and expenditures for such period and with such details and other information as the Minister may require.

196. (1) When charter to be forfeited for non-user or discontinuance — If an insurer incorporated under the law of Ontario, whether under this Act or under any general or special Act, does not go into actual operation within two years after incorporation, or if, after an insurer has undertaken contracts, such insurer discontinues business for one year, or it its licence remains suspended for one year, or is cancelled and is not revived within the period of sixty days, the insurer's corporate powers by reason of that fact cease and determine, except for the sole purpose of winding up its affairs, and in any action or proceeding in which such non-user is alleged, proof of user is upon the insurer, and the court, upon the petition of the Attorney General or of any person interested, may limit the time within which the insurer is to settle and close its accounts, and may, for that purpose or for the purpose of liquidation generally, appoint a receiver.

(2) Rights of creditors — No such forfeiture affects prejudicially the rights of creditors as they exist at the date of the forfeiture.

1997, c. 19, s. 31(2)

197. Definition — In sections 198 to 204, **"shareholder"** includes member and participating policyholder eligible to vote for a policyholder's director.

198. (1) Information laid before annual meetings of life insurers — The directors of an insurer undertaking and transacting life insurance shall lay before each annual meeting of shareholders,

(a) a financial statement for the period commencing on the date of incorporation and ending not more than six months before such annual meeting or commencing immediately after the period covered by the previous financial statement and ending not more than six months before such annual meeting, as the case may be, made up of,

(i) a statement of revenue and expenditure for such period,

(ii) a statement of surplus for such period,

(iii) a balance sheet made up to the end of such period;

(b) the report of the auditor to the shareholders;

(c) such further information respecting the financial position of the insurer as the letters patent, supplementary letters patent or by-laws of the insurer require.

(2) **Contents of financial statement** — The statements referred to in the subclauses of clause (1)(a) shall comply with and be governed by sections 199 to 203 but it is not necessary to designate them the statement of revenue and expenditure, statement of surplus and balance sheet.

(3) **Incorporation of statements** — The statement of surplus referred to in subclause (1)(a)(ii) and the information required by subsections 200(2) and (3) may be incorporated in and form part of the statement of revenue and expenditure referred to in subclause (1)(a)(i).

(4) **Auditor's report to be read** — The report of the auditor to the shareholders shall be read at the annual meeting and shall be open to inspection by any shareholder.

199. (1) **Statement of revenue and expenditure** — The statement of revenue and expenditure to be laid before an annual meeting shall be drawn up so as to present fairly the results of the operations of the insurer for the period covered by the statement and so as to distinguish severally at least,

(a) premium income;

(b) income from invested assets;

(c) profit or loss from sale of invested assets;

(d) amounts by which values of invested assets are increased or decreased;

(e) payments to policyholders and beneficiaries, other than the disbursement of moneys previously left on deposit;

(f) increase or decrease in actuarial liability under insurance and annuity contracts;

(g) total remuneration of directors as such from the insurer, including all salaries, bonuses, fees, contributions to pension funds and other emoluments;

(h) premium taxes;

(i) head office, agency, investment and other operating expenses;

(j) the amount transferred to or from general surplus.

(2) **Notes** — Despite subsection (1), items of the natures described in clauses (1)(d) and (g) may be shown by way of note to the statement of revenue and expenditure.

200. (1) **Statement of surplus** — The statement of surplus shall be drawn up so as to present fairly the transactions reflected in it and shall show separately a statement of general surplus and a statement of shareholders' surplus, howsoever designated.

(2) **General surplus** — The statement of general surplus shall be drawn up so as to distinguish at least the following items:

1. The balance of each amount making up the total of general surplus as shown in the balance sheet at the end of the preceding financial period.

2. The additions to and deductions from such surplus during the financial period and, without restricting the generality of the foregoing, at least the following:

    i. The amount shown on the statement of revenue and expenditure as transferred to or from general surplus.

ii. The amount of surplus arising from the issue of shares or the reorganization of the insurer's issued capital, including,

(a) the amount of premiums received on the issue of shares at a premium;

(b) the amount of surplus realized on the purchase for cancellation of shares.

iii. Donations of cash or other property by shareholders.

3. The balance of each amount making up such general surplus as shown in the balance sheet at the end of the financial period.

(3) Shareholders' surplus — The statement of shareholders' surplus shall be drawn so as to distinguish at least the following items:

1. The balance of such surplus as shown in the balance sheet at the end of the preceding financial period.

2. The additions to and deductions from such surplus during the financial period and, without restricting the generality of the foregoing, at least the following:

i. The amount transferred to or from general surplus.

ii. Provision for taxes on income.

iii. The amount of dividends declared on each class of shares.

3. The balance of each surplus as shown in the balance sheet at the end of the financial period.

201. (1) Balance sheet — The balance sheet to be laid before an annual meeting shall be drawn up so as to present fairly the financial position of the insurer as at the date to which it is made up and so as to distinguish severally at least the following:

1. The invested assets of the insurer as described in Part XVII of the *Insurance Act*, severally designated as follows:

i. Cash.

ii. Preference and common shares.

iii. Bonds and debentures.

iv. Mortgages.

v. Real estate held for sale.

vi. Real estate held for production of income.

vii. Head office buildings.

viii. Agreements for sale.

ix. Loans on policies.

x. Other invested assets stating their nature.

2. Other assets of the insurer distinguishing severally at least the following:

i. Net outstanding premiums due and deferred.

ii. Interest and rents due and accrued.

iii. Debts owing to the insurer from its shareholders except debts of reasonable amount arising in the ordinary course of the insurer's business that are not overdue having regard to the insurer's ordinary terms of credit.

iv. The aggregate amount of any outstanding loans under clauses 24(2)(c), (d) and (e).

3. The actuarial liability under insurance and annuity contracts.

4. Bank loans and overdrafts.

5. Provision for unpaid and unreported claims.

6. All other liabilities to policyholders.

7. Debts owing by the insurer on loans from its directors, officers or shareholders.

8. Commissions and other debts owing by the insurer segregating those that arose otherwise than in the ordinary course of business.

9. Deferred income.

10. Liability for taxes.

11. Dividends on capital stock declared but not paid.

12. The authorized capital, giving the number of each class of shares and a brief description of each such class and indicating therein any class of shares which is redeemable and the redemption price thereof.

13. The issued capital, giving the number of shares of each class issued and outstanding and the amount received therefor that is attributable to capital, and showing,

(a) the number of shares of each class issued since the date of the last balance sheet and the value attributed thereto, distinguishing shares issued for cash, shares issued for services and shares issued for other consideration; and

(b) where any shares have not been fully paid,

(i) the number of shares in respect of which calls have not been made and the aggregate amount that has not been called, and

(ii) the number of shares in respect of which calls have been made and not paid and the aggregate amount that has been called and not paid.

14. Reserves, as described in clauses 204(1)(a), (b) and (c) showing the amounts added thereto and the amounts deducted therefrom during the financial period.

15. The amounts making up the surplus of the insurer severally designated as follows:

i. General surplus.

ii. Shareholders' surplus.

iii. Other surplus balances indicating their nature.

(2) **Notes** — Despite subsection (1), particulars of the items described in paragraphs 12 and 13 of subsection (1) may be shown by way of note to the balance sheet.

(3) **Idem** — The basis of valuation of the invested assets of the insurer shall be shown by way of note to the balance sheet.

202. (1) **Notes to financial statement** — There shall be stated by way of note to the financial statement particulars of any change in accounting or actuarial principle or practice or in the method of applying any accounting or actuarial principle or practice made during the period covered that affects the comparability of any of the statements with any of those for the preceding period, and the effect, if material, of any such change upon the results of operations for the period.

(2) Idem — Where applicable, the following matters shall be referred to in the financial statement or by way of note thereto:

1. The basis of conversion of amounts from currencies other than the currency in which the financial statement is expressed.

2. Foreign currency restrictions that affect the assets of the insurer.

3. Contractual obligations that will require abnormal expenditures in relation to the insurer's normal businessrequirements or financial position or that are likely to involve losses not provided for in the accounts.

4. Contingent liabilities, stating their nature and, where practicable, the approximate amounts involved.

5. Any liability secured otherwise than by operation of law on any asset of the insurer, stating the liability so secured, but it is not necessary to specify the asset on which the liability is secured.

6. The gross amount of arrears of dividends on any class of shares and the date to which such dividends were last paid.

7. Where an insurer has contracted to issue shares or has given an option to purchase shares, the class and number of shares affected, the price and the date for issue of the shares or exercise of the option.

8. Any restriction by the letters patent, supplementary letters patent or by-laws of the insurer or by contract on the payment of dividends that is significant in the light of the insurer's financial position.

(3) Idem — Every note to a financial statement is an integral part of it.

203. Insignificant circumstances — Despite sections 199 to 202, it is not necessary to state in a financial statement any matter that in all the circumstances is of relative insignificance.

204. (1) Reserves — In a financial statement, the term **"reserve"** shall be used to describe only,

(a) amounts appropriated from surplus at the discretion of management for some purpose other than to meet a liability or contingency known or admitted or a commitment made as at the statement date or a decline in value of an asset that has already occurred;

(b) amounts appropriated from surplus pursuant to the instrument of incorporation, instrument amending the instrument of incorporation or by-laws of the insurer for some purpose other than to meet a liability or contingency known or admitted or a commitment made as at the statement date or a decline in value of an asset that has already occurred; and

(c) amounts appropriated from surplus in accordance with the terms of a contract and which can be restored to the surplus when the conditions of the contract are fulfilled.

(2) Idem — Despite subsection (1), the term **"reserve"** may be used to describe the actuarial liability under insurance and annuity contracts.

205. Auditor's report, joint stock insurance companies and cash mutuals — The auditor of a joint stock insurance company or a cash mutual insurance corporation shall in the report required to be made by subsection 96(2) also make such statements as the auditor considers necessary,

(a) if, in the case of corporations transacting other than life insurance, the provision for unearned premiums is not calculated as required by the *Insurance Act*;

(b) if the provision for unpaid claims in the auditor's opinion, is not adequate;

(c) if the financial statement includes as assets items prohibited by the *Insurance Act* from being shown in the annual statement required to be filed thereunder; or

(d) if any of the transactions of the corporation that have come to the auditor's notice have not been within its powers.

206. Delivery of by-laws to Superintendent — Every insurer shall deliver to the Superintendent within one month after passing thereof, a certified copy of its by-laws and of every repeal or addition to or amendment or consolidation thereof.

207. Balance sheets and statements — A copy of every balance sheet or other statement published or circulated by an insurer, purporting to show its financial condition, shall be mailed or delivered to the Superintendent, concurrently with its issue to its shareholders or policyholders, or to the general public.

208. Offence — A person who fails to comply with section 205, 206 and 207 shall be deemed to be guilty of an offence under the *Insurance Act*.

209. [Repealed 2006, c. 33, Sched. O, s. 25.]

210. (1) Shareholders' directors; policyholders' directors — A joint stock life insurance company may, by by-law, provide that the affairs of the company shall be managed by a board of directors of whom a specified number, herein called shareholders' directors, shall be elected by the shareholders of the company, and a specified number, herein called policyholders' directors, shall be elected by those persons, herein called participating policyholders, whose lives are insured for at least $2,000 upon which no premiums are due, whether or not any such person is a shareholder of the company.

(2) Number of directors; vacancies — A by-law passed under subsection (1) shall provide for the election of not fewer than nine and not more than twenty-one directors, of whom not fewer than one-third shall be policyholders' directors, and any vacancy occurring in the board of directors may be filled for the remainder of the term by the directors.

(3) Participating policyholders' right to vote — Participating policyholders are entitled to attend and vote in person and not by proxy at all general meetings of the company, but as such are not entitled to vote for the election of shareholders' directors, but this section does not confer rights or impose liabilities on such participating policyholders in a liquidation of the company.

(4) [Repealed 2006, c. 33, Sched. O, s. 26.]

(5) Annual meeting — Such a life insurance company shall have a fixed time in each year for its annual meeting and such time shall be printed in prominent type on each premium notice or each premium receipt issued by the company, and, in addition to all other notices required to be given by this Act, it shall give fifteen days notice of such meeting in two or more daily newspapers published at or as near as may be to the place where the company has its head office.

2006, c. 33, Sched. O, s. 26

211. Conversion of joint stock life companies into mutual companies — Despite anything in the letters patent incorporating the company or in its by-laws or in this Act, a joint stock life insurance company may, with the permission of the minister charged with the administration of the *Insurance Act,* establish and implement a plan for the conversion of the company into a mutual company by the purchase of shares of the capital stock of the company in accordance with the Schedule to this Act.

212. Definitions — In sections 213 to 224,

"deposit" [Repealed 1997, c. 19, s. 31(3).]

"insured person" means a person who enters into a subsisting contract of insurance with an insurer and includes,

(a) every person insured by a contract whether named or not,

(b) every person to whom or for whose benefit all or part of the proceeds of a contract of insurance are payable, and

(c) every person entitled to have insurance money applied toward satisfaction of the person's judgment in accordance with section 258 of the *Insurance Act;*

"loss" includes the happening of an event or contingency by reason of which a person becomes entitled to a payment under a contract of insurance of money other than a refund of unearned premiums;

"Minister" means the member of the Executive Council charged for the time being by the Lieutenant Governor in Council with the administration of the *Insurance Act;*

"Ontario contract" means a subsisting contract of insurance that,

(a) has for its subject,

(i) property that at the time of the making of the contract is in Ontario or is in transit to or from Ontario, or

(ii) the life, safety, fidelity or insurable interest of a person who at the time of the making of the contract is resident in Ontario or of an incorporated company that has its head office in Ontario, or

(b) makes provision for the payment thereunder primarily to a resident of Ontario or to an incorporated company that has its head office in Ontario;

"reciprocal deposit" [Repealed 1997, c. 19, s. 31(3).]

"reciprocating province" [Repealed 1997, c. 19, s. 31(3).]

1997, c. 19, s. 31(3)

213. (1) Application of Part VI — The provisions of Part VI relating to the winding up of corporations apply to insurers incorporated under or subject to this Act except where inconsistent with this Part.

(2) Definition — Where the company, corporation or society is not constituted exclusively or chiefly for insurance purposes and the insurance branch and fund are completely severable from every other branch and fund of the company, corporation or society, the word **"insurer"** for the purposes of sections 214 to 227 means only the insurance branch of the company, corporation or society.

214. (1) Winding up by order of court on application of Superintendent — An insurer incorporated in Ontario may also be wound up by order of the court on the application of the Superintendent, if the court is satisfied that,

(a) the insurer has failed to exercise its corporate powers during any continuous period of four years; or

(b) the insurer has not commenced business or gone into actual operation within four years after it was incorporated; or

(c) the insurer has discontinued business for one year after it has undertaken insurance contracts within the meaning of the *Insurance Act;* or

(d) the insurer's licence has been suspended for one year or more; or

(e) the insurer has carried on business or entered into a contract or used its funds in a manner or for a purpose prohibited or not authorized by the *Insurance Act* or by its Act of incorporation or by any special Act applicable thereto; or

(f) other sufficient cause has been shown.

(2) Approval of Lieutenant Governor in Council — No such application shall be made by the Superintendent without the approval of the Lieutenant Governor in Council.

(3) Application of Part VI — Upon the making of an order under this section, the provisions of Part VI relating to the winding up of a corporation, in so far as they are not inconsistent with this Part, apply.

215. (1) Provisional liquidator appointment — In the case of an insurer incorporated in Ontario,

(a) [Repealed 1997, c. 19, s. 31(4).]

(b) if its licence is cancelled, the Minister may appoint a provisional liquidator who shall take charge of the affairs of the company and may direct that it be wound up forthwith under this Act.

(2) Powers — Until a permanent liquidator is appointed, the provisional liquidator shall exercise all the powers of the insurer and none of the officers or servants of the insurer shall make any contract for, incur any liability on behalf of, or expend any moneys of, the insurer without the approval of the provisional liquidator.

(3) Petition by provisional liquidator for winding-up order — The provisional liquidator shall petition the court for a winding up order, and, if the court is of the opinion that it is just and equitable so to do, it may make an order winding up the company and thereupon the provisions of this Act relating to the winding up of a corporation, in so far as they are not inconsistent with this Part, apply.

(4) Sale of business — The provisional liquidator or the liquidator, notwithstanding this Act, but, subject to the approval of the court, may sell the business and undertaking of the company as a going concern.

1997, c. 19, s. 31(4)

216. (1) Remuneration of provisional liquidator — The remuneration to be paid to a provisional liquidator appointed under subsection 215(1) shall be fixed by the Minister.

(2) Payment of costs of provisional liquidator — The remuneration and all expenses and outlay in connection with the appointment of the provisional liquidator, together with all expenses and outlay of the provisional liquidator while the provisional liquidator acts in that capacity, shall be borne and paid by the insurer and form a first lien or charge upon the assets of the insurer.

(3) [Repealed 1997, c. 19, s. 31(6).]

1997, c. 19, s. 31(5), (6)

217. (1) Notice of intention to cease writing insurance or to consider voluntary liquidation — When an insurer incorporated under or subject to the law of Ontario proposes to cease writing insurance or to call a general meeting to consider a resolution for its voluntary liquidation under this Act, it shall give at least one month's notice in writing thereof to the Superintendent of Financial Services and the superintendent of insurance in each province, other than Ontario, in which the insurer is licensed.

(2) Notice to Superintendent of voluntary winding up — When an insurer has passed a resolution for voluntary winding up, the insurer shall notify the Superintendent thereof and of the date on which contracts of insurance will cease to be entered into by the insurer and of the name and address of its liquidator.

(3) Publication of notice — The notice under subsection (2) shall also be published by the insurer in two consecutive issues of *The Ontario Gazette* and the official gazette of each other province in which the insurer is licensed and in such newspapers and other publications as the Superintendent may require.

1997, c. 28, s. 50

218. (1) Reinsurance — The provisional liquidator or the liquidator, before the fixing of a termination date pursuant to section 220, may arrange for the reinsurance of the subsisting contracts of insurance of the insurer with some other insurer licensed in Ontario.

(2) Funds available for reinsurance — For the purpose of securing the reinsurance the following funds shall be available:

1. The entire assets of the insurer in Ontario except the amount reasonably estimated by the provisional liquidator or the liquidator as being required to pay.

    (a) the cost of the liquidation or winding up;

    (b) all claims for losses covered by the insurer's contracts of insurance of which notice has been received by the insurer or provisional liquidator or liquidator before the date on which the reinsurance is effected;

    (c) the claims of the preferred creditors who are the persons paid in priority to other creditors under the winding-up provisions of this Act,

   all of which shall be a first charge on the assets of the insurer.

2. [Repealed 1997, c. 18, s. 31(9).]

(3) [Repealed 1997, c. 19, s. 31(10).]

(4) Payments to creditors other than preferred creditors — The creditors of the insurer, other than the insured persons and the said preferred creditors, are entitled to receive a payment on their claims only if provision has been made for the payments mentioned in subsection (2) and for the reinsurance.

(5) **Reinsurance of part of contracts** — If, after providing for the payments mentioned in subsection (2), the balance of the assets of the insurer, is insufficient to secure the reinsurance of the contracts of the insured persons in full, the reinsurance may be effected for such portion of the full amount of the contracts as is possible.

(6) **Approval** — No contract of reinsurance shall be entered into under this section until it is approved by the court.

1997, c. 19, s. 31(7)–(11)

219. [Repealed 1997, c. 19, s. 31(12).]

220. (1) **Termination date, where reinsurance not arranged** — If the provisional liquidator or the liquidator fails to secure reinsurance, or is of the opinion that it is impracticable or inexpedient to arrange for reinsurance the provisional liquidator or the liquidator,

(a) with the approval of the court and subject to such terms as are prescribed by it; and

(b) for the purpose of securing the payment of existing claims and avoiding further losses,

may publish a notice fixing a termination date for the subsisting contracts of insurance of such insurer, and on and after that date coverage and protection under the Ontario contracts cease and the insurer is not liable under any such contract for a loss that occurs after that date.

(2) **Termination of Ontario contracts, where termination date fixed in another province** — Where a provisional liquidator or a liquidator has been appointed in another province to wind up an insurer incorporated in that province, and if such provisional liquidator or liquidator fixed a termination date for the contracts of insurance of the insurer, on and after that date coverage and protection under the Ontario contracts cease and determine and the insurer is not liable under any such contract for a loss that occurs after that date.

(3) [Repealed 1997, c. 19, s. 31(13).]

1997, c. 19, s. 31(13)

221. Publication of notice of termination date — The provisional liquidator or the liquidator shall cause the notice,

(a) to be published in *The Ontario Gazette* and in the official gazette of each other province in which the insurer is licensed and in such newspapers as the Supreme Court directs in order to give reasonable notice of the termination date so fixed; and

(b) to be mailed to each policyholder at the policyholder's address as shown on the books and records of the company.

222. (1) **Payment of claims for losses and preferred claims, etc.** — The liquidator shall pay or set aside from the assets of the insurer sums in the liquidator's opinion sufficient to pay.

(a) the costs of the liquidation or winding up;

(b) all claims for losses covered by the insurer's contracts of insurance that occurred before the termination date fixed under section 220 and of which notice has been received by the insurer or the liquidator;

(c) the full amount of the legal reserve in respect of each unmatured life insurance contract; and

(d) the claims of preferred creditors who are the persons paid in priority to other creditors under the winding-up provisions of this Act.

(2) Refund of unearned premiums — Except in the case of life insurance, the assets remaining after payment or making provision for payment of the amounts mentioned in subsection (1) shall be used to pay the claims of the insured persons for refunds of unearned premiums on a proportionate basis in proportion to the periods of their contracts respectively unexpired on the termination dates.

(3) Calculation of unearned premium claims — The claims of the insured persons for refunds of unearned premiums shall be calculated,

(a) as at the termination date fixed under section 220 of the Act; or

(b) as at the date the insured person cancelled the contract, whichever date is the earlier.

(4) Effect of refund — The refund of all or a portion of the premium does not destroy or defeat any other remedy the insured person may have against the insurer in respect thereof or for any other cause.

(5) Effect of section — Nothing in this section prejudices or affects the priority of any mortgage, lien or charge upon the property of the insurer.

1997, c. 28, s. 31(14)–(16)

223. Payment of provincial fees and taxes, etc. — The fees, taxes and costs payable by the insurer to each province shall be paid out of the assets of the insurer remaining after the reinsurance of the subsisting contracts of insurance of the insurer or after the payment of the claims of policyholders for refund of unearned premiums, as the case may be, and the balance shall be distributed among the creditors of the insurer other than the insured persons, preferred creditors and the several provinces.

224. (1) Filing of statements by liquidator — Unless otherwise ordered by the court, within seven days after the close of each period of three months and until the affairs of the insurer are wound up and the accounts are finally closed, the liquidator shall file with the court or other authority appointing him and also with the Superintendent detailed schedules, in such form as is required, showing,

(a) receipts and expenditures; and

(b) assets and liabilities.

(2) Production of books, etc., by liquidator — The liquidator, whenever required so to do by the authority appointing the liquidator or by the Minister, shall exhibit the office books and vouchers and furnish such other information respecting the affairs of the insurer as is required.

(3) Offence — Every liquidator refusing or neglecting to furnish such information is guilty of an offence and on conviction is liable to a fine of not less than $50 and not more than $200 and in addition is liable to be dismissed or removed.

225. (1) Distribution of endowment and expectancy funds — Where a fraternal society transacts endowment or expectancy insurance and has an endowment fund separate and distinct from its life insurance fund, the society may, by resolution duly passed at a general meeting, after at least one month's notice of such intended resolution, determine that the endowment or expectancy shall be discontinued, and that the endowment or expectancy fund shall be distributed proportionately among the members then in good standing who are contributing to such fund according to the total contribution to such member.

(2) Procedure — After the resolution has been assented to by the Superintendent and filed with the Minister, the executive officers may proceed to ascertain the persons intended to rank upon the fund and may distribute the fund among those so entitled, and such distribution discharges the society and all executive officers thereof from all further or other liability in respect of such fund and of the endowment or expectancy contracts undertaken by the society.

(3) Merger of funds — If all the members interested in the endowment or expectancy fund are also interested as holders of life insurance contracts, the general meeting, instead of determining to distribute the endowment or expectancy fund, may determine to convert it into or merge it in a life insurance fund, and after the resolution has been assented to and filed as provided in subsection (2), the endowment or expectancy fund becomes a life insurance fund.

226. [Repealed 1997, c. 19, s. 31(17).]

227. Books, etc., as evidence — The books, accounts and documents of an insurer and the entries in the books of its officers or liquidators are proof, in the absence of evidence to the contrary, of the matters to which they relate as between an alleged debtor or contributory and the insurer.

PART VI — WINDING UP

228. Definition — In this Part, **"contributory"** means a person who is liable to contribute to the property of a corporation in the event of the corporation being wound up under this Part.

229. Application — Subject to section 2, this Part applies,

(a) to every corporation incorporated by or under a general or special Act of the Parliament of the late Province of Upper Canada;

(b) to every corporation incorporated by or under a general or special Act of the Parliament of the late Province of Canada that has its head office and carries on business in Ontario and that was incorporated with objects to which the authority of the Legislature extends;

(c) to every corporation incorporated by or under a general or special Act of this Legislature;

(d) to every insurer within the meaning of Part V that is incorporated under or subject to this Act except where inconsistent with Part V,

but this Part does not apply to a corporation incorporated for the construction and working of a railway, incline railway or street railway, or to a corporation within the meaning of the *Loan and Trust Corporations Act* except as provided by that Act.

Proposed Repeal — 229

229. [Repealed 2010, c. 15, s. 211(8). Not in force at date of publication.]

230. (1) Voluntary winding up — Where the shareholders or members of a corporation by a majority of the votes cast at a general meeting called for that purpose pass a resolution requiring the corporation to be wound up, the corporation may be wound up voluntarily.

(2) Appointment of liquidator — At such meeting, the shareholders or members shall appoint one or more persons, who may be directors, officers or employees of the corporation, as liquidator of the estate and effects of the corporation for the purpose of winding up its affairs and distributing its property, and may at that or ay subsequent general meeting fix the liquidator's remuneration and the costs, charges and expenses of the winding up.

231. (1) Publication of notice of winding up — Notice of resolution requiring the voluntary winding up of a corporation shall be filed with the Minister and be published in *The Ontario Gazette* by the corporation within fourteen days after the resolution has been passed.

(2) Offence — A corporation that fails to comply with subsection (1) is guilty of an offence and on conviction is liable to a fine of not more than $200 and every director or officer who authorizes, permits or acquiesces in such failure is guilty of an offence and on conviction is liable to a like fine.

232. Inspectors — A corporation being wound up voluntarily may, in general meeting, by resolution, delegate to any committee of its shareholders or members, contributories or creditors, herein after referred to as inspectors, the power of appointing the liquidator and filling any vacancy in the office of liquidator, or may by a like resolution enter into any arrangement with its creditors with respect to the powers to be exercised by the liquidator and the manner in which they are to be exercised.

233. Vacancy in office of liquidator — If in a voluntary winding up a vacancy occurs in the office of liquidator by death, resignation or otherwise, the shareholders or members in general meeting may, subject to any arrangement the corporation may have entered into with its creditors upon the appointment of inspectors, fill such vacancy, and a general meeting for that purpose may be convened by the continuing liquidator, if any, or by any contributory, and shall be deemed to have been duly held if called in the manner prescribed by the by-laws of the corporation, or, in default thereof, in the manner prescribed by this Act for calling general meetings of the shareholders or members of the corporation.

234. Removal of liquidator — The shareholders or members of the corporation may by a majority of the votes cast at a general meeting called for that purpose, remove a liquidator appointed under section 230 or 232, and in such case shall appoint another liquidator.

235. Commencement of winding up — A voluntary winding up commences at the time of the passing of the resolution requiring the winding up.

236. Corporation to cease business — Where a corporation is being wound up voluntarily, it shall, from the date of the commencement of its winding up, cease to carry on its undertaking, except in so far as may be required for the beneficial winding up thereof, and all transfers of shares, except transfers made to or with the sanction of the liquidator, or alterations in the status of the shareholders or members of the corporation, taking place after the commencement of its winding up, are void, but its corporate existence and all its corporate powers, even if it is otherwise provided by its instrument of incorporation or by-laws, continue until its affairs are wound up.

237. No proceedings against corporation after voluntary winding up except by leave — After the commencement of a voluntary winding up,

(a) no action or other proceeding shall be commenced against the corporation; and

(b) no attachment, sequestration, distress or execution shall be put in force against the estate or effects of the corporation,

except by leave of the court and subject to such terms as the court may impose.

238. (1) Settlement of list of contributories — Upon a voluntary winding up, the liquidator shall settle the list of contributories, and any list so settled is proof, in the absence of evidence to the contrary, of the liability of the persons name therein to be contributories.

(2) Payment from contributories — Upon a voluntary winding up, the liquidator may, before having ascertained the sufficiency of the property of the corporation, call on all or any of the contributories for the time being settled on the list of contributories to the extent of their liability to pay any sum that the liquidator considers necessary to satisfy the liabilities of the corporation and the costs, charges and expenses of winding up, and for the adjustment of the rights of the contributories among themselves, and the liquidator may, in making a call, take into consideration the probability that some of the contributories upon whom the call is made may partly or wholly fail to pay their respective portions of the call.

239. (1) Meetings of corporation during winding up — The liquidator may, during the continuance of the voluntary winding up, call general meetings of the shareholders or members of the corporation for the purpose of obtaining its sanction by resolution, or for any other purpose the liquidator thinks fit.

(2) Where winding up continues more than one year — In the event of a voluntary winding up continuing for more than one year, the liquidator shall call a general meeting of the shareholders or members of the corporation at the end of the first year and of each succeeding year from the commencement of the winding up, and shall lay before the meeting an account showing the liquidator's acts and dealings and the manner in which the winding up has been conducted during the preceding year.

240. Arrangements with creditors may be authorized — The liquidator, with the sanction of a resolution of the shareholders or members of the corporation passed in general meeting or of the inspectors, may make such compromise or other arrangement as the liquidator considers expedient with any creditor or person claiming to be a creditor or having or alleging to have a claim, present or future, certain or contingent, ascertained or sounding only in damages, against the corporation or whereby the corporation may be rendered liable.

241. Power to compromise with debtors and contributories — The liquidator may, with the like sanction, compromise all calls and liabilities to call, debts and liabilities capable of resulting in debts, and all claims, whether present or future, certain or contingent, ascertained or sounding only in damages, subsisting or supposed to subsist between the corporation and any contributory, alleged contributory or other debtor or person apprehending liability to the corporation and all questions in any way relating to or affecting the property of the corporation, or the winding up of the corporation, upon the receipt of such sums payable at such times and generally upon such terms as are agreed upon, and the liquidator may take any security for the discharge of such calls, debts or liabilities and give a complete discharge in respect thereof.

242. (1) Power to accept shares, etc., as consideration for sale of property to another company — Where a corporation is proposed to be or is in the course of being wound up voluntarily and the whole or a portion of its business or property is proposed to be transferred or sold to another corporation, the liquidator of the first-mentioned corporation, with the sanction of a resolution of the shareholders or members passed in general meeting of the corporation by which the liquidator was appointed conferring either a general authority on the liquidator or an authority in respect of any particular arrangement, may receive, in compensation or in part compensation for such transfer or sale, cash or shares or other like interest in the purchasing corporation for the purpose of distribution among the shareholders or members of the corporation that is being wound up in the manner set forth in the arrangement, or may, in lieu of receiving cash or shares or other like interest, or in addition thereto, participate in the profits of or receive any other benefit from the purchasing corporation.

(2) Confirmation of sale or arrangement — A sale made or arrangement entered into by the liquidator under this section is binding on the shareholders or members of the corporation that is being wound up voluntarily if,

(a) in the case of a company, the shareholders or classes of shareholders, as the case may be, at a general meeting duly called for the purpose, by votes representing at least three-fourths of the shares or of each class of shares represented at the meeting; or

(b) in the case of a corporation without share capital, the members or classes of members, as the case may be, at a general meeting duly called for the purpose, by votes representing at least three-fourths of the members or of each class of members represented at the meeting,

approve the sale or arrangement and if the sale or arrangement is approved by an order made by the court on the application of the corporation.

(3) Where resolution not invalid — No resolution shall be deemed invalid of the purposes of this section because it was passed before or concurrently with a resolution for winding up the corporation or for appointing the liquidator.

243. Winding up by court — A corporation may be wound up by order of the court,

(a) where the shareholders or members by a majority of the votes cast at a general meeting called for that purpose pass a resolution authorizing an application to be made to the court to wind up the corporation;

(b) where proceedings have been begun to wind up voluntarily and it appears to the court that it is in the interest of contributories and creditors that the proceedings should be continued under the supervision of the court;

(c) where it is proved to the satisfaction of the court that the corporation, though it may be solvent, cannot by reason of its liabilities continue its business and that it is advisable to wind it up; or

(d) where in the opinion of the court it is just and equitable for some reason, other than the bankruptcy or insolvency of the corporation, that it should be wound up.

244. (1) **Who may apply** — The winding-up order may be made upon the application of the corporation or of a shareholder or of a member or, where the corporation is being wound up voluntarily, of the liquidator or of a contributory or of a creditor having a claim of $200 or more.

(2) **Notice** — Except where the application is made by the corporation, four days notice of the application shall be given to the corporation before the making of the application.

245. Power of court — The court may make the order applied for, may dismiss the application with or without costs, may adjourn the hearing conditionally or unconditionally or may make any interim or other order as is considered just, and upon the making of the order may, according to its practice and procedure, refer the proceedings for the winding up and may also delegate any powers of the court conferred by this Act to any officer of the court.

246. (1) **Appointment of liquidator** — The court in making the winding-up order may appoint one or more persons as liquidator of the estate and effects of the corporation for the purpose of winding up its affairs and distributing its property.

(2) **Remuneration** — The court may at any time fix the remuneration of the liquidator.

(3) **Vacancy** — If a liquidator appointed by the court dies or resigns or the office becomes vacant for any reason, the court may by order fill the vacancy.

(4) **Removal of liquidator** — The court may by order remove for cause a liquidator appointed by it, and in such case shall appoint another liquidator.

247. Costs and expenses — The costs, charges and expenses of a winding up by order of the court shall be assessed by an assessing officer.

248. Commencement of winding up — Where a winding-up order is made by the court without prior voluntary winding-up proceedings, the winding up shall be deemed to commence at the time of service of notice of the application, and, where the application is made by the corporation, at the time the application is made.

249. Winding up after order — Where a winding-up order has been made by the court, the winding up of the corporation shall be conducted in the same manner and with the like consequences as provided for a voluntary winding up, except that the list of contributories shall be settled by the court unless it has been settled by the liquidator prior to the winding-up order, in which case the list is subject to review by the court, and except that all steps in the winding up are subject to the order and direction of the court.

250. (1) **Meetings of members of company may be ordered** — Where a winding-up order has been made by the court, the court may direct meetings of the shareholders or members of the corporation to be called, held and conducted in such manner as the court deems fit for the purpose of ascertaining their wishes, and may appoint a person to act as chair of any such meeting and to report the result of it to the court.

(2) **Order for delivery by contributories and others of property, etc.** — Where a winding-up order has been made by the court, the court may require any contributory for the time being settled on the list of contributories, or any trustee, receiver, banker or agent or officer of the corporation to pay, deliver, convey, surrender or transfer forthwith, or within

such time as the court directs, to the liquidator any sum or balance, books, papers, estate or effects that are in the person's hands and to which the corporation appears to be entitled.

(3) Inspection of books — Where a winding-up order has been made by the court, the court may make an order for the inspection of the books and papers of the corporation by its creditors and contributories, and any books and papers in the possession of the corporation may be inspected in conformity with such order.

251. No proceedings against corporation after court winding up except by leave — After the commencement of a winding up by order of the court,

(a) no action or other proceeding shall be proceeded with or commenced against the corporation; and

(b) no attachment, sequestration, distress or execution shall be put in force against the estate or effects of the corporation,

except by leave of the court and subject to such terms as the court may impose.

252. Application of ss. 253–265, 268 — Sections 253 to 265 and 268 apply to corporations being wound up voluntarily or by order of the court.

253. (1) Where no liquidator — If from any cause there is no liquidator, the court may by order on the application of a shareholder or member of the corporation appoint one or more persons as liquidator.

(2) Idem — Where there is no liquidator, the estate and effects of the corporation shall be under the control of the court until the appointment of a liquidator.

254. (1) Consequences of winding up — Upon a winding up,

(a) the liquidator shall apply the property of the corporation in satisfaction of all its liabilities proportionately and, subject thereto, shall distribute the property rateably among the shareholders or members according to their rights and interests in the corporation;

(b) in distributing the property of the corporation, the wages of all employees, apprentices and other wage earners in the employment of the corporation due at the date of the commencement of the winding up or within one month before, not exceeding three months wages and for vacation pay accrued for not more than twelve months under the *Employment Standards Act* and the regulations thereunder or under any collective agreement made by the corporation, shall be paid in priority to the claims of the ordinary creditors, and such persons are entitled to rank as ordinary creditors for the residue of their claims;

(c) all the powers of the directors cease upon the appointment of a liquidator, except in so far as the liquidator may sanction the continuance of such powers.

(2) Distribution of property — Section 53 of the *Trustee Act* applies with necessary modifications to liquidators.

1993, c. 27, Sched.

255. Payment of costs and expenses — The costs, charges and expenses of a winding up, including the remuneration of the liquidator, are payable out of the property of the corporation in priority to all other claims.

256. (1) **Powers of liquidators** — The liquidator may,

(a) bring or defend any action, suit or prosecution, or other legal proceedings, civil or criminal, in the name and on behalf of the corporation:

(b) carry on the business of the corporation so far as is necessary for the beneficial winding up of the corporation;

(c) sell in whole or in parcels the real and personal property, effects and things in action of the corporation by public auction or private sale:

(d) do all acts and execute, in the name and on behalf of the corporation, all deeds, receipts and other documents, and for that purpose use the seal of the corporation;

(e) draw, accept, make and endorse any bill of exchange or promissory note in the name and on behalf of the corporation;

(f) raise upon the security of the property of the corporation any requisite money;

(g) take out in the liquidator's official name letters of administration to the estate of any deceased contributory and do in the liquidator's official name any other act that is necessary for obtaining payment of any money due from a contributory or from the contributory's estate and which act cannot be done conveniently in the name of the corporation;

(h) do and execute all such other things as are necessary for winding up the affairs of the corporation and distributing its property.

(2) **Bills of exchange, etc., to be deemed drawn in due course** — The drawing, accepting, making or endorsing of a bill of exchange or promissory note by the liquidator on behalf of the corporation has the same effect with respect to the liability of the corporation as if such bill or note had been drawn, accepted, made or endorsed by or on behalf of the corporation in the course of carrying on its business.

(3) **Where money deemed to be due to liquidator** — Where the liquidator takes out letters of administration or otherwise uses the liquidator's official name for obtaining payment of any money due from a contributory, such money shall be deemed, for the purpose of enabling the liquidator to take out such letters or recover such money, to be due to the liquidator personally.

257. Nature of liability of contributory — The liability of a contributory creates a debt accruing due from the contributory at the time the liability commenced, but payable at the time or respective times when calls are made for enforcing such liability.

258. Who liable in case of death — If a contributory dies before or after he or she has been placed on the list of contributories, the contributory's legal representatives are liable in due course of administration to contribute to the property of the corporation in discharge of the liability of such deceased contributory and shall be contributories accordingly.

259. (1) **Deposit in financial institution by liquidator** — The liquidator shall deposit in a financial institution described in subsection (1.1) all sums of money that the liquidator has belonging to the corporation if such sums amount to $100 or more.

(1.1) **Financial institutions** — A financial institution referred to in subsection (1) is,

(a) a bank or authorized foreign bank within the meaning of section 2 of the *Bank Act* (Canada);

(b) a corporation registered under the *Loan and Trust Corporations Act*;

(c) a credit union within the meaning of the *Credit Unions and Caisses Populaires Act, 1994*; or

(d) a retail association as defined under the *Cooperative Credit Associations Act* (Canada).

(2) **Approval of financial institution by inspectors** — If inspectors have been appointed, the financial institution shall be one approved by them.

(3) **Separate deposit account to be kept; withdrawal from account** — Such deposit shall not be made in the name of the liquidator individually, but a separate deposit account shall be kept of the money belonging to the corporation in the liquidator's name as liquidator of the corporation and in the name of the inspectors, if any, and such money shall be withdrawn only on the joint cheque of the liquidator and one of the inspectors, if any.

(4) **Liquidators to produce bank pass-book** — At every meeting of the shareholders or members of the corporation the liquidator shall produce a pass-book or statement of account showing the amount of the deposits, the dates at which they were made, the amounts withdrawn and the dates of withdrawal, and mention of such production shall be made in the minutes of the meeting, and the absence of such mention is admissible in evidence as proof, in the absence of evidence to the contrary, that the pass-book or statement of account was not produced at the meeting.

(5) **Idem** — The liquidator shall also produce the pass-book or statement of account whenever so ordered by the court upon the application of the inspectors, if any, or of a shareholder or member of the corporation.

2007, c. 7, Sched. 7, s. 183(2)

260. Proving claim — For the purpose of proving claims, sections 25, 26 and 27 of the *Assignments and Preferences Act* apply with necessary modifications except that, where the word "judge" is used therein, the word "court" as used in this Act shall be substituted.

261. Application or motion for direction — Upon the application or motion of the liquidator or of the inspectors, if any, or of any creditors, the court, after hearing such parties as it directs to be notified or after such steps as it prescribes have been taken, may by order give its direction in any matter arising in the winding up.

262. (1) Examination of persons as to estate — The court may at any time after the commencement of the winding up summon to appear before the court or liquidator any director or officer of the corporation or any other person known or suspected to possess any of the estate or effects of the corporation, or alleged to be indebted to it, or any person whom the court considers capable of giving information concerning its trade, dealings, estate or effects.

(2) **Damages against delinquent directors, etc.** — Where in the course of the winding up it appears that any person who has taken part in the formation or promotion of the corporation or that a past or present director or officer, employee, liquidator or receiver of the corporation has misapplied or retained in the person's own hands, or become liable or accountable for, money of the corporation, or has committed any misfeasance or breach of trust in relation to it, the court may, on the application or motion of the liquidator or of any creditor or contributory, examine into the conduct of such person and order the person to repay the money so misapplied or retained, or for which the person has become liable or

accountable, together with interest at such rate as the court considers just, or to contribute such sum to the property of the corporation by way of compensation in respect of such misapplication, retention, misfeasance or breach of trust as the court considers just.

263. (1) **Proceedings by shareholders** — If a shareholder or member of the corporation desires to cause any proceeding to be taken that, in the shareholder's or member's opinion, would be for the benefit of the corporation, and the liquidator, under the authority of the shareholders or members, or of the inspectors, if any, refuses or neglects to take such proceeding after being required so to do, the shareholder or member may obtain an order of the court authorizing the shareholder or member to take such proceeding in the name of the liquidator or corporation, but at the shareholder's or member's own expense and risk, upon such terms and conditions as toindemnity to the liquidator or corporation as the court prescribes.

(2) **Benefits, when for shareholders** — Thereupon any benefit derived from such proceeding belongs exclusively to the shareholder or member instituting the proceeding for that person's benefit and that of any other shareholder or member who has joined the shareholder or member in causing the institution of the proceedings.

(3) **When for corporation** — If before such order is granted, the liquidator signifies to the court the liquidators readiness to institute such proceeding for the benefit of the corporation, an order shall be made prescribing the time within which the liquidator is to do so, and in that case the advantage derived from the proceeding, if instituted within such time, belongs to the corporation.

264. **Rights conferred by Act to be in addition to other powers** — The rights conferred by this Act are in addition to any other right of instituting proceedings against any contributory, or against any debtor of the corporation, for the recovery of any call or other sum due from such contributory or debtor or such person's estate.

265. **Stay of winding-up proceedings** — At any time during a winding up, the court, upon the application or motion of any shareholder or member or creditor or contributory and upon proof of its satisfaction that all proceedings in relation to the winding up ought to be stayed, may make an order staying the proceedings altogether or for a limited time on such terms and subject to such conditions as the court considers fit.

266. (1) **Account of voluntary winding up to be made by liquidator to a general meeting** — Where the affairs of the corporation have been fully wound up voluntarily, the liquidator shall make up an account showing the manner in which the winding up has been conducted, and the property of the corporation disposed of, and thereupon shall call a general meeting of the shareholders or members of the corporation for the purpose of having the account laid before them and hearing any explanation that may be given by the liquidator, and the meeting shall be called in the manner provided by the by-laws for calling general meetings.

(2) **Notice of holding of meeting** — The liquidator shall within ten days after the holding of the meeting file a notice with the Minister stating that the meeting was held and the date thereof.

(3) **Dissolution** — On the expiration of three months from the date of the filing of the notice, the corporation is dissolved.

(4) Extension — At any time during the three-month period mentioned in subsection (3), the court may, on the application of the liquidator or any other person interested, make an order deferring the date on which the dissolution of the corporation is to take effect to a date fixed in the order, and in such event the corporation is dissolved on the date so fixed.

(5) Copy of extension order to be filed — The person on whose application the order was made shall within ten days after it was made file with the Minister a copy of it certified under the seal of the court.

(6) Offence — A person who fails to comply with any requirement of this section is guilty of an offence and on conviction is liable to a fine of not more than $200.

267. (1) Order for dissolution — Despite section 266, in the case of a voluntary winding up or in the case of a winding up by order of the court, the court at any time after the affairs of the corporation have been fully wound up may, upon the application of the liquidator or any other person interested, make an order dissolving it, and it is dissolved at and from the date of the order.

(2) Copy of dissolution order to be filed — The person on whose application the order was made shall within ten days after it was made file with the Minister a copy of it certified under the seal of the court.

(3) Offence — A person who fails to comply with any requirement of this section is guilty of an offence and on conviction is liable to a fine of not more than $200.

268. (1) Where shareholder unknown — Where the liquidator is unable to distribute rateably the property of the corporation among the shareholders or members because a shareholder or member is unknown or the person's whereabouts is unknown, the share of the property of the corporation of such shareholder or member may, by agreement with the Public Guardian and Trustee, be delivered or conveyed by the liquidator to the Public Guardian and Trustee to be held in trust for the shareholder or member, and thereupon subsections 319(5) and (6) apply thereto.

(2) Idem — A delivery or conveyance under subsection (1) shall be deemed to be a rateable distribution among the shareholders or members for the purposes of clause 254(1)(a).

(3) Where creditor unknown — Where the liquidator is unable to pay all the debts of the corporation because a creditor is unknown or the creditor's whereabouts is unknown, the liquidator may, by agreement with the Public Guardian and Trustee, pay to the Public Guardian and Trustee an amount equal to the amount of the debt due to the creditor to be held in trust for the creditor and thereupon subsections 319(5) and (6) apply thereto.

(4) Idem — A payment under subsection (3) shall be deemed to be in satisfaction of the debt for the purposes of clause 254(1)(a).

CTS 30 AU 10 – 1

269. (1) Disposal of books, etc., after winding up — Where a corporation has been wound up under this Act and is about to be dissolved, its books, accounts and documents and those of the liquidator may be disposed of as it by resolution directs in case of voluntary winding up, or as the court directs in case of winding up under order.

(2) Where responsibility as to custody of books, etc., to cease — After the lapse of five years from the date of the dissolution of the corporation, no responsibility rests on it or the liquidator, or anyone to whom the custody of such books, accounts and documents has been committed by reason that the same or any of them are not forthcoming to any person claiming to be interested therein.

270. (1) **Provision for discharge of liquidator and distribution by the court** — Where a corporation is being wound up under an order of the court and the realization and distribution of its property has proceeded so far that in the opinion of the court it is expedient that the liquidator should be discharged and that the property of the corporation remaining in the liquidator's hands can be better realized and distributed by the court, the court may make an order discharging the liquidator and for payment, delivery and transfer into court, or to such officer or person as the court may direct, of such property, and it shall be realized and distributed by or under the direction of the court among the persons entitled thereto in the same way as nearly as may be as if the distribution were being made by the liquidator.

(2) **Disposal of books and documents** — In such case, the court may make an order directing how the books, accounts and documents of the corporation and of the liquidator are to be disposed of, and may order that they be deposited in court or otherwise dealt with as it thinks fit.

271. Rules of procedure — The Lieutenant Governor in Council may make rules for the due carrying out of this Part, and, except as otherwise provided by this Act or by such rules, the practice and procedure in a winding up under the *Winding-up Act* (Canada) apply.

PART VII — CORPORATIONS, GENERAL

272. Application — Subject to section 2, this Part, except where it is otherwise expressly provided, applies,

(a) to every corporation incorporated by or under a general or special Act of the Parliament of the late Province of Upper Canada;

(b) to every corporation incorporated by or under a general or special Act of the Parliament of the late Province of Canada that has its head office and carries on business in Ontario and that was incorporated with objects to which the authority of the Legislature extends; and

(c) to every corporation incorporated by or under a general or special Act of the Legislature,

but this Part does not apply to a corporation incorporated for the construction and working of a railway, incline railway or street railway, or to a corporation within the meaning of the *Loan and Trust Corporations Act* except as provided by that Act.

Proposed Repeal — 272

272. [Repealed 2010, c. 15, s. 211(8). Not in force at date of publication.]

273. Incorporation subject to trusts — A corporation is, upon its incorporation, invested with all the property and rights, real and personal, theretofore held by or for it under any trust created with a view to its incorporation.

274. General corporate powers — A corporation, unless otherwise expressly provided in the Act or instrument creating it, has and shall be deemed to have had from its creation the capacity of a natural person and may exercise its powers beyond the boundaries of Ontario to the extent to which the laws in force where the powers are sought to be exercised permit, and may accept extra-provincial powers and rights.

275. Incidental powers — A corporation has power,

(a) to construct, maintain and alter any buildings or works necessary or convenient for its objects;

(b) to acquire by purchase, lease or otherwise and to hold any land or interest therein.

1994, c. 27, s. 78(8)

276. [Repealed 1994, c. 27, s. 78(9).]

277. (1) Head office — Subject to subsection (2), a corporation shall at all times have its head office in the place in Ontario where the letters patent provide that the head office is to be situate.

(2) Change of head office — A corporation may by special resolution change the location of its head office to another place in Ontario.

(3) Where municipality annexed or amalgamated — Where the location of the head office of a corporation is changed by reason only of the annexation or amalgamation of the place in which the head office is situate to or with another municipality, such change does not constitute and has never constituted a change within the meaning of subsection (2).

(4) [Repealed 1998, c. 18, Sched. E, s. 72.]

(5) [Repealed 1998, c. 18, Sched. E, s. 72.]

1998, c. 18, Sched. E, s. 72

278. [Repealed 1994, c. 27, s. 78(9).]

279. Seal — A corporation may, but need not, have a corporate seal.

1998, c. 18, Sched. E, s. 73

280. (1) Contracts in writing under seal — A contract that if made between individual persons would be by law required to be in writing and under seal may be made on behalf of a corporation in writing under the seal of the corporation.

(2) Contracts in writing not under seal — A contract that if made between individual persons would be by law required to be in writing signed by the parties to be charged therewith may be made on behalf of a corporation in writing signed by any person acting under its authority, express or implied.

(3) Parol contracts — A contract that if made between individual persons would be by law valid although made by parol only and not reduced into writing may be made by parol on behalf of a corporation by any person acting under its authority, express or implied.

281. Power of attorney by corporation — A corporation may, by writing under seal, empower any person, either generally or in respect of any specified mattes, as its attorney to execute on its behalf deeds to which it is a party in any capacity in any place situate in or outside Ontario, and every deed signed by such attorney on behalf of the corporation and under the attorney's seal binds the corporation and has the same effect as if it were under the seal of the corporation.

282. Authentication of documents, etc. — A document requiring authentication by a corporation may be signed by anydirector or by any authorized person and need not be under seal.

283. (1) Directors — The affairs of every corporation shall be managed by a board of directors howsoever designated.

(2) Number — The board of directors of a corporation shall consist of a fixed number of directors not fewer than three.

(3) Conduct of business — Subject to subsection 298(1) and subsection (3.1), no business of a corporation shall be transacted by its directors except at a meeting of directors at which a quorum of the board is present.

(3.1) Means of meetings — Unless the by-laws otherwise provide, if all the directors of a corporation present at or particiapting in the meeting consent, a meeting of directors or of a committee of diretors may be held by such telephone, electronic or other communication facilities as permit all persons participating in the meeting to communicate with each other simultaneously and instantaneously, and a director participating in the meeting by those means is deemed for the purposes of this Act to be present at the meeting.

(4) Idem — Where there is a vacancy or vacancies in the board of directors, the remaining directors may exercise all the powers of the board so long as a quorum of the board remains in office.

(5) Purchase of liability insurance — Subject to subsection (6), a corporation may purchase and maintain insurance for a director or officer of the corporation against any liability incurred by the director or officer, in the capacity as a director or officer of the corporation, except where the liability relates to the person's failure to act honestly and in good faith with a view to the best interests of the corporation.

(6) Charitable corporation — A corporation referred to in subsection 1(2) of the *Charities Accounting Act* may not purchase insurance described in subsection (5) unless

(a) the corporation complies with the *Charities Accounting Act* or a regulation made under that Act that permits the purchase; or

(b) the corporation or a director or officer of the corporation obtains a court order authorizing the purchase.

Proposed Repeal — 283(6)

(6) [Repealed 2010, c. 15, s. 211(8). Not in force at date of publication.]

1998, c. 18, Sched. E, s. 74

284. (1) First directors — The person named as first directors in the Act or instrument creating the corporation are the directors of the corporation until replaced by the same number of others duly elected or appointed in their stead.

(2) Idem — The first directors of the corporation have all the powers and duties and are subject to all the liabilities of directors.

(3) Definition — In the case of corporations incorporated before the 30th day of April, 1954, **"first directors"** in this section means provisional directors.

285. (1) Change in number of directors — A corporation may by special resolution increase or decrease the number of its directors.

(2) [Repealed 1998, c. 18, Sched. E, s. 75.]

(3) [Repealed 1998, c. 18, Sched. E, s. 75.]

1998, c. 18, Sched. E, s. 75

286. (1) Qualification of directors, must be shareholders — Subject to subsections (2) and (3), no person shall be a director of a corporation unless he or she is a shareholder or member of the corporation, and, if he or she ceases to be a shareholder or member, he or she thereupon ceases to be a director.

(2) Exception — A person may be a director of a corporation if he or she becomes a shareholder or member of the corporation within ten days after his or her election or appointment as a director, but, if the person fails to become a shareholder or member within such ten days, the person thereupon ceases to be a director and shall not be re-elected or reappointed unless he or she is a shareholder or member of the corporation.

(3) Exception, hospitals, stock exchanges and insurers — A corporation may by by-law provide that a person may, with his or her consent in writing, be a director of the corporation even though the person is not a shareholder or member of the corporation if the corporation,

(a) operates a hospital within the meaning of the *Public Hospitals Act*;

(b) operates a recognized stock exchange; or

(c) is an insurer to which Part V applies, other than a pension fund or employees' mutual benefit society.

Proposed Amendment — 286(3)

(3) Exception, insurers — A corporation may by by-law provide that a person may, with his or her consent in writing, be a director of the corporation even though the person is not a shareholder or member of the corporation if the corporation is an insurer to which Part V applies, other than a pension fund or employees' mutual benefit society.

2010, c. 15, s. 211(9) [Not in force at date of publication.]

(4) Age — A director shall be eighteen or more years of age.

(5) Bankrupts — No undischarged bankrupt shall be a director, and, if a director becomes a bankrupt, he or she thereupon ceases to be a director.

2006, c. 33, Sched. O, s. 27

287. (1) Election of directors — The directors shall be elected by the shareholders or members in general meeting and the election shall be by ballot or in such other manner as the by-laws of the corporation prescribe.

(2) Idem — Unless the by-laws otherwise provide, the election of directors shall take place yearly and all the directors then in office shall retire, but, if qualified, are eligible for re-election.

(3) **Exception** — Subsection (2) does not affect the operation of any by-law passed before the 30th day of April, 1954, that provides that the election of directors shall take place otherwise than yearly.

(4) **Continuance in office** — If an election of directors is not held at the proper time, the directors continue in office until their successors are elected.

(5) **Rotation of directors** — The by-laws may provide for the election and retirement of directors in rotation, but in that case no director shall be elected for a term of more than five years and at least three directors shall retire from office in each year.

1998, c. 18, Sched. E, s. 76

288. (1) **Quorum of directors** — Unless the letters patent, supplementary letters patent or a special resolution otherwise provides, a majority of the board of directors constitutes a quorum, but in no case shall a quorum be less than two-fifths of the board of directors.

(2) **Vacancies** — As long as there is a quorum of directors in office, any vacancy occurring in the board of directors may be filled for the remainder of the term by the directors then in office.

(3) **Idem** — Whenever there is not a quorum of directors in office, the director or directors then in office shall forthwith call a general meeting of the shareholders or members to fill the vacancies, and, in default or if there are no directors then in office, the meeting may be called by any shareholder or member.

289. (1) **President** — The directors shall elect a president from among themselves.

(2) **Other officers** — The directors shall appoint a secretary and may appoint one or more vice-presidents and other officers.

(3) **Corporations without share capital** — Despite subsections (1) and (2), in the case of a corporation without share capital, if the letters patent, supplementary letters patent or by-laws so provide, the officers of the corporation or any of them may be elected or appointed at a general meeting of the members duly called for that purpose.

(4) **Acting secretary** — If the office of secretary is vacant or if for any reason the secretary is unable to act, anything required or authorized to be done by the secretary may be done by an assistant secretary or, if there is no assistant secretary able to act, by any other officer of the corporation authorized generally or specifically in that behalf of the directors.

290. Chair of the board — A corporation may by special resolution provide for the election by the directors from among themselves of a chair of the board of directors and define his or her duties, and may assign to the chair of the board of directors any or all of the duties of the president or other officer of the corporation, and in that case the special resolution shall fix and prescribe the duties of the president.

291. (1) **Qualification of officers** — Except in the case of the president and the chair of the board of directors, no officer of the corporation need be a director or a shareholder or member of the corporation unless the by-laws so provide.

(2) **Application of subs. (1)** — Subsection (1) does not apply to a corporation operating a recognized stock exchange.

292. Validity of acts of directors, etc. — The acts of a director or of an officer are valid despite any defect that may afterwards be discovered in his or her appointment or qualification.

293. Annual meetings — A corporation shall hold an annual meeting of its shareholders or members not later than eighteen months after its incorporation and subsequently not more than fifteen months after the holding of the last preceding annual meeting.

294. General meetings — The directors may at any time call a general meeting of the shareholders or members for the transaction of any business, the general nature of which is specified in the notice calling the meeting.

295. (1) Requisition for meeting — Shareholders of a company holding not less than one-tenth of the issued shares of the company that carry the right to vote at the meeting proposed to be held, or not less than one-tenth of the members of a corporation without share capital entitled to vote at the meeting proposed to be held, as the case may be, may request the directors to call a general meeting of the shareholders or members for any purpose connected with the affairs of the corporation that is not inconsistent with this Act.

(2) Requisition — The requisition shall state the general nature of the business to be presented at the meeting and shall be signed by the requisitionists and deposited at the head office of the corporation and may consist of several documents in like form signed by one or more requisitionists.

(3) Duty of directors to call meeting — Upon deposit of the requisition, the directors shall call forthwith a general meeting of the shareholders or members for the transaction of the business stated in the requisition.

(4) Where requisitionists may call meeting — If the directors do not within twenty-one days from the date of the deposit of the requisition call and hold such meeting, any of the requisitionists may call such meeting which shall be held within sixty days from the date of the deposit of the requisition.

(5) Calling of meeting — A meeting called under this section shall be called as nearly as possible in the same manner as meetings of shareholders or members are called under the by-laws, but, if the by-laws provide for more than twenty-one days notice of meetings, twenty-one days notice is sufficient for the calling of such meeting.

(6) Repayment of expenses — Any reasonable expenses incurred by the requisitionists by reason of the failure of the directors to call such meeting shall be repaid to the requisitionists by the corporation and any amount so repaid shall be retained by the corporation out of any money due or to become due from the corporation by way of fees or other remuneration in respect of their services to such of the directors as were in default, unless at such meeting the shareholders or members by a majority of the votes cast reject the repayment to the requisitionists.

296. (1) Circulation of shareholders' resolutions, etc. — On the requisition in writing of the shareholders of a company holding not less than one-twentieth of the issued shares of the company that carry the right to vote at the meeting to which the requisition relates or not less than one-twentieth of the members of a corporation without share capital entitled to vote at the meeting to which the requisition relates, as the case may be, the directors shall,

(a) give to the shareholders or members entitled to notice of the next general meeting of shareholders or members notice of any resolution that may properly be moved and is intended to be moved at that meeting; or

(b) circulate to the shareholders or members entitled to vote at the next general meeting of shareholders or members a statement of not more than 1,000 words with respect to the matter referred to in any proposed resolution or with respect to the business to be dealt with at that meeting.

(2) The notice or statement or both, as the case may be, shall be given or circulated by sending a copy thereof to each shareholder or member entitled thereto in the same manner and at the same time as that prescribed by this Act for the sending of notice of meetings of shareholders or members.

(3) Idem — Where it is not practicable to send the notice or statement or both at the same time as the notice of the meeting is sent, the notice or statement or both shall be sent as soon as practicable thereafter.

(4) Deposit of requisition, etc. — The directors are not bound under this section to give notice of any resolution or to circulate any statement unless,

(a) the requisition, signed by the requisitionists, is deposited at the head office of the corporation,

(i) in the case of a requisition requiring notice of a resolution to be given, not less than ten days before the meeting,

(ii) in the case of a requisition requiring a statement to be circulated, not less than seven days before the meeting; and

(b) there is deposited with the requisition a sum reasonably sufficient to meet the corporation's expenses in giving effect thereto.

(5) Where directors not bound to circulate statement — The directors are not bound under this section to circulate any statement if, on the application of the corporation or any other person who claims to be aggrieved, the court is satisfied that the rights conferred by this section are being abused to secure needless publicity for defamatory matter, and on any such application the court may order the costs of the corporation to be paid in whole or in part by the requisitionists even though they are not parties to the application.

(6) Where no liability — A corporation and a director, officer, employee or person acting on its behalf, except a requisitionist, is not liable in damages or otherwise by reason only of the circulation of a notice or statement or both in compliance with this section.

(7) Duty to deal with requisitioned matter — Despite anything in the by-laws of the corporation, where the requisitionists have complied with this section, the resolution, if any, mentioned in the requisition shall be dealt with at the meeting to which the requisition relates.

(8) Repayment of expenses — The sum deposited under clause (4)(b) shall be repaid to the requisitionists by the corporation unless at the meeting to which the requisition relates the shareholders or members by a majority of the votes cast reject the repayment to the requisitionists.

(9) Offence — A director of a corporation who authorizes, permits or acquiesces in any contravention of any requirement of this section is guilty of an offence and on conviction is liable to a fine of not more than $200.

297. Court may direct method of holding meetings — If for any reason it is impracticable to call a meeting of shareholders or members of the corporation in any manner in which meetings of shareholders or members may be called or to conduct the meeting in the manner prescribed by this Act, the letters patent, supplementary letters patent or by-laws, the court may, on the application of a director or a shareholder or member who would be entitled to vote at the meeting, order a meeting to be called, held and conducted in such manner as the court thinks fit, and any meeting called, held and conducted in accordance with such an order shall for all purposes be deemed to be a meeting of shareholders or members of the corporation duly called, held and conducted.

298. (1) By-laws and resolutions — Any by-law or resolution signed by all the directors is as valid and effective as if passed at a meeting of the directors duly called, constituted and held for that purpose.

(2) Idem — Any resolution signed by all the shareholders or members is as valid and effective as if passed at a meeting of the shareholders or members duly called, constituted and held for that purpose.

(3) Alternative method of confirming by-laws — Any by-law passed at any time during a corporation's existence may, in lieu of confirmation at a general meeting, be confirming in writing by all the shareholders or members entitled to vote at such meeting.

(4) Evidentiary value of signatures — Where a by-law or resolution purports to have been passed or confirmed under this section by the signatures of all the directors, shareholders or members, as the case may be, of the corporation, the signatures to such by-law or resolution are admissible in evidence as proof, in the absence of evidence to the contrary, of the signatures of all the directors, shareholders or members, as the case may be, and are admissible in evidence as proof, in the absence of evidence to the contrary, that the signatories to the by-law or resolution were all the directors, shareholders or members, as the case may be, at the date that the by-law or resolution purports so to have been passed or confirmed.

1998, c. 18, Sched. E, s. 77

299. (1) Minute books — A corporation shall cause minutes of all proceedings at meetings of the shareholders or members and of the directors and of any executive committee to be entered in books kept for that purpose.

(2) Evidence — Any such minutes, if purporting to be signed by the chair of the meeting at which the proceedings were had or by the chair of the next succeeding meeting, are admissible in evidence as proof, in the absence of evidence to the contrary, of the proceedings.

(3) Validity — Where minutes in accordance with this section have been made of the proceedings of a meeting of the shareholders or members or of the directors or any executive committee, then, until the contrary is proved, the meeting shall be deemed to have been duly called, constituted and held and all proceedings had thereat to have been duly had and all appointments of directors, officers or liquidators made thereat shall be deemed to have been duly made.

300. Documents and registers — A corporation shall cause the following documents and registers to be kept:

1. A copy of the letters patent and any supplementary letters patent issued to the corporation and of the memorandum of agreement, if any, or, if incorporated by special Act, a copy of the Act.

2. All by-laws and special resolutions of the corporation.

3. A register of shareholders or members in which are set out the names alphabetically arranged of all persons who are shareholders or members or have been within ten years shareholders or members or have been within ten years shareholders or members of the corporation and the address of every such person while a shareholder or member and, in the case of a company, in which are set out also the number and class of shares held by each shareholder and the amounts paid up and remaining unpaid on their respective shares.

4. A register of directors in which are set out the names and addresses of all persons who are or have been directors of the corporation with the several dates on which each became or ceased to be a director.

2004, c. 19, s. 10(5)

301. Documents evidence — The documents and registers mentioned in sections 41 and 300 are admissible in evidence as, in the absence of evidence to the contrary, proof before and after dissolution of the corporation of all facts purporting to be stated therein.

302. Books of account — A corporation shall cause to be kept proper books of account and accounting records with respect to all financial and other transactions of the corporation and, without derogating from the generality of the foregoing, records of,

(a) all sums of money received and disbursed by the corporation and the matters with respect to which receipt and disbursement took place;

(b) all sales and purchases of the corporation;

(c) the assets and liabilities of the corporation; and

(d) all other transactions affecting the financial position of the corporation.

303. Untrue entries — A director, officer or employee of a corporation who makes or assists in making any entry in the minutes of proceedings mentioned in section 299, in the documents and registers mentioned in sections 41 and 300 or in the books of account or accounting records mentioned in section 302, knowing it to be untrue, is guilty of an offence and on conviction is liable to a fine of not more than $1,000 or to imprisonment for a term of not more than three months, or both.

304. (1) Records to be kept at head office — The minutes of proceedings mentioned in section 299, the documents and registers mentioned in sections 41 and 300, and the books of account and accounting records mentioned in section 302 shall, during the normal business hours of the corporation, be open to inspection by any director and shall, except as provided in section 43 and in subsections (2) and (3) of this section, be kept at the head office of the corporation.

(2) Records of account at branch — A corporation may keep at any place where it carries on business such parts of the accounting records as relate to the operations and assets and liabilities thereof or to such business of the corporation as was carried on or supervised or accounted for at such place, but there shall be kept at the head office of the corporation or such other place as is authorized under subsection (3) such records as will enable the directors to ascertain quarterly with reasonable accuracy the financial position of the corporation.

(3) Exemption — A corporation may keep any of the records mentioned in subsection (1) at a place other than the head office of the corporation if the records are available for inspection during regular office hours at the head office by means of a computer terminal or other electronic technology.

(4) Offence — A director, officer or employee of a corporation who contravenes subsection (1) is guilty of an offence and on conviction is liable to a fine of not more than $200.

(5) Rescission of orders made under subs. (3) — The Minister may by order upon such terms as the Minister sees fit rescind any made under subsection (3) or any order made by the Lieutenant Governor in Council under a predecessor of that subsection.

1998, c. 18, Sched. E, s. 78

305. (1) Records to be open for inspection — The minutes of proceedings at meetings of shareholders or members mentioned in section 299 and the documents and registers mentioned in sections 41 and 300, during the normal business hours of the corporation, shall, at the place or places where they are kept, be open to inspection by the shareholders or members and creditors of the corporation or their agents or legal representatives, and any of them may make extracts therefrom.

(2) Offence — Every person who refused to permit a person entitled thereto to inspect such minutes, documents or registers, or to make extracts therefrom, is guilty of an offence and on conviction is liable to a fine of not more than $200.

306. (1) List of shareholders — No shareholder or member or creditor or the agent or representative of any of them shall make or cause to be made a list of all or any of the shareholders or members of the corporation, unless the person has filed with the corporation or its agent an affidavit of such shareholder, member or creditor in the following form in English or French, and, where the shareholder, member or creditor is a corporation, the affidavit shall be made by the president or other officer authorized by resolution of the board of directors of such corporation;

Form of Affidavit

Province of Ontario

County of

In the matter of

..................................(*Insert name of corporation*)

I,................................, of the .... of .... in the .... of .... make oath and say (*or* affirm)

1. I am a shareholder (*or* member *or* creditor) of the above-named corporation.

(Where the shareholder, member or creditor is a corporation, indicate office and authority of deponent in paragraph 1.)

2. I am applying to make a list of the shareholders (*or* members) of the above-named corporation.

3. I require the list of shareholders (*or* members) only for the purposes connected with the above-named corporation.

4. The list of shareholders (*or* members) and the information contained therein will be used only for purposes connected with the above-named corporation.

SWORN, etc.

(2) **Offence** — Every person, other than a corporation or its agent, who uses a list of all or any of the shareholders or members of the corporation for the purpose of delivering or sending to all or any of such shareholders or members advertising or other printed matter relating to shares or securities of the corporation, or for purposes not connected with the corporation is guilty of an offence and on conviction is liable to a fine of not more than $1,000.

(3) **Purposes connected with the corporation, defined** — Purposes connected with the corporation include any effort to influence the voting of shareholders or members at any meeting of the corporation and include the acquisition or offering of shares to acquire control or to effect an amalgamation or reorganization and any other purpose approved by the Minister.

307. (1) **Where list of shareholders to be furnished** — Any person, upon payment of a reasonable charge therefor and upon filing with the corporation or its agent the affidavit referred to in subsection (2), may require a corporation, other than a private company, or its transfer agent to furnish within ten days from the filing of such affidavit a list setting out the names alphabetically arranged of all persons who are shareholders or members of the corporation, the number of shares owned by each such person and the address of each person as shown on the books of the corporation made up to a date not more than ten days prior to the date of filing the affidavit.

(2) **Affidavit** — The affidavit referred to in subsection (1) shall be made by the applicant and shall be in the following form in English or French:

Form of Affidavit

Province of Ontario

County of

In the matter of

.... (*Insert name of corporation*)

I, ..., of the .... of .... in the .... of .... make oath and say (*or* affirm)

(Where the applicant is a corporation, indicate office and authority of deponent.)

1. I hereby apply for a list of the shareholders (*or* members) of the above-named corporation.

2. I require the list of shareholders (*or* members) only for purposes connected with the above-named corporation.

3. The list of shareholders (*or* members) and the information contained therein will be used only for purposes connected with the above-named corporation.

Sworn, etc.

(3) **Idem, where applicant a corporation** — Where the applicant is a corporation, the affidavit shall be made by the president or other officer authorized by resolution of the board of directors of such corporation.

(4) Offence — Every person who uses a list of shareholders or members of a corporation obtained under this section,

(a) for the purpose of delivering or sending to all or any of such shareholders or members advertising or other printed matter relating to shares or securities other than the shares or securities of the corporation; or

(b) for any purpose not connected with the corporation,

is guilty of an offence and on conviction is liable to a fine of not more than $1,000.

(5) Offence — Every corporation or transfer agent that fails to furnish a list in accordance with subsection (1) when so required is guilty of an offence and on conviction is liable to a fine of not more than $1,000, and every director or officer of such corporation or transfer agent who authorized, permitted or acquiesced in such offence is also guilty of an offence and on conviction is liable to a like fine.

(6) Interpretation — Purposes connected with the corporation include any effort to influence the voting of shareholders or members at any meeting of the corporation, any offer to acquire shares in the corporation or any effort to effect an amalgamation or reorganization and any other purpose approved by the Minister.

308. Offence — Every person who offers for sale or sells or purchases or otherwise traffics in a list or a copy of a list of all or any of the shareholders or members of a corporation is guilty of an offence and on conviction is liable to a fine of not more than $1,000, and, where such person is a corporation, every director or officer of such corporation who authorized, permitted or acquiesced in such offence is also guilty of an offence and on conviction is liable to a like fine.

309. (1) Power of court to correct — If the name of a person is, without sufficient cause, entered in or omitted from the minutes of proceedings mentioned in section 299 or from documents or registers mentioned in sections 41 and 300, or if default is made or unnecessary delay takes place in entering therein the fact of any person having ceased to be a shareholder or member of the corporation, the person or shareholder or member aggrieved, or any shareholder or member of the corporation, or the corporation itself, may apply to the court for an order that the minutes, documents or registers, be rectified, and the court may dismiss such application or make an order for the rectification of the minutes, documents or registers, and may direct the corporation to compensate the party aggrieved for any damage the person has sustained.

(2) Decision as to title — The court may, in any proceeding under this section, decide any question relating to the entitlement of a person who is a party to such proceeding to have the person's name entered in or omitted from such minutes, documents or registers, whether such question arises between two or more shareholders or members or alleged shareholders or members, or between any shareholder or member or alleged shareholder or member and the corporation.

(3) Trial of issue — The court may direct an issue to be tried.

(4) Appeal — An appeal lies from the decision of the court as if it had been given in an action.

(5) Jurisdiction of courts not affected — This section does not deprive any court of any jurisdiction it otherwise has.

(6) **Costs** — The costs of any proceeding under this section are in the discretion of the court.

310. (1) **Investigations and audits** — Upon an application by the shareholders of a company holding shares representing not less than one-tenth of the issued capital of the company, or upon an application of at least one-tenth of the members of a corporation without share capital, the court may appoint an inspector to investigate the affairs and management of the corporation or may appoint a person to audit its books.

(2) **Evidence** — The application shall be supported by such evidence as the court requires for the purpose of showing that the applicants have good reason requiring the investigation of audit, as the case may be.

(3) **Security for costs** — The court may require the applicants to give security to cover the probable cost of the investigation or audit and may make rules and prescribe the manner in which and the extent to which the investigation or audit is to be conducted.

(4) **Report on and expense of investigation or audit** — Such inspector or auditor shall report thereon to the court and the expense of the investigation shall, in the discretion of the court, be defrayed by the corporation or by the applicants or partly by the corporation and partly by the applicants.

(5) **Corporation may appoint inspector for same purpose** — A corporation may, by resolution passed at an annual meeting or at a general meeting called for that purpose, appoint an inspector to investigate its affairs and management.

(6) **Powers and duties of inspector** — The inspector appointed under subsection (5) has the same powers and shall perform the same duties as an inspector appointed under subsection (1) and the inspector shall make his or her report in such manner and to such persons as the corporation by resolution directs.

(7) **Production of books and documents** — All officers and agents of the corporation shall produce for the examination of any inspector or auditor appointed under this section all books and records in their custody or power.

(8) **Examination on oath** — Any such inspector or auditor may examine upon oath the officers, agents and employees of the corporation in relation to its affairs and management.

(9) **Offence** — Every officer or agent who refuses to produce any book or record referred to in subsection (7) and every person so examined who refuses to answer any question relating to the affairs and management of the corporation is guilty of an offence and on conviction is liable to a fine of not more than $200.

(10) **Report admissible in proceedings** — A copy of the report of the inspector or auditor, as the case may be, authenticated by the court or under the seal of the corporation whose affairs and management the inspector or auditor has investigated, is admissible in any legal proceedings as evidence of the opinion of the inspector or auditor in relation to any matter contained in the report.

311. (1) **Corporation with fewer than three shareholders or members exercising corporate powers** — If a corporation exercises its corporate powers when its shareholders or members are fewer than three for a period of more than six months after the number has been so reduced, every person who was a shareholder or member of the corporation during the time that it so exercised its corporate powers after such period of six months and is aware

of the fact that it so exercised its corporate powers is severally liable for the payment of the whole of the debts of the corporation contracted during such time and may be sued for the debts without the joinder in the action of the corporation or of any other shareholder or member.

(2) **Shareholder or member may avoid liability** — A shareholder or member who has become aware that the corporation is so exercising its corporate powers may serve a protest in writing on the corporation and may by registered letter notify the Minister of such protest having been served and of the facts upon which it is based, and such shareholder or member may thereby and not otherwise, from the date of the protest and notification, exonerate himself, herself or itself from liability.

(3) **Revocation of charter** — If after notice from the Minister the corporation refuses or neglects to bring the number of its shareholders or members up to three, such refusal or neglect may be regarded by the Lieutenant Governor as sufficient cause for the making of an order under subsection 317(1).

312. (1) **Bringing corporations under this Act** — A corporation incorporated otherwise than by letters patent and being at the time of its application a subsisting corporation may apply for letters patent under this Act, and the Lieutenant Governor may issue letters patent continuing it as if it had been incorporated under this Act.

Proposed Repeal — 312(1)

(1) [Repealed 2010, c. 15, s. 211(10). Not in force at date of publication.]

(2) **Change of powers, etc.** — Where a corporation applies for issue of letters patent under subsection (1), the Lieutenant Governor may, by the letters patent, limit or extend the powers of the corporation, name its directors and change its corporate name, as the applicant desires.

Proposed Repeal — 312(2)

(2) [Repealed 2010, c. 15, s. 211(10). Not in force at date of publication.]

(3) **Transfer of foreign corporations** — A corporation incorporated under the laws of any jurisdiction other than Ontario may, if it appears to the Lieutenant Governor to be thereunto authorized by the laws of the jurisdiction in which it was incorporated, apply to the Lieutenant Governor for letters patent continuing it as if it had been incorporated under this Act, and the Lieutenant Governor may issue such letters patent on application supported by such material as appears satisfactory and such letters patent may be issued on such terms and subject to such limitations and conditions and contain such provisions as appear to the Lieutenant Governor to be fit and proper.

313. (1) **Transfer of Ontario corporations** — A corporation incorporated under the laws of Ontario other than an insurance company may, if authorized by a special resolution, by the Minister and by the laws of any other jurisdiction in Canada, apply to the proper officer of that other jurisdiction for an instrument of continuation continuing the corporation as if it had been incorporated under the laws of that other jurisdiction.

(1.1) **Same, insurance company** — An insurance company incorporated under this Act may, if authorized by special resolution, by the Superintendent of Financial Services appointed under section 5 of the *Financial Services Commission of Ontario Act, 1997* and by the laws of any other jurisdiction in Canada, apply to the proper officer of that other jurisdiction for an instrument of continuation continuing the insurance company as if it had been incoporated under the laws of that other jurisdiction.

(2) Notice — The corporation shall file with the Minister a notice of the issue of the instrument of continuation and on and after the date of the filing of such instrument this Act ceases to apply to that corporation.

(3) [Repealed 1999, c. 12, Sched. F, s. 22(3).]

1999, c. 12, Sched. F, s. 22

313.1 (1) Continuance as co-operative corporation — A corporation incorporated under this Act may, if authorized by a special resolution and by the Minister, apply under the *Co-operative Corporations Act* to be continued as a co-operative corporation.

(2) Certificate to be filed with Minister — The corporation must file with the Minister a copy of the certificate of continuance issued under the *Co-operative Corporations Act* within 60 days after the date of issuance.

(3) Act ceases to apply — This Act ceases to apply to the corporation on the date upon which the corporation is continued under the *Co-operative Corporations Act*.

1994, c. 17, s. 31

314. Rights of creditors preserved — All rights of creditors against the property, rights and assets of a corporation amalgamated under section 113 or continued under section 312, and all liens upon the property, rights and assets are unimpaired by such amalgamation or continuation, and all debts, contracts, liabilities and duties of the corporation thenceforth attach to the amalgamated or continued corporation and may be enforced against it.

315. (1) Forfeiture for non-user — If a corporation incorporated by letters patent does not go into actual operation within two years after incorporation or for any two consecutive years does not use its corporate powers, the Lieutenant Governor, after having given the corporation such notice as he or she considers proper, may by order declare such powers forfeited, except so far as is necessary for the winding up of the corporation.

(2) Rights of creditors not affected — No such forfeiture affects prejudicially the rights of creditors as they exist at the date of the forfeiture.

(3) Revival — Where the powers of a corporation have been forfeited under subsection (1) or a predecessor of subsection (1), the Lieutenant Governor on the application of the corporation may by order, on such terms and conditions as he or she sees fit to impose, revive the corporate powers.

316. Social clubs cause for cancellation — Despite anything to the contrary in any Act, in any letters patent or in any supplementary letters patent, if it is made to appear to thesatisfaction of the Minister that a corporation that has objects in whole or in part of a social nature,

(a) occupies and uses a house, room or place as a club that, except for paragraph 197(2)(a) of the *Criminal Code* (Canada), would be a common gaming house as defined in subsection 1 thereof; or

(b) occupies premises that are equipped, guarded, constructed or operated so as to hinder or prevent lawful access to and inspection by police or fire officers, or are found fitted or provided with any means or contrivance for playing any game of chance or any mixed game of chance and skill, gaming or betting or with any device for concealing, removing or destroying such means or contrivance,

the Lieutenant Governor may make an order under subsection 317(1).

317. (1) Termination of existence for cause — Where sufficient cause is shown, the Lieutenant Governor may by order, upon such terms and conditions as he considers fit,

(a) cancel the letters patent of a corporation and declare it to be dissolved on such date as the order may fix;

(b) declare the corporate existence of a corporation incorporated otherwise than by letters patent to be terminated and the corporation to be dissolved on such date as the order may fix; or

(c) cancel any supplementary letters patent issued to a corporation.

(2) Inquiry — The Minister, under such circumstances and at any time as the Minister in his or her discretion thinks advisable, may authorize any officer of the Ministry of the Minister to conduct an inquiry for the purpose of determining whether or not there is sufficient cause for the making of an order under subsection (1).

(3) Powers of inquiring officer — Every officer so authorized has the power to summon any person to appear before him or her as a witness in such inquiry and to require such person to give evidence on oath, touching any matter relevant to the purpose of the inquiry, and to produce such documents and things as such officer considers requisite for that purpose.

(4) Witnesses — Every such officer has the same power to enforce the attendance of witnesses and compel them to give evidence and to produce documents and things as is vested in any court in civil cases.

(5) Witness may be required to answer — Section 9 of the *Evidence Act* applies to any witness and to the evidence given by him or her before any such officer in any such inquiry.

(6) Appeal — An appeal lies from an order made under subsection (1) to the Divisional Court upon a question of law only.

(7) Minister to be heard — The Minister is entitled to be heard, by counsel or otherwise, upon the argument of any such appeal.

(8) No costs — No costs are payable by or to any person by reason of or in respect of any such appeal.

(9) Order for dissolution — Where it appears that a corporation is in default of a filing requirement under the *Corporations Information Act* and that notice of such default has been sent in accordance with section 324 to the corporation or has been published once in *The Ontario Gazette,* the Lieutenant Governor may by order, after ninety days after the notice has been sent or published,

(a) cancel the letters patent of the corporation and declare it to be dissolved on such date as the order may fix; or

(b) declare the corporate existence of the corporation, if it was incorporated otherwise than by letters patent, to be terminated and the corporation to be dissolved on such date as the order may fix.

(10) Revival — Where a corporation has been dissolved under subsection (9) or any predecessor thereof, the Lieutenant Governor, on the application of any interested person, may in his or her discretion by order, on such terms and conditions as he or she sees fit to impose, revive the corporation, and thereupon the corporation shall, subject to the terms and conditions of the order and to any rights acquired by any person after its dissolution, be restored to its legal position, including all its property, rights, privileges and franchises, and be subject to all its liabilities, contracts, disabilities and debts, as at the date of its dissolution, in the same manner and to the same extent as if it had not been dissolved.

1993, c. 16, s. 3; 1994, c. 27, s. 78(10), (11)

318. (1) Continuation of existence for particular purpose — Despite the dissolution of a corporation under this Act,

(a) a civil, criminal or administrative action or proceeding commenced by or against the corporation before its dissolution may be continued as if the corporation had not been dissolved;

(b) a civil, criminal or administrative action or proceeding may be brought as if the corporation had not been dissolved;

(c) any property that would have been available to satisfy any judgment or order if the corporation had not been dissolved remains available for such purpose; and

(d) title to land belonging to the corporation immediately before its dissolution remains available to be sold in power of sale proceedings.

(2) Interpretation — In this section and section 322,

"proceeding" includes a power of sale proceeding relating to land commenced pursuant to a mortgage.

(3) Service of process — For the purposes of this section, the service of any process on a corporation after its dissolution shall be deemed to be sufficiently made if it is made upon any person shown on the records of the Ministry as being a director or officer of the corporation immediately before the dissolution.

(4) Notice of action — A person who commences an action, suit or proceeding against a corporation after its dissolution, shall serve the writ or other document commencing the action, suit or proceeding on the Public Guardian and Trustee in accordance with the rules that apply generally to service on a party to an action, suit or proceeding.

(5) Notice of power of sale proceeding — A person who commences a power of sale proceeding relating to land against a corporation after its dissolution shall serve a notice of the proceeding on the Public Guardian and Trustee in accordance with the notice requirements in the *Mortgages Act* that apply with respect to a person with an interest in the land recorded in the records of the appropriate land registry office.

1998, c. 18, Sched. E, s. 79

319. (1) Surrender of charter — The charter of a corporation incorporated by letters patent may be surrendered if the corporation proves to the satisfaction of the Lieutenant Governor,

(a) that the surrender of its charter has been authorized,

(i) by a majority of the votes cast at a meeting of its shareholders or members duly called for that purpose or by such other vote as the letters patent or supplementary letters patent of the corporation provide, or

(ii) by the consent in writing of all the shareholders or members entitled to vote at such meeting;

(b) that it has parted with its property by distributing it rateably among its shareholders or members according to their rights and interests in the corporation;

(c) that it has no debts, obligations or liabilities or its debts, obligations or liabilities have been duly provided for or protected or its creditors or other persons having interests in its debts, obligations or liabilities consent; and

(d) that there are no proceedings pending in any court against it.

(2) **Acceptance of surrender and dissolution of corporation** — The Lieutenant Governor, upon due compliance with this section, may by order accept the surrender of the charter and declare the corporation to be dissolved on such date as the order may fix.

(3) **Where shareholder unknown** — When a corporation surrenders its charter and a shareholder or member is unknown or the whereabouts of a shareholder or member is unknown, it may, by agreement with the Public Guardian and Trustee, deliver or convey the person's share of the property to the Public Guardian and Trustee to be held in trust for the person, and such delivery or conveyance shall be deemed to be a rateable distribution among the shareholders or members for the purposes of clause (1)(b).

(4) **Where creditor unknown** — When a corporation surrenders its charter and a creditor is unknown or the whereabouts of a creditor is unknown, it may, by agreement with the Public Guardian and Trustee, pay to the Public Guardian and Trustee an amount equal to the amount of the debt due to the creditor to be held in trust for the creditor, and such payment shall be deemed to be due protection of the debt for the purposes of clause (1)(c).

(5) **Power to convert** — If the share of the property so delivered or conveyed to the Public Guardian and Trustee under subsection (3) is in a form other than money, the Public Guardian and Trustee may at any time, and within ten years after such delivery or conveyance shall, convert it into money.

(6) **Payment to person entitled** — If the share of the property delivered or conveyed under subsection (3) or its equivalent in money, or the amount paid under subsection (4), as the case may be, is claimed by the person beneficially entitled thereto within ten years after if was so delivered, conveyed or paid, it shall be delivered, conveyed or paid to the person, but, if not so claimed, it vests in the Public Guardian and Trustee for the use of Ontario, and, if the person beneficially entitled thereto at any time thereafter establishes the person's right thereto to the satisfaction of the Lieutenant Governor in Council, an amount equal to the amount so vested in the Public Guardian and Trustee shall be paid to the person.

(7) **Property now held by Public Guardian and Trustee** — When an order has been made before the 30th day of April, 1954, accepting the surrender of the charter of a corporation and the Public Guardian and Trustee is holding property of the corporation in trust for its shareholders, members or creditors, the corporation in trust for its shareholders, members or creditors, subsections (5) and (6) apply to the property so held, except that the ten-year period mentioned in subsection (6) commences on the 30th day of April, 1954.

1994, c. 27, s. 78(12); CTS 30 AU 10 – 1

320. Termination of existence of corporation not incorporated by letters patent — The corporate existence of a corporation incorporated otherwise than by letters patent may be terminated by order of the Lieutenant Governor upon application therefor by such corporation under like circumstances, in like manner and with like effect as a corporation incorporated by letters patent may surrender its charter.

321. (1) Liability of shareholders to creditors — Despite the dissolution of a corporation, the shareholders or members among whom its property has been distributed remain liable to its creditors to the amount received by them respectively upon such distribution, and an action may be brought in a court of competent jurisdiction to enforce such liability.

(2) Action against one shareholder as representing class — Where there are numerous shareholders or members, such court may permit an action to be brought against one or more shareholders or members as representatives of the class and, if the plaintiff establishes the plaintiff's claim as creditor, may make an order of reference and add as parties on the reference all such shareholders or members as are found and the referee shall determine the amount that each should contribute towards the plaintiff's claim and may direct payment of the sums so determined.

2002, c. 24, Sched. B, s. 31(2)

322. (1) Forfeiture of undisposed property — Any property of a corporation that has not been disposed of at the date of its dissolution is immediately on the dissolution forfeit to and vests in the Crown.

(2) Exception — Despite subsection (1), if a judgment is given or an order or decision is made or land is sold in an action, suit or proceeding commenced in accordance with section 318 and the judgment, order, decision or sale affects property belonging to the corporation before its dissolution, unless the plaintiff, applicant or mortgagee has not complied with subsection 318(4) or (5),

(a) the property shall be available to satisfy the judgment, order or other decision; and

(b) title to the land shall be transferred to a purchaser free of the Crown's interest, in the case of a power of sale proceeding.

(3) No notice — Despite clause (2)(b), a person who commences a power of sale proceeding relating to land before the dissolution of a corporation but the sale of the land was not completed until after the dissolution, is not required to serve the notice mentioned in subsection 318(5) and title to the land may be transferred to a purchaser free of the Crown's interest.

1998, c. 18, Sched. E, s. 80

323. Evidence of by-laws — A copy of any by-law of a corporation under its seal and purporting to be signed by an officer of the corporation, or a certificate similarly authenticated to the effect that a person is a shareholder or member of the corporation and that dues or other sums payable are due and have not been paid, or that a call or assessment that has been made is due and has not been paid, shall be received in all courts as proof, in the absence of evidence to the contrary, of the by-law or of the statements contained in such certificate.

324. (1) Service of notice — Subject to the letters patent, supplementary letters patent or by-laws, a notice or demand to be served or made by a corporation upon a shareholder or member may be served or made personally or sent by registered letter addressed to the shareholder or member at the person's last address as shown on the books of the corporation.

(2) Time of service — Subject to the letters patent, supplementary letters patent or by-laws, a notice or other document served by mail by a corporation on a shareholder or member shall be deemed to be served at the time when it would be delivered in the ordinary course of mail.

(3) Delivery of notices, etc. — A notice or other document that is required or permitted by this Act or the regulations to be sent by the Lieutenant Governor or the Minister may be sent by ordinary mail or by any method, including registered mail, certified mail or prepaid courier, where there is a record by the person who has delivered it that the notice or document has been sent.

(4) Same — A notice or other document referred to in subsection (3) may be sent by telephone transmission of a facsimile of the notice or other document or by another form of electronic transmission where there is a record that the notice or other document has been sent.

(5) Deemed delivery — A notice or other document sent by mail by the Lieutenant Governor or Minister shall be deemed to have been received by the intended recipient on the earlier of,

(a) the day the intended recipient actually receives it; or

(b) the fifth business day after it is mailed.

(6) Same — A notice or other document sent by a method referred to in subsection (4) shall be deemed to have been received by the intended recipient on the earlier of,

(a) the day the intended recipient actually receives it; or

(b) the first business day after the day the transmission is sent by the Lieutenant Governor or Minister.

1994, c. 27, s. 78(13)

325. Proof of matters under this Act — Proof of any matter that is necessary to be made under this Act may be made by certificate.

326. Reciprocal insurance — A corporation that insures property with or insures the property of other persons, where such insurance is reciprocal and for protection only and not for profit, shall not be deemed to be an insurer or an insurance corporation within the meaning of this Act.

326.1 (1) Powers of Minister — The Minister may make regulations prescribing the form and content of letters patent, supplementary letters patent, or other documents or notices that this Act requires to be filed.

(2) Fees — The Minister may by order require the payment of fees and approve the amount of the fees to be paid under this Act for,

(a) the filing of letters patent, supplementary letters patent and other documents or other services; and

(b) search reports, copies of documents and information, or other services.

1998, c. 18, Sched. E, s. 81

327. Regulations — The Lieutenant Governor in Council may make regulations,

(a) [Repealed 1998, c. 18, Sched. E, s. 82(1).]

(b) respecting any matter that the Lieutenant Governor in Council considers requisite for carrying out the objects of this Act, and, without limiting the generality of the foregoing, respecting names of corporations or classes thereof, objects of corporations, authorized capital of companies, the preferences, rights, conditions, restrictions, limitations or prohibitions attaching to share or classes of shares of companies, or any other matter pertaining to letters patent, supplementary letters patent or orders or the applications therefor.

1998, c. 18, Sched. E, s. 82

328. Fees to be paid in advance — No letters patent and no supplementary letters patent shall be issued and no order shall be made and no document shall be accepted for filing under this Act until all fees therefor have been paid.

329. Appeal — An appeal lies to the Divisional Court from any order made by a court under this Act.

330. (1) Untrue statements — Every person who makes or assists in making a statement in any return, certificate, financial statement or other document required by or for the purposes of this Act or the regulations made under this Act, knowing it to be untrue, is guilty of an offence and on conviction is liable to a fine of not more than $1,000 or to imprisonment for a term of not more than three months, or to both.

(2) Limitation of action — No prosecution under subsection (1) shall be commenced more than one year after the facts upon which the prosecution is based first came to the personal knowledge of the Minister or Deputy Minister.

331. General penalty — Every corporation that, and every person who, being a director or officer of the corporation, or acting on its behalf, commits any act contrary to this Act, or fails or neglects to comply with any such provision, is guilty of an offence and on conviction, if no penalty for such act, failure or neglect is expressly provided by this Act, is liable to a fine of not more than $200.

332. Aggrieved shareholders — Where a shareholder or member or creditor of a corporation is aggrieved by the failure of the corporation or a director, officer or employee of the corporation to perform any duty imposed by this Act, the shareholder, member or creditor, despite the imposition of any penalty and in addition to any other rights that he, she or it may have, may apply to the court for an order directing the corporation, director, officer or employee, as the case may be, to perform such duty, and upon such application the court may make such order or such other order as the court thinks fit.

333. (1) Order for compliance — Where it appears to the Commission that any person or company to which section 73, subsection 85(1) or subsection 86(1) applies has failed to comply with or is contravening any such provision, despite the imposition of any penalty in respect of such non-compliance or contravention, the Commission may apply to the court for an order directing such person or company to comply with such provision or for an order restraining such person or company from contravening such provision, and upon the application, the court may make such order or such other order as the judge thinks fit.

(2) Appeal — An appeal lies to the Divisional Court from an order made under subsection (1).

334. [Repealed 2004, c. 19, s. 10(6).]

SCHEDULE — CONVERSION OF JOINT STOCK LIFE COMPANIES INTO MUTUAL COMPANIES

1. Details of plan to be set forth in by-law — The terms and provisions of any plan referred to in section 211 of the *Corporations Act* shall be set forth in detail in a by-law made by the directors and confirmed at a special general meeting of the company duly called for the purpose of considering the by-law, and there shall be recorded in the minutes of the meeting the number of votes for and the number of votes against confirmation of the by-law, the votes of shareholders and the votes of policyholders being recorded separately.

2. Sanction of by-law by Lieutenant Governor in Council — No such by-law becomes effective until sanctioned by the Lieutenant Governor in Council, and in no case shall any such by-law be sanctioned unless the Lieutenant Governor in Council is satisfied that,

(a) the conversion of the company into a mutual company may reasonably be expected to be achieved under the terms of the by-law and in accordance with this paragraph;

(b) the paid-up capital of the company has ceased to be an important factor in safeguarding the interests of the policyholders of the company, having regard to the quality and amount of the company, having regard to the quality and amount of assets of the company, the surplus of the company relative to its liabilities, the nature of the business carried on by the company and any other considerations deemed by the Lieutenant Governor in Council to be relevant;

(c) the majority of the votes cast by shareholders and the majority of the votes cast by policyholders at the special general meeting referred to in paragraph 1, whether in person or by proxy, were in favour of confirmation of the by-law;

(d) the company holds offers from shareholders, in such terms as to preclude the withdrawal thereof prior to notice by the company in accordance with paragraph 13, to sell to the company, at a price fixed by the directors, not less than 25 per cent of all issued and outstanding shares of the capital stock of the company immediately upon the sanction of the by-law by the Lieutenant Governor in Council, or not less than 50 per cent of all issued and outstanding shares of the capital stock of the company within such period, commencing immediately upon the sanction of the by-law by the Lieutenant Governor in Council, as is specified in the by-law;

(e) the amount required to purchase 25 per cent of the issued and outstanding shares of the capital stock of the company at the price fixed by the directors for the purposes of clause (d) does not exceed the maximum amount, determined in accordance with paragraph 9, that may be applied by the company, immediately upon the sanction of the by-law by the Lieutenant Governor in Council, in payment for shares purchased under the terms of the by-law; and

(f) the price fixed by the directors for the purposes of clause (d) is fair and reasonable in the circumstances.

3. Prices to be paid for shares purchased under by-law — Upon the sanction of the by-law by the Lieutenant Governor in Council, the price fixed for the purposes of clause (d) of paragraph 2 shall continue to be the price that may be paid for shares purchased under the terms of the by-law until such price is changed by the directors in accordance with paragraph 4.

4. Change in price, when effective — The directors may from time to time change the price to be paid for shares purchased under the terms of the by-law, but no such change becomes effective until approved by the Minister on the report of the Superintendent.

5. Period for which price to remain in effect — The price fixed for the purposes of clause (d) of paragraph 2 and any subsequent change in price approved in accordance with paragraph 4 shall remain in effect for a period of not less than six months from the date of sanction of the by-law or the date of approval by the Minister, as the case may be.

6. Payment — All shares purchased under the terms of the by-law shall be paid for by the company in full at the time of the purchase thereof, but nothing in this paragraph shall be construed as prohibiting the company from applying, in payment for any shares so purchased, the full amount of the purchase price thereof by promissory note, payable at a fixed or determinable future time not later than ten years from the date of the making thereof and bearing a rate of interest fixed by the directors and approved by the Minister on the report of the Superintendent.

7. Date for commencement of purchase of shares — The by-law shall fix a day for the commencement of purchase of shares under the terms of the by-law, which day shall be not sooner than the day following the day the by-law is sanctioned by the Lieutenant Governor in Council.

8. Purchase of shares offered for sale — Subject to paragraph 9, the company shall purchase all shares offered for sale under the terms of the by-law on the day or days fixed by the terms of the offer in each case for the sale of those shares and at the price in effect on the day the offer was received or the day fixed by the by-law for the purposes of paragraph 7, whichever is the later, except that no such purchase shall be made prior to the day so fixed by the by-law.

9. Limitation — Despite anything in this Schedule, the maximum amount that may be applied by the company at any particular time in payment for shares purchased under the terms of the by-law is the amount by which,

(a) the aggregate of the surplus and general or contingency reserves of the company, after deducting the excess of the book value over the par value of any shares purchased under the terms of the by-law on or before the date as of which the condition and affairs of the company are required to be shown in the most recent annual statement as required by the *Corporations Act*,

exceeds the aggregate of,

(b) 6 per cent of the total assets of the company or such lesser percentage of the total assets of the company as may be approved by the Lieutenant Governor in Council, upon application by the company, as safe and reasonable in the circumstances having regard to the bases and methods used in the computation of the policy reserves of the company, the quality of its assets, the nature of the business transacted by the company, the earnings of the company and any other matters deemed by the Lieutenant Governor in Council to be relevant thereto; and

(c) the total amount applied by the company before that particular time in payment for any shares purchased under the terms of the by-law after the date referred to in clause (a).

10. Idem — For the purposes of paragraph 9, the assets, surplus and general or contingency reserves of the company and the book value of any shares purchased under the terms of the by-law shall be taken as shown in the annual statement referred to in clause (a) of paragraph 9.

11. Number of shares to be purchased from each shareholder offering shares — Where, by reason of paragraph 9, the company may, at any particular time, purchase some but not all of the shares in respect of which offers for sale at that time have been received, the amount that may be applied by the company at that time in payment for shares purchased under the terms of the by-law shall be applied by the company by apportionment among all of the shares so offered for sale at that time, or any of them, in such manner as specified in the by-law.

12. Register to be kept — The company shall cause a register to be kept in which shall be recorded the offers for sale of shares under the terms of the by-law in the order in which such offers are received by the company, showing, in respect of each such offer,

(a) the date of receipt by the company of the offer;

(b) the name and address of the shareholder making the offer;

(c) the number of shares so offered by the shareholder making the offer and the day or days fixed by the terms of the offer for the sale of those shares;

(d) the price at which each of the shares so offered may be purchased;

(e) the date of purchase, if any, of each of the shares so offered and the number of shares purchased; and

(f) the date of withdrawal, if any, of the offer and the number of shares affected thereby.

13. Notice to shareholders of discontinuation of purchases — Where, by reason of paragraph 9, the company is required to discontinue the purchase of shares under the terms of the by-law, the company shall give notice of such discontinuation to each shareholder on the register whose offer for the sale of shares has not been fully taken up by the company, but any such offer as regards shares not so purchased shall continue to be effective and shall maintain its place on the register until withdrawn by the shareholder by notice in writing to the company.

14. Shares purchased: general — Where the company has purchased any shares of the capital stock of the company under the terms of the by-law,

(a) the number of policyholders' directors of the company shall at all times thereafter be not less than,

(i) one-third of the total number of directors, or

(ii) that proportion of the total number of directors, as nearly as may be, that the total number of shares purchased under the terms of the by-law is of the total number of shares outstanding immediately prior to the sanction of the by-law by the Lieutenant Governor in Council, whichever is the greater, except that nothing in this clause shall be held to require an increase in the number of policyholders' directors except as vacancies occur among the shareholders' directors;

(b) the company shall not thereafter sell any of the shares so purchased, issue any new capital stock or make any calls on shares of the capital stock subscribed;

(c) any dividends thereafter payable to shareholders shall be at a rate not less than the average rate paid in the three years immediately preceding the sanction of the by-law by the Lieutenant Governor in Council, unless the company establishes to the satisfaction of the Minister that a reduction therein is justified by reason of the earnings and general financial condition of the company; and

(d) shares purchased under the terms of the by-law rank equally with other shares in the declaration of dividends to shareholders, but any dividends that may be payable in respect of shares so purchased shall be paid by transfer of the applicable amount from the shareholders' account to the insurance funds of the company.

15. Idem — In respect of each share purchased under the terms of the by-law, until the capital stock of the company has been cancelled in accordance with paragraph 20,

(a) the company may include in its assets shown in the annual statement required by the *Corporations Act* an amount not exceeding the purchase price of the share, minus one-fifth of the excess of the purchase price over the par value thereof for each complete year that has elapsed since the date of purchase of the share; and

(b) the policyholders' directors shall have additional voting rights corresponding to the voting rights that might have been exercised by the holder of the share if the holder had not sold it, and, unless the by-law otherwise provides, such additional voting rights shall be divided as nearly as may be equally among the policyholders' directors, and the remainder, if any, shall be exercised by such one of the policyholders' directors as designated for the purpose by resolution of all the directors.

16. Notice where 90 per cent or more of shares acquired by company — At such time as the company first acquires 90 per cent or more of the shares of its capital stock, it shall notify the Minister and each of the remaining shareholder's of the company to that effect, and, for the purposes of this paragraph, notice to any shareholder shall be deemed to have been given by the company if the company has forwarded to the shareholder by registered mail, at the shareholder's address shown in the book or books in which the names of the shareholder's of the company are recorded, the notice required by this paragraph.

17. Contents of notice — The notice required by paragraph 16 to be given to each of the remaining shareholders of the company shall request each such shareholder to offer the shareholders shares for sale forthwith to the company, and shall state therein the substance of paragraph 18.

18. Acquisition of remaining shares by company — All shares of a shareholder remaining outstanding at the expiration of six months from the date of the notice required by paragraph 16, or at the expiration of such further period as may be required by reason of paragraph 9, shall, upon tender by the company to the shareholder of an amount equal to the price in effect,

(a) in the case of shares in respect of which any offer for sale was received by the company prior to the date of the notice, on the day the offer was received; or

(b) in the case of any other shares, on the date of the notice, be deemed to have been purchased by the company, and, for the purposes of this paragraph, tender shall be deemed to have been made to a shareholder by the company if made to the shareholder in person or by registered mail forwarded to the shareholder at the shareholders address shown in the book or books referred to in paragraph 16.

19. Amount tendered to be retained for payment — Where tender of an amount in accordance with paragraph 18 has been made and the amount so tendered has not been accepted, the amount so tendered shall be retained by the company for payment to the person entitled thereto, and until so paid shall be shown on the books of the company as a liability.

20. Retirement and cancellation of capital stock — Where the company has purchased or is deemed by paragraph 18 to have purchased all of the shares of the capital stock of the company and the shares have been written down in the books of the company to their par value, the capital stock of the company shall thereupon be retired and cancelled by resolution of the board of directors, and the company shall then become a mutual company without capital stock, having for its members the participating policyholders and such other policyholders, if any, as may be authorized by by-law, and the directors shall take all necessary steps to reorganize the affairs of the company accordingly.

21. No change in by-law except with sanction of Lieutenant Governor in Council — No change in any by-law of a company described in paragraph 1 shall be made after the sanction of the by-law by the Lieutenant Governor in Council, except by a subsequent by-law of the company made by the directors and confirmed at a special general meeting of the company duly called for that purpose, and no such subsequent by-law becomes effective until sanctioned by the Lieutenant Governor in Council.

22. Interpretation — In this Schedule, **"Minister"** means the member of the Executive Council charged for the time being by the Lieutenant Governor in Council with the administration of the *Insurance Act*, and **"Superintendent"** means the Superintendent of Financial Services.

1997, c. 28, s. 51

Ont. Reg. 181 — General

made under the *Corporations Act*

R.R.O. 1990, Reg. 181, as am. O. Reg. 580/91; 596/92; 625/93; 177/94; 638/94; 294/95; 402/95; 310/96; 563/98; 189/99; 192/99; 43/00; 248/05; 301/05.

Names

1. (1) The following documents shall accompany any application for letters patent, supplementary letters patent, an extra-provincial licence or an amended extra-provincial licence containing a proposed name for a corporation or a change of corporate name.

1. An original Ontario biased or weighted computer printed search report for the same name as the proposed name from the new updated automated name search system (NUANS) owned by the Department of Consumer and Corporate Affairs, Canada, dated not more than ninety days before the submission of the application.
2. Any consent or consent and undertaking required by the Act or by the Minister.

(2) A computer printed search report referred to in subsection (1) shall accompany an application for revival under section 317 of the Act if the application changes the name of the corporation or at least ten years have elapsed since the corporation was dissolved.

(3) The computer printed search report referred to in subsection (1) is not required where the application is for letters patent, supplementary letters patent, reservation of a name or revival for a corporation incorporated under Part III of the Act if incorporation is required by a government authority as a condition to the awarding of financial assistance under a government program.

O. Reg. 625/93, s. 1; 638/94, s. 1; 402/95, s. 1; 248/05, s. 1

2. (1) [Revoked O. Reg. 625/93, s. 2(1).]

(2) No name that is identified in a computer printed search report as proposed in Ontario shall be used as a corporate name by a person other than the one who proposed the name unless a consent in writing has been obtained from the person who first proposed the name.

O. Reg. 625/93, s. 2

3. (1) The following words and expressions shall not be used in a corporate name:

1. "Amalgamated", "fusionné" or any other related word or expression in French, unless the corporation is an amalgamated corporation resulting from the amalgamation of two or more corporations.
2. [Revoked O. Reg. 625/93, s. 3(2).]
3. "College", "collège", "institute", "institut", "university" or "université", except with a consent in writing on behalf of the Ministry of Education and Training.

4. "Engineer", "ingénieur", "engineering", "génie" or "ingénierie" or any variation thereof, except with the consent in writing of the Association of Professional Engineers of Ontario.

5. [Repealed O. Reg. 248/05, s. 2.]

6. "Royal", where used as an adjective, unless the consent of the Crown has been obtained through the Secretary of State.

7. Numerals indicating the year of incorporation, unless the proposed corporation is the successor to a corporation the name of which is the same as or similar to the proposed corporation, or the year is the year of amalgamation of the corporation.

8. Any word or expression that would lead to an inference that the corporation is a business corporation.

(2) The name of a fraternal society incorporated under section 176 of the Act shall include the words "fraternal society" or "société fraternelle".

(3) The name of a pension fund or employees' mutual benefit society incorporated under section 185 of the Act shall include the words "pension fund society", "employees' mutual benefit society", "caisse de retraite" or "société de secours mutuel d'employés", as the case may be, and the name in whole or in part of the parent corporation.

(4) If the name of a corporation includes the word "veteran", "ancien combattant" or any abbreviation or derivation of those words, the letters patent of the corporation shall provide that at all times at least 95 per cent of the members of the corporation shall be composed of war veterans, their spouses or children, unless the name has been in continuous use for at least 20 years.

(5) In subsection (4), **"war veteran"** means a person who served in the armed forces of any country while that country was in a state of war. *("ancien combattant")*

"same-sex partner" [Repealed O. Reg. 301/05, s. 1(2).]

"spouse" means,

(a) a spouse as defined in section 1 of the *Family Law Act*, or

(b) either of two persons who live together in a conjugal relationship outside marriage. *("conjoint")*

O. Reg. 625/93, s. 3; 43/00, s. 1; 248/05, s. 2; 301/05, s. 1

4. The name of a corporation formed by the amalgamation of two or more corporations may be the same as the name of one of the amalgamating corporations, if the name is not a number name.

O. Reg. 625/93, s. 4

5. Unless the proposed corporate name has been in continuous use for at least twenty years before the date of filing the application, or unless the proposed corporate name has through use acquired a meaning that renders the name distinctive, a corporate name shall not be,

(a) too general;

(b) primarily or only a given name or surname used alone of an individual who is living or has died within thirty years preceding the date of filing an application for letters patent or supplementary letters containing the name;

(c) primarily or only a geographic name used alone.

6. (1) A corporate name shall not contain a word or expression, an element of which is the family name of a particular individual, who is living or who has died within the previous thirty years whether or not preceded by a given name or initials, unless the individual, his or her heir, executor, administrator, assigns or guardian consents in writing to the use of the name.

(2) Subsection (1) does not apply where the corporation that will use the proposed name is the successor or affiliate of another corporation that has, as an element of its name, the family name, if,

(a) the other corporation consents in writing to the use of the name; and

(b) where the proposed name would contravene clause 13(1)(a) of the Act, the other corporation undertakes in writing to dissolve itself or to change its name to a name that complies with clause 13(1)(a) of the Act within six months after the incorporation of the new corporation.

(3) Subsection (1) does not apply where,

(a) the required consent cannot be obtained; and

(b) the family name is of historic or patriotic significance and has a connection with the objects of the corporation.

7. A corporate name shall not contain any word or expression in any language that describes in a misleading manner the activities or services in association with which the corporate name is proposed to be used.

8. (1) Only letters from the Roman alphabet or Arabic numerals or a combination thereof, and punctuation marks and other marks set out in subsection (2), may form part of the name of a corporation.

(2) The following punctuation marks and other marks are permitted as part of a corporation name:

! “ ” << » # $ % & ’ ( ) * + , - . / \ : ; < = > ? [ ] < ^ « , ‘ ‘ ^ @

(3) A corporate name shall not consist only or primarily of a combination of marks set out in subsection (2) and at least the first three characters of the corporate name shall be letters from the Roman alphabet or Arabic numerals or a combination thereof.

O. Reg. 625/93, s. 5; 248/05, s. 3

9. (1) The name of a corporation shall not exceed 120 characters in length, including punctuation marks and spaces.

(2) The name of a corporation shall be set out in an application filed under the Act in block capital letters and with only one space between each word.

O. Reg. 248/05, s. 4

CAPITAL

10. Where preference shares of a class have attached thereto conditions, restrictions, limitations or prohibitions on the right to vote, the preferences, rights, conditions, restrictions, limitations or prohibitions attaching to that class of preference shares shall provide that the holders of that class are entitled to notice of any meeting of shareholders called for the purpose of authorizing the dissolution of the company or the sale of its undertaking or a substantial part thereof.

Objects

11. [Revoked O. Reg. 625/93, s. 6.]

12. (1) Where the proposed objects of a corporation include horse racing, the application for letters patent or supplementary letters patent shall be accompanied by the consent in writing of the Ontario Racing Commission.

(2) The proposed objects of a corporation shall not include dog racing, but may include the breeding of racing dogs.

Miscellaneous

13. Where the letters patent or supplementary letters patent of a corporation provide that the directors of the corporation shall be elected for a term of more than one year, the term shall be an integral number of years, not exceeding five.

14. The letters patent or supplementary letters patent of a private company may provide that an application for an order accepting the surrender of the charter of the company may be authorized at a general meeting of its shareholders duly called for that purpose by a majority of the votes cast at the meeting or by at least 50 per cent of the votes of all shareholders entitled to vote at the meeting.

15. (1) [Revoked O. Reg. 192/99, s. 1.]

(2) A notice of resolution requiring the voluntary winding up of a corporation required to be filed with the Minister under subsection 231(1) of the Act shall be signed manually by a director or officer of the corporation or by the liquidator.

(3) A notice required to be filed by a liquidator with the Minister under subsection 266(2) of the Act shall be signed manually by the liquidator.

(4) [Revoked O. Reg. 192/99, s. 1.]

(5) A notice signed by an agent or attorney on behalf of a director or officer of a corporation or a liquidator is not a notice signed manually by the director, officer or liquidator.

O. Reg. 192/99, s. 1

Form Of Documents

16. (1) All documents delivered to or filed with the Minister including all affidavits, applications, assurances, balance sheets, by-laws, consents, dissents, notices and statements shall be printed, typewritten or reproduced legibly, in a manner suitable for photographing on microfilm, on one side of good quality white paper that is,

(a) 210 millimetres by 297 millimetres with a margin of 30 millimetres on the left-hand side; or

(b) $8\frac{1}{2}$ inches by 11 inches, with a margin of $1\frac{1}{4}$ inches on the left-hand side.

(2) A document consisting of two or more pages shall have no backing or binding and shall be stapled in the upper left-hand corner and each page shall be numbered consecutively.

(3) Where a form is provided by the Minister, the form or a facsimile of the form reproduced on good quality white paper of the size set out in subsection (1) shall be used.

16.1 If a corporation has a seal, it may set out the seal on any form prescribed by this Regulation.

O. Reg. 189/99, s. 1

FORMS

17, 18 [Repealed O. Reg. 248/05, s. 5.]

19. (1) [Repealed O. Reg. 248/05, s. 6.]

(2) Where an application for supplementary letters patent is made under clause 34(1)(b) of the Act or under clause 131(1)(b) of the Act, the application shall contain a statement that the corporation is not insolvent within the meaning of subsection (4).

(3) Where the application is one to which section 35 of the Act applies, the application shall contain a statement that the corporation is not insolvent and, after the issue of the supplementary letters patent, will not be insolvent within the meaning of subsection (4).

(4) For the purposes of this section, a corporation is insolvent if its liabilities exceed the realizable value of its assets or if the corporation is unable to pay its debts as they become due.

O. Reg. 248/05, s. 6

20. [Revoked O. Reg. 402/95, s. 2.]

21. [Revoked O. Reg. 192/99, s. 2.]

22. [Repealed O. Reg. 248/05, s. 7.]

23. (1) An application for an order accepting the surrender of a charter of a corporation under subsection 319(1) of the Act or for an order terminating the existence of a corporation under section 320 of the Act shall be accompanied by,

(a) in the case of a company, a consent from the Corporations Tax Branch of the Ministry of Finance; and

(b) in the case of a company that is a reporting issuer under the *Securities Act*, a consent from the Ontario Securities Commission.

(2) [Repealed O. Reg. 248/05, s. 8(1).]

(3) Where a shareholder or member is unknown or the shareholder's or member's whereabouts is unknown and the corporation has delivered or conveyed the shareholder's or member's share of the property to the Public Guardian and Trustee to be held in trust for the shareholder or member or where a creditor is unknown or his, her or its whereabouts in unknown and the corporation has paid to the Public Guardian and Trustee an amount equal to the amount of the debt due to the creditor to be held in trust for the creditor, the application shall set out a statement to that effect.

O. Reg. 625/93, s. 7; 248/05, s. 8

24. The Minister may require that an application for an order to revive a dissolved corporation under subsection 317(10) of the Act be accompanied by,

(a) a statement in writing by the Public Guardian and Trustee that he or she has no objection to the revival of the corporation; and

(b) in the case of a company, a consent from the Corporations Tax Branch of the Ministry of Finance to the revival of the corporation.

O. Reg. 638/94, s. 2; 248/05, s. 9

25. [Repealed O. Reg. 248/05, s. 10.]

Continuation

26. [Repealed O. Reg. 248/05, s. 10.]

27. (1) [Repealed O. Reg. 248/05, s. 11.]

(2) Except in the case of continuance under the laws of another Canadian jurisdiction, the application for authorization to be continued as a corporation under the laws of another jurisdiction shall be accompanied by a legal opinion stating that the laws of the other jurisdiction provide that,

(a) the corporation's property continues as its property;

(b) the corporation continues to be liable for its obligations;

(c) an existing cause of action, claim or liability to prosecution is unaffected;

(d) the corporation may continue to prosecute a civil, criminal or administrative action or proceeding being prosecuted by or against it;

(e) a conviction, ruling, order or judgment against the corporation may be enforced against it and a ruling, order or judgment in favour of the corporation may be enforced by it.

O. Reg. 177/94, s. 3; 189/99, s. 2; 248/05, s. 11

27.1 [Repealed O. Reg. 248/05, s. 12.]

Insider Reporting

28. A report required to be filed by an insider under subsections 73(1) and (2) of the Act shall be prepared in accordance with Form 14.

29. A report of subsequent changes required to be filed by an insider under subsection 73(3) of the Act shall be prepared in accordance with Form 15.

Information Circular

30. (1) An information circular shall be prepared in accordance with Form 16.

(2) The information required by Form 16 shall be given as of a date specified in the circular, which date shall be a date occurring not more than thirty days before the date on which the information circular is first sent to any shareholders of the corporation.

(3) The information contained in an information circular shall be clearly presented and the statements contained therein shall be divided into groups according to subject-matter and each group of statements shall be preceded by an appropriate heading.

(4) The order of items set out in Form 16 need not be followed.

(5) Where practicable and appropriate, the information required by Form 16 shall be presented in tabular form.

(6) All amounts required by Form 16 shall be stated in figures.

(7) Information required to be set out under more than one item in Form 16 need only be set out under one of the items.

(8) No statement need be made in an information circular that an item is inapplicable and answers to items that are inapplicable may be omitted.

(9) Information that is not known by or is unavailable to the person on whose behalf an information circular is prepared and that is not reasonably within the power of that person to ascertain or obtain may be omitted from the information circular if a brief statement is made in the information circular indicating the reasons why the information is not known or is unavailable.

(10) An information circular prepared for a meeting need not contain any information contained in any other information circular, notice of meeting or form of proxy sent to a person whose proxies are being solicited for the same meeting if reference is made in the information circular to the document that contains the information.

31. Every person who sends or delivers to shareholders an information circular or proxy to which sections 83 to 89 of the Act apply in respect of a meeting of shareholders of a company shall forthwith file with the Ontario Securities Commission a copy of the information circular, proxy and all other material sent or delivered by the person in connection with the meeting.

Beneficial Ownership Of Shares

32. (1) For the purposes of section 73 of the Act, a report filed by a company that includes a statement of capital securities beneficially owned or deemed to be beneficially owned by a subsidiary of the company under clause 72(2)(c) of the Act or that includes a statement of changes in the subsidiary's beneficial ownership of capital securities shall be deemed to be a report filed by the subsidiary and the subsidiary need not file a separate report.

(2) For the purposes of section 73 of the Act, a report filed by an individual that includes a statement of capital securities beneficially owned or deemed to be beneficially owned under clause 72(2)(b) of the Act by a company controlled by the individual or by an affiliate, if any, of the controlled company or that includes a statement of changes in the beneficial ownership of the capital securities of the controlled company or affiliate shall be deemed to be a report filed by the controlled company or by the affiliate and the controlled company and the affiliate need not file a separate report.

SEARCHES

33. If a required fee is paid for a search requested in person, the Minister may produce for examination the original documents on file, if any, in which case no microfiche or microfiche copy of the documents will be supplied.

O. Reg. 177/94, s. 4; 192/99, s. 3

33.1 [Revoked O. Reg. 192/99, s. 3.]

34. [Revoked O. Reg. 192/99, s. 3.]

35. [Revoked O. Reg. 192/99, s. 3.]

36. [Revoked O. Reg. 192/99, s. 3.]

SCHEDULE FEES

[Revoked O. Reg. 192/99, s. 4.]

Forms 1–3

[Repealed O. Reg. 248/05, s. 13.]

Form 4

[Repealed O. Reg. 402/95, s. 3].

Forms 5–13.1

[Repealed O. Reg. 248/05, s. 13.]

Form 14 — Initial Report of Insider

Form 14

Corporations Act

INITIAL REPORT OF INSIDER

1. Name of the company of which the undersigned is an insider.

2. Full name of the undersigned.

3. Business or home address of the undersigned. Where the business address is given, the Director of the Ontario Securities Commission may request that the home address in full be furnished to the Commission.

4. Indicate in what capacity or capacities the undersigned qualifies as an insider.

5. Capital securities of the company,

   (a) beneficially owned, directly or indirectly, by the undersigned on ....
   day month year

   (b) over which the undersigned exercises control or direction ....
   day month year

DESIGNATION OF CAPITAL SECURITY	AMOUNT OR NO.	NATURE OF OWNERSHIP

6. Additional remarks.

   The undersigned hereby certifies that the information given in this report is true and complete in every respect.

....
DATE OF THE REPORT SIGNATURE

IT IS AN OFFENCE UNDER THE *CORPORATIONS ACT* TO FILE A FALSE OR MISLEADING REPORT.

Form 15 — Report of Insider on Changes in Ownership of, or Control or Direction Over, Capital Securities

Form 15

Corporations Act

REPORT OF INSIDER ON CHANGES IN OWNERSHIP OF, OR CONTROL OR DIRECTION OVER, CAPITAL SECURITIES

1. Name of company of which the undersigned is insider.

2. Full name of the undersigned.

3. Business or home address of the undersigned. Where the business address is given, the Director of the Ontario Securities Commission may request that the home address in full be furnished to the Commission.

4. Indicate in what capacity or capacities the undersigned qualifies as an insider.

5. Information given for calendar month of

6. Date of last Report filed.

7. Changes during the month in the undersigned's direct or indirect beneficial ownership, or control or direction over capital securities of the company.

Designation of Capital Security	Date of Transfer or Purchase or Sale Transaction	Amount or Number Purchased or Otherwise Acquired	Amount or Number Sold or Otherwise Disposed of	Price Per Capital Security at Which Sold or Purchased or Otherwise Acquired or Disposed of	Nature of Ownership or Control or Direction of Capital Security

8. As of the end of the month, list all capital securities of the company beneficially owned, directly or indirectly, by the undersigned and over which the undersigned exercised control or direction.

Designation of Capital Security	Balance at Date of Last Report Filed	Balance at End of Month	Nature of Ownership or Control or Direction over Capital Securities

9. Additional remarks.

The undersigned hereby certifies that the information given in this report is true and complete in every respect.

....

DATE OF THE REPORT SIGNATURE

IT IS AN OFFENCE UNDER THE *CORPORATIONS ACT* TO FILE A FALSE OR MISLEADING REPORT.

Form 16 — Information Circular

Form 16

Corporations Act

INFORMATION CIRCULAR

ITEM 1 REVOCABILITY OF PROXY

State whether the person giving the proxy has the power to revoke it. If any right of revocation is limited or is subject to compliance with any formal procedure, briefly describe the limitation or procedure.

ITEM 2 PERSONS MAKING THE SOLICITATION

(a) If solicitation is made by or on behalf of the management of the company, so state. Give the name of any director of the company who has informed the management in writing that he intends to oppose any action intended to be taken by the management and indicate the action that he intends to oppose.

(b) If a solicitation is made otherwise than by or on behalf of the management of the company, so state and give the name of the person by whom or on whose behalf it is made.

(c) If the solicitation is to be made otherwise than by mail, describe the method to be employed. If the solicitation is to be made by specially engaged employees or soliciting agents, state,

(i) the material features of any contract or arrangement for the solicitation and identify the parties to the contract or arrangement, and

(ii) the cost or anticipated cost thereof.

(d) State the name of the person by whom the cost of soliciting has been or will be borne, directly or indirectly.

ITEM 3 INTEREST OF CERTAIN PERSONS IN MATTERS TO BE ACTED UPON

Give brief particulars of any material interest, direct or indirect, by way of beneficial ownership of capital securities or otherwise of each of the following persons of any matter to be acted upon other than the election of directors or the appointment of auditors,

(a) if the solicitation is made by or on behalf of the management of the company, each person who has been a director or senior officer of the company at any time since the beginning of the last financial year of the company;

(b) if the solicitation is made otherwise than by or on behalf of the management of the company, each person on whose behalf, directly or indirectly, the solicitation is made;

(c) each proposed nominee for election as a director of the company;

(d) each associate or affiliate of any of the foregoing persons.

ITEM 4 EQUITY SHARES AND PRINCIPAL HOLDERS OF EQUITY SHARES

(a) State as to each class of equity shares of the company entitled to be voted at the meeting, the number of shares outstanding and the particulars of voting rights for each share of each such class.

(b) Give the record date as of which the shareholders entitled to vote at the meeting will be determined or particulars as to the closing of the share transfer register, as the case may be, and, if the right to vote is not limited to shareholders of record as of a specified record date, indicate the conditions under which shareholders are entitled to vote.

(c) If, to the knowledge of the directors or senior officers of the company, any person beneficially owns, directly or indirectly, or exercises control or direction over, equity shares carrying more than 10 per cent of the voting rights attached to any class of equity shares of the company, name each such person or company, state the approximate number of the shares beneficially owned, directly or indirectly, or over which control or direction is exercised, by each such person and the percentage of the class of outstanding equity shares of the company represented by the number of equity shares so owned, controlled or directed.

ITEM 5 ELECTION OF DIRECTORS

(a) If directors are to be elected, provide the following information, in tabular form to the extent practicable, for each person proposed to be nominated for election as a director and each other person whose term of office as a director will continue after the meeting:

(i) Name and identify as such each proposed director of the company and name each director of the company whose term of office will continue after the meeting.

(ii) State when the term of office for each director and proposed director will expire.

(iii) State whether the company has an executive committee of its Board of Directors or is required to have an audit committee and, if so, name those directors who are members of each such committee.

(iv) Where a director or officer has held more than one position in the company parent or subsidiary thereof, state only the first and last position held.

(v) State the present principal occupation, business or employment of each director and proposed director. Give the name and principal business of any person in which any such employment is carried on. Furnish similar information as to all of the principal occupations, businesses or employments of each proposed director within the five preceding years, unless he or she is now a director and was elected to his or her present term of office by a vote of shareholders at a meeting, the notice of which was accompanied by an information circular.

(vi) If the proposed director is or has been a director of the company, state the period or periods during which he has served as such.

(vii) State the number of shares of each class of equity shares of the company or of any subsidiary of the company, beneficially owned, directly or indirectly or over which control or direction is exercised by each proposed director.

(viii) If equity shares carrying more than 10 per cent of the voting rights attached to all equity shares of the company or of a subsidiary of the company are beneficially owned, directly or indirectly, or controlled or directed by any proposed director and his associates or affiliates, state the number of shares of each class of equity shares beneficially owned, directly or indirectly, or controlled or directed by the associates or affiliates, naming each associate or affiliate whose shareholdings are 10 per cent or more.

(b) If any proposed director is to be elected pursuant to any arrangement or understanding between the nominee and any other person except the directors and senior officers of the company acting solely in such capacity, name the other person and describe briefly the arrangement or understanding.

ITEM 6 DIRECTORS' AND OFFICERS' REMUNERATION

If action is to be taken with respect to:

— the election of directors,

— any bonus, profit sharing or other plan of remuneration, contract or arrangement in which any director or officer of the company will participate,

— any pension or retirement plan of the corporation in which any director or officer of the company will participate, or

— the granting to any director or officer of the company of any option or right to purchase any shares other than rights issued rateably to all shareholders or to all shareholders resident in Canada.

TABLE

REMUNERATION OF DIRECTORS AND OFFICERS

NATURE OF REMUNERATION

	From Office, Employment and Employer Contributions (Aggregate)	Cost Pension Benefits (Aggregate)	Other (Aggregate)
(I) DIRECTORS (Total Number: .....)			Last Completed Financial Year
(A) From issuer and wholly-owned subsidiaries:			Future Years
(B) From partially-owned subsidiaries (Provide Names):			
....			
....			
....			
TOTAL	$	$	$
(II) FIVE SENIOR OFFICERS:			Last Completed Financial Year
(A) From issuer and wholly-owned subsidiaries:			Future Years
(B) From partially-owned subsidiaries (Provide Names):			
....			
....			
....			
TOTAL	$	$	$

(III) OFFICERS WITH REMUNERATION OVER $50,000
(Total Number: .....)

			Last Completed Financial Year Future Years
(A) From issuer and wholly-owned subsidiaries:			
(B) From partially-owned subsidiaries (Provide Names):			
....			
....			
....			
TOTAL	$	$	$

(a) State in the form of the table shown above separately for each of the following the aggregate remuneration paid or payable by the company and its subsidiaries in respect of the company's last completed financial year to:—

(i) the directors of the company in their capacity as directors of the company and any of its subsidiaries,

(ii) the five senior officers of the company in receipt of the largest amounts of remuneration, in their capacity as officers or employees of the corporation and any of its subsidiaries, and

(iii) the officers of the company other than those in (ii) who received in their capacity as officers or employees of the corporation and any of its subsidiaries aggregate remuneration in excess of $50,000 in that year, provided that this disclosure shall not be required where the company has less than two such officers.

(b) State, where practicable, the estimated aggregate cost to the company and its subsidiaries in or in respect of the last completed financial year of all benefits proposed to be paid under any pension or retirement plan upon retirement at normal retirement age to persons to whom paragraph (a) applies, or, in the alternative, the estimated aggregate amount of all such benefits proposed to be paid upon retirement at normal retirement age to those persons.

(c) State, where practicable, the aggregate of all remuneration payments other than those of the type referred to in paragraphs (a) and (b) made in or in respect of the company's last completed financial year and, as a separate amount, proposed to be made in the future by the company or any of its subsidiaries pursuant to an existing plan to persons to whom paragraph (a) applies.

(d) State as to all options to purchase capital securities of the company or any of its subsidiaries that, since the commencement of the company's last financial year, were granted to directors or senior officers of the company, the following particulars:

(i) the description and number of capital securities included,

(ii) the dates of grant, the prices, expiration dates and other material provisions,

(iii) the consideration received for the granting thereof, and

(iv) where reasonably ascertainable, a summary showing the price range of the capital securities in the thirty-day period preceding the date of the grant and, where not reasonably ascertainable, a statement to that effect.

As to all options to purchase capital securities of the company or any of its subsidiaries that were exercised by directors or senior officers of the company since the commencement of the company's last financial year, state the following particulars:

(i) the description and number of capital securities purchased,

(ii) the purchase price, and

(iii) where reasonably ascertainable, a summary showing the price range of the capital securities in the thirty-day period preceding the date of purchase and, where not reasonably ascertainable, a statement to that effect.

ITEM 7 INDEBTEDNESS OF DIRECTORS AND SENIOR OFFICERS

In regard to,

(i) each director and each senior officer of the company,

(ii) each proposed nominee for election as a director of the company, and

(iii) each associate or affiliate of any such director, senior officer or proposed nominee, who is or has been indebted to the company or its subsidiaries at any time since the beginning of the last completed financial year of the company, state with respect to each such body corporate or subsidiary the largest aggregate amount of indebtedness outstanding at any time during the last completed financial year, the nature of the indebtedness and of the transaction in which it was incurred, the amount thereof presently outstanding, and the rate of interest paid or charged thereon, but no disclosure need be made of routine indebtedness.

1. In this item "routine indebtedness" means indebtedness described in any of the following clauses:

(a) if a company makes loans to employees generally whether or not in the ordinary course of business then loans shall be considered to be routine indebtedness if made on terms, including those as to interest or collateral, no more favourable to the borrower than the terms on which loans are made by the issuer to employees generally, but the amount at any time remaining unpaid under such loans to any one director, senior officer or proposed nominee together with his associates or affiliates that are treated as routine indebtedness under this clause (a) shall not exceed $25,000;

(b) whether or not the company makes loans in the ordinary course of business, a loan to a director or senior officer shall be considered to be routine indebtedness if,

(i) the borrower is a full-time employee of the company,

(ii) the loan is fully secured against the residence of the borrower, and

(iii) the amount of the loan does not exceed the annual salary of the borrower;

(c) where the company makes loans in the ordinary course of business, a loan shall be considered to be routine indebtedness if made to a person other than a full-time employee of the company, and if the loan,

(i) is made on substantially the same terms, including those as to interest rate and collateral, as were available when the loan was made to other customers of the company with comparable credit ratings, and

(ii) involves no more than usual risks of collectibility; and

(d) indebtedness arising by reason of purchases made on usual trade terms or of ordinary travel or expense advances, or for similar reasons shall be considered to be routine indebtedness if the repayment arrangements are in accord with usual commercial practice.

2. State the name and home address in full or, alternatively, solely the municipality of residence or postal address of each person whose indebtedness is described.

ITEM 8 INTEREST OF INSIDERS IN MATERIAL TRANSACTIONS

Where not previously disclosed in an information circular, describe briefly, and where practicable, state the approximate amount of any material interest, direct or indirect, of any insider of the company, any proposed nominee for election as a director of the company or any associate or affiliate of such insider or proposed nominee in any transaction since the commencement of the company's last financial year or in any proposed transaction which has materially affected or would materially affect the company or any of its subsidiaries.

ITEM 9 APPOINTMENT OF AUDITOR

If action is to be taken with respect to the appointment of an auditor, name the auditor of the company. If the auditor was first appointed within the last five years, state the date when the auditor was first appointed.

ITEM 10 MANAGEMENT CONTRACTS

Where management functions of the company or any subsidiary are to any substantial degree performed by a person other than the directors or senior officers of the company or subsidiary:

(i) give details of the agreement or arrangement under which the management functions are performed,including the name and address of any person who is a party to the agreement or arrangement or who is responsible for performing the management functions;

(ii) give the names and home addresses in full or, alternatively, solely the municipality of residence or postal address of the insiders of any person with which the company or subsidiary has any such agreement or arrangement and, if the following information is known to the directors or senior officers of the company, give the names and addresses of any person with which the company or subsidiary has any such agreement or arrangement if the person were a company;

(iii) with respect to any person named in answer to paragraph (i), state the amounts paid or payable by the company and its subsidiaries to the person since the commencement of the last financial year and give particulars; and

(iv) with respect to any person named in answer to paragraph (i) or (ii) and their associates or affiliates, give particulars of,

(a) any indebtedness of the person, associate or affiliate to the company or its subsidiaries that was outstanding, and

(b) any transaction or arrangement of the person, associate or affiliate with the company or subsidiary,

at any time since the commencement of the company's last financial year.

ITEM 11 PARTICULARS OF MATTERS TO BE ACTED UPON

If action is to be taken on any matter to be submitted to the meeting of shareholders, other than the approval of financial statements the substance of the matter, or related groups of matters, should be briefly described, except to the extent described pursuant to th foregoing items, in sufficient detail to permit shareholders to form a reasoned judgment concerning the matter. Without limiting th generality of the foregoing, such matters include alterations of share capital, charter amendments, property acquisitions or dispositions amalgamations, mergers or reorganizations. Where a reorganization or similar restructuring is involved, reference should be made to prospectus form or issuer bid form for guidance as to what is material.

If the matter is one that is not required to be submitted to a vote of shareholders, the reasons for submitting it to shareholders should b given and a statement should be made as to what action is intended to be taken by management in the event of a negative vote by th shareholders.

ONT. REG. 244/05 — FORMS

made under the *Corporations Act*

O. Reg. 244/05

1. Forms — The following forms shall be in the form approved by the Minister:

1. An application for incorporation of a company.

2. An application for incorporation of a corporation without share capital.

3. An application for supplementary letters patent.

4. An application for letters patent of amalgamation under subsection 113(4) of the Act.

5. An application for an order under subsection 304(5) of the Act rescinding an order made under a predecessor of subsection 304(3) of the Act permitting removal of records from the head office of the corporation.

6. An application for letters patent for continuation under subsection 312(1) of the Act.

7. An application for letters patent for continuation in Ontario of an extra-provincial corporation under subsection 312(3) of the Act.

8. An application for authorization to transfer to another jurisdiction under section 313 of the Act.

9. An application under section 313.1 of the Act for authorization to continue a corporation without share capital as a cooperative corporation under the *Co-operative Corporations Act.*

10. An application for an order to revive a dissolved corporation under subsection 317(10) of the Act.

11. An application for an order accepting the surrender of a charter of a corporation under subsection 319(1) of the Act.

12. An application for an order terminating the existence of a corporation under section 320 of the Act.

2. Signing — **(1)** An application for incorporation of a company and an application for incorporation of a corporation without share capital shall be signed by all of the applicants.

(2) An application for an order to revive a dissolved corporation under subsection 317(10) of the Act shall be signed by an interested person.

(3) All forms under this Regulation, other than the forms mentioned in subsection (1) and (2), shall be signed by two officers or directors of the applicant.

3. Filing — Two duplicate originals of a form under this Regulation shall be filed with the Minister.

CA Forms

Form 2 — Application for Incorporation of a Corporation Without Share Capital*

INSTRUCTIONS FOR COMPLETING APPLICATION FORM

FEE

$155.00 **BY MAIL** - Cheque or money order payable to the Minister of Finance.

IN PERSON - If you are delivering the application in person, you can also pay by cash, Visa, MasterCard, American Express or debit card. The address for personal delivery is 375 University Ave., 2nd floor, Toronto. Please note these documents are **not** checked while you wait, they take several weeks to process.

There will be a service charge payable for any cheque returned as non-negotiable by a bank or financial institution.

DOCUMENTS REQUIRED

1. Application for Incorporation of a Corporation without Share Capital, Form 2, as prescribed by the Ontario Regulations under the *Corporations Act*, completed in duplicate and bearing original signatures on both copies.
2. An original, Ontario-biased NUANS name search report for the proposed name of the corporation. The search report must be submitted with the application within 90 days of the production of the report.
3. A covering letter, setting out the name, address and telephone number of the person or firm to whom the Letters Patent, or any correspondence, should be mailed.
4. If the proposed name of the corporation is similar to the name of an existing corporation, organization, registered business or includes the name of a person, Central Production and Verification Services Branch may require consent to the use of the proposed name from the corporation, organization, business or individual.

APPEARANCE OF DOCUMENTS

The Application for Incorporation, and any supporting documents must be typewritten, or if completed by hand, printed in CAPITAL letters in black ink. All documents must be legible and suitable for microfilming.

Forms, extra pages and any supporting documents, must be printed on one side of good quality white bond paper 8 ½" by 11". Facsimile (Fax) applications, or supporting documents, cannot be accepted in lieu of original copies.

Pages are numbered 1 through 4; applications with missing pages cannot be accepted. If additional pages are required due to lack of space, they *should be numbered the same as the original page with the addition of letters of the alphabet to indicate sequence. For example, supplementary pages for the objects Item 4 on page 2, would be numbered 2A, 2B, etc. Do not attach schedules to the form. The last page should be the signing page.*

CORPORATE NAME

Prior to completing the form, the applicants should determine if the proposed corporate name is available for use. To do this they must obtain, from a name search company, an original Ontario-biased NUANS name search report for the name under which the corporation is to be incorporated.

Name search companies are listed in the Yellow Pages of the telephone directory under "Searchers of Records". The original, six-page name search report should be submitted with the application. The name set out in the application must be exactly the same as the name set out in the name search report. Reports received more than 90 days from the date they were produced will not be accepted and a new report will be required.

07109 (2011/05)

The Ministry will determine whether a proposed corporation name is acceptable. A name that is identical to another corporation or that contravenes the *Corporations Act or Regulations* will not be approved. If the proposed name is similar to that of an existing corporation, organization, business, or the name contains the name of an individual, the consent of the existing corporation, organization, business or the individual may be required. The name must reflect the objects of the corporation and should not be too general in character. It should contain a distinctive element and a descriptive element, for example:

HAPPY TIME *DAYCARE CENTRE*

(Distinctive) (*Descriptive*)

The name may include the word "Incorporated", "Incorporée" or "Corporation" or the corresponding abbreviations, but it is not required. A corporation without share capital cannot have "Limited", "Limitée" or the corresponding abbreviations as part of the name.

APPLICATION

Item 1 Set out the name of the corporation in block capital letters starting on the first line in the first box on the left with one letter per box and one empty box for a space. Punctuation marks are entered in separate boxes. Complete one line before starting in the first box of the next line. The name entered must be exactly the same as that on the name search report.

H	A	P	P	Y	T	I	M	E		R	E	C	R	E	A	T	I	O	N		A	N	D		D	A	Y	C	A
R	E		C	E	N	T	R	E		I	N	C	.																

Item 2 Set out the full address of the head office of the corporation, including the postal code. (If the address is a multi-office building, include the room or suite number). A post office box or *general delivery* is not acceptable for the address. The head office must be in Ontario.

Item 3 Set out the full name and address for service of all persons who are to be first directors of the corporation. The address should be in full, including postal code and room or suite number if applicable. A post office box or general delivery is not acceptable. *There must be at least three directors.* All of the directors must also be applicants under Item 6.

Item 4 Set out the objects of the corporation. The objects should be a concise statement of the ultimate purpose of the corporation. First describe the principal object, or primary undertaking of the corporation. Then set out the secondary objects, if any. It is advisable to keep the objects short but broad in nature. They should however, be sufficiently specific so as to avoid misinterpretation. You will find examples of these clauses in the Not-For-Profit Incorporator's Handbook (see the end of these instructions for information on obtaining this Handbook). Note that the objects of a corporation without share capital cannot contain a clause contrary to Section 126 of the *Corporations Act*, which states that a corporation shall be carried on without the purpose of gain for its members.

Item 5 In this item, you may include special provisions or ancillary powers of the corporation. For a non-profit **non-charitable** corporation the only special provision that **must be** set out is the "No Gain for Members" clause which is pre-printed on the form. However, you may include other provisions such as providing that on dissolution of the corporation and after payment of all debts and liabilities, any remaining property shall be distributed or disposed of to charities. For more information refer to the Not-for-Profit Incorporator's Handbook.

Ancillary powers are also listed under this item. There is usually no need to set out ancillary powers as all corporations without share capital automatically acquire ancillary or supplementary powers (Section 23(1)(a) to (p) and (s) to (v) of the *Corporations Act*) unless withheld in the Letters Patent or Supplementary Letters Patent.

Charities must include certain special provisions. For a list of the standard objects, special provisions and powers for **charities** contact Central Production and Verification Services Branch or the Office of the Public Guardian & Trustee website listed at the end of these instructions.

07109 (2011/05)

Item 6 Set out the full name, and the address for service of each of the applicants. All of the directors listed in Item 3 must be included as applicants.

EXECUTION

Both copies of the form must be signed by each of the applicants. The signatures must be original signatures. Photocopies will not be accepted.

CHARITABLE CORPORATIONS

To incorporate a charity you can use either pre-approved (standard) objects and special provisions or if none of the pre-approved objects accurately describe the objects of the organization you can draft your own objects (non-standard):

Pre-approved objects (standard)
The standard objects and special provisions are clauses that have been approved by the Office of the Public Guardian and Trustee. Applications for Incorporation using the pre-approved objects and special provisions should be sent directly to the Ministry of Government Services (the address is listed at the end of this form). As the Office of the Public Guardian and Trustee do not review these corporations, the only fee payable will be the incorporation fee. See the end of these instructions for information on obtaining a list of the pre-approved objects and special provisions. You cannot add extra objects or change the wording of the standard objects.

Objects that have not been pre-approved (non-standard)
If the corporation uses non-standard objects or special provisions they must be reviewed and approved by the Office of the Public Guardian & Trustee. There is a fee for this review, which must be paid, as well as the incorporation fee. The application, supporting documents and both fees should be sent to the Office of the Public Guardian and Trustee for review (the address is listed at the end of this form). The approval for a charity is not a guarantee that the Letters Patent will be issued. After the objects have been reviewed and approved by the Office of the Public Guardian and Trustee they will forward the application directly to the Central Production and Verification Services Branch. If the application and supporting documents are complete and comply with the *Corporations Act* the Letters Patent will be issued.

Not-for-Profit incorporation forms and the bulletin listing the pre-approved charitable objects are available from the Ministry of Government Services. The completed forms for not-for-profit corporations and charitable not-for-profit corporations that are using the standard objects should be sent, together with the name search, any supporting documents and incorporation fee, to:

Ministry of Government Services
Central Production and Verification Services Branch
393 University Ave, Suite 200
Toronto ON M5G 2M2
Tel: 416 314-8880 or in Ontario toll free 1 800 361-3223

Applications for charitable corporations that are not using the pre-approved objects should be filed together with the name search, any supporting documents, the incorporation fee and the fee for review, with the Office of the Public Guardian and Trustee:

Office of the Public Guardian & Trustee
Charitable Property Program
595 Bay Street, Suite 800
Toronto ON M5G 2M6
Tel: 416 326-1963 or in Ontario toll free 1 800 366-0335
Website: www.attorneygeneral.jus.gov.on.ca/english/family/pgt/charities/

NOT-FOR-PROFIT INCORPORATOR'S HANDBOOK

The Not-For-Profit Incorporator's Handbook contains general information as well as precedent clauses for objects and special provisions for both non-profit ***non-charitable*** corporations, and the pre-approved objects and provisions for non-profit ***charitable*** corporations.

The Handbook is available on the Office of the Public Guardian & Trustee website (see above).

07109 (2011/05)

INSTRUCTIONS

DROITS

155 $ **DÉPÔT PAR COURRIER** – Paiement par chèque ou mandat libellé à l'ordre du « Ministre des Finances ».

DÉPÔT EN PERSONNE – Si vous déposez la requête en personne, vous pouvez aussi payer les droits en argent comptant ou par carte Visa, MasterCard, American Express, ou par carte de débit. Adresse pour les dépôts en personne : 375, avenue University, 2ᵉ étage, Toronto. Toutefois, les documents ne seront pas traités immédiatement; le délai de traitement est de plusieurs semaines.

Des frais d'administration seront facturés pour tout chèque refusé par la banque ou l'institution financière.

DOCUMENTS À DÉPOSER

1. Requête en constitution d'une personne morale sans capital-actions, Formule 2, prescrite par les règlements de l'Ontario en application de la *Loi sur les personnes morales*. Le formulaire doit être rempli en double exemplaire et doit porter une signature originale sur chaque exemplaire.
2. L'original d'un rapport de recherche NUANS axé sur l'Ontario, qui permet de vérifier si la dénomination sociale proposée n'est pas déjà utilisée. Le rapport doit être soumis avec la requête dans les 90 jours suivant la production du rapport.
3. Lettre d'accompagnement indiquant le nom, l'adresse et le numéro de téléphone de la personne ou de l'entreprise à laquelle les Lettres patentes ou toute correspondance devraient être envoyées.
4. Si la dénomination sociale proposée est semblable à celle d'une personne morale ou d'une entreprise enregistrée existante ou si la dénomination renferme le nom d'un particulier, la Direction des services centraux de production et de vérification et des sûretés mobilières peut exiger de la part de l'entreprise ou de la personne intéressée un consentement autorisant l'utilisation du nom proposé par la future personne morale.

PRÉSENTATION DES DOCUMENTS

Dactylographier la requête et tout document à l'appui; si les documents sont remplis au stylo, écrire lisiblement en LETTRES MAJUSCULES, au stylo noir. Tous les documents doivent se prêter à la microphotographie.

La requête, les pages supplémentaires et les documents à l'appui doivent être remplis uniquement au recto d'un papier filigrané blanc de bonne qualité, de format 8 ½ po x 11 po. Les télécopies de requêtes ou de documents à l'appui ne seront pas acceptées.

La requête comporte 4 pages numérotées. S'il manque des pages, la requête sera rejetée. Si, faute d'espace, il faut insérer des pages supplémentaires, celles-ci doivent porter le même numéro que la page originale, suivi d'une lettre de l'alphabet pour en indiquer la séquence. Par exemple, des pages supplémentaires se rapportant à l'article 4 de la page 2 seront numérotées 2A, 2B, etc. Ne rien annexer à la fin du formulaire. La page des signatures doit rester la dernière page.

DÉNOMINATION SOCIALE

Avant de remplir la requête, les requérants doivent vérifier si la dénomination sociale proposée pour leur personne morale n'est pas déjà utilisée ailleurs. Pour ce faire, ils doivent demander l'original d'un rapport de recherche NUANS axé sur l'Ontario, auprès d'une maison de recherche de raisons sociales.

Les noms et adresses des maisons de recherche figurent dans les Pages jaunes de l'annuaire téléphonique, sous la rubrique « Titres et archives – Recherche » ou « Searchers of Records ». Il faut soumettre avec la requête l'original du rapport de recherche (6 pages). La dénomination sociale indiquée dans la requête doit être exactement la même que celle indiquée dans le rapport de recherche. Les rapports reçus plus de 90 jours après la date de leur production seront refusés, et les requérants devront obtenir un nouveau rapport de recherche.

07109 (2011/05)

Le ministère déterminera si la dénomination sociale proposée est acceptable. Il n'approuvera pas une dénomination qui est identique à celle d'une autre personne morale ou qui contrevient à la *Loi sur les personnes morales* ou aux règlements s'y rapportant. Si la dénomination sociale est semblable à celle d'une personne morale ou d'une entreprise enregistrée ou si elle renferme le nom d'un particulier, il se peut que l'on exige l'autorisation de l'entreprise ou de la personne intéressée.
La dénomination sociale doit refléter les objets de la personne morale et ne devrait pas être trop générale. Elle devrait comporter un élément descriptif et un élément distinctif. Par exemple :

L'OISEAU BLEU : GARDERIE FRANCOPHONE
(Distinctif) (Descriptif)

La dénomination sociale peut se terminer par les mots « Incorporated », « Incorporée », « Corporation » ou leur abréviation équivalente, mais cela n'est pas obligatoire. La dénomination d'une personne morale sans capital-actions ne peut pas comporter les mots « Limited », « Limitée » ou leur abréviation.

REQUÊTE

Section 1 Indiquer le nom complet de la personne morale en lettres majuscules, une lettre par case, en commençant à la première case de la première ligne de la grille. Laisser une case vide pour chaque espace entre les mots. Chaque signe de ponctuation occupe aussi une case distincte. Il faut remplir chaque ligne jusqu'au bout avant de commencer la suivante, même si un mot doit être coupé (voir exemple ci-dessous). Le nom entré ici doit être identique au nom indiqué sur le rapport de recherche NUANS.

L	'	O	I	S	E	A	U		B	L	E	U		:		G	A	R	D	E	R	I	E		F	R	A	N	C
O	P	H	O	N	E																								

Section 2 Indiquer l'adresse du siège social au complet, y compris le code postal. (Si le siège social est situé dans un édifice de bureaux, indiquer le numéro du bureau.) Une case postale ou une adresse *poste restante* ne sont pas acceptées. Le siège social doit être situé en Ontario.

Section 3 Inscrire le nom au complet de toutes les personnes appelées à devenir les premiers administrateurs de la personne morale. Inscrire, pour chacun, l'adresse complète du domicile élu, sans oublier le code postal et, au besoin, le numéro d'appartement. Une case postale ou une adresse *poste restante* ne sont pas acceptées.
Il doit y avoir au moins trois administrateurs. Tous les premiers administrateurs doivent aussi être des requérants et donc être inscrits à la section 6 de la requête.

Section 4 Indiquer les objets de la personne morale. Il s'agit ici d'énoncer brièvement le but ultime de la personne morale. Tout d'abord, présenter l'objet principal, c'est-à-dire le but premier de l'organisme. Ensuite, inscrire les objets secondaires, le cas échéant. Les objets décrits doivent être brefs et de portée générale. Toutefois, ils doivent être suffisamment précis pour éviter une interprétation erronée. Des exemples d'énoncés d'objets sont donnés dans le *Guide à l'intention des fondateurs de personnes morales sans but lucratif* (pour savoir comment obtenir le guide, voir les coordonnées à la fin des instructions présentes). À noter que les objets d'une personne morale sans capital-actions ne peuvent pas renfermer un énoncé qui enfreint l'article 126 de la *Loi sur les personnes morales*, qui stipule qu'une personne morale de cette nature doit exercer ses activités sans rechercher de gain pécuniaire pour ses membres.

Section 5 Indiquer ici les dispositions particulières ou les pouvoirs connexes de la personne morale. Si la personne morale sans but lucratif **n'est pas un organisme de bienfaisance**, la seule disposition **obligatoire** est celle concernant la non-recherche de gain pécuniaire, et cette disposition est déjà imprimée en haut de la page 3. Mais on peut, si l'on veut, inclure d'autres dispositions, comme celle qui, par exemple, prévoit qu'à la dissolution de la personne morale et après règlement de toutes ses dettes et autres obligations, les biens restants seront transmis, à titre gracieux ou non, à des organismes de bienfaisance. Pour d'autres renseignements à ce sujet, se reporter au *Guide à l'intention des fondateurs de personnes morales sans but lucratif.*

Les pouvoirs connexes sont aussi indiqués à cette section. Habituellement, il n'y pas lieu d'énoncer les pouvoirs connexes puisque les personnes morales sans capital-actions acquièrent d'office des pouvoirs connexes ou supplémentaires (aux termes des alinéas 23 (1) a) à p) et s) à v) de la *Loi sur les personnes morales*), à moins que ces pouvoirs soient suspendus dans les Lettres patentes ou les Lettres patentes supplémentaires.

Les **organismes de bienfaisance** doivent indiquer ici certaines dispositions particulières. Pour obtenir une liste d'énoncés d'objets standard et une liste des dispositions particulières et des pouvoirs pour un **organisme de bienfaisance**, contacter la Direction des services centraux de production et de vérification ou consulter le site Web du Bureau du Tuteur et curateur public (voir les coordonnées à ce sujet à la fin des instructions présentes).

07109 (2011/05)

Section 6 Inscrire le nom au complet des requérants et, pour chacun d'eux, l'adresse du domicile élu, autrement dit leur adresse personnelle. Tous les administrateurs déjà indiqués à la section 3 doivent être indiqués ici comme requérants.

SIGNATURE

Chacun des requérants doit signer les deux exemplaires de la requête. Les signatures doivent être originales. Toute requête portant des signatures photocopiées sera rejetée.

ORGANISMES DE BIENFAISANCE

Pour la constitution d'un organisme de bienfaisance, on peut utiliser des énoncés d'objets et des dispositions particulières préapprouvés (standard). Si aucun des objets standard ne décrit exactement les objets de l'organisme, on peut rédiger ses propres objets (non standard).

Objets préapprouvés (standard)

Les objets et les dispositions particulières standard sont des énoncés et des dispositions qui sont déjà approuvés par le Bureau du Tuteur et curateur public. Les requêtes indiquant des objets et des dispositions particulières standard doivent être envoyées directement au ministère des Services gouvernementaux (voir l'adresse à la fin des instructions présentes). Puisque ces requêtes ne sont pas examinées par le Bureau du Tuteur et curateur public, seuls les droits prescrits relatifs à la constitution sont prélevés. Voir à la fin des instructions présentes les contacts où l'on peut obtenir une liste d'objets et de dispositions particulières standard. On ne peut pas ajouter des objets à un énoncé d'objets standard ni en modifier le contenu.

Objets non préapprouvés (non standard)

Si l'organisme rédige ses propres objets ou ses propres dispositions particulières, ceux-ci doivent être soumis à l'examen et à l'approbation du Bureau du Tuteur et curateur public. Pour cet examen, des frais sont facturés. Il faut envoyer la requête, les documents à l'appui, les droits prescrits et les frais d'examen au Bureau du Tuteur et curateur public, qui examinera la demande (voir l'adresse à la fin des instructions présentes). L'approbation des objets et des dispositions par le Bureau ne garantit pas que les Lettres patentes seront délivrées. Une fois l'approbation donnée, le Bureau du Tuteur enverra la requête directement à la Direction des services centraux de production et de vérification. Si la requête et les documents à l'appui sont complets et conformes à la *Loi sur les personnes morales*, les Lettres patentes seront délivrées.

On peut se procurer le formulaire de la requête ainsi que la liste des objets standard (pour les organismes de bienfaisance) auprès du ministère des Services gouvernementaux. Les organismes de bienfaisance qui utilisent des objets standard et les organismes sans but lucratif autres que les organismes de bienfaisance doivent envoyer la requête et les documents à l'appui, y compris le rapport de recherche NUANS et les droits prescrits, à l'adresse suivante :

Ministère des Services gouvernementaux
Direction des services centraux de production et de vérification
393, av University, bureau 200
Toronto ON M5G 2M2
Tél. : 416 314-8880; ou sans frais en Ontario : 1 800 361-3223

Les organismes de bienfaisance qui n'utilisent pas les objets standard doivent envoyer la requête, les documents à l'appui, y compris le rapport de recherche NUANS, les droits prescrits et les frais d'examen au Bureau du Tuteur et curateur public, à l'adresse suivante :

Bureau du Tuteur et curateur public
Division des biens aux fins de bienfaisance
595, rue Bay, bureau 800
Toronto ON M5G 2M6
Tél. : 416 326-1963; ou sans frais en Ontario : 1 800 366-0335
Site Web : www.attorneygeneral.jus.gov.on.ca/french/family/pgt/charities

GUIDE À L'INTENTION DES FONDATEURS DE PERSONNES MORALES SANS BUT LUCRATIF

Le *Guide à l'intention des fondateurs de personnes morales sans but lucratif* donne des renseignements généraux, mais aussi des modèles d'objets et de dispositions particulières déjà utilisés pour les organismes sans but lucratif **autres que les organismes de bienfaisance** et les objets et les dispositions particulières préapprouvés pour les **organismes de bienfaisance**.

On peut obtenir le guide au site Web du Bureau du Tuteur et curateur public (voir ci-dessus, sous l'adresse du Bureau).

07109 (2011/05)

This space is for
Ministry Use Only
Espace réservé à l'usage
exclusif du ministère

Ontario Corporation Number
Numéro de la société en Ontario

Form 2
Corporations Act

Formule 2
Loi sur les personnes morales

APPLICATION FOR INCORPORATION OF A CORPORATION WITHOUT SHARE CAPITAL
REQUÊTE EN CONSTITUTION D'UNE PERSONNE MORALE SANS CAPITAL-ACTIONS

1. The name of the corporation is: (Set out in BLOCK CAPITAL LETTERS)
   Dénomination sociale de la société : (Écrire en LETTRES MAJUSCULES SEULEMENT)

2. The address of the head office of the corporation is:
   Adresse du siège social:

   (Street & Number or R.R. Number & if Multi-Office Building give Room No.)
   (Rue et numéro ou numéro de la R.R. et, s'il s'agit d'un édifice à bureaux, numéro du bureau)

   Ontario

   (Name of Municipality or Post Office)
   (Nom de la municipalité ou du bureau de poste)

   (Postal Code)
   (Code postal)

3. The applicants who are to be the first directors of the corporation are:
   Requérants appelés à devenir les premiers administrateurs de la personne morale :

First name, middle names and surname Prénom, autres Prénoms et nom de famille	Address for service, giving Street & No. or R.R. No., Municipality, Province, Country and Postal Code Domicile élu, y compris la rue et le numéro, le numéro de la R.R. ou le nom de la municipalité, la province, le pays et le code postal

07109 (2011/05)

Page 1 of/de 4

4. The objects for which the corporation is incorporated are:
Objets pour lesquels la personne morale est constituée:

07109 (2011/05)

Page 2 of/de 4

5. The special provisions are:
Dispositions particulières:

The corporation shall be carried on without the purpose of gain for its members, and any profits or other accretions to the corporation shall be used in promoting its objects.

La personne morale doit exercer ses activités sans rechercher de gain pécuniaire pour ses membres, et tout bénéfice ou tout accroissement de l'actif de la personne morale doit être utilisé pour promouvoir ses objets.

6. The names and address for service of the applicants:
Nom et prénoms et domicile élu des requérants :

First name, middle names and surname Prénom, autres Prénoms et nom de famille	Address for service, giving Street & No. or R.R. No., Municipality, Province, Country and Postal Code Domicile élu, y compris la rue et le numéro, le numéro de la R.R. ou le nom de la municipalité, la province, le pays et le code postal

This application is executed in duplicate.
La présente requête est faite en double exemplaire.

Signatures of applicants
Signature des requérants

Form 3 — Application for Supplementary Letters Patent*

INSTRUCTIONS FOR COMPLETING

A corporation may apply for Supplementary Letters Patent to change its name, to amend the objects or provisions set out in the original Letters Patent or an earlier Supplementary Letters Patent or any other matter set out in Section 131 of the *Corporations Act*. Applications should be mailed or delivered to the address listed above. ***Please note these documents are reviewed by the Central Production and Verification Services Branch (CPVSB) and take several weeks to process***.

FEE

$130 BY MAIL - Cheque or money order payable to the Minister of Finance.

IN PERSON - If you are delivering the application in person, you can also pay by cash, Visa, MasterCard, American Express or debit card. If the corporation is a charity there is an additional fee for review by the Public Guardian and Trustee.

(See below, "Charities")

There will be a service charge payable for any cheque returned as non-negotiable by a bank or financial institution.

DOCUMENTS REQUIRED

1. Application for Supplementary Letters Patent (Form 3, under the *Corporations Act*) completed in duplicate with original signatures on both copies.
2. A covering letter, setting out the name, address and telephone number of the person or firm to whom the Supplementary Letters Patent, or any correspondence, should be mailed.
3. If the application is being made to change the name of the corporation, an original, Ontario-biased NUANS name search report, dated not more than 90 days before the submission of the application, is required for the proposed name.
4. If the proposed name is similar to the name of a known corporation, association, partnership, individual, or business, or contains the family name of an individual the CPVSB may require consent in writing to the use of the proposed name from the individual or the existing entity. CPVSB may require that the existing entity dissolve or change its name before issuing the Supplementary Letters Patent.

APPEARANCE OF DOCUMENTS

The Application for Supplementary Letters Patent and any supporting documents must be typewritten, or if completed by hand, printed in BLOCK CAPITAL letters in black ink. All documents must be legible and suitable for microfilming.

Forms, extra pages and any supporting documents must be printed on one side of good quality white bond paper 8½" by 11". Pages are numbered 1 and 2; applications with missing pages cannot be accepted. If additional pages are required due to lack of space, they should be numbered the same as the original page with the addition of letters of the alphabet to indicate sequence. For example, supplementary pages for item 5 on page 1 would be numbered 1A, 1B, etc. Do not attach schedules to the form. The last page must be the signing page.

NAME CHANGE

For a name change request, the Central Production and Verification Services Branch requires an original Ontario-biased NUANS search for the proposed new name. The NUANS name search must be obtained from a private name search company and cannot be dated more than 90 days before the submission of the application. For example, applications submitted on November 28th could be accompanied by a NUANS name search report dated as early as August 30th, but not dated earlier. If the report is dated earlier, a new report will be required. Name search companies are listed in the Yellow Pages under the heading "Searchers of Records". The name set out in the application must be exactly the same as the name set out in the name search report.

07108 (2011/05)

The Ministry will not grant a name that is identical to another corporation or that contravenes the *Corporations Act* or Regulations. If the proposed name is similar to that of a known corporation, association, partnership, individual or business, or contains the family name of an individual, the consent in writing of the existing corporation, assocation, partnership, individual or business may be required or CPVSB may require that the existing entity dissolve or change its name. The name must reflect the objects of the corporation and should not be too general in character or imply the corporation is a business corporation. It should contain a distinctive element and a descriptive element, for example:

WESTWAY ROAD COMMUNITY CENTRE
(Distinctive) (Descriptive)

The name may include the word "Incorporated" or "Corporation" or the corresponding abbreviations, but it is not required. A corporation without share capital cannot have "Limited", "Limitée" or the corresponding abbreviations as part of the name.

In the case of an application for a name change, subsection 19(2) of Regulation 181 under the *Corporations Act* requires that the Application for Supplementary Letters Patent contain a statement that the corporation is not insolvent within the meaning of subsection 19 (4) of Regulation 181. This statement should be included under item 5 on the form. (see below, "item 5")

APPLICATION

ITEM 1 Set out the current name of the corporation in BLOCK CAPITAL letters starting on the first line in the first box on the left, with one letter per box and one empty box for a space. Punctuation marks are entered in separate boxes. Complete one line before starting in the first box of the next line. The name entered must be exactly the same as it appeared on the original Letters Patent or if there has been a name change, the most recent Supplementary Letters Patent changing the name.

H	A	P	P	Y		T	I	M	E		R	E	C	R	E	A	T	I	O	N		A	N	D		D	A	Y		C	A
R	E		C	E	N	T	R	E		I	N	C	.																		

ITEM 2 If this is an application for a name change, set out the new name in BLOCK CAPITAL letters starting on the first line in the first box on the left, with one letter per box and one empty box for a space. Punctuation marks are entered in separate boxes. Complete one line before starting in the first box of the next line. The name entered must be exactly the same as that on the NUANS name search report submitted with the application. **If the name is not to be changed, leave this item blank.**

ITEM 3 Set out the date of incorporation or amalgamation of the corporation.

ITEM 4 Set out the date the resolution authorizing the application for Supplementary Letters Patent was approved by the members/shareholders of the corporation.

ITEM 5 This item must contain an extract from the Resolution passed by the corporation setting out the change, or changes, which are to be made to the original, or previously amended, Letters Patent of the corporation. The application should clearly set out in what way the existing Letters Patent would be changed. For example:

RESOLVED that the corporation apply for Supplementary Letters Patent

To delete object 4(a) from the original Letters Patent which reads

(a) *To promote the sport of soccer for children aged 15 and under.*
and replace it with the following:
(a) *To promote the sport of soccer for children and adults.*

To change the objects of the corporation by adding the following paragraph after object (c),

(d) *To arrange soccer competitions and social functions for the members of the corporation.*

To change the name of the corporation from:
West Bay Youth Soccer Club
to
West Bay Soccer Club

07108 (2011/05)

If the application includes a proposed new name (as shown in item 5 on the previous page), the following statement must be included in item 5,

"The corporation is not insolvent within the meaning of subsection 19(4) of Ontario Regulation 181."

EXECUTION Both copies of the application must be signed by two officers, two directors or one officer and one director of the corporation. The signatures must be original signatures. Photocopies of signatures will not be accepted. Also set out the office of each person who signs (e.g.,

President, Director, Secretary). The current name of the corporation should be set out above the signatures. If the corporation has a seal it should be affixed to both copies of the form beside the signatures. Under the *Corporations Act* the corporation may have a seal but it is not required.

CHARITABLE CORPORATIONS

Applications for Supplementary Letters Patent to change the objects or provisions of a charitable corporation must be reviewed and approved by the office of the Public Guardian and Trustee. This would also apply to a not-for-profit, non-charitable corporation that was applying to change its objects to those of a charity.

If the applicant is filing an application for Supplementary Letters Patent only to change the corporate name, the application should be sent directly to Central Production and Verification Services Branch, as the Public Guardian and Trustee does not have to approve the new name.

The Public Guardian and Trustee charges a fee of $150.00 to review the new objects and/or provisions of the corporation. Both the fee for the Public Guardian and Trustee and the $130.00 filing fee for Central Production and Verification Services Branch should be sent with the completed application to the Office of the Public Guardian and Trustee. Both fees should be paid by a single cheque in the amount of $280.00 payable to the "Public Guardian and Trustee". After the application has been reviewed and approved as a charity the Public Guardian and Trustee will forward the forms, filing fee and name search (if applicable) to the Central Production and Verification Services Branch. If the application and supporting documents are complete and comply with the *Corporations Act*, the Supplementary Letters Patent will be issued.

Applications to amend the objects or provisions of a **charity** should be mailed to:

The Ministry of the Attorney General
Office of the Public Guardian and Trustee
Charitable Property Program
595 Bay Street, Suite 800
Toronto ON M5G 2M6

Phone: 416 326-1963 or toll free 1 800 366-0335
Internet: www/attorneygeneral.jus.gov.on.ca/english/family/pgt/charities

Applications for non-profit **non-charitable** corporations or charitable corporations that are only changing the name of the corporation, should be mailed in duplicate together with the name search (if applicable), any supporting documents and fee of $130.00, to:

Ministry of Government Services
Central Production and Verification Services Branch
393 University Avenue, Suite 200
Toronto ON M5G 2M2

375 University Avenue, 2nd Floor (In Person)

07108 (2011/05)

INSTRUCTIONS

Une personne morale peut présenter une requête pour obtenir des lettres patentes supplémentaires en vue de changer sa dénomination sociale, de modifier ses objets ou des dispositions de ses lettres patentes d'origine ou de ses lettres patentes supplémentaires antérieures, ou en vue d'autres mesures prévues à l'article 131 de la *Loi sur les personnes morales*. La requête peut être envoyée par courrier ou délivrée à l'adresse susmentionnée. ***La Direction des services centraux de production et de vérification (la Direction) devant examiner les documents, il faut compter un délai de plusieurs semaines pour leur traitement.***

DROITS

130 $ **DÉPÔT PAR COURRIER** – Paiement par chèque ou mandat libellé à l'ordre du Ministre des Finances.

DÉPÔT EN PERSONNE – Si vous déposez la requête en personne, vous pouvez aussi payer les droits en argent comptant ou par carte Visa, MasterCard, American Express ou par carte de débit.

Si la personne morale est un organisme de bienfaisance, des droits supplémentaires sont perçus pour l'examen des documents par le Bureau du Tuteur et curateur public (voir plus loin *Organismes de bienfaisance*).

Des frais d'administration seront facturés pour tout chèque refusé par la banque ou l'institution financière.

DOCUMENTS À DÉPOSER

1. Le formulaire Requête en vue d'obtenir des lettres patentes supplémentaires (Formule 3 requise aux termes de la *Loi sur les personnes morales*). Le formulaire doit être rempli en double exemplaire et doit porter une signature originale sur chaque exemplaire.
2. Une lettre d'accompagnement indiquant le nom, l'adresse et le numéro de téléphone de la personne ou de l'entité à laquelle les lettres patentes supplémentaires ou toute correspondance devraient être envoyées.
3. Seulement si la requête a pour but de modifier la dénomination sociale : un rapport de recherche NUANS axé sur l'Ontario portant sur la nouvelle dénomination proposée. Ce rapport ne peut pas porter une date antérieure de plus de 90 jours à la date du dépôt de la requête.
4. Si la nouvelle dénomination proposée est semblable au nom d'une personne morale, d'une entreprise enregistrée ou d'une personne physique connue, ou si elle renferme le nom de famille d'une personne, la Direction peut exiger de la part de la personne ou de l'entité existante un consentement écrit autorisant l'utilisation de la nouvelle dénomination proposée. La Direction peut aussi, avant de délivrer les lettres patentes supplémentaires, ordonner à l'entité existante de se dissoudre ou de changer sa dénomination sociale.

PRÉSENTATION DES DOCUMENTS

Dactylographier la requête et tout document à l'appui. Si les documents sont remplis au stylo, écrire lisiblement en LETTRES MAJUSCULES, au stylo noir. Tous les documents doivent se prêter à la microphotographie.

La requête, les pages supplémentaires et les documents à l'appui doivent être remplis uniquement au recto d'un papier filigrané blanc de bonne qualité, de format 8 ½ po x 11 po. La requête comporte 2 pages numérotées. S'il manque des pages, la requête sera rejetée. Si, faute d'espace, il faut insérer des pages supplémentaires, celles ci doivent porter le même numéro que la page originale, suivi d'une lettre de l'alphabet pour en indiquer la séquence. Par exemple, des pages supplémentaires se rapportant à l'article 5 de la page 1 seront numérotées 1A, 1B, etc. Ne pas joindre d'annexes (listes préimprimées). La page des signatures doit rester la dernière page du formulaire.

CHANGEMENT DE DÉNOMINATION SOCIALE

Si la requête a pour but de changer la dénomination sociale, la personne morale doit soumettre un rapport de recherche NUANS axé sur l'Ontario, qu'elle doit obtenir auprès d'une maison de recherche de raisons sociales. Elle doit remettre l'original du rapport. Le rapport ne peut pas porter une date antérieure de plus de 90 jours à la date du dépôt de la requête. Par exemple, une requête présentée le 28 novembre pourrait être accompagnée d'un rapport NUANS portant une date antérieure pouvant remonter jusqu'au 30 août précédent seulement. Si le rapport porte une date remontant à plus de 90 jours, la Direction exigera un nouveau rapport.

07108 (2011/05)

Les maisons de recherche figurent dans les Pages jaunes de l'annuaire téléphonique, sous la rubrique « Titres et archives – Recherche » ou « Searchers of Records ». La dénomination indiquée dans la requête doit être identique à celle indiquée dans le rapport de recherche. Le ministère n'autorisera pas une dénomination sociale qui est identique à celle d'une autre personne morale ou qui contrevient à la *Loi sur les personnes morales* ou aux règlements s'y rapportant. Si la dénomination proposée est semblable au nom d'une personne morale, d'une entreprise enregistrée ou d'une personne physique connue ou si elle renferme le nom de famille d'une personne, il se peut que l'on exige le consentement écrit de la personne ou de l'entité existante; il se peut aussi que la Direction demande à l'entité existante de se dissoudre ou de changer son nom. La dénomination sociale doit refléter les objets de la personne morale et ne doit pas être trop générale ou impliquer que la personne morale est une société par actions. Elle devrait comporter un élément distinctif et un élément descriptif. Par exemple :

L'OISEAU BLEU: GARDERIE FRANCOPHONE
(Distinctif) (Descriptif)

La dénomination sociale peut se terminer par les mots « Incorporated », Incorporée », « Corporation » ou leur abréviation équivalente, mais cela n'est pas obligatoire. La dénomination d'une personne morale sans capital-actions ne peut pas comporter les mots « Limited », « Limitée » ou leur abréviation.

Si la requête porte sur un changement de dénomination sociale, il faut, conformément au paragraphe 19(2) du Règlement 181 (*Loi sur les personnes morales*), inclure une déclaration indiquant que la personne morale n'est pas insolvable au sens du paragraphe 19(4) du Règlement 181. Cette déclaration doit être incluse sous l'article 5 de la requête (voir ci-dessous).

REQUÊTE

SECTION 1 Indiquer en lettres majuscules le nom actuel de la personne morale, une lettre par case, en commençant à la première case de la première ligne. Laisser une case vide pour chaque espace entre les mots. Chaque signe de ponctuation occupe aussi une case distincte. Il faut remplir chaque ligne jusqu'au bout avant de commencer la suivante. La dénomination entrée ici doit être identique à celle figurant aux lettres patentes d'origine ou, s'il y a eu un changement de nom, elle doit être identique au nom figurant aux lettres patentes supplémentaires les plus récentes.

L	'	O	I	S	E	A	U		B	L	E	U	:		G	A	R	D	E	R	I	E		F	R	A	N	C	O	P	H
O	N	E																													

SECTION 2 Si le but de la requête est un changement de nom, indiquer la nouvelle dénomination en lettres majuscules, une lettre par case, en commençant à la première case de la première ligne. Laisser une case vide pour chaque espace. Chaque signe de ponctuation occupe aussi une case distincte Il faut remplir chaque ligne jusqu'au bout avant de commencer la suivante. La dénomination entrée ici doit être identique à celle figurant au rapport de recherche NUANS. **Si la requête ne porte pas sur un changement de nom, sauter cette section.**

SECTION 3 Indiquer la date de la constitution ou de la fusion de la personne morale.

SECTION 4 Inscrire la date à laquelle la résolution autorisant la demande de lettres patentes supplémentaires a été ratifiée par les actionnaires ou les membres.

SECTION 5 Reproduire ici un extrait de la résolution que la personne morale a adoptée au sujet des modifications qui doivent être apportées aux lettres patentes originales ou précédemment modifiées. La requête doit énoncer clairement comment les lettres patentes existantes seront modifiées. Par exemple :

RÉSOLUTION : La personne morale demande des lettres patentes supplémentaires dans les buts suivants :

Supprimer dans les lettres patentes originales l'objet 4 a) :

a) *Promouvoir le soccer auprès des jeunes de moins de 15 ans*

et le remplacer par l'objet suivant :

a) *Promouvoir le soccer auprès des jeunes et des adultes*

Modifier les objets en ajoutant le paragraphe suivant après l'objet c) :

d) *Organiser des compétitions de soccer et des activités sociales pour les membres de la personne morale*

07108 (2011/05)

Changer la dénomination sociale :
Club de soccer Jeunes de Carleton
et la remplacer par :
Club de soccer de Carleton

De plus, si la requête vise un changement de la dénomination sociale (comme l'indique l'exemple donné à la page précédente), il faut ajouter ensuite, toujours à la section 5, la déclaration suivante :

« La personne morale n'est pas insolvable au sens du paragraphe 19(4) du Règlement 181 de l'Ontario. »

SIGNATURE Chacun des deux exemplaires de la requête doit être signé par deux dirigeants ou deux administrateurs, ou un dirigeant et un administrateur. Les signatures doivent être originales. Toute requête portant des signatures photocopiées sera rejetée. Ne pas oublier d'indiquer la fonction de chaque signataire ainsi que la dénomination sociale actuelle de la personne morale. Si celle ci a un sceau (non obligatoire en vertu de la Loi), on doit l'apposer près des signatures sur chaque exemplaire.

ORGANISMES DE BIENFAISANCE

Si le but de la requête (lettres patentes supplémentaires) est de modifier les objets ou des dispositions se rapportant à un organisme de bienfaisance, la requête doit être examinée et approuvée par le Bureau du Tuteur et curateur public. Cette mesure s'appliquerait aussi à une personne morale sans but lucratif autre qu'un organisme de bienfaisance qui présenterait une requête en vue de modifier ses objets pour les remplacer par des objets de bienfaisance.

Si le but de la requête est de changer la dénomination socialeq de l'organisme de bienfaisance, la requête doit être envoyée directement à la Direction des services centraux de production et de vérification, l'approbation du Bureau du Tuteur et curateur public n'étant pas requise dans ces cas.

Le Bureau du Tuteur et curateur public perçoit des droits de 150 $ pour l'examen de nouveaux objets ou de nouvelles dispositions. La requête envoyée au Bureau du Tuteur et curateur public doit être accompagnée d'un chèque de 280 $ (150 $ + droits de dépôt de 130 $) libellé au nom du Tuteur et curateur public. Une fois la requête examinée et approuvée, le Bureau du Tuteur et curateur public remettra la requête, le paiement des droits de dépôt et le rapport de recherche NUANS (le cas échéant) à la irection des services centraux de production et de vérification. Si la requête et les documents à l'appui sont complets et conformes à la *Loi sur les personnes morales*, la Direction délivrera les lettres patentes supplémentaires.

Les requêtes visant à modifier les objets ou des dispositions se rapportant à un **organisme de bienfaisance** doivent être envoyées à l'adresse suivante :

Ministère du Procureur général
Bureau du Tuteur et curateur public
Division des biens aux fins de bienfaisance
595, rue Bay, bureau 800
Toronto ON M5G 2M6

Téléphone : 416 326-1963, ou sans frais : 1 800 366-0335
Internet : www.attotneygeneral.jus.gov.on.ca/french/family/pgt/charities/

Les requêtes se rapportant à des personnes morales sans but lucratif **autres que des organismes de bienfaisance** ou à des organismes de bienfaisance qui changent seulement leur dénomination sociale, doivent être envoyées, accompagnées d'un rapport de recherche NUANS (s'il y a lieu), des documents nécessaires et du paiement de 130 $ (droits de dépôt), à l'adresse suivante :

Ministère des Services gouvernementaux
Direction des services centraux de production et de vérification
393, avenue University, bureau 200
Toronto ON M5G 2M2

375, avenue University, 2e étage (dépôt en personne)

07108 (2011/05)

For Ministry Use Only
À l'usage exclusif du ministère

Ontario Corporation Number
Numéro de la société en Ontario

Form 3
Corporations Act

Formule 3
Loi sur les personnes morales

APPLICATION FOR SUPPLEMENTARY LETTERS PATENT
REQUÊTE EN VUE D'OBTENIR DES LETTRES PATENTES SUPPLÉMENTAIRES

1. Name of the applicant corporation: (Set out in BLOCK CAPITAL LETTERS)
   Dénomination sociale de la personne morale : (écrire en LETTRES MAJUSCULES SEULEMENT)

2. The name of the corporation is changed to (if applicable): (Set out in BLOCK CAPITAL LETTERS)
   La dénomination sociale de la personne morale devient (le cas échéant) : (écrire en LETTRES MAJUSCULES SEULEMENT)

3. Date of incorporation/amalgamation:
   Date de la constitution ou de la fusion
   Year/Année Month/Mois Day/Jour

4. The resolution authorizing this application was confirmed by the shareholders/members of the corporation on:
   La résolution autorisant la présente requête a été ratifiée par les actionnaires ou membres de la personne morale le :
   Year/Année Month/Mois Day/Jour

   under section 34 or 131 of the *Corporations Act*.
   aux termes de l'article 34 ou 131 de la *Loi sur les personnes morales*.

5. The corporation applies for the issue of supplementary letters patent to provide as follows:
   La personne morale demande la délivrance de lettres patentes supplémentaires qui prévoient ce qui suit :

07108 (2011/05) Page 1 of/de 2

This application is executed in duplicate
La présente requête est faite en double exemplaire.

Current Name of Corporation
Dénomination sociale actuelle de la personne morale

By
Par :

Signature Signature	Description of Office Fonction
Signature Signature	Description of Office Fonction

07108 (2011/05)

Page 2 of/de 2

Corporations Information Act

R.S.O. 1990, c. C.39, as am. S.O. 1994, c. 17, ss. 33–43 [s. 36 Cannot be applied.]; 1994, c. 27, s. 79 [s. 79(2) as it enacts s. 7.2 repealed 2004, c. 19, s. 11(3).]; 1995, c. 3 [s. 2(2) Cannot be applied.]; 1998, c. 18, Sched. E, ss. 83–85; 1999, c. 12, Sched. F, s. 23; 2001, c. 9, Sched. D, ss. 13, 14; 2004, c. 16, Sched. D, s. 1, Table (Fr.); 2004, c. 19, s. 11 [s. 11(1), (2) Cannot be applied.]; 2007, c. 11, Sched. B, s. 1; 2011, c. 1, Sched. 5, s. 3.

1. Definitions — In this Act,

"business" includes non-profit activities;

"corporation" means any corporation with or without share capital wherever or however incorporated and includes an extra-provincial corporation;

"court" means the Superior Court of Justice presided over by a judge designated by the Chief Justice of Ontario to hear applications under this Act;

"extra-provincial corporation" means a corporation, with or without share capital, incorporated or continued otherwise than by or under the authority of an Act of the Legislature;

"Minister" means the Minister of Government Services or such other member of the Executive Council to whom the administration of this Act may be assigned;

"Ministry" means the Ministry of the Minister;

"prescribed" means prescribed by the regulations;

"regulations" means the regulations made under this Act;

"resident Canadian" means an individual who is a Canadian citizen or has been lawfully admitted to Canada for permanent residence and who is ordinarily resident in Canada.

1994, c. 27, s. 79(1); 2001, c. 9, Sched. D, ss. 13, 14; 2007, c. 11, Sched. B, s. 1(1)

2. (1) Initial return — Every corporation other than an extra-provincial corporation or a corporation of a class exempted by the regulations shall file with the Minister an initial return setting out the prescribed information as of the date of filing.

(2) Idem — The initial return shall be filed within sixty days after the date of incorporation, amalgamation or continuation of the corporation.

1994, c. 17, s. 33

3. (1) Initial return, extra-provincial corporation — Every extra-provincial corporation, other than a corporation of a class exempted by the regulations, that begins to carry on business in Ontario shall file with the Minister an initial return setting out the prescribed information as of the date of filing.

(2) Idem — The initial return shall be filed within sixty days after the date the corporation begins to carry on business in Ontario.

1994, c. 17, s. 34

3.1 (1) Annual return — Every corporation, other than a corporation of a class exempted by the regulations, shall file a return each year with the Minister in accordance with the regulations, by delivering it to the prescribed person or entity in the prescribed manner and within the prescribed time.

(2) Receipt — If the person or entity prescribed for the purposes of subsection (1) is not the Minister, the person or entity shall receive the return on behalf of the Minister.

(3) Exception — If the person or entity prescribed for the purposes of subsection (1) is not the Minister, a corporation that delivers the return to the Minister shall be deemed to comply with the requirement in subsection (1) to deliver the return to the prescribed person or entity, if the prescribed circumstances exist and the prescribed requirements are met.

(4) Contents — The return must set out the prescribed information as of the prescribed date.

(5) Form — The return must be in a form approved by the Minister.

(6) Incomplete return — The Minister may accept a return from a corporation for filing even if the return does not comply with the information requirements of subsection (4), but the corporation shall not be considered to have complied with this section until it has satisfied all of the requirements of this section.

(7)-(11) [Repealed 2007, c. 11, Sched. B, s. 1(2).]

1994, c. 17, s. 35; 1995, c. 3, s. 1; 1999, c. 12, Sched. F, s. 23; 2007, c. 11, Sched. B, s. 1(2)

4. (1) Notice of change — Every corporation shall file with the Minister a notice of change for every change in the information filed under this Act, within 15 days after the day the change takes place.

(2) Same — The notice of change shall set out the prescribed information and shall specify any changes that have taken place and the dates of the changes.

(3) Exception — It is not necessary to file a notice of change in respect of a director's retirement and subsequent re-election for the next term of office.

(4) Same — A corporation incorporated under the laws of Ontario that changes only its name does not need to file a notice of change.

2007, c. 11, Sched. B, s. 1(3)

5. (1) Verification — Every return filed under subsection 2(1) or 3(1) or section 3.1 and every notice filed under subsection 4(1) or (2) shall be verified by the certificate of an officer or director of the corporation or other individual having knowledge of the affairs of the corporation.

(2) Record and examination — A corporation shall maintain an up-to-date paper or electronic record of the prescribed information set out in returns and notices that it has filed under this Act and make the record available for examination by any shareholder, member, director, officer or creditor of the corporation during its normal business hours at its registered office or principal place of business in Ontario.

(3) Idem — A person examining a document under subsection (2) may make copies of or take extracts from it.

1994, c. 17, s. 37; 1995, c. 3, s. 3(2)

6. (1) Special filing — The Minister may at any time by written notice require any corporation other than a corporation of a class exempted by the regulations to make a special filing for the purposes of establishing or maintaining an electronic record database under section 9.

(2) Idem — Upon receipt of the notice, a corporation shall make the special filing in the prescribed form and manner within the prescribed time.

(3) Idem — The special filing shall contain the information required by subsection 2(1) or 3(1), whichever is applicable.

7. Further return or notice — The Minister may, at any time by request in writing sent by prepaid mail or otherwise, require any corporation to file within 30 days after the date of the request a return or notice for any or all of the matters contained in section 2, 3, 3.1, 4 or 6.

1994, c. 17, s. 38

7.1 (1) Delivery of notices, etc. — A notice or other document that is required or permitted by this Act to be sent by the Minister may be sent by ordinary mail or by any other method, including registered mail, certified mail or prepaid courier, if there is a record by the person who has delivered it that the notice or document has been sent.

(2) Same — A notice or other document referred to in subsection (1) may be sent by telephone transmission of a facsimile of the notice or other document or by another form of electronic transmission where there is a record that the request has been sent.

(3) Deemed delivery — A notice or other document sent by mail under subsection (1) shall be deemed to be received by the intended recipient on the earlier of,

(a) the day the intended recipient actually receives it; or

(b) the fifth business day after it is mailed.

(4) Same — A notice or other document sent by a method referred to in subsection (2) shall be deemed to be received by the intended recipient on the earlier of,

(a) the day the intended recipient actually receives it; or

(b) the first business day after the day the transmission is sent by the Minister.

1994, c. 27, s. 79(2)

7.2 [Repealed 2004, c. 19, s. 11(3).]

8. (1) Record — The Minister shall enter into a record the information from every return and notice received under this Act.

(2) Effective date — The effective date of filing for every notice and return received under this Act shall be the date determined under the regulations.

1994, c. 17, s. 39; 1995, c. 3, s. 4; 2007, c. 11, Sched. B, s. 1(4)

9. (1) Form of records — Records required by this Act to be prepared and maintained by the Minister may be in bound or loose-leaf or electronic form or in a photographic film form or may be entered or recorded by any system of mechanical or electronic data processing or by any other information storage device that is capable of reproducing any required information in an accurate and intelligible form within a reasonable time.

(2) Idem — If records maintained by the Minister are prepared and maintained otherwise than in written or other form, the Minister shall furnish any copy required to be furnished under subsection 10(2) in an intelligible written form.

(3) Idem — A report reproduced from records prepared and maintained otherwise than in written form that purports to be certified by the Minister is, without proof of the Minister's office or signature, admissible in evidence.

(4) Copies — The Minister is not required to produce the original of a document if a copy is furnished in compliance with subsection (2).

(5) Idem — For the purposes of this section, a document is a copy of an original if it contains all the information contained in the original.

1994, c. 27, s. 79(3)–(5)

10. (1) Examination by public — Upon payment of the required fee, any person is entitled to examine the record of any document filed under section 2, 3, 3.1, 4, 6 or 7 or any predecessor of those sections, and to make extracts from it.

(2) Copies — Upon payment of the required fee, the Minister shall furnish any person with a certified copy of the contents of any document filed under section 2, 3, 3.1, 4, 6 or 7 or any predecessor of those sections.

1998, c. 18, Sched. E, s. 83

11. (1) Information required by Minister — The Minister may at any time by notice in writing, given by prepaid mail or otherwise, require any corporation to file within the time specified in the notice a return upon any subject connected with its affairs and relevant to the administration or enforcement of this Act, the *Business Corporations Act*, the *Corporations Act* or the *Co-operative Corporations Act*.

(2) Confidentiality — The Minister or any employee of the Ministry shall not disclose any information contained in a return made under subsection (1) except where the disclosure is necessary for the administration or enforcement of this Act, the *Business Corporations Act*, the *Corporations Act* or the *Co-operative Corporations Act* or where disclosure is required by a court for the purposes of any proceeding.

12. Delegation by Minister — The Minister may delegate in writing any of his or her duties or powers under this Act to any public servant employed under Part III of the *Public Service of Ontario Act, 2006*.

2011, c. 1, Sched. 5, s. 3(1)

13. (1) Offence — Every person who makes a statement in any document, material, evidence or information submitted or required by or for the purposes of this Act that, at the time and in the light of the circumstances under which it is made, is false or misleading with respect to any material fact or that omits to state any material fact, the omission of which makes the statement false or misleading, is guilty of an offence and on conviction is liable to a fine of not more than $2,000 or to imprisonment for a term of not more than one year, or to both, or, if such person is a corporation, to a fine of not more than $25,000.

(2) Knowledge as element of offence — No person is guilty of an offence under subsection (1) if the person did not know the statement was false or misleading and, in the exercise of reasonable diligence, could not have known that the statement was false or misleading.

(3) Responsibility of directors and officers — Where a corporation is guilty of an offence under subsection (1), every director or officer of such corporation who authorized, permitted or acquiesced in such offence is also guilty of an offence and, on conviction, is liable to a fine of not more than $2,000 or to imprisonment for a term of not more than one year, or to both.

14. (1) General offence — Every person who,

(a) contravenes this Act or the regulations; or

(b) fails to observe or comply with an order, direction, or other requirement made under this Act or the regulations,

is, except where such conduct constitutes an offence under section 13, guilty of an offence and on conviction is liable to a fine of not more than $2,000 or, if such person is a corporation, to a fine of not more than $25,000.

(2) Responsibility of directors and officers — Where a corporation is guilty of an offence under subsection (1), every director or officer of the corporation, and, where the corporation is an extra-provincial corporation, every person acting as his or her representative in Ontario, who authorized, permitted or acquiesced in such offence is also guilty of an offence and on conviction is liable to a fine of not more than $2,000.

15. (1) Consent to prosecute — No proceeding under section 13 or 14 shall be commenced except with the consent of or under the direction of the Minister.

(2) Limitation — No proceeding under section 13 or 14 shall be commenced more than two years after the facts upon which the proceeding is based first came to the knowledge of the Minister as certified by him or her.

16. Order for compliance — Where it appears to the Minister or to any shareholder, member, creditor, director or officer of the corporation that the corporation has not complied with any provision of this Act or the regulations or any order, direction or other requirement made under this Act or the regulations, despite the imposition of any penalty in respect of such non-compliance and in addition to any other rights he or she may have, he or she may apply to the court for an order directing the corporation or any director or officer or employee, as the case may be, to comply with such provision, order, direction or other requirement or for an order restraining such person from contravening such provision, order, direction or requirement and upon such application the court may make such order, or such other order as the court thinks fit.

17. Late filing fee — A corporation that files a return or notice after the time set out in this Act or the regulations shall pay the prescribed late filing fee.

1994, c. 17, s. 40

18. (1) Ability to sue — A corporation that is in default of a requirement under this Act to file a return or notice or that has unpaid fees or penalties is not capable of maintaining a proceeding in a court in Ontario in respect of the business carried on by the corporation except with leave of the court.

(2) Idem — The court shall grant leave if the court is satisfied that,

(a) the failure to file the return or notice or pay the fees or penalties was inadvertent;

(b) there is no evidence that the public has been deceived or misled; and

(c) at the time of the application to the court, the corporation has filed all returns and notices required by this Act and has no unpaid fees or penalties.

(3) Contracts valid — No contract is void or voidable by reason only that it was entered into by a corporation that was in contravention of this Act or the regulations at the time the contract was made.

1994, c. 17, s. 41

19. Certificate of Minister — The Minister may issue a certificate certifying,

(a) as to the filing or non-filing of any document or material required or permitted to be filed under this Act;

(b) as to the time when the facts upon which proceedings are based first came to the knowledge of the Minister;

(c) that a person named in the certificate on the date or during the period specified in the certificate is shown on the records of the Ministry as a director, officer, manager or attorney for service of the corporation named in the certificate;

(d) that information set out in the certificate has been filed under this Act and is contained in the records of the Ministry; or

(e) information relating to the corporation based on the records of the Ministry.

2004, c. 19, s. 11(4)

20. (1) Execution of certificate of Minister — Where this Act requires or authorizes the Minister to issue a certificate or certify any fact, the certificate shall be issued under the seal of the Minister and shall be signed by him or her or by such officer of the Ministry as is designated by the regulations.

(2) Certificates as evidence — Any certificate purporting to be under the seal of the Minister and signed by a person authorized by or under subsection (1), or any certified copy, shall be received in evidence in any prosecution or other proceeding as proof, in the absence of evidence to the contrary, of the facts so certified without personal appearance to prove the seal, the signature or the official position of the person appearing to have signed the certificate.

21. Duty of Minister — The Minister may accept the information contained in any return or notice filed under this Act without making any inquiry as to its completeness or accuracy.

1994, c. 17, s. 42

21.1 Powers of Minister — (0.1) Minister's regulations — The Minister may make regulations,

(a) respecting the form, period of retention and destruction of any document required to be filed under this Act or a predecessor of this Act;

(b) prescribing the manner in which special filings under section 6 shall be made;

(c) prescribing the time within which special filings under section 6 shall be made;

(d) prescribing alternative methods of filing documents under this Act and governing the filing of documents by each method, including the manner of acceptance of documents and the determination of the date of receipt;

(e) for the purpose of subsection 8(2), governing the effective date of filing for every notice and return received under this Act;

(f) designating officers of the Ministry who may sign certificates for the purposes of section 20.

(1) **Fees** — The Minister may by order require the payment of fees for search reports and copies of documents and information, or other services under this Act and may approve the amount of those fees.

1998, c. 18, Sched. E, s. 84; 2011, c. 1, Sched. 5, s. 3(2)

21.2 (1) **Corporations information agreement** — The Minister may enter into an agreement with a prescribed person or entity, providing for the person or entity to receive returns required to be filed under section 3.1 and to transmit the information in every return to the Minister for the purposes of recording under section 8, in accordance with the terms and conditions of the agreement.

(2) **Supplemental agreements authorized** — The Minister may enter into one or more agreements amending an agreement entered into under this section.

(3) **Payment of fees under agreement** — All fees and other amounts payable by Ontario pursuant to an agreement entered into under this section are a charge upon and payable out of the Consolidated Revenue Fund.

2007, c. 11, Sched. B, s. 1(5)

21.3 **Director's regulations** — The Director appointed under section 278 of the *Business Corporations Act* may make regulations prescribing forms and providing for their use.

2011, c. 1, Sched. 5, s. 3(3)

22. **Regulations** — (1) The Lieutenant Governor in Council may make regulations,

(a) exempting any class or classes of corporations from filing returns or notices under section 2, 3, 3.1 or 6;

(b) [Repealed 1998, c. 18, Sched. E, s. 85(1).]

(c) [Repealed 2011, c. 1, Sched. 5, s. 3(4).]

(d) [Repealed 2011, c. 1, Sched. 5, s. 3(4).]

(e) prescribing the information required by subsections 2(1) and 3(1) and section 3.1;

(f) [Repealed 1998, c. 18, Sched. E, s. 85(3).]

(g) [Repealed 2011, c. 1, Sched. 5, s. 3(4).]

(h) [Repealed 2011, c. 1, Sched. 5, s. 3(4).]

(i) [Repealed 2011, c. 1, Sched. 5, s. 3(4).]

(i.1) [Repealed 2004, c. 19, s. 11(6).]

(i.2) [Repealed 2004, c. 19, s. 11(6).]

(i.3) [Repealed 2011, c. 1, Sched. 5, s. 3(4).]

(j) prescribing anything referred to in this Act as prescribed for which a specific power is not otherwise provided.

(2) **General or particular** — A regulation made under subsection (1) that applies for the purposes of section 3.1 may be general or particular and may contain different rules, requirements and provisions for different classes of corporations.

1994, c. 17, s. 43; 1994, c. 27, s. 79(6); 1998, c. 18, Sched. E, s. 85; 2004, c. 19, s. 11(5), (6); 2007, c. 11, Sched. B, s. 1(6), (7); 2011, c. 1, Sched. 5, s. 3(4), (5)

ONT. REG. 182 — GENERAL

made under the *Corporations Information Act*

R.R.O. 1990, Reg. 182, as am. O. Reg. 12/91; 123/91; 255/92; 256/92; 597/92; 628/93; 178/94; 59/95; 311/96, ss. 1, 2 (Fr.), 3, 4; 564/98; 193/99; 575/99; 249/05; 49/08; 262/08; 12/09; CTR 15 JA 09 – 1.

1. (1) An initial return, notice of change and a return or notice required under section 7 of the Act shall be in a form provided or approved by the Minister.

(2) The information required to be set out in a return or notice mentioned in subsection (1) shall be typewritten or printed legibly in capital letters in dark ink.

O. Reg. 12/91, s. 1; 59/95, s. 1

1.1 (1) An initial return under subsection 2(1) of the Act shall set out the following information in respect of a corporation:

1. The name of the corporation.

2. The Ontario corporation number of the corporation.

3. The date of its incorporation or amalgamation, whichever is the most recent.

4. The names and addresses for service of the corporation's directors, including municipality, street and number, if any, and postal code.

5. The date on which each director became a director and, where applicable, the date on which a director ceased to be a director.

6. If the corporation is a corporation with share capital, a statement as to whether each director is or is not a resident Canadian.

7. The names and addresses for service, including municipality, street and number, if any, and postal code, of the corporation's five most senior officers.

8. The date on which each person referred to in paragraph 7 became a senior officer, and, where applicable, the date on which a person ceased to be a senior officer.

9. The address of the corporation's head or registered office, including municipality, street and number, if any, and postal code.

10. [Revoked O. Reg. 564/98, s. 1(2).]

11. [Revoked O. Reg. 59/95, s. 2.]

12. Whether the language of preference for communication with the corporation is English or French.

(2) For the purposes of paragraph 3 of subsection (1), the date of incorporation of a corporation that has been continued in Ontario from another jurisdiction is the date of its incorporation in its original jurisdiction.

(3) An initial return under subsection 2(1) of the Act may set out a mailing address of the corporation.

O. Reg. 12/91, s. 1; 255/92, s. 1; 178/94, s. 1; 59/95, s. 2; 564/98, s. 1; 262/08, s. 1; CTR 15 JA 09 – 1

2. An initial return under subsection 3(1) of the Act shall set out the following information in respect of an extra-provincial corporation:

1. The name of the corporation.
2. The Ontario corporation number of the corporation.
3. The date of its incorporation or amalgamation, whichever is the most recent.
4. The name of the jurisdiction in which the corporation was incorporated, continued or amalgamated, whichever is the most recent.
5. The address of the corporation's head or registered office, including municipality, street and number, if any, and postal code.
6. The date on which the corporation commenced activities in Ontario, and, where applicable, the date on which it ceased activities in Ontario.
7. The name and office address of the corporation's chief officer or manager in Ontario, if any, including municipality, street and number, if any, and postal code, the date on which the person assumed this position, and, where applicable, the date on which the person ceased to hold this position.
8. The address of the corporation's principal office in Ontario, if any, including municipality, street and number, if any, and postal code.
9. If the corporation is required by law to have an agent for service in Ontario, the name and address of its agent, including municipality, street and number, if any, and postal code, and the Ontario corporation number of the agent, if the agent is a corporation.
10. [Repealed O. Reg. 249/05, s. 1.]
11. [Revoked O. Reg. 59/95, s. 3.]
12. Whether the language of preference for communication with the corporation is English or French.
13. [Revoked O. Reg. 59/95, s. 3.]
14. The immediate former name of the corporation.
15. [Revoked O. Reg. 59/95, s. 3.]

O. Reg. 12/91, s. 2; 255/92, s. 2; 178/94, s. 2; 59/95, s. 3; 193/99, s. 1; 249/05, s. 1; 262/08, s. 2

2.1 [Repealed O. Reg. 12/09, s. 1.]

2.2 [Repealed O. Reg. 12/09, s. 1.]

2.3 (1) A corporation that is required to file an annual return under section 3.1 of the Act shall deliver the return to the person or entity and in the manner and within the time specified in this section.

(2) A corporation that is required to file a tax return under section 150 of the *Income Tax Act* (Canada) or an information return under subsection 149.1(14) of the *Income Tax Act* (Canada) shall deliver the annual return to the Canada Revenue Agency.

(3) Instead of delivering an annual return to the Canada Revenue Agency, a corporation referred to in subsection (2) may deliver the return to the Minister in electronic format in accordance with subsection 3(1) or in such other manner as the Minister approves.

(4) A corporation that is required to file a tax return under section 150 of the *Income Tax Act* (Canada) shall,

(a) deliver the annual return, together with its tax return for its last completed taxation year, within the time period for delivery of the tax return; or

(b) deliver the annual return within the time period for delivery of the tax return, if it delivers the annual return to the Minister under subsection (3).

(5) A corporation that is required to file an information return under subsection 149.1(14) of the *Income Tax Act* (Canada) shall,

(a) deliver the annual return, together with its information return for its last completed taxation year, within the time period for delivery of the information return; or

(b) deliver the annual return within the time period for delivery of the information return, if it delivers the annual return to the Minister under subsection (3).

(6) A corporation that is required to file both a tax return under section 150 of the *Income Tax Act* (Canada) and an information return under subsection 149.1(14) of the *Income Tax Act* (Canada) in a year, or more than one tax return or information return in a year, is required to file the annual return only within the time period that it is required to file its first tax return or information return during the year.

(7) In this section,

"information return" means a return for a taxation year that subsection 149.1(14) of the *Income Tax Act* (Canada) requires a corporation to file with the Minister of National Revenue;

"tax return" means a return for a taxation year that section 150 of the *Income Tax Act* (Canada) requires a corporation to file with the Minister of National Revenue.

O. Reg. 262/08, s. 3; 12/09, s. 2

2.4 An annual return delivered under section 2.3 shall set out the following information in respect of the corporation as of the date of delivery:

1. If the corporation is delivering the annual return to the Minister, the year of the return.

2. The name of the corporation.

3. The Ontario corporation number of the corporation.

4. The date of the corporation's incorporation or amalgamation, whichever is the most recent.

5. The address of the corporation's head or registered office, including municipality, street and number, if any, and postal code, or, if applicable, an indication that the address pre-printed on the form provided by the Minister is correct.

6. If the corporation is an extra-provincial corporation, the name of the jurisdiction in which it was incorporated, continued or amalgamated, whichever is the most recent.

7. An indication as to whether there has been a change in the information set out in the notice or return that the corporation most recently filed under the Act and, if applicable, all changes in the information.

O. Reg. 262/08, s. 3

2.5 (1) Section 2.3 of this Regulation does not apply in respect of an annual return that a corporation was required to deliver before October 1, 2009 under section 2.1 of this Regulation as it read on or after January 1, 2009 and before October 1, 2009 or that a corporation was required to deliver before January 1, 2009 under section 3.1 of the Act as it read before that date, but that the corporation did not deliver within the required time.

(2) A corporation may deliver the annual return referred to in subsection (1) to the Minister if the return is in electronic format in accordance with subsection 3(1).

(3) A corporation may not deliver the annual return referred to in subsection (1) to the Canada Revenue Agency or to the Minister of Revenue.

(4) An annual return delivered under this section shall set out the information listed in paragraphs 1 to 7 of section 2.4 in respect of the corporation as of the date of delivery.

O. Reg. 262/08, s. 3; 12/09, s. 3

2.6 A notice or return filed with the Minister under the Act in respect of a corporation shall set out the name of the corporation with only one space between each word.

O. Reg. 262/08, s. 3

3. (1) A notice or return to be filed with the Minister under the Act may be submitted in electronic format if,

(a) the person submitting the notice or return satisfies the technical requirements established by the Minister;

(b) the Minister has approved the electronic format of the notice or return; and

(c) the person submitting the notice or return to the Minister submits it during business hours approved by the Minister.

(2) A filing made under subsection (1) is effective on the date assigned by the computer system that the Ministry has established for filings.

(3), (4) [Repealed O. Reg. 262/08, s. 4.]

O. Reg. 12/91, s. 3; 564/98, s. 2; 575/99, s. 2; 262/08, s. 4

4. For the purposes of subsection 4(2) of the Act, the notice of change shall repeat the information required under subsection 2(1) or 3(1) of the Act, whichever is applicable, and shall specify any changes that have taken place and the dates of the changes.

O. Reg. 123/91, s. 1; 262/08, s. 5

5. For the purposes of subsection 8(2) of the Act, the effective date of filing for every notice and return received under the Act shall be the date that the Minister records it.

O. Reg. 123/91, s. 1; 262/08, s. 5

6. (1) The following classes of corporation are exempt from filing under sections 2 and 3 of the Act:

1. Corporations subject to the *Bank Act* (Canada).

2. Corporations that operate railways or telegraph lines or carry on the business of a railway express company or the business of leasing or hiring railway sleeping, parlour or dining cars in Ontario.

3. Corporations subject to the *Telephone Act*.

4, 5 [Revoked O. Reg. 12/91, s. 4.]

6. International Bank for Reconstruction and Development approved by the *Bretton Woods and Related Agreements Act* (Canada).

7. Municipalities within the meaning of the *Municipal Affairs Act*.

(2) All corporation are exempt from filing under section 3.1 of the Act except for the following classes:

1. Corporations subject to the *Business Corporations Act*.

2. Corporations subject to the *Corporations Act*.

3. Foreign corporations which have a licence endorsed under the *Extra-Provincial Corporations Act*.

(3) Despite subsection (2), a corporation is exempt from filing under section 3.1 of the Act in a year if the corporation is required to file a tax return under section 150 of the *Income Tax Act* (Canada) but is not required to file a tax return in that year.

O. Reg. 12/91, s. 4; 59/95, s. 4; 575/99, s. 3; 262/08, s. 6

7. A director, deputy director or manager of the Ministry whose duties relate to the administration of the Act may sign any certificate for the purposes of section 20 of the Act.

O. Reg. 12/09, s. 4

8. The following persons or entities are prescribed for the purposes of section 21.2 of the Act:

1. The Minister of Finance.

2. The Minister of Revenue.

3. The Canada Revenue Agency.

O. Reg. 193/99, s. 2; 49/08, s. 1

9. (1) The Notice for the Special Filing required under section 6 of the Act shall be in a form provided or approved by the Minister.

(2) The Notice may, at any time, be sent by prepaid mail or otherwise.

(3) The corporation to which the Notice is sent shall make the Special Filing within thirty days after the day the Notice is sent by the Minister.

O. Reg. 255/92, s. 3

SCHEDULE — FEES

[Revoked O. Reg. 193/99, s. 3.]

Forms 1, 2

[Revoked O. Reg. 12/91, s. 5.]

CIA Forms

Form 1 — Initial Return/Notice of Change by an Ontario Corporation*

Instructions for Completion

The attached form is to be used by a corporation that is incorporated, continued or amalgamated in Ontario:

(A) as an Initial Return to be filed within 60 days of the date of incorporation, continuation or amalgamation;

OR

(B) as a Notice of Change that must be filed within 15 days after the change or changes take place in the information previously filed.

It is not necessary to file a notice of change in respect of a director's retirement and subsequent re-election for consecutive terms of office.

A duplicate copy of the return/notice must be kept at the Corporation's registered/head office in Ontario and must be available for examination.

Please type or print all information in block capital letters using black ink.

Only information completed within the input boxes will be captured and reflected in the Public Record.

All items on Form 1 and Schedule A must be completed in full, unless otherwise indicated.

Documents filed with the Central Production and Verification Services Branch must be legible. Documents that do not conform to this standard will be returned to the corporation.

All **dates** must be completed using the following numeric format:
For example:

December 3, 2001 would be:

Year	Month	Day
2001	12	03

Addresses must be completed in full, including the street number and name, the city or town and the unit or suite number, if applicable. The province or state, country and postal code must be included when required. **Do not use abbreviations for provinces, states or countries. Post office box numbers cannot be used.**

Please note that any handwriting or typing outside the designated boxes will be ignored because it is not part of the approved form.

FEE

There is no fee for the filing of an initial return or notice of change.

PENALTIES

Sections 13 and 14 of the *Corporations Information Act* provide penalties for contravening the Act or Regulations.

Section 18(1) of the Act provides that a corporation that is in default of a requirement under this Act to file a return/notice or that has unpaid fees or penalties is not capable of maintaining a proceeding in a court in Ontario in respect of the business carried on by the corporation except with leave of the court.

07200 (2011/06)

COMPLETION OF FORM 1

Item 1: **Initial Return/Notice of Change:**
Indicate whether a business corporation or not-for-profit corporation is filing an initial return or a notice of change by placing an **X** in the appropriate box. (Choose **one** box only.)

Item 2: **Ontario Corporation Number:**
Insert the Ontario Corporation Number. This number appears in the top right corner of your Certificate of Incorporation /Continuation or Amalgamation or your Letters Patent.

Item 3: **Date of Incorporation or Amalgamation:**
Insert the full date of incorporation or amalgamation, whichever applies.

Item 4: **Corporation Name:**
Insert the name of the corporation, including all punctuation and correct spacing.

Item 5: **Address of Registered or Head Office in Ontario:**
Complete the full address of the Registered or Head Office in Ontario. Post office box numbers cannot be used. A street address or lot and concession number is required.

Item 6: **Mailing Address:**
Do not leave this item blank.
If the address is the same as the registered or head office address, place an **X** in the box provided.
If the address is different from the registered or head office in Ontario, you must set out the address in full.
If you do not wish to set out a mailing address, place an **X** in the "Not Applicable" box.

Item 7: **Language of Preference:**
Specify whether you prefer to receive correspondence from Central Production and Verification Services Branch in English or French.

Item 8: **Number of Schedule A(s) submitted:**
Schedule A must be submitted with your form. Specify the number of Schedule A(s) you are submitting.
NOTE:
A blank Schedule A may be photocopied if required.

Item 9: **Person Authorizing Filing:**
Print the name of the person authorizing the filing. This must be a director, officer or other individual having knowledge of the affairs of the corporation. The name of the individual must be completed in the box provided and an **X** must be placed in the appropriate box to indicate whether the individual is a director, officer or other individual having knowledge of the affairs of the corporation.

07200 (2011/06)

COMPLETION OF SCHEDULE A

Complete all applicable items on Schedule A in full, including the Ontario Corporation Number and Date of Incorporation or Amalgamation.

Schedule A must report all information pertaining to directors and the five most senior officers of the corporation and must include all changes that have taken place since the filing of the initial return, special notice, annual return or most recent notice of change.

One director/senior officer information section must be completed for each individual who is a director and/or senior officer of the corporation.

There must be a minimum of one director in a non-offering business corporation and a minimum of three directors in a not-for-profit corporation or an offering business corporation.

Not-for-profit corporations must also have a minimum of two senior officers, namely a president and a secretary, plus three directors.

DIRECTOR/OFFICER INFORMATION

The following two sections must be completed for each individual:

NAME
Complete the name in full, providing last, first, and middle name or initials.

ADDRESS
A full address for service is required for the individual. A box number is not acceptable.

Director Information

If the individual is a director, the next three sections must be completed.

Resident Canadian
This information is required for directors of business corporations only.

Specify whether the individual is a Resident Canadian by checking **yes** or **no**.

Date Elected
Complete the date on which the individual became a director.

Date Ceased
Insert the date the director ceased to hold his/her position.

If the date ceased has been completed, the date the director assumed his/her position must also be completed.

Officer Information

If the individual is one of the five most senior officers, the next two sections must be completed:

Date Officer Appointed
Complete the date the individual was appointed as a senior officer under the appropriate title(s).

If the senior officer is not the president, secretary, treasurer or general manager, select the appropriate position(s) from the pre-printed « **Other Titles** » list and include the proper date appointed.

Date Officer Ceased

Insert the date the senior officer ceased to hold his/her position, or
Insert the date an officer ceased to be one of the five most senior officers (as applicable).

If the date ceased has been completed, the date the officer assumed his/her position must also be completed.

The completed form must be mailed or delivered to:

Ministry of Government Services
Central Production and Verification Services Branch
393 University Ave, Suite 200
Toronto ON M5G 2M2

07200 (2011/06)

Directives pour remplir la formule

La formule ci-jointe est à l'usage des personnes morales constituées, prorogées ou fusionnées en Ontario :

A) soit à titre de rapport initial; elle doit être déposée dans les soixante (60) jours de la date de constitution, de prorogation ou de fusion;

OU

B) soit à titre d'avis de modification; elle doit être déposée dans les quinze (15) jours après la ou les modification(s) aux renseignements produits antérieurement.

Il n'est pas nécessaire de déposer un avis de modification quand il s'agit de la retraite et de la réélection immédiate d'un administrateur pour un nouveau mandat.

Un double du rapport de l'avis doit être conservé au siège social en Ontario de la personne morale et doit être disponible pour examen.

Prière de dactylographier les renseignements ou de les écrire en caractères d'imprimerie, à l'encre noire.

Seuls les renseignements indiqués dans les cases ou sections prévues à cet effet seront saisis et consignés aux dossiers publics.

Toutes les rubriques de la Formule 1 et de l'Annexe A doivent être dûment remplies, sauf indication contraire.

Les documents déposés auprès de la Direction des services centraux de production et de vérification doivent être propres et lisibles. Les documents non conformes seront retournés.

Les **dates** doivent être écrites dans l'ordre numérique suivant :
Par exemple :

Le 3 décembre 2001 s'écrirait

année	mois	jour
2001	12	03

Indiquer **l'adresse** au complet, y compris le numéro civique et le nom de la rue, la ville, le numéro d'unité ou de bureau, le cas échéant. Inclure également la province ou l'état, le pays et le code postal, le cas échéant. **Ne pas utiliser d'abréviations pour la province, l'état ou le pays. Une case postale ne constitue pas une adresse.**
NOTE : Les renseignements inscrits au stylo ou à la machine hors des cases ou des sections désignées ne seront pas pris en compte.

DROITS

Aucun droit n'est exigible pour le dépôt d'un rapport initial, ni pour un avis de modification.

INFRACTIONS ET PEINES

Les articles 13 et 14 de la *Loi sur les renseignements exigés des personnes morales* prévoient des peines pour la contravention à la présente loi ou à ses règlements.

Le paragraphe 18(1) prévoit que la personne morale qui a omis de déposer un rapport/avis conformément aux exigences de la présente loi ou d'acquitter des droits ou pénalités ne peut introduire ni continuer une instance devant un tribunal de l'Ontario à l'égard des activités exercées par cette personne morale, sauf avec l'autorisation du tribunal.

07200 (2011/06)

COMMENT REMPLIR LA FORMULE 1

Rubrique 1. Rapport initial/Avis de modification :
Indiquer si une société par actions ou une personne morale sans but lucratif dépose un rapport initial ou un avis de modification en cochant **(x)** la case appropriée. (Ne cocher qu' **une seule** case.)

Rubrique 2. Numéro matricule de la personne morale en Ontario :
Le numéro matricule de la personne morale en Ontario apparaît dans le coin supérieur droit du Certificat de constitution, de prorogation ou de fusion de la personne morale ou de ses lettres patentes.

Rubrique 3. Date de constitution ou de fusion :
Indiquer la date au complet de la constitution ou de la fusion, le cas échéant.

Rubrique 4. Raison sociale de la personne morale :
Indiquer la raison sociale de la personne morale, y compris la ponctuation et les espaces appropriées.

Rubrique 5. Adresse du siège social :
Indiquer l'adresse du siège social. Une case postale ne constitue pas une adresse. Il faut indiquer un numéro et un nom de rue ou un numéro de lot et de concession.

Rubrique 6. Adresse postale :
Ne pas laisser cette rubrique en blanc.
Si l'adresse est la même que celle du siège social, cocher **(x)** la case prévue à cette fin.
Si l'adresse est différente de celle du siège social, il faut inscrire l'adresse au complet.
Si on ne veut pas inscrire une adresse postale, cocher **(x)** la case << Ne s'applique pas >>.

Rubrique 7. Langue préférée :
Indiquer si vous préférez recevoir la correspondance de la Direction des services centraux de production et de vérification en français ou en anglais.

Rubrique 8. Nombre d'annexes A présentées :
L'annexe A doit être présentée avec votre formule. Préciser le nombre d'annexes A présentées avec votre formule.
REMARQUE :
Utiliser une annexe A vierge pour faire le nombre de photocopies requis.

Rubrique 9. Personne autorisant l'enregistrement :
Dans la case prévue, indiquer en lettres majuscules le nom complet de la personne autorisant le dépôt de la formule. Indiquer ensuite si cette personne est un administrateur, un dirigeant ou une personne ayant connaissance des activitiés de la personne morale, en cochant **(x)** la case appropriée, à droite.

07200 (2011/06)

COMMENT REMPLIR L'ANNEXE A

Remplir toutes les rubriques pertinentes au complet dans l'Annexe A, y compris le numéro matricule de la personne morale en Ontario, et la date de constitution ou de fusion.

Sur l'Annexe A, on doit indiquer tous les renseignements se rapportant aux administrateurs et aux cinq cadres dirigeants les plus importants; si c'est un Avis de modification, il faut modifier les renseignements conformément aux changements qui sont intervenus dans la société depuis le dépôt du Rapport initial, d'un Avis spécial, d'un Rapport annuel ou du dernier Avis de modification.

La section des renseignements relatifs aux administrateurs/dirigeants doit être remplie pour chacun des administrateurs et dirigeants de la personne morale.

Il doit y avoir au moins un administrateur pour une société par actions qui ne fait pas d'appel public à l'épargne, et au moins trois administrateurs pour une personne morale sans but lucratif ou une société par actions qui fait un appel public à l'épargne.

Les personnes morales sans but lucratif doivent avoir un minimum de deux dirigeants, c'est-à-dire un président et un secrétaire, en plus de trois administrateurs.

RENSEIGNEMENTS RELATIFS AUX ADMINISTRATEURS/DIRIGEANTS :

Les deux sections suivantes doivent être remplies pour chaque personne :

NOM
Indiquer le nom au complet, en donnant le nom de famille, le prénom et, le cas échéant, un autre prénom.

ADRESSE
Une adresse complète du domicile élu est requise pour chacun des administrateurs/dirigeants. Une case postale ne constitue pas une adresse.

Renseignements relatifs aux administateurs

Si la personne est un administrateur, les trois sections suivantes doivent être remplies :

Résident canadien
Ce renseignement est exigé des administrateurs des sociétés par actions seulement.

Préciser si la personne est un résident canadien en cochant **oui** ou **non**.

Date d'élection
Indiquer la date à laquelle la personne est devenue administrateur.

Date de cessation des fonctions à titre d'administrateur
Inscrire la date à laquelle l'administrateur a cessé ses fonctions à titre d'administrateur.

Si la date de cessation des fonctions a été indiquée, la date à laquelle l'administrateur est entré en fonction doit également être indiquée.

Renseignements relatifs aux dirigeants

Si la personne est l'un des cinq plus importants membres de la haute direction, les deux sections suivantes doivent être remplies :

Date de nomination de la personne
Indiquer la date à laquelle la personne a été nommée dirigeant sous le titre approprié. Si le dirigeant à enregistrer n'est pas président, secrétaire, trésorier ou directeur général, cocher le(s) titre(s) approprié(s) dans la liste « **Autres titres** » et indiquer, sous la liste, la date de sa nomination.

Date de cessation
Indiquer la date à laquelle le dirigeant a cessé ses fonctions.
Indiquer la date à laquelle un dirigeant a cessé d'être l'un des cinq plus importants dirigeants.

Si la date de cessation est indiquée, la date à laquelle le dirigeant a pris ses fonctions doit aussi être indiquée.

La formule dûment remplie doit être envoyée par la poste ou livrée à l'adresse suivante :

Ministère des Services gouvernementaux
Direction des services centraux de production et de vérification
393, av University, bureau 200
Toronto ON M5G 2M2

07200 (2011/06)

For Ministry Use Only
À l'usage du ministère seulement
Page/Page 1 of/de ______

Form 1 - Ontario Corporation Initial Return / Notice of Change
Formule 1 - Personnes morales de l'Ontario Rapport initial / Avis de modification
Corporations Information Act / Loi sur les renseignements exigés des personnes morales

Please type or print all information in block capital letters using black ink.
Prière de dactylographier les renseignements ou de les écrire en caractères d'imprimerie à l'encre noire.

1.	Initial Return / Rapport initial	Notice of Change / Avis de modification
Business Corporation/ Société par actions	☐	☐
Not-For-Profit Corporation/ Personne morale sans but lucratif	☐	☐

2. Ontario Corporation Number / Numéro matricule de la personne morale en Ontario

3. Date of Incorporation or Amalgamation/ Date de constitution ou fusion — Year/Année Month/Mois Day/Jour

For Ministry Use Only
À l'usage du ministère seulement

4. Corporation Name Including Punctuation/Raison sociale de la personne morale, y compris la ponctuation

5. Address of Registered or Head Office/Adresse du siège social

c/o / a/s

Street No./N° civique Street Name/Nom de la rue Suite/Bureau

Street Name (cont'd)/Nom de la rue (suite)

City/Town/Ville **ONTARIO, CANADA**

Postal Code/Code postal

For Ministry Use Only/
À l'usage du ministère seulement

6. Mailing Address/Adresse postale

☐ Same as Registered or Head Office/ Même que siège social

☐ Not Applicable/ Ne s'applique pas

Street No./N° civique

Street Name/Nom de la rue Suite/Bureau

Street Name (cont'd)/Nom de la rue (suite)

City/Town/Ville

Province, State/Province, État Country/Pays Postal Code/Code postal

7. Language of Preference/Langue préférée English - Anglais ☐ French - Français ☐

8. **Information on Directors/Officers must be completed on Schedule A as requested.** If additional space is required, photocopy Schedule A./**Les renseignements sur les administrateurs ou les dirigeants doivent être fournis dans l'Annexe A, tel que demandé.** Si vous avez besoin de plus d'espace, vous pouvez photocopier l'Annexe A.

Number of Schedule A(s) submitted/Nombre d'Annexes A présentées ☐ (At least one Schedule A must be submitted/Au moins une Annexe A doit être présentée)

9. (Print or type name in full of the person authorizing filing / Dactylographier ou inscrire le prénom et le nom en caractères d'imprimerie de la personne qui autorise l'enregistrement)

I/Je

certify that the information set out herein, is true and correct.
atteste que les renseignements précités sont véridiques et exacts.

Check appropriate box
Cocher la case pertinente

D) ☐ Director/Administrateur

O) ☐ Officer /Dirigeant

P) ☐ Other individual having knowledge of the affairs of the Corporation/Autre personne ayant connaissance des activités de la personne morale

Note/Remarque : Sections 13 and 14 of the *Corporations Information Act* provide penalties for making false or misleading statements or omissions. Les articles 13 et 14 de la *Loi sur les renseignements exigés des personnes morales* prévoient des peines en cas de déclaration fausse ou trompeuse, ou d'omission.

07200 (2011/06) Page 1 of/de 3

Form 1 - Ontario Corporation/Formule 1 - Personnes morales de l'Ontario
Schedule A/Annexe A

For Ministry Use Only
À l'usage du ministère seulement
Page/Page _____ of/de _____

Please type or print all information in block capital letters using black ink. Prière de dactylographier les renseignements ou de les écrire en caractères d'imprimerie à l'encre noire.	Ontario Corporation Number / Numéro matricule de la personne morale en Ontario	Date of Incorporation or Amalgamation / Date de constitution ou fusion (Year/Année Month/Mois Day/Jour)

DIRECTOR / OFFICER INFORMATION - RENSEIGNEMENTS RELATIFS AUX ADMINISTRATEURS/DIRIGEANTS

Full Name and Address for Service/Nom et domicile élu

Last Name/Nom de famille | First Name/Prénom | Middle Names/Autres prénoms

Street Number/Numéro civique | Suite/Bureau

Street Name/Nom de la rue

Street Name (cont'd)/Nom de la rue (suite)

City/Town/Ville

Province, State/Province, État | Country/Pays | Postal Code/Code postal

*OTHER TITLES (Please Specify)
*AUTRES TITRES (Veuillez préciser)

- Chair / Président du conseil
- Chair Person / Président du conseil
- Chairman / Président du conseil
- Chairwoman / Présidente du conseil
- Vice-Chair / Vice-président du conseil
- Vice-President / Vice-président
- Assistant Secretary / Secrétaire adjoint
- Assistant Treasurer / Trésorier adjoint
- Chief Manager / Directeur exécutif
- Executive Director / Directeur administratif
- Managing Director / Administrateur délégué
- Chief Executive Officer / Directeur général
- Chief Financial Officer / Agent en chef des finances
- Chief Information Officer / Directeur général de l'information
- Chief Operating Officer / Administrateur en chef des opérations
- Chief Administrative Officer / Directeur général de l'administration
- Comptroller / Contrôleur
- Authorized Signing Officer / Signataire autorisé
- Other (Untitled) / Autre (sans titre)

Director Information/Renseignements relatifs aux administrateurs

Resident Canadian/Résident canadien ☐ YES/OUI ☐ NO/NON (Resident Canadian applies to directors of business corporations only.)/ (Résident canadien ne s'applique qu'aux administrateurs de sociétés par actions)

Date Elected/Date d'élection — Year/Année Month/Mois Day/Jour
Date Ceased/Date de cessation — Year/Année Month/Mois Day/Jour

Officer Information/Renseignements relatifs aux dirigeants

	PRESIDENT/PRÉSIDENT	SECRETARY/SECRÉTAIRE	TREASURER/TRÉSORIER	GENERAL MANAGER/ DIRECTEUR GÉNÉRAL	*OTHER/AUTRE
Date Appointed/ Date de nomination	Year/Année Month/Mois Day/Jour	Year/Année Month/Mois Day/Jour	Year/Année Month/Mois Day/Jour	Year/Année Month/Mois Day/Jour	Year/Année Month/Mois Day/Jour
Date Ceased/ Date de cessation	Year/Année Month/Mois Day/Jour	Year/Année Month/Mois Day/Jour	Year/Année Month/Mois Day/Jour	Year/Année Month/Mois Day/Jour	Year/Année Month/Mois Day/Jour

DIRECTOR / OFFICER INFORMATION - RENSEIGNEMENTS RELATIFS AUX ADMINISTRATEURS/DIRIGEANTS

Full Name and Address for Service/Nom et domicile élu

Last Name/Nom de famille | First Name/Prénom | Middle Names/Autres prénoms

Street Number/Numéro civique | Suite/Bureau

Street Name/Nom de la rue

Street Name (cont'd)/Nom de la rue (suite)

City/Town/Ville

Province, State/Province, État | Country/Pays | Postal Code/Code postal

*OTHER TITLES (Please Specify)
*AUTRES TITRES (Veuillez préciser)

- Chair / Président du conseil
- Chair Person / Président du conseil
- Chairman / Président du conseil
- Chairwoman / Présidente du conseil
- Vice-Chair / Vice-président du conseil
- Vice-President / Vice-président
- Assistant Secretary / Secrétaire adjoint
- Assistant Treasurer / Trésorier adjoint
- Chief Manager / Directeur exécutif
- Executive Director / Directeur administratif
- Managing Director / Administrateur délégué
- Chief Executive Officer / Directeur général
- Chief Financial Officer / Agent en chef des finances
- Chief Information Officer / Directeur général de l'information
- Chief Operating Officer / Administrateur en chef des opérations
- Chief Administrative Officer / Directeur général de l'administration
- Comptroller / Contrôleur
- Authorized Signing Officer / Signataire autorisé
- Other (Untitled) / Autre (sans titre)

Director Information/Renseignements relatifs aux administrateurs

Resident Canadian/Résident canadien ☐ YES/OUI ☐ NO/NON (Resident Canadian applies to directors of business corporations only.)/ (Résident canadien ne s'applique qu'aux administrateurs de sociétés par actions)

Date Elected/Date d'élection — Year/Année Month/Mois Day/Jour
Date Ceased/Date de cessation — Year/Année Month/Mois Day/Jour

Officer Information/Renseignements relatifs aux dirigeants

	PRESIDENT/PRÉSIDENT	SECRETARY/SECRÉTAIRE	TREASURER/TRÉSORIER	GENERAL MANAGER/ DIRECTEUR GÉNÉRAL	*OTHER/AUTRE
Date Appointed/ Date de nomination	Year/Année Month/Mois Day/Jour	Year/Année Month/Mois Day/Jour	Year/Année Month/Mois Day/Jour	Year/Année Month/Mois Day/Jour	Year/Année Month/Mois Day/Jour
Date Ceased/ Date de cessation	Year/Année Month/Mois Day/Jour	Year/Année Month/Mois Day/Jour	Year/Année Month/Mois Day/Jour	Year/Année Month/Mois Day/Jour	Year/Année Month/Mois Day/Jour

07200 (2011/06) Page 2 of/de 3

This information is being collected under the authority of The *Corporations Information Act* for the purpose of maintaining a public database of corporate information.

La *Loi sur les renseignements exigés des personnes morales* autorise la collecte de ces renseignements pour constituer une banque de données accessible au public.

The completed form must be mailed or delivered to:
Ministry of Government Services
Central Production and Verification Services Branch
393 University Ave, Suite 200
Toronto ON M5G 2M2

La formule dûment remplie doit être envoyée par la poste ou livrée à l'adresse suivante :
Ministère des Services gouvernementaux
Direction des services centraux de production et de vérification
393, av University, bureau 200
Toronto ON M5G 2M2

07200 (2011/06) Page 3 of/de 3

Form 2 — Initial Return/Notice of Change by an Extra-Provincial Corporation*

Instructions for Completion

The attached form is to be used by a corporation that is incorporated, continued or amalgamated **in a jurisdiction other than Ontario:**

(A) as an Initial Return to be filed within 60 days of the date of commencing business activity in Ontario;

OR

(B) as a Notice of Change to be filed within 15 days after the change or changes take place in the information previously filed.

A duplicate copy of this return/notice must be kept at the corporation's registered office or principal place of business in Ontario and must be available for examination.

Please type or print all information **in block capital letters using black ink.**

All items on Form 2, page 1 and page 2 must be completed in full, unless otherwise indicated.

Documents filed with the Central Production and Verification Services Branch must be neat, legible and suitable for microfilming. Documents that do not conform to this standard will be returned to the corporation.

All **dates** must be completed using the following numeric format:

January 3, 1999 would be:

Year	Month	Day
1999	01	03

Addresses must be completed in full, including the street number and name, the city or town and the unit or suite number, if applicable. The province or state, country and postal code must be included when required. **Do not use abbreviations for provinces, states or countries. Post office box numbers cannot be used.**
Please note that any handwriting or typing outside the designated boxes will be ignored; it is not part of the approved form.

FEE

There is no fee for the filing of an initial return or notice of change.

PENALTIES

Sections 13 and 14 of the *Corporations Information Act* provide penalties for contravening the Act or Regulations.

Section 18(1) of the Act provides that a corporation that is in default of a requirement under this Act to file a return/notice or that has unpaid fees or penalties is not capable of maintaining a proceeding in a court in Ontario in respect of the business carried on by the corporation except with leave of the court.

07201 (2011/06)

COMPLETION OF PAGE 1

Item 1: **Initial Return/Notice of Change by a business corporation/not-for-profit corporation:**
Indicate whether an extra-provincial corporation is filing an Initial Return or a Notice of Change by placing an **X** in the appropriate box. (Choose **one** box only.)

Item 2: **Ontario Corporation Number:**
Insert the Ontario Corporation Number. This number appears in the top right corner of the Extra-Provincial Licence issued to the corporation. If the corporation does not require a licence, the number will be assigned upon filing the Initial Return.

Item 3: **Date of Incorporation or Amalgamation:**
Insert the full date of incorporation or amalgamation, whichever is the most recent.
Where an amalgamation has taken place since last filing, please submit a photocopy of the Certificate of Amalgamation with Form 2.

Item 4: **Corporation Name:**
Insert the name of the corporation, including punctuation and spacing.

Item 5: **Address of Registered or Head Office:**
Do not leave this blank.
Complete the full address of the Registered or Head Office. Post Office box numbers cannot be used. A street address or lot and concession number is required.

Item 6: **Address of Principal Office in Ontario:**
If the address is the same as the address of the Registered or Head Office, place an **X** in the box provided.
If this item is not applicable, place an **X** in the box provided.
If the address of the principal office is different from the address of the registered or head office, complete this item in full.

Item 7: **Language of Preference:**
Specify whether you prefer to receive correspondence from Central Production and Verification Services Branch in English or French.

Item 8: **Former Corporation Name:**
Insert the most recent former name of the corporation, including spacing and punctuation.

Item 9: **Date Commenced Business Activity in Ontario:**
Insert the date the corporation commenced business activity in Ontario.

Item 10: **Date Ceased Carrying on Business Activity in Ontario:**
Insert the complete date on which the corporation ceased carrying on business activity in Ontario.
If not applicable, place an **X** in the box provided.

Item 11: **Jurisdiction of Incorporation, Amalgamation or Continuation:**
The jurisdiction of incorporation, continuation or amalgamation (whichever is most recent) must be indicated by placing an **X** in the appropriate box. If the jurisdiction is one other than those listed, set out the name of the jurisdiction in full in the space provided.

COMPLETION OF PAGE 2

Complete the Ontario Corporation Number and the Date of Incorporation or Amalgamation (whichever is most recent).

Item 12: **Name and office address of the Chief Officer/Manager in Ontario:**
If this item is not applicable to your corporation, place an **X** in the box provided.
If applicable, complete the name in full, providing the last name, first name, and middle name/initials. Complete the full office address of the Chief Officer/Manager in Ontario.

Date Effective:
Insert the date the Chief Officer/Manager in Ontario assumed his/her position.

Date Ceased:
Insert the date the Chief Officer/Manager in Ontario ceased to hold his/her position.
If the date ceased has been completed, the date the Chief Officer/Manager assumed his/her position must also be completed.

Item 13: **Name and office address of Agent for Service in Ontario:**
If the corporation is incorporated outside of Canada, an agent for service is required.
If the requirement for an agent for service is not applicable, place an **X** in the box provided.
If Item 14 is applicable, indicate if the agent is an individual or a corporation with its registered office address in Ontario. If the agent is an individual, complete section (a) his/her last name, first name, middle name/initials and section (c) full address.

If the agent is a corporation, complete section (b) the Ontario Corporation Number and the full Corporation name, including punctuation and spacing, and section (c) full address.

Please Note: For a foreign corporation, (business corporation incorporated or continued under the laws of a jurdisdiction outside of Canada), to change information about an Agent for Service, a completed Form 2, Revised Appointment of Agent for Service under the *Extra-Provincial Corporations Act* (Ontario) must accompany the document you are presently completing.

Not -for-Profit corporations incorporated outside of Canada do not require an Agent for Service and therefore a Revised Appointment of Agent for Service is not required for these corporations.

Item 14: **Person Authorizing Filing:**
Print the name of the person authorizing this filing. This must be a director, officer or other individual having knowledge of the affairs of the corporation. The name of the individual must be completed in the box provided and an **X** must be placed in the appropriate box to indicate whether the individual is a director, officer or other individual having knowledge of the affairs of the corporation.

The completed form must be mailed or delivered to:
Ministry of Government Services
Central Production and Verification Services Branch
393 University Ave, Suite 200
Toronto ON M5G 2M2

07201 (2011/06)

Directives pour remplir la formule

La formule ci-jointe est à l'usage des personnes morales constituées, prorogées ou fusionnées **dans tout ressort autre que l'Ontario:**

A) soit à titre de rapport initial, et elle doit être déposée dans les soixante (60) jours du début des activités en Ontario;

OU

B) soit à titre d'avis de modification, et elle doit être déposée dans les quinze (15) jours qui suivent toute modification aux renseignements produits antérieurement.

Un double du rapport est conservé au bureau d'affaires principal de la personne morale en Ontario et doit être disponible pour examen.

Prière de dactylographier les renseignements ou de les écrire **en caractères d'imprimerie à l'encre noire.**

Toutes les rubriques de la formule 2, pages 1 et 2, doivent être dûment remplies, sauf indication contraire.

Les documents déposés auprès de la Direction des services centraux de production et de vérification sont microfilmés; ils doivent, par conséquent, être propres, lisibles et adaptés à cette opération. Les documents qui ne répondent pas à cette norme seront renvoyés à la personne morale.

Les **dates** doivent être écrites dans l'ordre numérique suivant :

Par exemple :

le 3 janvier 1999 s'écrirait

année	mois	jour
1999	01	03

Indiquer **l'adresse** au complet, y compris le numéro civique et le nom de la rue, la ville, le numéro d'unité ou de bureau, le cas échéant. Inclure également la province ou l'État, le pays et le code postal, le cas échéant. **Ne pas utiliser d'abréviations pour la province, l'État ou le pays. Une case postale ne constitue pas une adresse.**
NOTE : Tous renseignements inscrits au stylo ou à la machine hors des cases ou des sections désignées ne seront pas pris en compte.

DROITS

Aucun droit n'est exigible pour le dépôt d'un rapport initial, ni pour un avis de modification.

INFRACTIONS ET PEINES

Les articles 13 et 14 de la *Loi sur les renseignements exigés des personnes morales* prévoient des peines pour la contravention à la présente loi ou à ses règlements d'application.

Le paragraphe 18 (1) prévoit que la personne morale qui a omis de déposer un rapport/avis conformément aux exigences de la présente loi ou d'acquitter des droits ou pénalités ne peut introduire ni continuer une instance devant un tribunal de l'Ontario à l'égard des activités exercées par cette personne morale, sauf avec l'autorisation du tribunal.

07201 (2011/06)

COMMENT REMPLIR LA PAGE 1

Rubrique 1. **Rapport initial/Avis de modification par une société par actions/une personne morale sans but lucratif :**
Indiquer si la personne morale extra-provinciale dépose un rapport initial ou un avis de modification en cochant **(x)** la case appropriée.

Rubrique 2. **Numéro matricule de la personne morale en Ontario :**
Le numéro matricule de la personne morale en Ontario apparaît dans le coin supérieur droit du Permis extraprovincial de la personne morale.

Lorsqu'aucun permis n'est exigible pour la personne morale, le numéro matricule sera donné au moment où le rapport initial sera déposé.

Rubrique 3. **Date de constitution ou fusion :**
Inscrire la date au complet de constitution ou de fusion (celle qui est la plus récente).
Lorsqu'une fusion a eu lieu depuis le dernier dépôt, une photocopie du certificat de fusion doit être déposée avec la formule 2.

Rubrique 4. **Raison sociale de la personne morale :**
Indiquer la raison sociale de la personne morale, y compris la ponctuation et les espaces.

Rubrique 5. **Adresse du siège social :**
Ne pas laisser cet espace en blanc.
Indiquer l'adresse du siège social. Une case postale ne constitue pas une adresse. Il faut indiquer un numéro et un nom de rue ou un numéro de lot ou de concession, s'il y a lieu.

Rubrique 6. **Adresse du bureau principal en Ontario :**
Si l'adresse est la même que celle du siège social, cocher **(x)** la case appropriée.
Si cette rubrique ne s'applique pas, cocher **(X)** la case appropriée.
Si l'adresse du bureau principal est différente de celle du siège social, remplir cette rubrique au complet.

Rubrique 7. **Langue préférée :**
Indiquer si vous préférez recevoir la correspondance de la Direction des services centraux de production et de vérification en français ou en anglais.

Rubrique 8. **Raison sociale antérieure :**
Indiquer la raison sociale antérieure, y compris les espaces et la ponctuation. Si cela ne s'applique pas, cocher **(x)** la case appropriée.

Rubrique 9. **Date de début des activités en Ontario :**
Indiquer la date de début des activités en Ontario.

Rubrique 10. **Date de cessation des activités en Ontario :**
Indiquer la date au complet à laquelle l'entreprise a cessé ses activités en Ontario. Si cela ne s'applique pas, cocher **(x)** la case appropriée.

Rubrique 11. **Ressort de constitution / de fusion ou prorogation :**
Pour indiquer le plus récent ressort de constitution, de prorogation ou de fusion (le plus récent), cocher **(x)** la case pertinente.
Si le ressort n'est pas parmi les ressorts qui sont mentionnés, indiquer le nom du ressort au complet dans l'espace prévu à cet effet.

COMMENT REMPLIR LA PAGE 2
Indiquer le numéro matricule de la personne morale en Ontario et la date de constitution ou de fusion (celle qui est la plus récente).

Rubrique 12. **Nom et adresse du bureau du directeur général /gérant en Ontario :**
Si cette rubrique ne s'applique pas, cocher **(x)** la case appropriée.
Si elle s'applique, indiquer le nom au complet en donnant le nom de famille et le(s) prénom(s). Indiquer l'adresse complète du bureau du directeur général ou gérant en Ontario.
Date d'entrée en vigueur :
Indiquer la date où le directeur général ou gérant en Ontario est entré en fonction.
Date de cessation :
Indiquer la date où le directeur général ou gérant a cessé ses fonctions en Ontario.
Si la date de cessation des fonctions a été indiquée, la date où le directeur général ou gérant est entré en fonction doit également être indiquée.

Rubrique 13. **Nom et adresse du bureau du mandataire aux fins de signification en Ontario :**
Si la personne morale a été constituée à l'extérieur du Canada, un mandataire aux fins de signification est exigé.
Si l'exigence d'un mandataire aux fins de signification n'est pas applicable, cocher **(x)** la case appropriée.
Si la rubrique 14 s'applique, indiquer si le mandataire est un particulier ou une personne morale dont l'adresse du siège social est en Ontario.

Si le mandataire est un particulier, remplir la partie a), son nom de famille et son (ses) prénom(s) et la partie c), son adresse complète.

Si le mandataire est une personne morale, remplir la partie b), le numéro matricule de la personne morale en Ontario et le nom de la personne morale au complet, y compris la ponctuation et les espaces et la partie c), son adresse complète.

Remarque : Pour modifier des renseignements concernant le mandataire aux fins de signification, une personne morale étrangère (société à but lucratif constituée ou maintenue en vertu des lois d'une compétence législative extérieure au Canada) doit remplir la Formule 2 - Modification de la désignation de mandataire requise aux termes de la *Loi sur les personnes morales extraprovinciales* (Ontario) et la soumettre avec le présent document.

Les personnes morales à but non lucratif constituées à l'extérieur du Canada ne peuvent pas désigner ou constituer de mandataire aux fins de signification : par conséquent, elle n'ont pas à soumettre la Formule 2 - Modification de la désignation de mandataire.

Rubrique 14. **Personne autorisant l'enregistrement :**
Dans la case prévue, indiquer en lettres majuscules le nom complet de la personne autorisant le dépôt de la formule.
Indiquer ensuite si cette personne est un administrateur, un dirigeant ou une personne ayant connaissance des activitiés de la personne morale, en cochant **(x)** la case appropriée à droite.

La formule dûment remplie doit être envoyée par la poste ou livrée à l'adresse suivante :
Ministère des Services gouvernementaux
Direction des services centraux de production et de vérification
393, av University, bureau 200
Toronto ON M5G 2M2

07201 (2011/06)

Form 2- Extra-Provincial Corporations / Initial Return / Notice of Change
Formule 2 - Personnes morales extra-provinciales / Rapport initial/Avis de modification
Corporations Information Act / Loi sur les renseignements exigés des personnes morales

Please type or print all information in block capital letters using black ink.
Prière de dactylographier les renseignements ou de les écrire en caractères d'imprimerie à l'encre noire.

For Ministry Use Only / À l'usage du ministère seulement	2. Ontario Corporation Number / Numéro matricule de la personne morale en Ontario	3. Date of Incorporation or Amalgamation / Date de constitution, ou fusion — Year/Année Month/Mois Day/Jour	1.	Initial Return / Rapport initial	Notice of Change / Avis de modification
			Business Corporations/ Société par actions	☐	☐
			Not-For-Profit Corporation/ Personne morale sans but lucratif	☐	☐

4. Corporation Name Including Punctuation/Raison sociale de la personne morale, y compris la ponctuation

For Ministry Use Only
À l'usage du ministère seulement

5. Address of Registered or Head Office/Adresse du siège social

c/o / a/s

Street No./Nº civique Street Name/Nom de la rue Suite/Bureau

Street Name (cont'd)/Nom de la rue (suite)

City/Town/Ville Province, State/Province, État

Country/Pays Postal Code/Code postal

For Ministry Use Only
À l'usage du ministère seulement

6. Address of Principal Office in Ontario/Adresse du bureau principal en Ontario

Street No./Nº civique

☐ Same as Above/ Même que celle ci-dessus ☐ Not Applicable/ Ne s'applique pas

Street Name/Nom de la rue Suite/Bureau

Street Name (cont'd)/Nom de la rue (suite)

City/Town/Ville **ONTARIO, CANADA**

Postal Code/Code postal

7. Language of Preference / Langue préférée English/Anglais ☐ French/Français ☐

8. Former Corporation Name if applicable/Raison sociale antérieure de la personne morale, le cas échéant.

Not Applicable / Ne s'applique pas ☐

9. Date commenced business activity in Ontario/ Date de début des activités en Ontario
Year/Année Month/Mois Day/Jour

10. Date ceased carrying on business activity in Ontario/ Date de cessation des activités en Ontario
Year/Année Month/Mois Day/Jour

Not Applicable / Ne s'applique pas ☐

11. Jurisdiction of Incorporation/Amalgamation or Continuation. (Check appropriate box) Do not check more than one box.
Ressort de constitution/de fusion ou prorogation (cocher la case pertinente). Ne cocher qu'une seule case.

1. ☐ ALBERTA ALBERTA 2. ☐ CANADA CANADA 3. ☐ NEW BRUNSWICK NOUVEAU-BRUNSWICK 4. ☐ NOVA SCOTIA NOUVELLE-ÉCOSSE 5. ☐ QUEBEC QUÉBEC 6. ☐ YUKON YUKON 7. ☐ BRITISH COLUMBIA COLOMBIE-BRITANNIQUE

8. ☐ MANITOBA MANITOBA 9. ☐ NEWFOUNDLAND TERRE-NEUVE 10. ☐ PRINCE EDWARD ISLAND ÎLE-DU-PRINCE-ÉDOUARD 11. ☐ SASKATCHEWAN SASKATCHEWAN 12. ☐ NORTHWEST TERRITORIES TERRITOIRES DU NORD-OUEST 13. ☐ NUNAVUT NUNAVUT

If other please specify / Si autre, veuillez préciser

This information is being collected under the authority of *The Corporations Information Act* for the purpose of maintaining a public data base of corporate information. / La *Loi sur les renseignements exigés des personnes morales* autorise la collecte de ces renseignements pour constituer une banque de données accessible au public.

FOR MINISTRY USE ONLY/À L'USAGE DU MINISTÈRE ☐ See deficiency letter enclosed/Voir l'avis d'insuffisance ci-joint

07201 (2011/06) Page 1 of/de 2

Form 2 - Extra-Provincial Corporations / Initial Return / Notice of Change
Formule 2 - Personnes morales extra-provinciales / Rapport initial/Avis de modification
Corporations Information Act / Loi sur les renseignements exigés des personnes morales

Please type or print all information in block capital letters using black ink.
Prière de dactylographier les renseignements ou de les écrire en caractères d'imprimerie à l'encre noire.

FOR MINISTRY USE ONLY À L'USAGE DU MINISTÈRE SEULEMENT	Ontario Corporation Number/ Numéro matricule de la personne morale en Ontario	Date of Incorporation or Amalgamation Date de constitution ou fusion Year/Année Month/Mois Day/Jour	For Ministry Use Only À l'usage du ministère seulement

12. Name and Office Address of the Chief Officer/Manager in Ontario/
Nom et adresse du bureau du directeur général/gérant en Ontario

☐ Not Applicable/Ne s'applique pas

Last Name/Nom de famille | First Name/Prénom | Middle Name/Autres prénoms

Street Number/Numéro civique

Street Name/Nom de la rue

Street Name (cont'd)/Nom de la rue (suite) | Suite/Bureau

City/Town/Ville | **ONTARIO, CANADA** | Postal Code/Code postal

Date Effective / Date d'entrée en vigueur — Year/Année Month/Mois Day/Jour

Date Ceased / Date de cessation des fonctions — Year/Année Month/Mois Day/Jour

13. Name and Office Address of Agent for Service in Ontario - Check One box
Nom et adresse du bureau du mandataire aux fins de signification en Ontario. Cocher la case pertinente.

☐ Not Applicable/Ne s'applique pas

Only applies to foreign business corporations
S'applique seulement aux personnes morales étrangères

a) ☐ Individual or / un particulier ou   b) ☐ Corporation / une personne morale

Complete appropriate sections below/Remplir les parties pertinentes ci-dessous.

a) Individual Name/Nom du particulier

Last Name/Nom de famille | First Name/Prénom | Middle Name/Autres prénoms

b) Ontario Corporation Number/Numéro matricule de la personne morale en Ontario

Corporation Name including punctuation/Raison sociale, y compris la ponctuation

c) Address/Adresse

c/o / a/s

Street No./N° civique | Street Name/Nom de la rue | Suite/Bureau

Street Name (cont'd)/Nom de la rue (suite) | City/Town/Ville

ONTARIO, CANADA | Postal Code/Code postal

14. (Print or type name in full of the person authorizing filing./ Dactylographier ou inscrire le prénom et le nom en caractères d'imprimerie de la personne qui autorise l'enregistrement.

I / Je

certify that the information set out herein, is true and correct.
atteste que les renseignements précités sont véridiques et exacts.

Check appropriate box / Cocher la case pertinente

D) ☐ Director/Administrateur

O) ☐ Officer/Dirigeant

P) ☐ Other individual having knowledge of the affairs of the Corporation/Autre personne ayant connaissance des activités de la personne morale

NOTE/REMARQUE: Section 13 and 14 of the *Corporations Information Act* provide penalties for making false or misleading statements, or omissions.
Les articles 13 et 14 de la *Loi sur les renseignements exigés des personnes morales* prévoient des peines en cas de déclaration fausse ou trompeuse, ou d'omission.

This information is being collected under the authority of The *Corporations Information Act* for the purpose of maintaining a public data base of corporate information. /
La *Loi sur les renseignements exigés des personnes morales* autorise la collecte de ces renseignements pour constituer une banque de données accessible au public.

FOR MINISTRY USE ONLY/À L'USAGE DU MINISTÈRE   ☐ See deficiency letter enclosed/Voir l'avis d'insuffisance ci-joint

07201 (2011/06) Page 2 of/de 2

EXTRA-PROVINCIAL CORPORATIONS ACT

R.S.O. 1990, c. E.27, as am. S.O. 1994, c. 17, s. 44; 1994, c. 27, s. 82; 1998, c. 18, Sched. E, ss. 87–92; 1999, c. 12, Sched. F, ss. 25, 26; 2001, c. 9, Sched. D, s. 6; 2011, c. 1, Sched. 5, s. 4.

1. (1) **Definitions** — In this Act,

"business" includes undertaking and non-profit activities; *("activités")*

"court" means the Superior Court of Justice; *("tribunal")*

"Director" means the Director appointed under section 3; *("directeur")*

"endorse" includes imprinting a stamp, in accordance with section 5, on the face of an application sent to the Director; *("apposer")*

"extra-provincial corporation" means a corporation, with or without share capital, incorporated or continued otherwise than by or under the authority of an Act of the Legislative Assembly; *("personne morale extraprovinciale")*

"Minister" means the Minister of Consumer and Business Services; *("ministre")*

"Ministry" means the Ministry of the Minister; *("ministère")*

"prescribed" means prescribed by the regulations; *("prescrit")*

"regulations" means the regulations made under this Act; *("règlements")*

"send" includes deliver or mail. *("envoyer")*

(2) **Carrying on business in Ontario** — For the purposes of this Act, an extra-provincial corporation carries on its business in Ontario if,

(a) it has a resident agent, representative, warehouse, office or place where it carries on its business in Ontario;

(b) it holds an interest, otherwise than by way of security, in real property situate in Ontario; or

(c) it otherwise carries on its business in Ontario.

(3) **Idem** — An extra-provincial corporation does not carry on its business in Ontario by reason only that,

(a) it takes orders for or buys or sells goods, wares and merchandise; or

(b) offers or sells services of any type,

by use of travellers or through advertising or correspondence.

2001, c. 9, Sched. D, s. 6(1), (2)

2. (1) Classes of extra-provincial corporations — Extra-provincial corporations shall be classified into the following classes:

- Class 1. Corporations incorporated or continued by or under the authority of an Act of a legislature of a province of Canada.
- Class 2. Corporations incorporated or continued by or under the authority of an Act of the Parliament of Canada or of the legislature of a territory of Canada.
- Class 3. Corporations incorporated or continued under the laws of a jurisdiction outside of Canada.

(2) Class 1 — Corporations incorporated under the laws of the Northwest Territories or of Nunavut but governed by the corporation laws of a province are corporations within Class 1.
1999, c. 12, Sched. F, s. 25

3. Director — There shall be a Director appointed by the Minister who shall perform such duties and have such powers as are assigned to him or her by this Act.

4. (1) Where licence not required — Subject to this Act, the *Corporations Information Act* and any other Act, an extra-provincial corporation within class 1 or 2 may carry on any of its business in Ontario without obtaining a licence under this Act.

(2) Carrying on business without licence prohibited — No extra-provincial corporation within class 3 shall carry on any of its business in Ontario without a licence under this Act to do so, and no person acting as representative for or agent for any such extra-provincial corporation shall carry on any of its business in Ontario unless the corporation has a licence under this Act.

5. (1) Application for licence, etc. — An extra-provincial corporation may make an application for a licence, an amended licence or a termination of licence by sending to the Director two originals of the application signed by a director or officer of the corporation, all other required documents and the required fee.

(2) Where Director endorses — Where the Director receives an application in accordance with subsection (1) he or she may endorse on each original a licence, amended licence or a termination of the licence, setting out the day, month and year of endorsement and a corporation number and, where the Director so endorses, he or she shall,

(a) file one original of the application with the endorsement; and

(b) send to the corporation or its representative one original of the application with the endorsement thereon.

(3) Date of endorsement — An endorsement under subsection (2) may be dated as of the date the Director receives the originals of any application together with all other required documents executed in accordance with this Act and the prescribed fees or as of any later date acceptable to the Director specified by the person who submitted the application.

(4) When endorsement effective — An endorsement under subsection (2) is effective on the date shown thereon although any action required to be taken by the Director under this Act with respect to the endorsement of the application and filing by the Director is taken at a later date.

(5) Restrictions on licence — The Director may make a licence or an amended licence subject to restrictions on the business of a corporation and to such other limitations or conditions as are specified in the licence or amended licence.

1994, c. 27, s. 82(1); 1998, c. 18, Sched. E, s. 87

6. (1) Where endorsement refused — Where the Director refuses to endorse any application required by this Act to be endorsed by the Director before it becomes effective, he or she shall give written notice to the person who delivered the application of the refusal, specifying the reasons therefor.

(2) Idem — Where, within six months after an application referred to in subsection 5(1) has been sent to the Director, the Director has not endorsed the application, the Director shall be deemed for the purposes of section 8 to have refused to endorse it.

7. (1) Director may cancel licence — Where sufficient cause is shown, the Director, after giving an extra-provincial corporation within class 3 an opportunity to be heard, may by order cancel the licence of the corporation upon such date as is fixed in the order.

(2) Review by Director — If no proceedings have been taken under section 8, the Director may at any time review an order made under subsection (1) and may affirm, revoke or vary any such order if in the Director's opinion it is appropriate to do so.

(3) Definition — In this section, **"sufficient cause"** includes,

(a) failure to pay any required fee;

(b) failure to comply with section 19;

(c) failure to comply with a filing requirement under the *Corporations Information Act*; and

(d) a conviction of the extra-provincial corporation for an offence under the *Criminal Code* (Canada) or an offence as defined in the *Provincial Offences Act* in circumstances where cancellation of the licence is in the public interest.

1994, c. 17, s. 44(1); 1998, c. 18, Sched. E, s. 88

8. (1) Appeal — A person aggrieved by a decision of the Director,

(a) to refuse to endorse an application;

(b) to make or refuse to make an order under section 11;

(c) to cancel a licence under section 7 or subsection 12(2);

(d) to require that a corrected licence be endorsed under section 13; or

(e) to impose conditions on a licence or amended licence,

may appeal to the Divisional Court.

(2) Certification by Director — The Director shall certify to the Divisional Court,

(a) the decision of the Director together with a statement of the reasons therefor;

(b) the record of any hearing; and

(c) other material that is relevant to the appeal.

(3) Director may be heard — The Director is entitled to be heard by counsel or otherwise upon the argument of an appeal under this section.

(4) Court order — Where an appeal is taken under this section, the court may direct the Director to make such decision or do such other act that the Director is empowered to do under this Act, as the court thinks proper, having regard to the material and submissions before it.

(5) Further orders by Director — Despite an order of the court under subsection (4), the Director has power to make any further decision where he or she is presented with new material or where there is a material change in the circumstances and every such decision is subject to this section.

9. Use of other name — An extra-provincial corporation may, subject to its incorporating instrument, the *Corporations Information Act* and any other Act, use and identify itself in Ontario by a name other than its corporate name.

1999, c. 12, Sched. F, s. 26

10. (1) Where name, etc., likely to deceive — Despite section 9 and subject to subsection (2), an extra-provincial corporation within class 1 or 3 shall not use or identify itself in Ontario by a name,

(a) that contains a word or expression prohibited by the regulations;

(b) that is the same as or, except where a number name is used, similar to,

(i) the name of a known,

(A) body corporate,

(B) trust,

(C) association,

(D) partnership,

(E) sole proprietorship, or

(F) individual,

whether in existence or not, or

(ii) the known name under which any body corporate, trust, association, partnership, sole proprietorship or individual carries on its business or identifies itself,

if the use of that name would be likely to deceive; or

(c) that does not meet the requirements prescribed by the regulations.

(2) Exception — An extra-provincial corporation within class 1 or 3 may use or identify itself in Ontario by a name described in clause (1)(b) upon compliance with such conditions as may be prescribed.

(3) Filing material — An extra-provincial corporation to which this section applies shall file with the Director such documents relating to the name or proposed name as may be prescribed.

11. (1) Where contravention — If an extra-provincial corporation within class 1 or 3, through inadvertence or otherwise, uses or identifies itself by a name contrary to section 10, the Director may, after giving the extra-provincial corporation an opportunity to be heard, order it to cease using the name in Ontario and, where the name is contained in a licence, the Director may order that the corporation apply for an amended licence under a different name within the time specified in the order.

(1.1) Written hearing — A hearing under subsection (1) shall be in writing in accordance with rules made by the Director under the *Statutory Powers Procedures Act*.

(2) Director may apply for order under s. 14 — Where an extra-provincial corporation within class 1 fails to comply with an order made under subsection (1), the Director may apply to the Court for an order under section 14.

(3) Director may cancel licence — Where an extra-provincial corporation within class 3 fails to apply for an amended licence pursuant to an order under subsection (1), the Director may cancel the licence.

1998, c. 18, Sched. E, s. 89

12. (1) Where change of name or jurisdiction — An extra-provincial corporation within class 3 shall make application for an amended licence where,

(a) it has changed its name or has been ordered to change its name under section 11; or

(b) it has continued under the laws of another jurisdiction.

(2) Where corporation ceases to carry on business — Where an extra-provincial corporation within class 3 has not carried on any of its business in Ontario for any two consecutive years, the extra-provincial corporation shall make application for termination of its licence or, if it does not do so, the Director, upon giving the corporation an opportunity to be heard, may by order cancel the licence.

13. (1) Where error in respect of licence — Where a licence contains an error,

(a) the corporation shall, upon the request of the Director, return the licence; or

(b) the corporation may apply to the Director for a corrected licence and shall return the licence.

(2) Endorsement of corrected licence — After giving the corporation an opportunity to be heard, where the Director is of the opinion that it is appropriate to so do and is satisfied that such steps have been taken by the corporation as the Director required, the Director shall endorse a corrected licence.

(3) Date on corrected licence — A corrected licence endorsed under subsection (2) may bear the date of the licence it replaces.

(4) [Repealed 1994, c. 27, s. 82.]

1994, c. 27, s. 82

14. (1) Court order — The Director may apply to the court for an order prohibiting an extra-provincial corporation within class 1 from carrying on its business in Ontario or such other order as the Director may think fit and, where sufficient cause exists, the court may make an order under subsection (2).

(2) Idem — Upon an application under this section the court may make any interim or final order it thinks fit.

(3) Definition — In subsection (1), **"sufficient cause"** includes,

(a) failure to comply with a filing requirement under the *Corporations Information Act*;

(b) a conviction of the extra-provincial corporation for an offence under the *Criminal Code* (Canada) or an offence as defined in the *Provincial Offences Act*, in circumstances where an order of prohibition is in the public interest; and

(c) failure to comply with an order made under section 11.

1994, c. 17, s. 44(2)

15. Notice not deemed — No person is affected by or is deemed to have knowledge of the contents of a document concerning an extra-provincial corporation by reason only that the document has been filed with the Director.

16. Certificate — The Director shall, on payment of the required fee, issue a certificate certifying,

(a) as to the endorsement or non-endorsement of a licence for any corporation;

(b) as to the filing or non-filing of any document or material required or permitted to be filed under this Act; or

(c) that a person named in the certificate on the date or during the period specified in the certificate is shown on the records of the Ministry as an officer or agent for service of the corporation named in the certificate.

1998, c. 18, Sched. E, s. 90

17. (1) Delegation by Director — The Director may delegate in writing any of the Director's duties or powers under this Act to any public servant employed under Part III of the *Public Service of Ontario Act, 2006.*

(2) Signing — Where this Act requires or authorizes the Director to endorse a licence or to certify any fact, the licence or certificate shall be signed by the Director or any other person designated for the purpose by the regulations.

(3) Evidence — A licence or certificate referred to in subsection (2) or a certified copy thereof when introduced as evidence in any civil, criminal or administrative action or proceeding is proof, in the absence of evidence to the contrary, of the facts so certified without personal appearance to prove the signature or official position of the person appearing to have signed the endorsed licence or certificate.

(4) Reproducing signature — For the purposes of subsections (2) and (3), any signature authorized under this section may be printed or otherwise mechanically reproduced.

2011, c. 1, Sched. 5, s. 4(1)

18. (1) Verification by affidavit — The Director may require any fact relevant to the performance of his or her duties under this Act or the regulations to be verified by affidavit or otherwise.

(2) Evidence under oath — For the purpose of holding a hearing under this Act, the Director may administer oaths to witnesses and require them to give evidence under oath.

19. (1) Agent for service — Every extra-provincial corporation within class 3 that carries on its business in Ontario shall ensure the continuing appointment, at all times, of an individual, of the age of eighteen years or older, who is resident in Ontario or a corporation having its head office or registered office in Ontario as its agent for service in Ontario on whom service of process, notices or other proceedings may be made and service on the agent shall be deemed to be service on the corporation.

(2) Appointment form — The appointment shall be in the prescribed form and shall accompany the application for a licence.

(3) **Revised appointment** — Where the name, address or any other particular set out in the appointment of an agent changes or where an agent is substituted, the extra-provincial corporation shall forthwith file a revised appointment in the prescribed form with the Director.

(4) **Delivery of notices** — A notice or other document that is required or permitted by this Act to be sent by the Director may be sent by ordinary mail or by any other method, including registered mail, certified mail or prepaid courier, if there is a record by the person who has delivered it that the notice or document has been sent.

(5) **Same** — A notice or other document referred to in subsection (4) may be sent by telephone transmission of a facsimile of the notice or other document or by another form of electronic transmission where there is a record that the notice or other document has been sent.

(6) **Deemed delivery** — A notice or other document sent by mail by the Director to an agent or extra-provincial corporation and addressed as provided in subsection (7) shall be deemed to have been received on the earlier of,

(a) the day the agent or corporation actually receives it; or

(b) the fifth day after the day it is mailed.

(7) **Same** — Subsection 6 applies if the notice or document is addressed,

(a) to the agent referred to in subsection (1) at the agent's latest address shown on the records of the Director; or

(b) to the head or registered office of the extra-provincial corporation at the latest address shown on the records of the Director.

(8) **Same** — A notice or other document sent by the Director by a method referred to in subsection (5) shall be deemed to be received by the intended recipient on the earlier of,

(a) the day the intended recipient actually receives it; or

(b) the first business day after the day the transmission is sent by the Director.

1994, c. 27, s. 82(3)

20. (1) **Penalty** — Every person who, without reasonable cause,

(a) contravenes this Act or the regulations;

(b) contravenes a condition of a licence; or

(c) fails to observe or comply with an order, direction or other requirement made under this Act or the regulations,

is guilty of an offence and on conviction is liable to a fine of not more than $2,000 or if such person is a corporation to a fine of not more than $25,000.

(2) **Idem** — Where an extra-provincial corporation is guilty of an offence under subsection (1), every director or officer of the corporation and every person acting as its representative in Ontario who authorized, permitted or acquiesced in such offence is also guilty of an offence and on conviction is liable to a fine of not more than $2,000.

21. (1) **Ability to maintain action** — An extra-provincial corporation within class 3 that is not in compliance with section 19 or has not obtained a licence when required by this Act, is not capable of maintaining any action or any other proceeding in any court or tribunal in Ontario in respect of any contract made by it.

(2) Correcting default — Where a default referred to in subsection (1) has been corrected, an action or other proceeding may be maintained as if the default had been corrected before the institution of the action or other proceeding.

22. Power to hold land — Every corporation,

(a) within class 1 or 2;

(b) within class 3 that has a licence under this Act; or

(c) that is exempt from the licensing requirement under this Act,

has power to acquire, hold and convey any land or interest therein in Ontario necessary for its actual use and occupation or for carrying on its undertaking.

23. (1) Effect of licence under previous Act — Where a licence has been issued to an extra-provincial corporation within class 3 under Part VIII of the *Corporations Act*, being chapter 95 of the Revised Statutes of Ontario, 1980, or a predecessor thereof,

(a) the licence remains in effect and shall be deemed to have endorsed under this Act;

(b) the powers of the extra-provincial corporation shall be deemed to be restricted as set out in the existing licence; and

(c) the attorney for service previously appointed continues in office and the provisions of this Act with respect to agents for service apply.

(2) Licences cancelled — All extra-provincial licences issued under Part VIII of the *Corporations Act*, being chapter 95 of the Revised Statutes of Ontario, 1980, or a predecessor thereof except licences referred to in subsection (1) are cancelled on the 1st day of March, 1985.

(3) Same, exempt corporation — The Director may cancel a licence issued under this Act or a predecessor of it to an extra-provincial corporation that is not required to have a licence under this Act.

2001, c. 9, Sched. D, s. 6(3)

24. (1) References in other Acts — In any other Act, unless the context otherwise requires,

(a) a reference to an extra-provincial corporation is deemed to be a reference to an extra-provincial corporation under this Act; and

(b) a reference to an extra-provincial corporation that is licensed or required to be licensed under Part VIII of the *Corporations Act*, being chapter 95 of the Revised Statutes of Ontario, 1980, means an extra-provincial corporation within class 1 or 3.

(2) Where corporation deemed to have licence — Where a corporation within class 1 or 2 would enjoy an exemption or a benefit under another Act if it had an extra-provincial licence, the corporation shall be deemed to have a licence for the purpose of the other Act.

24.1 Powers of Minister — (1) Minister's regulations — The Minister may make regulations,

(a) designating officers of the Ministry for the purposes of endorsing licences and issuing certificates as to any fact or certifying true copies of documents required or authorized under this Act;

(b) prescribing the documents relating to names to be filed with the Director under subsection 10(3);

(c) respecting the evidence required upon the application for a licence under this Act, including evidence as to the incorporation of the extra-provincial corporation, its powers, objects and existence as a valid and subsisting corporation;

(d) respecting the appointment and continuance by extra-provincial corporations of an agent for service on whom service or process notices or other proceedings may be made and the powers to be conferred on such an agent;

(e) prescribing the form and content of any documents to be filed under this Act.

(2) Fees — The Minister may by order require the payment of fees for search reports and copies of documents and information, or other services under this Act and may approve the amount of those fees.

1998, c. 18, Sched. E, s. 91; 2011, c. 1, Sched. 5, s. 4(2)

24.2 Director's regulations — The Director may make regulations prescribing forms and providing for their use.

2011, c. 1, Sched. 5, s. 4(3)

25. Regulations — The Lieutenant Governor in Council may make regulations respecting any matter he or she considers necessary for the purposes of this Act, including, without limiting the generality of the foregoing, regulations,

(a) [Repealed 1998, c. 18, Sched. E, s. 92(1).]

(b) [Repealed 1998, c. 18, Sched. E, s. 92(1).]

(c) [Repealed 2011, c. 1, Sched. 5, s. 4(4).]

(d) respecting names of extra-provincial corporations or classes thereof;

(e) prohibiting the use of any words or expressions in a corporate name;

(f) defining any word or expression used in clause 10(1)(b);

(g) prescribing requirements for the purposes of clause 10(1)(c);

(h) prescribing conditions for the purposes of subsection 10(2);

(i) [Repealed 2011, c. 1, Sched. 5, s. 4(4).]

(j) [Repealed 2011, c. 1, Sched. 5, s. 4(4).]

(k) [Repealed 2011, c. 1, Sched. 5, s. 4(4).]

(l) prescribing the conditions and limitations that may be specified in licences;

(m) prescribing classes of extra-provincial corporations and exempting any class of extra-provincial corporation from all or any part of the provisions of this Act upon such terms and conditions, if any, as may be prescribed;

(n) prescribing any matter required by this Act to be prescribed for which a specific power is not otherwise provided.

1998, c. 18, Sched. E, s. 92; 2011, c. 1, Sched. 5, s. 4(4), (5)

ONT. REG. 365 — GENERAL

made under the *Extra-Provincial Corporations Act*

R.R.O. 1990, Reg. 365, as am. O. Reg. 581/91; 598/92; 626/93; 312/96; 565/98; 194/99; 251/05; 11/09.

NAMES

1. Sections 2 to 7 apply only to corporations within class 1 and class 3.

2. (1) For the purposes of clause 10(1)(b) of the Act, **"if the use of that name would be likely to deceive"** includes,

(a) a name that is likely to cause a person or class of persons who ordinarily might be expected to deal with either the extra-provincial corporation or another person to believe that the business, undertaking or activities carried on or intended to be carried on by the extra-provincial corporation under the name and the business, undertaking or activities carried on by that other person are one business, one undertaking or one activity, whether or not the nature of the business, undertaking or activity of the extra-provincial corporation and the other person is generally the same;

(b) a name that is likely to cause a person or a class of persons who ordinarily might be expected to deal with either the extra-provincial corporation or another person to believe that the extra-provincial corporation bearing the name or proposed name is or would be associated or affiliated with such other person if the extra-provincial corporation and such person are not or will not be associated or affiliated; or

(c) a name that is so similar to that of a person that it is likely to cause someone who had an interest in dealing or reason to deal with the person to deal with the extra-provincial corporation bearing the name in the belief that he or she was dealing with the person.

(2) For the purposes of subsection (1),

"person" means a known body corporate, trust, association, partnership, sole proprietorship or individual, whether in existence or not, and includes the known name or known trademark under which any of them carry on business or identify themselves;

"use" means actual use by a person that carries on business or an undertaking in Canada or elsewhere.

3. An extra-provincial corporation shall not use or identify itself by a name in Ontario that contains any word or expression or abbreviation thereof in any language,

(a) that is obscene or connotes a business, undertaking or activity that is scandalous, obscene or immoral or that is otherwise objectionable on public grounds;

(b) that describes in a misleading manner the business, undertaking or activity in association with which the name is proposed to be used; or

(c) the use of which is prohibited or restricted under an Act or regulation of the Parliament of Canada or a province or territory of Canada, unless the restriction is satisfied.

4. An extra-provincial corporation shall not use or identify itself in Ontario by a name that contains the following words:

1. "Amalgamated", "fusionné" or any other related word or expression in French, unless the extra-provincial corporation is an amalgamated corporation resulting from the amalgamation of two or more corporations.

2. "Architect", "architecte", "architectural", "d'architecture" or any variation thereof, where the use suggests the practice of the profession, except with the written consent of the Council of the Ontario Association of Architects.

3. "Condominium", "condominial" or any abbreviation or derivation thereof.

4. "Co-operative", "coopérative" or any abbreviation or derivation thereof; except with the written consent of the Minister under the *Co-operative Corporations Act.*

5. "Engineer", "ingénieur", "engineering", "génie", "ingénierie" or any variation thereof, except with the written consent of the Association of Professional Engineers of Ontario.

6. [Repealed O. Reg. 251/05, s. 1.]

7. "Royal" where the use suggests that the extra-provincial corporation is sponsored by or connected with the Crown, except with the written consent of the Crown through the Secretary of State.

O. Reg. 626/93, s. 1; 251/05, s. 1

5. No word or expression that suggests that an extra-provincial corporation,

(a) is connected with the Government of Canada, the government of a province or a territory of Canada or a municipal government or any department, ministry, branch, bureau, service, board, agency, commission or activity of any of them; or

(b) is sponsored or controlled by or is associated or affiliated with a university or an association of accountants, architects, engineers, lawyers, physicians, surgeons or any other professional association recognized by the laws of Canada or a province or territory of Canada,

shall be used by an extra-provincial corporation in its name without the consent in writing of the appropriate person referred to in clause (a) or (b).

5.1 An application made under the Act in respect of an extra-provincial corporation shall set out the name of the corporation with only one space between each word.

O. Reg. 251/05, s. 2

LICENCES

6. (1) Where an extra-provincial corporation within class 3 applies for an extra-provincial licence, the following documents shall accompany the application:

1. An original Ontario biased or weighted computer printed search report from the automated name search system owned by the Department of Consumer and Corporate Affairs, Canada, dated not more than ninety days prior to the submission of the application.

2. A certificate of status, signed by an official of the governing jurisdiction who is authorized to so certify, setting out,

(i) the name of the extra-provincial corporation,

(ii) the date of its incorporation or amalgamation,

(iii) the jurisdiction to which the corporation is subject, and

(iv) that the corporation is a valid and subsisting corporation.

3. An appointment of an agent for service in Form 2 duly executed by the corporation.

(2) Where the Director is not satisfied on the basis of the material filed with him or her under subsection (1) that the extra-provincial corporation is a valid and subsisting corporation in the jurisdiction in which it purports to be incorporated, the extra-provincial corporation shall provide the Director with a legal opinion in writing from a lawyer authorized to practice in that jurisdiction that the extra-provincial corporation is a valid and subsisting corporation in that jurisdiction.

(3) No name that is identified in an Ontario biased or weighted computer printed search report as "proposed" shall be used by an extra-provincial corporation unless a consent in writing is obtained from the person who first proposed the name.

7. Where an extra-provincial corporation within class 3 applies for an amended extra-provincial licence, the application shall be accompanied by the documents referred to in section 6 that are relevant to the application.

Delegation of Duties

8. A director, deputy director, manager or examiner of the Ministry whose duties relate to the administration of the Act may sign or endorse any licence or certificate required or authorized by the Act.

O. Reg. 11/09, s. 1

9-12 [Repealed O. Reg. 251/05, s. 3.]

Fees

13. [Revoked O. Reg. 194/99, s. 1.]

Refunds

14. [Revoked O. Reg. 194/99, s. 1.]

Exemptions

15. The following classes of extra-provincial corporations are exempt from the Act:

1. Corporations licensed or registered under the *Insurance Act*, the *Investment Contracts Act* or the *Loan and Trust Corporations Act*.

2. Corporations incorporated for the purpose of operating,

i. a banking business or the business of a savings bank,

ii. a railway,

iii. the business of a telegraph company,

iv. the business of an express company over a railway, or

v. the business of leasing or hiring sleeping or parlour or dining cars run upon a railway.

3. Corporations engaged in the brewing, distilling or the making of wine that are licensed under the *Liquor Licence Act*.

4. Corporations not having a gain for any of their objects.

SCHEDULE — FEES

[Revoked O. Reg. 194/99, s. 2.]

Forms 1–4

[Repealed O. Reg. 251/05, s. 4.]

ONT. REG. 245/05 — FORMS

made under the *Extra-Provincial Corporations Act*

O. Reg. 245/05

1. Forms — The following forms shall be in the form approved by the Minister:

1. An application for an extra-provincial licence.
2. An appointment of an agent for service or a revised appointment of an agent for service.
3. An application for an amendment to an extra-provincial licence.
4. An application for termination of an extra-provincial licence.

EPCA FORMS

Form 1 — Application for Extra-Provincial Licence*

Instructions for Completing

FEE

The fee for an extra-provincial licence is $330.00, payable in Canadian funds. Cheques or money orders are to be made payable to the Minister of Finance. **Where a cheque is tendered in payment, the name of the corporation must be entered on the face of the cheque.** Do not send cash through the mail.

FORMAT

The application must be in **duplicate** in Form 1 prescribed in Ontario Regulations made under the *Extra-Provincial Corporations Act*. Applications which do not conform to Form 1 cannot be accepted and will be returned to the applicant submitting the application.

APPEARANCE OF DOCUMENTS

Applications and any supporting documents which are to be filed with the Ministry must be typewritten, or, if completed by hand, printed in BLOCK CAPITAL letters, and must be legible and compatible with microfilming process. Applications and supporting documents must be upon one side of good quality white bond paper 210 mm. x 297 mm. with a margin of 30 mm. on the left hand side or 8 1/2" x 11" with a margin of 1 1/4" on the left hand side. Documents which do not conform to this standard cannot be accepted and will be returned to the applicant submitting the application.

PAGES

The pages are numbered 1 to 3 and must remain in that order. Pages must not be removed. If any item is inapplicable, state "nil" or "not applicable".

Applications with missing pages will not be accepted and will be returned to the applicant.

SUPPLEMENTARY PAGES

If additional pages are required due to lack of sufficient space they must be the same size as all other pages, must have a margin of 30 mm. or 1 1/4" on the left hand side and must be numbered the same as the original with the addition of letters of the alphabet to indicate sequence. For example, supplementary pages for Item 9 would be numbered 2A, 2B, etc. See instructions for **Appearance of Documents.**

SUPPORTING DOCUMENTS

The application must be accompanied by:

a) an **Appointment of Agent for Service** (Form 2);

b) a **Certificate of Status** issued under the seal of office and signed by the proper officer (Director, Corporations Branch, etc) of the jurisdiction to which the corporation is subject, setting out the following:
   (i) the name of the corporation;
   (ii) date of incorporation/amalgamation or merger;
   (iii) jurisdiction to which the corporation is subject;
   (iv) that the corporation is a valid and subsisting corporation; and

c) **the original NUANS name search report** (See instructions re: Corporate Name).

CORPORATE NAME

Prior to completing the application the officers of the corporation should satisfy themselves that the corporate name is available for use in Ontario. To do this the applicants must obtain from a private search house an **Ontario biased or weighted** NUANS computer printed search report on the name which is to be **cleared** by the Companies Branch of the Ministry. The names and addresses of private search houses are listed in the yellow pages of telephone directories under the heading "Searchers of Records".

The **original** NUANS report dated not more than 90 days before submission of the application must accompany the application. Failure to obtain the NUANS report, or submission of a stale dated report will delay processing of the application.

07065(2011/06)

APPLICATION

ITEM 1 The name of the corporation must be set out in BLOCK CAPITAL letters in the spaces provided and must commence on the first line in the first space.

ITEM 2 Set out in BLOCK CAPITAL letters the name **other than** the corporate name under which the corporation is to be licenced in Ontario. If not applicable, please state "none". If this Item is completed, a Form 2 under the Business Names Act must also be filed for the business name with the prescribed fee.

ITEM 3 State the jurisdiction to which the corporation is subject, for example, State of New York, U.S.A., etc.

ITEM 4 State the full date (year, month, day) on which the corporation came into existence either by incorporation, amalgamation or merger, as the case may be.

ITEM 5 The address (where multi-office building include room or suite number) of the head office of the corporation must be set out in full including the **postal/zip code.** Post office box is not an acceptable address for head office. The name of the State and Country must also be set out.

ITEM 6 The full date (year, month, day) on which the corporation was authorized to make the application must be set out.

ITEM 7 The address (where multi-office building, include room or suite number) of the chief place of business in Ontario (if determined) of the corporation must be set out in full including the **postal code.** Post office box is not an acceptable address for principal office. If none, state so.

ITEM 8 Set out one first name, initials and last name and full residence address or address for service (including suite number, if applicable) of the Chief Officer or Manager in Ontario (if determined).

ITEM 9 Set out the business which the corporation intends to carry on in Ontario.

ITEM 10 to 13 incl. must appear in all applications.

EXECUTION

Both copies of the application must be signed by an officer or a director of the corporation and the signatures must be original signatures and not photocopies. Applications containing photocopied signatures will not be accepted. The name of the corporation must be set out above the signature.

The corporate seal must be affixed to both copies of the application. If the jurisdiction to which the corporation is subject does not require its corporations to have a corporate seal, please so indicate when submitting the application.

The application (in duplicate), Appointment of Agent for Service and Consent to Act as Agent for Service (Form 2), together with the fee, Ontario biased NUANS computer printed search report and Certificate of Status should be mailed or delivered to:

Ministry of Government Services
Central Production and Verification Services Branch
393 University Avenue, Suite 200
Toronto ON M5G 2M2

375 University Avenue, 2nd Floor (In Person)

07065(2011/06)

Pour remplir la formule

DROITS

Le paiement des droits est de 330 $, à acquitter en dollars canadiens, se fait par chèque ou par mandat, libellé à l'ordre du ministre des Finances. **En cas de paiement par chèque, la dénomination social de la personne morale doit figurer au recto de ce dernier.** Prière de ne pas envoyer d'espèces par le courrier.

FORMAT

Présenter la demande **en double exemplaire** sur la formule 1 prescrite par les règlements de l'Ontario pris en application de la *Loi sur les personnes morales extraprovinciales*. Les demandes qui ne sont pas conformes à la formule 1 seront rejetées et renvoyées aux requérants.

PRÉSENTATION DES DOCUMENTS

Dactylographier ou écrire lisiblement en LETTRES MAJUSCULES les demandes et les documents à l'appui qui sont déposés au ministère, en vue de la microphotographie. Les demandes et les documents à l'appui doivent être remplis uniquement au recto d'un papier filigrané blanc de bonne qualité, de format 210 mm x 297 mm avec une marge de 30 mm à gauche, ou de format 8 1/2 po x 11 po avec une marge de 1 1/4 po à gauche. Les documents qui ne sont pas conformes à cette norme seront rejetés et renvoyés aux requérants.

PAGES

Les pages sont numérotées de 1 à 3 et doivent rester dans cet ordre. Ne pas enlever de page. Si certaines sections ne concernent pas les requérants, indiquer "néant" ou << sans objet >> (s/o).

S'il manque des pages, les demandes seront rejetées et renvoyées aux requérants.

PAGES SUPPLÉMENTAIRES

Si faute d'espace, il faut insérer des pages supplémentaires, elles doivent être du même format que les autres, comporter une marge de 30 mm ou de 1 1/4 po à gauche et porter le même numéro que la page originale suivi d'une lettre de l'alphabet pour en indiquer l'ordre. Par exemple, on numérotera les pages supplémentaires pour la section 9 2A, 2B, etc. Voir les instructions au paragraphe **Présentation des documents.**

DOCUMENTS À L'APPUI

Les documents suivants doivent accompagner la demande :

a) une **Désignation du mandataire aux fins de signification** (formule 2);

b) un **Certificat de statut légal** portant le sceau officiel et signé par l'agent responsable (directeur, des corporations etc.) de la compétence législative dont relève la personne morale, et indiquant :
   (i) la dénomination sociale de la personne morale;
   (ii) la date de constitution ou de fusion;
   (iii) la compétence législative dont relève la personne morale;
   (iv) que la personne morale conserve sa validaté et son existence juridique, et

c) **le rapport de recherche NUANS original, approuvé par le ministère** (voir les instructions sur les dénominations sociales).

DÉNOMINATION SOCIALE

Avant de remplir la demande, les dirigeants de la personne morale sont priés de vérifier si la dénomination social est disponible en Ontario. Pour ce faire, ils doivent obtenir d'une maison de recherche privée un rapport de recherche informatique NUANS sur la dénomination sociale **portant principalement sur l'Ontario.** Cette dénomination social doit être **acceptée** par la Direction des compagnies du ministère. Les noms et adresses des maisons de recherche privées figurent dans les pages jaunes de l'annuaire téléphonique sous le titre << Searchers of Records/Titres et archives - Recherche >>.

L' **original** du rapport NUANS, daté de 90 jours au plus avant le dépôt de la demande, doit accompagner celle-ci. Le défaut de présentation du rapport ou la présentation d'un rapport périmé retardera le traitement de la demande.

07065(2011/06)

DEMANDE

SECTION 1 Inscrire la dénomination sociale de la compagnie EN LETTRES MAJUSCULES à l'endroit réservé à cet effet, en commençant par la première case de la première ligne.

SECTION 2 Indiquer EN LETTRES MAJUSCULES le nom **autre que** la dénomination sociale qui figurera sur le permis ontarien délivré à la compagnie. S'il n'y a pas lieu de remplir cette section, inscrire "sans objet". Sinon, remplir et présenter également la formule 2 en vertu de la *Loi sur les noms commerciaux* et y joindre les droits prescrits.

SECTION 3 Indiquer la compétence législative dont relève la compagnie, par exemple, État de New York, (É.-U.).

SECTION 4 Inscrire la date complète (année, mois et jour) de constitution ou de fusion de la compagnie.

SECTION 5 Inscrire l'adresse au complet (s'il s'agit d'un immeuble de bureaux, préciser le numéro du bureau) du siège social de la compagnie, **code postal/zip** compris. L'indication d'une case postale n'est pas une adresse acceptable pour le siège social. Ne pas oublier de donner le nom de l'état et du pays.

SECTION 6 Indiquer la date complète (année, mois et jour) à laquelle la compagnie a reçu la permission de faire une demande de permis extraprovincial.

SECTION 7 Inscrire l'adresse au complet (s'il s'agit d'un immeuble de bureaux, préciser le numéro du bureau) de l'établissement principal de la compagnie en Ontario (si elle y est établie), **code postal** compris. L' indication d'une case postale n'est pas une adresse acceptable pour l'établissement principal. Si la compagnie n'a pas de case postale, le préciser.

SECTION 8 Indiquer les prénoms, le nom de famille et l'adresse au complet du domicile du directeur ou du gérant en Ontario (s'il est désigné) ou l'adresse où l'on peut le joindre aux fins de signification.

SECTION 9 Décrire les activités que la compagnie compte exercer en Ontario.

Toutes les demandes doivent comprendre les sections 10 à 13.

SIGNATURE

Un dirigeant ou un administrateur de la compagnie doit signer de sa main la demande en double exemplaire. Les demandes portant des signatures photocopiées seront rejetées. Les signatures doivent toujours apparaître en dessous de la dénomination sociale de la compagnie.

La compagnie doit apposer son sceau aux deux exemplaires de la demande. Si la compagnie n'est pas tenue d'avoir un sceau par la compétence législative dont elle relève, elle doit l'indiquer dans sa demande.

Envoyer ou remettre la demande (en double exemplaire), la désignation du mandataire et l'acceptation du mandataire aux fins de signification (formule 2), les droits, le rapport de recherche informatique NUANS portant principalement sur l'Ontario et le certificat de statut légal au :

Ministère des Services gouvernementaux
Direction des services centraux de production et de vérification
393, avenue University, bureau 200
Toronto ON M5G 2M2

375, avenue University, 2e étage (dépôt en personne)

07065(2011/06)

Ontario Corporation Number
Numéro de la compagnie en Ontario

Form 1
Extra-Provincial Corporations Act

Formule 1
Loi de 1984 sur les compagnies extraprovinciales

APPLICATION FOR EXTRA-PROVINCIAL LICENCE/ DEMANDE EN VUE D'OBTENIR UN PERMIS EXTRAPROVINCIAL

1.

1. The name of the Corporation is (Print in UPPER CASE ONLY) :
Dénomination sociale de la compagnie (Écrire en LETTRES MAJUSCULES SEULEMENT) :

2. Business name or style, other than the corporate name, under which the corporation is to be licensed in Ontario, if any (if none, state so): / Nom, autre que la dénomination sociale, sous lequel un permis doit être délivré à la compagnie en Ontario, le cas échéant (si ce n'est pas le cas, veuillez l'indiquer) :

3. Jurisdiction to which subject:/
Compétence législative :

(Name of Province, State or Country) / (Province, État ou pays)

4. Date of incorporation/amalgamation:/
Date de la constitution ou de la fusion :

year / année month / mois day / jour

5. Full address of the head or registered office: / Adresse du siège social :

(Street & Number or R.R. Number & if Multi-Office Building give Room No.) / (Rue et numéro ou numéro de la R.R. et numéro du bureau)

(Name of Municipality or Post Office) / (Municipalité ou bureau de poste)

Postal/Zip Code / Code postal/zip

(Name of State or Country) / (État ou pays)

6. The corporation has been authorized to make this application by a resolution passed by the directors of the corporation at a meeting held on: / La compagnie est autorisée à présenter cette demande au moyen d'une résolution adoptée par ses administrateurs le :

year / année month / mois day / jour

07065(2011/06)

2.

7. Full address (including postal code) of the principal office or chief place of business in Ontario, if determined (if not, state so): / Adresse de l'établissement principal en Ontario, si elle est établie (si ce n'est pas le cas, l'indiquer) :

(Street & Number or R.R. Number & if Multi-Office Building give Room No.) / (Rue et numéro ou numéro de la R.R. et numéro du bureau)

(Name of Municipality or Post Office) / (Municipalité ou bureau de poste)

Postal/Zip Code / Code postal/zip

8. Chief officer or manager in Ontario, if determined (if none, state so): /
Premier dirigeant ou gérant en Ontario, s'il est désigné (si ce n'est pas le cas, l'indiquer) :

Name in full, including all first and middle names / Nom et prénoms	Residence address, giving Street & No. or R.R. No. & Municipality or Post Office and Postal Code: / Adresse personnelle y compris la rue et le numéro ou le numéro de la R.R., et le nom de la municipalité ou du bureau de poste et le code postal

9. The business which the corporation intends to carry on in Ontario is: /
Les activités commerciales que la compagnie entend exercer en Ontario sont les suivantes :

07065(2011/06)

3.

10. The corporate existence of the corporation is not limited in any way by statute or otherwise and the corporation is a valid and subsisting corporation. / La personnalité morale de la compagnie n'est restreinte d'aucune manière notamment par l'effet de la loi et la compagnie conserve sa validité et son existence juridique.

11. The corporation has the capacity to carry on business in Ontario. / La compagnie est habilitée à exercer ses activités commerciales en Ontario.

12. The corporation has the capacity to hold land without conditions or limitations. / La compagnie est habilitée à posséder des biens-fonds sans condition ni restriction.

13. The corporation hereby acknowledges that upon the licence being issued the corporation shall be subject to the provisions of the *Extra-Provincial Corporations Act*, the *Corporations Information Act*, the *Corporations Tax Act* and to such further and other legislative provisions as the Legislature of Ontario may deem expedient in order to secure the due management of the corporation's affairs and the protection of its creditors within Ontario. /
La compagnie reconnaît par la présente que dès la délivrance du permis, elle sera assujettie aux dispositions de la *Loi sur les compagnies extraprovinciales*, de la *Loi sur les renseignements exigés des compagnies et associations*, de la *Loi sur l'imposition des personnes morales* ainsi qu'aux autres dispositions législatives ultérieures que la Législature de l'Ontario peut juger opportunes afin d'assurer la saine gestion des affaires de la compagnie et la protection de ses créanciers en Ontario.

This application is executed in duplicate. / La présente demande est signée en double exemplaire.

____
(Name of Corporation) / (Dénomination sociale de la compagnie)

By: / Signé : ______________________________
(Signature) / (Signature)

____
(Description of Office) / (Fonctions)

(Corporate Seal) / (Sceau de la compagnie)

07065(2011/06)

Form 2 — Appointment of Agent for Service/Revised Appointment of Agent for Service*

Instructions for Completing

FEES

There is no fee payable for filing an Appointment of Agent for Service/Revised Appointment of Agent for Service.

FORMAT OF DOCUMENTS

The Appointment of Agent for Service or Revised Appointment of Agent for Service must be in Form 2 prescribed by Ontario Regulations made under the *Extra-Provincial Corporations Act*.

GENERAL

An Agent for Service must be a natural person 18 years of age or older, having his/her residence in the Province of Ontario or a corporation (other than the applicant) having its registered office in the Province of Ontario.

Where the Agent is a corporation, the Consent to Act as Agent for Service shall be executed in the name of the corporation under the signature of an officer or a director of the corporation which is to act as the agent.

All information must be typewritten or, if completed by hand, be printed in BLOCK CAPITAL letters. All documents filed with the Branch are microfilmed and must therefore be neat, legible and suitable for microfilming. Documents which do not conform to this standard will be returned to the corporation. We recommend the form be completed using heavy black typewriter ribbon or black pen.

ONTARIO CORPORATION NUMBER

"Ontario Corporation Number" appears in the top right corner of the extra-provincial licence issued to the corporation. Where a Revised Appointment of Agent for Service is prepared, the Ontario corporation number must be set out by the appointing corporation.

EXECUTION STATEMENT

The form must be in duplicate and both copies must have original signatures.

The **Original** Appointment or **Revised** Appointment is to be mailed or delivered to:

Ministry of Government Services
Central Production and Verification Services Branch
393 University Ave, Suite 200
Toronto ON M5G 2M2

375 University Avenue, 2nd Floor (In Person)

07064 (2011/05)

Pour remplir la formule

DROITS
Aucuns droits ne sont perçus pour le dépôt de la présente formule.

FORMULE À DÉPOSER
La désignation du mandataire aux fins de signification doit être présentée sur la Formule 2 -- Désignation du mandataire aux fins de signification / Modification de la désignation de mandataire — prescrite par le Règlement de la *Loi sur les personnes morales extraprovinciales* de l'Ontario.

GÉNÉRALITÉS
Le mandataire désigné aux fins de signification doit être une personne âgée d'au moins 18 ans et résidant en Ontario, ou une personne morale (autre que le demandeur) ayant son siège en Ontario.

Si le mandataire est une personne morale, le Consentement à agir en qualité de mandataire aux fins de signification doit être signé par un dirigeant ou un administrateur de la personne morale, au nom de celle-ci.

Tous les renseignements doivent être tapés à la machine ou, s'ils sont indiqués au stylo, inscrits en LETTRES MAJUSCULES. Tous les documents déposés auprès de la Direction des compagnies sont microfilmés; l'écriture doit donc être soignée et lisible. Les documents non conformes à cette règle seront renvoyés à la société. Pour une présentation soignée, nous recommandons l'utilisation d'un ruban de machine épais noir ou d'un stylo noir.

NUMÉRO DE LA SOCIÉTÉ EN ONTARIO

Le numéro de la société en Ontario est indiqué dans le coin supérieur droit du permis extraprovincial délivré à la société. Si on remplit la présente formule pour modifier la désignation du mandataire, la société doit inscrire le numéro de la société en Ontario.

SIGNATURE

La Formule doit être signée en double exemplaire. Les signatures doivent être originales.

La Désignation du mandataire aux fins de signification, **originale** ou **modifiée**, doit être envoyée par la poste ou livrée à l'adresse suivante :

Ministère des Services gouvernementaux
Direction des services centraux de production et de vérification
393, avenue University, bureau 200
Toronto ON M5G 2M2

375, avenue University, 2e étage (dépôt en personne)

07064 (2011/05)

Form 2
Extra-Provincial Corporations Act
Formule 2
Loi sur les personnes morales extraprovinciales

Check (X) the appropriate box
Cochez (X) la case appropriée

☐ APPOINTMENT OF AGENT FOR SERVICE
DÉSIGNATION DU MANDATAIRE AUX FINS DE SIGNIFICATION

or/ou

☐ REVISED APPOINTMENT OF AGENT FOR SERVICE
MODIFICATION DE LA DÉSIGNATION DE MANDATAIRE

Ontario Corporation Number
Numéro de la société en Ontario

(Name of appointing corporation)
(Dénomination sociale de la société désignant le mandataire)

(hereinafter called the "Corporation") hereby nominates, constitutes and appoints
(ci-après appelée la « société ») constitue

(Name of agent giving first name, initials and surname; or full Corporate Name)
(Mandataire : prénom, initiale et nom de famille; ou dénomination sociale complète)

(Business address of the agent, including Street Number, Suite or Room Number and Municipality)
(Adresse d'affaires du mandataire : numéro et rue, bureau et municipalité)

Postal/Zip Code / Code postal/zip

its true and lawful agent for service, to act as such, and as such to sue and be sued, plead and be impleaded in any court in Ontario and generally on behalf of the corporation within Ontario to accept service of process and to receive all lawful notices and, for the purposes of the corporation, to do all acts and to execute all deeds and other instruments relating to the matters within the scope of this appointment. Until due lawful notice of the appointment of another and subsequent agent has been given to and accepted by the Director under the *Extra-Provincial Corporations Act*, service of process or of papers and notices upon the said agent for service shall be accepted by the corporation as sufficient service.
son mandataire aux fins de signification, qui agira en cette qualité, soutiendra à titre de demandeur ou de défendeur les actions en justice intentées en Ontario et, de manière générale, recevra et acceptera en Ontario, au nom de la société, tous actes de procédure et tous avis requis ou autorisés par la loi, accomplira toutes actions et signera tous actes et autres instruments relativement aux affaires entrant dans le cadre du présent mandat. Tant qu'un avis en bonne et due forme visant à désigner un autre mandataire n'aura pas été donné au directeur et accepté par lui, conformément à la *Loi sur les personnes morales extraprovinciales*, la société accepte comme suffisante la signification au mandataire susmentionné desdits actes de procédure, avis et autres documents.

(Name of Corporation / Dénomination sociale de la société)

Dated
Date ________ year / année month / mois day / jour

BY: ________ (Signature) ________ (Description of Officer / Titre)

(Corporate Seal)
(Sceau de la société)

________ (Signature) ________ (Description of Officer / Titre)

CONSENT TO ACT AS AGENT FOR SERVICE
CONSENTEMENT À AGIR EN QUALITÉ DE MANDATAIRE AUX FINS DE SIGNIFICATION

I / Je soussigné(e), ________
(Name of Agent in full; if Corporation, full Corporate Name)
(Nom complet du mandataire; si personne morale, dénomination sociale complète)

of / dont l'adresse d'affaires est : ________,
(Business address including Street Number, Suite or Room Number and Municipality)
(Adresse d'affaires : numéro et rue, numéro du bureau et municipalité)

Ontario, hereby consent to act as the agent for service in the Province of Ontario of
en Ontario, consens par les présentes à agir, dans la Province de l'Ontario, en qualité de mandataire aux fins de signification de

(Name of Corporation / Dénomination sociale de la société)

pursuant to the appointment executed by the said corporation on the
en vertu du présent mandat que ladite société a signé le

________ day of / jour de ________, year / année ________;

authorizing me to accept service of process and notices on its behalf.
ledit mandat m'autorise à recevoir et à accepter au nom de la société tous actes de procédure, avis et autres documents.

Dated
Date ________ year / année month / mois day / jour

(Signature of witness / Signature du témoin)

(Signature of the consenting person or Officer/Director of Corporation)
(Signature du mandataire; si personne morale, signature du dirigeant / administrature agissant en son nom)

07064 (2011/05)

Page 1 of/de 1

Form 3 — Application for Amendment to Extra-Provincial Licence*

Instructions for Completing

FEE

The fee for an amended extra-provincial licence is $150.00, payable in Canadian funds. Cheques or money orders are to be made payable to the Minister of Finance. **Where a cheque is tendered in payment, the name of the corporation must be entered on the face of the cheque.** Do not send cash through the mail.

FORMAT

The application must be in **duplicate** in Form 3 prescribed in Ontario Regulations made under the *Extra-Provincial Corporations Act*. Applications which do not conform to Form 3 cannot be accepted and will be returned to the applicant submitting the application.

APPEARANCE OF DOCUMENTS

Applications and any supporting documents which are to be filed with the Ministry must be typewritten, or, if completed by hand, printed in BLOCK CAPITAL letters, and must be legible and compatible with microfilming process. Applications and supporting documents must be upon one side of good quality white bond paper 210 mm. x 297 mm. with a margin of 30 mm. on the left hand side or 8 1/2" x 11" with a margin of 1 1/4" on the left hand side. Documents which do not conform to this standard cannot be accepted and will be returned to the applicant submitting the application.

PAGES

The pages are numbered 1 to 2 and must remain in that order. Pages must not be removed. If any item is inapplicable, state "nil" or "not applicable".

Applications with missing pages will not be accepted and will be returned to the applicant.

SUPPLEMENTARY PAGES

If additional pages are required due to lack of sufficient space they must be the same size as all other pages, must have a margin of 30 mm. or 1 1/4" on the left hand side and must be numbered the same as the original with the addition of letters of the alphabet to indicate sequence. For example, supplementary pages for Item 7 would be numbered 1A, 1B, etc. See instructions for **Appearance of Documents.**

CHANGE OF NAME

A corporation which holds an extra-provincial licence in Ontario may use in Ontario only the corporate name in which the licence is issued. Where the corporation has changed its corporate name in its home jurisdiction since the date of the issue of the extra-provincial licence or since the date of last amendment to the extra-provincial licence, it must obtain an amendment to its extra-provincial licence within 30 days of the date of change, authorizing it to use its new name in Ontario.

Prior to completing the application the officers of the corporation should satisfy themselves that the corporate name is available for use in Ontario. To do this the applicants must obtain from a private search house an original **Ontario biased** NUANS computer printed search report on the name which is to be **cleared** by the Central Production and Verification Services Branch of the Ministry. The names and addresses of private search houses are listed in the yellow pages of telephone directories under the heading "Searchers of Records".

SUPPORTING DOCUMENTS

Where the corporation has changed its corporate name in its home jurisdiction the application must be accompanied by:

a) a **Certificate of Status** issued under the seal of office and signed by the proper officer (Director, Corporations Branch, etc) of the jurisdiction to which the corporation is subject, setting out the following:
   - (i) the name of the corporation;
   - (ii) date of incorporation/amalgamation or merger;
   - (iii) jurisdiction to which the corporation is subject;
   - (iv) that the corporation is a valid and subsisting corporation; and

b) An original **Ontario biased** computer printed name search on its new name obtained from a private search house and produced by the NUANS System not more than 90 days prior to the date of delivery of the application **which is to be cleared** by the Central Production and Verification Services Branch of the Ministry. The names, addresses and telephone numbers of private search houses are listed in the yellow pages of telephone directories under the heading "Searchers of Records".

   The original cleared NUANS report must accompany the application. Failure to obtain the NUANS report when required, or submission of a stale dated report will delay the processing of the application.

07066E (2011/05)

APPLICATION

ITEM 1 The name of the corporation which is currently licenced in Ontario must be set out in BLOCK CAPITAL letters in the spaces provided and must commence on the first line in the first space.

ITEM 2 Set out in BLOCK CAPITAL letters the name **other than** the corporate name under which the corporation presently is authorized to carry on business in Ontario. If not applicable, please state "none".

ITEM 3 State the jurisdiction to which the corporation is subject, for example, State of New York, U.S.A., etc.

ITEM 4 State the full date (year, month, day) on which the corporation came into existence either by incorporation, amalgamation or merger, as the case may be.

ITEM 5 State the full date, (year, month, day) of the original extra-provincial licence issued to the corporation which is presently in force.

ITEM 6 Where the corporation has changed its corporate name in its home jurisdiction since the date of the issue of the extra-provincial licence set out the new name of the corporation in BLOCK CAPITAL letters commencing in the first space of the first line. Where there is no change in the name, state "Not Applicable".

ITEM 7 State in point form the amendment(s) desired. Where space provided in Item 7 is not sufficient, supplementary pages should be inserted following page 1. See instructions for **Supplementary Pages**.

ITEM 8 State the full date (year, month, day) on which the corporation was authorized to make an application for amendment to its extra-provincial licence in Ontario.

EXECUTION

Both copies of the application must be signed by an officer or a director of the corporation and the signatures must be original signatures and not photocopies. Applications containing photocopied signatures will not be accepted. The name of the corporation must be set out above the signature.

The corporate seal must be affixed to both copies of the application. If the jurisdiction to which the corporation is subject does not require its corporations to have a corporate seal, please so indicate when submitting the application.

The application (in duplicate), together with the fee, (Ontario biased NUANS computer printed search report and Certificate of Status, if required) should be mailed or delivered to:

Ministry of Government Services
Central Production and Verification Services Branch
393 University Ave, Suite 200
Toronto ON M5G 2M2

375 University Avenue, 2nd Floor (In Person)

07066E (2011/05)

Pour remplir la formule

DROITS

Le paiement des droits est de 150 00 $, à acquitter en dollars canadiens, se fait par chèque ou par mandat, libellé à l'ordre du Ministre des Finances. **En cas de paiement par chèque, la dénomination sociale doit figurer au recto de ce dernier.** Prière de ne pas envoyer d'espèces par le courrier.

FORMAT

Présenter la demande **en double exemplaire** sur la formule 3 prescrite par les règlements de l'Ontario pris en application de la *Loi sur les compagnies extraprovinciales*. Les demandes qui ne sont pas conformes à la formule 3 seront rejetées et renvoyées aux requérants.

PRÉSENTATION DES DOCUMENTS

Dactylographier ou écrire lisiblement en LETTRES MAJUSCULES les demandes et les documents à l'appui qui sont déposés au ministère, en vue de la microphotographie. Les demandes et les documents à l'appui doivent être remplis uniquement au recto d'un papier filigrané blanc de bonne qualité, de format 210 mm x 297 mm avec une marge de 30 mm à gauche, ou de format 8 1/2 " x 11" avec une marge de 1 1/4" à gauche. Les documents qui ne sont pas conformes à cette norme seront rejetés et renvoyés aux requérants.

PAGES

Les pages sont numérotées de 1 à 2 et doivent rester dans cet ordre. Ne pas enlever de page. Si certaines sections ne concernent pas les requérants, indiquer « néant » ou « sans objet » (s/o).

S'il manque des pages, les demandes seront rejetées et renvoyées aux requérants.

PAGES SUPPLÉMENTAIRES

Si, faute d'espace, il faut insérer des pages supplémentaires, elles doivent être du même format que les autres, comporter une marge de 30 mm ou de 1 1/4" à gauche et porter le même numéro que la page originale suivi d'une lettre de l'alphabet pour en indiquer l'ordre. Par exemple, on numérotera les pages supplémentaires pour la section 7 1A, 1B, etc. Voir les instructions au paragraphe **Présentation des documents.**

CHANGEMENT DE DÉNOMINATION SOCIALE

Une compagnie qui détient un permis extraprovincial en Ontario ne peut utiliser en Ontario que la dénomination sociale figurant sur le permis qui lui a été délivré. Si elle a changé de dénomination sociale dans sa compétence législative d'origine depuis la date de délivrance du permis extraprovincial ou depuis la date de la dernière modification de son permis extraprovincial, elle doit faire modifier son permis extraprovincial dans les trente jours suivant l'entrée en vigueur de la nouvelle dénomination sociale pour pouvoir l'utiliser en Ontario.

Avant de remplir la demande, les dirigeants de la compagnie sont priés de vérifier si la dénomination sociale est disponible en Ontario. Pour ce faire, ils doivent obtenir d'une maison de recherche privée un rapport de recherche informatique NUANS sur la dénomination sociale **portant principalement sur l'Ontario.** Cette dénomination sociale doit être **acceptée** par la Direction des services centraux de production et de vérification du ministère. Les noms et adresses des maisons de recherche figurent dans les Pages jaunes de l'annuaire téléphonique, sous larubrique
« Titres et archives – Recherche » ou « Searchers of Records » .

DOCUMENTS À L'APPUI

Toute compagnie qui a changé sa dénomination sociale dans sa compétence législative d'origine doit présenter avec sa demande les documents suivants :

a) un **Certificat de statut légal** portant le sceau officiel et signé par l'agent responsable (directeur des compagnies, etc.) de la compétence législative dont relève la compagnie, et indiquant :
   (i) la dénomination sociale de la compagnie;
   (ii) la date de constitution ou de fusion;
   (iii) la compétence législative dont relève la compagnie;
   (iv) que la compagnie continue d'exister, et

b) un rapport de recherche informatique NUANS sur la nouvelle dénomination sociale **portant principalement sur l'Ontario**; ce rapport doit être établi par une maison de recherche privée, daté de 90 jours au plus avant le dépôt de la demande et **approuvé** par la Direction des services centraux de production et de vérification du ministère. Les noms, adresses et numéros de téléphone des maisons de recherche privées figurent dans les pages jaunes de l'annuaire téléphonique sous le titre "Searchers of Records/Titres et archives - Recherche".

   La demande doit être accompagnée de l'original du rapport NUANS approuvé. Tout défaut de présentation du rapport ou la présentation d'un rapport périmé retardera le traitement de la demande.

07066F (2011/05)

DEMANDE

SECTION 1 Inscrire la dénomination sociale de la compagnie qui détient actuellement un permis en Ontario.

EN LETTRES MAJUSCULES à l'endroit réservé à cet effet, en commençant par la première case de la première ligne.

SECTION 2 Indiquer EN LETTRES MAJUSCULES le nom **autre que** la dénomination sociale sous lequel la compagnie exerce actuellement ses activités en Ontario. S'il n'y a pas lieu de remplir cette section, inscrire « sans objet ».

SECTION 3 Indiquer la compétence législative dont relève la compagnie, par exemple, État de New York (É.-U.).

SECTION 4 Inscrire la date complète (année, mois et jour) de constitution ou de fusion de la compagnie.

SECTION 5 Indiquer la date complète (année, mois et jour) de délivrance du permis extraprovincial original de la compagnie, lequel est toujours en vigueur.

SECTION 6 Si la compagnie a changé de dénomination sociale dans sa compétence législative d'origine depuis la date de délivrance du permis extraprovincial ou depuis la date de la dernière modification du permis extraprovincial, indiquer cette nouvelle dénomination EN LETTRES MAJUSCULES en commençant par la première case de la première ligne. Sinon, écrire « sans objet » (s/o).

SECTION 7 Indiquer point par point les modifications souhaitées. Si l'espace réservé à la section 7 n'est pas suffisant, ajouter des pages supplémentaires à la suite de la page 1. Voir les instructions au paragraphe **Pages supplémentaires**.

SECTION 8 Indiquer la date complète (année, mois et jour) à laquelle la compagnie a reçu la permission de faire une demande de permis extraprovincial modifié en Ontario.

SIGNATURE

Un dirigeant ou un administrateur de la compagnie doit signer de sa main la demande en double exemplaire. Les demandes portant des signatures photocopiées seront rejetées. Les signatures doivent toujours apparaître en dessous de la dénomination sociale de la compagnie.

La compagnie doit apposer son sceau aux deux exemplaires de la demande. Si la compagnie n'est pas tenue d'avoir un sceau par la compétence législative dont elle relève, elle doit l'indiquer dans sa demande.

Envoyer ou remettre la demande (en double exemplaire), les droits, (le rapport de recherche informatique NUANS portant principalement sur l'Ontario et le certificat de statut légal, le cas échéant) au :

Ministère des Services gouvernementaux
Direction des services centraux de production et de vérification
393 avenue University, bureau 200
Toronto ON M5G 2M2

375, avenue University, 2e étage (dépôt en personne)

07066F (2011/05)

Ontario Corporation Number
Numéro de la compagnie en Ontario

Form 3
Extra-Provincial Corporations Act

Formule 3
Loi sur les personnes morales extraprovinciales

APPLICATION FOR AMENDED EXTRA-PROVINCIAL LICENCE/ DEMANDE EN VUE D'OBTENIR UN PERMIS EXTRAPROVINCIAL MODIFIÉ

1. The name of the Corporation which is currently licensed in Ontario (Print in UPPER CASE ONLY) :
Dénomination sociale de la compagnie présentement autorisé en Ontario (Écrire en LETTRES MAJUSCULES SEULEMENT :

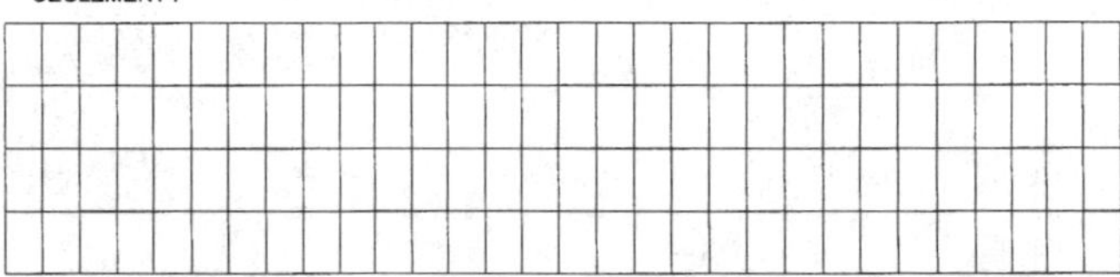

2. Name, other than the corporate name, under which the corporation is currently licensed to carry on business in Ontario, if different from above: / Nom, autre que la dénomination sociale, sous lequel la compagnie est présentement autorisée à exercer ses activités commerciales en Ontario, s'il diffère de celui qui est mentionné ci-dessus :

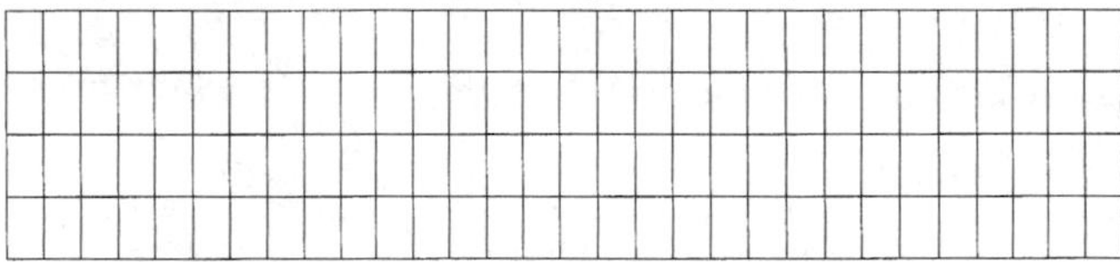

3. Jurisdiction to which subject:/
Compétence législative :

(Name of Province, State or Country) / (Province, État ou pays)

4. Date of incorporation/amalgamation:/
Date de la constitution ou de la fusion :

year / année month / mois day / jour

5. Date of original extra-provincial licence: /
Date du permis extraprovincial original :

year / année month / mois day / jour

6. The name of the corporation has been changed in its home jurisdiction to: /
La dénomination sociale de la compagnie, dans la compétence législative de sa constitution, a été modifée de la façon suivante :

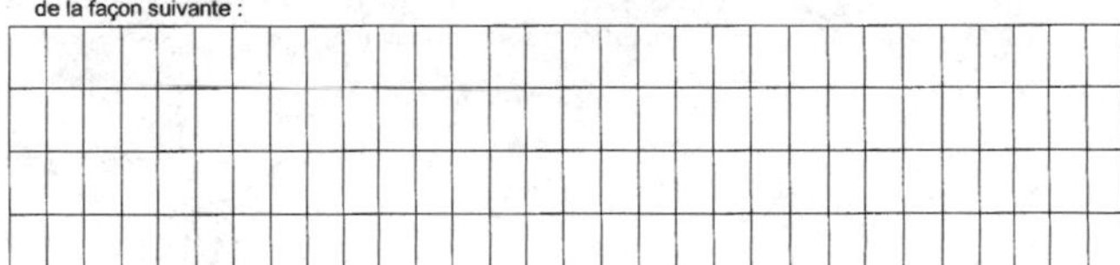

and the corporation requests that it be permitted to use this name in Ontario./
et la compagnie demande l'autorisation d'utiliser cette dénomination sociale en Ontario .

07066 (2011/05)

Page 1 of/de 2

7. The corporation requests amendments to its provincial licence as follows: /
La compagnie demande que son permis extraprovincial soit modifé de la façon suivante :

8. The corporation has been authorized to make this application by a resolution passed by the directors of the corporation on /
La compagnie est autorisée à faire la présente demande au moyen d'une résolution adoptée par ses administrateurs le

year / année month / mois day / jour

This application is executed in duplicate. / La présente demande est signée en double exemplaire.

(Name of Corporation) / (Dénomination sociale de la compagnie)

By: / Signé : ______________________

(Signature) / (Signature)

(Description of Office) / (Fonctions)

(Corporate Seal) / (Sceau de la compagnie)

07066 (2011/05)

Page 2 of/de 2

Form 4 — Application for Termination of Extra-Provincial Licence*

INSTRUCTIONS FOR COMPLETING

FEE

There is no fee payable for Termination of Extra-Provincial Licence.

FORMAT

The application must be in **duplicate** in Form 4 prescribed in Ontario Regulations made under the *Extra-Provincial Corporations Act*. Applications which do not conform to Form 4 cannot be accepted and will be returned to the applicant submitting the application.

APPEARANCE OF DOCUMENTS

Applications and any supporting documents which are to be filed with the Ministry must be typewritten, or, if completed by hand, printed in BLOCK CAPITAL letters, and must be legible and compatible with the microfilming process. Applications and supporting documents must be upon one side of good quality white bond paper 210 mm. x 297 mm. with a margin of 30 mm. on the left hand side or 8 ½" x 11" with a margin of 1¼" on the left hand side. Documents which do not conform to this standard cannot be accepted and will be returned to the applicant submitting the application.

APPLICATION

ITEM 1 The name of the corporation must be set out in BLOCK CAPITAL letters in the spaces provided and must commence on the first line in the first space.

ITEM 2 Set out in BLOCK CAPITAL letters the name **other than** the corporate name under which the corporation is licensed in Ontario. If not applicable, please state "none".

ITEM 3 State the jurisdiction to which the corporation is subject, for example, State of New York, U.S.A., etc.

ITEM 4 State the full date (year, month, day) on which the corporation came into existence either by incorporation, amalgamation or merger, as the case may be.

ITEM 5 State the full date (year, month, day) on which the corporation ceased to carry on business in Ontario.

EXECUTION

Both copies of the application must be signed by an officer or a director of the corporation and the signatures must be original signatures and not photocopies. Applications containing photocopied signatures will not be accepted. The name of the corporation must be set out above the signature.

The corporate seal must be affixed to both copies of the application. If the jurisdiction to which the corporation is subject does not require its corporations to have a corporate seal, please so indicate when submitting the application.

The application (in duplicate) should be mailed or delivered to:

Ministry of Government Services
Central Production and Verification Services Branch
393 University Avenue, Suite 200
Toronto ON M5G 2M2

375 University Avenue, 2nd Floor (In Person)

07067 (2011/06) Français au verso

POUR REMPLIR LA FORMULE

DROITS

Aucuns droits ne sont perçus pour le dépôt d'une demande de résiliation d'un permis extraprovincial.

FORMAT

Présenter la demande **en double exemplaire** sur la formule 4 prescrite par les règlements de l'Ontario pris en application de la *Loi sur les personnes morales extraprovinciales*. Les demandes qui ne sont pas conformes à la formule 4 seront rejetées et renvoyées aux requérants.

PRÉSENTATION DES DOCUMENTS

Dactylographier ou écrire lisiblement en LETTRES MAJUSCULES les demandes et les documents à l'appui qui sont déposés au ministère, en vue de la microphotographie. Les demandes et les documents à l'appui doivent être remplis uniquement au recto d'un papier filigrané blanc de bonne qualité, de format 210 mm sur 297 mm avec une marge de 30 mm à gauche, ou de format 8 ½ po sur 11 po avec une marge de 1¼ po à gauche. Les documents qui ne sont pas conformes à cette norme seront rejetés et renvoyés aux requérants.

DEMANDE

SECTION 1 Inscrire la dénomination sociale de la personne morale en LETTRES MAJUSCULES à l'endroit réservé à cet effet, en commençant par la première case de la première ligne.

SECTION 2 Indiquer en LETTRES MAJUSCULES le nom **autre que** la dénomination sociale qui figure sur le permis ontarien délivré à la personne morale. S'il n'y a pas lieu de remplir cette section, inscrire « sans objet ».

SECTION 3 Indiquer la compétence législative dont relève la personne morale, par exemple, État de New York, (É.-U.).

SECTION 4 Inscrire la date complète (année, mois et jour) de constitution ou de fusion de la personne morale.

SECTION 5 Indiquer la date complète (année, mois et jour) à laquelle la personne morale a cessé d'exercer ses activités en Ontario.

SIGNATURE

Un dirigeant ou un administrateur de la personne morale doit signer de sa main la demande en double exemplaire. Les demandes portant des signatures photocopiées seront rejetées. Les signatures doivent toujours apparaître en dessous de la dénomination sociale de la personne morale.

Par ailleurs, la personne morale doit apposer son sceau aux deux exemplaires de la demande. Si la personne morale n'est pas tenue d'avoir un sceau par la compétence législative dont elle relève, elle doit l'indiquer dans sa demande.

Envoyer par la poste ou livrer la demande (en double exemplaire) au :

Ministère des Services gouvernementaux
Direction des services centraux de production et de vérification
393, avenue University, bureau 200
Toronto ON M5G 2M2

375, avenue University, 2e étage (dépôt en personne)

07067 (2011/06) English on reverse

For Ministry Use Only
À l'usage exclusif du ministère

Ontario Corporation Number
Numéro de personne morale en Ontario

Form 4
Extra-Provincial Corporations Act

Formule 4
Loi sur les personnes morales extraprovinciales

APPLICATION FOR TERMINATION OF EXTRA-PROVINCIAL LICENCE
DEMANDE DE RÉSILIATION D'UN PERMIS EXTRAPROVINCIAL

1. Name of the Corporation (Print in UPPER CASE ONLY):
Dénomination sociale de la personne morale (Écrire en LETTRES MAJUSCULES SEULEMENT) :

2. Business name or style, other than the corporate name, under which the corporation is licensed in Ontario, if any (if none, state so) (Print in UPPER CASE ONLY):
Nom, autre que la dénomination sociale, sous lequel un permis a été délivré à la personne morale en Ontario, le cas échéant (si ce n'est pas le cas, veuillez l'indiquer) (Écrire en LETTRES MAJUSCULES SEULEMENT) :

3. Jurisdiction to which subject:
Compétence législative :

(Name of Province, State or Country)
(Province, État ou pays)

4. Date of incorporation/amalgamation:
Date de la constitution ou de la fusion :

year / année month / mois day / jour

5. The corporation has ceased to carry on business in Ontario within the meaning of the *Extra-Provincial Corporations Act* on:
La personne morale a cessé d'exercer ses activités commerciales en Ontario au sens de la *Loi sur les personnes morales extraprovinciales* le :

year / année month / mois day / jour

6. The corporation therefore requests that the extra-provincial Licence and any amended extra-provincial Licence obtained by the corporation be terminated.
La personne morale demande par conséquent la résiliation du permis extraprovincial ainsi que de tout permis extraprovincial modifié qu'elle a obtenus.

(Name of Corporation) / (Dénomination sociale de la personne morale)

By: / Signé :

(Signature) / (Signature)

(Description of Office) / (Fonctions)

(Corporate Seal) / (Sceau de la personne morale)

07067 (2011/06)

LIMITED PARTNERSHIPS ACT

R.S.O. 1990, c. L.16, as am. S.O. 1994, c. 27, s. 87 [s. 87(1) not in force at date of publication. Repealed 2004, c. 19, s. 15(1).]; 1998, c. 18, Sched. E, ss. 161–165; 2001, c. 9, Sched. D, s. 14; 2004, c. 19, s. 15; 2009, c. 33, Sched. 2, s. 44; 2011, c. 1, Sched. 5, s. 6.

1. Definitions — In this Act,

"business" includes every trade, occupation and profession;

"extra-provincial limited partnership" means a limited partnership organized under the laws of a jurisdiction other than Ontario;

"person" includes an individual, sole proprietorship, partnership, unincorporated association, unincorporated syndicate, unincorporated organization, trust, body corporate, and a natural person in his or her capacity as trustee, executor, administrator or other legal representative;

"prescribed" means prescribed in the regulations;

"Registrar" means the Registrar appointed under the *Business Names Act*.

2. (1) Limited partnership — A limited partnership may, subject to this Act, be formed to carry on any business that a partnership without limited partners may carry on.

(2) Whom to consist — A limited partnership shall consist of one or more persons who are general partners and one or more persons who are limited partners.

3. (1) Formation — A limited partnership is formed when a declaration is filed with the Registrar in accordance with this Act.

(2) Declaration — A declaration shall be signed by all of the general partners desiring to form a limited partnership and shall state the prescribed information.

(3) Expiry of declaration — Every declaration filed under subsection (1), including a declaration filed by an extra-provincial limited partnership, expires five years after its date of filing unless the declaration is cancelled by filing a declaration of dissolution or the declaration is replaced by filing a new declaration before the expiry date.

(4) Subsequent filing — A limited partnership is not dissolved if a declaration expires, but an additional fee in the required amount is payable for the subsequent filing of a new declaration.

1998, c. 18, Sched. E, s. 161

4. (1) Record of limited partners — The general partners of every limited partnership other than an extra-provincial limited partnership shall maintain a current record of the limited partners stating, for each limited partner, the prescribed information.

(2) **Where record to be kept** — The record of limited partners shall be kept at the limited partnership's principal place of business in Ontario.

(3) **Rights to inspect** — Upon request and without charge, any general partner must permit any person to inspect the record of limited partners during the normal business hours of the limited partnership and to make copies or take extracts from them.

(4) **Registrar may require copy of record** — The Registrar may at any time by written notice require any general partner to provide to the Registrar or any other person a copy of the record of limited partners.

(5) **Copy of record to be provided** — Upon receipt of the Registrar's notice, the general partner to whom it is directed shall, within the time specified in the notice, provide a copy of the record of limited partners to the Registrar or any other person specified in the notice.

1994, c. 27, s. 87(2)

5. (1) **General and limited partners** — A person may be a general partner and a limited partner at the same time in the same limited partnership.

(2) **Idem** — A person who is at the same time a general partner and a limited partner in the same limited partnership has the rights and powers and is subject to the restrictions and liabilities of a general partner except that in respect of the person's contribution as a limited partner the person has the same rights against the other partners as a limited partner.

6. (1) **Restriction in name of partnership** — The surname or a distinctive part of the corporate name of a limited partner shall not appear in the firm name of the limited partnership unless it is also the surname or a distinctive part of the corporate name of one of the general partners.

(2) **Liability if limited partner** — Where the surname or a distinctive part of the corporate name of a limited partner appears in the firm name contrary to subsection (1), the limited partner is liable as a general partner to any creditor of the limited partnership who has extended credit without actual knowledge that the limited partner is not a general partner.

(3) **Use of term limited** — Despite any Act, the word "Limited" may be used in the firm name but only in the expression "Limited Partnership".

7. (1) **Contribution of limited partner** — A limited partner may contribute money and other property to the limited partnership, but not services.

(2) **Personal property** — A limited partner's interest in the limited partnership is personal property.

8. **Rights of general partners** — A general partner in a limited partnership has all the rights and powers and is subject to all the restrictions and liabilities of a partner in a partnership without limited partners except that, without the written consent to or ratification of the specific act by all the limited partners, a general partner has no authority to,

(a) do any act in contravention of the partnership agreement;

(b) do any act which makes it impossible to carry on the ordinary business of the limited partnership;

(c) consent to a judgment against the limited partnership;

(d) possess limited partnership property, or assign any rights in specific partnership property, for other than a partnership purpose;

(e) admit a person as a general partner;

(f) admit a person as a limited partner, unless the right to do so is given in the partnership agreement; or

(g) continue the business of the limited partnership if a general partner dies, retires or becomes incapable as defined in the *Substitute Decisions Act, 1992* or a corporate general partner is dissolved, unless the right to do so is given in the partnership agreement.

2009, c. 33, Sched. 2, s. 44(1)

9. Liability of limited partner — Subject to this Act, a limited partner is not liable for the obligations of the limited partnership except in respect of the value of money and other property the limited partner contributes or agrees to contribute to the limited partnership, as stated in the record of limited partners.

10. Rights of limited partner — A limited partner has the same right as a general partner,

(a) to inspect and make copies of or take extracts from the limited partnership books at all times;

(b) to be given, on demand, true and full information concerning all matters affecting the limited partnership, and to be given a complete and formal account of the partnership affairs; and

(c) to obtain dissolution of the limited partnership by court order.

11. (1) Share of profits — A limited partner has, subject to this Act, the right,

(a) to a share of the profits or other compensation by way of income; and

(b) to have the limited partner's contribution to the limited partnership returned.

(2) When profit may not be paid — No payment of a share of the profits or other compensation by way of income shall be made to a limited partner from the assets of the limited partnership or of a general partner if the payment would reduce the assets of the limited partnership to an amount insufficient to discharge the liabilities of the limited partnership to persons who are not general or limited partners.

12. (1) Business dealings by limited partner with partnership — A limited partner may loan money to and transact other business with the limited partnership and, unless the limited partner is also a general partner, may receive on account of resulting claims against the limited partnership with general creditors a prorated share of the assets, but no limited partner shall, in respect of any such claim,

(a) receive or hold as collateral security any of the limited partnership property; or

(b) receive from a general partner or the limited partnership any payment, conveyance or release from liability if at the time the assets of the partnership are not sufficient to discharge partnership liabilities to persons who are not general or limited partners.

(2) Rights of limited partner — A limited partner may from time to time,

(a) examine into the state and progress of the limited partnership business and may advise as to its management;

(b) act as a contractor for or an agent or employee of the limited partnership or of a general partner; or

(c) act as a surety for the limited partnership.

13. (1) Limited partner in control of business — A limited partner is not liable as a general partner unless, in addition to exercising rights and powers as a limited partner, the limited partner takes part in the control of the business.

(2) Additional rights and powers — For the purposes of subsection (1), a limited partner shall not be presumed to be taking part in the control of the business by reason only that the limited partner exercises rights and powers in addition to the rights and powers conferred upon the limited partner by this Act.

14. (1) Limited partners' rights as between themselves — Subject to subsection (2), limited partners, in relation to one another, share in the limited partnership assets,

(a) for the return of contributions; and

(b) for profits or other compensation by way of income on account of their contributions,

in proportion to the respective amounts of money and other property actually contributed by the limited partners to the limited partnership.

(2) Priority agreement — Where there are several limited partners, the partners may agree that one or more of the limited partners is to have priority over other limited partners,

(a) as to the return of contributions;

(b) as to profits or other compensation by way of income; or

(c) as to any other matter,

but the terms of this agreement shall be set out in the partnership agreement.

(3) Idem — Where the partnership agreement does not contain an agreement referred to in subsection (2), the shares of the limited partners in the partnership assets shall be determined in accordance with subsection (1).

15. (1) Return of limited partner's contribution — A limited partner has the right to demand and receive the return of the limited partner's contribution,

(a) upon the dissolution of the limited partnership;

(b) when the time specified in the partnership agreement for the return of the contribution occurs;

(c) after the limited partner has given six months notice in writing to all other partners, if no time is specified in the partnership agreement for the return of the contribution or for the dissolution of the limited partnership; or

(d) when all partners consent to the return of the contribution.

(2) Idem — Despite subsection (1), a limited partner is not entitled to receive any part of the limited partner's contribution out of the limited partnership assets or from a general partner until,

(a) all liabilities of the limited partnership, except liabilities to general partners and to limited partners on account of their contributions, have been paid or there remains sufficient limited partnership assets to pay them; and

(b) the partnership agreement is terminated or so amended, if necessary, to set forth the withdrawal or reduction of the contribution.

(3) **Idem** — A limited partner has, irrespective of the nature of the limited partner's contribution, only the right to demand and receive money in return therefor, unless,

(a) the partnership agreement provides otherwise; or

(b) all the partners consent to some other manner of returning the contribution.

(4) **Dissolution** — A limited partner is entitled to have the limited partnership dissolved and its affairs wound up where,

(a) the limited partner is entitled to the return of the limited partner's contribution but, upon demand, the contribution is not returned to the limited partner; or

(b) the other liabilities of the limited partnership have not been paid or the limited partnership assets are insufficient for their payment as required by clause (2)(a) and the limited partner seeking dissolution would otherwise be entitled to the return of the limited partner's contribution.

16. (1) **Limited partner's liability to partnership** — A limited partner is liable to the limited partnership for the difference, if any, between the value of money or other property actually contributed by the limited partner to the limited partnership and the value of money or other property stated in the record of limited partners as being contributed or to be contributed by the limited partner to the limited partnership.

(2) **Limited partner as trustee** — A limited partner holds as trustee for the limited partnership,

(a) specific property stated in the partnership agreement as contributed by the limited partner, but which has not in fact been contributed or which has been returned contrary to this Act;

(b) money or other property paid or conveyed to the limited partner on account of the limited partner's contribution contrary to this Act.

(3) **Idem** — Where a limited partner has received the return of all or part of the limited partner's contribution, the limited partner is nevertheless liable to the limited partnership or, where the limited partnership is dissolved, to its creditors for any amount, not in excess of the amount returned with interest, necessary to discharge the liabilities of the limited partnership to all creditors who extended credit or whose claims otherwise arose before the return of the contribution.

17. **Admission of additional limited partners** — After the formation of the limited partnership, additional limited partners may be admitted by amendment of the record of limited partners.

18. (1) **Interest assignable** — A limited partner's interest is assignable.

(2) **Limited partner** — A substituted limited partner is a person admitted to all the rights and powers of a limited partner who has died or who has assigned the limited partner's interest in the limited partnership.

(3) **Rights of assignee** — An assignee who is not a substituted limited partner has no right,

(a) to inspect the limited partnership books;

(b) to be given any information about matters affecting the limited partnership or to be given an account of the partnership affairs,

but is entitled only to receive the share of the profits or other compensation by way of income or the return of the contribution to which the assignor would otherwise be entitled.

(4) **Manner of becoming a substituted limited partner** — An assignee may become a substituted limited partner,

(a) if all the partners, except the assignor, consent in writing thereto; or

(b) if the assignor, being so authorized by the partnership agreement, constitutes the assignee a substituted limited partner.

(5) **Idem** — An assignee, who is otherwise entitled to become a substituted limited partner, becomes a substituted limited partner when the record of limited partners is amended.

(6) **Rights, liabilities of substituted limited partner** — A substituted limited partner has all the rights and powers and is subject to all the restrictions and liabilities of the limited partner's assignor, except any liability of which the limited partner did not have notice at the time the limited partner became a limited partner and which could not be ascertained from the partnership agreement, the declaration or the record of limited partners.

(7) **Liability of assignor** — The substitution of an assignee as a limited partner does not release the assignor from liability under section 16 or 30.

19. (1) **Change of firm name** — Where the firm name of a limited partnership is to be changed, a new declaration shall be filed with the Registrar under subsection 3(1).

(2) **Declaration of change** — A declaration of change shall be filed with the Registrar for every change in information, other than a change in the firm name, required to be stated in the declaration under subsection 3(1).

(3) **Signing of declaration** — A declaration of change shall be signed by at least one of the general partners.

(4) **Change not effective** — For the purposes of this Act, a change referred to in subsection (2) does not take effect until a declaration of change is filed with the Registrar.

(5) **Expiry** — A declaration of change expires upon the expiry, replacement or cancellation of the declaration amended by the declaration of change.

(6) **Change of address** — If there is a change in an address set out in a declaration, the declaration of change referred to in subsection (2) shall be filed within 15 days after the change takes place.

1994, c. 27, s. 87(3), (4)

20. (1) **Ability to sue** — No limited partnership that has unpaid fees or penalties or in respect of which a declaration has not been filed as required by this Act and no member thereof is capable of maintaining a proceeding in a court in Ontario in respect of the business carried on by the limited partnership except with leave of the court.

(2) **Idem** — The court shall grant leave if the court is satisfied that,

(a) the failure to pay the fees or penalties or file the declaration was inadvertent;

(b) there is no evidence that the public has been deceived or misled; and

(c) at the time of the application to the court, the limited partnership has no unpaid fees or penalties and has filed all declarations required by this Act.

(3) **Contracts valid** — No contract is void or voidable by reason only that it was entered into by a limited partnership that was in contravention of this Act or the regulations at the time the contract was made.

21. **Dissolution of limited partnership** — A general partner's retirement, death or incapacity to manage property within the meaning of the *Substitute Decisions Act, 1992* or a corporate general partner's dissolution dissolves a limited partnership unless the business is continued by the remaining general partners,

(a) pursuant to a right to do so contained in the partnership agreement; and

(b) with the consent of all the remaining partners.

2009, c. 33, Sched. 2, s. 44(2)

22. (1) **Death of limited partner** — The executor or administrator of the estate of a limited partner has,

(a) all the rights and powers of a limited partner for the purpose of settling the estate of the limited partner; and

(b) whatever power the limited partner had under the partnership agreement to constitute the limited partner's assignee a substituted limited partner.

(2) **Liability** — The estate of a limited partner is liable for all the liabilities of the limited partner as a limited partner.

23. (1) **Declaration of dissolution** — A declaration of dissolution shall be filed with the Registrar when,

(a) the limited partnership is dissolved; or

(b) all of the limited partners cease to be limited partners.

(2) **Idem** — The declaration of dissolution shall be signed by at least one of the general partners.

(3) **Declaration cancelled** — When the declaration of dissolution is filed, the declaration filed under subsection 3(1) is cancelled.

1994, c. 27, s. 87(5)

23.1 (1) **Delivery of notices** — A notice or other document that is required or permitted by this Act to be sent by the Registrar may be sent by ordinary mail or by any other method, including registered mail, certified mail or prepaid courier, if there is a record by the person who has delivered it that the notice or document has been sent.

(2) **Same** — A notice or other document referred to in subsection (1) may be sent by telephone transmission of a facsimile of the notice or other document or by another form of electronic transmission where there is a record that the notice or other document has been sent.

(3) Deemed delivery — A notice or other document sent by mail by the Registrar shall be deemed to be received by the intended recipient on the earlier of,

(a) the day the intended recipient actually receives it; or

(b) the fifth day after the day it is mailed.

(4) Same — A notice or other document sent by a method referred to in subsection (2) shall be deemed to be received by the intended recipient on the earlier of,

(a) the day the intended recipient actually receives it; or

(b) the first business day after the day the transmission is sent by the Registrar.

1994, c. 27, s. 87(6)

23.2 Cancellation of declaration — The Registrar may cancel a declaration filed under subsection 3(1) for failure to pay the required fee if the limited partnership is given 21 days notice of the intention to cancel.

1994, c. 27, s. 87(7); 1998, c. 18, Sched. E, s. 162

24. Settling accounts on dissolution — In settling accounts after the dissolution of a limited partnership, the liabilities of the limited partnership to creditors, except to limited partners on account of their contributions and to general partners, shall be paid first, and then, unless the partnership agreement or a subsequent agreement provides otherwise, shall be paid in the following order:

1. To limited partners in respect of their share of the profits and other compensation by way of income on account of their contributions.
2. To limited partners in respect of their contributions.
3. To general partners other than for capital and profits.
4. To general partners in respect of profits.
5. To general partners in respect of capital.

25. (1) Declaration — No extra-provincial limited partnership shall carry on business in Ontario unless it has filed a declaration with the Registrar that sets forth the information required by subsection 3(2) and states the jurisdiction in which the extra-provincial limited partnership is organized.

(2) Carry on business — For the purposes of this section, an extra-provincial limited partnership carries on business in Ontario if,

(a) it solicits business in Ontario;

(b) its name is listed in a telephone director for any part of Ontario;

(c) its name is included in any advertisement in which an address in Ontario is given for the limited partnership;

(d) it has a resident agent or representative or a warehouse, office or place of business in Ontario;

(e) it owns real property situate in Ontario;

(f) it effects a distribution of securities in Ontario by way of a prospectus or offering memorandum in compliance with the *Securities Act* and the regulations made thereunder; or

(g) it otherwise carries on business in Ontario.

(3) **Signing of declaration** — The declaration filed under subsection (1) shall be signed by all of the general partners.

(4) **Power of attorney** — An extra-provincial limited partnership shall execute a power of attorney in the prescribed form appointing a person resident in Ontario or a corporation having its head or registered office in Ontario to be the attorney and representative in Ontario of the extra-provincial limited partnership.

(5) **Same** — The attorney and representative in Ontario of the extra-provincial limited partnership shall keep the power of attorney referred to in subsection (4) at its address set out in the declaration filed under subsection (1).

(6) **Same** — Upon request and without charge, the attorney and representative shall permit any person to inspect the power of attorney during the normal business hours of the attorney and representative and to make a copy of it.

(6.1) **Change of firm name** — Where there is a change in the firm name of an extra-provincial limited partnership, a new declaration shall be filed with the Registrar under this section.

(6.2) **Exemption** — Subsections (4), (5) and (6) do not apply to an extra-provincial limited partnership formed in another Canadian jurisdiction that has an office or other place of business in Ontario.

(7) **Declaration of change** — An extra-provincial limited partnership shall file a declaration of change with the Registrar for every change in the information, other than a change in the firm name, contained in the declaration filed under subsection (1) and the declaration shall be signed in the manner described in section 19.

(8) **Declaration of withdrawal** — An extra-provincial limited partnership may cancel the declaration and the power of attorney by filing with the Registrar a declaration of withdrawal signed by at least one of the general partners.

1994, c. 27, s. 87(8); 1998, c. 18, Sched. E, s. 163

26. (1) **Record of limited partners** — The general partners of every extra-provincial limited partnership that has filed a declaration under subsection 25(1) shall maintain a current record of the limited partners stating, for each limited partner, the prescribed information.

(2) **Where record to be kept** — Subject to subsection (3), the record of limited partners shall be kept at the limited partnership's principal place of business in Ontario.

(3) **Idem** — If an extra-provincial limited partnership does not have a principal place of business in Ontario, the record of limited partners shall be kept by the attorney and representative in Ontario of the extra-provincial limited partnership at the address stated in the power of attorney filed under subsection 25(4).

(4) **Right to inspect** — Any person may inspect the record of limited partners during the normal business hours of the limited partnership or the limited partnership's attorney and representative and may make copies of and take extracts from it.

(5) **Registrar may require copy of record** — The Registrar may at any time by written notice require any general partner or a limited partnership's attorney and representative to provide to the Registrar or any other person a copy of the record of limited partners.

(6) Copy of record to be provided — Upon receipt of the Registrar's notice, the person to whom it is directed shall, within the time specified in the notice, provide a copy of the record of limited partners to the Registrar or other person specified in the notice.

27. (1) Liability of limited partner — A limited partner of an extra-provincial limited partnership is not liable in Ontario as a general partner of the extra-provincial limited partnership by reason only that it carries on business in Ontario without filing the declaration and power of attorney required by this Act.

(2) Laws applicable to extra-provincial limited partnerships — The laws of the jurisdiction under which an extra-provincial limited partnership is organized govern its organization and internal affairs and the limited liability of its limited partners.

28. (1) Ability to sue — No extra-provincial limited partnership that has unpaid fees or penalties or in respect of which a declaration or power of attorney has not been filed as required by this Act and no member thereof is capable of maintaining a proceeding in a court in Ontario in respect of the business carried on by the extra-provincial limited partnership except with leave of the court.

(2) Idem — The court shall grant leave if the court is satisfied that,

(a) the failure to pay the fees or penalties or file the declaration or power of attorney was inadvertent;

(b) there is no evidence that the public has been deceived or misled; and

(c) at the time of the application to the court, the extra-provincial limited partnership has no unpaid fees or penalties and has filed all declarations and powers of attorney required by this Act.

(3) Contracts valid — No contract is void or voidable by reason only that it was entered into by an extra-provincial limited partnership that was in contravention of this Act or the regulations at the time the contract was made.

29. Effect of false statement in declaration — Where a declaration contains a false or misleading statement, any person suffering loss as a result of relying upon the statement may hold liable,

(a) every general partner who knew when signing the declaration that the statement was false or misleading; and

(b) every general partner who became aware after signing the declaration that the statement was false or misleading and failed within a reasonable time to file a declaration of change.

30. Effect of false statement in record of limited partners — Where a record of limited partners contains a false or misleading statement, any person suffering loss as a result of relying upon the statement may hold liable,

(a) every general partner; and

(b) every limited partner who became aware that the statement was false or misleading and failed within reasonable time to take steps to cause the record of limited partners to be corrected.

31. Liability of person mistakenly believing the person is a limited partner — A person who contributes to the capital of a business carried on by a person or partnership erroneously believing that the person has become a limited partner in a limited partnership,

(a) is not, by reason only of exercising the rights of a limited partner, a general partner with the person or in the partnership carrying on the business; and

(b) is not bound by the obligations of the person or partnership carrying on the business,

if, upon ascertaining the fact that the person is not a limited partner, promptly,

(c) renounces the person's interest in the profits or other compensation by way of income from the business; or

(d) takes steps to cause the record of limited partners to be amended to show the person to be a limited partner.

32. (1) Authority to sign — A general or limited partner may give written authority to any other person to sign on the partner's behalf any document referred to in this Act.

(2) Idem — A person who signs a document to be filed with the Registrar under an authority referred to in subsection (1) shall indicate in the document that the person signs on behalf of a general or limited partner.

33. (1) Access to documents — Every limited partnership shall keep at its principal place of business in Ontario,

(a) a copy of the partnership agreement;

(b) a copy of the declaration and a copy of each declaration of change amending the declaration;

(c) a copy of any court order made under section 34;

(d) a copy of any written authority given under subsection 32(1); and

(e) in the case of an extra-provincial limited partnership, a copy of the power of attorney filed with the Registrar.

(2) Where no principal place of business — Where an extra-provincial limited partnership does not have a principal place of business in Ontario, the documents referred to in subsection (1) shall be kept by the attorney and representative in Ontario of the extra-provincial limited partnership at the address stated in the power of attorney filed under subsection 25(4).

(3) Right to inspect — Any partner may inspect any of the documents referred to in subsection (1) during the normal business hours of the partnership or the partnership's attorney and representative.

(4) Idem — Any person who has a business relationship with the partnership may inspect any of the documents referred to in clauses (1)(b), (c), (d) and (e) during the normal business hours of the partnership or the partnership's attorney and representative.

34. (1) Definition — In this section, **"Court"** means the Superior Court of Justice.

(2) Order for compliance — Where a person who is required by this Act to sign or permit inspection of a document refuses to do so, a person who is aggrieved by the refusal may apply to the Court for an order directing the person to comply with the provisions of this Act and upon such application, the Court may make such order or any other order that the Court considers appropriate in the circumstances.

(3) **Application** — An application may be made under subsection (2) despite the imposition of a penalty in respect of the refusal and in addition to any other rights the applicant may have at law.

2001, c. 9, Sched. D, s. 14

35. (1) **Offences** — Every person who,

(a) contravenes any provision of this Act or the regulations; or

(b) makes a statement in any document, material, evidence or information submitted or required by or for the purposes of this Act that, at the time and in the light of the circumstances under which it is made, is false or misleading with respect to any material fact or that omits to state any material fact, the omission of which makes the statement false or misleading,

is guilty of an offence and on conviction is liable to a fine of not more than $2,000 or, if such person is a corporation, to a fine of not more than $20,000.

(2) **False statements wilful** — No person is guilty of an offence referred to in clause (1)(b) if the person did not know that the statement was false or misleading and in the exercise of reasonable diligence could not have known that the statement was false or misleading.

(3) **Liability of directors and officers** — Where a corporation is guilty of an offence under subsection (1), every director or officer of such corporation, and where the corporation is an extra-provincial corporation, every person acting as its representative in Ontario, who authorized, permitted or acquiesced in such an offence is also guilty of an offence and on conviction is liable to a fine of not more than $2,000.

35.1 **Powers of Minister** — (0.1) **Minister's regulations** — The Minister may make regulations,

(a) prescribing alternative methods of filing documents under this Act and governing the filing of documents by each method, including the manner of acceptance of documents, the determination of the date of receipt and the form of electronic signatures;

(b) waiving any of the signature requirements under this Act.

(1) **Fees** — The Minister may by order require the payment of fees for search reports, copies of documents or information, the filing of documents or other services under this Act and may approve the amount of those fees.

1998, c. 18, Sched. E, s. 164; 2011, c. 1, Sched. 5, s. 6(1)

35.2 **Registrar's regulations** — The Registrar may make regulations prescribing forms and providing for their use.

2011, c. 1, Sched. 5, s. 6(2)

36. **Regulations** — The Lieutenant Governor in Council may make regulations,

(a) [Repealed 1998, c. 18, Sched. E, s. 165.]

(b) prescribing information to be set out in a declaration filed under this Act and information to be set out in a record of limited partners;

(c) [Repealed 2011, c. 1, Sched. 5, s. 6(3).]

(d) [Repealed 2011, c. 1, Sched. 5, s. 6(3).]

(e) [Repealed 2011, c. 1, Sched. 5, s. 6(3).]

(f) [Repealed 2004, c. 19, s. 15(3).]

1994, c. 27, s. 87(9); 1998, c. 18, Sched. E, s. 165; 2004, c. 19, s. 15(2), (3); 2011, c. 1, Sched. 5, s. 6(3)

ONT. REG. 713 — GENERAL

made under the *Limited Partnerships Act*

R.R.O. 1990, Reg. 713, as am. O. Reg. 11/91; 582/91; 599/92; 629/93; 176/94; 313/96; 566/98; 195/99; 250/05; CTR 15 JA 09 – 2.

1. (1) A declaration, a declaration of change and a declaration of dissolution or withdrawal shall be in the form provided or approved by the Minister of Consumer and Commercial Relations.

(2) If a declaration is filed on or after April 1, 1994, the business identification number assigned by the Registrar to the declaration must be set out on a declaration of change, a declaration of dissolution or withdrawal or a new declaration filed under subsection 3(3), 19(1) or 25(5) of the Act.

(3) If a declaration was filed before April 1, 1994, the business identification number assigned by the Registrar to the first new declaration filed on or after that date must be set out on a declaration of change, a declaration of dissolution or withdrawal or on any subsequent new declaration.

(4) A power of attorney shall be in Form 4.

(5) A declaration filed in respect of a limited partnership shall set out the firm name of the partnership with only one space between each word.

O. Reg. 11/91, s. 1; 176/94, s. 1; 250/05, s. 1

1.1 A declaration filed under subsection 3(2) or 25(1) of the Act shall set out the following information:

1. The firm name under which the limited partnership is to be conducted.

2. The general nature of the business of the limited partnership.

3. For each general partner who is an individual, the partner's surname, the given name by which the partner is commonly known, another given name, if any, and the partner's residential address or address for service, including municipality, street and number, if any, and postal code.

4. For each general partner that is not an individual, the partner's name and address or address for service, including municipality, street and number, if any, and postal code, and the partner's Ontario corporation number, if any.

5. The address of the limited partnership's principal place of business in Ontario, including municipality, street and number, if any, and postal code, and the mailing address of the limited partnership.

6. An indication that there is a power of attorney, in the case of an extra-provincial limited partnership.

7. For the attorney of an extra-provincial limited partnership who is an individual, the attorney's surname, the given name by which the attorney is commonly known, another

given name, if any, and the attorney's residential address or address for service, including municipality, street and number, if any, and postal code.

8. For the attorney of an extra-provincial limited partnership that is not an individual, the attorney's name and address or address for service including municipality, street and number, if any, and postal code, and the attorney's Ontario corporation number if any.

O. Reg. 11/91, s. 2; 629/93, s. 1; CTR 15 JA 09 – 2

2. The information required to be set out in a form mentioned in section 1 shall be clearly, neatly and legibly typewritten or printed on the form in a manner suitable for photographing on microfilm and the form shall not be folded or otherwise damaged.

3. All declarations and other forms under the Act shall be filed in the central registry established in the office of the Registrar.

4. A record of limited partners required by subsection 4(1) or 26(1) of the Act shall set out the following information for each limited partner:

1. If the partner is an individual, the partner's surname, the given name by which the partner is commonly known, the first letters of the partner's other given names and the partner's residential address or address for service, including municipality, street and number, if any, and postal code.

2. If the partner is not an individual, the partner's name and address or address for service, including municipality, street and number, if any, and postal code, and the partner's Ontario corporation number, if any.

3. The amount of money and the value of other property contributed or to be contributed by the partner to the limited partnership.

O. Reg. 11/91, s. 2; CTR 15 JA 09 – 2

SCHEDULE — FEES

[Revoked O. Reg. 195/99, s. 2.]

Form 1

[Revoked O. Reg. 11/91, s. 3(1).]

Form 1A

[Revoked O. Reg. 11/91, s. 3(2).]

Form 2

[Revoked O. Reg. 11/91, s. 3(1).]

Form 2A

[Revoked O. Reg. 11/91, s. 3(2).]

Form 3

[Revoked O. Reg. 11/91, s. 3(1).]

Form 3A

[Revoked O. Reg. 11/91, s. 3(2).]

Form 4 — Power Of Attorney — The *Limited Partnerships Act/Procuration — Loi sur les sociétes en commandite*

Limited Partnerships Act/Loi sur les sociétés en commandite

Know all persons by these presents that/*Faisons savoir par les présentes que*

....

(Name of appointing extra-provincial limited partnership/*Nom de la société en commandité extraprovinciale qui nomme le procureur*) (hereinafter called the "Partnership"/*ciaprés appelée la "Société"*)

hereby nominates, constitutes and appoints/*nomme*

....

(Name of attorney in full/*Nom au complet du procureur*)

...., Ontario ❑❑❑❑❑❑

(Business address of the attorney including street, municipality and postal code/*Adresse d'affaires du procureur sans omettre la rue, la municipalité et le code postal*)

its true and lawful attorney, to act as such, and as such to sue and be sued, plead and be impleaded in any court in Ontario, and generally on behalf of the partnership within Ontario to accept service of process and to receive all lawful notices and, for the purposes of the partnership to do all acts and to execute all deeds and other instruments relating to the matters within the scope of this power of attorney. Until the Registrar appointed under the *Business Names Act* has received and accepted a due and lawful notice naming another and subsequent attorney, the partnership shall accept as sufficient service of process and other documents upon the said:/

son procureur légitime et le charge d'agir en cette qualité et d'intenter des poursuites, d'être poursuivi et de plaider devant n'importe quel tribunal de l'Ontario au nom de la Société, ainsi que d'accepter au nom de la Société les significations des actes et de recevoir au nom de la Société tous les avis légaux relatifs à l'Ontario et aussi de faire toutes les démarches et de passer tous les actes et autres documents relatifs aux questions entrant dans le champ de la procuration. Jusqu'à ce que le registrateur nommé aux termes de la Loi sur les noms commerciaux *ait reçu et accepté un avis en bonne et due forme nommant un autre procureur, la Société considérera comme suffisante la signification des actes et autres documents et avis audit:*

....

(name of attorney in full/*Nom au complet du procureur*)

Dated/*Fait le* [*month, day, year*]

....

(Name of extra-provincial limited partnership)/(*Nom de la société en commandite extraprovinciale*)

By/Par..

(Signature/*Signature*) (General Partner/*Commandité*)

Consent To Act As Attorney — The *Limited Partnerships Act/Consentement du procureur — Loi sur les sociétés en commandite*)

I/*Je soussigné(e),*

....

(name of attorney in full/*Nom au complet du procureur*), of/*au*

....(Business address including street number municipality and postal code/*Adresse d'affaires sans omettre le numéro et la rue, la municipalité et le code postal*), Ontario,

hereby consent to act as the attorney in the province of Ontario of/*consens par la présente à agir dans la province de l'Ontario en qualité de procureur de*

....

(Name of extra provincial limited partnership/*Nom de la sociéte en commandite extraprovinciale*)

pursuant to the Power of Attorney in that behalf executed by the said limited partnership on /*conformément à la procuration passée à cet effet par ladite société en commandite, le*

[*month, day, year*], authorizing me to accept service of process and notices on its behalf /*qui m'autorise à accepter la signification des actes et autres avis en son nom.*

Dated this/*Fait le* [*month, day, year*]

....

(Signature of witness/*Signature du témoin*)

....

(Signature of the consenting person or corporation/*Signature de la personne physique ou morale consentante*)

LPA FORMS

Form 3 — Declaration*

INSTRUCTIONS **It is important to read these notes before completing the attached form.**

Print all information clearly in CAPITAL LETTERS using black ink.

Complete all applicable sections of the form. Incomplete forms will be returned. When filing a declaration of any type, including a change, complete all items on the form, including information regarding all current general partners.

Fees:
- **$210 - New declaration, name change or renewal**
- **$360** ($210 + $150 penalty) – **Late renewal**
- By Mail - money order or cheque payable to the Minister of Finance
- In Person – cash, money order or cheque payable to the Minister of Finance, Visa, MasterCard, American Express or debit card
- There will be a service charge payable for any cheque returned as non-negotiable by a bank or other financial institution.

This form must be completed in duplicate.
Please forward both copies of the enclosed form to the Ministry of Government Services.
The "client copy" will be returned, with a validation including the declaration date, expiry date and the Business Identification Number.

Return completed forms to:
Ministry of Government and Consumer Services
Companies and Personal Property Security Branch
393 University Avenue, Suite 200
Toronto ON M5G 2M2

375 University Avenue, 2nd Floor (In Person)

Please do not separate the form.

1. **Declaration Type – Check the appropriate box:**

   A - New (Fee $210)
   Check box "A" if this is the first filing of a declaration to form an Ontario limited partnership or the first filing of an Extra-Provincial Limited Partnership permitting it to carry on business in Ontario

   B - Name Change (Fee $210)
   For a name change check box "B". Because a name change is a new declaration filed under s. 3(1) or s. 25(1) of the Act, the expiry date will be extended by five years. For example, if the name is changed two years before the expiry date, the expiry date will be extended to seven years.

   C - Change – other than name change (No fee payable)
   Check the change box for a change in information – for example, address, activity or information regarding general partners.

   D & E - Renewal (Fee $210)
   A declaration expires after five years. A limited partnership must be renewed before the expiry date set out on the registration. **There is a penalty fee of $150 for late renewals.**

   D - Renewal Without Name Change
   Check box "D" to renew a declaration that is about to expire and the firm is not changing its name.

   E - Renewal With Name Change
   If the firm name is changing at the time of renewal check box "E".

   F - Dissolution (No fee payable)
   Check box "F" to file a declaration of dissolution of a limited partnership formed in Ontario.

   G - Withdrawal (No fee payable)
   Check box "G" to file a declaration of withdrawal to cancel the declaration and power of attorney of an extra-provincial limited partnership in Ontario.

   BIN (Business Identification Number)
   The Business Identification Number must be entered for a name change, renewal (with or without a name change), change of information, dissolution or withdrawal. This number is recorded on the validation stamp on the original declaration or most recent declaration of renewal or change.

2. **Firm Name** - Please print the firm name of the limited partnership. The firm name must be set out in BLOCK CAPITAL LETTERS in the squares provided and must commence on the first line of the grid in the first square. Each square of the grid represents a letter of the alphabet, a punctuation mark or a space.

3. **Mailing Address of Registrant** - Include street and number or post office box, municipality, province, country and postal code. *Your copy of the registration will be mailed to this address.*

4. **Address of Principal Place of Business in Ontario** - Include street name and number (if any), municipality and postal code. A post office box alone is not acceptable in a business address. If there is more than one place of business, select one as the principal place of business. Extra-provincial limited partnerships are not required to have a business address in Ontario. If this is the case check the box provided.

5. **General Nature of Business** - Include a brief description (maximum 40 characters) of the business activity being carried on by the firm.

6. **Information Regarding General Partners**

   New Declaration, Name Change or Renewal,
   Item 6 must be completed and signed by **all** the general partners or their attorneys. If there is more than one general partner set out the total number of general partners in the box provided and attach additional **Schedules** as required.

   Change (other than name change), Withdrawal or Dissolution
   Item 6 must be completed and signed by at least one general partner.

6. **Information Regarding General Partners** - Continued

   (A) Individual - If the general partner is an individual set out his/her last name, first name and middle names in the space provided.

   (B) Corporation, Partnership, etc. - If the general partner is not an individual, set out the name of the corporation, partnership, etc.

   Ontario Corporation Number - If the general partner is a corporation, set out the Ontario corporation number in the space provided. An extra-provincial corporation must obtain an Ontario corporation number by filing an initial return under the *Corporations Information Act* (domestic corporations) or by obtaining a licence under the *Extra-Provincial Corporations Act* (foreign corporations) before it can be a general partner.

   Address - Include the residential address, registered or head office address, or address for service for each general partner. This includes the street name and number, municipality, province, country and postal code. A post office box alone is not acceptable.

   Signature - Each general partner or a person signing as attorney on behalf of the general partner must sign the form. In the case of a corporation, the office of the individual who is signing on behalf of the corporation should be set out below the signature.

   Name of Signatory - Print the name of the person who is signing as general partner. If the person is signing as attorney pursuant to written authority under Section 32, of the *Limited Partnership Act* check the box provided.

7. **Jurisdiction of Formation** - state the jurisdiction in which the limited partnership is organized. For example, Ontario, British Columbia, Delaware, California, etc.

8. **Information Regarding Attorney /Representative for an Extra-Provincial Limited Partnership:**
   This item applies to all extra-provincial limited partnerships formed in a jurisdiction outside Canada carrying on business in Ontario. It also applies to extra-provincial limited partnerships within Canada that carry on business in Ontario but do not have an office or other place of business in Ontario.

   Power of Attorney - Form 4 under the *Limited Partnerships Act*
   Check the box to confirm that there is an executed Form 4 under the *Limited Partnerships Act* appointing the person/corporation named in item 8 to be the attorney and representative of the limited partnership in Ontario. The attorney and representative in Ontario is required to keep an executed Power of Attorney available for inspection at the address set out in the declaration.

   (A) Individual - complete this box if the attorney is an individual.

   (B) Corporation, Partnership, etc. - complete this box if the attorney is a corporation or other type of organization.

   Ontario Corporation Number - if the attorney is a corporation, set out the Ontario corporation number from its incorporation documents or, if an extra-provincial corporation, set out the Ontario corporation number assigned under the *Corporations Information Act or Extra-Provincial Corporations Act.*

   Address - Enter the attorney's residential address or address for service, or in the case of a corporation the registered/head office address or address for service including municipality, street and number (if any), and postal code. **The address must be in Ontario. A post office box alone is not acceptable.**

Information Regarding Limited Partners
The general partners of every Ontario limited partnership must maintain a current record of the limited partners at the principal place of business in Ontario. The general partners of every extra-provincial limited partnership carrying on business in Ontario shall maintain a current record of the limited partners at the principal place of business in Ontario or, if the limited partnership does not have a principal place of business in Ontario, the record must be kept by the attorney and representative in Ontario at the attorney/representative address set out in the declaration.

07191 (2014/11)

INSTRUCTIONS Il est important de lire ces remarques avant de remplir le formulaire

Inscrivez les renseignements clairement en LETTRES MAJUSCULES, au stylo noir.

Remplissez toutes les sections. Les formulaires incomplets seront retournés. Quel que soit le type de déclaration que vous déposez, y compris un changement, fournissez tous les renseignements demandés dans le formulaire, notamment ceux qui portent sur tous les commandités actuels.

Droits :
- **210 $ – Nouvelle Déclaration, modification de la raison sociale, ou renouvellement**
- **360 $ (210 $ + frais de retard de 150 $) – Renouvellement en retard**
- Par courrier – Mandat ou chèque établi à l'ordre du « Ministre des Finances »
- En personne – Espèces; mandat ou chèque établi à l'ordre du « Ministre des Finances »; carte Visa, MasterCard, American Express ou carte de débit
- Des frais administratifs seront facturés pour tout chèque non négociable retourné par la banque ou tout autre établissement financier

Il faut remplir cette formule en double exemplaire.
Envoyez les deux copies du formulaire au ministère des Services gouvernementaux. La copie Client sera retournée avec une mention de validation indiquant la date de la Déclaration, la date d'expiration et le numéro d'identification de l'entreprise.

Retournez le formulaire rempli au : Ministère des Services gouvernementaux et des Services aux consommateurs
Direction des compagnies et des sûretés mobilières
393, avenue University, bureau 200
Toronto ON M5G 2M2

En personne : 375, avenue University, 2e étage

Ne séparez pas les pages du formulaire

1. **Types de déclaration – Cochez la case appropriée :**

A - Nouvelle (Droits de 210 $)
Cochez la case A si vous déposez pour la première fois une Déclaration pour former une société en commandite de l'Ontario ou pour autoriser une société en commandite extraprovinciale à mener des activités en Ontario

B - Modification de la raison sociale (Droits de 210 $))
Cochez la case B. Étant donné qu'une modification de la raison sociale constitue une nouvelle déclaration aux termes du par. 3 (1) ou 25 (1) de la Loi, la date d'expiration de la déclaration sera repoussée de cinq ans. Par exemple, si la raison sociale est modifiée deux ans avant l'expiration de la déclaration en cours, la déclaration expirera au bout de sept ans.

C - Changement (autre que modification de la raison sociale) [Service gratuit]
Cochez la case C si vous modifiez des renseignements déjà fournis. Par exemple : changement d'adresse, d'activités, modification des renseignements sur les commandités.

D & E Renouvellement (Droits de 210 $)
Une déclaration expire au bout de cinq ans. Elle doit être renouvelée avant la date d'expiration indiquée sur l'enregistrement. **Des frais de 150 $ sont facturés pour les renouvellements déposés en retard.**

D - Renouvellement sans modification de la raison sociale
Cochez la case D pour renouveler une Déclaration si la société ne modifie pas son nom.

E - Renouvellement avec modification de la raison sociale
Cochez la case E pour renouveler une Déclaration si la société modifie en même temps son nom.

F - Dissolution (Service gratuit)
Cochez la case F pour déposer une Déclaration de dissolution pour une société en commandite formée en Ontario.

G - Retrait (Service gratuit)
Cochez la case G si vous déposez une Déclaration de retrait pour annuler la Déclaration et la Procuration d'une société en commandite extraprovinciale menant des activités en Ontario.

NIE (N° d'identification de l'entreprise)
Il faut entrer le numéro d'identification de l'entreprise pour une Modification de la raison sociale, un Renouvellement avec ou sans modification de la raison sociale, un Changement (de renseignements), une Dissolution ou un Retrait. Ce numéro figure sur le timbre de validation apposé sur la Déclaration originale ou sur la Déclaration de renouvellement ou de modification la plus récente.

2. **Raison sociale de la société en commandite –** Inscrivez en MAJUSCULES la raison sociale, une lettre par case, en commençant à la première case de la première ligne. Utilisez aussi une case pour chaque signe de ponctuation et pour chaque espace entre les mots.

3. **Adresse postale de Registrant –** Entrez l'adresse complète, telle que demandée, y compris le numéro de case postale, au besoin. *Votre document d'enregistrement sera envoyé à cette adresse.*

4. **Adresse de l'établissement principal en Ontario –** Entrez l'adresse complète (numéro et nom de la rue, le cas échéant). Une adresse composée d'une case postale seule n'est pas acceptée. S'il y a plus d'un établissement, choisissez en un comme établissement principal. Une société en commandite extraprovinciale n'est pas tenue d'avoir une adresse d'affaires en Ontario. Si c'est le cas, cochez la case correspondante.

5. **Nature générale de l'activité exercée –** Donnez une brève description (40 caractères au maximum) de l'activité que la société exerce.

6. **Renseignements sur le ou les commandités**

Nouvelle déclaration, Modification de la raison sociale ou Renouvellement : Remplissez la section 6 pour chacun des commandités. **Chaque commandité** ou son procureur doit signer les renseignements le concernant. S'il y a plus d'un commandité, indiquez le nombre total de commandités dans la case prévue, puis remplissez et joignez à la Déclaration une ou des **annexes**, selon les besoins.

6. **Renseignements sur le ou les commandités** (suite)

Changement (autre que raison sociale), Dissolution ou Retrait
Remplissez la section 6, qui doit être signée par au moins un commandité.

(A) **Personne physique -** Si le commandité est une personne, indiquez son nom de famille, prénom et autre prénom.

(B) **Personne morale, société en nom collectif, etc. -** Si le commandité est une entreprise, indiquez le nom de l'entreprise.

N° matricule de la personne morale en Ontario - Si le commandité est une personne morale, indiquez son numéro matricule de l'Ontario. Avant de pouvoir être un commandité, une personne morale extraprovinciale doit obtenir un numéro matricule de l'Ontario en déposant le Rapport initial requis par la *Loi sur les renseignements exigés des personnes morales* (sociétés canadiennes) ou en demandant un permis aux termes de la *Loi sur les personnes morales extraprovinciales* (sociétés étrangères).

Adresse - Indiquez, pour chaque commandité, l'adresse du domicile, ou celle du siège social, ou le domicile élu. Indiquez l'adresse complète, telle que demandée. Une adresse composée d'une case postale seule n'est pas acceptée.

Signature - Chaque commandité ou son procureur doit signer le formulaire. Dans le cas d'une personne morale, la personne signant au nom de la société devrait indiquer son titre sous la signature.

Nom du signataire - Indiquez en lettres moulées le nom de la personne qui signe en tant que commandité. Si la personne signe en tant que procureur nommé en vertu d'une procuration écrite (art. 32 de la Loi), cochez la case prévue à cet effet.

7. **Territoire d'origine -** Indiquez au complet le territoire de compétence où la société en commandite a été formée. Par exemple : Ontario, Colombie-Britannique, Delaware, Californie, etc.

8. **Renseignements sur le procureur / représentant de la société en commandite extraprovinciale**
Ne remplissez cette section que dans le cas d'une société en commandite extraprovinciale d'un pays étranger qui mène des activités en Ontario ou d'une société en commandite extraprovinciale du Canada qui mène des activités en Ontario mais qui n'a pas d'établissement d'affaires en Ontario.

Procuration - Formule 4 requise aux termes de la *Loi sur les sociétés en commandite*
Cochez la case pour confirmer qu'il existe une Procuration signée aux termes de la *Loi sur les sociétés en commandite* qui nomme la personne ou la société désignée à la section 8 comme procureur et représentant de la société en Ontario. Cette personne doit tenir la Procuration à disposition aux fins d'examen à l'adresse indiquée dans la Déclaration.

(A) **Personne physique** - Remplissez ce segment si le procureur est une personne physique.

(B) **Personne morale, société en nom collectif, etc**. - Remplissez ce segment si le procureur est une entreprise.

N° matricule de la personne morale en Ontario - Si le procureur est une personne morale, entrez son numéro matricule de l'Ontario qui figure dans ses documents constitutifs ou, s'il s'agit d'une personne morale extraprovinciale, entrez le numéro matricule de l'Ontario attribué aux termes de la *Loi sur les renseignements exigés des personnes morales* ou de la *Loi sur les personnes morales extraprovinciales.*

Adresse - Entrez l'adresse du domicile ou du domicile élu du procureur dans le cas d'une personne physique ou, dans le cas d'une personne morale, l'adresse de son siège social ou du domicile élu. Indiquez la rue et le numéro (le cas échéant), la ville, la province, le pays et le code postal. **L'adresse doit être située en Ontario. Une adresse composée d'une case postale seule n'est pas acceptée.**

Renseignements sur les commandités
Dans une société en commandite de l'Ontario, les commandités doivent avoir et tenir et à jour un registre des commanditaires à l'établissement principal de la société en Ontario. Dans une société en commandite extraprovinciale menant des activités en Ontario, les commandités doivent aussi avoir et tenir à jour un registre des commanditaires à l'établissement principal de l'Ontario ou, si la société extraprovinciale n'a pas d'établissement en Ontario, le registre doit être conservé à l'adresse du procureur et représentant de la société en Ontario.

07191 (2014/11)

Page ______ of / de ______

Print clearly in CAPITAL LETTERS / Écrivez clairement en LETTRES MAJUSCULES

1. **Declaration Type / Type de déclaration**
   A. ☐ New / Nouvelle B. ☐ Name Change / Modification de la raison sociale C. ☐ Change (other than name change) / Changement (autre que modification de la raison sociale)
   D. ☐ Renewal Without Name Change / Renouvellement sans modification de la raison sociale E. ☐ Renewal With Name Change / Renouvellement avec modification de la raison sociale F. ☐ **Dissolution / Dissolution** G. ☐ **Withdrawal / Retrait**
   Enter the Business Identification Number (BIN) for all Declaration Types except Type A. / Entrez le nº d'identification de l'entreprise (NIE) pour tous les types de déclaration, sauf pour le type A. **BIN (Business Identification No.) / NIE Nº d'identification de l'entreprise**

2. **Firm Name / Raison sociale de la société en commandite**

3. **Mailing Address of Registrant / Adresse postale de registrant**
   Street No. / Nº de rue | Street Name / Nom de la rue | Suite No. / Bureau nº
   City / Town / Ville | Province / Province | Country / Pays | Postal Code / Code postal

4. **Address of Principal Place of Business in Ontario / Adresse de l'établissement principal en Ontario**
   ☐ Same as above / comme ci-dessus ☐ Extra-Provincial Limited Partnership without business address in Ontario / Société en commandite extraprovinciale sans établissement en Ontario
   Street No. / Nº de rue | Street Name / Nom de la rue | Suite No. / Bureau nº (PO Box not acceptable / CP non acceptés)
   City / Town / Ville | Province / Province | Country / Pays | Post al Code / Code postal

5. **General Nature of Business / Nature générale de l'activité exercée**

6. **Information Regarding General Partner(s) / Renseignements sur le ou les commandités**
   (A) Individual / Personne physique - Last Name / Nom de famille | First Name / Prénom | Middle Name / Autre prénom
   (B) Corporation, Partnership etc. / Personne morale, société en nom collectif etc. - Name / Raison sociale | Ontario Corporation Number / Nº matricule de la personne morale en Ontario
   Street No. / Nº de rue | Street Name / Nom de la rue | Suite No. / Bureau nº
   City / Town / Ville | Province / Province | Country / Pays | Post al Code / Code postal
   Signature of General Partner or Attorney for the General Partner/ Signature du commandité ou de son procureur
   X
   Print Name of Signatory / Nom du signataire en lettres moulées
   Check if signing as **attorney** on behalf of the general partner pursuant to s. 32 of the *Limited Partnerships Act*. Cochez la case ci contre si le signataire est le **procureur** du commandité (art. 32 de la Loi) ☐
   For a new Declaration, name change or renewal, Item 6 must be completed and signed by all the general partners or their attorneys. If there is more than one general partner, set out the total number of partners in the box and attach additional schedule(s) / Pour une nouvelle Déclaration, une modification de la raison sociale ou un renouvellement, il faut remplir la section 6 pour chaque commandité, et chaque commandité ou son procureur doit signer la section 6. S'il y a plus d'un commandité, entrez le nombre total de commandités dans la case ci contre et remplissez et joignez une ou des annexes.
   Number of General Partners / Nombre de commandités ☐

7. **Jurisdiction of Formation / Territoire d'origine**

Extra-Provincial Limited Partnership Carrying on Business in Ontario / Société en commandite extraprovinciale menant des activités en Ontario

8. **Information Regarding Attorney/Representative for an Extra-Provincial Limited Partnership - (Does not apply to limited partnerships formed in another Canadian jurisdiction that have an office or other place of business in Ontario) / Renseignements sur le procureur / représentant de la société en commandite extraprovinciale - (Ne s'applique pas aux sociétés en commandite d'un autre territoire canadien qui ont un établissement en Ontario)**
   Power of Attorney - Check the box to confirm there is an executed Power of Attorney (Form 4) appointing the person/corporation listed below to be the attorney and representative in Ontario. The attorney/representative is required to keep the executed Form 4 available for inspection at the address set out below. / Procuration – Cochez la case ci-contre pour confirmer qu'il y a une Procuration signée (Formule 4) nommant la personne physique ou morale indiquée ci dessous à titre de procureur et représentant en Ontario. Celui ci doit tenir la Formule 4 signée à disposition aux fins d'inspection à l'adresse ci dessous. ☐
   Attorney / Representative – Procureur / représentant
   (A) Individual / Personne physique - Last Name / Nom de famille | First Name / Prénom | Middle Name / Autre prénom
   (B) Corporation, Partnership etc. / Personne morale, société en nom collectif etc. - Name / Raison sociale | Ontario Corporation Number / Nº matricule de la personne morale en Ontario
   Street No. / Nº de rue | Street Name / Nom de la rue | Suite No. / Bureau nº
   City / Town / Ville | Province / Province
   Country / Pays | Postal Code / Code postal
   MINISTRY USE ONLY - RÉSERVÉ AU MINISTÈRE

07191 (2014/11)

SCHEDULE - To Form 3, Declaration Under the *Limited Partnerships Act*
ANNEXE à la Formule 3 - Déclaration *Loi sur les sociétés en commandite*
Information Regarding General Partners
Renseignements sur le ou les commandités

Page ____ of / de ____

Only complete this schedule if the limited partnership has more than one general partner. All general partners must be listed and must sign a new declaration, name change, or renewal. Complete as many Schedules as required. A change other than a name change, withdrawal or dissolution must be signed by at least one general partner.

Ne remplissez cette Annexe que si la société en commandite a plus d'un commandité. Tous les commandités doivent être déclarés et chacun doit signer la Déclaration si vous remplissez une nouvelle déclaration, une modification de la raison sociale ou un renouvellement. Utilisez d'autres annexes, si nécessaire. Si vous remplissez une Déclaration pour un changement autre qu'une modification de la raison sociale, ou pour un retrait ou une dissolution, la Déclaration doit être signée par au moins un commandité.

BIN (Business Identification No.)/NIE Nº d'identification de l'entreprise

Firm Name / Raison sociale de la société en commandite

9. Information Regarding General Partner(s) / Renseignements sur le ou les commandités

(A) Individual / Personne physique - Last Name / Nom de famille First Name / Prénom Middle Name / Autre prénom

(B) Corporation, Partnership etc. / Personne morale, société en nom collectif etc. - Name / Raison sociale

Ontario Corporation Number
Nº matricule de la personne morale en Ontario

Street No. / Nº de rue Street Name / Nom de la rue Suite No. / Bureau nº

City / Town / Ville Province / Province Country / Pays Post al Code / Code postal

Signature of General Partner or Attorney for the General Partner/
Signature du commandité ou de son procureur

X

Print Name of Signatory / Nom du signataire en lettres moulées

Check if signing as **attorney** on behalf of the general partner pursuant to s. 32 of the *Limited Partnerships Act*.

Cochez la case ci contre si le signataire est le **procureur** du commandité (art. 32 de la Loi) ☐

(A) Individual / Personne physique - Last Name / Nom de famille First Name / Prénom Middle Name / Autre prénom

(B) Corporation, Partnership etc. / Personne morale, société en nom collectif etc. - Name / Raison sociale

Ontario Corporation Number
Nº matricule de la personne morale en Ontario

Street No. / Nº de rue Street Name / Nom de la rue Suite No. / Bureau nº

City / Town / Ville Province / Province Country / Pays Post al Code / Code postal

Signature of General Partner or Attorney for the General Partner/
Signature du commandité ou de son procureur

X

Print Name of Signatory / Nom du signataire en lettres moulées

Check if signing as **attorney** on behalf of the general partner pursuant to s. 32 of the *Limited Partnerships Act*.

Cochez la case ci contre si le signataire est le **procureur** du commandité (art. 32 de la Loi) ☐

(A) Individual / Personne physique - Last Name / Nom de famille First Name / Prénom Middle Name / Autre prénom

(B) Corporation, Partnership etc. / Personne morale, société en nom collectif etc. - Name / Raison sociale

Ontario Corporation Number
Nº matricule de la personne morale en Ontario

Street No. / Nº de rue Street Name / Nom de la rue Suite No. / Bureau nº

City / Town / Ville Province / Province Country / Pays Post al Code / Code postal

Signature of General Partner or Attorney for the General Partner/
Signature du commandité ou de son procureur

X

Print Name of Signatory / Nom du signataire en lettres moulées

Check if signing as **attorney** on behalf of the general partner pursuant to s. 32 of the *Limited Partnerships Act*.
Cochez la case ci contre si le signataire est le **procureur** du commandité (art. 32 de la *Loi*) ☐

MINISTRY USE ONLY - RÉSERVÉ AU MINISTÈRE

07191 (2014/11)

Form 4 — Power of Attorney — The Limited Partnerships Act*

Know all persons by these presents that / Faisons savoir par les présentes que

____

(Name of appointing extra-provincial limited partnership / Nom de la société en commandite extraprovinciale qui nomme le procureur)

(hereinafter called the "Partnership" / ci-après appelée la Société)
hereby nominates, constitutes and appoints / nomme.

____

(Name of attorney in full / Nom au complet du procureur)

____ Ontario ☐☐☐☐☐☐

(Business address of the attorney including street, municipality and postal code /
Adresse d'affaires du procureur sans omettre la rue, la municipalité le code postal)

its true and lawful attorney, to act as such, and as such to sue and be sued, plead and be impleaded in any court in Ontario, and generally on behalf of the partnership within Ontario to accept service of process and to receive all lawful notices and, for the purposes of the partnership to do all acts and to execute all deeds and other instruments relating to the matters within the scope of this power of attorney. Until the Registrar appointed under the *Business Names Act* has received and accepted a due and lawful notice naming another and subsequent attorney, the partnership shall accept as sufficient service of process and other documents upon the said:

son procureur légitime et le charge d'agir en cette qualité et d'intenter des poursuites, d'être poursuivi et de plaider devant n'importe quel tribunal de l'Ontario au nom de la Société, ainsi que d'accepter au nom de la Société les significations des actes et de recevoir au nom de la Société tous les avis légaux relatifs à l'Ontario et aussi de faire toutes les démarches et de passer tous les actes et autres documents relatifs aux questions entrant dans le champ de la procuration. Jusqu' à ce que le registrateur nommé aux termes de la *Loi sur les noms commerciaux* ait reçu et accepté un avis en bonne et due forme nommant un autre procureur, la Société considérera comme suffisante la signification des actes et autres documents et avis audit :

____

(name of attorney in full / Nom au complet du procureur)

Dated
Date ______________________________
year / année month / mois day / jour

____

(Name of extra-provincial limited partnership)
(Nom de la société en commandite extraprovinciale)

By / Par ______________________________
(Signature/Signature) / (General Partner/commanditeé)

07262 (2009/11)

CONSENT TO ACT AS ATTORNEY - THE *LIMITED PARTNERSHIPS ACT*
CONSENTEMENT DU PROCUREUR - *LOI SUR LES SOCIÉTÉS EN COMMANDITE*

I/Je soussigné(e) ____
(Name of attorney in full / Nom au complet du procureur)

of / au ____
(Business address including street number,
(Adresse d'affaires sans omettre le numéro et la rue,

______________________________, Ontario, hereby consent to act as the
municipality and postal code) , (Ontario) consens par la présente à agir dans
la municipalité et le code postal)

attorney in the province of Ontario of
la province de l'Ontario en qualité de procureur de ______________________________
(Name of extra-provincial limited partnership)
(Nom de la société en commandite extraprovinciale)

____

pursuant to the Power of Attorney in that behalf executed by the said limited partnership on the ______________
conformément à la procuration passée à cet effet par ladite société en commandite, le

day of
jour de ______________, year
année ______________ authorizing me to accept service of process and notices on its behalf.
qui m'autorise à accepter la signification des actes et autres avis en son nom.

Dated
Date ____
year / année month / mois day / jour

______________________________ ______________________________
(Signature of witness / Signature du témoin) (Signature of the consenting person or corporation)
(Signature de la personne physique ou morale consentante)

07262 (2009/11)

PARTNERSHIPS ACT

R.S.O. 1990, c. P.5, as am. S.O. 1998, c. 2, ss. 1–8; 1999, c. 6, s. 52; 2005, c. 5, s. 55; 2006, c. 19, Sched. G, s. 7; 2006, c. 34, s. 19; 2009, c. 33, Sched. 2, s. 57.

1. (1) **Definitions** — In this Act,

"business" includes every trade, occupation and profession;

"court" includes every court and judge having jurisdiction in the case.

"extra-provincial limited liability partnership" means a limited liability partnership formed under the laws of another jurisdiction but does not include an extra-provincial limited partnership with the meaning of the *Limited Partnerships Act*;

"limited liability partnership" means a partnership, other than a limited partnership, that is formed or continued as a limited liability partnership under section 44.1 or that is an extra-provincial limited liability partnership.

(2) **Idem** — A person is deemed to be "insolvent" within the meaning of this Act if the person is adjudged a bankrupt under the *Bankruptcy Act* (Canada) or if the person makes an assignment for the general benefit of his or her creditors, and "insolvency" has a meaning corresponding with "insolvent".

1998, c. 2, s. 1

NATURE OF PARTNERSHIP

2. Partnership — Partnership is the relation that subsists between persons carrying on a business in common with a view to profit, but the relation between the members of a company or association that is incorporated by or under the authority of any special or general Act in force in Ontario or elsewhere, or registered as a corporation under any such Act, is not a partnership within the meaning of this Act.

3. Rules for determining existence of partnership — In determining whether a partnership does or does not exist, regard shall be had to the following rules:

1. Joint tenancy, tenancy in common, joint property, common property, or part ownership does not of itself create a partnership as to anything so held or owned, whether the tenants or owners do or do not share any profits made by the use thereof.
2. The sharing of gross returns does not of itself create a partnership, whether the persons sharing such returns have or have not a joint or common right or interest in any property from which or from the use of which the returns are derived.
3. The receipt by a person of a share of the profits of a business is proof, in the absence of evidence to the contrary, that the person is a partner in the business, but the receipt

of such a share or payment, contingent on or varying with the profits of a business, does not of itself make him or her a partner in the business, and in particular,

(a) the receipt by a person of a debt or other liquidated amount by instalments or otherwise out of the accruing profits of a business does not of itself make him or her a partner in the business or liable as such;

(b) a contract for the remuneration of a servant or agent or a person engaged in a business by a share of the profits of the business does not of itself make the servant or agent a partner in the business or liable as such;

(c) a person who,

(i) was married to a deceased partner immediately before the deceased partner died,

(ii) was living with a deceased partner in a conjugal relationship outside marriage immediately before the deceased partner died, or

(iii) is a child of a deceased partner,

and who receives by way of annuity a portion of the profits made in the business in which the deceased partner was a partner is not by reason only of such receipt a partner in the business or liable as such;

(d) the advance of money by way of loan to a person engaged or about to engage in a business on a contract with that person that the lender is to receive a rate of interest varying with the profits, or is to receive a share of the profits arising from carrying on the business, does not of itself make the lender a partner with the person or persons carrying on the business or liable as such, provided that the contract is in writing and signed by or on behalf of all parties thereto;

(e) a person receiving by way of annuity or otherwise a portion of the profits of a business in consideration of the sale by him or her of the goodwill of the business, is not by reason only of such receipt a partner in the business or liable as such.

1999, c. 6, s. 52; 2005, c. 5, s. 55

4. Insolvency — In the event of a person to whom money has been advanced by way of loan upon such a contract as is mentioned in section 3, or of a buyer of the goodwill in consideration of a share of the profits of the business, becoming insolvent or entering into an arrangement to pay his or her creditors less than 100 cents on the dollar or dying in insolvent circumstances, the lender of the loan is not entitled to recover anything in respect of the loan, and the seller of the goodwill is not entitled to recover anything in respect of the share of profits contracted for, until the claims of the other creditors of the borrower or buyer, for valuable consideration in money or money's worth, are satisfied.

5. Meaning of "firm" — Persons who have entered into partnership with one another are, for the purposes of this Act, called collectively a firm, and the name under which their business is carried on is called the firm name.

Relation Of Partners To Persons Dealing With Them

6. Power of partner to bind firm — Every partner is an agent of the firm and of the other partners for the purpose of the business of the partnership, and the acts of every partner who does any act for carrying on in the usual way business of the kind carried on by the firm of which he or she is a member, bind the firm and the other partners unless the partner so acting has in fact no authority to act for the firm in the particular matter and the person with whom the partner is dealing either knows that the partner has no authority, or does not know or believe him or her to be a partner.

7. Partners bound by acts on behalf of firm — An act or instrument relating to the business of the firm and done or executed in the firm name, or in any other manner showing an intention to bind the firm by a person thereto authorized, whether a partner or not, is binding on the firm and all the partners, but this section does not affect any general rule of law relating to the execution of deeds or negotiable instruments.

8. Partner using credit of firm for private purposes — Where one partner pledges the credit of the firm for a purpose apparently not connected with the firm's ordinary course of business, the firm is not bound, unless he or she is in fact specially authorized by the other partners, but this section does not affect any personal liability incurred by an individual partner.

9. Effect of notice that firm not bound by act of partner — If it is agreed between the partners to restrict the power of any one or more of them to bind the firm, no act done in contravention of the agreement is binding on the firm with respect to persons having notice of the agreement.

10. (1) Liability of partners — Except as provided in subsection (2) every partner in a firm is liable jointly with the other partners for all debts and obligations of the firm incurred while the person is a partner, and after the partner's death the partner's estate is also severally liable in a due course of administration for such debts and obligations so far as they remain unsatisfied, but subject to the prior payment of his or her separate debts.

(2) Limited liability partnerships — Subject to subsections (3) and (3.1), a partner in a limited liability partnership is not liable, by means of indemnification, contribution or otherwise, for,

(a) the debts, liabilities or obligations of the partnership or any partner arising from the negligent or wrongful acts or omissions that another partner or an employee, agent or representative of the partnership commits in the course of the partnership business while the partnership is a limited liability partnership; or

(b) any other debts or obligations of the partnership that are incurred while the partnership is a limited liability partnership.

(3) Limitations — Subsection (2) does not relieve a partner in a limited liability partnership from liability for,

(a) the partner's own negligent or wrongful act or omission;

(b) the negligent or wrongful act or omission of a person under the partner's direct supervision; or

(c) the negligent or wrongful act or omission of another partner or an employee of the partnership not under the partner's direct supervision, if,

(i) the act or omission was criminal or constituted fraud, even if there was no criminal act or omission, or

(ii) the partner knew or ought to have known of the act or omission and did not take the actions that a reasonable person would have taken to prevent it.

(3.1) Same — Subsection (2) does not protect a partner's interest in the partnership property from claims against the partnership respecting a partnership obligation.

(4) Partner not proper party to action — A partner in a limited liability partnership is not a proper party to a proceeding by or against the limited liability partnership for the purpose of recovering damages or enforcing obligations arising out of the negligent acts or omissions described in subsection (2).

(5) Extra-provincial limited liability partnerships — This section does not apply to an extra-provincial limited liability partnership.

1998, c. 2, s. 2; 2006, c. 34, s. 19

11. Liability of firm for wrongs — Where by any wrongful act or omission of a partner acting in the ordinary course of the business of the firm, or with the authority of the co-partners, loss or injury is caused to a person not being a partner of the firm, or any penalty is incurred, the firm is liable therefor to the same extent as the partner so acting or omitting to act.

12. Misapplication of money or property received for or in custody of the firm — In the following cases, namely,

(a) where one partner, acting within the scope of the partner's apparent authority, receives the money or property of a third person and misapplies it; and

(b) where a firm in the course of its business receives money or property of a third person, and the money or property so received is misapplied by one or more of the partners while it is in the custody of the firm,

the firm is liable to make good the loss.

13. Liability for wrongs joint and several — Except as provided in subsection 10(2) every partner is liable jointly with the co-partners and also severally for everything for which the firm, while the person is a partner therein, becomes liable under section 11 or 12.

1998, c. 2, s. 3

14. Improper employment of trust property for partnership purposes — If a partner, being a trustee, improperly employs trust property in the business or on the account of the partnership, no other partner is liable for the trust property to the persons beneficially interested therein, but,

(a) this section does not affect any liability incurred by any partner by reason of the partner having notice of a breach of trust; and

(b) nothing in this section prevents trust money from being followed and recovered from the firm if still in its possession or under its control.

15. (1) Persons liable by "holding out" — Every person, who by words spoken or written or by conduct represents himself or herself or who knowingly suffers himself or herself to be represented as a partner in a particular firm, is liable as a partner to any person who has on the faith of any such representation given credit to the firm, whether the representation has or has not been made or communicated to the persons so giving credit by or with the knowledge of the apparent partner making the representation or suffering it to be made.

(2) Continuing business after death of partner — Where after a partner's death the partnership business is continued in the old firm name, the continued use of that name or of the deceased partner's name as part thereof does not of itself make his or her executor's or administrator's estate or effects liable for any partnership debts contracted after his or her death.

16. Admissions and representations of partners — An admission or representation made by a partner concerning the partnership affairs and in the ordinary course of its business is evidence against the firm.

17. Notice to acting partner to be notice to the firm — Notice to a partner who habitually acts in the partnership business of any matter relating to partnership affairs operates as notice to the firm, except in the case of a fraud on the firm committed by or with the consent of that partner.

18. (1) Liability commences with admission to firm — A person who is admitted as a partner into an existing firm does not thereby become liable to the creditors of the firm for anything done before the person became a partner.

(2) Liability for debts, etc., incurred before retirement — A partner who retires from a firm does not thereby cease to be liable for partnership debts or obligations incurred before the partner's retirement.

(3) Agreement discharging retiring partner — A retiring partner may be discharged from any existing liabilities by an agreement to that effect between the partner and the members of the firm as newly constituted and the creditors, and this agreement may be either express or inferred as a fact from the course of dealing between the creditors and the firm as newly constituted.

19. Revocation of continuing guaranty by change in firm — A continuing guaranty or cautionary obligation given either to a firm or to a third person in respect of the transactions of a firm is, in the absence of agreement to the contrary, revoked as to future transactions by any change in the constitution of the firm to which, or of the firm in respect of the transaction of which, the guaranty or obligation was given.

Relation Of Partners To One Another

20. Variation by consent of terms of partnership — The mutual rights and duties of partners, whether ascertained by agreement or defined by this Act, may be varied by the consent of all the partners, and such consent may be either expressed or inferred from a course of dealing.

21. (1) Partnership property — All property and rights and interests in property originally brought into the partnership stock or acquired, whether by purchase or otherwise, on account of the firm, or for the purposes and in the course of the partnership business, are called in this Act "partnership property", and must be held and applied by the partners exclusively for the purposes of the partnership and in accordance with the partnership agreement.

(2) Devolution of land — The legal estate or interest in land that belongs to a partnership devolves according to the nature and tenure thereof and the general rules of law thereto applicable, but in trust, so far as necessary, for the persons beneficially interested in the land under this section.

(3) Co-owners of land — Where co-owners of an estate or interest in land, not being itself partnership property, are partners as to profits made by the use of that land or estate, and purchase other land or estate out of the profits to be used in like manner, the land or estate so purchased belongs to them, in the absence of an agreement to the contrary, not as partners, but as co-owners for the same respective estates and interests as are held by them in the land or estate first mentioned at the date of purchase.

22. Property bought with partnership money — Unless the contrary intention appears, property bought with money belonging to the firm shall be deemed to have been bought on the account of the firm.

23. Conversion of land bought with partnership money into personalty — Where land or any heritable interest therein becomes partnership property, unless the contrary intention appears, it is to be treated as between the partners, including the representatives of a deceased partner, and also as between the heirs of a deceased partner and his or her executors or administrators as personal or movable and not real or heritable estate.

24. Rules as to interests and duties of partners — The interests of partners in the partnership property and their rights and duties in relation to the partnership shall be determined, subject to any agreement express or implied between the partners, by the following rules:

1. All the partners are entitled to share equally in the capital and profits of the business, and must contribute equally towards the losses, whether of capital or otherwise, sustained by the firm, but a partner shall not be liable to contribute toward losses arising from a liability for which the partner is not liable under subsection 10(2).

2. The firm must indemnify every partner in respect of payments made and personal liabilities incurred by him or her,

(a) in the ordinary and proper conduct of the business of the firm; or

(b) in or about anything necessarily done for the preservation of the business or property of the firm.

2.1 A partner is not required to indemnify the firm or other partners in respect of debts or obligations of the partnership for which a partner is not liable under subsection 10(2).

3. A partner making, for the purpose of the partnership, any actual payment or advance beyond the amount of capital that he or she has agreed to subscribe is entitled to interest at the rate of 5 per cent per annum from the date of the payment or advance.

4. A partner is not entitled, before the ascertainment of profits, to interest on the capital subscribed by the partner.

5. Every partner may take part in the management of the partnership business.

6. No partner is entitled to remuneration for acting in the partnership business.

7. No person may be introduced as a partner without the consent of all existing partners.

8. Any difference arising as to ordinary matters connected with the partnership business may be decided by a majority of the partners, but no change may be made in the nature of the partnership business without the consent of all existing partners.

9. The partnership books are to be kept at the place of business of the partnership, or the principal place, if there is more than one, and every partner may, when he or she thinks fit, have access to and inspect and copy any of them.

1998, c. 2, s. 4

25. Expulsion of partner — No majority of the partners can expel any partner unless a power to do so has been conferred by express agreement between the partners.

26. (1) **Retirement from partnership at will** — Where no fixed term is agreed upon for the duration of the partnership, any partner may determine the partnership at any time on giving notice of his or her intention to do so to all the other partners.

(2) **Notice of retirement** — Where the partnership was originally constituted by deed, a notice in writing, signed by the partner giving it, is sufficient for that purpose.

27. (1) **Presumption of continuance after expiry of term** — Where a partnership entered into for a fixed term is continued after the term has expired and without any express new agreement, the rights and duties of the partners remain the same as they were at the expiration of the term, so far as is consistent with the incidents of a partnership at will.

(2) **Arises from continuance of business** — A continuance of the business by the partners or such of them as habitually acted therein during the term without any settlement or liquidation of the partnership affairs shall be presumed to be a continuance of the partnership.

28. Duty as to rendering accounts — Partners are bound to render true accounts and full information of all things affecting the partnership to any partner or the partner's legal representatives.

29. (1) **Accountability for private profits** — Every partner must account to the firm for any benefit derived by the partner without the consent of the other partners from any transaction concerning the partnership or from any use by the partner of the partnership property, name or business connection.

(2) **Extends to survivors and representatives of deceased** — This section applies also to transactions undertaken after a partnership has been dissolved by the death of a partner and before its affairs have been completely wound up, either by a surviving partner or by the representatives of the deceased partner.

30. Duty of partner not to compete with firm — If a partner, without the consent of the other partners, carries on a business of the same nature as and competing with that of the firm, the partner must account for and pay over to the firm all profits made by the partner in that business.

31. (1) **Rights of assignee of share in partnership** — An assignment by a partner of the partner's share in the partnership, either absolute or by way of mortgage or redeemable charge, does not, as against the other partners, entitle the assignee, during the continuance of the partnership, to interfere in the management or administration of the partnership business or affairs, or to require any accounts of the partnership transactions, or to inspect the partnership books, but entitles the assignee only to receive the share of profits to which the assigning partner would otherwise be entitled, and the assignee must accept the account of profits agreed to by the partners.

(2) **On dissolution** — In the case of a dissolution of the partnership, whether as respects all the partners or as respects the assigning partner, the assignee is entitled to receive the share of the partnership assets to which the assigning partner is entitled as between the assigning partner and the other partners, and, for the purpose of ascertaining that share, to an account as from the date of the dissolution.

DISSOLUTION OF PARTNERSHIP

32. Dissolution by expiry of term or notice — Subject to any agreement between the partners, a partnership is dissolved,

(a) if entered into for a fixed term, by the expiration of that term;

(b) if entered into for a single adventure or undertaking, by the termination of that adventure or undertaking; or

(c) if entered into for an undefined time, by a partner giving notice to the other or others of his or her intention to dissolve the partnership, in which case the partnership is dissolved as from the date mentioned in the notice as the date of dissolution, or, if no date is so mentioned, as from the date of the communication of the notice.

33. (1) Dissolution by death or insolvency of partner — Subject to any agreement between the partners, every partnership is dissolved as regards all the partners by the death or insolvency of a partner.

(2) **Where partner's share charged for separate debt** — A partnership may, at the option of the other partners, be dissolved if any partner suffers that partner's share of the partnership property to be charged under this Act for that partner's separate debt.

34. By illegality of business — A partnership is in every case dissolved by the happening of any event that makes it unlawful for the business of the firm to be carried on or for the members of the firm to carry it on in partnership.

35. (1) By the court — On application by a partner, the court may order a dissolution of the partnership,

(a) when a partner is found to be incapable as defined in the *Substitute Decisions Act, 1992*;

(b) when a partner, other than the partner suing, becomes in any other way permanently incapable of performing the partner's part of the partnership contract;

(c) when a partner, other than the partner suing, has been guilty of such conduct as, in the opinion of the court, regard being had to the nature of the business, is calculated to prejudicially affect the carrying on of the business;

(d) when a partner, other than the partner suing, wilfully or persistently commits a breach of the partnership agreement, or otherwise so conducts himself or herself in matters relating to the partnership business that it is not reasonably practicable for the other partner or partners to carry on the business in partnership with the partner;

(e) when the business of the partnership can only be carried on at a loss; or

(f) when in any case circumstances have arisen that in the opinion of the court render it just and equitable that the partnership be dissolved.

(2) **Application where incapacity** — In the case of an application under clause (1)(a), the application may be made by the litigation guardian of the partner found to be incapable, on the partner's behalf.

2009, c. 33, Sched. 2, s. 57

36. (1) **Rights of persons dealing with firm against apparent members** — Where a person deals with a firm after a change in its constitution, the person is entitled to treat all apparent members of the old firm as still being members of the firm until the person has notice of the change.

(2) **Notice** — An advertisement in The Ontario Gazette shall be notice as to persons who had not dealings with the firm before the dissolution or change so advertised.

(3) **Estate of dead or insolvent partner, how far liable** — The estate of a partner who dies, or who becomes insolvent, or of a partner who, not having been known to the person dealing with the firm to be a partner, retires from the firm, is not liable for partnership debts contracted after the date of the death, insolvency, or retirement.

37. **Right to give notice of dissolution** — On the dissolution of a partnership or retirement of a partner, any partner may publicly given notice of the same, and may require the other partner or partners to concur for that purpose in all necessary or proper acts, if any, that cannot be done without his, her or their concurrence.

38. **Continuing authority of partners for purposes of winding up** — After the dissolution of a partnership, the authority of each partner to bind the firm and the other rights and obligations of the partners continue despite the dissolution so far as is necessary to wind up the affairs of the partnership and to complete transactions begun but unfinished at the time of the dissolution, but not otherwise; provided that the firm is in no case bound by the acts of a partner who has become insolvent; but this proviso does not affect the liability of a person who has, after the insolvency, represented himself or herself or knowingly suffered himself or herself to be represented as a partner of the insolvent.

39. **Rights of partners as to application of partnership property** — On the dissolution of a partnership every partner is entitled, as against the other partners in the firm and all persons claiming through them in respect of their interests as partners, to have the property of the partnership applied in payment of the debts and liabilities of the firm and to have the surplus assets after such payment applied in payment of what may be due to the partners respectively after deducting what may be due from them as partners to the firm, and for that purpose any partner or the partner's representative may, on the termination of the partnership, apply to the court to wind up the business and affairs of the firm.

40. **Apportionment of premium on premature dissolution** — Where one partner paid a premium to another on entering into a partnership for a fixed term and the partnership is dissolved before the expiration of that term otherwise than by the death of a partner, the court may order the repayment of the premium, or of such part thereof as it thinks just,

having regard to the terms of the partnership contract and to the length of time during which the partnership has continued, unless,

(a) the dissolution is, in the judgment of the court, wholly or chiefly due to the misconduct of the partner who paid the premium; or

(b) the partnership has been dissolved by an agreement containing no provision for a return of a part of the premium.

41. Rights where partnership dissolved for fraud or misrepresentation — Where a partnership contract is rescinded on the ground of fraud or misrepresentation of one of the parties thereto, the party entitled to rescind is, without prejudice to any other right, entitled,

(a) to a lien on, or right of retention of, the surplus of the partnership assets, after satisfying the partnership liabilities, for any sum of money paid by the party for the purchase of a share in the partnership and for any capital contributed by him or her; and

(b) to stand in the place of the creditors of the firm for any payments made by the party in respect of the partnership liabilities; and

(c) to be indemnified by the person guilty of the fraud or making the representation against all the debts and liabilities of the firm.

42. (1) Right of outgoing partner as to share in profits after dissolution — Where any member of a firm dies or otherwise ceases to be a partner and the surviving or continuing partners carry on the business of the firm with its capital or assets without any final settlement of accounts as between the firm and the outgoing partner or his or her estate, then, in the absence of an agreement to the contrary, the outgoing partner or his or her estate is entitled, at the option of the outgoing partner or his or her representatives, to such share of the profits made since the dissolution as the court finds to be attributable to the use of the outgoing partner's share of the partnership assets, or to interest at the rate of 5 per cent per annum on the amount of his or her share of the partnership assets.

(2) Proviso as to option of remaining partners to purchase share — Where by the partnership contract an option is given to surviving or continuing partners to purchase the interest of a deceased or outgoing partner and that option is duly exercised, the estate of the deceased partner, or the outgoing partner or his or her estate, as the case may be, is not entitled to any further or other share of profits, but if any partner, assuming to act in exercise of the option, does not in all material respects comply with the terms thereof, he or she is liable to account under the foregoing provisions of this section.

43. Retiring or deceased partner's share to be a debt — Subject to any agreement between the partners, the amount due from surviving or continuing partners to an outgoing partner or the representatives of a deceased partner in respect of the outgoing or deceased partner's share, is a debt accruing at the date of the dissolution or death.

44. Rules for distribution of assets on final settlement of accounts — In settling accounts between the partners after a dissolution of partnership, the following rules shall, subject to any agreement, be observed:

1. Losses, including losses and deficiencies of capital, are to be paid first out of profits, next out of capital, and lastly, if necessary, by the partners individually in the proportion in which they were entitled to share profits, but a partner is not required to pay any loss arising from a liability for which the partner is not liable under subsection 10(2).

2. The assets of the firm, including the sums, if any, contributed by the partners to make up losses or deficiencies of capital, are to be applied in the following manner and order,

(a) in paying the debts and liabilities of the firm to persons who are not partners therein;

(b) in paying to each partner rateably what is due from the firm to him or her for advances as distinguished from capital;

(c) in paying to each partner rateably what is due from the firm to him or her in respect of capital.

3. After making the payments required by paragraph 2, the ultimate residue, if any, is to be divided among the partners in the proportion in which profits are divisible.

1998, c. 2, s. 5

LIMITED LIABILITY PARTNERSHIPS

44.1 (1) Formation — A limited liability partnership that is not an extra-provincial limited liability partnership is formed when two or more persons enter into a written agreement that,

(a) designates the partnership as a limited liability partnership; and

(b) states that this Act governs the agreement.

(2) Continuance — A partnership may be continued as a limited liability partnership that is not an extra-provincial limited liability partnership if all of the partners,

(a) enter into an agreement that continues the partnership as a limited liability partnership and states that this Act governs the agreement; or

(b) if there is an existing agreement between the partners that forms the partnership, amend the agreement to designate the partnership as a limited liability partnership and to state that this Act governs the agreement.

(3) Effect of continuance — Upon the continuance of a partnership as a limited liability partnership under subsection (2),

(a) the limited liability partnership possesses all the property, rights, privileges and franchises and is subject to all liabilities, including civil, criminal and quasi-criminal, and all contracts, disabilities and debts of the partnership which were in existence immediately before the continuance; and

(b) all persons who were partners immediately before the continuance remain liable for all debts, obligations and liabilities of the partnership or all partners with respect to the other partners that arose before the continuance.

1998, c. 2, s. 6

44.2 Limitation on business activity — A limited liability partnership may carry on business in Ontario only for the purpose of practising a profession governed by an Act and only if,

(a) that Act expressly permits a limited liability partnership to practise the profession;

(b) the governing body of the profession requires the partnership to maintain a minimum amount of liability insurance; and

(c) the partnership complies with section 44.3 if it is not an extra-provincial limited liability partnership or section 44.4 if it is an extra-provincial limited liability partnership.

1998, c. 2, s. 6

44.3 (1) Business name — No limited liability partnership formed or continued by an agreement governed by this Act shall carry on business unless it has registered its firm name under the *Business Names Act*.

(2) Amendments, cancellations and renewals — To amend, renew or cancel a registration of its firm name, a limited liability partnership mentioned in subsection (1) shall register an amendment, renewal or cancellation of a registration in accordance with the requirements of the *Business Names Act*.

(3) Firm name — The firm name of a limited liability partnership mentioned in subsection (1) shall contain the words "limited liability partnership" or "société à responsabilité limitée" or the abbreviations "LLP", "L.L.P." or "s.r.l." as the last words or letters of the firm name.

(3.1) Same — A limited liability partnership mentioned in subsection (1) may have a firm name that is in,

(a) an English form only;

(b) a French form only;

(c) a French and English form, where the French and English are used together in a combined form; or

(d) a French form and an English form, where the French and English forms are equivalent but are used separately.

(3.2) Same — A limited liability partnership mentioned in subsection (1) that has a firm name described in clause (3.1)(d) may be legally designated by the French or English version of its firm name.

(4) Use of registered name only — No limited liability partnership mentioned in subsection (1) shall carry on business under a name other than its registered firm name.

(5) Right to carry on business outside of Ontario — Nothing in this Act prevents a limited liability partnership mentioned in subsection (1) from carrying on its business and exercising its powers in any province or territory of Canada or any other country.

1998, c. 2, s. 6; 2006, c. 19, Sched. G, s. 7(1), (2)

44.4 (1) Extra-provincial limited liability partnerships — No extra-provincial limited liability partnership shall carry on business in Ontario unless it has registered its firm name under the *Business Names Act*.

(2) Amendments, cancellations and renewals — To amend, renew or cancel a registration of its firm name, an extra-provincial limited liability partnership shall register an amendment, renewal or cancellation of a registration in accordance with the requirements of the *Business Names Act*.

(3) Use of registered name only — No extra-provincial limited liability partnership shall carry on business under a name other than its registered firm name.

(4) **Laws of other jurisdiction** — The laws of the jurisdiction under which an extra-provincial limited liability partnership is formed shall govern,

(a) its organization and internal affairs; and

(b) the liability of its partners for debts, obligations and liabilities of or chargeable to the partnership or any of its partners.

(5) **Service** — A person may serve a notice or document on an extra-provincial limited liability partnership at its Ontario place of business, if any, or its address required to be maintained under the laws of the jurisdiction of formation or its principal office address.

1998, c. 2, s. 7; 2006, c. 19, Sched. G, s. 7(3)

General

45. Saving as to rules of equity and common law — The rules of equity and of common law applicable to partnership continue in force, except so far as they are inconsistent with the express provisions of this Act.

46. Construction — This Act is to be read and construed as subject to the *Limited Partnerships Act* and the *Business Names Act*.

COMPANIES SERVICE STANDARDS AND FEES

COMPANIES SERVICE STANDARDS AND FEES
As of April 1, 2011

CORPORATE DOCUMENTS:	ServiceOntario				SERVICE PROVIDERS (SPs) **	
Corporate Filing Services / ***Business Corporations Act (For-Profit)***	**OVER-THE COUNTER SERVICE TIME**	**FEE**	**MAILED-IN/ DROP-OFF SERVICE TIME**	**FEE**	**ELECTRONIC SERVICE TIME**	**FEE ***
Incorporation	Immediate	$360	15 bus. days	$360	Immediate	$300
Amalgamation (10 or fewer amalgamating corporations)	Immediate	$330	15 bus. days	$330	Not Available	---
Amalgamation (more than 10 amalgamating corporations)	Immediate	$500	15 bus. days	$500	Not Available	---
Amendment	Immediate	$150	15 bus. days	$150	Not Available	---
Restated Articles	Immediate	$150	15 bus. days	$150	Not Available	---
Dissolution	Immediate	$25	15 bus. days	$25	Not Available	---
Winding-Up (first filing)	Not Available	---	15 bus. days	$25	Not Available	---
Continuation in Ontario	48 hours	$330	15 bus. days	$330	Not Available	---
*** **Expedited Service for Continuation in Ontario**	24 hours	$500	Not Available	---	Not Available	---
Authorization to Continue in Another Jurisdiction	Immediate	$330	15 bus. days	$330	Not Available	---
Revival	Immediate	$330	15 bus. days	$330	Not Available	---
Reorganization	48 hours (minimum)	$150	15 bus. days	$150	Not Available	---
Arrangement	48 hours (minimum)	$330	15 bus. days	$330	Not Available	---
*** **Expedited Service for Arrangements**	24 hours	$500	Not Available	---	Not Available	---
Corrected Certificate	Not available	---	4 – 6 weeks	$500	Not Available	---
**** **Multiple transactions special service**	Immediate	$25	Not Available	---	Not Available	---
Corporations Act (Not-For-Profit)						
Incorporation/Amalgamation/Continuation	Not Available	---	35 bus. days	$155	Not Available	---
*** **Expedited Letters Patent** (Incorporation only)	Not Available	---	7 bus. days	$255	Not Available	---
Supplementary Letters Patent	Not Available	---	35 bus. days	$130	Not Available	---
Surrender of Charter	Not Available	---	35 bus. days	No Fee	Not Available	---
Revival	Immediate	$100	15 bus. days	$100	Not Available	---
Corrected Letters Patent/Supplementary Letters Patent	Not Available	---	4 – 6 weeks	$155	Not Available	---
Extra-Provincial Corporations Act (Foreign Corporation)						
Extra-Provincial Licence	Not Available	---	10 bus. days	$330	Not Available	---
Amended Extra-Provincial Licence	Not Available	---	10 bus. days	$150	Not Available	---
Termination of Extra-Provincial Licence	Not Available	---	10 bus. days	No Fee	Not Available	---
Corrected Extra-Provincial Licence	Not Available	---	4 – 6 weeks	$330	Not Available	---
***Corporations Information** Act (CIA)*						
Initial Return/Notice of Change (Form 1 – Ontario Corporations)	Not Available	---	25 bus. days	No Fee	Immediate	No Gov't Fee
Initial Return/ Notice of Change (Form 2 – Foreign Corporations or Extra-Provincial Domestic Corporations)	Not Available	---	25 bus. days	No Fee	Not Available	---
**CIA Annual Return - Integrated with T2 Tax Return (Ont./EP corps) or with Registered Charity Information Return (Ont. corps).	Not Available	---	Via Canada Revenue Agency	No Fee	Not Available	---
**CIA Annual Return – Standalone (Form 1 – Ontario Corporations)	Not Available	---	Not Available		Immediate	No Gov't Fee
**CIA Annual Return – Standalone (Form 2 – Extra-Provincial Foreign Corporations) (without T2 Tax Return or Registered Charity Information Return (Ont. Corps).	Not Available		Not Available		Immediate	No Gov't Fee

PLEASE NOTE:

Payment Information:

Payments may be made by cash, Visa, MasterCard, AMEX , Interac, certified cheque, money order or personal cheque payable to the Minister of Finance. Personal cheques must include pre-printed name, address, bank transit number and account number on the front of the cheque. Please do not send cash in the mail. You cannot pay by Visa, MasterCard or AMEX when using the mail-in service.

The Federal Goods and Services Tax (GST) does not apply to government fees.

N.B. A $35.00 fee will be charged for any cheque returned as non-negotiable.

* This chart only displays the government fees. Please contact the Service Providers directly for information about their charges for the online service they provide.

Service times are subject to change

*** The expedited service fee is for the review of articles/applications within the specific service time. When documents are deficient, they will be returned to the client for amendment and the expedited service time no longer applies.

**** By appointment for filing more than 3 over-the-counter BCA documents. $25 fee in addition to filing fee for each transaction over 3.

***** CIA Annual Returns integrated with the federal T2 or charities return are filed with the Canada Revenue Agency.

****** CIA Annual Returns standalone may be filed with the Service Providers under contract with the Ontario government. As of October 1, 2009 it is no longer possible to file the CIA Annual Returns with the Ontario Ministry of Revenue.

** For information about Service Providers under contract with the Ontario government, visit: www.Ontario.ca

COMPANIES SERVICE STANDARDS AND FEES
As of April 1, 2011

BUSINESS NAME, LIMITED PARTNERSHIP	ServiceOntario				SERVICE PROVIDERS (SPs) **		eCHANNEL***	
	OVER THE COUNTER		MAILED-IN		ELECTRONIC		ELECTRONIC	
Registration / Filing Services	**SERVICE TIME**	**FEE**	**SERVICE TIME**	**FEE**	**SERVICE TIME**	**FEE ***	**SERVICE TIME**	**FEE**
Business Names Act								
Registration (Sole Proprietorship, General Partnership and Business Name for Corporations)								
New Registration	Immediate	$80	20 bus. days	$80	Immediate	$60	Immediate	$60
Renewal	Immediate	$80	20 bus. days	$80	2 weeks	$60	2 weeks	$60
Amendment or Cancellation	Immediate	No Fee	20 bus. days	No Fee	Not Available		3 weeks (via OBC website only)	No fee
Registration Partnership/Limited Partnership Registration (Limited Liability Partnership, Extra-Provincial Limited Liability Partnership, Extra-Provincial Limited Liability Company)								
New / Renewal	Immediate	$80	20 bus. days	$80	Not Available		Not Available	
Amendment or Cancellation	Immediate	No Fee	20 bus. days	No Fee	Not Available		Not Available	
Limited Partnerships Act								
Declaration								
New / Renewal	Immediate	$210	20 bus. days	$210	Not Available		Not Available	
Late Renewal ($210 + $150 penalty)	Immediate	$360	20 bus. days	$360	Not Available		Not Available	
Change	Immediate	No Fee	20 bus. days	No Fee	Not Available		Not Available	
Dissolution	Immediate	No Fee	20 bus. days	No Fee	Not Available		Not Available	
Withdrawal	Immediate	No Fee	20 bus. days	No Fee	Not Available		Not Available	

PLEASE NOTE:

Payment Information:

Payments may be made by cash, Visa, MasterCard, AMEX, Interac, certified cheque, money order or personal cheque payable to the Minister of Finance. Personal cheques must include pre-printed name, address, bank transit number and account number on the front of the cheque. Please do not send cash in the mail. You cannot pay by Visa, MasterCard or AMEX when using the mailed-in service.

The Federal Goods and Services Tax (GST) does not apply to government fees.

N.B. A $35.00 fee will be charged for any cheque returned as non-negotiable.

* This chart only displays the government fees. Please contact the Service Providers directly for information about their charges for the online service they provide.

Service times are subject to change.

** You may register or renew your business name through Service Providers under contract with the Ontario government. For information about Service Providers, visit: www.Ontario.ca
***You may register, renew, amend or cancel your business name via the Internet at: www.Ontario.ca

COMPANIES SERVICE STANDARDS AND FEES
As of April 1, 2011

CORPORATE SEARCH PRODUCTS / SERVICES	ServiceOntario				SERVICE PROVIDERS (SPs)**	
Corporate Search Products and Services:	**FEE**	**OVER-THE-COUNTER SERVICE TIME**	**FAXED-IN SERVICE TIME**	**MAILED-IN SERVICE TIME**	**SERVICE TIME**	**FEE***
Corporation Profile Report	$12	Immediate	Not Available	5 bus. days	Immediate	$8
Corporation Point-In-Time Report	$12	Immediate	Not Available	5 bus. days	Immediate	$8
Corporation Document List	$5	Immediate	Not Available	5 bus. days	Immediate	$3
List of Business Names Registered by a Corporation	$12	Immediate	Not Available	5 bus. days	Immediate	$8
For certification of the above electronic products, add $8.00 to the product fee						
Certificate of Status	$30	Immediate	Not Available	5 bus. days	Immediate	$26
Certificate of No Record	$30	Immediate	Not Available	5 bus. days	Immediate	$26
Certificate of Non-Filing	$30	Immediate	Not Available	5 bus. days	Immediate	$26
Statement of No Record	$12	Immediate	Not Available	5 bus. days	Immediate	$8
Electronic Data Extraction Report	---	Not Available	Not Available	Not Available	Immediate	$8
Microfiche	$10	3 business days	3 business days	4 – 6 weeks	3 business days (pick up at the Branch)	$10
Certified Microfiche	$36	3 business days	3 business days	4 – 6 weeks		$36
Photocopy of Notice / Return (only if Profile Report is not available)	$14	10 business days (if film on site)	10 business days (if film on site)	4 –6 weeks	Not Available	---
Certified Copy of Notice / Return (from microfilm only)	$40	10 business days (if film on site)	10 business days (if film on site)	4 – 6 weeks	Not Available	---
TC/RC paper files (old files not kept on site)	$25	10 business days (minimum) -depending on number of copies	10 business days	4 –6 weeks	Not Available	---
For certification of TC/RC paper file, add $26.00 to the product fee						

PLEASE NOTE:

Payment information:

Payments may be made by cash, Visa, MasterCard, AMEX, Interac, certified cheque, money order or personal cheque payable to the Minister of Finance. Personal cheques must include pre-printed name, address, bank transit number and account number on the front of the cheque. Please do not send cash in the mail. You cannot pay by Visa, MasterCard or AMEX when using the mailed-in service.

The Federal Goods and Services Tax (GST) does not apply to government fees.

N.B. A $35.00 fee will be charged for any cheque returned as non-negotiable.

* This chart only displays the government fees. Please contact the Service Providers directly for information about their charges for the online service they provide.

Service times are subject to change.

**For information about Service Providers under contract with the Ontario government, visit: www.Ontario.ca

COMPANIES SERVICE STANDARDS AND FEES
As of April 1, 2011

BUSINESS NAME, LIMITED PARTNERSHIP SEARCH PRODUCTS	ServiceOntario				SERVICE PROVIDERS (SPs) **		eCHANNEL	
		OVER-THE COUNTER	FAXED-IN	MAILED-IN	ELECTRONIC		PUBLIC ACCESS WORKSTATION - INTERNET	
Business Names & Limited Partnership Search Products:	**FEE**	**SERVICE TIME**	**SERVICE TIME**	**SERVICE TIME**	**SERVICE TIME**	**FEE***	**SERVICE TIME**	**FEE**
Business Names Report	$12	Immediate	Not Available	5 bus. days	Immediate	$8	Workstation/ Internet	$8
Limited Partnerships Report	$12	Immediate	Not Available	5 bus. days	Immediate	$8	Not Available	--
Document Replica	$12	Immediate	Not Available	5 bus. days	Immediate	$8	Not Available	--
Partnership Business Names List	$12	Immediate	Not Available	5 bus. days	Immediate	$8	Not Available	--
BNLP Document List	$5	Immediate	Not Available	5 bus. days	Immediate	$3	Not Available	--
For certification of the above electronic products, add $8.00 to the product fee								
Certificate of Non-Registration	$30	Immediate	Not Available	5 bus. days	Immediate	$26	Immediate	$26
Statement of No Match	$12	Immediate	Not Available	5 bus. days	Immediate	$8	Immediate	$8
Expired Search Registration has expired. The name was registered more than 5 years ago, but less than 20 years prior to date of search	$40	5 days	5 days	5 bus. days	Not Available	---	Not Available	

PLEASE NOTE:

Payment information:

Payments may be made by cash, Visa, MasterCard, AMEX, Interac, certified cheque, money order or personal cheque payable to the Minister of Finance. Personal cheques must include pre-printed name, address, bank transit number and account number on the front of the cheque. Please do not send cash in the mail. You cannot pay by Visa, MasterCard or AMEX when using the mailed-in service.

The Federal Goods and Services Tax (GST) does not apply to government fees.

N.B. A $35.00 fee will be charged for any cheque returned as non-negotiable.

* This chart only displays the government fees. Please contact the Service Providers directly for information about their charges for the online service they provide.

Service times are subject to change.

**For information about Service Providers under contract with the Ontario government, visit: www.Ontario.ca

April 1, 2011

Aussi disponible en français

LEGISLATIVE INDEX

All references are to section numbers of Acts and Regulations, and not to page numbers.

The following abbreviations are used in this Index:

BCA — *Business Corporations Act*, R.S.O. 1990, c. B.16.
BNA — *Business Names Act*, R.S.O. 1990, c. B.17.
BRPA — *Business Records Protection Act*, R.S.O. 1990, c. B.19.
BRR — *Business Regulation Reform Act, 1994*, S.O. 1994, c. 32.
CA — *Corporations Act*, R.S.O. 1990, c. C.38.
CIA — *Corporations Information Act*, R.S.O. 1990, c. C.39.
EPCA — *Extra-Provincial Corporations Act*, R.S.O. 1990, c. E.27.
LPA — *Limited Partnerships Act*, R.S.O. 1990, c. L.16.
PA — *Partnerships Act*, R.S.O. 1990, c. P.5.
Reg. 62 — Business Corporations Act Regulation — General, R.R.O. 1990, Reg. 62.
O. Reg. 665/05 — Business Corporations Act Regulation — Health Profession Corporations.
O. Reg. 121/91 — Business Names Act Regulation — General.
O. Reg, 122/91 — Business Names Act Regulation — Restrictions Respecting Names.
O. Reg. 18/07 — Business Names Act Regulation — Refund of Fee for Electronic Application for New Registration.
O. Reg. 442/95 — Business Regulation Reform Act, 1994 Regulation — General.
Reg. 181 — Corporations Act Regulation — General, R.R.O. 1990, Reg. 181.
O. Reg. 244/05 — Corporations Act Regulation — Forms.
Reg. 182 — Corporations Information Act Regulation — General, R.R.O. 1990, Reg. 182.
Reg. 365 — Extra-Provincial Corporations Act Regulation — General, R.R.O. 1990, Reg. 365.
O. Reg. 245/05 — Extra-Provincial Corporations Act Regulation — Forms.
Reg. 713 — Limited Partnerships Act Regulation — General, R.R.O. 1990, Reg 713.

A

T

W